# Information Systems Development

Chris Barry • Kieran Conboy • Michael Lang
Gregory Wojtkowski • Wita Wojtkowski
Editors

# Information Systems Development

## Challenges in Practice, Theory and Education

Volume 1

*Editors*

Chris Barry
Business Information Systems Group
J.E. Cairnes School of Business & Economics
National University of Ireland, Galway
University Road
Galway
Ireland

Kieran Conboy
Business Information Systems Group
J.E. Cairnes School of Business & Economics
National University of Ireland, Galway
University Road
Galway
Ireland

Michael Lang
Business Information Systems Group
J.E. Cairnes School of Business & Economics
National University of Ireland, Galway
University Road
Galway
Ireland

Gregory Wojtkowski
Boise State University
Department of Electrical & Computer
  Engineering
1910 University Dr.
MEC 202C
Boise, ID 83725-2075
USA

Wita Wojtkowski
Boise State University
Department of Electrical & Computer
  Engineering
1910 University Dr.
MEC 202C
Boise, ID 83725-2075
USA

ISBN: 978-1-4419-4022-3            e-ISBN: 978-0-387-68772-8

DOI: 10.1007/978-0-387-68772-8

Printed on acid-free paper

springer.com

# Preface

This two-volume book is the published proceedings of the 16th International Conference on Information Systems Development (ISD2007) that was hosted by the Cairnes Graduate School of Business & Public Policy at National University of Ireland, Galway, from 29–31 August 2007. The theme of the conference was "Challenges in Practice, Theory and Education." The theme is not a new one – we chose to reproduce that used in Lithuania in 2004 because it encapsulates our ideals for the profession we are in: Teaching ISD practice and theory is what we all must aspire to achieve.

In total, 120 delegates from 27 different countries registered for the conference, making it a truly international event. Papers presented at the conference strongly reflected the three pillars of our conference theme. Of 131 papers submitted, 84 were presented at the conference, representing an acceptance rate of ~64%. All papers were double-blind, peer reviewed by at least two referees. Over the course of 3 days, 29 sessions were held, covering a range of areas such as agile methods, usage of systems development methods, method tailoring, users and usability, web development methods, requirements analysis, business process modelling, systems analysis and design, ISD in developing nations, ISD in public sector organisations, socio-technical aspects of ISD, human resources issues in ISD, knowledge management in ISD, ERP systems development and implementation, legal and ethical dimensions of ISD, management of ISD, information systems security, ISD education and training, e-learning technologies, project and requirements management, data quality and integrity, database design, practical applications of database technologies, Web services, automation of software development, and information systems engineering. The book is organised by the order of the conference sessions.

Reviewing papers, which is key to ensuring quality and fairness, is not generally a task that is acknowledged at a conference. It is done as part of a sense of collegiality and duty. At our conference a remarkable 95% of reviews were completed. In recognition of the reviewer who applied the most diligence and penned the most extensive review with both critical and constructive feedback, a *Best Reviewer Award* was given. Of course, a *Best Paper Award* was given as well. Details of these awards can be found on the conference Web site at http://isd2007.nuigalway.ie.

Our gratitude is extended first to all those who attended and authored work for the conference. The contribution of the International Program Committee was invaluable in identifying track chairs and reviewers to commit to doing vital work. Although volunteering to host a conference is a highly personal undertaking, without institutional support it would be impossible. Thus, a special thanks to Professor Jim Browne, the Registrar and Deputy-President of NUI, Galway, who opened the conference and welcomed the delegates to the Cairnes Graduate School. Our local organising committee laboured industriously to make the conference a success, especially Laura Regan, our conference secretary, who worked tirelessly to ensure harmony in all affairs. We also received invaluable advice from our conference office and assistance from the Centre for Education and Learning Technologies (CELT). Our sincere thanks are also extended to Mike Roche of IBM Dublin Software Laboratory and Professor Stefan Decker of the Digital Enterprise Research Institute (DERI) in Galway, who delivered the keynote addresses. Finally, we thank our sponsors for their financial support and other aid.

The ISD conference community has developed over the years a real sense of collegiality and friendliness, perhaps unusually so for a conference. At the same time it has been a stimulating forum where a free exchange of views and perspectives is encouraged. Perhaps what brings the community together is a belief that the process of systems development is important; whether it is systematic or structured or improvised or spontaneous, there is something about the process and the outcomes that excites us. We form a spectrum of thought from those who see the activity as somewhat scientific to others that see it as wholly sociological; we span a divide between abstract and conceptual, to hard code and artefacts – somewhere in-between lies the truth. If our work is to make a meaningful contribution to both practice (by teaching students) and research (by sharing our experiences and studies with others), then hopefully this conference will have done a little of the former and much for the latter.


Chris Barry and Michael Lang
ISD2007 Programme Chairs


Kieran Conboy
ISD2007 Organising Chair

# Conference Organisation

The 16th International Conference on Information Systems Development was hosted by the Business Information Systems Group, Cairnes Graduate School of Business & Public Policy, National University of Ireland, Galway, from 29 to 31 August 2007. The organisation and management of such a major international conference requires the collaboration and dedication of very many people. We are especially grateful to our international programme committee who voluntarily gave their time to review the submissions. The excellent standard of papers contained within this volume bears testimony to the diligence and rigour of the peer review process. We are also very appreciative of the efforts of all the conference officers and the tremendous support provided by the local organising committee.

## Programme Chairs

| | | |
|---|---|---|
| Chris Barry | National University of Ireland, Galway | Ireland |
| Michael Lang | National University of Ireland, Galway | Ireland |

## Organising Chair

| | | |
|---|---|---|
| Kieran Conboy | National University of Ireland, Galway | Ireland |

## International Advisory Committee

| | | |
|---|---|---|
| Gregory Wojtkowski | Boise State University | USA |
| Wita Wojtkowski | Boise State University | USA |
| Stanislaw Wrycza | University of Gdansk | Poland |
| Joze Zupancic | University of Maribor | Slovenia |

## Local Organising Committee

| | | |
|---|---|---|
| Tom Acton | National University of Ireland, Galway | Ireland |
| Annmarie Curran | National University of Ireland, Galway | Ireland |
| Brian Donnellan | National University of Ireland, Galway | Ireland |
| Willie Golden | National University of Ireland, Galway | Ireland |
| Mairéad Hogan | National University of Ireland, Galway | Ireland |
| Martin Hughes | National University of Ireland, Galway | Ireland |
| Séamus Hill | National University of Ireland, Galway | Ireland |
| Orla McHugh | National University of Ireland, Galway | Ireland |

| Anatoli Nachev | National University of Ireland, Galway | Ireland |
|---|---|---|
| Laura Regan | National University of Ireland, Galway | Ireland |
| Murray Scott | National University of Ireland, Galway | Ireland |
| Patricia Walsh | National University of Ireland, Galway | Ireland |
| Eoin Whelan | National University of Ireland, Galway | Ireland |

# Track Chairs

## Managing Information Systems Development

| Brian O'Flaherty | University College Cork | Ireland |
|---|---|---|
| Gaye Kiely | University College Cork | Ireland |

## Innovation in Information Systems Development

| Brian Donnellan | National University of Ireland, Galway | Ireland |
|---|---|---|
| Séamas Kelly | University College Dublin | Ireland |

## Enterprise Systems Development & Adoption

| Anders G. Nilsson | Karlstad University | Sweden |
|---|---|---|
| Odd Fredriksson | Karlstad University | Sweden |

## Public Information Systems Development

| Michael Lang | National University of Ireland, Galway | Ireland |
|---|---|---|

## Agile and High-Speed Systems Development Methods

| Pär Ågerfalk | University of Limerick | Ireland |
|---|---|---|
| Kieran Conboy | National University of Ireland, Galway | Ireland |

## Information Systems Engineering

| Norah Power | University of Limerick | Ireland |
|---|---|---|

## Business Systems Analysis & Design

| Larry Stapleton | Waterford Institute of Technology | Ireland |
|---|---|---|
| Chris Barry | National University of Ireland, Galway | Ireland |

## Data and Information Modelling

| | | |
|---|---|---|
| Markus Helfert | Dublin City University | Ireland |

## ISD Education

| | | |
|---|---|---|
| Lorraine Fisher | University College Dublin | Ireland |
| Murray Scott | National University of Ireland, Galway | Ireland |

## ISD in Developing Nations

| | | |
|---|---|---|
| John Traxler | University of Wolverhampton | UK |

## Legal and Administrative Aspects of ISD

| | | |
|---|---|---|
| Rónán Kennedy | National University of Ireland, Galway | Ireland |

## Service Oriented Modelling and Semantic Web Technologies

| | | |
|---|---|---|
| William Song | University of Durham | UK |
| Remigijus Gustas | Karlstad University | Sweden |
| Yuansheng Zhong | Jiangxi University of Finance & Economy | China |

# International Programme Committee

| | | |
|---|---|---|
| Witold Abramowicz | Economic University, Poznan | Poland |
| Tom Acton | National University of Ireland, Galway | Ireland |
| Pär Ågerfalk | University of Limerick | Ireland |
| Majed Al-Mashari | King Saud University | Saudi Arabia |
| Scott W. Ambler | IBM Rational | Canada |
| Viveca Asproth | Mid Sweden University | Sweden |
| David Avison | ESSEC Business School | France |
| Karin Axelsson | Linköping University | Sweden |
| Per Backlund | University of Skovde | Sweden |
| Akhilesh Bajaj | The University of Tulsa | USA |
| Chris Barry | National University of Ireland, Galway | Ireland |
| Janis Barzdins | University of Latvia, Riga | Latvia |
| Richard Baskerville | Georgia State University | USA |
| Dinesh Batra | Florida International University | USA |
| Frances Bell | University of Salford | UK |
| Paul Beynon-Davies | Cardiff Business School | UK |
| Juris Borzovs | Information Technology Institute | Latvia |
| Deborah Bunker | University of New South Wales | Australia |
| Adriana Schiopiu Burlea | University of Craiova | Romania |
| Dave Bustard | University of Ulster, Jordanstown | UK |

| | | |
|---|---|---|
| Tom Butler | University College Cork | Ireland |
| Rimantas Butleris | Kaunas University of Technology | Lithuania |
| Albertas Caplinskas | Institute of Mathematics and Informatics | Lithuania |
| Sven Carlsson | Lund University | Sweden |
| Michael Cavanagh | Balmoral Consulting | UK |
| Antanas Cenys | Semiconductor Physics Institute, Vilnius | Lithuania |
| Des Chambers | National University of Ireland, Galway | Ireland |
| Deren Chen | Zhejiang University | China |
| Rodney Clarke | University of Wollongong | Australia |
| Jenny Coady | Heriot-Watt University | UK |
| Gerry Coleman | Dundalk Institute of Technology | Ireland |
| Kieran Conboy | National University of Ireland, Galway | Ireland |
| Heitor Augustus Xavier Costa | Universidade Federal de Lavras | Brazil |
| Darren Dalcher | Middlesex University | UK |
| Gert-Jan de Vreede | University of Nebraska at Omaha | USA |
| Brian Donnellan | National University of Ireland, Galway | Ireland |
| Liam Doyle | Waterford Institute of Technology | Ireland |
| Jim Duggan | National University of Ireland, Galway | Ireland |
| Seán Duignan | Galway-Mayo Institute of Technology | Ireland |
| Dalé Dzemydiené | Law University, Vilnius | Lithuania |
| Phillip Ein-Dor | Tel-Aviv University | Israel |
| Owen Eriksson | Dalarna University College, Borlänge | Sweden |
| Chris Exton | University of Limerick | Ireland |
| Joe Feller | University College Cork | Ireland |
| Pat Finnegan | University College Cork | Ireland |
| Julie Fisher | Monash University, Melbourne | Australia |
| Lorraine Fisher | University College Dublin | Ireland |
| Brian Fitzgerald | University of Limerick | Ireland |
| Guy Fitzgerald | Brunel University | UK |
| Owen Foley | Galway-Mayo Institute of Technology | Ireland |
| Marko Forsell | SESCA Technologies Oy | Finland |
| Odd Fredriksson | Karlstad University | Sweden |
| Chris Freyberg | Massey University | New Zealand |
| Matt Glowatz | University College Dublin | Ireland |
| Goran Goldkuhl | Linköping University | Sweden |
| Gary Griffiths | University of Teesside | UK |
| Janis Grundspenkis | Riga Technical University | Latvia |
| Remigijus Gustas | Karlstad University | Sweden |
| Hele-Mai Haav | Tallinn Technical University | Estonia |
| G. Harindranath | University of London | UK |
| Igor Hawryszkiewycz | University of Technology, Sydney | Australia |
| John Healy | Galway-Mayo Institute of Technology | Ireland |
| Kevin Heffernan | Galway-Mayo Institute of Technology | Ireland |
| Markus Helfert | Dublin City University | Ireland |
| Brian Henderson-Sellers | University of Technology, Sydney | Australia |
| Ola Henfriddson | Viktoria Institute | Sweden |

| | | |
|---|---|---|
| Alan Hevner | University of South Florida | USA |
| Séamus Hill | National University of Ireland, Galway | Ireland |
| Mairéad Hogan | National University of Ireland, Galway | Ireland |
| Jesper Holck | Copenhagen Business School | Denmark |
| Helena Holmstrom | University of Limerick | Ireland |
| Debra Howcroft | Manchester Business School | UK |
| Joshua Huang | E-Business Technology Institute, Hong Kong | China |
| Magda Huisman | North-West University | South Africa |
| Sergey Ivanov | George Washington University | USA |
| Mirjana Ivanovic | University of Novi Sad | Serbia and Montenegro |
| Letizia Jaccheri | Norwegian University of Science and Technology | Norway |
| Marius A. Janson | University of Missouri – St. Louis | USA |
| Sherif Kamel | American University in Cairo | Egypt |
| Roland Kaschek | Massey University | New Zealand |
| Karlheinz Kautz | Copenhagen Business School | Denmark |
| Felicity Kelleher | Waterford Institute of Technology | Ireland |
| Séamas Kelly | University College Dublin | Ireland |
| Rónán Kennedy | National University of Ireland, Galway | Ireland |
| Gaye Kiely | University College Cork | Ireland |
| Marite Kirikova | Riga Technical University | Latvia |
| Gábor Knapp | Budapest University of Technology and Economics | Hungary |
| John Krogstie | Norwegian University of Science and Technology | Norway |
| Rein Kuusik | Tallinn University of Technology | Estonia |
| Sergei Kuznetsow | Russian Academy of Science | Russia |
| Michael Lane | University of Southern Queensland | Australia |
| Michael Lang | National University of Ireland, Galway | Ireland |
| John Lannon | University of Limerick | Ireland |
| Mauri Leppänen | University of Jyväskylä | Finland |
| Xia Li | Shenzhen University | China |
| Mikael Lind | University of Borås | Sweden |
| Henry Linger | Monash University | Australia |
| Steven Little | Open University Business School | UK |
| Jan Ljungberg | Göteborg University | Sweden |
| Jo Lee Loveland Link | Volvox Inc. | USA |
| David Lowe | University of Technology, Sydney | Australia |
| Audrone Lupeikiene | Institute of Mathematics and Informatics | Lithuania |
| Leszek A. Maciaszek | Macquarie University | Australia |
| Lars Mathiassen | Georgia State University | USA |
| Orla McHugh | National University of Ireland, Galway | Ireland |
| Ulf Melin | Linköping University | Sweden |
| Elisabeth Métais | CNAM University, Paris | France |

| | | |
|---|---|---|
| Peter Middleton | Queen's University Belfast | UK |
| Owen Molloy | National University of Ireland, Galway | Ireland |
| Robert Moreton | University of Wolverhampton | UK |
| Phelim Murnion | Galway-Mayo Institute of Technology | Ireland |
| Anatoli Nachev | National University of Ireland, Galway | Ireland |
| Lina Nemuraite | Kaunas Technical University | Lithuania |
| Peter Axel Nielsen | Aalborg University | Denmark |
| Anders G. Nilsson | Karlstad University | Sweden |
| Ovidiu Noran | Griffith University | Australia |
| Jacob Nørbjerg | Copenhagen Business School | Denmark |
| Briony Oates | University of Teesside | UK |
| Mel Ó Cinnéide | University College Dublin | Ireland |
| Gerard O'Donovan | Cork Institute of Technology | Ireland |
| Brian O'Flaherty | University College Cork | Ireland |
| Lorne Olfman | Claremont Graduate University | USA |
| Phil O'Reilly | University College Cork | Ireland |
| Malgorzata Pankowska | University of Economics in Katowice | Poland |
| George A. Papadopoulos | University of Cyprus | Cyprus |
| Jeff Parsons | Memorial University of Newfoundland | Canada |
| Oscar Pastor | University of Valencia | Spain |
| Anne Persson | University of Skövde | Sweden |
| Graham Pervan | Curtin University | Australia |
| John Sören Pettersson | Karlstad University | Sweden |
| Alain Pirotte | University of Louvain | Belgium |
| Jaroslav Pokorny | Charles University, Prague | Czech Republic |
| Norah Power | University of Limerick | Ireland |
| Jan Pries-Heje | The IT University of Copenhagen | USA |
| Boris Rachev | Technical University of Varna | Bulgaria |
| Vaclav Repa | Prague University of Economics | Czech Republic |
| Karel Richta | Czech Technical University | Czech Republic |
| Kamel Rouibah | Kuwait University | Kuwait |
| Alice Rupe | AR IT Solutions | USA |
| Steve Sawyer | Pennsylvania State University | USA |
| Murray Scott | National University of Ireland, Galway | Ireland |
| Keng Siau | University of Nebraska – Lincoln | USA |
| Klaas Sikkel | University of Twente | Netherlands |
| Guttorm Sindre | Norwegian University of Science and Technology | Norway |
| Piotr Soja | Cracow University of Economics | Poland |
| William Song | University of Durham | UK |
| Carsten Sorensen | London School of Economics | UK |

| Tor Stålhane | Norwegian University of Science and Technology | Norway |
| Ioannis Stamelos | Aristotle University | Greece |
| Larry Stapleton | Waterford Institute of Technology | Ireland |
| Uldis Sukovskis | Riga Technical University | Latvia |
| Håkan Sundberg | Mid Sweden University | Sweden |
| Bo Sundgren | Mid Sweden University | Sweden |
| Witold Suryn | Université du Québec | Canada |
| István Szakadát | Budapest University of Technology & Economics | Hungary |
| Janis Tenteris | Riga Technical University | Latvia |
| John Traxler | University of Wolverhampton | UK |
| Tuure Tuunanen | The University of Auckland | New Zealand |
| Olegas Vasilecas | Vilnius Gediminas Technical University | Lithuania |
| Ramesh Venkataraman | Indiana University | USA |
| Richard Veryard | Veryard Projects | UK |
| Richard Vidgen | University of Bath | UK |
| Jiri Vorisek | Prague University of Economics | Czech Republic |
| Gottfried Vossen | University of Münster | Germany |
| David Wainwright | University of Northumbria | UK |
| Hongbing Wang | Southeast University | China |
| Leoni Warne | Defence Science and Technology Organisation | Australia |
| Dave Wastell | University of Salford | UK |
| Brian Webb | Queen's University Belfast | UK |
| Eoin Whelan | National University of Ireland, Galway | Ireland |
| Edgar Whitley | London School of Economics | UK |
| Roel Wieringa | University of Twente | Netherlands |
| Gregory Wojtkowski | Boise State University | USA |
| Wita Wojtkowski | Boise State University | USA |
| Carson C. Woo | University of British Columbia | Canada |
| Stanislaw Wrycza | University of Gdansk | Poland |
| Judy Wynekoop | Florida Gulf Coast University | USA |
| Karen Young | National University of Ireland, Galway | Ireland |
| Yuansheng Zhong | Jiangxi University of Finance and Economy | China |
| Jozef Zurada | University of Louisville | USA |

# Contents

# A Failure to Learn in a Software Development Team: The Unsuccessful Introduction of an Agile Method

John McAvoy and Tom Butler

Business Information Systems, University College of Cork, Cork, Ireland
j.mcavoy@ucc.ie, tbutler@afis.ucc.ie

**Abstract**  This paper presents an investigation of the failures associated with the introduction of a new software development methodology in a software project team. The failure to adopt the new methodology is seen as a failure to learn by the team. This paper posits that learning is more than the cognitive process of acquiring a new skill; learning also involves changes in behaviours, attitudes and opinions. As methodology adoption involves changes to a team's activities, values and norms, this study investigates the introduction of an Agile method by a software team as a learning experience. Researchers use the concepts of single- and double-loop learning to explain how social actors learn to (a) perform tasks efficiently and (b) decide on the best task to perform. The theory of triple-loop learning explains how a learning process can be ineffective; accordingly, it is employed to examine why the introduction of a new methodology was ineffective in the team studied. The theory illustrates how power factors influence learning. This study focuses on one specific power factor – the power inherent in the desire for cohesion and conformity within a team. Ineffective decision-making and related actions occur because of the desire to conform among group members; this was shown as the cause of ineffective learning in the software team. The findings illustrate how the values inherent in the Agile methodologies, primarily the desire for cohesion within the team, ultimately led to the failure of the team to learn.

## 1 Introduction

The deployment of a new software development methodology is an exercise in change – a change in actions that lead to new behaviours (Larsen 2001). Such change is, in effect, an exercise in learning. This study examines the introduction of an Agile method in a software development team as a learning activity, and determines why this learning experience was ineffectual and, ultimately, failed.

C. Barry et al. (eds.), *Information Systems Development: Challenges in Practice, Theory, and Education, Vol.1*, doi: 10.1007/978-0-387-68772-8_1,

The remainder of this paper is as follows. The second section presents an overview of Agile software development. This is followed by an examination of how learning occurs among individuals and groups, and a relationship between the values of Agile and learning behaviours is posited. The case study of the adoption of an Agile method is then presented, the findings of which illustrate that a core value of Agile inhibited learning in the team. The final section offers several conclusions and recommendations for future research.

## 2 The Introduction of Agile in a Project Team

The deployment of a new software development methodology is an exercise in change – change in actions that lead to new behaviours (Larsen 2001). Researchers and authors have described the introduction of Agile as a culture change. Such change is, in effect, an exercise in learning. In a review of research on the changes brought about by the introduction of an Agile method, Larsen (2001) concludes that there is a need to learn from such change. This paper notes this observation and therefore concentrates on the change brought about by the introduction of Agile specifically through the lens of the learning experiences of team members.

### 2.1 The Principle and Behaviours of Agile

Agile places a much greater emphasis on people and the team than do other methodologies by concentrating on the social aspects of software development (Stephen and Rosenberg 2003). This is evident from the Agile principles and values. Allied with this, Agile's technical practices (or processes) also drive social interaction in teams (Robinson and Sharp 2003; Hazzan and Tomayko 2004), by invoking a sense of community (Cockburn and Highsmith 2001). People issues are at the core of the Agile methodologies and this is evident in the levels of empowerment that team members possess (Boehm and Turner 2004). For example, research has shown that collective ownership and collective responsibility are key features of teams adopting Agile (Robinson and Sharp 2003); in fact, collective ownership is one of the twelve practices in Extreme Programming (XP), which is one of the most popular Agile methodologies (Cohn 2004; Sharp and Robinson 2004; Stephens and Rosenberg 2003). The move to empowerment of teams acts in tandem with new attitudes towards change; change is a positive aspect of a project as opposed to being perceived as a problem (Riehle 2001).

## 2.2 Introducing Agile as an Experience in Learning

Argyris (1976) describes learning as the detection and correction of errors. In a later work, Argyris (1995) adds that learning also occurs when there is an initial match between people's intentions and the consequences of their actions. Organisations and teams introduce Agile with the aim of creating better software faster; this is achieved by following the values of the Agile manifesto. In terms of Argyris's learning theory, this can be considered to be a learning process in which an error has been detected with existing software development methods and Agile is introduced to correct these errors. Before examining potential mismatches between the intention to introduce Agile and the reality of the consequences of its introduction, it is necessary to further examine the different forms of learning.

### 2.2.1 Single and Double-Loop Learning

Argyris (1994, 1995, 1997, 2002) argues that there are two forms of learning – single and double loop. Argyris uses the often-cited example of a thermostat to demonstrate single-loop learning. In this scenario, temperature is measured against a predefined value and the thermostat turns on or off the heat source to maintain the temperature at this value. In single-loop learning, the norms and beliefs that chose the temperature are unchanged – for example, the reason why the temperature is set to 28 degrees as opposed to 32 degrees. Double-loop learning occurs when strategies are examined, along with the assumptions behind those strategies. Using the original analogy of a thermostat to demonstrate single-loop learning, the analogy of the thermostat is further developed by stating that if the thermostat could question why it was set to a temperature, or to examine why it worked a certain way, then the thermostat would be engaged in double-loop learning (Argyris 1997, 2002; Blackman et al. 2004; Denhardt et al. 2002). Double-loop learning not only questions the facts, it questions the logic behind the facts; thus, norms and values are questioned, leading to the emergence of new theories in use (Argyris and Schon 1978; Argyris 1995; Blackman et al. 2004; Bokeno 2003; Easterby-Smith and Lyles 2003).

The use of an Agile methodology appears to promote opportunities for double-loop learning as opposed to single-loop learning – this is, in theory, a positive benefit of adopting Agile. It should be noted that this can only be implied, as there is no extant research showing a link between Agile and double-loop learning. Despite this, existing literature on single- and double-loop learning could be interpreted as implying the existence of a positive link. (This study concludes that the implied link between Agile and double-loop learning can actually be negative; however, existing literature strongly suggests a positive link.). Single-loop learning is predominant in bureaucratic organisations where employees are expected to keep to pre-defined roles and tasks (Yeomans 2000). As the Agile methodologies advocate a move away from traditional bureaucratic management to one of empowerment and ownership, the opportunities for double-loop learning appear to be increased. Argyris (1976) argues that groups and organisations can achieve stability but in doing so they may limit learning. Again, this should not have major implications for the adoption and use of Agile, which embraces change as one of its core values. Furthermore, single-loop learning is relevant for the achievement of individual goals. Team goals are more relevant to double-loop learning, as inquiry and feedback must be more dynamic (Yeo 2002). The relevance of team goals to double-loop learning appears to match the emphasis placed on teams by Agile methodologies. Additional links between Agile and double-loop learning can be seen in the argument that single-loop learning involves learning how to effectively perform a task, whereas double-loop learning involves determining which is the best task to perform and when change is required (Clegg et al. 2005; Wardhaugh et al. 2003). Agile teams reflect on their work and make changes as required (Schatz and Abdelshafi 2005).

For learning to occur, there needs to be a match between an individual's intentions and their consequences. Argyris and Schon (1978) illustrate the relationship between intentions and consequences by connecting learning and behaviour through theories in use (consequences) and espoused theories (intentions). Espoused theories are the beliefs that individuals describe themselves as having – for example, the belief in the benefits of introducing Agile to their projects. Theories in use guide how individuals actually behave, as opposed to what they profess guides them. Theories in use, therefore, describe the actual behaviour of social actors. Human behaviour can be categorised as following a particular theory in use, typically model I behaviour. Model I behaviour is operationalised as the need to win at any cost, the suppression of negative feelings, an emphasis of rationality, stability, and the avoidance of risk. This type of behaviour leads to the desire to protect the individual or the group from criticism, which leads to individuals being overly defensive. Agyris (1976, 1994, 1995, 1997, 2002) describes this behavioural model as being underpinned by single-loop learning, as by censoring what is said and heard, learning is prevented. Model II behaviour moves away from the repressive censoring behaviours of model I. The governing variables of model II behaviour are valid information, free and informed choice, and commitment to decision and actions. This model is based on double-loop learning and is a move away from the concept of winning to one of open debate. The governing variables for model II behaviour, and the double-loop learning it is based on, are compared with Agile values in Table 1; this indicates the relationship between the two.

It would appear from Table 1 that the use of an Agile methodology seems to favour and enhance opportunities for double-loop learning by permitting developers to transcend the limitations of model I behaviour. In addition, Bokeno (2003) associates group cohesion with model II behaviour. In an ideal situation, therefore, the use of Agile should demonstrate double-loop learning seen through model II behaviour.

Although Agile promotes, and appears to assist, model II behaviour, not all Agile projects are successful and could thus be considered as learning failures. The C3 project (Chrysler Comprehensive Compensation) was the first attempt at applying Agile practices, yet it was ultimately cancelled (Boehm and Turner 2004;

Stephens and Rosenberg 2003). In some cases, therefore, there can be ineffective learning in Agile projects. To examine why such failures occur, whether related to the use of Agile or otherwise, it is necessary to examine why learning can be ineffective.

**Table 1.** Double-loop learning and Agile values

| Model II governing variables | Agile values |
| --- | --- |
| Valid information | "The agile manager fosters an environment where members of a team are able to make decisions and base them on the best information available" (Schuh 2004, p. 164). |
| Free and informed choice/open debate | Agile projects should have rules governing behaviour, including the following: Everyone should have an equal voice; everyone's contribution is valuable; attack issues, not people; respect each other and your differences; everyone participates (Highsmith 2004). |
| Commitment to decisions and actions | As everyone is involved in decision-making, the team will implement the decisions that are made (Highsmith 2004). |

## 2.2.2 Triple-Loop Learning

The highest level of learning is what Bateson (1972) refers to as deutero learning and Flood and Romm (1996) refer to as triple-loop learning. Flood and Romm (1996) describe the first loop of their triple-loop learning as concerning the "how" question: How are organisations and processes designed? If no structures are in place to assist in task-oriented design decisions, then inefficiencies may be introduced. In contrast, if there are too many structures in place, then rules may stifle choices.  Flood and Romm liken this to a bureaucratic system; hence, traditional bureaucratic structures need to be overcome if learning is to occur in organisations (Wang and Ahmed 2003). As Agile advocates a move away from overly restrictive bureaucratic structures, it follows that the replacement of such structures with Agile methods can help achieve the type of learning associated with the first loop.

The second loop of Flood and Romm's (1996) triple-loop learning concerns the question of what decisions will be made? The first loop is based on how things should be done, whereas the second loop is based on what should be done. Learning is achieved here through debate and discussion on the course(s) of action to be taken, and the freedom to debate these issues. While too little reflection and debate in the decision-making process leads to inaction, the opposite of this is not necessarily better. At the other extreme to limited debate are "superdecisions", which are based on assumptions that are not challenged. This type of dysfunctional situations arise where, for example, a subject matter expert expresses an opinion on a design choice and this is not debated by software team as they are deferring to the assumed superior knowledge of the "expert". In such situations "forced decisions" result, which although are arrived at through consensus, involve the tacit acceptance of unchallenged assumptions. Flood and Romm therefore argue that suboptimal learning outcomes occur when social actors have little control over, and influence on, decision-making (cf. Finnegan et al. 2003).

By combining these first two loops, double-loop learning can be achieved. The third loop is a reflexive loop, where the important factor is how people effectively undertake the first two (Flood and Romm 1996). Politics and power relations are of primary concern here as they can greatly influence learning in the first two loops. The question to be answered here is, "do people have the power and freedom to make the choices required in the first two loops?" Alternatively, do social actors have too much power, in which case decisions can also be flawed?

### 2.2.3 Groupthink

If, as argued herein, the attributes of Agile match those of model II behaviours and double-loop learning, then a failure to adopt Agile by a software development project team is essentially a failure to learn. Wenger (1999) argues that learning is a social phenomenon; hence, learning failures can be caused by social factors. As indicated, Flood and Romm (1996) propose that social power has an impact on learning. While power is traditionally viewed as an individual asserting authority over a subordinate, the power of a group to make members conform is equally strong. As Agile advocates empowered teams with collective ownership, the cohesion of the Agile team is vital to the success of its activities. However, strong cohesion within a team can lead to the emergence of power-related dysfunctional-ity, wherein pressures on team members to conform become a concern. Research on groupthink illustrates how a desire for cohesion in a team can ultimately lead to ineffective or sub-optimal decision-making, where the need for unanimity and consensus becomes paramount to the acceptance of alternative or critical opinion (Cartwright 2002; Griffin 1997; Janis 1972; Moorhead et al. 1998).

Ineffective decision-making, such as groupthink, has the potential to prohibit double-loop learning. When groupthink exerts its influence, individual social actors feel that they should not "go against the grain"; their opinions are either voluntarily or involuntarily suppressed. The group as a whole therefore runs the risk of making uninformed decisions. The power relationships within the team, as demonstrated through groupthink, therefore have the potential to adversely affect learning within Agile project teams. It should be noted that groupthink emerged from this research: it was not initially looked for, rather it became the conclusion.

# 3 Research Approach

This paper's basic premise is that the successful adoption and use of Agile methods is related to the ability of software teams to adopt model II behaviors and achieve triple-loop learning. The objective of this study was, therefore, to examine how learning occurred, or did not occur, in software development teams that introduced an Agile method. Factors that aided team-based learning and, also, those that constrained learning were to be identified and explained. Klein and Myers (1999, p. 75) maintain that in the interpretivist mode of research "theory is used ... more as a 'sensitizing device' to view the world in a certain way", and hence the inclusion of previous sections on learning theory. However, the section on groupthink was included herein as it emerged from the findings.

Learning or the lack thereof, in organisations, teams and individuals, is often hidden, even from those involved in the process. Individuals, for a variety of social and psychological reasons, are usually not able to determine why and when learning does not occur; this is true whether it is themselves or others. This situation calls for the application of research approaches that are sensitive to such issues. To investigate learning problems in software development teams necessitates a research approach that permits the team to be examined in context over an extended period. Furthermore, the investigation of the social factors that inhibit learning involves the examination of phenomena that would be normally hidden from, or not observable by, outsiders; indeed, individual team members themselves may not be aware of the existence of such influences. Argyris (1976) illustrates how individuals are able to discern the difference between another social actor's espoused theory vs. their theory in use better than they identify the dissonance between their theories. To overcome these difficulties, an interpretive research approach utilising participant observation was adopted for the study. A number of studies have used participant observation to conduct research on agile software development projects. For example, a qualitative approach involving participant observation was used by researchers to investigate the characteristics of an agile team and provided rich insights that could not be obtained by other research methods (Robinson and Sharp 2005).

A purposeful sampling strategy was adopted (Patton 1990), which saw a software development project team chosen for study: importantly, this team had recently decided to introduce Agile in order to undertake a new project. This project team designed and developed an information system within a large telecommunications company. A team of six developers and a team lead were involved in the project, which lasted 1 year. Participant observation was chosen as the primary research technique to investigate the phenomenon of interest, as it is a particularly relevant approach when "the phenomenon is obscured from the view of outsiders" (Jorgensen 1989, p. 12). The failure of social actors to translate espoused theory into theory in use (i.e., a failure to learn) is one such pheno- menon. Participant observation of the development team occurred at regular intervals over the year, in what was a longitudinal research study. A researcher joined the team, primarily to help in their adoption of Agile, and was therefore able to participate in team meetings, formal and informal discussions, and so on. Such activities are argued to be vital in participant observation (Ezey 2003), as it "allows you to experience activities directly to get a feel of what events are like, and to record your own perceptions" (Spradley 1980, p. 51). Rather than being an outsider looking in, the researcher was an insider working with the team while researching the phenomena – he was, as Bødker and Pedersen (1991) put it, a cultural insider. Detailed field notes were taken throughout the research process and these were reflexively analysed and recorded by the researchers. The theories presented herein acted as a lens in the interpretation and analysis of the data, which began at the point of collection. Various themes, issues, and group interactions were identified as the study progressed and initial observations subsequently confirmed.

## 4 Field Observations

The year-long investigation into the introduction of Agile into the project team commenced with the decision by team members to adopt an Agile method (XP in this case) and continued through its introduction and use. The field research examined the learning processes inherent in the introduction of XP and highlighted a problem with the changeover to this new Agile process.

The team members exhibited the type of core values that aligned well with those expressed in the Agile Manifesto. The team leader empowered the team to perform their tasks; in addition, ownership of the tasks rested with the team as a unit, as opposed the individual. He ensured that the development team had access to all the information they required to fulfil their roles and responsibilities, and included team members in all decisions – nothing was hidden from the team. Because of this, the developers regarded the team leader as "one of the team", as opposed to an outsider operating in a command and control structure. The team evolved their own language, with terms and phrases unique to the group, and demonstrated an ability to ensure that disagreements were accepted and never got out of hand. From the outset of the project, cohesion was important to the team.

The team lead originally suggested, and the team agreed with, the use of agile software development for this new project. Prior to this, a more traditional formal software development approach was used, following the waterfall model; this was the usual approach to software development in this company. Prior to the adoption of the new methodology, one of the authors provided an overview of XP to the team and suggested additional reading material. Some of the team were already familiar with Agile, without specifically having used it before.

Early on into the life of the project, it was observed that the initial commitment to the use of Agile decreased. When the project commenced, the team (both developers and team lead) agreed that a new process, or methodology, was required. It was felt that the existing methodology had problems, and that these problems could be fixed or mitigated through the use of XP. This was a demonstration of single-loop learning – a realisation that "how" things were done needed to change. Initially, the entire project team enthusiastically welcomed the use of XP. The team espoused their belief in the value of XP and were determined to make use of it in the project. Resistance to change would imply an initial negative reaction against the use of Agile techniques, such as user stories or iterations, for example. This was not the case though as there was initial acceptance, followed by a dilution in commitment to the use of XP. The espoused beliefs were therefore not translated into theories in use, thus demonstrating a failure to learn.

It should be noted that the team gradually progressed from initially espousing their belief in the value of Agile to its eventual abandonment in just over 5 months: the effect was similar to a gradual "chipping away at" support for the use of Agile. What made this interesting was that most of the developers stated at the end of the project that they believed in the value of the Agile method. Attitudes to Agile did not change overnight: observations noted subtle changes over a long time period, changes that could not be pin-pointed to a specific date, rather a time period (such as first 2 months, last 2 months).

The longitudinal aspect of the study showed how the team had gone full circle – espousing the benefit of Agile, failing to convert this into practice, and then back to espousing the benefit of Agile. This failure to translate espoused theories to theories in use (a failure to learn) appeared to oppose the model II behaviour that Agile appeared to promote. An examination of the variables of model II behaviour showed how the team, at times, demonstrated behaviour that was the antithesis of model II behaviour (Table 2).

Five months into the project, it was clear that double-loop learning was not happening in the project team. Single-loop learning was demonstrated by the team

Table 2. Double-loop learning and observed behaviours

| Model II/Double-loop learning | Observed behaviours |
| --- | --- |
| Valid information | This behaviour was actually demonstrated, as all information was available to the team. The team leader ensured that nothing was hidden from the team. It could be argued, though, that by concentrating on team unity the team restricted the information they were willing to discuss. |
| Free and informed choice/Open debate | At times, it was more important to display team unity than to have an open debate. The team leader strived to ensure unity in the team, suppressing his own views, on occasion, if they went against the group. Debates usually ended early in compromise rather than continuing discussions. |
| Commitment to decisions and actions | The team espoused commitment to Agile, yet they were not translated into use. The team leader "backed down" on Agile as he preferred team unity rather than forcing Agile upon the team. |

in that they decided to change how they developed software. Although Agile practices appear to promote model II behaviours, as demonstrated by double-loop learning, this behaviour was not apparent in the team. The underlying forces preventing effective learning, and the move to model II behaviour, were not apparent. Interestingly, triple-loop learning theory posits that power issues prevent double-loop learning, but it was not initially clear which power issues were present in the Agile project and how they might be negating the positive influence of Agile values.

Evidence at project team meetings and observations of group interactions indicated that groupthink might be playing a role. One of the primary symptoms of groupthink is a pressure among group members to conform to the group's views (Cartwright 2002; Griffin 1997; Janis 1972; Moorhead et al. 1998). This appeared to be of relevance, as initially the group accepted the values and benefits of Agile. Over time, however, the group failed to translate this into action – the group's collective opinion had changed.

Reinterpreting the field notes made during the year-long observation of the project provided an explanation. The team leader was liked and respected by the team. Unlike some team leaders, he was regarded as part of the development team, as opposed to an outsider – several developers specifically stated this. The majority of the team had worked under this individual on previous projects and enjoyed the trust and empowerment given to them by him. The team leader had originally suggested the change from traditional development methods to Agile software development. At this stage, the development team agreed to the change and were committed to the use of Agile. In follow-up interviews, the developers were asked about the failure to translate the initial optimism for Agile into a tangible reality. Each developer stated that the developers on the team felt that the team leader was not very committed to the use of Agile, and so they did not pursue the matter. Interestingly, the team leader stated that he did not want to impose his view of the benefits of Agile on the team, and so he left the adoption to the developers – he said that he had empowered them to do so, and left the matter in their collective hands. It is interesting that the developers and team leader did not discuss why the adoption slowly failed, and so neither side knew that they both actually wanted to use Agile. In fact, both the team leader and the developers assumed that the other did not wish to pursue the adoption; so, to maintain team cohesion, they gradually reduced their commitment to the use of Agile. In regard to triple-loop learning theory and the influence of power factors in inhibit learning, for this Agile project team, the pressure to conform is the power factor observed. The desire to conform prevented double-loop learning in the team; on the other hand, Agile requires cohesive teams, empowered to take collective ownership and responsibility. This desire for cohesion did have positive benefits for the team, as was evident over the year of the study, but it also led to ineffective learning.

## 5 Discussion and Conclusion

This paper's first conclusion is that the values associated with Agile methods possess a previously unobserved negative side affect. In software development teams, as with other groups, there exist pressures to conform to group norms and beliefs. While such forces exert positive influences in getting groups to cohere and work together, once this is achieved such forces act to maintain the status quo. Thus there is a desire to conform among team members and this leads to an unwillingness to offer contrary opinions. It is necessary, therefore, to ensure a degree of conflict exists. This observation is supported by Euchner ct al. (1993), who report that the dialectical nature of conflict can be beneficial for the IS development process. Thus while Agile argues for team cohesion, which appears to be the antithesis of conflict, it should still be possible to maintain team cohesion while introducing low levels of conflict. One solution to this could involve the team leader taking on the role of devil's advocate in team meetings. In the present study, the team leader was very much part of the software development team, working day to day with the team, and socialising with the team outside of work. Perhaps the team lead could have controlled for groupthink by adopting a position that was more removed from the team, and by questioning decisions and choices, as opposed to being part of the decision-making process.

A potential flaw with qualitative studies is that they tend towards detailed examinations of specific issues or cases. Researchers argue that it is difficult to generalise from the findings of a single case study. The authors accept this, but it was not this study's aim to do so. A further potential flaw with the choice of participant observation is the possibility of bias and a lack of objectivity. This has to be accepted as a potential problem. Participant observation will always tend towards a subjective view, but the longitudinal aspect of the study does provide sufficient data to challenge any a priori assumptions.

It is accepted by the authors that groupthink does not provide an all-encompassing explanation for the failure to learn in all Agile projects. What is clear, however, is that the use of Agile and the values it embraces does have the potential to affect the ability of a team to negotiate the gulf that separates stated beliefs and their application in practice (i.e., from espoused theories to theories in use). This may therefore create a situation where, while Agile embraces change, the Agile team may work against it.

## References

Argyris, C. (1976) Single-loop and double-loop models in research on decision making. Administrative Science Quarterly. 21(3). 363–375.

Argyris, C. and Schon, S. (1978) *Organizational learning: A theory of action perspective.* Addison-Wesley, MA, USA.

Argyris, C. (1994) Good communication that blocks learning. Harvard Business Review. 72(4). 77–85.

Argyris, C. (1995) Action science and organizational learning. Journal of Managerial Psychology. 10(6). 20–26.

Argyris, C. (1997) Double loop learning in organizations. Harvard Business Review. 55(5). 115–125.

Argyris, C. (2002) Double loop learning, teaching, and research. Academy of Management Learning and Education. 1(2). 206–218.

Bateson, G. (1972) *Steps to an ecology of mind.* Ballantine Books, New York, USA.

Blackman, D. Connelly, J. and Henderson, S. (2004) Does double loop learning create reliable knowledge? The Learning Organization. 11(1). 11–27.

Bødker, K. and Pedersen, J. (1991). Workplace Cultures: Looking at artifacts, symbols and practices. In Greenbaum, J., King, M. (eds.) *Design at work: Collaborative design of computer systems.* Erlbaum, Mahwah, NJ, pp. 121–136.

Boehm, B. and Turner, R. (2004) *Balancing agility and discipline.* Pearson Education, MA, USA.

Bokeno, R. (2003) The work of Chris Argyris as critical organization practice. Journal of Organizational Change Management. 16(6). 633–649.

Cartwright, R. (2002) *Mastering team leadership.* Palgrave Macmillan, Wales.

Clegg, S., Kornberger, M. and Pitsis, T. (2005) *Managing and organizations: An introduction to theory and practice.* Sage, London, UK.

Cockburn, A. and Highsmith, J. (2001) Agile software development: The people factor. IEEE Computer. 34(11). 131–133.

Cohn, M. (2004) *User stories applied for agile software development.* Addison-Wesley, MA, USA.

Denhardt, R., Denhardt, J. and Aristigeuta, M. (2002) *Managing behaviour in public and nonprofit organizations.* Sage, CA, USA.

Easterby-Smith, M. and Lyles, M. (2003) Re-reading organizational learning: Selective memory, forgetting, and adaptation. Academy of Management Executive. 17(2). 51–55.

Euchner, J. Sachs, P. and The NYNEX Panel (1993) The benefits of internal tension. Communications of the ACM. 36(4). 53.

Ezey, P. (2003) Integration and its challenges in participant observation. Qualitative Research. 3(2). 191–205.

Finnegan, P., Galliers, R. and Powell, P. (2003) Applying triple loop learning to planning electronic trading systems. Information Technology and People. 16(4). 461–483.

Flood, R. and Romm, N. (1996) *Diversity management: Triple loop learning.* Wiley, London, UK.

Griffin, E. (1997) *A first look at communication theory.* McGraw-Hill, NY, USA.

Hazzan, O. and Tomayko, J. (2004) Human aspects of software engineering. In Proceedings of extreme programming and agile processes in software engineering. 5th International conference, Germany. Springer-Verlag, Heidelberg, pp. 303–311.

Highsmith, J. (2004) *Agile project management.* Pearson Education, MA, USA.

Janis, I. (1972) *Victims of groupthink.* Houghton Mifflin, Boston, MA, USA.

Jorgensen, D. (1989) *Participant observation: A methodology for human studies.* Sage, CA, USA.

Klein, K. and Myers, M. (1999) A set of principles for conducting and evaluating interpretive field studies in information systems. MIS Quarterly. 23(1). 67–94.

Larsen, T. (2001) The phenomenon of diffusion. In Ardis, M., Marcolin, B. (eds.) *Diffusing software product and process innovations.* Kluwer, MA, USA, pp. 35–50.

Moorhead, G., Neck, C. and West, M. (1998) The tendency towards defective decision making with self-managing teams: The relevance of groupthink. Organizational Behaviour and Human Decision Process. 73(2/3). 327–351.

Patton, M. (1990) *Qualitative evaluation and research methods.* Sage, London.

Riehle, D. (2001) A comparison of the value systems of Adaptive Software Development and Extreme Programming: How methodologies may learn from each other. In Succi, G.,

Marchesi, M. (eds) *Extreme Programming explained*. Addison-Wesley, Boston, USA, pp. 35–50.

Robinson, H. and Sharp, H. (2003) XP Culture: Why the twelve practices both are and are not the most significant thing. In *Proceedings of Agile development conference, Salt Lake City*. IEEE Computer Society, pp. 12–21.

Robinson, H. and Sharp, H. (2005) The social side of technical practices. In *Proceedings of 6th international conference on Extreme Programming and Agile processes in software engineering (XP2005), Sheffield, UK*. Springer-Verlag, Heidelberg, pp. 100–108.

Schatz, B. and Abdelshafi, I. (2005) Primavera gets Agile: A successful transition to Agile development. IEEE Software 22(3), 36–42.

Schuh, P. (2004) *Integrating agile development in the real world*. Delmar Thomson Learning, New York, USA.

Sharp, H. and Robinson, H. (2004) An ethnographic study of XP practice. Empirical Software Engineering. 9(4). 353–375.

Spradley, J. (1980) *Participant observation*. Holt, Rinehard, and Winston, New York, USA.

Stephens, M. and Rosenberg, D. (2003) *Extreme Programming refactored: The case against XP*. Springer-Verlag, Heidelberg, Germany.

Wang, C. and Ahmed, C. (2003) Organizational learning: A critical review. The Learning Organisation. 10(1). 8–17.

Wardhaugh, R., Shani, A. and Docherty, P. (2003) *Learning by design*. Blackwell, Oxford, UK.

Wenger, E. (1999) Learning as social participation. Knowledge Management Review. 1(6). 30–33.

Yeo, R. (2002) From individual to team learning. Team Performance Management: An International Journal. 8(7/8). 157–170.

Yeomans, L. (2000) Does reflective practice have relevance for innovation in public relations? Journal of Communications Management. 5(1). 72–81.

# Using Visual Risk Assessment to Uncover Subtle Team Performance Issues

**Philip S. Taylor[1], Gerry Coleman[1], Kevin McDaid[1], Frank Keenan[1] and Dave Bustard[2]**

[1]Computing and Mathematics Department, Dundalk Institute of Technology, philtay@acm.org; {gerry.coleman; kevin.mcdaid; frank.keenan}@dkit.ie

[2]School of Computing and Information Engineering, University of Ulster, dw.bustard@ulster.ac.uk

**Abstract** Developing software systems is predominantly a team endeavour. The importance of the team is heightened when using an agile development approach that relies on open and frequent communication between team members. It is important for software companies to assess their readiness for an agile development approach and this necessarily includes an assessment of the performance of their teams. This work-in-progress report presents an approach for assessing key software engineering risks in relation to agile or plan-driven development approaches. Importantly, this assessment can be used to uncover subtle team performance issues which have a bearing on how well a particular development approach can be enacted. Assessments performed to date suggest a sufficiently good correlation of subjective rating and actual team performance.

## 1 Introduction

Agile methods have become a viable option in the last 5 years for many software development organisations in numerous product domains. The literature related to agility in general and specific agile methods is voluminous given its recent origins. In addition to standard texts, there is an increasing number of research papers presented at conferences, such as the International Conference on eXtreme Programming and Agile Processes in Software Engineering and the Agile International Conference, and in journals such as *IEEE Software* (IEEE Software 2003) and *Crosstalk* (Crosstalk 2002).

Ceschi et al. (2005) provide indicative results, suggesting that adopting agile methods improves management of the development process and customer relationships, and Syed-Abdullah et al. (2006) indicate that agile methods can lead to more enthusiastic development teams. Enthusiasm and happiness at work are

C. Barry et al. (eds.), *Information Systems Development: Challenges in Practice, Theory, and Education, Vol.1*, doi: 10.1007/978-0-387-68772-8_2,
© Springer Science+Business Media, LLC 2009

closely linked to better company performance (Gavin and Mason 2004). However, agile methods do not suit every problem domain, and careful planning is required to determine how much agility and planning are needed for each project (Boehm and Turner 2004; Taylor et al. 2006).

Although the literature on agile methods is mostly based on real-world case studies, there is often a misconception that adopting and tailoring agile methods are straightforward. In practice, however, the empirical nature of agile methods means that practitioners need to be careful and disciplined when adopting and tailoring them. This is particularly the case with small software companies (SSCs) who, in comparison to many large software companies, are less able to absorb the impact of failed experimentation (Börjesson et al. 2006; Fitzgerald et al. 2006).

Limited in scale and resources, SSCs find software process improvement a major challenge. Early-stage software companies focus on time to market, innovation and creativity (Sutton 2000) and thus often ignore SPI models such as CMMI and Spice, whose primary initial emphasis is on achieving stability and predictability. So, to realize their business goals, small companies are increasingly attracted to agile methods, which promise shorter development schedules and greater delivery flexibility. One cautious approach to adopting agile methods is to assess an organisation's risks and what it does to manage those risks. The understanding gained from such an assessment can then be used to inform process improvement (Iversen et al. 2004).

The practice of agile development relies on a form of team work that emphasises frequent, open communication and collective ownership of successes and failures. Team effectiveness can be influenced by factors such as team membership, composition, structure, processes, psychology, tasks and task design, organisational context, resources, structure and environment (Cohen and Bailey 1997). The influence of these factors on team performance can be obvious. For example, a character clash amongst team members often leads to communication breakdown and the subsequent lengthening of problem-solving time. In agile software development teams a character clash can lead to a blame culture when system faults occur. The principle of collective ownership quickly degrades. However, some team performance issues, and the factors that influence them, can be more subtle. For example, it is not immediately clear how team members' differing views of who constitutes their team influence performance, yet, the agility/discipline assessments (ADAs) performed by the authors indicate that it does affect team performance.

It is because of such factors that adopting, tailoring and practicing agile development approaches is more difficult than many software teams realise and requires careful assessment and planning. In Sect. 2 an overview of an agility/discipline assessment is provided, with a brief description of how such an assessment is performed. Sect. 3 describes how the assessment results are interpreted with specific reference to subtle team performance issues. Sect. 4 concludes the paper and provides possible directions for how this work-in-progress may proceed.

## 2 Agility/Discipline Risk Assessment

After using the original ADA developed by Boehm and Turner (Boehm 2002; Boehm and Turner 2003a,b, 2004) in a number of software companies, it was adapted and improved (Taylor et al. 2006; McCaffery et al. 2007) to help SSCs take a reasoned step towards process and quality improvement through adopting and tailoring agile methods. There were two main aims when adjusting the assessment. First, the assessment was to be efficient, considering the limited time and resources available to many SSCs. Second, the assessment was to involve all employees directly related to software product development. Many software process assessments and risk assessments are conducted exclusively by management level staff. It is believed that this impoverishes the assessments, as all staff directly related to software product development have important perspectives for process improvement and risk mitigation.

The assessment, as adapted by the authors, is conducted in three stages. First, an overview of agile and plan-driven methods is provided so that all team members are aware of what each offers. Then each team member is provided with a critical factors diagram with an accompanying explanation and asked to produce a plot. Finally, the results are collated and presented to the company.

### 2.1 Assessment Technique

The main part of the assessment technique summarizes the strengths and weaknesses of agile and plan-driven methods using six critical factors:

- *Criticality* – loss suffered because of defects in the software system
- *Team size* – number of personnel in the team, including developers, project leads and management
- *Client involvement* – nature of the client's involvement with the development team
- *Team distribution* – geographic distribution of the development team
- *Requirements churn* – percentage of requirements change per month
- *Personnel ability* – competencies of the development team

Boehm and Turner (2004) originally had five critical factors that were summarised from the strengths and weaknesses they saw in agile and plan-driven methods: *criticality, team size, dynamism, personnel* and *culture*. After some initial assessments with the original five factors and with feedback from assessment participants, the authors introduced *client involvement* and *team distribution* as important factors in agile and plan-driven methods for SSCs. These new factors were consistently evident for software development teams, particularly those who were just beginning to take an agile development approach. The *culture* factor was deemed least useful, and hence removed, as most participants were in the middle of the scale preferring a balance between chaos and order. The rather abstract *dynamism* factor was replaced with the more concrete *requirements churn*.

There are also other factors that seem important, such as team sociotechnical organisation (Sawyer 2004), and that may need to be incorporated after further industrial assessment. Figure 1 shows the diagram used by the team members to capture their opinions of the critical factors. The meaning of most of the critical factors is self-evident but *personnel ability* and *client involvement* require further explanation.

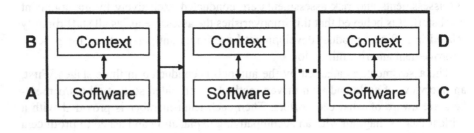

**Fig. 1.** Six critical factors for determining software process strategy

## *2.2 Personnel Ability*

This is an important part of self-assessment. All team members are required to give an honest assessment of themselves and each other using the levels devised by Cockburn (2005):

- *Level 3* – able to revise a method (break its rules) to fit an unprecedented situation
- *Level 2* – able to tailor a method to fit a precedented new situation
- *Level 1A* – with training, able to perform discretionary method steps
- *Level 1B* – with training, able to perform procedural method steps
- *Level 1* – may have technical skill, but unable or unwilling to collaborate or follow shared methods

In Fig. 1 the outer solid line indicates that the team has two level 2 or 3 members and eight level 1B members. Given a team size of 100 the figure indicates 90 level 1A members. Such a ratio of abilities is more suited to a plan-driven approach as the level 2 or 3 members will be spending most of their time working with the level 1A members and hence not free enough to focus on agile development. The dashed line in Fig. 1 indicates that in a team of 15 members there are ten level 2 or 3 and one level 1B, leaving four level 1A members. Such an ability ratio is ideally suited to agile development, as the most experienced team members are largely free to focus on the task of product delivery.

## 2.3 Client Involvement

The *client involvement* factor was added by the authors, along with *team distribution*, as crucial risks affecting the ability of an SSC to adopt an agile development approach. Each software company that has undergone assessment agrees that lack of client involvement is fatal for their agile development efforts. Agile methods advocate close client involvement, a concept that includes client attitude and physical location. A client's involvement in daily stand-up meetings and the day-to-day requirements elicitation and negotiation will make an agile approach more successful. An "agile believer", that is, one who is convinced of the benefits of agile methods, who is not on site at least some of the time will introduce some problems, though not insurmountable ones. This is why an on-site agile believer (*On AB*) is followed by an off-site agile believer (*Off AB*). Both are good clients, *On AB* being slightly better than *Off AB* for agile development. Likewise, an on-site agile sceptic (*On AS*) is someone who may be potentially won over by an agile approach as they get drawn into its successes and is therefore frequently better to have on an agile project than an off-site agile sceptic (*Off AS*). However, clients who are *Off AS* may correspondingly show the strengths required for a plan-driven development approach.

- *On AB* – Clients are on-site and agile believers. This is the ideal when clients are fully persuaded of the agile approach and make themselves available on-site to work with the team.
- *Off AB* – Clients are off-site, but are agile believers. Although off-site, the clients fully understand the nature of agile development and are open to frequent communication.
- *On AS* – Clients are on-site, but are agile sceptics. They may be on-site but they are not convinced about the agile development approach. This is more problematic than Off AB because the relationship is one of resistance rather than facilitation.
- *Off AS* – Same as On AS except the problem is compounded by the clients being off-site.
- *Off Uninvolved* – Not only are the clients off-site, but they want no involvement between providing the initial requirements and getting the right product delivered.

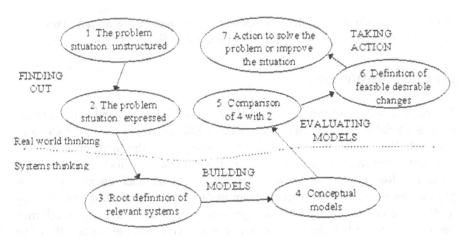

**Fig. 2.** Six critical factors for one team of four people

## 3 Interpretation of Results

In Fig. 1, an example diagram given to all assessment participants, the outer solid line would suggest suitability to a plan-driven approach whereas the inner solid line would suggest suitability to an agile approach. The dashed line suggests a general suitability to an agile approach but with significant risk on the *criticality* factor requiring careful planning.

Figure 2 shows the critical factors for one team of four people. From this and other data a risk mitigation plan and a process improvement plan are developed and reassessed at an agreed time subsequent to the original assessment. However, it was discovered almost incidentally during presentation of the Critical Factors results that some subtle team performance issues were being uncovered and discussed by the team in question. Recognising the subjective nature of the Critical Factors measurements is important, but initial assessments suggest a sufficiently good correlation of subjective rating and actual team performance.

The key to interpreting the team Critical Factors diagram is to look for commonality and variation. Higgs et al. (2005) suggest that team diversity may be beneficial for teams when engaged in non-routine tasks because of the higher level of creative potential. However, they suggest that a number of potential disadvantages are evident, which may outweigh the advantages, e.g., more conflicts, reduced group cohesion, higher risk of communication problems, and so forth. The advice is that homogenous teams are more suited to repeatable and relatively straightforward tasks (Higgs et al. 2005) such as those that comprise most of the software development effort. With regard to the Critical Factors, if there is significant commonality then the team will likely be performing well and maintains a good shared understanding of the project (Coetzer and Bushe 2006). If there is significant variation, as in Fig. 2, then the team will not be performing at an opti-mal level, with team members somewhat unaware of each other.

For example, in Fig. 2 the responses indicated significant differences regarding *team distribution*. This suggests some confusion about the membership of the team. The difference plotted for *team size* supported this conclusion. There was also wide variation in the perceived amount of *requirements churn*. Again, this suggested confusion over what constituted a requirement change, and indicated a weakness in how changes are recorded and made visible to the team. It is also im-portant to determine whether the workload is balanced reasonably well across the team as a lack of balance can decrease morale (Gavin and Mason 2004). *Client in-volvement* also exhibited variance for this team. This suggested that the team was unsure about the identity of the client and therefore who should be contacted for requirements elicitation and negotiation.

There is more commonality shown for *criticality* and *personnel ability*. This can indicate that the team understands the project domain and that it has a realistic assessment of each other's ability. Understanding the project domain will lead to a more suitable software testing approach. Understanding each other's ability will help determine who can solve particular problems and how the project work can be allocated most appropriately.

## 4 Conclusion and Further Work

The advantages of the visual risk assessment technique primarily lie in the ex-planatory power of the Critical Factors diagram. When presented with the results, team members often resolve some of the issues instantly and determine to work on other issues over the ensuing weeks. Such self-directed learning and improvement is welcomed by software companies. From a management perspective, it becomes clear where training needs to be directed and if issues related to client involvement need to be resolved and improved.

Approximately 3 h is required to complete the assessment, with the result being a team-directed improvement path driven by all relevant members of staff. This improvement path will help address the subtle team performance issues uncovered through the visual Critical Factors diagram. Although this research focuses pri-marily on software engineering companies, the critical factors approach could be tailored to many business and engineering domains, with similar beneficial results expected. Ways of linking with more detailed but lightweight process appraisal techniques, such as the Express Process Appraisal (Wilkie et al. 2007; McCaffery et al. 2007), are also being considered.

As noted, the use of the Critical Factors diagram to address team performance issues was almost incidental to the purposes of the adapted ADA. To date, four SSCs have undergone assessment and in each case team performance issues have been exposed. Further work will seek to establish whether there is any valid correlation exhibited between the subjective ratings supplied by individuals and actual team performance. A starting point for this is to use the method adopted by Higgs et al. (2005). Further work may also investigate the performance of software development teams who have undergone some form of improvement by using a nonlinear dynamics model of positivity and connectivity (Losada and Heaphy 2004), both of which have a bearing on agile teams. Another perspective to consider is that of the role that shared mental models have on team effectiveness (Kang et al. 2006).

# References

Boehm, B. (2002) Get ready for Agile methods, with care. *IEEE Computer*, 35(1), 64–69.

Boehm, B. and Tuner, R. (2003a) Rebalancing your organization's discipline and agility. In: F. Maurer and D. Wells. (eds.) *XP/Agile Universe 2003*. Springer-Verlag, Heidelberg, pp. 1–8.

Boehm, B. and Tuner, R. (2003b) Using risk to balance Agile and plan-driven methods. *IEEE Computer*, 36(6), 57–66.

Boehm, B. and Tuner, R. (2004) *Balancing Agility and Discipline – A Guide for the Perplexed.* Addison-Wesley, Reading, MA.

Börjesson, A., Martinsson, F. and Timmerås, M. (2006) Agile improvement practices in software organizations. *European Journal of Information Systems*, 15(2), 169–182.

Ceschi, M., Sillitti, A., Succi, G. and De Panfilis, S. (2005) Project management in plan-based and Agile companies. *IEEE Software*, 22(3), 21–27.

Cockburn, A. (2005) *Crystal Clear: A Human-Powered Methodology for Small Teams.* Addison-Wesley, Reading, MA.

Coetzer, G. H. and Bushe, G. R. (2006) Using discrepancy theory to examine the relationship between shared cognition and group outcomes. *Team Performance Management*, 12(5/6), 155–161.

Cohen, S. G. and Bailey, D. E. (1997) What makes teams work?: Group effectiveness research from the shop floor to executive suite. *Journal of Management*, 23(3), 239–290.

Crosstalk. (2002) *Crosstalk: The Journal of Defense Software Engineering*, 15(10).

Fitzgerald, B., Hartnett, G. and Conboy, K. (2006) Customising agile methods to software practices at Intel Shannon. *European Journal of Information Systems*, 15(2), 200–213.

Gavin, J. H. and Mason, R. O. (2004) The virtuous organization: The Value Of Happiness In The Workplace. *Organizational Dynamics*, 33(4), 379–392.

Higgs, M., Plewnia, U., and Ploch, J. (2005) Influence of team composition and task complexity on team performance. *Team Performance Management*, 11(7/8), 227–250.

IEEE Software. (2003) *IEEE Software*, 20(3).

Iversen, J. H., Mathiassen, L., and Nielsen, P A. (2004) Managing risk in software process improvement: An action research approach. *MIS Quarterly*, 28(3), 395–433.

Kang, H.-R., Yang, H.-D., and Rowley, C. (2006) Factors in team effectiveness: Cognitive and demographic similarities of software development team members. *Human Relations*, 59(12), 1681–1710.

Losada, M. and Heaphy, E. (2004) The role of positivity and connectivity in the performance of business teams: A nonlinear dynamics model. *American Behavioral Scientist*, 47(6), 740–765.

McCaffery, F., Taylor, P. S., and Coleman, G. (2007) Adept: A unified assessment method for small software companies. *IEEE Software*, 24(1), 24–31.

Sawyer, S. (2004) Software development teams. *Communications of the ACM*, 47(12), 95–99.

Sutton Jr., S. M. (2000) The role of process in a software start-up. *IEEE Software*, 17(4), 33–39.

Syed-Abdullah, S., Holcombe, M., and Gheorge, M. (2006) The impact of an Agile methodology on the well being of development teams. *Empirical Software Engineering*, 11(1), 143–167.

Taylor, P. S., Greer, D., Sage, P., Coleman, G., McDaid, K., Lawthers, L., and Corr, R. (2006) Applying an Agility/Discipline assessment for a small software organisation. In: J. Münch and M. Vierimaa (eds.) *Product-Focused Software Process Improvement.* PROFES'2006 – 7th international conference on product focused software process improvement, Amsterdam, The Netherlands, June 2006. Lecture notes in computer science, vol. 4034. Springer-Verlag, Heidelberg, pp. 290–304.

Wilkie, F. G., McCaffery, F., McFall, D., Lester, N., and Wilkinson, E. (2007) A low-overhead method for software process appraisal. *Software Process: Improvement and Practice*, 12(4), 339–349.

# Soft Systems Methodology: An Aid to Agile Development?

**D. Bustard[1] and F. Keenan[2]**

[1]School of Computing and Information Engineering, University of Ulster,
dw.bustard@ulster.ac.uk

[2]Department of Mathematics and Computing, Dundalk Institute of Technology,
frank.keenan@dkit.ie

**Abstract** In principle, an agile approach to information systems development has the potential to improve the efficiency and effectiveness of the development process. One apparent disadvantage, however, is that agile methods tend to be strongly "product-focused", meaning that they place greater emphasis on creating and modifying information systems than on understanding the context in which they are to be used. As a result, higher level requirements and issues can be less well understood. This paper argues for the use of more context analysis in agile development, while acknowledging that any extra effort required must be modest to stay within the general agile ethos. In particular, the paper considers the extent to which soft systems methodology might be a suitable way to perform such analysis. It is concluded that although this methodology is generally perceived as time-consuming, it is essentially sympathetic to the agile approach and is flexible enough to integrate with existing agile techniques.

## 1 Introduction

The agile movement continues to grow in strength (Larson 2006). Obvious indicators include (1) the increasing numbers of papers, books and other publications in the area; (2) the use of the approach by larger organizations – the companywide adoption by British Telecom being particularly significant (Evans 2006); and (3) the spread of the concept into related areas, such as database (Ambler 2003) and information systems development (Conboy et al. 2005; Desouza 2006).

Agile methods emphasise development productivity over process rigour, attempting to deliver business value quickly and accommodate changing user requirements (Abrahamsson et al. 2003). Generally, agile methodologies promote personal communication, collaboration and response to change, over formality in following a defined process and producing comprehensive documentation.

C. Barry et al. (eds.), *Information Systems Development: Challenges in Practice, Theory, and Education, Vol.1,* doi: 10.1007/978-0-387-68772-8_3,
© Springer Science+Business Media, LLC 2009

Agile methods seem to have the potential to improve both the efficiency and effectiveness of software development by using just enough process to achieve the desired result, and refining the software produced through feedback from incremental releases. One apparent disadvantage for information systems, however, is the agile movement's strong focus on the software product, characterised by the principle that "working software is the primary measure of progress" (Beck et al. 2001). By implication, less attention is paid to wider issues that are traditionally important in information systems, such as the influence of the business context in which the software will be used, and an analysis of how the software will affect that context. Typically, such concerns are expected to be handled by following the agile principle that "business people and developers must work together daily throughout the project." Unfortunately, this may mean that developers acquire their understanding of the context in a piecemeal fashion, and so find it difficult to take account of all relevant factors. For example, if developers focus on a single information system in a context where there are multiple systems in use (or required) they may miss opportunities for integration. More important, there is no single shared understanding of system development.

This paper argues for the introduction of an initial analysis to set the context for development, so that all stakeholders start with the same basic collaborative vision of what is required, including an appreciation of some of the business and sociotechnical issues involved. This is still consistent with the highest priority agile principle "to satisfy the customer…" (Beck et al. 2001), as such an analysis can help highlight what is truly needed for a customer to be "satisfied". It is recognised, however, that to be acceptable to the agile community, such analysis must have agile characteristics and build on the existing learning cycle of iterative development.

The paper looks specifically at the use of soft systems methodology (SSM) (Checkland and Scholes 1990; Checkland 1999; Checkland and Poulter 2006; Wilson 1990, 2001; Mingers 2002) as a means of performing the wider analysis. The first section discusses the role of context analysis in agile software development. This is followed by an overview of SSM and then an assessment of its potential role in agile software development.

## 2 Basic Model of Software Development

At the heart of agile development is the notion of software being delivered in evolutionary releases. Each release is designed to provide valuable functionality, with users giving feedback on its effectiveness, which is then taken into account in the design of the next cycle. In general, this is a process of *co-evolutionary change*, as suggested in Fig. 1. Each new release may involve an adjustment to the software, its context or both.

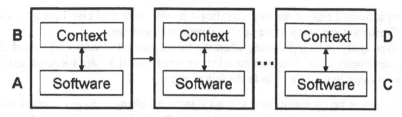

**Fig. 1.** Co-evolutionary software development

The letters on the sides of the diagram (A–D) identify four possible starting positions for analysis (Bustard and Keenan 2005). These are the variations of two choices:

1. Analysis can either be *top-down*, starting with a context analysis (B and D), or *bottom-up*, focusing on the software to be produced (A and C).
2. Analysis can either be *goal-oriented*, developing a vision of what the context (and its supporting software) could or should become (C and D), or *problem-oriented*, focusing on current shortcomings (or opportunities) and determining how they might be addressed (A and B).

The goal-oriented approach seems particularly appropriate for agile software development as it helps define the target to which releases progress. Also, the top-down approach seems necessary for information systems, to ensure a good understanding of the business context for change. Thus, approach D, in effect, appears to be the best for the agile development of information systems. In the agile spirit, however, each of the other options should be examined more closely in case there are circumstances in which one or other would be sufficient. These are discussed in the subsections that follow.

## 2.1 A-Type: Software Focus, Immediate Needs

The focus in the A-type approach to analysis is the definition of software to meet immediate needs. Here, the context is mainly understood in terms of its relevance to that software, taking account of any constraints imposed and identifying the services that need to be provided (software functions). An iterative sequence of implementation phases would be planned if the work could not be completed conveniently in one project.

This is the classic product-focused approach to software development that has been common practice since software was first developed. It is potentially very efficient in that only those aspects of the context that have direct relevance to software development need be investigated and documented. The weakness of the approach is difficulties and vulnerabilities resulting from having only a partial appreciation of the context. In particular, this incomplete understanding can make discussion with stakeholders difficult. Also, it will be harder to identify requirements, with an increased risk of missing significant needs; there will also be a knock-on cost of readjustment when those needs subsequently emerge.

A-type analysis is appropriate when the target context is well understood and future development is either unimportant or appreciated to an adequate extent. Particular cases that apply include the following:

- Software is being maintained and no significant changes have occurred since the original analysis was done. This also applies to the successive implementation of planned increments.
- The software is not expected to evolve and the developers have good understanding of the development context. A relevant example is the production of digital games. Here developers are nearly always games players themselves and have a strong appreciation of not only game requirements but the relative strengths and weaknesses of competitors.
- The software is already well defined. This includes compilers and other software being implemented against standard specifications. This category of application also includes certain types of embedded system where little appreciation of user needs or other context information is required.

In principle, A-type analysis can also be used for simple one-off developments to meet a short-term need. Even here, however, it is usually better to spend a few minutes, at least, considering the context and speculating on the life expectancy of the software, before starting its definition and implementation.

## 2.2 B-Type: Context Focus, Immediate Needs

The initial focus in the B-type approach to analysis is the understanding of the current context in which software is to be developed or enhanced. It can be interpreted as the A-type approach, with a preceding context analysis. This is what has become the traditional information systems approach to software development, involving the analysis and modelling of the environment to provide a context for identifying software requirements. This approach overcomes some of the potential problems associated with the A-type strategy. In particular, the developed appreciation of the context will improve communication with stakeholders and, overall, enhance the quality of the software requirements identified. This has to be balanced, however, against the cost of the analysis and modelling involved.

B-type analysis is appropriate when a context needs to be examined but future development is obvious, of low importance or already defined. Particular cases that apply include the following:

- Software is being developed for an information system and the associated business process is well established; that is, the process is both stable and effective, with no obvious requirement for enhancement or adjustment.
- During planned incremental development, the context is confirmed on each increment to ensure that it has not changed significantly.

- During maintenance, a change to the software is needed because of small context changes.

B-type analysis may not seem necessary in cases where the analyst has experienced similar situations, but Jackson (2004) warns that it is dangerous to ignore the environment (context) before development, even in situations that appear familiar. A brief B-type analysis can confirm such understanding with modest effort.

## 2.3 C-Type: Software Focus, Long-Term Goal

The focus in the C-type approach to analysis is the development of a long-term vision of what the software could or should become. Implementation steps are then defined to advance the software in that direction. Gilb's Evolutionary Delivery method (1988) is the classic example of this strategy. In principle, his approach has been adopted by Extreme Programming (Beck 1999), but the part that is usually given most emphasis is short delivery cycles, with little said about the definition of the target state of the software. Without such a documented view, and an initial plan for the steps involved, the approach effectively degenerates to A-type analysis.

C-type analysis is appropriate in an environment that is stable and well understood, but where it is important to have a plan for how the software might evolve. Particular cases that apply include the following:

- Software is being developed in planned increments and these have to be identified.
- Software is being developed for the marketplace, where the strategy for handling competitors is to have a useful version of the product available as quickly as possible, followed by the timely release of versions that offer significant enhancements.

## 2.4 D-Type: Environment Focus, Long-Term Goal

As indicated, the focus in the D-type approach to analysis is the development of a long-term vision of the context in which the software will be used. This helps determine organisational changes as well as the identification of the desirable supporting technology. Once the target context has been established, it is relatively straightforward to identify corresponding computing support, and from there produce a co-evolutionary plan for incremental change. Note that, initially, this would be in outline form, with the relevant details resolved at the beginning of each increment.

D-type analysis seems like the best general approach for the agile development of information systems. It is particularly valuable when the long-term context for development has to be understood, as, for example, when

- the current context or the need for software is unclear. In practice, that may mean that there are a range of issues in the context that need to be explored, leading to a mixture of organizational and computing changes being identified.
- business process re-engineering is required to make substantial changes to current operational processes and the way that they are supported by technology.

Despite these arguments in favour of a D-type analysis, it is currently the least-used approach. On the positive side, however, it is supported directly by soft systems methodology (SSM), which is a well-established approach to problem-solving in organisations and has been of particular interest to the information systems community (Mingers and Taylor 1992; Stowell 1995; Mathiassen and Nielsen 2000). Commonly, SSM is linked with other analysis techniques to create a multi-methodology approach (Munro and Mingers 2002).

The general impression from the literature, however, is that SSM is more associated with thoroughness than with speed, with analysis appearing to take the order of weeks and months. Indeed, survey responses indicate that a main reason for lack of widespread adoption is that it is so "time consuming" (Mingers and Taylor 1992). This appears to make SSM unattractive for agile software developers, but further analysis is needed before conclusions can be drawn. The next section summarises the SSM process with respect to software development, illustrating the modelling involved through a simple example.

## 3 SSM Analysis: An Illustration

Prior to the recent book by Checkland and Poulter (2006), it was surprisingly difficult to find a simple straightforward account of SSM and how to apply it. There were certainly several texts available that presented the methodology and illustrated aspects of it in the context of "systems thinking", but most novices would have preferred a more direct, mechanical description before being made aware of the subtleties of the approach. The next subsection presents a summary of SSM, based on the experience of the authors, taking the perspective of those wishing to use it as a way of helping to develop information systems or computing systems, in general.

### 3.1 Computing-Oriented Summary of SSM

Essentially, there are three stages in the creation of a co-evolutionary change plan:

1. Understand the context where software seems desirable
2. Understand the need or potential for computing support
3. Define the change plan based on that understanding

SSM is used in the first stage to build an understanding of the context by mod-elling it as a "system". The classic seven-stage model of SSM is illustrated in Fig. 2. It identifies seven activities that are largely followed in sequence, but with some iteration, as necessary. The upper five activities are associated with so-called real world thinking, the first two of which are concerned with building an understand-ing of a *problem situation* (1, 2) (i.e. context), and the other three for deriving change recommendations and taking action to improve that situation (5, 6 and 7). There are also two activities (below the dotted line) concerned with "systems thinking" (3, 4), in which relevant models (*root definitions* and *SSM conceptual models*) are developed to help understand the purpose of the system and the activi-ties involved.

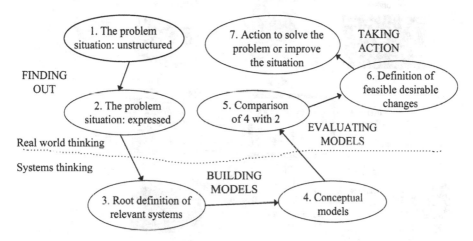

**Fig. 2.** Seven-stage soft systems methodology model

As an example, consider the (fictional) case of a bed and breakfast (B&B) business (The Full Irish!) where it is assumed that there is an initial problem statement of the form "*the owners believe that computing facilities could improve their business by attracting more customers and making it more efficient. Custom-ers might be attracted through greater visibility on the Web and efficiency achieved by having software to facilitate bookings.*" The context here is "*the op-eration of a (B&B) business in a competitive market*" and the "problem" is that "*the business is currently less successful than desired by its owners*".

In the first two activities of SSM (Fig. 2), the creation of a *rich picture* (Lewis 1992) is the traditional way to help document a problem situation. There are no rules for the creation of such diagrams but they tend to identify people associated with the situation (the *stakeholders*), issues of concern, and key activities and places. For example, Fig. 3 shows a rich picture associated with the B&B busi-ness, drawn up using Microsoft PowerPoint.

Ideally this diagram would be prepared by the analyst in consultation with the owner of the B&B and other relevant stakeholders. SSM is not prescriptive, how-ever, and so the use of rich pictures is optional. In other words, the form of modelling is flexible, combining what the analyst finds comfortable with what works most effectively in a given situation.

Once a situation is understood and documented adequately, it can be modelled as one or more *systems*. For each system, a root definition is created to describe its purpose and an SSM Conceptual model used to identify the activities necessary to achieve that purpose. So, for example, for the B&B business, the main system to consider is the one associated with the provision of a successful B&B service. A root definition for this viewpoint might take the following form:

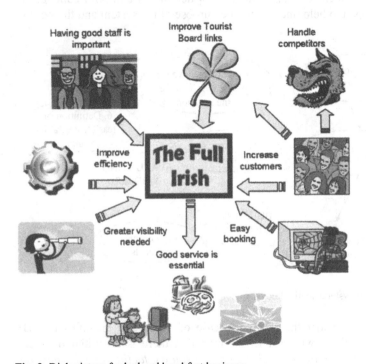

**Fig. 3.** Rich picture for bed and breakfast business

*A system, operated by the B&B owners and other staff, to facilitate those visiting the area by providing accommodation, breakfast and other services, taking account of the expectation of visitors and the need to be competitive with other providers.*

Such a description can be assembled in a largely mechanical way from six components that should be present or implied in any root definition (Checkland 1999). These spell out the mnemonic CATWOE, as indicated in Table 1. The *Weltanschauung*, or viewpoint, identifies "why" a system exists, and the *transformation* defines "what" the system does to achieve its purpose.

In general, there may be several viewpoints to explore in any given situation. For example, a university can be modelled from a teaching, research or enterprise perspective. For a B&B business, however, one viewpoint is sufficient to take account of the main concerns involved.

**Table 1.** Bed and breakfast (B&B) root definition

| Component | Entry | Meaning |
|---|---|---|
| Customers | Visitors | The beneficiaries or victims of a system |
| Actors | B&B owners and other staff | The agents who carry out, or cause to be carried out, the main activities of the system |
| Transformation | Provide accommodation, breakfast and other services | The process by which defined inputs are transformed into defined outputs |
| Weltanschauung | Facilitate those visiting the area | A viewpoint, framework, image or purpose, which makes a particular root definition meaningful |
| Owner | Proprietor of B&B | Those who own a system (have the power to close it down) |
| Environment | Expectation of visitors; competition from other providers | Influences external to a system that affect its operation |

A Conceptual model effectively expands a root definition to identify the necessary activities involved and their interrelationship. For example, one activity in the B&B system is "accept a booking" and another is "take in guests", where the first normally precedes the second. Figure 4 shows a Conceptual model for the B&B business. The activities have been labelled for convenience. The model includes the transformation taken directly from the root definition (A5). This is essentially the central activity of the model. Another important activity is A13, which monitors that the defined *Weltanschauung* (viewpoint) is achieved, taking control action if necessary (TCA), which can affect any other activity in the model. Activities are also added to handle the environmental constraints listed in the root definition (A10, A11) and to cover consequential or implied activities (A1–A4, A6–A9, A12). These may be identified by putting down necessary activities and asking if any preparation activities are needed. Note that all activities start with a verb and that enough text is put into each box to make it self-explanatory. If necessary, individual activities at the top level may be expanded into similar lower-level diagrams. The corollary is that if diagrams become too large, activities can be grouped to hide some of the detail. A final point to note is that although Conceptual models are more formal than rich pictures, there is still considerable flexibility in their creation and representation. Traditionally, for example, the diagrams are usually presented as if they are hand drawn, unlike Fig. 4. This is also an indication that very little tool support has been developed for SSM modelling.

Although Conceptual models are largely informal – in that the meaning of each activity identified is described solely by the text displayed in the diagram, and the linking arrows simply imply relationships between activities with no accompanying labels or explanations – they do provide a good basis for debate about the meaning and implementation of individual activities. This analysis can be facilitated by putting each activity into a table and then assessing it in terms of its potential for improvement and the use of computing technology to achieve that improvement (Hassan et al. 2006).

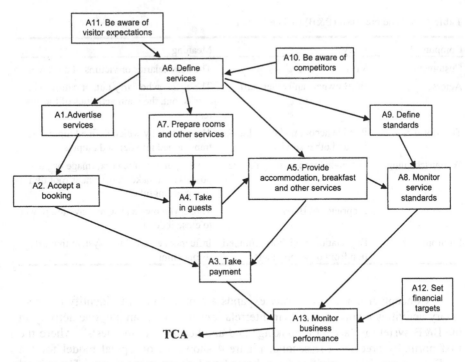

**Fig. 4.** Conceptual model for bed and breakfast business

**Table 2.** Activity analysis for bread and breakfast system

| Activity | Improvement | Computing support |
|---|---|---|
| 1. Advertise services | The business is advertised locally and is in tourist brochures but would benefit from increased visibility. | The business could be advertised on accommodation Web sites and a Web site created specifically for it. |
| 2. Accept a booking | The main way of booking is by telephone. Many people seem to hang up rather than leave a message. | An e-mail booking arrangement (with guaranteed 24 h response) might be introduced; also, a computer-based booking system could keep track of regular customers. |
| 3. Take payment | Arrangements for payment are a bit too lax. Sometimes people cancel at short notice, with income lost. | A finance application could keep track of payments for accounting purposes. |
| 4. Take in guests | Handling arriving guests seems okay. Some arrive very late, but it is not clear how this can be improved. | No special computing support needed but a booking system and/or finance system would be updated on arrival. |

Table 2 shows the first four activities in the Conceptual model for the B&B business. Alongside each activity, in separate columns, are an analysis of what might be done to improve each activity and the potential for computing support. In relation to the first activity, A1 – *advertise services*, for example, it is noted that the visibility of the B&B should be improved and that the use of Web sites might be helpful.

After completing the analysis to identify the opportunities for improvement, it is now relatively straightforward to consider what might be included in a first release. This may be, for example, to set up a Web site and an e-mail address for bookings. This has obvious implications for the owners and staff of the B&B, who would then have to make arrangements to handle the resulting e-mail communication.

## 4 Assessment of SSM in Agile Software Development

The issue of whether or not SSM can be used effectively in agile software development can be broken down into three sub-questions: (1) Is explicit context analysis needed in agile development?; (2) Is SSM an appropriate technique for that analysis?; and (3) Can SSM integrate effectively with existing agile techniques?

### 4.1 Is Explicit Context Analysis Needed?

Section 2 of this paper made the case for a type of analysis that seems best suited to agile development: one that focuses on the environment and takes a long-term view of how the software and its environment are likely to evolve. If that argument is accepted, then SSM is certainly a suitable technique for performing such an analysis.

Traditionally in agile development, context knowledge is usually the responsibility of an "onsite customer", and so using SSM may appear to be an unnecessary overhead. In practice, however, the role of the onsite customer is not always filled adequately; so explicit analysis may be necessary in such circumstances. Also, even if the onsite customer is suitable, using SSM collaboratively could be an effective way of building a shared understanding of the problem situation among the development team.

### 4.2 Is SSM Appropriate for That Analysis?

Section 3 of this paper presented an example of the use of SSM in a simple situation. Its purpose was to provide enough detail to allow someone new to the approach to draw conclusions about its relevance, efficiency and effectiveness. The longevity of SSM suggests that it has a strong basic appeal, but its lack of widespread adoption indicates some difficulty with its use. On reflection, this is perhaps not surprising in that although SSM is an aid to analysing complex situations, achieving meaningful results still relies on the skill of those performing the analysis.

Thus, while many can understand the results of an SSM analysis, fewer can facilitate the creation of insightful models. In practice, this means that it may be much easier to find an onsite customer than a suitable SSM analyst. On the other hand, if this type of analysis is important to agile development, namely, to produce a shared vision of the direction of development, then some process is needed to help create that vision. SSM is particularly strong in this respect, in that many other techniques tend to focus on the analysis of what current exists rather than produce models of a desired position.

## 4.3 Can SSM Integrate Effectively with Existing Agile Techniques?

If it is believed that a visionary context analysis is needed and that SSM is a suitable technique for that purpose, there is still the potential issue of how well SSM fits into an agile development framework. The Agile Manifesto (Beck et al. 2001) identifies four principles of agile development in valuing: (1) individuals and interactions over processes and tools, (2) working software over comprehensive documentation, (3) customer collaboration over contract negotiation, and (4) responding to change over following a plan. There is nothing in SSM that conflicts with any of these principles: it is a strong people-oriented technique, is flexible in its application, has no dependence on tools and uses minimal documentation, as indicated in the models shown in Sect. 3.

Where it is expected to be problematic is in the time taken to perform the analysis itself. It is important to recognise, however, that SSM's reputation as time-consuming is based on the analysis of situations wherein organizational change is the main focus. For agile software development, the organisational context need not be investigated in depth as the main concern is to identify information systems and their interdependence. This will reduce the time required for analysis.

Also, the time taken to produce the models themselves is surprisingly short once a reasonable level of experience and expertise has been developed. The reason for the speed-up is that there are commonly occurring patterns in the models, which can be built upon during analysis. For example, the models produced for the B&B business are largely common to all such businesses and, indeed, have elements that are common to all service providers. Once an analyst is aware of these patterns, SSM Conceptual models can be created almost as quickly as the analyst can put the ideas down on paper (or onto a white board). What takes time is then to refine them for presentation or to reconfigure them if they become too cluttered. Similarly, root definitions can be created quickly through the identification of their six constituent elements.

A further way to improve the cost-benefit of SSM is to link it with an existing agile technique so that SSM models are built upon directly in defining software releases. This option is currently being explored by us through work combining the use of SSM and XP (Keenan and Bustard 2007).

## 5 Conclusion

Behind this paper is a belief that soft systems methodology (SSM) is a significant aid to the improvement of organisations, with an expectation that some of that improvement will almost certainly involve computing technology. The longevity of SSM is evidence of its value, but its lack of widespread adoption also indicates that there are issues to be resolved before business analysts and IT professionals can accept it as a routine technique. The growth of the agile movement can appear to be a disadvantage for such adoption in that SSM is perceived to be time-consuming. As this paper has suggested, however, SSM does not conflict with agile expectations and indeed is rapid to apply once an analyst has acquired knowledge of commonly occurring patterns in the activities of organisations.

More fundamentally, the paper argues that for effective agile development it is necessary to appreciate the target context towards which evolutionary development proceeds. This is not simple to determine without methodological help, and SSM has been precisely developed for this purpose.

Current work on linking SSM and XP is expected to provide further insights into the potential of using SSM for routine agile software development, together with a clarification of the benefits and limitations involved.

**Acknowledgements** This work was undertaken through the Centre for Software Process Technologies, which is supported by the EU Programme for Peace and Reconciliation in Northern Ireland and the Border Region of Ireland (PEACE II).

## References

Abrahamsson, P., Warsta, J., Siponen, M. and Ronkainen, J. (2003) New directions on agile methods: A comparative analysis. In Proceedings of ICSE 2003, pp. 244–254.

Ambler, S. (2003) *Agile Database Techniques: Effective Strategies for the Agile Software Developer*. Wiley, New York.

Beck, K. (1999) *Extreme Programming Explained*. Addison-Wesley, Reading, MA.

Beck, K. et al. (2001) Principles behind the Agile Manifesto. agilemanifesto.org/principles.html (last accessed on 14 April 2007).

Bustard, D.W. and Keenan, F. (2005) Strategies for systems analysis: Groundwork for process tailoring. In Hinchey, M. et al. (eds), 12th IEEE international conference and workshops on the engineering of computer-based systems (ECBS '05), Greenbelt, Washington, USA, 4–7 April 2005. pp. 357–362.

Checkland, P. (1990) *Soft Systems Methodology in Action*. Wiley, New York.

Checkland, P. (1999) *Systems Thinking, Systems Practice (with 30-year retrospective).* Wiley, New York.

Checkland, P. and Poulter, J. (2006) *Learning for Action: A Short Definitive Account of Soft Systems Methodology.* Wiley, New York.

Conboy, K., Fitzgerald, B. and Golden, W. (2005) Agility in information systems development: A three-tiered framework. In Baskerville, R. et al. (eds), *Business Agility and Information Technology Diffusion.* IFIP TC8 WG 8.6 international working conference, Atlanta, Georgia, USA, 8–11 May 2005. Springer, Heidelberg.

Desouza, K.C. (ed) (2006) *Agile Information Systems: Conceptualization, Construction, and Management.* Butterworth-Heinemann, Woburn, MA.

Evans, I. (Summer 2006) Agile delivery at British Telecom. Methods and Tools, 20–27.

Gilb, T. (1988) *Principles of Software Engineering Management.* Addison-Wesley, Reading, MA.

Hassan, S., Bustard, D.W. and McSherry, D.M.G. (2006) Soft systems methodology in autonomic computing analysis. Systemist, 28(2), 106–115.

Jackson, M. (2004) Seeing more of the world. IEEE Software, 21(6), 83–85.

Keenan, F. and Bustard, D.W. (Feb 2007) Enhancing Extreme Programming (XP) with environment analysis. Proceedings of software engineering, Innsbruck, Austria, Feb 2007. ACTA Press, Calgary, AB, Canada, pp. 72–77.

Larson, D. (2006) Agile alliance survey: Are we there yet? www.infoq.com/articles/agile-alliance-survey-2006 (last accessed on 14 April 2007).

Lewis, P.J. (1992) Rich picture building in the soft systems methodology. European Journal of Information Systems, 1(5), 351–360.

Mathiassen, L. and Nielsen, P.A. (2000) Interaction and transformation in SSM. Systems Research and Behavioural Sciences, 17(3), 243–253.

Mingers, J. (2002) An idea ahead of its time: The history and development of soft systems methodology. Systemist, 24(2), 113–139.

Mingers, J. and Taylor, S. (1992) The use of soft systems methodology in practice. Journal of the Operational Research Society, 43(4), 321–332.

Munro, I. and Mingers, J. (2002) The use of multimethodology in practice – Results of a survey of practitioners. Journal of the Operational Research Society, 369–378.

Stowell, F.A. (ed) (1995) *Information Systems Provision: The Contributions of SSM.* McGraw-Hill, London.

Wilson, B. (1990) *Systems: Concepts, Methodologies and Applications,* 2nd ed. Wiley, New York.

Wilson, B. (2001) *Soft Systems Methodology: Conceptual Model Building and Its Contribution.* Wiley, New York.

# Methodology Usage by Virtual Information Systems Development Teams

**Brenda Mullally[1] and Larry Stapleton[2]**

[1]Computing, Mathematics and Physics Department, Waterford Institute of Technology,
bmullally@wit.ie

[2]Waterford Institute of Technology, Computing, Mathematics & Physics Department,
lstapleton@wit.ie

**Abstract** Organisational globalisation has strengthened the popularity of virtual information systems development (ISD) teams, by maximising the availability of resources. However, few studies investigate the practices of virtual ISD teams. This paper presents findings from a survey on the use of ISD methodologies by virtual ISD teams. Virtual ISD teams appear to employ the use of methodologies to a greater extent than do colocated teams. Teams employed a structured approach to the ISD process, following a methodology with clear emphasis on the importance of documentation and constant communication between team members. Conversely, ISD literature on colocated teams presents a view that methodologies are not wholly used and where they are used, a tailoring of the methodology takes place. The virtual teams involved in this study did not engage in a tailoring of methods during development. Most teams utilised an internally developed methodology specific to the organisation. The results lead to recommendations for future research into virtual ISD teams.

## 1 Introduction

Advances in technology and the expansion of the Internet have facilitated significant changes to organisational structures. A virtual team is one of these new organisational structures. A team is a collection of people working on interdependent tasks to collectively achieve a common goal for which they are accountable (Furst et al. 1999). A virtual team is one which accomplishes its goal using technological means to communicate while distributed across multiple locations (Lipnack and Stamps 2000). Management of a virtual team requires an understanding of the impact time and space separation have on the team members (Connaughton and Daly 2004).

Information systems development (ISD) demands specialised resources at a minimum cost to the customer. A virtual team reduces costs by facilitating access

C. Barry et al. (eds.), *Information Systems Development: Challenges in Practice, Theory, and Education, Vol.1*, doi: 10.1007/978-0-387-68772-8_4,
© Springer Science+Business Media, LLC 2009

to distanced resources and limiting the need to travel. In today's ISD environment the team must work interdependently across organisational and geographic boundaries. Much research exists on coordinating this type of work (Cramton 2002; Kraut et al. 2002; Mortensen and Hinds 2002) and the impact computer-mediated communication has on the communication practices of virtual teams (McGrath and Hollingshead 1994; Sproull and Kiesler 1991; Daft and Lengel 1986). However, little research specifically addresses ISD teams. Those studies that do, concentrate on the team processes such as knowledge exchange (Walz et al. 1993), coordination of activities (Ovaska et al. 2003; Faraj and Sproull 2000), and communication (Layman et al. 2006; Andres 2002). According to Andriessen and Verburg's (2004) model for the analysis of virtual teams, the context dimension of a virtual team determines the quality of group processes. The context dimension includes people, tools, tasks, structures, culture and the setting. A gap exists in the literature addressing the contextual dimension of virtual ISD teams. This paper addresses that gap through investigation of the methodology practices of virtual ISD teams.

The paper is structured as follows. The first section describes the virtual information systems team environment and the theoretical background to the use of ISD methodologies. The second section details the research methodology, followed by the third section containing the findings. The paper concludes with a discussion of the findings and directions for future research.

## 2 Virtual Information Systems Development

ISD is a complex process that requires business, technical, quality and testing expertise. This expertise may exist within an organisation but at different locations. Consequently, a virtual team can facilitate access to these resources. For example, Microsoft and Dell now seek developers with experience working in multicultural and multinational development teams, along with project managers who demonstrate the ability to lead a virtual team (http://www.irishjobs.ie Web search, April 2007). Ultimately, managers, users, analysts, programmers and testers must communicate and coordinate effectively across locations to succeed in ISD (McManus and Wood-Harper 2003; Mathiassen and Purao 2002). However, the understanding of how these virtual ISD teams operate is limited. According to Jackson (1999), the assumption that virtual teams work in a way similar to collocated teams is mistaken.

### 2.1 Virtual Team Challenges

Computer-mediated communication tools (such as video conferencing, e-mail, group support systems, intranets and online chat) present challenges to the users.

Messages can be misunderstood, and behaviour misinterpreted (Cramton 2001); increased conflict (Mannix et al. 2002) and poor levels of trust are common (Kanawattanachai and Yoo 2002; Meyerson et al. 1996). Online co-ordination, communication and collaboration on complex ambiguous tasks are difficult when conducted across a distance (Ahuja and Galvin 2003; Yoo and Alavi 2001; McKenny et al. 1992). The reliance on computer-mediated communication means that team messages lack the physical and auditory cues present in face-to-face communication. Without these cues, it is necessary to be more obvious and explicit when communicating online (Fiore et al. 2003). Kiesler and Cummings (2002) theorize that additional structured management may produce more effective virtual teams. In support of their theory, the research of Lurey and Raisinghani (2001) found that the formalisation of work processes positively relates to virtual team performance. In the case of virtual ISD teams, ISD methodologies should support the team's effort to communicate and coordinate effectively. However, the literature lacks research on the methodological practices of virtual ISD teams. This study addresses that gap by investigating the use of methodologies, their purpose, and their benefit to virtual ISD teams.

## 2.2 Methodology Usage

The development environment has changed considerably since the inception of ISD. The move from large colocated teams of programmers to smaller multidisciplinary distributed teams presents new challenges. For clarity, the term methodology will be used in this paper to mean "a set of goal-orientated procedures supported by tools and techniques" (Iivari and Hirschheim 1996). ISD methodologies based on traditional organisational structures and processes do not reflect the current need for adaptability and flexibility. To be competitive, organisations must react quickly to changes in their business environment. Consequently, there is a need for faster turnaround times to meet the demands of the business. Businesses therefore opt for small-scale projects such as the customisation of existing systems (Fitzgerald 1998).

Methodologies can introduce rigour and scientific method into the development process (Baskerville et al. 1992). However, in practice, studies show that methodologies can restrict the natural evolution of the project development (Ovaska 2005). Fitzgerald (1998) found that almost 60% of respondents in his study of colocated teams did not use a development methodology. In a similar study, Chatzoglou and Macaulay (1996) found that 47% of the project teams surveyed did not use a methodology. Research also shows that methodologies are used in principle but in reality ignored or adopted in a piecemeal fashion (Ovaska 2005; Nandhakumar and Avison 1999). It is believed that no one methodology can support all the development needs of an organisation; to this end, more than one methodology is utilised (Russo et al. 1996). Literature supports the view that a mixing of methodologies and the pragmatic use of methodologies are to be employed (Coleman 2005; Clarke and Lehaney 2000; Truex et al. 2000; Wynekoop and Russo 1997). Mixing of methods may produce a true representation of the real world rather than narrowing the field of vision by using a single methodology. However, Ovaska (2005) reported the need for excellent communication between team members in order to utilise methodologies successfully. Mixing methodologies across distances without face-to-face contact may be very difficult.

Recent methodological advancements provide agile methodologies as an alternative to traditional methodologies. Agile methodologies focus on the fast production of code through iterative and incremental software development. Examples include extreme programming (XP), dynamic system development methodology (DSDM) and Scrum and the Agile Unified Process (Turk et al. 2005; Ambler 2002). All agile methodologies emphasise close collaboration between the developer and the client. Frequent face-to-face communication is seen as more efficient than written documentation. It is unclear how appropriate this type of methodology is to the virtual context.

As discussed in Sect. 2.1, virtual teams encounter difficulties in relation to communication, coordination and collaboration. This section examined the use of methodologies by colocated teams. In many cases, no methodology was in place or a pragmatic mixing of methodologies occurred. This research posed the following key questions: What methodology practices exist for virtual ISD teams? Who determines the use or non-use of methodologies by virtual ISD teams? And what types of projects do virtual ISD teams undertake?

Based on the literature, the following questions were tested through the survey:

- RQ1. How do virtual ISD teams use ISD methodologies to support the management of the team?
- RQ2. Do virtual ISD teams pragmatically choose and mix methodologies that suit the situation at hand during development?
- RQ3. Do the majority of virtual ISD teams engage in the customisation of existing systems?

The following section presents the research methodology used by this study, detailing the instrument and measures applied.

# 3 Research Methodology

A cross-sectional study where measures were taken at a single point in time formed the basis for the research (Robson 2002). As with many studies within the information systems field, a random sampling process was not possible. Access to professionals in virtual ISD teams was challenging. Purposeful sampling allowed the selection of suitable projects across a variety of industries and countries. Of the 20 organisations approached, 13 became involved. Each team met the following criteria. First, a virtual team should have completed an ISD project within the previous 12 months. Second, a minimum of three team members had to complete the survey. Finally, one member of each team was a project leader, enabling access to data on project scheduling, budget and team characteristics.

The following quantitative and qualitative techniques were used to confirm that the sample gathered was valid and that response bias was kept to a minimum:

- The online survey was available to the respondents any time day or night, reducing participant error.
- All team members were targeted, with at least three from each team required to complete the survey to ensure consistency of answers across a team.
- Each team received a summary report. It contained a description of the project, the methodologies used and a request for validation and feedback.

A potential sample of 214 participants arose from the 15 teams. A total of 60 surveys were completed. In many Internet surveys, it is extremely difficult to calculate a realistic sample size. The formula of De Vaus (2002) allows ineligible and unreachable respondents to be removed from the sample size. There were 8 contract employees and 80 unreachable employees due to job transfers and reassignment to new virtual teams. The formula yields a return rate of 47.6%, which accurately reflects the number of people that were accessible and agreeable to partake in the study. The 60 respondents represent a diverse group of virtual team members.

Face-to-face or telephone interviews with ISD professionals located in different time zones would have been problematic. An online survey accommodated participants and maximised the number of teams involved. Participants completed the survey at their convenience during or after work; their only requirement was an Internet connection. Section one of the survey captured background information necessary for differentiation in analysis. Section two captured ISD methodology usage through a six-part Likert scale influenced by studies previously carried out on colocated teams (Ovaska 2005; Fitzgerald 1997). Structured and open-ended qualitative questions provided insights into the methodology practices of the teams.

# 4 Findings

Table 1 summarises background information on the ISD project teams. The 15 teams existed across one or more countries. There were 3 teams in four countries, 1 team in three countries, 9 teams in two countries and 2 teams in one country. The distribution of industry category is similar to that found in Fitzgerald's study (1998). All but three teams came from large organisations of more than 250 employees. Each of these large organisations conducted in-house development. The remaining three teams came from small- to medium-sized software development companies. Project teams were predominately small, with 9 of the teams surveyed having less than 10 members. Teams consisted of members distributed across 2, 3 or 4 locations, with the majority having no more than three locations. Team members held a variety of positions. Of the 60 respondents, 15 held a management or team leader role, 14 were software developers, 14 analysts, 7 testers and the remaining 10 held other roles such as operations and technical support.

**Table 1.** Background information on information systems development project teams

| Team size | (<10) | (10–30) | (30–60) | |
|---|---|---|---|---|
| (no. of members) | 9 | 3 | 3 | |
| No. of locations | (2) | (3) | (4) | |
| | 11 | 1 | 3 | |
| Job category | (Analyst) | (Manager/leader) | (Testing/quality) | (Software developer) |
| | 14 | 15 | 7 | 14 |
| Industry category | (Service/ communications) | (Construction/ manufacturing/ distribution) | (Consultants/ software house) | (Financial/ insurance/ real estate) |
| | 1 | 5 | 5 | 2 |
| Organisation size | (<20) | (21–100) | (101–250) | (250+) |
| (no. of employees) | 1 | 1 | 1 | 10 |

## 4.1 ISD Methodological Practices

Research question 1 asked how methodologies provide support to virtual ISD. It is clear from the findings that the majority of the teams surveyed utilise some form of methodology. Table 2 shows that only 2 teams did not employ a methodology. None of the teams followed a single commercial methodology developed by a third party. The remaining 13 teams created their own methodology. Of these, 6 created a methodology based on one or more commercial methodologies, and 7 created a bespoke methodology. Many team members described their methodology as a tool for "global consistency". The methodology "provided processes, roles and responsibilities", and "ensured same standards were used in all sites". Team members described the purpose of their methodology through the terms *planning, scheduling, standards, framework*, and *formalise*. The methodology supported collaboration with distanced team members through "a single reference source for information". Information was "sent back and forth efficiently" and stored so that "a common language and set of processes... allowed team members to understand each other". This study found that ISD methodologies provided a common method for design and deployment of information systems across an organisation. The methodologies supported the management of the virtual ISD team through structure and control of communication, collaboration and coordination.

**Table 2.** Methodology usage by virtual ISD teams

|  | Commercial method | Internal (based on 1 method) | Internal (based on >1 method) | Internal (bespoke) | No formal method | *Total* |
|---|---|---|---|---|---|---|
| New system | 0 | 3 | 1 | 1 | 0 | 5 |
| Customisation |  | 1 | 1 | 6 | 2 | 10 |
| *Total* | 0 | 4 | 2 | 7 | 2 | 15 |

Research question 2 concerned methodology mixing in the virtual ISD context. Table 3 summarises the use of other methods during the development project. Eleven teams did not mix methodologies during development and a further 2 teams only did so occasionally. Mixing of methodologies occurred only to a small degree during development. Primarily, it took place at the creation of the internal methodology. One third of the teams used an internally developed methodology based on one or more commercial methodologies. Only 1 team that engaged in mixing methodologies during development chose the methods to mix. The remaining teams used methods determined by management, or the client.

**Table 3.** Methodology mixing

| Were other methods used during the ISD project? | Frequency |
|---|---|
| Not at all | 11 |
| Occasionally | 2 |
| Neutral | 1 |
| Often | 1 |
| Always | 0 |
| *Total* | 15 |

*ISD* information systems development

Research question 3 concerned the type of development project undertaken by virtual ISD teams. Ten teams developed new functionality for an existing or a newly implemented packaged system. The remaining 5 teams consisted of software development companies creating new systems for specific customers. The customisations conducted by the majority of teams involved systems such as SAP, Oracle, enterprise learning management system (ELMS), and proprietary applications for payroll, human resources and technical support. Table 2 shows that of the 10 teams involved in customisations, 6 used an internally developed methodology not based on any commercial methodology and 2 used no formal methodology. Conversely, 3 of the 5 teams that created new systems used an internal methodology based on a commercial methodology.

The majority of teams followed a structured approach to the development or customisation of the information system. Many of the internally developed methodologies in this study incorporated business standards. These included the Capability Maturity Model Integrated for Software (SEI/CMMI), the International Organisation for Standardisation (ISO9126) and the Institute of Electrical and

Electronics Engineers (IEEE) standards. Other methods used included unified modelling language (UML), bug tracking systems, formal methods and compliance with the Sarbanes-Oxley Act. Team members stated that adherence to the methodology was important and beneficial to the project success. The methodology provided a framework upon which all team members could work.

## 5 Discussion

One of the key research questions posed by this study concerned the methodological practices of virtual ISD teams. The literature suggested that virtual ISD teams may use methodologies to place structure on the process. The findings of this study support this theory. Project teams managed their communication, collaboration and coordination using a structured approach through an ISD methodology. The consistent use of documents by all team members throughout each stage in the development process placed rigour and structure on the information exchanged, the interactions between team members, and the coordination of tasks. Documentation provided clear specifications of process and product. Distribution of team members across countries can result in language and cultural barriers. Team members stated that the methodology helped "reach agreement", "clarity of definition, scope and execution", "accuracy", and "sharing information". These findings are in line with the literature discussed in Sect. 2.1, indicating that greater structure and management are a priority for effective virtual teams. Only 2 of the 15 (13%) project teams did not use a methodology. This is significantly lower than the values found by studies on colocated teams such as Chatzoglou and Macaulay's (1996) 47% and Fitzgerald's (1998) 60%. The difference may be attributed to the virtual context of the study; or perhaps new trends have emerged in the use of methodologies in ISD.

The second research question addressed methodology mixing in virtual ISD teams. Past research presented in Sect. 2.2 found that colocated ISD teams include members who adapt and construct the rules to fit their needs. Ovaska's (2005) study highlighted the need for good communication between team members in order to best utilise methodologies. Mixing methodologies by virtual teams during development would require even greater communication abilities. This study found that 11 teams (73%) did not mix methodologies during development and a further 2 teams only did so occasionally. This contradicts findings in colocated ISD team literature. Russo et al. (1996) found that 60% adapted their methodology to suit the project in hand. Wynekoop and Russo (1993) found that 89% of organisations reported adapting systems development methods on a project-by-project basis. Coleman (2005) found that 66% of organisations adapted their software processes depending on the customer, situation, team size, product model and participating staff. Pragmatic mixing of methodologies did not take place during the development cycle of the ISD teams involved in this study. However, mixing did occur prior to the project inception. The internally developed methodology in many cases comprised of more than one methodology.

This study also investigated the type of development project undertaken by virtual teams as posed by the third research question. Fitzgerald (1998) reported that 40% of colocated projects were customisations. This study found a significant increase where 10 (63%) of the virtual ISD teams surveyed were customising existing systems. This increase may be attributed to the virtual context of the study, or perhaps a general reduction of new development projects over the past decade has occurred. There are also indications that the type of project may influence the use of methodologies. Those teams involved in the development of new systems relied on the guidance of a commercially developed methodology. Two of the new systems development teams used agile methods as the basis for their internal methodology. Those teams involved in the customisation of existing systems employed internal methodologies, which in most cases were not based on a commercial methodology. Organisations may develop bespoke methodologies that suit their type of development.

The methodological practices of virtual ISD teams differ somewhat from those of colocated teams. Ultimately, the methodologies created appeared to fall within the structured approach. Further investigation may lead to a greater understanding of the implications of these findings. The following section offers directions for future research and concluding remarks.

# 6 Conclusion

The use of a structured methodological approach with no pragmatic mixing of methods is a clear indication that virtual teams do not operate in the same manner as colocated teams. This structured approach includes the use of a commercially based methodology for new project development and an internally developed methodology for the customisation of packages or existing systems. A comparison of the trends in methodology usage by colocated and virtual teams would add to this study. To complete the comparison, it would be necessary to investigate the type of development projects undertaken by colocated ISD teams. The decision to use a methodology by a virtual ISD team occurs at an organisational level, removing the involvement of the project team. Consequently, little mixing of methodologies occurs during the development cycle. Identification of the appropriateness of the chosen methodology could provide insights into this phenomenon. Many of the teams used internally developed methodologies. Further investigation into the design of internally developed methodologies is necessary, particularly in the virtual context. New development projects appear to use commercial methodologies as the basis for development. In this study, those teams showed a preference towards Agile methodologies. It is however unclear how appropriate Agile methods are to the virtual development environment, as few studies address their suitability (Armour 2007; Layman et al. 2006). Future longitudinal studies are needed to examine the use of methodologies during the life of a virtual ISD project. By further understanding the creation and application of internally developed ISD methodologies, virtual ISD teams may benefit from this form of structured management. For the success of virtual ISD teams more research in the area is essential.

# References

Ahuja, M. K. and Galvin, J. E. (2003). Socialization in virtual groups, Journal of Management, Vol. 29, Iss. 2, pp. 161–185.

Ambler, S. (2002). Agile development best dealt with in small groups, Computing Canada, Vol. 28, Iss. 9, pp. 9.

Andres, H. P. (2002). A comparison of face-to-face and virtual software development teams, Team Performance Management, Vol. 8, Iss. 1/2, pp. 39.

Andriessen, J. H. E. and Verburg, R. M. (2004). 'A model for the analysis of virtual teams', In Virtual and Collaborative Teams. Process, Technologies and Practice, Edited by Godar, S. H. and Ferris, S. P., Idea Group, London.

Armour, P. G. (2007). Agile... and Offshore, Communications of the ACM, Vol. 50, Iss. 1, pp. 13–16.

Baskerville, R., Travis, J. and Truex, D. (1992). 'Systems without method: The impact of new technologies on information systems development projects', In The Impact of Computer Supported Technologies on Information Systems Development, Edited by Kendall, J. E. and Kendall, K. E., Elsevier, Holland.

Chatzoglou, P. D. and Macaulay, L. A. (1996). Requirements capture and IS methodologies, Information Systems Journal, Vol. 6, pp. 209–225.

Clarke, S. and Lehaney, B. (2000). Mixing methodologies for information systems development and strategy: A higher education case study, Journal of Operational Research Society, Vol. 51, pp. 542–556.

Coleman, G. (2005). 'An empirical study of software process in practice', In Proceedings of 38th Hawaii International Conference on System Sciences, IEEE, Hawaii.

Connaughton, S. L. and Daly, J. A. (2004). 'Leading from afar: Strategies for effectively leading virtual teams', In Virtual and Collaborative Teams. Process, Technologies and Practice, Edited by Godar, S. H. and Ferris, S. P., Idea Group Publishing, London.

Cramton, C. D. (2001). The mutual knowledge problem and its consequences for dispersed collaboration, Organization Science, Vol. 12, Iss. 3, pp. 346.

Cramton, C. D. (2002). Finding common ground in dispersed collaboration, Organizational Dynamics, Vol. 30, Iss. 4, pp. 356–367.

Daft, R. L. and Lengel, R. H. (1986). Organisational information requirements, media richness and structural design, Management Science, Vol. 32, Iss. 5, pp. 554–571.

De Vaus, A. D. (2002). Surveys in Social Research, Allen & Unwin, Crows Nest, NSW, Australia.

Faraj, S. and Sproull, L. (2000). Coordinating expertise in software development teams, Management Sciences, Vol. 46, Iss. 12, pp. 1554–1568.

Fiore, S. M., Salas, E., Cuevas, H. M. and Bowers, C. A. (2003). Distribution coordination space: Toward a theory of distributed team process and performance, Theoretical Issues in Ergonomics Science, Vol. 4, Iss. 3/4, pp. 340–364.

Fitzgerald, B. (1997). The use of systems development methodologies in practice: A field study, Info Systems Journal, Vol. 7, pp. 201–212.

Fitzgerald, B. (1998). An empirical investigation into the adoption of systems development methodologies, Information and Management, Vol. 34, pp. 317–328.

Furst, S., Blackburn, R. and Rosen, B. (1999). Virtual team effectiveness: a proposed research agenda, Information Systems Journal, Vol. 9, Iss. 4, pp. 249–269.

Iivari, J. and Hirschheim, R. (1996). Analyzing information systems development: A comparison and analysis of eight IS development approaches, Information Systems, Vol. 21, Iss. 7, pp. 551–575.

Jackson, P. J. (1999). Organizational change and virtual teams: strategic and operational integration, Information Systems Journal, Vol. 9, Iss. 4, pp. 313–332.

Kanawattanachai, P. and Yoo, Y. (2002). Dynamic nature of trust in virtual teams, The Journal of Strategic Information Systems, Vol. 11, Iss. 3/4, pp. 187–213.

Kiesler, S. and Cummings, J. N. (2002). 'What do we know about proximity and distance in work groups? A legacy of research', In *Distributed Work*, Edited by Hinds, P. J. and Kiesler, S., MIT Press, London.

Kraut, R. E., Fussell, S. R., Brennan, S. E. and Siegel, J. (2002). 'Understanding effects of proximity on collaboration: Implications for technologies to support', In *Distributed Work*, Edited by Hinds, P. J. and Kiesler, S., MIT Press, London.

Layman, L., Williams, L., Damian, D. and Bures, H. (2006). Essential communication practices for Extreme Programming in a global software development team, Information and Software Technology, Vol. 48, pp. 781–794.

Lipnack, J. and Stamps, J. (2000). *Virtual Teams. People working across boundaries with technology*, Wiley, New York.

Lurey, J. S. and Raisinghani, M. S. (2001). An empirical study of best practices in virtual teams, Information and Management, Vol. 38, pp. 523–544.

Mannix, E. A., Griffith, T. and Neale, M. A. (2002). 'The phenomenology of conflict in distributed work teams', In *Distributed Work*, Edited by Hinds, P. J. and Kiesler, S., MIT Press, London.

Mathiassen, L. and Purao, S. (2002). Educating reflective systems developers, Information Systems Journal, Vol. 12, Iss. 2, pp. 81–102.

McGrath, J. E. and Hollingshead, A. B. (1994). *Groups Interacting with Technology*, Sage, California.

McKenny, J. L., Zack, M. H. and Doherty, V. S. (1992). 'Complementary communication media: A comparison of electronic mail and face-to-face communication in a programming team', In *Networks and Organizations: Structure, Form, and Action*, Edited by Nohria, N. and Eccles, R. G., Harvard Business School Press, Boston.

McManus, J. and Wood-Harper, T. (2003). Information systems project management: The price of failure, Management Services, Vol. 47, Iss. 5, pp. 16.

Meyerson, D., Weick, K. E. and Kramer, R. M. (1996). 'Swift trust and temporary groups', In *Trust in Organisations: Frontiers of theory and research*, Edited by Kramer, R. M. and Tyler, T. R., Sage, Thousand Oaks, pp. 166–195.

Mortensen, M. and Hinds, P. J. (2002). 'Fuzzy teams: Boundary disagreement in distributed and collocated teams', In *Distributed Work*, Edited by Hinds, P. J. and Kiesler, S., MIT Press, London, pp. 283.

Nandhakumar, J. and Avison, D. E. (1999). The fiction of methodological development: A field study of information systems development, Information Technology and People, Vol. 12, Iss. 2, pp. 176–191.

Ovaska, P. (2005). 'Working with methods: Observations on the role of methods in systems development', In *Information Systems Development: Advances in Theory, Practice and Education*, Edited by Vasilecas, O., Springer, Heidelberg.

Ovaska, P., Rossi, M. and Marttiin, P. (2003). Architecture as a coordination tool in multi-site software development, Software Process Improvement and Practice, Vol. 8, pp. 233–247.

Robson, c. (2002). *Real World Research. A Resource for Social Scientists and Practitioner-Researchers*, Blackwell, London.

Russo, N. L., Hightower, R. and Pearson, J. M. (1996). 'The failure of methodologies to meet the needs of current development environments', In Proceedings of 4th Annual Conference on Information Systems Methodologies, British Computer Society Information Systems Methodologies Specialist Group, University College Cork, Ireland, 12–14 Sept. 1996.

Sproull, L. and Kiesler, S. (1991). *Connections. New Ways of Working in the Networked Organization*, MIT Press, London.

Truex, D., Baskerville, R. and Travis, J. (2000). Amethodical systems development: The deferred meaning of systems development methods, Accounting, Management and Information Technology, Vol. 10, pp. 53–79.

Turk, D., France, R. and Rumbe, B. (2005). Assumptions underlying agile software-development processes, Journal of Database Management, Vol. 16, Iss. 4, pp. 62.

Walz, D. B., Elam, J. J. and Curtis, B. (1993). Inside a software design team: Knowledge acquisition, sharing and integration, Communications of the ACM, Vol. 36, Iss. 10, pp. 63.

Wynekoop, J. L. and Russo, N. L. (1993). 'System development methodologies: Unanswered questions and the research-practice gap', In Proceedings of International Conference on Information Systems, Orlando, Florida.

Wynekoop, J. L. and Russo, N. L. (1997). Studying system development methodologies: An examination of research methods, Information Systems Journal, Vol. 7, pp. 47–65.

Yoo, Y. and Alavi, M. (2001). Media and group cohesion: Relative influences on social presence, task participation, and group consensus, MIS Quarterly, Vol. 25, Iss. 3, pp. 371–391.

# Research of the Use of Agile Methodologies in the Czech Republic

**A. Buchalcevova**

Department of Information Technologies, University of Economics, Prague, Czech Republic,
buchalc@vse.cz

**Abstract** Agile methodologies have recently been widely gaining ground. We assumed another situation in the Czech Republic. Therefore we decided to conduct our own research based on a survey. The research objective was to determine the rate of agile approaches usage and practical experience with these approaches in companies in the Czech Republic. This paper presents the results of that research.

## 1 Introduction

Agile software development evolved in the mid-1990s when some "lightweight methodologies" were defined and used as a part of the reaction against "heavyweight" methodologies. Since 2001, when the Agile Manifesto was created, these methodologies, such as Extreme Programming, Feature-driven Development, Scrum, Crystal, Dynamic Systems Development Method, and others were denoted as agile. Agile software development is an iterative process that allows small development teams to build software functionality in a collaborative environment that is responsive to business change. Development is done in short iterations (typically weeks to months) ending with working increment of software.

Advantages of the agile software development include faster time-to market, lower development costs and better quality. But we must realize that agile methodologies do not suite to all projects. According to agile evangelists, books and case studies, agile methodologies are more suitable when requirements are emergent and rapidly changing, the corporate culture supports negotiation, people are competent, skilled and trusted and projects are implemented by small teams with fewer than 20–40 people. Other limitations of agile software development, according to Tur et al. (2002), are as follows: limited support for distributed development environment, subcontracting, building reusable artefacts, developing safety-critical, large and complex software.

Although we saw broad adoption of agile practices worldwide, we assumed another situation in the Czech Republic. Our previous research made in 2002

C. Barry et al. (eds.), *Information Systems Development: Challenges in Practice, Theory, and Education, Vol.1*, doi: 10.1007/978-0-387-68772-8_5,
© Springer Science+Business Media, LLC 2009

exposed that the use of software development methodologies in our country was high below the world's level. We defined some research questions. First, we wanted to know whether the situation with low level of formal methodologies usage had changed with expansion of agile approaches. Second, when we decided to conduct our survey in 2005, only few researches about the use of agile methodologies had been presented, which were evidently not focused on the Czech environment. Third, we wanted to examine the extent of knowledge about agile methodologies in the practical software development. From the time I presented principles of agile methodologies first at the Objects 2002 Conference in Prague (Buchalcevova 2002), agile topics have appeared more often in the programs of software conferences in the Czech Republic. After many English books, Czech original books about agile methodologies came out (Buchalcevova 2005; Kadlec 2004). But we did not have feedback from practical software development. Therefore we decided to conduct our own survey, which was based on these assumptions:

- A substantial part of IT professional community has a low level of knowledge about software development methodologies.
- A substantial part of IT companies in the Czech Republic does not implement any formal methodology.
- Agile methodologies are used by small companies and small teams.

This paper presents the results of the survey that was carried out in 2006 as part of the dissertation (Leitl 2006).

## 2 Research Characteristics

The research objective was to determine the rate of agile approaches usage and practical experience with these approaches in companies in the Czech Republic. The aim was to carry out the research for a wide spectrum of companies involved in software development.

## 2.1 Questionnaire

The research was carried out over a period of about 6 months, from December 2005 to April 2006, and was based on a survey. We prepared a questionnaire consisting of 18 questions. Each question contained the following:

- The exact wording of the question and possible answers.
- The reason why this question was included in the questionnaire.
- Information on how the answer would influence the overall agility index (see Sect. 3.1) and its calculation.

As we assumed a limited awareness of methodologies in general, and agile methodologies in particular, the questionnaire was supplemented with a presentation of agile principles and the questions were formulated in such a way that they would be comprehensible to respondents with low level of knowledge on methodologies. The questionnaire thus not only was a part of the research but it also provided some basic information about agile methodologies and contributed to their publicity. The respondents were contacted by direct mailing and then they were offered a personal appointment to fill out the questionnaire. They could choose to have the company data processed anonymously. The whole questionnaire ran to about 15 pages, and so I present only its abbreviated form in the appendix to this paper.

## 2.2 The Structure of the Sample

Fifty companies involved in software development were chosen from the database of companies maintained by the Czech Society for System Integration (CSSI) and from the "Top 100 companies in the Czech Republic". These companies were addressed by e-mail or were personally visited. Although the response rate was relatively high (42%), the final sample was only 21 companies.

The respondents represented companies of all sizes, small development companies with 4–15 employees (10 companies), middle-sized companies with 16–70 software developers (4 companies), and big companies with more than 70 developers (7 companies). Seventeen companies had software development as their main activity, of which 9 focused primarily on custom-made software development, 4 specialized in commercial off-the-shelf solutions and 4 developed solutions primarily for their own needs.

## 3 Research Results

## 3.1 The Rate of Agile Methodologies Use

To compare the rate in which agile methodologies or practices were used in individual companies, we have defined an indicator called the "total agility index". This indicator has evaluated software development in a complex manner according to the significance given to all fundamental principles of the agile development. We have defined the algorithm for calculation which is based on answers to questions 1, 2, 4–6. In the appendix to this paper, where the survey instrument is presented, you can see impact on agility index calculation for each question, e.g., number of points according to each offered answer. These values are then counted up and in this way we get the "total value of agility", which ranges from 19.2 (no agile approach) to 148.2 (maximum agility). Owing to the greater clarity, we present the agility index in a percentage form: 0% stands for non-agility development and 100% represents totally agile development (see Fig. 1). Most respondents scored between 48 and 62%, which means a balanced compromise between agile and traditional development, with moderate dominance of agile features. Calculating the agility index for a certain company enables to draw a general conclusion about whether the company uses agile approaches and whether it is more or less agile in comparison to other companies.

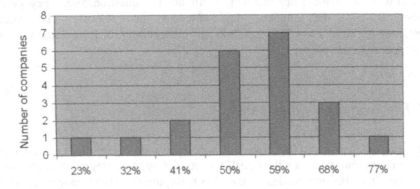

**Fig. 1.** The agility index for companies in the sample

## 3.2 Methodologies Used in Software Development

The research objective was to find out what specific methodologies, traditional but particularly agile, had been used in software development companies. Figure 2 shows the results.

The research has confirmed the assumption that most Czech companies do not use any public methodology. Of 21 respondents, 3 stated that they do not use any methodology, and these were not just small companies. Of 21 companies, 12 use company standards. As for agile methodologies, Extreme programming was used in 1 company.

The questionnaire included the question whether the company is considering any alteration to its existing methodology or introducing a methodology if it has not yet used any. Only in two cases did the respondents say that they were considering such an alteration. To sum up, companies (at least those included in the investigated sample) can hardly be expected to adopt more agile approaches.

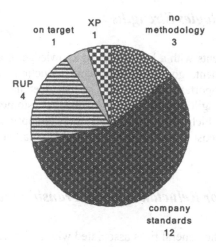

**Fig. 2.** Use of methodologies

## 3.3 Level of Knowledge about Agile Methodologies

The research was based on the assumption that the level of knowledge about methodologies in general and about agile methodologies in particular, is relatively limited. This assumption was confirmed (see Fig. 3). Five respondents stated that they had a basic knowledge of agile methodologies; 8 respondents stated a low level of knowledge; 4 respondents considered their knowledge advanced and the same number admitted this is the first time they have heard about agile methodologies. Given the fact that the respondents were carefully chosen and they had either university degree in informatics or working experience in this field, the result is rather unsatisfactory.

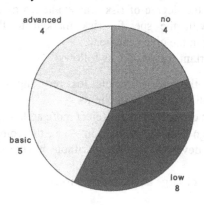

**Fig. 3.** Level of knowledge of agile methodologies

## 3.4 Agile Methodologies Strengths

Generally, the respondents with a lower level of knowledge of agile methodologies stated rapid development, good feedback, cost reduction and flexible change processing as most important advantages. On the other hand, respondents with better knowledge of agile methodologies stressed customer involvement and reduced error rate, which they considered more important than quantitative characteristics such as cost reduction and faster time-to market.

## 3.5 The Reasons for Reluctance to the Transition to Agile Concept

First we investigated the general risks associated with an implementation of a new methodology or replacing a current methodology (see question 13). By far the greatest risk, that was stated, is that the new mental approach might not be accepted by all employees. People often tend towards stereotypes and accept new methods reluctantly and with certain self-denial. Another risk that was perceived as significant was the fear of the customer outflow after application of a new methodology. On the other hand, the risk of high costs connected with the transition to a new methodology was perceived as rather low. This risk could be relatively easily prevented by creating substantial monetary reserves and by a thorough planning of the transition.

Then we investigated the risks associated with an implementation of an agile methodology (see question 14). The respondents could check off multiple offered reasons (risks) leading to the rejection of the more agile concept of development or directly to rejection of the agile methodology implementation. They could also add additional risks they considered serious in that case. Figure 4 indicates both the general reception of risks by all respondents, as well as the differences between more agile and more traditional companies (according to the agility index). The respondents were given the opportunity to check off multiple offered reasons, and therefore, the degree of risk was evaluated as the proportion of the number of answers with the specific risk marked to the total number of respondents responding in the given category.

The four most important reasons are as follows:

- Legal reasons – i.e., the risk of financial loss resulting from the lower level of legal protection of all contracts with clients.
- The risk that current customers might reject more agile approaches.
- Low stress on design and documentation – i.e., the companies fear that they will not be able to develop effectively without having carried out a detailed analysis and design.
- Lower applicability for large and complex projects.

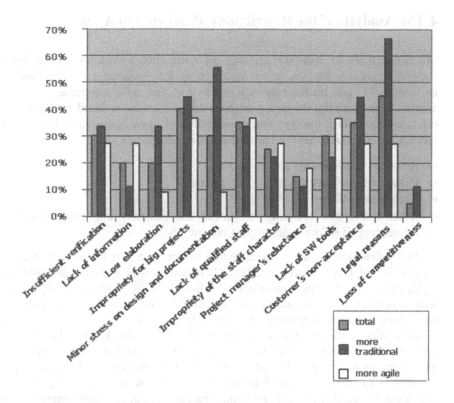

**Fig. 4.** Risks of agile software development

The results show a substantial difference in the perception of some risks between more agile and more traditional companies. The most perceptible difference is for "Minor stress on design and documentation", "Legal reasons" and "Insufficient verification". These are generally promoted drawbacks of agile development that are perceived especially by more traditional companies that do not have enough knowledge and practical experience with agile methodologies.

A somewhat strange result is presented for issues such as "Lack of information", "Lack of qualified staff", "Impropriety of the staff character", "Project manager's reluctance", and "Lack of SW tools", where the companies that are more agile are reporting greater objections than do the companies that are more traditional. We can explain it in such a way that companies that have used some agile practises perceive more strongly the lack of qualified staff with necessary character features and the lack of software tools. When the survey was conducted, there was only limited software tools support for agile development. Nowadays the situation is much better as some software tools such an agile development lifecycle management platform V1: Agile Enterprise from VersionOne or Microsoft's new MSF integrated with Visual studio have started to appear.

# 4 The Analysis of the Restrictions of Moving to Agile

The research results show that one can see quite often some agile approaches in Czech companies. On the other hand, from the evaluation of the level of knowledge of agile methodologies it is obvious that agile approaches are often applied unconsciously. We analyzed respondent answers in detail to deduce the principal restrictions that prevent a wider use of agile approaches. For greater lucidity we structured these restrictions into four categories:

- Restrictions influencing the developers
- Restrictions influencing the project managers
- Restrictions influencing other roles
- Other restrictions operating not inside the company but rather externally influencing all software-developing companies

In the first category the main restriction is represented by the unwillingness or incapability of programmers to extend their activities in software development. Agile development requires developers with wide skills, from the ability to deal with customers, to detail analysis, design, implementation and testing. There are two main paths to overcome this restriction. In the first order, it is the responsibility of universities to educate widely skilled developers. They have to take this into account when building their computing curricula. Also, companies have their own responsibility of permanent staff education. The second path consists in systematic approach to staff self-education and knowledge sharing, which can be achieved, e.g., through patterns application, pair programming, team code revisions and knowledge management.

As for the "project managers influencing restrictions", we can name the fear of negative consequences of the simplification and speed-up of the analysis and design stage, again insufficient qualification and not corresponding character of developers. Minor stress on design is generally presented drawback of the agile development that is perceived especially by traditionalists and is often misinterpreted. The agile development does not mean uncontrolled development but highly disciplined process. Agile is based on permanent design and code quality improving instead of big design up front. Some methodologies, such as Feature-driven Development, have placed design phase producing overall domain model in the beginning of development lifecycle.

Into the category "Restrictions influencing other roles", we can include maybe the most important restriction of agile methodologies use – e.g., the risk of agile approach rejection on the customer side. This risk presents a real barrier against agile approaches adoption, which is perceived worldwide. Therefore most agile projects, even the greatest one – e.g., project Eclipse, are realized in the field of the open source development and the commercial off-the-shelf solutions. In the field of the custom-made software development, we must carry out systematic work on the customer side to improve customer maturity in the sense of customer knowledge of agile methodologies and their advantages, realizing the necessity of customers' involvement in software development and their co-responsibility for project success. That is also the responsibility of universities, whose target must be to produce business people well qualified in cooperation with software developers.

Other restrictions in this category are, e.g., the fear of loss of the competitiveness after the replacement of development methodology and the risk of the lower level of legal protection of the relationships with customers. The "loss of competitiveness" risk was stated only by more traditional companies (see Fig. 4), and we deduce that these respondents have hardly any knowledge of agile principles, as the aim of agile approaches is to support the change during the development process and in this way to contribute to keep or to increase the competitive level. As to legal restrictions, legal issues might to be a permanent problem in IS/ICT. Law is always delayed compared to technology, which is true especially for countries such as the Czech Republic, where information technology progress was blocked for a long time. ICT sector must drive change in legislation to support technology and methodology changes.

We can state the low level of knowledge of formal methodologies generally, and agile methodologies especially, as restrictions externally influencing the software development field in the Czech Republic. I think one of the reasons for this is the language. Czech Republic is a non-native-English-speaking country, where knowledge of the English language, especially in the older part of the population, is not very good. Most methodologies originate from English environment. Books about methodologies are mostly written in English; many agile conferences take place in USA, and for Czech companies and universities, it is difficult to travel there. As with the restriction of low-skilled developers, there is also the responsibility of universities to include special courses about software development methodologies into their computing curricula and that of companies to carry on the permanent staff education. If we want to increase the level of knowledge of agile methodologies that was indicated in our survey, students must be taught agile approaches to software development. I personally think that it is worth to teach traditional approaches first and then to introduce agile approaches.

## 5 Comparisons with Other Studies

As I have mentioned earlier, when we decided to conduct our survey in 2005, only few researches about the use of agile methodologies had been presented. Almost at the same time, Agile Alliance and VersionOne conducted the survey focused on using agile methodologies. Results of that survey presented at the Agile 2006 Conference show that agile methodologies are gaining ground on a worldwide scale. On the basis of about 1,000 responses from people in small to large corporations, it was found that 75% of the companies surveyed deploy agile processes (Larsen 2006).

Ambler also performed an Agile Adoption Rate Survey in March 2006 and presented his early findings at Agile 2006 Conference and then complete results in the paper (Ambler 2006). He repeated the same survey in March 2007. Ambler's survey was sent out to the combined mailing lists from *Dr. Dobb's Journal* and Software Development and reached a large number of people (4,232). Ambler (2006) summarizes the survey results as "Agile Works in Practice. Agile software development methods and techniques are gaining acceptance within the IT industry. Adoption of agile techniques (65%) is further ahead than adoption of agile methods (41%), but that should come as no surprise – most organizations choose to perform software process improvement on an incremental basis." The most popular agile methodologies are Extreme programming and Scrum, but other methodologies such as the Agile MSF, Agile Unified Process, and, in particular, FDD had strong showings. These survey results seem to be very optimistic, but we must realize that the links to that survey are provided by a number of agile sources, and thus the survey would tend to reach only those who either are using agile or have knowledge of agile methods.

# 6 Conclusion

To sum up the results of our survey and consecutive analysis, we can conclude that the use of agile methodologies and approaches in the Czech Republic is only at the starting line and much more development projects could work in a more agile manner. On the other hand, this late-movement to agile could bring some advantages, as agile methodologies have matured recently and have been scaling along a number of dimensions, especially geographic distribution and global development, team size, project size, mission criticality, and involvement with legacy systems. Companies that switch to the agile development later can use the above-mentioned researches in order to choose the methodology that is most used in the world. They can use even the software tools supporting agile development that have appeared recently. In addition, the much larger source of information in the form of books, papers, panel discussions and conferences are available nowadays.

It is necessary to draw attention to the limitations of our research, especially to the dimension of the examined sample (21 companies). For this reason, it is not possible to deduce general conclusions about the situation in the Czech Republic. Nevertheless, the results of the research reflect, in my opinion, the situation of the software development practice in our country, and it is necessary to learn a lesson from it and to take into consideration especially the deduced conclusions.

These conclusions, especially the identification of restrictions preventing the greater expansion of agile approaches and the means to overcome them, are applicable to other countries as well. It is also possible to use there the survey instrument and the way of the assessment of the agility rate on the basis of the agility index.

The number of agile projects in the world is increasing every quarter of the year, and therefore it is appropriate to repeat the research of the use of agile approaches. In this context, our research represents a very good starting basis.

I am convinced that the number of agile projects would nowadays be definitely higher than that presented in our research.

# References

Ambler, S. (2006) Agile software development methods and techniques are gaining traction. http://www.ddj.com/dept/architect/191800169

Buchalcevova, A. (2002) Agile methodologies, In *Objects 2002 conference, Prague, 2003* (pp. 53–61).

Buchalcevova, A. (2005) *Methodologies for IS development and operation, categorization, agile methodologies, methodology patterns*, Grada, Prague.

Kadlec, V. (2004) *Agile programming*, Computer Press, Prague.

Larsen, D. (2006) Agile Alliance Survey: Are we here yet? http://www.infoq.com/articles/agile-alliance-survey-2006

Leitl, M. (2006) *Research of the use of agile methodologies in the CR*, diploma thesis, University of Economics, Prague.

Tur, D., France, R. and Rumpe, B. (2002) Limitations of agile software process. http://www.agilealliance.org/system/article/file/1096/file.pdf

# Appendix – The Survey Instrument

The questionnaire consisted of 18 questions, which are presented here in an abbreviated form. Offered answers are listed here only if they have an impact on the agility index.

1. Order the four parameters of a software development project (time, quality, cost, project scope) according to their priority and to how important you think it is to observe them. Please start with the most important parameter. *Impact on the agility index*: Total of values according to Table 1.

**Table 1.** Values for the agility index calculation

| Parameters order | 1 | 2 | 3 | 4 |
|---|---|---|---|---|
| Time | 3 | 2 | 1 | 0 |
| Cost | 3 | 2 | 1 | 0 |
| Scope | 0 | 1 | 2 | 3 |
| Quality | 0 | 0 | 1 | 0 |

2. How do you deal with requirements changes?

(a) Changes are rejected (*0 points*)
(b) All changes are under the change management (*1 point*)
(c) Small changes are implemented, bigger ones under the change management (*4 points*)
(d) Only coarse grained requirements initially, further changes are accepted (*6 points*)
   *Impact on the agility index:* Number of points for a certain answer in brackets.

3. Do you use any software development methodology? (one of listed answers)
   *No impact on the agility index*
4. Do you adapt your methodology to individual projects (e.g. according to the project scope or criticality)? (multiple answers allowed)

(a) No adaptation. (*0 points*)
(b) We do not adapt it because our projects have similar character (*1 point*)
(c) We scale our manner of work for large projects to more formality (*2 points*)
(d) We make our manner of work for small projects more flexible (*1 point*)
(e) We adapt our manner of work according to the particular client (*2 points*)
(f) Our methodology itself provides adaptation. (*2 points*)
   *Impact on the agility index:* Total of points for certain answer (max 3 points)

5. What principles are considered crucial in your methodology? If you are not using any specific methodology what do you personally consider crucial? To each question you can attach from 1 point (*not included*) to 7 points (*CSF for the methodology*)

(a) Sequence of development phases (analysis → design → implementation → deployment → maintenance) (*indicator weight = 1*)
(b) Big design up front (*indicator weight = 1*)
(c) Sophisticated change management (*indicator weight = 0.3*)
(d) Sophisticated requirements management (*indicator weight = 0.8*)
(e) Frequent delivery of functional software versions (*indicator weight = 1*)
(f) Source code quality (*indicator weight = 0.6*)
(g) Start programming as soon as possible (*indicator weight = 0.8*)
(h) Continuous testing (*indicator weight = 1*)
(i) Detailed project documentation ( (*indicator weight = 1*)
(j) Effective communication among team members and user (*indicator weight = 0.4*)
(k) User is integrated into development process (*indicator weight = 1*)
(l) People motivation (*indicator weight = 0.6*)
(m) Decision power (*indicator weight = 1*)
(n) Maximum compliance with original requirements (*indicator weight = 1*)
(o) User satisfaction (*indicator weight = 0.3*)
(p) Methodology adaptation (*indicator weight = 0.6*)

*Impact on the agility index:* The assessment of the answers to questions which are important for traditional methodologies (a, b, c, d, i, n) is reversed. Values are then multiplied by an indicator weight and totaled up.

6.  What are the weaknesses of the methodology you are using? To each question you can attach from 1 point (*not a problem*) to 7 points (*critical problem*)
(a) Low level of detail (*indicator weight = 0.3*)
(b) Large scope, very complicated (*indicator weight = 0.5*)
(c) Low level of this methodology knowledge (*indicator weight = 0.2*)
(d) Low flexibility (*indicator weight = 1*)
(e) User is not involved (*indicator weight = 1*)
(f) Methodology is concentrated mainly on technology (*indicator weight = 0.3*)
(g) Methodology demands highly qualified people (*indicator weight = 0.7*)
(h) No description of SW processes (*indicator weight = 0.2*)
(i) High skilled project manager (*indicator weight = 0.7*)
(j) Slight stress on design quality (*indicator weight = 0.5*)
(k) Strong stress on design quality (*indicator weight = 0.8*)

*Impact on the agility index:* The assessment of the answers to questions which are important for traditional methodologies (b, d, e, f, k) is reversed. Values are then multiplied by an indicator weight and totaled up.

7.  Do you know the terms "agile methodologies" or agile approaches to software development, and do you know what they mean? (one of listed answers). *No impact on the agility index.*
8.  What do you think the advantages of agile methodologies are? *No impact on the agility index.*
9.  What do you regard as being the disadvantages of agile methodologies? *No impact on the agility index.*

10. Assess the methodology you use in your company (if you do not use any specific methodology, assess your style of software development) according to the degree of its agility. *No impact on the agility index.*
11. Are you considering using any specific methodology in the future (if you do not use any) or are you considering any alteration to your current methodology? (one of listed answers). *No impact on the agility index.*
12. Assess the possible future methodology according to the degree of its agility. *No impact on the agility index.*
13. What risks do you see in the transition to a new methodology? (multiple answers allowed). *No impact on the agility index.*
14. What risks can you see in using agile approaches and what are your reasons for refusing them? (multiple answers allowed). *No impact on the agility index.*
15. Agile methodologies often have more significant demands on people. Do you consider your employees' level of knowledge and readiness to agile development to be sufficient? *No impact on the agility index.*
16. Agile methodologies often lead to a significant increase in the "creative freedom" of programmers. Do you consider your employees' character to be sufficient? *No impact on the agility index.*
17. Based on your experience, is there any difference between Czech and foreign employees as far as the use of agile methodologies is concerned? Choose the relevant option and give a brief description of where you see any differences. If possible, give a simple example from your practice. *No impact on the agility index.*
18. Do you consider the method and quality of software development methodologies education at Czech universities to be sufficient? If you do not, please give a brief explanation of any possible deficiencies. *No impact on the agility index.*

# Method Deployment in Small- and Medium-Sized Firms: Addressing the Organizational Context

T. Päivärinta[1], E.Å. Larsen[2], L. Ingulfsvann and Ø. Kristiansen

Department of Information Systems, School of Management, Agder University College, Grimstad, Norway
[1]tero.paivarinta@hia.no, [2]even.larsen@hia.no

**Abstract** This paper presents results from a grounded theory analysis of method deployment in five small- and medium-sized system development organizations. The study confirms some observations from earlier research, such as the impact of project size and individual attitude and experience of developers. In addition, organizational factors, such as type of business, development goals, history of method use, employee turnover, geographical distribution and customer relationship, may explain method deployment decisions.

## 1 Introduction

Information systems development (ISD) researchers have discussed the role of methods in systems and software development work for decades. Traditionally, formal systems development methods (SDMs) were regarded as normative prescriptions for development work (e.g., Humphrey et al. 1991; Jarke et al. 1994). However, in the last 15 years, a few researchers have started to examine the actual use and deployment of methods (Stolterman 1992; Fitzgerald 1997; Whitley 1998; Khalifa and Verner 2000; Fitzgerald et al. 2002, 2003; Hardgrave et al. 2003; Madsen et al. 2006; Päivärinta et al. 2007). Among them, the traditional view on prescribed method deployment or formal, even situational, method engineering (Brinkkemper et al. 1996), in which developers would rationally elaborate local SDMs to fit the project contingencies at hand (Kumar and Welke 1992), has been largely abandoned. Research shows that in many cases methods undergo a great extent of pragmatic adaptation in use (Stolterman 1992; Fitzgerald 1998; Päivärinta et al. 2007). One stream of research has even suggested that so-called amethodical systems development prevails in contemporary ISD organizations. That is, methods have no prescribed role at all, and ISD practice emerges purely through contextual interaction and improvisation of individual developers to meet the project exigencies (Truex et al. 2000).

C. Barry et al. (eds.), *Information Systems Development: Challenges in Practice, Theory, and Education, Vol.1*, doi: 10.1007/978-0-387-68772-8_6,
© Springer Science+Business Media, LLC 2009

Introna and Whitley (1997) address the importance of "background knowledge", which affects success (or failure) of SDMs in practice. In this regard, contemporary research has largely focused on the viewpoint of individual systems developers, on how they perceive the relevance of methods and utilize them in their work. Prominent examples of this include works on the relationship between developer experience in relation to modes of SDM use, or determinants of developer intentions to use methods (Hardgrave et al. 2003). The education of future professionals, into "reflective systems developers", with regard to SDMs has also received attention (Mathiassen and Purao 2002). Alongside the developer-centric unit of analysis, a few case studies have discussed ISD project exigencies in relation to method adoption, where the unit of analysis has been a project (e.g. Madsen et al. 2006).

Few studies discuss about method deployment in the organizational context. The exceptions include work by Fitzgerald et al. (2003, 2006), which focused on internal software development in large IT industry organizations. Päivärinta et al. (2007) studied how a particular method was deployed and evolving in a consulting organization. However, these studies mainly focus on how methods have been tailored and evolved in the organizations in question, rather than study issues in the background of decisions to adopt and deploy methods in the first place.

Even fewer reports focus on method deployment in small- and medium-sized enterprises (SMEs). Whitley (1998) gives a sketch of three contemporary Web developer organizations, two of them being pretty small ones, giving insight into the reason they practice mostly amethodical development of Web sites. These organizations had rather explicit grounds not to use methods: the nature of systems developed (Web-based in the 1990s) did not fit to the traditional methods, or the designers were allowed to be creative and free with regard to hypermedia design. Our personal motivation to study determinants of method deployment in ISD SMEs resides in the fact that a great proportion of candidates trained in our institution have their first jobs in small software firms – and it is thus useful for our training to know more about the actual role of method knowledge and method deployment in such companies.

Hence, we focus on the question: Which issues relate to deployment of ISD methods in small- and medium-sized systems development firms and consultancies?

The next section summarizes the research process. Section 3 summarizes the results and Sect. 4 discusses them in light of previous research. We conclude with suggestions for future research in Sect. 5.

## 2 Research Process

We chose the grounded theory approach (Strauss and Corbin 1990), because of a lack of previous theory of method deployment in ISD SMEs, and because of our hopes of finding issues not previously studied in research done in bigger firms (such as Khalifa and Verner 2000; Hardgrave et al. 2003). Two researchers had

access to five firms, listed in Table 1. The firms were selected based on accessibility – without any preknowledge of their method deployment. The only criterion
was the fit to the European Union definition of SMEs (less than 250 employees
and annual turnover less than €50 m). One target organization (A) may be categorized as "micro", three (B–D) are small, and one company (E) is medium-sized.
The interviewees were experienced developers and managers (Table 1).

**Table 1.** Target organizations

| Firm | Employees | Business | Turnover 2004 (€) | Interviewees |
|------|-----------|----------|-------------------|--------------|
| A | 6, one site | Small Web-based e-business solutions | 370,000 (3 m NOK) | • Sr. developer (13 years of work experience) |
| B | 8 (Norway, one site) + 10 (India) | Logistics solution for electricity networks | 1 m (8 m NOK) | • Developer (5 y exp.) • Development manager (well-experienced) |
| C | 42, one site | System development and administration | 4.8 m (38 m NOK) | • Developer (8 y exp.) • Project manager (30 y experience) |
| D | 25 (Norway, one site) + 3 (Serbia) | Systems development and consulting | 1.8 m (13.5 m NOK) | • Developer and project manager (12 y exp.) • Developer (13 y exp.) |
| E | 184 (in Norway altogether, 4 in the local office in question) | Systems development and con-sulting | 25 m (200 m NOK) | • Developer/consultant (8 y exp.) • Deveoper/consultant/ project manager (8 y exp.) |

Nine interviews (Table 1) were tape-recorded and transcribed. We focused on
the theme of utilizing methods for systems development work in the organization.
The interviews relied on open questions covering the general-level idea of the ISD
methods held by the interviewees, whether and how methods are used in the organization, pros and cons of method use, and the concrete use of methods in actual
projects.

This paper reports results from two data analysis procedures: open coding and
axial coding (Strauss and Corbin 1990). The open-coding phase produced conceptual categories of issues we found to relate to method deployment (or nondeploy-
ment) in the organization in question. The axial coding divided further "categories
to their subcategories, linking categories at the level of properties and dimensions"
(Strauss and Corbin 1990, p. 123). However, we do not yet have sufficient data for
selective coding, by which we could propose a well-elaborated theory. This would
require further, targeted, research on the selected relationships so far only weakly
indicated by the data. However, we summarize the analysis at the level of a few
emerging concepts and their dimensions, which already gives food for thought in
relation to the previous literature and can suggest new avenues for future research
efforts.

# 3 Results

## 3.1 Company A

Company A focuses on implementing small-scale Web-based e-business systems for their customers. The company aims at quick deliveries with no support.

"It is better for us to be done with the customer when the project is over. It is really awkward with previous customers who call for fixes."

The company has low employee turnover. They manage risk by avoiding complex projects. No explicitly defined method is used, beyond some checklists and practices for pricing and contracting. The company offers three predefined solution categories to their customers, priced at around €1,500, €4,500, and €9,000. Many of the customers contact the company through a marketing consultancy, with which they cooperate. In case the customer needs do not fit with the predefined solution types, the organization mainly would not take the project in question.

"If we're unsure, we just price ourselves out."

The attitude on methods is generally such that they could be usable in big projects, which, however, are outside the very business scope of the company.

"I am not for use of methods at all... It is time-consuming. It is really difficult to coordinate more than one programmer at a time. It takes a lot of time."

Recently, the company has become concerned about the quality of the delivered product, and is considering more systematic testing practices before the delivery.

## 3.2 Company B

Company B is a software vendor in the energy sector, providing a logistics system for electrical power networks. In addition to 8 employees at the Norway headquarters, the company has a team of 10 software developers in India. This seems to require more standardized specifications between the sites in the future, which, however, are not seen to replace person-to-person interactions to solve the emerging problems.

Employee turnover has been very low. The company interacts closely with their main customers, developing and maintaining the system continuously.

"We're not project-oriented, we're product oriented, and our product has a life-cycle beyond one project... in addition, we have deliveries of add-on modules... but the functionality will live on." (Development manager)

The educational background of most of the developers in the company is in engineering, and the very concept of SDMs has remained remote to them. The interviewees stated clearly that the company did not have any predefined method in use.

"We use no formal method tools, such as UML to coordinate the development process." (Development manager)

"There are no formal guidelines here... every developer is actually pretty free. I try for my part to think that if I disappear, that the others could understand the things I have done." (Developer)

The development work focuses on reuse of components. The interviewees reported that they had previously used a design tool, but dropped it out because of its cost.

"We have used some, for example Rational Rose, for a period. The cost and benefit to use such a tool is clearly an element..." (Development manager)

To summarize, company B also could be as well characterized as practicing mainly "amethodical" systems/software development. They consider experience of developers more valuable than explicit adherence to methods. However, they have been trying to elaborate company-based practices for product specifications. Prototyping has a prominent role in the work practices as well.

"You will always use a method... if you say you don't use one, you will use one anyhow... For example, design of a user interface starts with a suggestion of how it should look like, then we go through iterations and hearing process to find out if this is how we wish to use it or if our customers are happy with the way we do it, so that there is an iteration which results in a clearer specification of what it should look like." (Development manager)

## 3.3 Company C

Company C was started by former IBM employees when IBM closed the local office. It provides consultancy and organizational implementation on a niche product family. The company has a handful of big, long-term customers (including IBM). Employee turnover is low, as the company is now owned by the employees. The projects focus on product updates, consulting, and implementation for the customers.

The firm has an explicit in-house method in use, which is largely based on the standard practice from their IBM time.

"We use it from requirements specification, design, implementation, to testing. It is from A to Z."(Developer)

"The big difference to IBM is that we can be more flexible here. If something in our quality system does not work, so we just change it right away and tell everyone that now that routine is changed."(Project manager)

The method, in turn, is a part of a quality system that documents the system development activities, and provides a model for project coordination and templates and techniques for deliveries. The projects are typically involving 4–5 persons for a few months, whereas the biggest projects have included 15 employees. People can also work across projects. The interviewees highlighted that method use leads to better quality and project coordination and fewer errors in the system.

"We have few errors and good quality. Customers are happy." (Developer)

However, the interviewees addressed that the method use should not become an end in itself. Moreover, the organization reflects continuously over the method, and the method-in-use is decided in detail for each project. A group of 3–4 persons periodically discuss the standard method and decide whether any changes are necessary.

"We have not found a good method which covers the whole cycle. When we come to code and development, we think the methods are at their best. There should be a method which would follow up the whole way, but it is not easy to find." (Project manager)

In all, we can conclude that company C simply has continued their method-oriented approach inherited from the previous mother corporation.

"I cannot see any cons to use methods, so far the method wouldn't be there only for its own sake." (Project manager)

## 3.4 Company D

Company D is a small consultancy, where 17 people work on systems development projects. In addition, the company has recently hired a small team of 5 programmers from Serbia. They have specialized on two technical platforms to provide tailored application development and system integration projects for their customers. Business is project based, mostly one-off projects for varying customers.

"Our core competence is consulting...We do it all from requirements analysis, system development, design, to delivery. We deal with every possible technology in existence... but mostly .NET or Java." (Project manager)

The projects vary in size, ranging from 1,000 to 2,000 man hours. Earlier, poor markets forced the organization to involve in smaller projects, which they can now avoid.

Although having some established organizational practices in place, e.g., for project coordination, version control, document storage, and code documentation, the organization has not deployed any formal or commercial method.

"Yes, we use work methods, but it is actually in a form of... we do not use any specific method beyond the experience of the person in question... For example, I and a couple of colleagues had experience of a general method, and then agreed to do it like this. We have the design phase and then we start with system development, then we have testing etc... But ultimately we want to have control over development by having early deliveries... a form of incremental delivery."

They have considered adoption of commercial methods. However, the methods seemed to limit project flexibility, as the project characteristics vary from one context to another. Another problem is that requirements change during the project, which was seen as incompatible with the methods. There had been discussions about a "more flexible method", suggested by one of the consultants and to be tried out with a customer willing to test it. Methods are also seen to have positive implications for project coordination, whereas they may have negative effects on speed.

To summarize, company D mostly represents the "amethodical" view to IS development, though they reflect on their practices continuously.

"We use, as said, no specific method we can name, but we use 'the method' we have experienced on the way in the work life. It is always a dialogue with colleagues and if there is something new, we discuss that." (Project manager)

## 3.5 Company E

Company E is a local office (4 employees) of a nationwide consultancy, which altogether employs 184 people. The business is tailor-made IT consulting and implementation projects for varying customers. The project size and complexity, as well as customer preferences and requirements, vary greatly.

The company uses an in-house method, which covers the "whole ISD cycle". The method has been combined with commercial tools, e.g. Rational Rose, in parts of the company. Formal adherence to the method is seen to increase the quality of the project and end-product, although adding cost and reducing speed especially in smaller projects. Hence, the method-in-use is tailored project-by-project.

"The customers' willingness to pay is central. As a rule, it costs more with more documentation." (Project manager)

"It depends on what needs to be solved, customer preferences, complexity... whether you have only experienced people... customer preferences... often the customer's own methods fit better than ours, as they know it from before." (Developer)

Moreover, existence of an explicitly documented, organization-standard method is regarded to have a positive effect on the general-level image of the organization.

"You cannot be a serious actor in consulting without having a method to refer to... It is a necessity in itself. It is." (Developer)

The interviewees, while seemingly happy with the "methodical" approach to ISD in general, criticized current practices to train and continuously improve the method.

"We could have had much better training in the method framework." (Project manager)

"Maintenance and further development of the method takes often place too late... when we have a problem, there is no framework we can use [to improve the method], so we need to invent it from scratch and often 180 consultants each invent it again... and that is a bit stupid. So that is clearly a challenge." (Developer)

Company E thus can be characterized as a user of an in-house method, while tailoring the extent to use the method depending on the project exigencies.

"It is a clear weakness if methods are not used. It happens that they are dropped out from smaller projects, but you use anyhow techniques which you can find from the method framework... whether you think about it or not." (Developer)

## 3.6 Summary: Issues of Method Adoption in SMEs

Our analysis of the five cases is summarized in Fig. 1. The issues can be categorized under three main topics: The organization/business context, the ISD process, and prevailing opinions of ISD methods. These topics and categories interact with each other, forming the context for contemporary method deployment. Under each concept, we identify dimensions characterizing the concept.

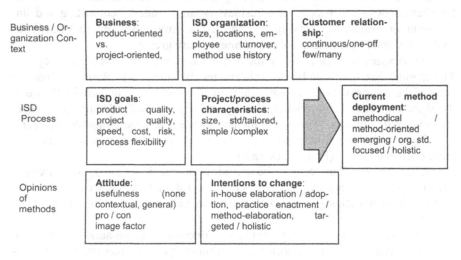

**Fig. 1.** Summary of Method Deployment Issues

The business could be product-oriented (B), dealing with organizational implementation on particular software; project-oriented (D, E), tailoring the projects for customer needs; or a "hybrid" approach in which the companies deliver a particular solution or solution type, but tailor that to their customers according to predefined moulds (A) or implement new product extensions (C). The characteristics of the ISD organization also varied, e.g., size (from 6 to 184 developers), locations (from distributed to 1 site), method use history (from no method use to long-term use), and employee turnover (A–C highlighted this issue). Customer relationship varied along two dimensions. The companies could focus either on one-off projects (A, D) or on long-term relationships, including product support (B, C). Second, some companies sold their development work to many and varying customers (A, D, E), whereas others focused on particular domains and the main actors there (B, C).

The goal combinations for the ISD process varied accordingly. Company A focused on speed and cost issues with low risk, while product quality awareness was increasing. B focused on product quality, and C on project quality and efficiency. Company D indicated that their main goal would be process flexibility, e.g., with regard to changing customer needs, whereas company E indicated a contingency approach, where the customers needed to define the prioritizations of development work.

With regard to ISD project/process characteristics, company A focused on one-man projects fitting predefined solution categories, while company E could take on projects of variable size and type. Another dimension here was whether projects were following a standard or tailored process. For example, company B followed a pretty standard process. So did company A (although A did not use any explicit method), whereas D and E could adapt their project process to the contextual needs.

Concerning the attitudes to methods, company A considered methods unusable in general. Companies C and E saw methods as beneficial if adapted to the context. No company, however, considered any method as "universally useful". Company E mentioned that method use improved the company image. Intentions of deploying methods varied. Company D had plans to try a 3rd-party method, supposed to allow project flexibility. The others were more inclined to elaborate their practices in-house, without specific references to commercial or academic methods. Another dimension here was whether such deployment would be method-oriented or simply enactment of emerging practices. Company C tried to capture good practices systematically and include them in their quality system framework. Companies A and B had, in turn, perhaps the most emerging practice, which were enacted, sometimes documented, without reference to any method framework. Company D, despite its current nonmethodical position, had considered several available methods, and was now planning to try another one. Company E also had a covering method framework which which to develop, but would deviate from that in individual projects. The third issue of intentions concerns whether deployment would be targeted (e.g., on some particular and constrained tasks) or aiming at a holistic framework. Here, companies A and B would develop their practices in the targeted manner, whereas company C was clear about the holistic role of potential method frameworks.

Our research question culminates in the current method deployment box (Fig. 1). Our analysis clearly suggests that some organizations (A, B) are deliberately amethodical, Company B being so very consciously (and managing the projects based on other parameters), whereas in B the interviewees had less personal relationship to the very concept of method in itself. On the other hand, C and E were more method-oriented, considering them as very useful tools for organizing ISD work. Company D was clearly aware of methods as potentially useful. However, with previous history of perceived misfits of available methods to their type of operations, it had only a cautious interest in more explicit method deployment. Another dimension here is whether methods or practices are predefined or emerging. Although company A was clearly amethodical in general, the enacted practices for contracting and pricing formed guidelines for the sales and project operations. On the other hand, while company E had very method-like deployment prevailing, emerging practices in projects were accepted. Finally, the scope of deployment of methods or enacted practices could vary. Companies A and B had very focused practices, while companies C and E had a more overall scope for their method/practice deployment. Company D, again, falls between these extremes here, as they were discussing challenges of particular practices, such as project communication between managers and designers, but were also considering a test of a more covering method framework.

# 4 Discussion

Consensus prevailed on the need for flexible and pragmatic contextual adoptions of practices rather than adoption of complete "universal" methods. However, we observed at least two organization-level approaches to this: the amethodical approach in which practices emerge without reference to any method framework (A, B, D) and an approach in which an organization-standard method is kept up and documented to reflect on emerging practices (C, E). In our data, the biggest organizations (with 42 and 184 employees) followed the method-oriented approach, and the smallest were clearly amethodical, whereas company D intended to adopt a 3rd-party "flexible method" and had considered other methods previously. Despite the deliberate "amethodicality", even the micro firm A saw a need for more systematic practices for quality assurance, however. So did organization B with regard to their interface and functionality specifications to communicate among the development teams.

Previous studies have found developer attitudes (Khalifa and Verner 2000), perceived usefulness of method, compatibility to the problem at hand, organizational mandate legitimating the method use (Hardgrave et al. 2003), and project/development team size to have an effect on method deployment (Cockburn 2002; Khalifa and Verner 2000). The social pressure factor (Hardgrave et al. 2003) did not emerge in our data, which may indicate that in smaller companies people may have greater individual freedom to decide on their work practices. Support for method use from organization (Khalifa and Verner 2000) was mentioned by company E, where one interviewee hoped for better training for the method.

The data revealed a few additional organization-level issues, which have been less prominent in previous research. The *ISD goals* of the organizations varied. Here, company A deliberately avoids large projects, keeping the project size at the level of one person. Whereas, e.g., Lyytinen and Rose (2006) discuss variance in ISD process goals (innovative content, risk, quality, cost, speed) in relation to ISD agility, our results thus propose that such process goals may also explain some of the variation in practical method deployment in general. In the consultancies D and E, we found a new type of ISD process goal – the flexibility of the ISD process itself to adapt to customer preferences. This indicates that in consulting business the "goal interactions" may vary within one firm, project by project, highlighting other goals differently in different development contexts.

In addition to size, a number of other factors in the ISD organization may relate to method deployment decisions, such as *type of business*, *previous history of method use*, *geographical distribution*, *employee turnover*. As well, *customer relationship* may explain (lack of) method deployment. In one-off customer relationships, the amethodical approach was favored (although company B was also amethodical with a solid customer base). This could also explain method deployment in bigger organizations. For example, Fitzgerald et al. (2003, 2006) discuss method deployment in Motorola and Intel, where the "customer" relationship naturally is more continuous than in one-off microfirms. Altogether, our results suggest that the issues of business/organization context should inform future research on method deployment.

Our study confirms that the attitude of individual developers is a significant issue. In the companies favoring the organization-standard method, the individual attitudes to methods appeared more positive than in those that had not used them. This suggests that the relationship of these concepts is a two-way one, unlike in some simplified models (e.g. Khalifa and Verner 2000), which have implied that a method deployment decision is a one-way consequence from preconceptions. Only the interviewee from company A had a clear stance on method uselessness, unlike the others who seemed to weigh the pros and cons of method in a more fine-grained way. In C and E, methods were institutionalized at the level of the organization. This suggests that we should not discuss SDM deployment *only* in relation to the preferences and experience of individual developers (e.g., Stolterman 1992; Fitzgerald 1997; Mathiassen and Purao 2002; Hardgrave et al. 2003). The organization context may provide alternative explanations for the phenomenon – as individual employees, especially novices (cf. Päivärinta et al. 2007), seldom decide on their work practices without more generic guidelines. Company E also highlighted the "image-issue" of having an organization-standard method, in line with the company described by Päivärinta et al. (2007). Our results thus suggest a more fine-grained concept to describe developer attitude on method usefulness than reported in previous research.

Finally, all organizations intended to develop their ISD practices. Hence, some enacted practices seem to be needed, at least occasionally, even in so-called amethodical organizations. It varied whether such development would be incorporated in a holistic method framework or whether it should be targeted on specific practices. The amethodical approach is content with identifying emerging practices while issues occur, whereas the method-oriented stance still considers methods as useful to increase project and product quality and as a framework for improving the practice.

## 5 Conclusions and Further Research

We studied method deployment in five ISD SMEs, in response to calls by Introna and Whitley (1997) and Russo and Stolterman (2000), who state that SDM "research must focus on in-depth studies of practice, create rich descriptions of practice, and come up with interpretations and analysis of this practice" (p. 325). The results highlight the role of organization-related issues in explaining why and how methods are deployed (or not) in practice. However, the organization-specific stories of method deployment were in our cases very contextual, a sum of a good number of intertwined issues. Hence, it remains to be studied whether these factors and relationships are generally significant. Alternatively, future research could aim at developing a few stereotypical scenarios of method deployment, which could give qualitative guidance for future decision-makers and educators of ISD methods, with regard to issues to scrutinize in connection with their organizational adoption.

A word of caution is in place. This piece of research does not represent a full-fledged grounded theory study. We have not reached the "theoretical saturation" (Glaser and Strauss 1967) of sampling – each case has so far brought in new ideas and categories/dimensions to our model. The theoretical sampling must be improved to improve our model. Moreover, we address the need for selective coding to cultivate our results further. For example, we could study the two modes of method deployment – the amethodical approach vs. the organizational-method-oriented approach, by collecting data from organizations that deliberately practice one or another of those, or we could do longitudinal studies of select organizations.

## References

Brinkkemper, S., Lyytinen, K. & Welke, R. K. (eds.) (1996) *Method Engineering: Principles of Method Construction and Tool Support*. Chapman & Hall, London.

Cockburn, A. (2002) *Agile Software Development*. Pearson Education, NJ.

Fitzgerald, B. (1997) The use of systems development methodologies in practice: A field study. *The Information Systems Journal*, 7 (3), 201–212.

Fitzgerald, B. (1998) An empirical investigation into the adoption of systems development methodologies. *Information and Management*, 34, 317–328.

Fitzgerald, B., Russo, N. L. & Stolterman, E. (2002) *Information Systems Development: Methods in Action*. McGraw-Hill, New York.

Fitzgerald, B., Russo, N. & O'Kane, T. (2003) Software development method tailoring at Motorola. *Communications of the ACM*, 46 (4), 65–70.

Fitzgerald, B., Hartnett, G. & Conboy, K. (2006) Customising agile methods to software practices at Intel Shannon. *European Journal of Information Systems*, 15, 200–213.

Glaser, B. G. & Strauss, A. L. (1967) *The Discovery of Grounded Theory*. Aldine, Chicago.

Hardgrave, B., Davis, F. D. & Riemenschneider, C. K. (2003) Investigating determinants of software developers' intentions to follow methodologies. *Journal of Management Information Systems*, 20 (1), 123–151.

Humphrey, W., Snyder, T. & Willis, R. (1991) Software process improvement at Hughes Aircraft. *IEEE Software*, **8** (4), 11–23.

Introna, L. D. & Whitley, E. A. (1997) Against method-*ism*: Exploring the limits of method. *Information Technology and People*, **10** (1), 31–45.

Jarke, M., Pohl, K., Rolland, C. & Shmitt, J.-R. (1994) Experience-based method evaluation and improvement: A process modeling approach. In: *Proceedings of the IFIP WG8.1 Working Conference on Methods and Associated Tools for the Information Systems Life Cycle*, Verrijn-Stuart, A. A. & Olle, T. W. (eds.), pp. 1–27. Elsevier, New York.

Khalifa, M. & Verner, J. (2000) Drivers for software development method usage. *IEEE Transactions on Engineering Management*, **47** (3), 360–369.

Kumar, K. & Welke, R. J. (1992) Methodology engineering: A proposal for situation-specific methodology construction. In: *Challenges and Strategies for Research in Systems Development*, Cotterman, W. W. & Senn, J. A. (eds.), pp. 257–270. Wiley, Chichester.

Lyytinen, K. & Rose, G. M. (2006) Information system development agility as organizational learning. *European Journal of Information Systems*, **15**, 183–199.

Madsen, S., Kautz, K. & Vidgen, R. (2006) A framework for understanding how a unique and local IS development method emerges in practice. *European Journal of Information Systems*, **15**, 225–238.

Mathiassen, L. & Purao, S. (2002) Educating reflective systems developers. *Information Systems Journal*, **12**, 81–102.

Päivärinta, T., Sein, M. K. & Peltola, T. (2007) From ideals towards practice: Paradigmatic mismatches and drifts in method deployment. *Information Systems Journal*, doi: 10.1111/j.1365-2575.2007.00256.x [online] [Accessed 22, Nov. 2007].

Russo, N. L. & Stolterman, E. (2000) Exploring the assumptions underlying information systems methodologies. *Information Technology and People*, **13** (4), 313–327.

Stolterman, E. (1992) How system developers think about design and methods. *Scandinavian Journal of Information Systems*, **3** (1), 137–150.

Strauss, A. L. & Corbin, J. M. (1990) *Basics of Qualitative Research: Grounded Theory Procedures and Techniques*. Sage, Newbury Park, CA.

Truex, D., Baskerville, R. & Travis, J. (2000) Amethodical systems development: The deferred meaning of systems development methods. *Accounting, Management and Information Technologies*, **10** (1), 53–79.

Whitley, E. A. (1998) Method-ism in practice: Investigating the relationship between method and understanding in Web page design. In: *Proceedings of the Nineteenth International Conference on Information Systems*, Hirschheim, R., Newman, M. & DeGross, J. I. (eds.), pp. 68–75. ICIS.

# Method Construction by Goal Analysis

C. Gonzalez-Perez[1], P. Giorgini[2] and B. Henderson-Sellers[3]

[1]Department of Software Engineering, University of Technology, Sydney, Australia, cesargon@verdewek.com

[2]Department of Information and Communication Technology, University of Trento, Trento, Italy, paolo.giorgini@unitn.it

[3]Department of Software Engineering, University of Technology, Sydney, Australia, brian@it.uts.edu.au

**Abstract** Method engineering proposes the construction of methodologies by selecting method fragments from a repository and assembling them in an appropriate way. However, the rules by which the "optimal" method fragments are chosen are not clear, and such chores are usually done manually by an expert. This paper presents a goal analysis technique for the selection of the optimal method fragments from a repository, using backward reasoning to obtain the set of fragments that satisfy the desired goals with minimum effort. By using this technique, a methodologist can determine the goals that the organisation wants the methodology to satisfy, and then, preferably, rely on automated tools for the selection of the optimal solution.

## 1 Introduction

It is well accepted that no single software development methodology (or method; we will consider them here as synonyms) serves all purposes (Cockburn 2000). Different project, product and organisational characteristics call for different methodologies, which are often further tweaked or customised to fit the particular idiosyncrasies of their users (Bajec et al. 2007). One quick way to obtain a customised methodology is to adopt an existing one and change it as necessary. However, this entails significant risks since the methodologists making the changes are not necessarily aware of the interconnections and dependencies between different components of the methodology. The situational method engineering (SME) paradigm (Brinkkemper 1996; Henderson-Sellers et al. 2004b) offers a solution to this problem: instead of adopting an existing methodology and changing it as necessary, a custom methodology is created by selecting the appropriate method fragments from an existing repository and combining them appropriately. This approach is used in methodological frameworks such as OPF (Firesmith and

C. Barry et al. (eds.), *Information Systems Development: Challenges in Practice, Theory, and Education, Vol.1*, doi: 10.1007/978-0-387-68772-8_7,
© Springer Science+Business Media, LLC 2009

Henderson-Sellers 2002), OOSPICE (Henderson-Sellers et al. 2002) and FIPA (Cossentino et al. 2007), and is advocated in the recent ISO/IEC (2007) 24744 International Standard "Software Engineering Metamodel for Development Methodologies".

Despite an increasing and broadening interest in SME, some areas are still to be fully explored. For example, how are the method fragments to be selected from the repository? A complete methodology is likely to be composed of hundreds of method fragments, and each of these must be carefully chosen to (a) fit the purpose of the methodology being constructed and (b) be compatible with other method fragments. Usually, this task is performed by a methodologist, who uses his or her expert judgement to handcraft an "optimal" solution. This approach has a number of drawbacks. First of all, it can be extremely time-consuming. Second, there is no way to demonstrate that the chosen collection of method fragments is the best; i.e., no guarantee can be given on the quality of the result (other than that given by the trust on the methodologist's expertise). Typically, an organisation willing to adopt the method engineering paradigm will need to recruit a methodologist or hire a consultant to compose a methodology each time.

This paper presents a solution to these drawbacks in which a project manager will be able to create a profile of the methodology to be constructed in terms of the *goals that it must achieve*, and then use a goal analysis technique, ideally implemented by a tool, to extract the optimal combination of method fragments from the repository that fulfils the goals at minimum effort.

Section 2 of this paper introduces some important concepts of method engineering; Sect. 3 explains the basic concepts of goal analysis and Sect. 4 its application to methodology construction.

## 2 Background for Situational Method Engineering

As explained earlier, the SME approach needs the existence of a method fragment repository. This repository is usually a database that contains method fragments of different kinds. Method fragments are self-contained, relatively independent specifications of some aspect of a methodology, such as a task to be performed, a technique that may be employed, a product that can be generated or a team that can be formed. Different kinds of method fragments have different properties: for example, task specifications have a purpose (that declares what the task intends to achieve) and a description (that specifies the steps that may be followed in order to achieve it); work product specifications, on the other hand, have a name (such as "Requirements Specification Document" or "Class Diagram") and a description. In turn, different kinds of method fragments are related to each other; for example, task specifications may be linked to the work products that they generate when executed.

The structure of the repository, i.e., the kinds of method fragments, their properties and the relationships between them, is usually given by a metamodel. A *metamodel* is a formal description of the concepts that can be used to construct a methodology and the relationships amongst them. Here, we will adopt the International Standard ISO/IEC (2007) 24744 "Software Engineering Metamodel for Development Methodologies" (SEMDM). SEMDM defines 68 concrete classes, instances of which can potentially be stored in a method fragment repository. Not all the method fragment classes are relevant for this paper; we will concentrate on the following:

- *PhaseKind.* Specification of a managed timeframe within a project for which the objective is the transition between levels of abstraction. Phase kinds specify the "when" of a methodology, i.e., its temporal ordering and organisation.
- *ProcessKind.* Specification of a discrete, large-grained job performed within a project that operates within a given area of expertise. Process kinds specify the "what and why" of a methodology at an abstract level, i.e., the methodology's job structure.
- *TaskKind.* Specification of a small-grained job performed within a project that focuses on what must be done in order to achieve a given purpose. Task kinds specify the "what and why" of a methodology at a detailed level.
- *TechniqueKind.* Specification of a small-grained job performed within a project that focuses on how the given purpose may be achieved. Technique kinds specify the "how" of a methodology, i.e., the specific means of achieving the associated task.
- *WorkProductKind.* Specification of an artefact of interest for the project. Work product kinds specify what is created and consumed during a project.
- *ActionKind.* Specification of how a given task kind acts upon a particular work product kind.

These classes are interrelated in the following way (Fig. 1); i.e., each phase kind is composed of process kinds, which give "content" to it. The phase kind specifies when something must be done, while the associated process kinds define what to do. In turn, each process kind contains a number of task kinds, which flesh out and refine the purpose of process. In turn, each task kind may be associated with a number of technique kinds, since there is often a choice from several techniques, each of which can be used to achieve the goals of the same task, and different tasks can use the same technique. Finally, each task kind may be mapped to a number of work product kinds via action kinds. These mappings involve different action types: a task can *create, modify, delete* or *read* a work product. Typically, each task kind will read work products of some kinds and perhaps create a new work product of a different kind.

## 2.1 Sample Method Fragment Repository

Consider the following (simplified) example. Two phase kinds are defined in a repository: "System Definition" and "System Construction". The first is intended to be performed at the beginning of a project and defines the system to be built. The second is meant to be executed at the end of a project in order to construct the system previously defined. A number of process kinds are also defined: "Requirements Engineering", "Coding", "Acceptance Testing", "Quality Assurance" and "Process Improvement". Each of these process kinds specifies, from an abstract point of view, what can be done at some point in the project. Some of these process kinds are associated to the "System Definition" phase kind, some to "System Construction", and some to both (Table 1). Then, some task kinds can be introduced, such as "Elicit requirements", "Analyse requirements", "Validate requirements", "Develop service models" and "Determine work product defects" (Table 2). These task kinds, together with many more, would be associated to different process kinds. A number of technique kinds can also be introduced, such as "Prototyping", "Peer reviewing" and "Threat modelling" (Table 3). These technique kinds would be mapped to task kinds in a many-to-many fashion. Finally, some work product kinds can be introduced into the repository, such as "Requirements Specification Document", "Service Diagram", "Source Programme" and "Report" (Table 4). Each of these work product kinds would be associated to a number of task kinds with a particular action type; for example, "Requirements Specification Document" can be mapped to "Document requirements" via an action kind with a "create" type and to "Develop service models" via a different action kind with a "read" type. In turn, "Service Diagram" can be mapped to "Develop service models" via an action kind with a "create" type.

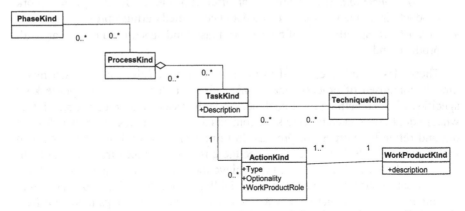

**Fig. 1.** Metamodel fragment (a subset of ISO/IEC 24744). Only relevant classes, attributes and associations are depicted. Here the *diamond* indicates a generic whole-part relationship

Relevant life cycle models are created by instantiating the class TimeCycle-Kind from ISO/IEC 24744. This is a subtype of StageWithDurationKind (also the supertype of PhaseKind). Selection of the lifecycle is a stylistic decision much akin to the choice of architectural style for a software application. Although it is possible to represent this selection process in terms of a soft goal, it is more likely that the choice will be made based on other, external factors and influences. (Life cycle selection is a topic for future research – not discussed further here.)

**Table 1.** Sample process kinds

| Name | Mapped to phase kinds |
| --- | --- |
| Requirements engineering | System definition |
| Coding | System construction |
| Acceptance testing | System construction |
| Quality assurance | System definition, system construction |
| Process improvement | System definition, system construction |

**Table 2.** Sample task kinds

| Name | Mapped to process kinds |
| --- | --- |
| Elicit requirements | Requirements engineering |
| Analyse requirements | Requirements engineering |
| Validate requirements | Requirements engineering |
| Document requirements | Requirements engineering |
| Develop class models | High-level modelling |
| Develop service models | High-level modelling |
| Sketch user interface | High-level modelling |
| Develop interaction models | Detailed modelling |
| Write code | Coding |
| Unit test class | Coding |
| Demonstrate the system | Acceptance testing |
| Obtain stakeholder feedback | Acceptance testing, quality assurance |
| Determine work product defects | Quality assurance |
| Prepare defect report | Quality assurance |
| Test build system | Quality assurance |

**Table 3.** Sample technique kinds

| Name | Mapped to task kinds |
| --- | --- |
| Prototyping | Develop service models, sketch user interface |
| Text analysis | Analyse requirements, develop class models |
| CRC cards | Develop class models |
| Peer reviewing | Validate requirements, determine work product defects |
| Test-first development | Unit test class |
| In-house customer | Demonstrate the system, obtain stakeholder feedback |
| Automated builds | Test build system |
| Threat modelling | Analyse requirements |

**Table 4.** Sample work product kinds with action types

| Name | Mapped to task kinds | Action type |
|---|---|---|
| Stakeholders statement | Elicit requirements | Create |
| | Analyse requirements, validate requirements | Modify |
| | Document requirements | Read |
| Requirements specification document | Document requirements | Create |
| | Develop class models, develop service models, sketch user interface | Read |
| Service diagram | Develop service models | Create |
| | Develop interaction models | Modify |
| | Sketch user interface | Read |
| User interface sketch | Sketch user interface | Create |
| | Develop service models | Modify |
| | Write code | Read |
| Source programme | Write code | Create |
| | Unit test class | Modify |
| | Test build system | Read |
| Report | Test build system, determine work product defects, prepare defect report | Create |

From the sample method fragments in Tables 1–4, it can be seen that the dependency network that can arise from the method fragments in a repository can be extremely intricate. For example, selecting the "High-Level Modelling" process kind would usually imply bringing along the "Develop service models" task kind, which "creates" a "Service Diagram" work product and "reads" a "Requirements Specification Document" work product. To provide the necessary input (i.e., a requirements specification document), we need to select a task kind that creates it, namely, "Document Requirements". This task kind, in turn, may bring along the whole "Requirements Engineering" process kind together with additional task kinds.

Technique selection is usually more flexible, since a number of technique kinds are often available for each individual task kind. Which is selected depends only on the characteristics of the project (e.g., time or budget constraints), the product context (e.g., safe-criticality) and the organisation (e.g., culture and skills). Although we can assume that any of the technique kinds mapped to a given task kind is appropriate to achieve the task's purpose, the particular technique kinds that are chosen will likely influence overall project properties such as time consumed or defect injection rate as well as providing a different level of risk and associated costs. From this perspective, we can say that some techniques are better than others for some particular purposes.

## 2.2 Requirements for Method Construction

The design and construction of a methodology can be seen as any other engineering activity: some requirements are given and a suitable artefact that satisfies them must be developed. Therefore, we can assume that some requirements exist when methodologists face the task of constructing a methodology from a method fragment repository. These requirements can be described in terms of the capabilities and qualities of the intended outcome of the engineering effort, namely, the future methodology. In turn, method capabilities and qualities may refer to the kind of products that the method can construct, the type of projects used to tackle such activities and the characteristics of the organisations where these projects may take place. If we can characterise products, projects and organisations with measurable attributes, we will have a solid starting point on which requirements for method construction can be defined. These can be seen as defining the requirements *for the construction of the methodology* (as opposed to the requirements for the construction of the software application, which is the target of the software development project) (Ralyté 2002). Factors that influence these requirements are many, including organizational maturity level, skills set of development team members, type of domain (e.g., information systems, real-time control, e-business), project size, team size, level of criticality, interface style, level of resources allocated to project and whether or not the system is to be a distributed application (Nguyen and Henderson-Sellers 2003).

**Table 5.** Product, project and organisation attributes for method construction

| Area | Attribute | Description |
|---|---|---|
| Product | Reliability | The product must offer high reliability; i.e., its users will depend on it for critical operations. |
| | Changeability | The product will need to be changed, and so it will need to offer the appropriate mechanisms to achieve this with ease. |
| | Usability | The product must be easy to use. |
| Project | Cost constraints | The project has cost constraints; so it must be completed at the lowest cost possible. |
| | Time constraints | The project has time constraints; so it must be completed in the shortest time possible. |
| | Staffing constraints | The project has staffing constraints; so it must be completed with the lowest possible number of staff. |
| | Visibility | The project needs high visibility; so all the work must be properly documented. |
| Organisation | Formal culture | The development team's culture promotes formal, high-ceremony work. |
| | Agile culture | The development team's culture promotes agile-style, low-ceremony work. |
| | Experience | The development team has got extensive experience in the kind of project and product to be developed. |

Table 5 shows a list of the attributes that we have identified for the purpose of illustration in this paper. We have only included attributes that may be directly affected by the choice of method fragments when constructing a methodology. We are aware that many other attributes (such as product correctness or readability) are also of interest to software engineering, but they have been left out from this experiment since they are not likely to be directly affected by the choice of method fragments.

# 3 Goal Analysis Concepts

In goal analysis, the final goal of each process step is considered from the point of view of a specific actor. There are three relevant reasoning techniques that are useful: means-end analysis, contributions analysis and AND/OR decomposition (Bresciani et al. 2004). In means-end analysis, the following are performed iteratively until an acceptable solution is reached: "Describe the current state, the desired state (the goal) and the difference between the two; Select a promising procedure for enabling this change of state by using this identified difference between present and desired states; Apply the selected procedure and update the current state" (Henderson-Sellers et al. 2004a).

Contributions analysis helps to identify goals that may contribute towards the partial fulfilment of the final goal and is sometimes used as an alternative to means-end analysis, particularly useful for soft goals. Positive or negative influences towards attainment of the goal are identified and quantified on a (usually 5-point) Likert scale. In particular, contributions analysis has been shown to be very effective for soft goals used for eliciting non-functional (quality) requirements.

Finally, AND/OR decomposition changes a root goal into a finer goal structure, i.e., a set of subgoals – either alternatives (OR decomposition) or additive (AND decomposition).

Goal analysis has been used in a number of ways to support software development, e.g., in the design of systems, especially for documenting early requirements, as in the Tropos methodology (Bresciani et al. 2004), in business process reengineering (Grau et al. 2005) and in the support of ISO/IEC 15504 assessments (Rifaut 2005). Here, we present the first application of goal analysis to method construction in the context of method engineering.

# 4 Applying Goal Analysis to Method Construction

To use goal analysis for method construction, we need to determine how each of the method fragments in the sample repository affects each of the above-listed attributes. For example, we can say that performing the Quality Assurance process (see Table 1) enhances product reliability. For each method fragment plus attribute

**Table 6.** Mappings between attributes and method fragments. For each mapping, a value is included indicating how the choice of the method fragment affects the attribute.

| Attribute | | Method fragment | | Value |
|---|---|---|---|---|
| Area | Name | Class | Name | |
| Product | Reliability | Process kind | Quality assurance | Strongly enhances |
| | | Task kind | Unit test class | Enhances |
| | | Technique kind | Test-first development | Enhances |
| | | | In-house customer | Enhances |
| | | | Threat modelling | Strongly enhances |
| | Changeability | Process kind | Configuration management | Enhances |
| | | Task kind | Document requirements | Enhances |
| | Usability | Process kind | Acceptance testing | Strongly enhances |
| | | Task kind | Demonstrate the system | Enhances |
| | | | Obtain stakeholder feedback | Strongly enhances |
| Project | Cost constraints | Phase kind | System definition | Deteriorates |
| | | Process kind | Quality assurance | Deteriorates |
| | | | Process improvement | Deteriorates |
| | Time constraints | Phase kind | System definition | Deteriorates |
| | | Process kind | Process improvement | Deteriorates |
| | | Task kind | Unit test class | Deteriorates |
| | | Technique kind | Prototyping | Deteriorates |
| | | | Automated builds | Enhances |
| | Staffing constraints | Process kind | Quality assurance | Deteriorates |
| | | Technique kind | Peer reviewing | Deteriorates |
| | | | Pair programming | Deteriorates |
| | Visibility | Task kind | Prepare defect report | Enhances |
| | | | Prepare process quality report | Enhances |
| Organisation | Formal culture | Phase kind | System definition | Strongly enhances |
| | | Task kind | Measure process quality | Enhances |
| | Agile culture | Phase kind | System definition | Strongly deteriorates |
| | | Process kind | Process improvement | Deteriorates |
| | | Task kind | Document requirements | Deteriorates |
| | | | Elicit requirements | Enhances |
| | | Technique kind | In-house customer | Enhances |
| | | | Test-first development | Enhances |
| | Experience | Phase kind | System definition | Strongly enhances |
| | | Process kind | Requirements engineering | Enhances |
| | | | Acceptance testing | Enhances |
| | | Task kind | Elicit requirements | Enhances |
| | | Technique kind | Focus groups | Strongly enhances |
| | | | Prototyping | Strongly enhances |
| | | | Walkthroughs | Enhances |
| | | | In-house customer | Enhances |

pair, one of five possible values has been determined: strongly enhances, enhances, neutral, deteriorates and strongly deteriorates.

Table 6 shows these (non-neutral) mappings between method fragments and attributes. Please note that we are not claiming that these mappings are optimal or even correct; these are a sample collection of reasonable mappings for the purpose of this paper. A separate study would be necessary in order to determine how each method fragment in a production repository affects each attribute of interest.

Suppose we have two options for a software engineering process (SEP) and each has several tasks, each implemented by a technique chosen from a list. The two options are shown graphically in Fig. 2.

Looking at the Techniques, we have a table (akin to Table 6) that links Techniques to impact factors (-ilities). The Techniques are labelled as X1–X6, where X1 denotes Test first; X2, In house customer; X3, Prototyping; X4, Automated builds; X5, Threat modelling and X6, Peer reviewing. Then the two processes can be described in terms of these terminal Techniques as follows:

SEP1 is (X1 or X2); (X3 or X4)

SEP2 is (X1 or X2); (X1 or X2 or X5 or X6)

We consider just two examples. The impact on the Reliability and Agility factors:

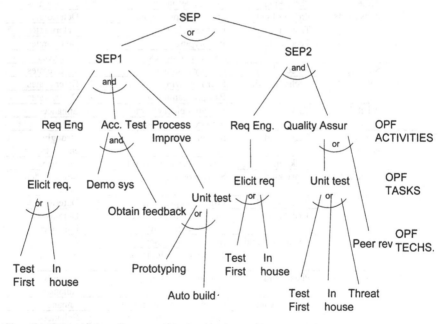

**Fig. 2.** Hierarchical tree depicting activities, tasks and techniques for two hypothetical software engineering processes

1. *Reliability*

| | |
|---|---|
| Test-first development (X1) | Enhances (+) |
| In-house customer (X2) | Enhances (+) |
| Prototyping (X3) | Neutral (0) |

| Automated builds (X4) | Deteriorates (−) |
|---|---|
| Threat modelling(X5) | Strongly enhances (++) |
| Peer reviewing (X6) | Strongly enhances (++) |

2. *Agility*

| Test-first development (X1) | Enhances (+) |
|---|---|
| In-house customer (X2) | Enhances (+) |
| Prototyping (X3) | Deteriorates (−) |
| Automated builds (X4) | Strongly deteriorates (—) |
| Threat modelling(X5) | Strongly deteriorates (—) |
| Peer reviewing (X6) | Strongly enhances (++) |

Then the impact is as follows:

| Option | Reliability | Agility |
|---|---|---|
| SEP1 option 1 is X1; X3 | +/0 | +/− |
| SEP1 option 2 is X1; X4 | +/− | +/— |
| SEP1 option 3 is X2; X3 | +/0 | +/− |
| SEP1 option 4 is X2; X4 | +/− | +/— |
| SEP2 option 1 is X1; X1 | +/+ | +/+ |
| SEP2 option 2 is X1; X2 | +/+ | +/+ |
| SEP2 option 3 is X1; X5 | +/++ | +/— |
| SEP2 option 4 is X1; X6 | +/++ | +/++ |
| SEP2 option 5 is X2; X1 | +/+ | +/+ |
| SEP2 option 6 is X2; X2 | +/+ | +/+ |
| SEP2 option 7 is X2; X5 | +/++ | +/— |
| SEP2 option 8 is X2; X6 | +/++ | +/++ |

We conclude that from a reliability viewpoint, the best choice would be SEP2, options 3, 4, 7 or 8. On the other hand, from an agility perspective, the best choice would be SEP2, option 4 or 6.

This analysis is fully supported and automated in Tropos (Giorgini et al. 2005). In particular, backward reasoning allows the analyst to search for possible method fragments from the repository that satisfy the desired goal. Moreover, by assigning a cost to each fragment, backward reasoning also produces the solution with the minimum cost.

# 5 Conclusions and Future Work

With the aim of creating a high-quality software development methodology from those method fragments selected from an existing repository, we have examined a new idea based on goal analysis. Rather than select the elements of the methodology "top-down" by considering what seems reasonable in a particular situation using what might be termed "intuition" (the current approach in SME), we suggest that a more objective process can be created in which the main focus becomes the goal rather than the means of achieving that goal (the process element). The goal analysis approach proposed here permits the creation of an optimized methodology; importantly, one that is optimized for a particular characteristic such as reliability or agility. A hierarchical tree is constructed (Fig. 2), and for each element, we identify whether there is a positive or negative impact *for the chosen optimization characteristic*. We have demonstrated this approach with a simple example of a small tree in which fragments for activities, tasks and techniques from the OPF repository have been selected, considering the impacts on two different software engineering processes, SEP1 and SEP2 (Fig. 2). That these processes have different optima under different evaluation criteria (here agility and reliability) suggests that this approach is worthy of further investigation, including practical trials in industry and the development of a prototype support tool. We are currently planning such industry trials within the Italian-ministry-funded project MEnSA (http://www.mensa-project.org) and anticipate building appropriate support tools in due course.

**Acknowledgements** We acknowledge financial support of both the Australian Research Council and the Italian ministry for research through its PRIN-MEnSA project.

# References

Bajec, M., Vavpotič, D. and Krisper, M. (2007) Practice-driven approach for creating project-specific software development methods. Inf. Software Technol. 49, 345–365.

Bresciani, P., Perini, A., Giorgini, P., Giunchiglia, F. and Mylopolous, J. (2004) Tropos: an agent-oriented software development methodology. Auton. Agents Multi-Agent Syst. 8(3), 203–236.

Brinkkemper, S. (1996) Method engineering: engineering of information systems development methods and tools. Inf. Software Technol. 38(4), 275–280.

Cockburn, A.S. (2000) Selecting a project's methodology. IEEE Software 17(4), 64–71.

Cossentino, M., Gaglio, S., Garro, A. and Seidita, V. (2007) Method fragments for agent design methodologies: from standardization to research. Int. J. Agent-Oriented Software Eng. 1(1), 91–121.

Firesmith, D.G. and Henderson-Sellers, B. (2002) *The OPEN Process Framework*. Addison-Wesley, London.

Giorgini, P., Mylopoulous, J. and Sebastiani, R. (2005) Goal-oriented requirements analysis and reasoning in the Tropos methodology. Eng. Appl. Artif. Intell. 18(2), 159–171.

Grau, G., Franch, X. and Maiden, N.A.M. (2005) A goal-based round-trip method for system development. In: *Proceedings of 11th International Conference on Requirements Engineering: Foundations for Software Quality (REFSQ'05)*, pp. 67–82.

Henderson-Sellers, B., Stallinger, F. and Lefever, B. (2002) Bridging the gap from process modelling to process assessment: the OOSPICE process specification for component-based software engineering. In: *Proceedings of 28th EUROMICRO Conference*, Dortmund, Germany, 4–6 Sept. 2002. IEEE Computer Society, Los Alamos, CA, USA, pp. 324–331.

Henderson-Sellers, B., Giorgini, P. and Bresciani, P. (2004a) Enhancing Agent OPEN with concepts used in the Tropos methodology. In: A. Omicini, P. Pettra and J. Pitt (Eds.), *Engineering Societies in the Agents World IV*. 4th International Workshop, ESAW 2003. LNAI 3071, Springer-Verlag, Berlin, Germany, pp. 328–345.

Henderson-Sellers, B., Serour, M., McBride, T. Gonzalez-Perez, C. and Dagher, L. (2004b) Process construction and customization. J. Univers. Comput. Sci. 10(4), 326–358.

ISO/IEC (2007) *Software Engineering Metamodel for Development Methodologies* (ISO/IEC 24744). International Organization for Standardization, Geneva, Switzerland.

Nguyen, V.P. and Henderson-Sellers, B. (2003) Towards automated support for method engineering with the OPEN Process Framework. In: M.H Hamza (Ed.), *Proceedings of 7th IASTED International Conference on Software Engineering and Applications*. ACTA Press, Anaheim, CA, USA, pp. 691–696.

Ralyté, J. (2002) Requirements definition for the situational method engineering. In: C. Rolland, S. Brinkkemper and M. Saeki (Eds.), *Engineering Information Systems in the Internet Context*. Kluwer, Boston, USA, pp. 127–152.

Rifaut, A. (2005) Goal-driven requirements engineering for supporting the ISO 15504 assessment process. In: I. Richardson, P. Abrahamsson and R. Messnarz (Eds.), *Software Process Improvement*. 12th European Conference, EuroSPI 2005. LNCS 3792, Springer, Heidelberg, pp. 151–162.

# The Agile Development of Rule Bases

**Valentin Zacharias**

FZI – Research Center for Information Technologies, IPE-WIM, University of Karlsruhe, Karlsruhe, Germany, zacharias@fzi.de

**Abstract** Recently, with the large-scale practical use of business rule systems and the interest of the Semantic Web community in rule languages, there is an increasing need for methods and tools supporting the development of rule-based systems. Existing methodologies fail to address the challenges posed by modern development processes in these areas, namely, the increasing number of end-user programmers and the increasing interest in iterative methods. To address these challenges, we propose and discuss the adoption of agile methods for the development of rule-based systems. The main contribution of this paper is three development principles for and changes to the Extreme Programming development process to make it suitable for the development of rule-based systems.

## 1 Introduction

Recently, with the large-scale practical use of business rule systems (Seer 2005) and the interest of the Semantic Web community in rule languages (Kifer et al. 2005), there is an increasing need for methods and tools supporting the development of rule based-systems.

There already exists a large body of research into this topic, but most of it is older and does not account for (1) changes in the training of the developers of such systems and (2) the shifting nature of projects that creates rule-based systems.

### 1.1 Changes in Programmers Training

In the early days of rule-based systems, these systems were created by a small number of highly trained knowledge engineers who could easily work with logic and highly formal models. Many methodologies and tools still assume this kind of user. These days, however, software artefacts are often created by end-user programmers – people trained for a non-programming area who just need a programme, script of spreadsheet, as a tool for some task; in fact end-user programmers are estimated to outnumber professional programmers by four to one (Scaffidi et al. 2005). End-user programmers are particularly important for the Semantic Web and the business rule community:

- Business rules are usually small parts of larger systems that allow customizing of an application for a particular company/organisation. Business rules are used to represent that part of business applications that changes in time or from company to company. The prospect of business rules is to allow the quick adaptation of applications to (changing) business needs. To fully realize this prospect, business rules need to be changeable by the same people who use them and hence often end-user programmers.
- The Semantic Web is a candidate for the next development stage of the World Wide Web and it will have to be built largely by the same people who build and maintain the current Web – a high percentage of these people are known to be end-user programmers (Rossen et al. 2004; Harrison 2004).

## 1.2 Changes in Project Structure

Current best practices stipulates that rule bases form only a part of a larger application – only that part concerned with changing or complex logical relations (Merrit 2004). This tends to result in smaller rule bases. Also, the fact that end-user programmers are expected to maintain rule sets means that these have to remain relatively small.

Recent years also saw the increasing adoption and acceptance of iterative and evolutionary development methodologies (Larman and Basili 2003) – they are now widely believed to be superior to waterfall-like models (MacCormack 2001). This development too is not reflected in most current methodologies for the development of rule-based systems.

## 1.3 Overview

Current methodologies for the development of rule-based systems do not adequately address the challenges posed by end-user programmers and smaller projects; they also often do not take advantage of the ideas of iterative application development. To address this shortcoming, we propose an adoption of the ideas of agile software development for the development of rule bases.

Even with the existence of agile development methodologies many end-user programmers will undoubtedly continue to tinker, to create programmes without any clear process. However, we have supported end user developers in the creation of ontologies and rule bases and found that they did ask for methodological guidance; in particular because they were very unfamiliar with the task of creating a knowledge base. Also, it seems likely that many projects will in fact be performed by both professional and end-user programmers – an approach that is common in the business rule community. Here, professional programmers and knowledge engineers set up the system, create the basic structure and are called in for major changes. They also define and set up the processes for changes done by end-user programmers – processes that are partly enforced by the business rule management system. In conclusion, it can be said that some projects will always remain unstructured and that some projects will be done with heavyweight methods; however, it seems obvious that in between there is considerable space for the use of lightweight, agile methods. In addition, even an end-user programmer working purely by trial-and-error could profit from an environment set up to support the principles detailed below.

This paper starts with a short overview of the existing methodologies for the creation of knowledge base. After that, the core principles of agile software development and Extreme Programming (XP) are presented. The main part of the paper then consists of the discussion of why and how it needs to be adapted for the development of rule bases.

## 2 Methodologies for Knowledge Base Creation

CommonKADS (Schreiber et al. 1999) is to date the most influential academic methodology for the development of knowledge-based systems. It understands the development of knowledge-based systems mainly as a modeling task. It emphasizes the construction of conceptual models of the knowledge, the entire system and the context of the application. CommonKADS stipulates the definition of a KBS in a series of six interconnected models: the organization, the task, agent, knowledge, communication and design model. CommonKADS claims to support the iterative development of KBS but requires a large up front analysis phase for the initial definition of these models. Because of this large, formal analysis phase, it is not well suited for the kind of end-user-driven, smaller projects that are the topic of this paper (Kingston 1992). It imposes too much of an overhead and end-user programmers with no prior experience in building KBS cannot be expected to build correct, formal specifications; they can also not be expected to learn CML as another formal language just for the specification.

The approach to build a KBS in a top-down fashion, as the stepwise refinement of interconnected models, is not unique to CommonKADS and is in fact used in many methodologies (Stokes 2001; Plant and Gamble 1997; Yen and Lee 1993), but they all suffer from the problems described earlier. PragmaticKADS is a variant of the initial KADS methodology that tries to address this problem of the large initial overhead, but it is defined only at a very high abstraction level, makes no allowance for refinement steps and has almost no discussion of validation and verification activities (Kingston 1992).

Another group of methodologies arose from the attempt to reconcile the building of KBS as a series of rapidly created prototypes with the need for formal processes to monitor and control a project's progress (Miller 1990; Weitzel and Kerschberg 1989; ANSI 1992). All of these methodologies have prototypes at their centre, but also have some structure to allow monitoring and controlling. These methodologies see the different prototypes created during the development as different from the actual application (that is created by re-implementing the prototypes) and some have only a fixed number of stages. In this sense they are not real iterative methods.

Another related thread of research is methodologies for the development of ontologies, in particular the On-To-Knowledge (OTK) methodology (Sure and Studer 2002). OTK proposes a relatively lightweight, multi-stage approach that allows for some iterative cycles. However, this too is not really an iterative method since it considers the refinement steps only when a final product fails the evaluation. OTK also focuses on ontologies as tools for navigation and retrieval, less for inferences – hence there is, for example, no notion of "test" in the OTK methodology.

# 3 Agile Software Development and XP

Agile software development is based on the core ideas of simplicity and speed. An agile method is one that defines software developments as follows (Abrahamsson et al. 2002):

- Incremental: Software is created in an evolutionary, iterative way with many small software releases in rapid succession.
- Cooperative: Software developers and customers are constantly working together in close cooperation.
- Straightforward: The method itself is easy to understand and easy to apply.
- Adaptive: The method makes it easy to react to late braking changes.

Many agile methods for software development have been proposed, such as XP, Scrum, FDD or DSDM (Beck 1999; Schwaber and Beedle 2002; Palmer and Felsing 2002; Stapleton 1997). The description in this paper is based on the well-known XP methodology, although most of the ideas presented are applicable to the general problem of adopting agile methods to the development of rule bases. For brevity only a short overview of XP can be given here; the interested reader can find more complete descriptions in the works by Beck (1999) and Beck and Andres (2004).

A simplified view of the XP methodology is shown in Fig. 1. XP can be understood as being structured in six phases (Abrahamsson et al. 2002):

- In the *exploration phase* the customers create the requirements for the software system by specifying "User Stories" – things the system needs to do for them. At the same time the developers familiarize themselves with the technology needed for the project and investigate any critical parts by creating prototypes.

- In the *release planning phase* the user stories are prioritized and a rough cost estimate is made for them. Also in the planning phase customers and developers agree on the user stories to be included in the first release.
- In the *iteration phase* a planned release is first broken down into multiple iterations. Within each iteration the user stories are broken down into programming tasks. The iterations are time boxed (typically 1–3 weeks), and user stories are added or removed to arrive at a plan realizable in this time. A quick design is done at the beginning of each iteration and testing is used as a tool for verification and validation. Code is integrated continuously and run against acceptance tests representing user stories (that are ideally created directly by customers). XP also stipulates a number of best practices for development, such as stand-up meetings, pair programming, collective code ownership or the recommendation to refactor mercilessly.
- In the *release phase* further tests are made to ensure that the system is fast and reliable enough to be deployed. Feedback from the released and deployed system influences the release planning. Work on the next release then commences.
- The *maintenance* and *death phases* not shown here deal with later development stages when further development takes second place to customer support.

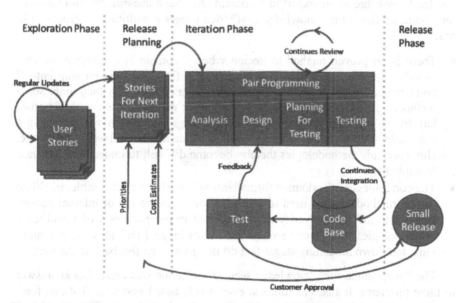

**Fig. 1.** A simplified view of XP according to Abrahamsson (2004). The maintenance and death phases have been omitted for brevity

Extreme programming is a general software development methodology that can be applied to the development of rule-based systems. However, it was created from experiences mainly in object-oriented programming and its application to rule-based systems is not always straight forward and warrants discussion. On the basis of our experiences with the development of multiple rule bases, we therefore propose three new principles, changes to the iteration planning phase and two new best practices for the actual development.

# 4 Core Principles

We propose three guiding principles for the development of rule bases with XP.

## 4.1 Programme First, Knowledge Second

Many existing methodologies for the creation of rule bases systems put at their core the idea that rule bases are not only programmes but first and foremost attempts to capture the knowledge in one domain. This idea imposes new validation criteria on the development of such systems: no longer is it possible to validate a system by showing that it completes the tasks it was created for; rather such systems must be validated by showing/proofing some mapping between the systems and the knowledge of the expert in a domain. Although unassailable from a theoretic point of view, this "knowledge first" idea causes a multitude of problems in practice:

- There is no proven method to decide when a domain is completely or adequately captured, when the modelling task is finished. This missing cut-off point can lead to the modelling process dragging on for a very long time. Some methodologies (see the related work section for details) try to assail this problem by giving excessive guidance on knowledge acquisition and proposing a multitude of interconnected formal models to identify the relevant knowledge. However, this methodologies thereby become difficult to understand and hard to implement.
- The correctness of the domain formalization is posing similar problems. While formal methods can be used to at least show some notion of internal consistency, it is still hard to verify rule-based system independently of actual tests. Methodologies that centre around the "knowledge first" idea often require long, top-down modelling stages that do not give much feedback to the user.

The "programme first, knowledge second" principle was created as an answer to these problems. It states as follows: even a rule-based system is first and foremost created to solve, and evaluated against a number of tasks. The idea that it represents the knowledge in a domain is secondary to that: it is only a guideline on how this task is to be solved.

## 4.2 Interactive Rule Creation

End-user programmers tend to build software system in a trial-and-error, incremental way, learning while they are building the system (Myers et al. 2006). Many development environments for object-oriented or script languages have long offered support for this kind of working: compiling programmes on the fly while they are edited, allowing starting of a programme at the touch of a button and some even allowing changes to the code while a programme is running. For current development environments for rule-based systems similar support is not always offered. Hence the need for the "interactive rule creation" principle: the agile development of rule bases must be supported by an environment that enables the developers to instantly try out their rules and see how they interact with the rest of the rule base. To try out a rule can mean both to see which (new) inferences a rule enables and to pose queries to the entire rule base. Debugging support must be available for the cases where the results do not match the user's expectations.

## 4.3 Explanation Is Documentation

Rule-based systems are often created for high-level task, tasks that have not been implemented before and for which there is no clear algorithm. With these application scenarios comes the need for explanation subsystems. It has long been realized that in order to gain acceptance for such systems they need to somehow explain the process that leads to an answer. For example, a typical application for rule-based systems is the rating of applicants for loans based on their credit history and other data; the decision on whether to grant or deny a loan is then based on this rating. For such systems an explanation of the reasoning process is important to gain acceptance by the users and possibly to help the user deal with an upset customer. For these reasons explanation subsystems were part of many rule-based systems since the days of the early expert systems. The explanation facilities differ between systems but usually allow investigation of the proof after a result has been created. To make the proof better understandable and more informative, rules are often augmented with human readable templates, provenance information. In some systems meta-rules are used to aggregate or hide certain parts of the proof for a more concise representation.

The important observation here is that the data added to the rules for the purpose of explanation are a kind of documentation. This leads directly to the "explanation is documentation" principle: in rule bases that support explanations the data added for the explanation are (most of) the documentation. Explanation data and documentation are managed as one.

## 5 Iteration Planning

XP stipulates that at the beginning of each iteration the user stories are broken down into programming tasks. This informal analysis phase needs to be adapted for rule bases systems for three reasons:

- Rule bases are often only parts of larger systems; hence the system architecture has to be used to identify what a user story means for the rule base.
- Rule bases are often built to represent complex high-level knowledge that is not widely available in an organisation; hence a systematic attempt must be made to identify sources for this knowledge.
- It is prerogative for the creation of rule bases that the entities the rules work on are well defined; e.g., it causes havoc when one rule assumes employees to include retirees and another assumes the contrary.

To address these challenges, we propose to prefix the decomposition of user stories into programming task with a refinement process (see Fig. 2).

The starting points are the user stories for an iteration and the system architecture – some notion of how the rule base is integrated into the overall system. Based on this information query stories are created. A query story describes what kind of query is asked to the rule base in order to enable a user story. Query stories (rather than user stories) are used to create the acceptance tests for the rule base.

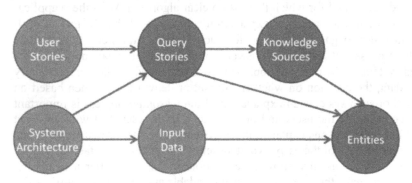

**Fig. 2.** A high-level view of the revised iteration planning stage

In the next step the query stories are evaluated on whether the knowledge needed to implement them is available within the project group creating the system. If not, knowledge sources must be identified to fill this gap. Knowledge sources can be for example

- additional experts available to help;
- documents such as text books, manuals, documented procedures;
- reusable data such as Web ontologies.

In parallel, based on the overall system architecture, the input data is identified. Input data are the data a rule base is meant to process, such as tables in existing databases or messages arriving from other programme parts. The purpose of collecting the input data is to use them for the identification of the entities in the domain. Other inputs for the identification of the domain entities are the query stories and the knowledge sources. The output of this process is a description of the entities the rule base should work with. This description can be informal or be a formal ontology that can be used for verification throughout the creation of the rules. In many cases the description of the entities can be largely derived from the schema for– and the documentation of – the input data.

Query stories, knowledge sources and the identified entities form the input for the rest of the iteration that commences with the decomposition of user stories in programming tasks.

# 6 Development

In object-oriented or procedural programming the overall structure of the programme is explicitly created by the developers and often directly visualized, which is not so in rule-based systems. In object-oriented programmes the overall structure is given by the class hierarchy, links between objects and method calls. In rule-based systems the connections between rules are made by the inference engine on an on-demand basis depending on data and the query asked. This automatic interaction between rules makes rule-based systems very flexible; however, the hidden nature of the rule interactions also causes problems:

- It makes it difficult for developers to see the overall structure of the programme. In particular this causes problems during refactoring where it cannot easily be seen which other rules are affected by a change.
- It makes it hard to verify that the rule interactions work as intended and complicates the diagnosis for the cases where it does not.

Another problem is that often rule languages do not have an equivalent for the strong typing of many programming languages and hence fewer errors can be found at compile time.

These challenges mandate some additions to the methods and best practices of the actual development stage. A view of the development stage is shown in Fig. 3. At its core it shows the test, debug and programme activities directly interconnected – as mandated by the interactive principle described earlier. These activities are supported by test coverage, anomaly detection and visualization. Test coverage plays a similar rule as it does in the development of object-oriented systems; visualization and anomaly detection, however, are unique additions for the development of rule bases and are discussed in the next two sections.

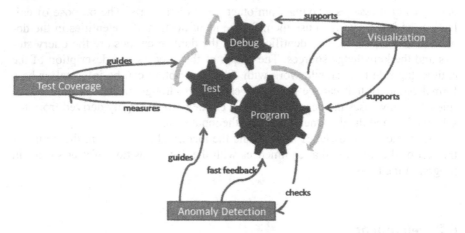

**Fig. 3.** A high-level view of the revised development stage

## 6.1 Anomaly Detection

Anomalies are symptoms of probable errors in the knowledge base (Preece and Shinghal 1994). Anomaly detection is a static verification technique to identify and show these anomalies to the user. Anomalies are often concerned with the hidden interaction structure between rules – one of the most commonly identified anomalies is a rule cycle. Anomaly detection is a well-established tool for the development of rule bases. Anomalies are commonly divided into four large categories (Preece and Shinghal 1994):

- Circularity – rules that can cause inference engines to run indefinitely.
- Ambivalence – in particular contradictory rules.
- Deficiency – input data never used in rules or other symptoms of missing parts in the rule base.
- Redundancy – rules that conclude statements that are never used, duplicate rules, subsumed rules, unsatisfiable rules, etc.

Anomaly detection heuristics should be used constantly to check the rules as they are formulated. The anomalies found form a fast feedback to the developer during programming and allow to quickly correct mistakes. Anomalies in the rule base that the developer does not understand as error can form a guidance for parts of the rule base that should be thoroughly tested.

In accordance with the paradigm of "interactivity" stated earlier, the anomalies should be calculated without requiring specific attention of the user and should instantly reflect the changes done by the developers.

## 6.2 Visualization

The introduction of this section has established that the invisibility of the overall structure of rule bases is a major impediment for their creation. One way to alleviate this problem is to attempt to identify and visualize this structure. This can be done based on the static or the dynamic structure of the rule base (Zacharias 2007):

- The static structure is based solely on the rules (and not the facts) and tries to identify the interactions between rules that could happen, if the rule base were to be used with the right facts.
- The dynamic structure of a rule base is based on the actual rule interactions that happen during queries to the rule base.

Such visualizations that show the actual/possible interactions between rules can then be used by the developers to aid programming, debugging and in particular refactoring.

## 7 Conclusion and Future Work

Current methodologies for the creation of rule-based systems fail to address the challenges posed by changes in project structure and in developers training. Agile methods from the world of object-oriented programming seem better suited to meet these challenges but cannot be applied to rule-based systems without considerable changes. To facilitate the application of agile methods for the development of rule-based systems, we propose three new development principles and changes to the iteration planning and development stages. The three principles are "interactive rule creation", "explanation is documentation" and "programme first, knowledge second". The iteration planning stage is changed to account for (1) the embedded nature of rule bases, (2) the need to identify the domain entities before rules are created and (3) the problem that the knowledge needed to create a rule base may not be easily available. The development stage is extended with anomaly detection and rule base visualization to deal with the invisibility of the overall rule base structure that hinders programming, debugging and refactoring.

In future we plan to further develop the application of agile methods for rule-based systems, in particular to account more clearly for projects where developers and customers are in fact the same people. Also, there are still considerable technical challenges in creating anomaly detection heuristics that are fast enough to support interactive rule creation. Finally, the overall visualizations of rule bases are a question that has been largely ignored by the research community and that hence knows only few approaches and implementations.

# References

Abrahamsson, P., Salo, O. & Ronkainen, J. (2002) *Agile software development methods Review and analysis*, VTT Finland, Espoo.

ANSI (1992) Life cycle development of knowledge-based systems using DoD-Std 2167A. ANSI/AIAA G-031-1992.

Beck, K. (1999) Embracing change with Extreme Programming. IEEE Computer 32(10), pp. 70–77.

Beck, K. & Andres, C. (2004) *Extreme Programming Explained*, Addison Wesley, Boston.

Harrison, W. (July–Aug. 2004) The dangers of end-user programming. IEEE Software 21(4), pp. 5–7.

Kifer, M. & de Bruijn, J. & Boley, H. & Fensel, D (2005) A realistic architecture for the semantic web. *Proceedings of the First International Conference on Rules and Rule Markup Languages for the Semantic Web* (RuleML 2005).

Kingston, J. (1992) Pragmatic KADS: A methodological approach to a small knowledge-based systems project. International Journal of Knowledge Engineering 9(4), pp. 171–180.

Larman, C. & Basili, V.R. (2003) Iterative and incremental development: A brief history. IEEE Computer 36(6), pp. 47–56.

MacCormack, A. (2001) Product-development practices that work. MIT Sloan Management Review 42(2), pp. 75–84.

Merrit, D. (January 2004) Best practices for rule-based application development. The Architecture Journal 1(1), http://msdn.microsoft.com/en-us/arcjournal/aa480018.aspx.

Miller, L. (1990) A realistic industrial strength life cycle model for knowledge-based systems development and testing. AAAI Workshop Notes: Validation and Verification.

Myers, B., Ko, A. & Burnett, M. (2006) Invited research overview: End-user programming. *ACM Conference on Human–Computer Interaction (CHI'06)*.

Palmer, S.R. & Felsing, J.M. (2002) *A Practical Guide to Feature-Driven Development*, Prentice Hall, Upper Saddle River, NJ.

Plant, R.T. & Gamble, R. (1997) A multilevel framework for KBS development. International Journal of Human-Computer Studies 46, pp. 523–547.

Preece, A.D. & Shinghal, R. (1994) Foundation and application of knowledge base verification. International Journal of Intelligent Systems 9(8), pp. 683–701.

Rossen, M.B., Balling, J. & Nash, H. (2004) Everyday programming: Challenges and opportunities for informal Web development. *Proceedings of the 2004 IEEE Symposium on Visual Languages and Human Centric Computing*.

Scaffidi, C., Shaw, M. & Myers, B. (2005) Estimating the number of end user programmers In *Proceedings of the 2005 IEEE Symposium on Visual Languages and Human-Centric Computing*, pp. 207–214.

Schreiber, G., Akkermanns, H., Aniewierden, A., de Hoog, A., Shadbolt, N., Van de Velde, W. & Weilinger, B. (1999) *Knowledge Engineering and Management: The CommonKADS Methodology*, MIT Press, Cambridge, MA.

Schwaber, K. & Beedle, M. (2002) *Agile Software Development with Scrum*, Prentice Hall, Upper Saddle River, NJ.

Seer, K. (August 2005) The business rules awareness survey. Business Rule Journal 6(8), http://www.brcommunity.com/b242.php.

Stapleton, J. (1997) *Dynamic Systems Development Method – The Method in Practice*, Addison Wesley Longman, Harlow, Essex, UK.

Stokes, M. (ed.) (2001) *Managing Engineering Knowledge, MOKA: Methodology for Knowledge Based Engineering Applications*, Professional Engineering and Publishing Limited, London, UK.

Sure, Y. & Studer R. (2002) On-To-Knowledge methodology [Technical report], University of Karlsruhe, Germany.

Weitzel, H.R. & Kerschberg, L. (1989) Developing knowledge-based systems: Reorganizing the system development life cycle. Communications of the ACM 45(11), pp. 16–19.

Yen, J. & Lee, J. (1993) A task based methodology for specifying expert systems. IEEE Intelligent Systems 8(1), pp. 8–15.

Zacharias, V. (2007) Visualizing Rule Bases – The Overall Structure. *7th International Conference on Knowledge Management I-Know 2007*. Special Track on Knowledge Visualization and Discovery.

# Is There Only One Systems Development Life Cycle?

J. Hedman and M. Lind

School of Business and Informatics, University College of Borås, Sweden
jonas.hedman@hb.se, mikael.lind@hb.se

**Abstract** This paper contributes to the literature on information systems development life cycle (SDLC) by presenting an enhanced SDLC model, which integrated three interdependent and complementary, but different SDLCs. It is based on integration of the traditional and well-established idea of custom development with package development and commercially off the shelf (COTS) selection and implementation. Package development includes all software made for a market, whereas COTS selection and implementation refers to the selection and implementation of package software. Although there are many similarities between the life cycles, many differences are important to understand. We highlight both the differences and the intersection between the life cycles and outline an integrated SDLC model, which will be used to discuss future research and curricula issues.

## 1 Introduction

The traditional information systems development life cycle (SDLC) is one of the more influential concepts within the information systems discipline (Avison and Fitzgerald 2006). It has had a tremendous impact on our conceptual thinking and understanding of information systems curricula, research, and practice. It is one of our discipline's selling points. The SDLC is a process model that describes and prescribes the phases that have to (or at least should) be carried out in the process of developing an information system for specific usage situations. It can be conceived as a generic model or a grand theory. In its purest form it includes five straightforward phases – planning and problem identification, analysis, design, realization, and use and maintenance, and is often referred to as the Waterfall model. This model is the basis of contemporary methods. If we, for example, consider Rational Unified Process (RUP), one of the dimensions for distinguishing increments is the phases according to the Waterfall model.

There are several potential strengths of the SDLC. It is simple and easy to understand; it is well established; there exists methodological support; it includes concrete deliverables and milestones, and support tools for each phase (Avison and Fitzgerald 2006). Meanwhile, the SDLC model has been criticized. For

C. Barry et al. (eds.), *Information Systems Development: Challenges in Practice, Theory, and Education, Vol.1*, doi: 10.1007/978-0-387-68772-8_9,

instance, Boehm (1988) claimed that the Waterfall model lacked relevance, since information systems and software are not developed through a straightforward stage process. It includes iterations, reviews, and feedback loops. There are several other issues with the traditional SDLC, such as failure to address the needs of management, strong technical emphasis leading to user dissatisfaction, and an assumption of and emphasis on custom development (Avision and Fitzgerald 2006). However, our main argument for writing this paper is that organizations of today are increasingly developing information systems through an acquisition process of packaged software (also so-called Commercially Off The Shelf (COTS), shrink wrap, or application package) (Sawyer 2000; Andersson and Nilsson 1996). These packages are configured and adapted to the user's requirements or the user has to adapt to the package. This way of developing information systems can be compared with the traditional SDLC (Sawyer 2001; Rosemann 2001; Markus and Tanis 2000).

In the beginning, development of information systems only meant one thing – in-house development of solutions from scratch. Hardware and software were uniquely designed and developed for a specific situation for an organization, e.g., Lyons Electronic Office and General Electric's payroll system (George 2000). Since the first package software was sold, the share of custom (unique) development in the software market has decreased (Sawyer 2000; George 2000). According to Sawyer's (2000), OECD (1998) estimates the software market in 1998 to $200 billion, of which $140 billion is related to package software. Today, organizations acquire software packages from the market, such as office packages, antivirus program, or ERP systems. We argue that this process is a type of SDLC, which is not sufficiently covered by the traditional SDLC. Whether a consequence of or a precondition for the change in how organizations develop information systems has created a new market or whether it is the market that has changed the way organizations develop information system is up for debate. Regardless of what, a new super market involving the largest software companies, such as Mircosoft, Oracle, and SAP, has established since the mid-1960s. Their core business process comprises also a SDLC, but with a different terminology and goals than custom development or COTS selection and implementation (Carmel and Becker 1995).

In sum, there are three interrelated, complementary, and simultaneously existing SDLCs. The first is custom development supporting the process of developing a custom-made information system for specific users. The second is the development of package software. The last is COTS selection and implementation. There are several similarities and differences regarding concepts and terminology used, phases, and goals and outputs between the different life cycles. Sawyer (2000, 2001) and Carmel and Becker (1995) call for further research into the differences and similarities between these three SDLCs.

A generic SDLC has several strengths in its potential in giving a good overview. We do however claim that the three processes identified have their own certain characteristics, but at the same time they give an expression for a variance of a more generic SDLC. This level of granularity is important to reach in order to get a comprehensive understanding of what the information systems field is characterized of today. Thus, the purpose of this paper is to present an integrated SDLC model, including custom development, package development, and COTS selection and implementation. The integrated model will accordingly reflect different SDLCs in contemporary practice, and is to be used for stimulating a broadening of the perspective in the information systems community. The only type of software development that is beyond this paper is embedded systems, i.e., software made for hardware.

The structure of the paper is as follows. In the next section we will begin with our legacy, i.e., custom development, followed by package software and COTS selection and implementation. The section is then concluded with a summary where the differences are highlighted. The third section outlines the integrated SDLC model. In the fourth section, we discuss the validity of models. We then conclude the paper.

## 2 Information Systems Development Processes

In this section, we will briefly introduce the three life cycles with an emphasis on distinguishing features (adopted from Sawyer 2000), including *industry pressure, labeling of phases in the development process, outcome of the development process, work roles*, and *degree of methodological support*. A note of caution though: The vast number of books, articles, approaches, methods, tools, types of information systems, etc., makes this task close to mission impossible. However, we hope that we are able to highlight some of the main characteristics of each SDLC in order to create a basis for a fruitful discussion.

### *2.1 Custom Development*

The history of information systems development (ISD) is about 60 years old, since the first software was developed in the 1940s (George 2000). Today, custom development is carried out by an internal IT department or with the assistance of external software companies (Sawyer 2000) or through a combination thereof (George 2000). A distinguishing aspect of custom development is that information systems are made-to-order for specific users. Sawyer (2000) characterizes custom development as follows: (1) industry cost pressures and focus on satisfaction, user acceptance, and return on investment; (2) the development is done by staff position in support units, user participation is desired, mature development process, separation between design and development; (3) the culture is bureaucratic and less individualistic; and (4) development teams are project focused, people work in many projects, paid by salary, and rely on formal specifications. The process of developing custom-made information system is illustrated by one of many classical SDLC, namely, the Waterfall model. It has five phases that capture the basic structure of a systems life cycle (George 2000).

1. *Planning* is the first phase and includes the activities that identify the need for a system, such as problem identification and feasibility study.

2. *Analysis* is the next phase, where the existing systems/IS should be analyzed and the requirements should be specified.
3. The *design* phase investigates whether a solution can be realized. This involves logical and physical designs.
4. *Realization* is the fourth phase and this is when the solution is programmed and installed. This is also commonly referred to as roll-out.
5. The *use and maintenance* phase includes keeping the system up and running and continuous updates. This proceeds until a new life cycle begins. A life cycle perspective on the system means that the introduction of a new life cycle implies a liquidation of the old system.

Custom development begins with a decision to develop an information system to solve a specific problem or meet some new requirements. The reason for this decision may vary between organizations and situations, but an underlying rationality is that we can design and build something better than buying the solution from someone else. To support this process, there is a large number of approaches (such as SSM, Speech Act, Decision Support, and Agile), methods (such as RUP, SCRUM, and SSAD), and techniques (such as ER diagram, Use Cases, and EPC models) (Iivari et al. 1998). Systems analysts, systems designers, and programmers do the work, and the output is an information system or software. Many of our legacy systems were built through custom development (Carmel and Sawyer 1998). Today, custom development is common in new application areas, such as e-commerce (George 2000) and m-commerce (Andersson and Hedman 2006), or in certain governmental areas (Sawyer 2000), e.g., defense, customs, and police force.

Custom development takes advantage of several components from package development, such as Web browsers for managing user interaction, protocols for managing computer-to-computer interaction, databases, software development tools, operating systems, application-programming interfaces for integration, and custom-developed information systems with package software.

## 2.2 Package Development

Owing to a number of reasons, such as market opportunities, efficiency in development, and economics of scale, the development of tradable software products has continuously grown since the late 1960s. The development of tradable software products includes all types of software that can be bought from a store, vendor, or distributor (Andersson and Nilsson 1996; Carmel 1997; Carmel and Sawyer 1998). There are two broad categories of package software. First, there are system-related packages, for example, operating systems, anti-virus tools, network operating systems. The other category is application packages, which are designed to support specific business problems, such as word processing, financial, human resource, and sales (Sawyer 2000).

Sawyer (2000) characterizes package development (compare with custom development earlier) as follows: (1) industry time to market pressures and focus on profit and market share; (2) the development is done by line position, users are not involved, immature process controlled through coordination; (3) the culture is entrepreneurial and individualistic; and (4) development teams are product focused, incentive systems, and rely on visions as specifications. Most packages are customizable. They can be adapted to a certain degree to specific user requirements (George 2000). The degree of adaptation of the system has to be taken into account in the development of a package (Regnell et al. 2001). When designing a package, the designer must foresee areas in which the package must be flexible in. The output of package development is a generic product that can be used by many users (Hedman 2003). Therefore, requirements specifications are market driven. The phases of package development have different labeling and goals than custom development. Carmel and Becker (1995) and Sawyer (2001) outlined such life cycles. According to Carmel and Becker (1995), the following phases can be distinguished:

1. The first phase is *business idea formulation*, when a package vendor starts up. The underlying reason for developing the package is a business plan, which is the justification for starting a package-developing firm. The driven forces are technology push/pull or market pull.
2. The second phase is *proof of concept* (POC), where the initial ideas are translated into some preliminary requirements and technical specifications, followed by prototype building and testing of concept.
3. The third phase is *realization*, including design, coding, and intermediary testing, followed by final testing.
4. The fourth phase is *production*, when the software is packaged for distribution.
5. The final phase is *sales*, i.e., the activities done to sell the package in the market.

Termination of this life cycle may occur because of changes in the market demand decreases or because of technology changes. This may lead to a new and improved version or even a totally new package.

The process of developing package software leads to some new work roles. The most distinguishing are the business innovator and the sales and marketing staff (Carmel and Becker 1995). These roles are not traditionally covered by IS curricula, but are essential for package development. We can also assume that there is need for requirements on new skills and capabilities of the work force.

## 2.3 COTS Selection and Implementation

We now turn to the point of view of the buyers of package software, i.e., COTS selection and implementation. The selection and implementation of COTS is often based on a strategic or policy decision, which states that the organization should buy software, not build them. There are several reasons for selecting a package software, e.g., technical (replacement of old and outdated IS), integration of disparate IS, business (changes of production mode, e.g., make-to-order vs. make-to-stock), organizational (new organizational structure), strategic (to gain competitive advantage), and due to difficulties with in-house development. The user organization configures the package to its requirements or adapts to the logic of the package. Compared with traditional systems development, one of the differences lie in the initial phases where an evaluation of the functionality takes place instead of a traditional analysis and design phase. Thus, evaluation becomes critical in the process of selecting COTS systems.

Research into COTS has mainly addressed Enterprise Systems implementation. There is some research focusing on life cycles (Markus and Tanis 2000), but there are fewer research attempts focusing on the difference between COTS selection and implementation and custom development on one hand or package development on the other hand. Some of the exceptions are Rosemann (2001), Hedman (2003), and Sawyer (2001). Sawyer (2001) labeled the phases as system planning, selection, initiation, needs analysis, function analysis, gap-fit comparison, installation, and support and upgrade. Depending on the type of package software, i.e., system or application, the installation phase can be very different in scope and workload. For instance, the installation of large ERP systems comprehends unique product-specific methods for managing the entire project; configures the package to user requirements, and implements the package in its user context. This type of method is labeled as COTS methods (Hedman 2004). For instance, consulting and package vendors, such as SAP AG and Accenture, provide the package-adopting firm with methods, e.g., AcceleratedSAP (ASAP) by SAP AG, Method R/3 by Accenture (this method is Accenture's own proprietary method for implementing R/3), and Implex provided by Intentia to implement the Movex system. These methods do not cover the selection, since they are product-specific and thus begin at the design phase. An illustration of this type of method is ASAP, which is based on best practice from a number of implementation projects, primarily in USA (Hedman 2004). It incorporates the knowledge and consulting practices from previous projects and in part from information systems literature. The method is packaged as a computer-based project management and implementation method that comprises five phases:

1. *Project preparations*, in which project mission and scope are defined.
2. *Business blueprint* includes a complete and comprehensive analysis of requirements and business processes.
3. *Realization* when the system is configured and tested.
4. *Final preparation* includes transfer of data from the old systems and end-user training. This is also commonly referred as roll-out.
5. *The go live and support phase* is when the actual installations take place.

Each of the phases includes a large number of tools and utilities to simplify the work, such as Concept Check Tool for handling data volume conflicts and Implementation Guide for supporting the configuration of the system (Hedman 2004). Third parties, not developers, typically implement COTS. ASAP follows the same overall stages and phases as in the system life cycles described for developing information systems from scratch. However, there is one important exception: the Business Blueprint phase comprises both requirements analysis and system specification and design, but in reverse order. ASAP may in some cases be useful, but it has some limitations. Since the method focuses on installing the system, it is not complete in generating suggestions for use of information technology for supporting organizations and businesses. ASAP is technically oriented and the goal is to install the system. The steps and procedures of this type of ISD method change, in particular, the requirements specification, which is addressed in the next section. This does however mean that there is also a need for considering how a life cycle for COTS (package) development is to be constituted and intertwined with a life cycle for COTS selection and implementation.

## 2.4 Distinguishing Features of the Three Life Cycles

There are many similarities between custom development, package development, and COTS selection and implementation, including the fact that they all involve a life cycle and are all related to information systems and software. Custom and package developments share the realization phase, and custom development and COTS selection and implementation have the same concluding phases. The obvious intersection point between package development and COTS selection and implementation is sales people and procurer of package software; i.e., the output of package development is the input in COTS selection and implementation. Nevertheless, there are many differences as well, including different industry pressure, phases, overall outcome, work roles, and degree of methodological support. Table 1 summaries the similarities and differences.

**Table 1.** Different characteristics of the three different information systems development processes

| | Industry pressure | Phases | Overall outcome | Work roles | Degree of methodological support |
|---|---|---|---|---|---|
| Custom development | Cost pressure | Planning Analysis Design Realization Use and maintenance | To solve a problem through the development of an information system | System analyst System designer Programmer | Large |
| Package development | Market pressure | Business idea Proof of concept Realization Production Sales and marketing Termination | To develop and sell a package | Innovator Sales person | Some |
| COTS selection and implementation | NA | Initiation Selection and configuration Implementation Use and maintenance | To buy and install a pre-made information system | ERP consultants | Product specific methods |

*COTS* commercially off the shelf

## 3 Towards an Enhanced Model of Information Systems
   Development Life Cycle

On the basis of the above-mentioned review of the widely ramified literature, we would propose an enhanced SDLC model that includes the following interrelated SDLCs, starting with our legacy of custom development, followed by package development to be concluded with COTS selection and implementation. Each of these SDLCs co-exists, but can be studied individually. It is however our intention to put forward that such co-existence also means that there is a need to understand these three SDLCs as parts of development processes in practice. To pinpoint such wholeness, several links between the SDLCs to illustrate both feedback loops and path dependencies are also included. Do however note that all three SDLCs are variances of the more generic SDLC.

Figure 1 shows these SDLCs, and dependencies between them are illustrated. The first concerns custom development or the process of developing unique information systems that are typically built for specific users. The second ISD process concerns package software, i.e., activities performed by vendors or suppliers for the development of COTS products. The last concerns the selection, configuration, implementation, and use and maintenance of COTS products. The logic of the expanded SDLC framework is as follows. Information systems are developed and implemented through these three unique, but similar and interdependent life cycles. The first supports the process of solving uniquely identified problems through the design of new information systems from scratch. It begins with planning and problem identification, followed by analysis, design, realization, and use and maintenance. The realized information system can then form the basis for the development of a business idea in package development. Package development begins either as an exploitation process of a previously built customer-unique system or as an identified market opportunity. The package is an offer to the market, among other competing offers, and part of COTS selection and implementation. COTS selection and implementation converts a software package through configuration and implementation to a usable information system. In cases where the package needs modification or customization, new or adjusted functionality is added, using the SDLC from custom development or maintenance activities during COTS selection and implementation.

Each of the three SDLCs is built upon the logic that a SDLC comprises several phases managing a task based on a clearly defined input (prerequisite) and output (result). On a generic level we acknowledge that the phases in all the SDLCs could be seen as (1) one (or several) initial phase(s), (2) analysis and design phase, (3) a phase of realization, and (4) a phase of maintenance. We also acknowledge the iterative and incremental steps within a SDLC as identified in the spiral model (c.f. Boehm 1988). This aspect is however not emphasized in this paper since we are more concerned with the identification of, the constituents of, and the relation between three essential SDLCs.

Another important foundation for distinguishing between the three SDLCs is that custom development and COTS selection and implementation are aimed towards particular clients while package development is aimed towards potential clients. Lind (2002) has earlier propagated for such distinction for process definitions. This means that the logic of the ordering and initiation of the work to be performed within the processes differs when the work is performed, in particular, for potential clients. Therefore, package development is more driven by seeing a potential in a future business case rather than specific needs from a client (as the case in custom development and COTS selection and implementation). An underlying perspective in the development of the model depicted in Fig. 1 is the acknowledgment of both a producer (supplier) and a procurer (customer) perspective.

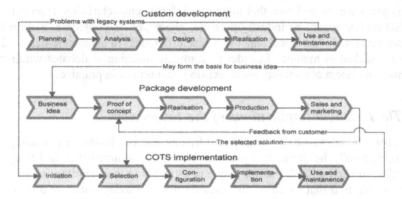

**Fig. 1.** Three different systems development life cycles and their interrelationships

# 4 Discussion

The validity of the model can be assessed by three particular criteria: the integration of the model (logical coherence), relative explanatory power, and its practical and theoretical relevance. The integration of the model will not be further elaborated here; we refer to the previous section.

## 4.1 The Extended SDLC Model in Comparison

The extended SDLC model is characterized by an integration of custom development, package development, and COTS selection and implementation, and shows the interdependency between the three different SDLCs. There are several competing models, such as Alter's (1999) generic system life cycle model, Carmel and Becker's (1995) process model for packaged software development, Sawyer's (2000) comparison of custom development and package development, Hedman's (2003) and Rosemann's (2001) enhanced ERP life cycle models. These papers address only one of the SDLC or two of them. The only paper that discusses or at least acknowledges the existence of all three SDLCs is the one by Sawyer (2001), who discusses changes in system development from a market perspective. Sawyer (2000) compares traditional SDLC or custom development with market-oriented SDLC, which includes both package development and COTS selection and development. However, instead of our proposed terminology, he uses consumer SDLC for COTS selection and implementation and producer SDLC for package development and does not integrate them. Our proposal, which we find necessary, is to acknowledge the dependencies between the three SDLCs. Furthermore, Sawyer's (2000) ambition is not to present an enhanced model, but to increase the awareness of market-driven SDLCs. By our acknowledgment of these three similar but different interrelated SDLCs a higher level of precision in stating requirements on methods to be used in the different phases could be achieved. Thus, we strongly object to Alter (1999), who claims that there is only need for one general SDLC. In this paper we have shown that there are different characteristics dependent on the ISD context regarding industry pressure, phases, overall outcome, work roles, and degree of methodological support. These differences in characteristics need to be distinguished in methods in order to stimulate meaningful debates within the information system community about existing phenomena in practice.

## 4.2 The Practical Implications of the Framework

How about the relevance of the proposed framework, i.e., its theoretical and practical usefulness? The framework provides a structure of how different life cycles interrelate to each other by identifying and articulating their similarities and differences. We find that much of the research reported today does not discuss the variety of SDLCs as discussed in this paper. It is, however, an existing phenomenon in practice that different kinds of life cycles do co-exist. We therefore believe that research must reflect upon these phenomena in practice.

Consequently, since much of the research reported upon (c.f. Sect. 2) covers SDLC for custom development, there is a great need for research on the two "new" SDLCs. Examples of research questions are as follows:

1. What triggers package development or how does it begin? Is this a process of exploitation or exploration, each with its unique theoretical frame of reference?
2. How should user involvement be handled during package development?
3. What methodological support is desired for selecting packages (as part of COTS selection and implementation)?

Furthermore, we should question the proposed model – whether we should strive for a single conception of SDLC or should we expand on those three proposed included in the framework or are even more SDLCs desired? For instance, two types of information systems projects could either be included in existing frameworks or form the basis for new SDLCs as modification or customization on one hand and integration of information systems on the other hand.

The second area of implications is related to information system curricula. We will pose some questions with answers that hopefully will stimulate further debate. The first one is, do we need to adopt existing information system courses and curricula? Yes, we believe so; for instance, courses in introduction to ISD should include the different SDLCs in order to provide the student with a deeper and diversified understanding of information systems development in practice. In addition to that, we foresee new information systems curricula addressing the specific issues involved in COTS selection and implementation and package development. This is motivated by the need for specific requirements for skills and capabilities related to each SDLC. For instance, a person working with COTS implementation needs more knowledge related to business than a person involved in the development of a package does. However, that person needs much more technical skills and capabilities. We probably need to educate people who sell packages. In addition, we need to focus more on requirements specification in general, but also for the specific SDLCs. There is probably a need for more than one IS model curricula, since each of the life cycles requires in part different skills and capabilities of the workforce.

## 5. Conclusions

In this paper, we have presented an enhanced SDLC model that is broader than the traditional conception of SDLC. It is broader in the sense that it acknowledges the different characteristics of three interrelated SDLCs: (1) COTS selection and implementation, (2) package development, and (3) custom development. It is not a radical departure from the traditional conception of SDLC, but offers a broader and more relevant view of the information systems development process. Our stance is that there is a need to acknowledge instances of a generic SDLC in order to achieve a more comprehensive view of systems development of today. The strengths of this model are as follows. First, it is a synthesis of three streams of information systems literature captured in one coherent model that previously have not been integrated, with a few exceptions (e.g. Sawyer 2001). Thus, it is possible to continue to cumulate knowledge in relation to each life cycle as well as to the whole field. Second, it highlights the differences and similarities between the SDLCs, which may be a foundation for formulating new research questions and stimulate curricula development. In relation to research we first suggest that research in particular focuses on the intersection between custom development, package development, and COTS selection and implementation. For instance, integration projects are such a research area. It can be between several packages or between packages and custom-made information systems. A second research area is method engineering along the entire COTS selection and implementation process and in particular to support selection and use, and user involvement in package development. Third, it shows the relationship and interdependencies between the life cycles, which may help practitioners and researchers to reach a common understanding.

**Acknowledgements** The authors appreciate the helpful comments from the anonymous reviewers.

# References

Alter, S. (1999) A general, yet useful theory of information systems. Communications AIS 1(13).

Andersson, B. and Hedman, J. (2006) Issues in the development of a mobile based communication platform for the Swedish Police Force and appointed security guards. 3rd International Conference on Information Systems for Crisis Response and Management, Newark.

Andersson, R. and Nilsson, A. (1996) The standard application package market – An industry in transition? In: M. Lundeberg and B. Sundgren (Eds.). *Advancing Your Business: People and Information Systems in Consert*. Sweden: EFI, Stockholm School of Economics.

Avison, D.E. and Fitzgerald, G. (2006) *Information Systems Development: Methodologies, Techniques, and Tools*, 4th ed. New York, NY: McGraw-Hill.

Boehm, B.W. (1988) A spiral model of software development and enhancement. IEEE Computer 21(5), 61–72.

Carmel, E. (1997) American hegemony in packaged software trade and the culture of software. The Information Society 13(1), 125–142.

Carmel, E. and Becker, S. (1995) A process model for packaged software development. IEEE Transactions of Engineering Management 41(5), 50–61.

Carmel, E. and Sawyer, S. (1998) Packaged software development teams: What makes them different? Information Technology and People 11(1), 7–19.

George, J. (2000) The origins of software: Acquiring systems at the end of the century. In R. Zmud (Ed.). *Framing the Domains of IT Management: Projecting the Future...Through the Past*. Cincinnati, Ohio: Pinnaflex Educational Resources, pp. 263–284.

Hedman, J. (2003) On enterprise systems artifacts: Changes in information systems development and evaluation, Doctoral thesis, Department of Informatics, School of Economics and Management, Lund University, Sweden.

Hedman, J. (2004) Understanding ERP implementation methods: The case of ASAP. 27th IRIS, Falkenberg.

Iivari, J., Hirschheim, R. and Klein, H. (1998) A paradigmatic analysis contrasting information systems development approaches and methodologies. Information Systems Research 9(2), 164–193.

Lind, M. (2002) Dividing businesses into processes – Foundations for modelling essentials. In: K. Liu, R.J. Clarke, P.B. Andersen, R.K. Stamper, E. Abou-Zeid (Eds.). *IFIP TC8/WG8.1 Working Conference on Organizational Semiotics: Evolving a Science of Information Systems*. Boston: Kluwer.

Markus, L. and Tanis, C. (2000) The enterprise systems experience – From adoption to success. In: R. Zmud (Ed.). *Framing the Domains of IT Management: Projecting the Future...Through the Past*. Cincinnati, Ohio: Pinnaflex Educational Resources, pp. 173–207.

Regnell, B., Höst, M., Dag och Natt, J., Beremark, P. and Hjelm, T. (2001) An industrial case study on distributed prioritisation in market driven requirements engineering for packaged software. Requirements Engineering 6, 51–62.

Rosemann, M. (2001) Requirements engineering for enterprise systems. 7th Americas Conference on Information Systems, Boston, MA.

Sawyer, S. (2000) Packaged software: Implications of the differences from custom approaches to software development. European Journal of Information Systems 9, 47–58.

Sawyer, S. (2001) A market-based perspective on information system development. Communication of the ACM 44(11), 97–102.

# Age Differences in Technophobia: An Irish Study

M. Hogan

Business Information Systems Group, Cairnes Graduate School of Business and Public Policy, National University of Ireland, Galway, Ireland, mairead.hogan@nuigalway.ie

**Abstract** This study examined levels of technophobia in a sample of 150 older adults who are members of active retired associations in Ireland and 291 undergraduate students. Technophobia was assessed using Rosen and Weil's Measuring Technophobia Instruments, which determine anxiety, cognitions and attitudes towards computer technology. Technophobia levels were tested for differences between (1) the older adults and students, and (2) the genders. A significant difference in levels of technophobia was found between the two groups, with older adults having higher levels of technophobia than do students. Some gender differences were also evident in the study, with older women showing higher levels of anxiety and technophobia than do the female students.

## 1 Introduction

The number of older adults is growing worldwide, with the term older adult being used to describe various age groups. For the purpose of this study, an older adult is defined as an adult older than 50 years because the sample used comprised members of active retired associations (ARAs) and ranged in age from early 50s to older than 75. The United Nations Population Division (2002) estimates that by the year 2015 the adults older than 60 years will represent 23.7% of the population of the more developed regions, with the figures for Europe representing 24%. This population represents an important segment of computer users, as evidenced by a survey which states that older adults represent the fastest growing online population in the USA (Greenspan 2003). However, this is increasing from a low base, as in 2001 only 22.1% of American adults older than 65 years used a computer at home, work or school, while 19.8% used the Internet (United States Census Bureau 2001). These figures increased to 27.7% and 25.1% respectively in 2003 (United States Census Bureau 2003). Internet usage in the EU 15 (the member countries before expansion in 2004) has increased for adults older than 55 years from 11.5% to 16.9% between 2001 and 2003, although older adults still lag behind younger adults (Commission of the European Communities 2005). This is supported by data from the UK which also suggest that older adults lag behind younger adults in terms of computer usage (Selwyn et al. 2003).

As aspects of daily life continue to become increasingly reliant on information technology, it is important that older adults be able and willing to use it (Morrell et al. 2000). This could be particularly important for the older adults as they become less mobile, as the Internet can be used to enhance their quality of life by developing friendships and accessing a wide variety of Web sites that can mentally stimulate them  (Swindell 2001). The Internet can also be of benefit to older adults by allowing access to government information and services (e-Government) (Phang et al. 2006). They can also utilise a wide variety of health Web sites, which may help those who suffer from illness and who may otherwise have difficulty accessing health information (Swindell 2001; Becker 2004). Tatnall and Lepa (2003) state that older adults who are less mobile could benefit from the use of e-commerce. However, they also note that only a small percentage of older adults use e-commerce, perhaps because of the barriers in place that prevent them from easily using these technologies.  Becker (2004) also states that many health Web sites that would be of interest to older adults are not, in fact, "senior-friendly". This suggests that many older adults are not availing themselves of the potential benefits of using ICT (information and communication technologies). Perhaps the best way to increase older adults' willingness to use information technology may be to "involve them in changing ICT" (Selwyn et al. 2003). This could result in older adults realising the potential benefits of ICT.

## 2 Computer Anxiety

Computer anxiety may prevent older adults from taking full advantage of computers. Research has shown that computer anxiety can adversely affect performance (Dyck and Al-Awar Smither 1994; Anderson 1996; Laguna and Babcock 1997; Brosnan 1998) and acceptance of computer technology (Dyck and Al-Awar Smither 1994; Fagan et al. 2004), a finding that is further supported by a meta-analysis carried out by Chua et al. (1999), who state that computer anxiety causes computer use avoidance. Research into computer anxiety has predominantly looked at younger adults, with students making up the main research cohort. Some researchers have looked beyond students and examined computer anxiety over a wide age range (Dyck and Al-Awar Smither 1992; Dyck and Al-Awar Smither 1994; Laguna and Babcock 1997; Broos 2005; Zhang 2005), while others have concentrated on computer anxiety in older adults exclusively (Morris 1992; Ellis and Allaire 1999; Karavidas et al. 2005; Hogan 2006). Overall, however, older adults have been a neglected cohort in this area of research.

Rosen et al. (1992) developed a series of measurement instruments to assess levels of technophobia, which they describe as anxiety about present or future interactions with computers or computer-related technology; negative global attitudes about computers, their operation or their societal impact; and/or specific negative cognitions or self-critical internal dialogues during actual computer interaction or when contemplating future computer interaction (pp. 7–8). These research instruments have been used and validated in more recent studies (Anthony et al. 2000; McIlroy et al. 2001; Gordon et al. 2003; Hogan 2006) and are used in this study in order to assess levels of technophobia in both older adults and students.

The central question of this research is whether there are differences in levels of technophobia in older and younger adults. A study by Anthony et al. (2000) suggests that technophobia, as measured using the scales developed by Rosen et al. (1992), is correlated with age. This result is supported by both Zhang (2005) and Ellis and Allaire (1999), who found that computer anxiety increases with age, albeit using a measurement scale different from the one used in this study. In contrast to these above-reported studies, studies by Bozionelos (2001) and Dyck et al. (1994) found that older adults displayed lesser computer anxiety than did younger adults, while Chua et al. (1999) found that the effect of age on computer anxiety is not easily observed when the age range is narrow.

The study also examined whether there are gender differences in levels of technophobia between the two groups. Some studies suggest that technophobia, as measured using the scales developed by Rosen et al. (1992), is not related to gender (Anderson 1996; Anthony et al. 2000; Havelka et al. 2004; Korukonda 2005) or that the effect is small (McIlroy et al. 2001). In contrast, a study by Hogan (2006) found a gender difference in levels of technophobia in older adults. Other studies have been carried out using a variety of measurement instruments. However, the results are conflicting, some indicating a gender difference (generally small to moderate) in computer anxiety (Whitley 1996; Broos 2005; Zhang 2005) and others indicating no significant difference in computer anxiety or attitudes (Orr et al. 2001). Chua et al. (1999), in their meta-analysis of relationships between computer anxiety and its three correlates (age, gender and computer experience), found that females are generally more anxious than males among a university undergraduate population, but that the strength of this relationship is not conclusive. Anthony et al. (2000) suggest that the reason for a reduced gender gap in technophobia over the last number of years is the increased exposure of women to computers at college level.

However, all the studies cited (bar those by Broos (2005) and Zhang (2005), both of whom looked at a wide age range, and that by Hogan (2006), who looked exclusively at older adults) dealt with students and younger adults, rather than older adults. A study of older adult computer users (Karavidas et al. 2005) suggest that there is a gender difference in anxiety levels in older adult computer users, with women displaying more anxiety and reporting less computer knowledge, despite the fact that males and females reported similar levels of computer usage.

# 3 Methodology

## 3.1 Participants

The participants in the study consisted of older adults who were members of active retired associations (ARAs) in the west of Ireland and young adults who were first year business undergraduates. The senior participants ranged in age from early 50s to 75+, with 96.2% aged 60 or older. The group consisted of 32 men and 128 women. Their level of computer experience ranged from none to extensive. The ARAs generally had reasonably similar profiles in terms of age, education and computer experience, although the larger groups had a higher percentage of male members than did the smaller groups.

The students ranged in age from 17 to 49, with 92.5% of students younger than 20 years. There were 141 male and 150 female students involved in the study. The students generally had higher levels of computer experience than did the older adults, as all bar 4 of the students who responded had at least some computer experience, while 72 of the older adults who responded had none. However, many of the students had little computer experience prior to starting college. Although the students were all required to attend computer tutorials as part of their course work, the tutorials had just begun and so, little experience had been gained at the time of the study.

## 3.2 Measuring Technophobia

The study was conducted using Rosen et al.'s (1992) *Measuring Technophobia Instruments* and a demographic questionnaire. The questionnaires developed by Rosen et al. (1992) consisted of the following:

1. Computer Anxiety Rating Scale Form C (CARS-C)
   This consists of 20 questions that refer to activities and experiences with computers that might cause anxiety. Respondents are required to indicate how anxious or nervous each situation would make them feel by selecting one of "Not at all", "A little", "A fair amount", "Much", or "Very much".
2. Computer Thoughts Survey Form C (CTS-C)
   This consists of 20 statements, reflecting both positive and negative cognitions while using a computer or thinking about using a computer. Respondents are required to indicate the extent to which they would have each of these thoughts by selecting one of "Not at all", "A little", "A fair amount", "Much", or "Very much".
3. General Attitudes Towards Computers Scale Form C (GATCS-C)
   This consists of 20 statements, reflecting both positive and negative attitudes towards computers. Respondents are required to indicate their level of agreement with the statements using a 5-point Likert scale.

The demographic questionnaire requested information such as gender, age, education, and computer experience.

## 3.3 The Procedure

The demographic questionnaire was prepared and pilot tested. This was then administered in conjunction with the CARS-C, CTS-C and GATCS-C. The CARS-C, CTS-C and GATCS-C were counterbalanced with each appearing first, second and third equally often while the demographic questionnaire appeared last in order to minimize hypothesis guessing on the part of the research participants (Rosen et al. 1992).

The questionnaires were designed to be self-administering. Participants were told to carefully read the instructions on each questionnaire as they vary for each. They were also assured that (1) their responses would remain anonymous and be kept confidential, (2) that they should answer honestly and candidly and (3) that the questionnaires are not a test and that there are no right answers (Rosen et al. 1992). The researcher was also on hand to answer any questions that the respondents might have regarding their understanding of questions. No time limits were imposed on the questionnaires but they were generally completed within 30 min.

# 4 Results

## 4.1 Computer Use

A large percentage of the respondents were computer users, with 99% of students using computers, 0.7% not using computers and 0.3% of students not answering the question ($n = 291$). For the older adults, the percentage of computer users and non-users was reasonably evenly split, with 44.7% of older adults not using computers, 46% using computers and 9.3% not responding to the question ($n = 160$). There was very little difference in the percentages of male and female computer users within each of the two groups, although the differences between the two groups were considerable (100% of male students and 98.7% of female students used computers while 51.5% of older males and 49.6% of older females used computers – see Fig. 1). Within the older adult grouping, the older the study participants in the older adult grouping were, the less likely they were to use computers (see Table 1)

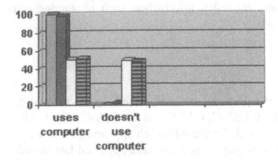

**Fig. 1.** Percentage of computer users in the study

**Table 1.** Computer usage and age for older adults

| Age range (years) | % Who use computers |
|---|---|
| <65 | 61.3 ($n = 34$) |
| 65–69 | 51.6 ($n = 31$) |
| 70–74 | 47.4 ($n = 57$) |
| 75+ | 46.2 ($n = 26$) |

**Table 2.** Reliability coefficients for measurement instruments

| Instrument | Cronbach's alpha coefficient |
|---|---|
| CARS-C (Computer Anxiety Rating Scale) | 0.884 |
| CTS-C (Computer Thoughts Survey) | 0.881 |
| GATCS-C (General Attitude Towards Computers) | 0.388 |

## 4.2 Reliability of the Measures

Although the reliability of the measures has been established previously by Weil and Rosen (1995), it was decided to confirm this since their study did not exclusively involve older adults. Cronbach's alpha coefficient was calculated for each of the research instruments. As can be seen in Table 2, the CARS-C and CTS-C both exhibited a high degree of reliability, whereas the GATCS-C did not. This finding corresponds with those of other studies of participants who were not from the United States (Weil and Rosen 1995; Anthony et al. 2000; Hogan 2006). Owing to its questionable reliability, the GATCS-C data were excluded from subsequent statistical analysis in this study.

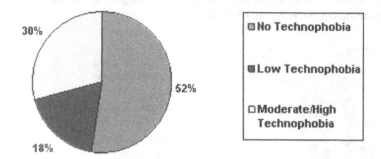

**Fig. 2.** Technophobia levels for students

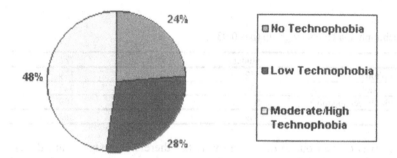

**Fig. 3.** Technophobia levels for older adults

## 4.3 Technophobia and Age

Rosen et al. (1992) partitioned each of the three measures (Computer Anxiety, Computer Thoughts, and General Attitudes Towards Computers) into three levels of technophobia: No Technophobia, Low Technophobia and Moderate/High Technophobia. They also defined an overall measure of technophobia based on a combination of the measures (see Figs. 2 and 3).

Given the differences in the percentage of computer users in the two groups, all subsequent comparisons are done on computer users only. The levels of technophobia for the controlled group of older adults can be seen in Fig. 4. The small number of students who have not used computers means that, with rounding, the levels of technophobia for students are the same as in Fig. 2. These controlled groups consisted of 141 male students and 148 female students and 17 older males and 57 older females. Although the two groups were disparate in terms of size, in each case where ANOVA was carried out, the test for homogeneity of variance indicated that the results of the tests can be used.

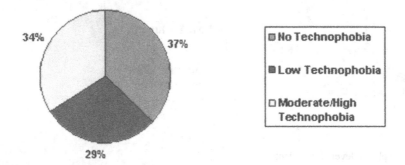

**Fig. 4.** Technophobia levels for older adults who use computers

**Table 3.** Technophobia levels by group ($p = 0.039$)

|                              | Student | Older adult | Total |
|------------------------------|---------|-------------|-------|
| No technophobia              | 152     | 27          | 179   |
| Low technophobia             | 53      | 21          | 74    |
| Moderate/high technophobia   | 84      | 25          | 109   |
| *Total*                      | *289*   | *73*        | *362* |

ANOVA was carried out to determine whether there was a significant difference between the older adults and the students in terms of computer anxiety and computer cognitions. There was a significant difference ($p = 0.003$) between the two groups (older adults and the students) for computer anxiety but no significant difference for computer cognitions ($p = 0.155$).

Chi-square analysis was carried out to determine whether students and older adults differed in terms of their levels of technophobia. The results show a significant difference between students and older adults in their overall level of technophobia ($p < 0.05$; see Table 3).

## 4.4 Technophobia and Gender

ANOVA was carried out to determine whether there were gender differences in computer anxiety or computer cognitions. When looking at females only, there was a significant difference in the levels of computer anxiety between the older females and the female students ($p \leq 0.001$). There was no significant difference for computer cognitions.

However, for males only, there was no significant difference between the older and student males for computer anxiety or computer cognitions. As there were only 16 males in the controlled group of older adults, Welch and Brown–Forsythe tests were carried out. These also showed no significant differences for computer anxiety and computer cognitions. Brown and Forsythe (1974) state that both of these tests perform well with group sample sizes as small as 10 and possibly even 5.

**Table 4.** Technophobia levels by gender

| Gender | | | Students | Older adults | *Total* |
|---|---|---|---|---|---|
| Male ($p = 0.715$) | Technophobia | No techno-phobia | 80 | 10 | 90 |
| | | Low techno-phobia | 25 | 4 | 29 |
| | | Moderate/high technophobia | 36 | 3 | 39 |
| | | *Total* | *141* | *17* | *158* |
| Female ($p = 0.048$) | Technophobia | No techno-phobia | 72 | 17 | 89 |
| | | Low techno-phobia | 28 | 17 | 45 |
| | | Moderate/high technophobia | 48 | 22 | 70 |
| | | *Total* | *148* | *56* | *204* |

Chi-square analysis was also carried out on the overall levels of technophobia. When the groups were broken down by gender (see Table 4), there was no significant difference between the overall level of technophobia of older men and male students but there was a significant difference between older women and female students. However, the small number of older males means that the figures for older males cannot be taken as reliable.

# 5 Discussion

## 5.1 Computer Use

In this study, the vast majority of students were computers users (99%) while the older adults were more evenly split, with a very small majority of older adults using computers (50.7% of those who responded). The figure for older adults is at odds with the figures for this population generally. Selwyn et al. (2003) reported only 22.4% of older adults having used a computer within the previous 12 months. Although the Commission of the European Communities (2005) does not report on computer use per se, it indicates that the EU 15 Internet usage in adults older than 55 years was 16.9% in 2003. In Ireland, the Information Society Commission defined 90% of retired people as "late adopters", that is, "adults without Internet access or using it less than once a month" (Information Society Commission 2003). The higher level of computer usage in this group is presumably due to the fact that the ARAs are offering computer courses on a regular basis.

Selwyn et al. (2003) found that most older computer users were male, well-educated and in the younger cohort of older adults; similarly, Morrell et al. (2000) also found that Web users were more likely to be in the younger cohort of older adults and better educated than non-users. This study showed that computer users were more likely to be more highly educated and in the younger cohort of participants, but the percentage of male and female computer users was similar (51.5% vs. 50.4% respectively).

## 5.2 Levels of Technophobia

Fig. 2 and 3 show that approximately half of the older adults show moderate to high levels of technophobia while less than a third of the students show moderate to high levels of technophobia. Studies in other countries (Weil and Rosen 1995; Anthony et al. 2000) show a range of technophobia levels, with the ~50% level displayed here for older adults not being atypical. In fact, the Weil and Rosen (1995) study showed ~40% of respondents in Northern Ireland with a moderate to high level of technophobia.

However, when only computer users were considered, the percentage of older adults with moderate to high levels of technophobia is lower, and although still higher than the percentage of students with moderate to high levels of technophobia (34% and 29.5% respectively), it is not substantially higher.

## 5.3 Technophobia and Age

The results of this study show significant differences between older adults and students in computer anxiety and overall technophobia levels. This concurs with the results of a number of other studies (Ellis et al. 1999; Anthony et al. 2000; Zhang 2005) which found that computer anxiety increased with age. However, it contrasts with the results of other studies (Dyck et al. 1994; Bozionelos 2001) that found that older adults displayed less computer anxiety than did younger adults. The differences with the study by Bozionelos (2001) may be because the older adults in his study were considerably younger than those in this study.

The higher levels of computer anxiety and technophobia in older adults in this study suggest that in order to help older adults fully realize the benefits of technology, some means of lowering computer anxiety and technophobia would be beneficial, as research has shown that computer anxiety can adversely affect performance (Dyck et al. 1994; Anderson 1996; Laguna et al. 1997; Brosnan 1998; Phang et al. 2006) and acceptance of computer technology (Dyck et al. 1994; Fagan et al. 2004), a finding that is further supported by a meta-analysis carried out by Chua et al. (1999), who state that computer anxiety causes computer use avoidance.

## 5.4 Technophobia and Gender

The results suggest that there are some gender differences in levels of technophobia, with older females being more anxious than younger females and older females being more technophobic than student females. Previous studies (Rosen and Maguire 1990; Weil et al. 1995; Anthony et al. 2000; Havelka et al. 2004) have shown mixed results, with some showing gender differences while others do not. Anthony et al. (2000) suggest that the lack of gender difference they found could be due to the increased exposure to computers amongst females at college level, resulting in the gender differences of the past no longer being evident. This would seem to concur with the findings in this study to an extent, as older females showed higher levels of computer anxiety and technophobia than did student females while older men and male students showed no significant difference in computer anxiety or technophobia. The findings with regard to gender seem to suggest that despite higher levels of computer anxiety and technophobia, older females are still willing to use computers.

## 5.5 Dealing with Technophobia

A high level of technophobia was found in the participants in this study, with higher levels being evident in older adults. The differences are particularly evident in older females. Older adults as a whole had higher levels of technophobia than did older adults who used computers (Hogan 2006), suggesting that those with higher levels of technophobia were less likely to use computers. This would suggest that an important area for further study would be interventions to treat computer anxiety and technophobia in older adults. This is particularly important if older adults are to contribute in a meaningful way to changing ICT (as suggested by Selwyn et al. (2003)) in order to fully realize the benefits of information technology. It is also important that those who provide services to older adults through IT-based applications (such as e-Government) must also understand the factors that will encourage acceptance of information systems as well as how to increase utilisation of such systems (Phang et al. 2006). Phang et al. (2006) suggest that a reduction in computer anxiety can increase the likelihood of older adults using e-Government services.

Appropriate intervention techniques (such as those suggested by Rosen et al. (1993)) could be incorporated into computer courses offered to older adults, allowing those that are more technophobic to deal with this as part of their learning process. This is supported by a number of studies (Beckers and Schmidt 2001; Wilfong 2006), suggesting that training programmes that enhance self-efficacy (one's confidence in one's own abilities) and computer literacy may reduce computer anxiety.

Although the results of this study suggest that older adults, despite high levels of technophobia, still use computers, developers of information systems should still consider options, in addition to the above-mentioned training, that would help older adults to realise the full potential benefits of ICT. One option is to include older adults in the development process, as user involvement generally has a positive impact on user satisfaction (Kujala 2003), which may then result in lower levels of anxiety, as according to McIlroy et al. (2001), a positive first experience can lead to lower levels of anxiety.

# 6 Further Research

The older individuals who participated in this study were all members of ARAs. As such, they may be different from the general population of older adults, as those willing and able to join such an organization may be more open to new experiences. The sample used also had considerably higher levels of computer usage than did the older population in general. Therefore, the study needs to be replicated across a broader population to assess whether the findings are consistent for the population at large.

The General Attitudes Towards Computers Scale (GATCS-C) was deemed to be unreliable, and has previously been found to be unreliable for participants outside the United States (Weil et al. 1995; Anthony et al. 2000; Hogan 2006). Weil et al. (1995) suggest that its unreliability outside the United States may be because it used a standard 5-point Likert scale (*strongly agree* to *strongly disagree*) and that this format may not be appropriate for assessing technophobia outside the United States, although they offer no supporting evidence for this premise. The GATCS should be redeveloped, perhaps by changing the rating scale so that it uses a similar scale to the other measures, and re-assessed for reliability in order to determine whether Weil et al.'s (1995) premise is correct. If their premise is not correct, then the reasons for the unreliability of the GATCS-C outside the United States should be investigated.

# References

Anderson, A. A. (1996). "Predictors of computer anxiety and performance in information systems." Computers in Human Behavior 12(1): 61–77.

Anthony, L. M., M. C. Clarke and S. J. Anderson (2000). Technophobia and personality subtypes in a sample of South African university students." Computers in Human Behavior 16(1): 31–44.

Becker, S. A. (2004). "A study of Web usability for older adults seeking online health resources." ACM Transactions on Computer–Human Interaction 11(4): 387–406.

Beckers, J. J. and H. G. Schmidt (2001). "The structure of computer anxiety: A six-factor model." Computers in Human Behavior 17(1): 35–49.

Bozionelos, N. (2001). "Computer anxiety: relationship with computer experience and prevalence." Computers in Human Behavior 17: 213–224.

Broos, A. (2005). "Gender and information and communication technologies (ICT) anxiety: Male self-assurance and female hesitation." Cyberpsychology and Behavior 8(1): 21–31.

Brosnan, M. J. (1998). "The impact of computer anxiety and self-efficacy upon performance." Journal of Computer Assisted Learning 14(3): 223–234.

Brown, M. B. and A. B. Forsythe (1974). "The small sample behavior of some statistics which test the equality of several means." Technometrics 16(1): 129–132.

Chua, S. L., D.-T. Chen and A. F. L. Wong (1999). "Computer anxiety and its correlates: a meta-analysis." Computers in Human Behavior 15(5): 609–623.

Commission of the European Communities (2005). "eInclusion revisited: The local dimension of the Information Society [Report]." Available at http://europa.eu.int/comm/employment_social/news/2005/feb/einclocal_en.html.

Dyck, J. L. and J. Al-Awar Smither (1992). "Computer anxiety and the older adult: Relationships with computer experience, gender, education and age." Proceedings of the Human factors Society 36th Annual Meeting, 1992.

Dyck, J. L. and J. Al-Awar Smither (1994). "Age differences in computer anxiety: The role of computer experience, gender and education." Journal of Educational Computing Research 10(3): 239–248.

Ellis, R. D. and J. C. Allaire (1999). "Modeling computer interest in older adults: The role of age, education, computer knowledge, and computer anxiety." Human Factors 41(3): 345–355.

Fagan, M. H., S. Neill and B. R. Wooldridge (2004). "An empirical investigation into the relationship between computer self-efficacy, anxiety, experience, support and usage." Journal of Computer Information Systems 44(2): 95–104.

Gordon, M., M. Killey, M. Shevlin, D. McIlroy and K. Tierney (2003). "The factor structure of the Computer Anxiety Rating Scale and the Computer Thoughts Survey." Computers in Human Behavior 19(3): 291–298.

Greenspan, R. (2003). "Senior surfing surges." http://www.nielsen-netratings.com/pr/pr_031120.pdf. Accessed 12 Oct. 2006.

Havelka, D., F. Beasley and T. Broome (2004). "A study of computer anxiety among business students." Mid-American Journal of Business 19(1): 63–71.

Hogan, M. (2006). "Technophobia amongst older adults in Ireland." The Irish Journal of Management 26: 57–78. Special Issue based on selected best papers from the 2005 Irish Academy of Management Conference.

Information Society Commission (2003). "eInclusion: Expanding the information society in Ireland." http://www.isc.ie/downloads/einclusion.pdf.

Karavidas, M., N. K. Lim and S. L. Katsikas (2005). "The effects of computers on older adult users." Computers in Human Behavior 21(5): 697–711.

Korukonda, A. R. (2005). "Personality, individual characteristics, and predisposition to technophobia: Some answers, questions and points to ponder about." Information Sciences 170(2–4): 309–328.

Kujala, S. (2003). "User involvement: A review of the benefits and challenges." Behaviour and Information Technology 22(1): 1–16.

Laguna, K. and R. L. Babcock (1997). "Computer anxiety in young and older adults: Implications for human–computer interactions in older populations." Computers in Human Behavior 13(3): 317–326.

McIlroy, D., B. Bunting, K. Tierney and M. Gordon (2001). "The relation of gender and background experience to self-reported computing anxieties and cognitions." Computers in Human Behavior 17(1): 21–33.

Morrell, R. W., C. B. Mayhorn and J. Bennet (2000). "A survey of World Wide Web use in middle-aged and older adults." Human Factors 42(2): 175–182.

Morris, J. M. (1992). "The effects of an introductory computer course on the attitudes of older adults towards computers." ACM SIGCSE Bulletin 24(1): 72–75.

Orr, C., D. Allen and S. Poindexter (2001). "The effect of individual differences on computer attitudes: An empirical study." Journal of End User Computing 13(2): 26–39.

Phang, C. W., J. Sutanto, A. Kankanhalli, Y. Li, B. C. Y. Tan and H.-H. Teo (2006). "Senior citizens' acceptance of Information Systems: A study in the context of e-Government services." IEEE Transactions on Engineering Management 53(4): 555–569.

Rosen, L. D. and P. Maguire (1990). "Myths and realities of computerphobia: A meta-analysis." Anxiety Research 3(1): 175–191.

Rosen, L. D., D. C. Sears and M. M. Weil (1992). *Measuring technophobia.* A manual for the administration and scoring of three instruments: Computer Anxiety Rating Scale (Form C), General Attitudes Toward Computers Scale (Form C) and Computer Thoughts Survey (Form C). California State University, Dominguez Hills, CA, USA. Computerphobia Reduction Program.

Rosen, L. D., D. C. Sears and M. M. Weil (1993). "Treating technophobia: A longitudinal evaluation of the computerphobia reduction program." Computers in Human Behavior 9(1): 27–50.

Selwyn, N., S. Gorard, J. Furlong and L. Madden (2003). "Older adult's use of information and communications technology in everyday life." Aging and Society 23(5): 561–582.

Swindell, R. (2001). "Technology and the over 65s? Get a life." Social Alternatives 20(1): 17–23.

Tatnall, A. and J. Lepa (2003). "The Internet, e-commerce and older people: An actor-network approach to researching reasons for adoption and use." Logistics Information Management 16(1): 56–63.

United Nations Population Division (2002). "World population prospects: The 2002 revision." http://esa.un.org/unpp.

United States Census Bureau (2001). "United States Census 2001." http://www.census.gov/population/www/socdemo/computer/ppl-175.html. Accessed 12 Mar. 2007.

United States Census Bureau (2003). "United States Census 2003." http://www.census.gov/population/www/socdemo/computer/2003.html. Accessed 12 Mar. 2007.

Weil, M. M. and L. D. Rosen (1995). "The psychological impact of technology from a global perspective: A study of technological sophistication and technophobia in university students from twenty-three countries." Computers in Human Behavior 11(1): 95–133.

Whitley, B. E. (1996). "Gender differences in computer-related attitudes: It depends on what you ask." Computers in Human Behavior 12(2): 275–289.

Wilfong, J. D. (2006). "Computer anxiety and anger: The impact of computer use, computer experience and self-efficacy beliefs." Computers in Human Behavior 22: 1001–1011.

Zhang, Y. (2005). "Age, gender and Internet attitudes among employees in the business world." Computers in Human Behavior 21(1): 1–10.

# Usability Evaluation of Information Systems: A Review of Five International Standards

**Dorina Marghescu**

Department of IT, Turku Centre for Computer Science, Åbo Akademi University,
dmarghes@abo.fi

**Abstract** In this chapter, we review five international standards that are concerned with defining and evaluating usability of information technology and interactive systems. The aim is to investigate the extent to which the international standards provide guidelines for planning and conducting usability evaluation of information systems. We first compare the standards in order to uncover the differences and relationships between the guidelines provided. Then, based on the guidelines, we provide a framework that highlights the activities required for usability evaluation of information systems. In the end, we discuss the way in which the standards cover the usability evaluation of information systems from the perspective of users, technology, system and phase in system's life-cycle.

## 1 Introduction

Evaluation of information systems (IS) represents an important topic among practitioners and researchers of information systems development (ISD) field. The evaluation of an IS may regard different aspects of the system, for example, performance, cost-benefit analysis, user acceptability, usability, reliability, functionality, efficiency, job satisfaction, etc. In this chapter, we will focus on usability evaluation (UE) of information systems.

UE is concerned with planning and conducting the measuring of the usability attributes of the user interface and identifying specific problems (Ivory and Hearst, 2001). Dix et al. (1998) point out that UE should be done throughout the design life-cycle and planned as providing results that can be used for improving the design. There are many models of usability that define the usability attributes that have to be measured. For example, Nielsen (1993) highlights the following usability attributes: learnability, efficiency, memorability, error rate and satisfaction. However, the literature provides several other attributes as well as methods, techniques and metrics that can be used for measurement (see, for example, Hornbæk, 2006).

C. Barry et al. (eds.), *Information Systems Development: Challenges in Practice, Theory, and Education, Vol.1*, doi: 10.1007/978-0-387-68772-8_11,

Though UE is extensively discussed in literature, especially from the perspective of usability models, methods, techniques and metrics used in evaluation, in the ISD methodologies, evaluation, in general, and usability evaluation, in particular, are not well addressed. Comparing different ISD methodologies, Avison and Fitzgerald (2003) identified only a small number of the existing methodologies that address in detail the system evaluation at the post-implementation stage. The other methodologies mention the post-implementation evaluation as being important or do not address evaluation at all. An exception is Merise methodology that considers the usability and acceptance criteria in the decision cycle, when users together with system developers and senior managers are involved in discussing various options for the technical part (i.e., software and hardware) of the information system. However, Merise does not address a post-implementation evaluation.

Motivated by this lack of details that Avison and Fitzgerald (2003) pointed out regarding the evaluation of IS in the ISD methodologies, we address in this chapter one important aspect of IS evaluation, namely, usability evaluation. We review five standards, developed by the International Organisation for Standardization (ISO), that address usability of information technology (IT) and interactive systems. The standards that we review are: ISO/IEC 9126-1, ISO/IEC 14598-1, ISO 9241-11, ISO 13407 and ISO 18529. We study these standards because they are intended to provide guidelines and general principles for planning and conducting evaluation during product/system development life-cycle. We do not analyse the standards that guide the assessment of the UE process capability (e.g., ISO/IEC 15504-1).

Other studies concerned with analysing the international standards that address usability are, for example, Jokela et al. (2003) and Seffah et al. (2006). In an interpretative study, Jokela et al. analysed ISO 13407 against ISO 9241-11 with the aim to find whether the two standards are consistent. Seffah et al. reviewed three ISO standards (ISO 9241-11, ISO/IEC 9126 – Parts 1 and 4 and ISO/IEC 14598-1) and other usability models from literature. Their aim was to highlight the need for a unified theory of usability measurement and propose a model for usability measurement. Nielsen (1993) describe and compare the advantages of using interface standards (national, international, industry or in-house built standards) when designing interactive systems.

Our aim is to identify how the ISO standards address the UE *process* of IS. We do not focus on the measurement component of the evaluation process (that is, on methods, usability models and metrics used in evaluation), but on the phases and activities that are required in planning and conducting UE. The research question is to what extent the standards provide guidance for planning and conducting UE of information systems. We study the guidelines provided by the standards with respect to planning and conducting UE of information systems. We first compare the standards to uncover differences and relationships between the guidelines provided. Then, based on the guidelines, we provide a framework that highlights the activities required for UE of IS.

The definition of an information system in Avison and Fitzgerald (2003) emphasizes that people and technology are equally important for the success of an information system: users and IT interact in order to accomplish a function, goal or task in a specified environment. Therefore the evaluation of the information system has to take into account the users, the technology (software) and the systems as whole. Having in mind this definition of an information system, we try also to examine the way in which the standards cover the UE from the perspective of the users, technology and the system as a whole. Moreover, the system has to be evaluated throughout the system's life-cycle, and we will analyse whether the standards provide guidelines for UE in different stages of system's life-cycle (requirements, design, implementation, use and maintenance).

The paper is organized as follows. Section 2 introduces the five ISO standards under analysis. Section 3 compares the scopes of the standards. Section 4 presents the definitions of usability encountered in international standards. Section 5 compares the usability evaluation approaches provided by the international standards. Section 6 discusses the comparative analysis of international standards and provides a framework for usability evaluation of information systems based on the standards' guidelines. It also discusses the way in which the standards cover the usability evaluation from the perspective of the users, technology, the system as a whole and the system's life-cycle. Section 7 concludes the paper.

# 2 International Standards that Address Usability

International standards provide practitioners with a common technical language necessary in development, acquisition, supply and evaluation of products and services and in communicating to other parties. They are also a means to ensure that the final product attains the desired quality. There are five ISO standards that address usability of information technology and interactive systems:

ISO/IEC 9126 – Part 1 (2000) – Information Technology – Software product quality – Part 1: Quality model

ISO/IEC 14598 – Part 1 (1999) – Information Technology – Software product evaluation – Part 1: General overview

ISO 9241 – Part 11 (1998) – Ergonomic requirements for office work with visual display terminals. Part 11: Guidance on usability

ISO 13407 (1999) – Human-centred design processes for interactive systems

ISO 18529 (2000) – Ergonomics – Ergonomics of human-system interaction – Human-centred life-cycle process descriptions.

ISO/IEC 9126 defines a software product quality model, characteristics and metrics, and Part 1 of this standard focuses on defining the quality model. ISO/IEC 14598 describes the process of evaluation of software product quality, and Part 1 of this standard provides a general overview of this process. A new series, namely, ISO/IEC 25000 (2005) – Software Engineering – Software product quality requirements and evaluation (SQuaRE) – Guide to SQuaRE, is intended to replace and integrate the multipart standards ISO/IEC 9126 and 14598. However, only ISO/IEC 25000 from the new series has been released and published, while other parts that detail the quality model and process of evaluation are currently under development. ISO/IEC 25000 introduces the other parts of SQuaRE and provides an overview of software quality modelling and evaluation as well as the relationships between current standards (ISO/IEC 9126 and ISO/IEC 14598) and the new SQuaRE series of standards. Until the other parts of the new series SQuaRE are published, the multipart ISO/IEC 9126 and ISO/IEC 14598 are applicable and therefore they are appropriate for analysis.

ISO 9241 – Part 11 addresses the definition and evaluation of usability in the context of visual display terminals or other products with which a user interacts in order to achieve a goal. ISO 13407 addresses the process of human-centred design for interactive systems and uses the definition of usability from ISO 9241 -11. Finally, ISO 18529 defines a model of the human-centred processes described in ISO 13407. It is intended to be used in the specification, assessment and improvement of the human-centred processes in system development and operation.

To uncover the relationships and differences between these standards with respect to usability evaluation, we analyse comparatively the standards focusing on:

Scope of the standard,
Definition of usability adopted by a standard and
The evaluation approach proposed by the standard.

## 3 Scopes of International Standards

The analysis of the scope of the standards aims at identifying three elements: (1) the entity under evaluation (e.g., software product, hardware and system), (2) the main stakeholders to whom the standard is addressed and (3) the phase in life-cycle at which the product or system is evaluated (e.g., during development, use, acquisition, etc.). Table 1 presents the scope of each standard.

**Table 1.** Scopes of ISO/IEC 9126-1, ISO/IEC 14598-1, ISO 9241-11, ISO 13407, ISO 18529

| Standard | Entity | Stakeholders | Phase in life-cycle |
|---|---|---|---|
| ISO/IEC 9126-1 ISO/IEC 14598-1 | Software product | Designers, developers, evaluators, maintainers, acquirers | Requirements, development, use, evaluation, support, maintenance, quality assurance, audit of software, acquisition |
| ISO 9241-11 | Software, hardware or service product in interactive systems | Designer, developer, evaluator, acquirer | Design, development, evaluation, procurement |
| ISO 13407 | Computer-based interactive system | Project managers, All parties involved in human-centred system development | Throughout the system development life-cycle |
| ISO 18529 | Life-cycle process of computer-based interactive system, software and hardware | Those involved in design, use and assessment of life-cycle processes | Design, development, use and assessment of life-cycle process of system, software and hardware |

By comparing the standards with respect to their scopes, the following observations can be made:

ISO/IEC 9126-1 and ISO/IEC 14598-1 (ISO/IEC 25000, respectively) focus on defining and evaluating *quality* of any kind of *software products* (including computer programs, data contained in firmware). They are, on the one hand, narrower in scope than the other standards, because they focus on the software product; while the others take into account both hardware and software of an interactive system. On the other hand, they are broader in scope than the other standards because they cover all quality characteristics of the software product, not just usability.

ISO 9241-11 focuses on defining and evaluating *usability* of any *product* that is part of an *interactive system* and can be of nature software, hardware or service (e.g., visual display terminals).

ISO/IEC 9126-1, ISO/IEC 14598-1 and ISO 9241-11 are addressed to *stakeholders* involved in all phases of product/system life-cycle: development, procurement or evaluation of software products and interactive systems, respectively. ISO/IEC 9126-1 and ISO/IEC 14598-1 are addressed to maintainers too.

ISO 13407 focuses on *designing* computer-based interactive systems and evaluating different *design solutions throughout the system development life-cycle* and is addressed mainly to *project managers*, and to other stakeholders involved in system's development life-cycle too.

ISO 18529, unlike the other standards, addresses the system's life-cycle *process* (how this process should be designed, used and assessed). The others standards address the software, hardware or systems (how these should be designed, implemented, used and assessed). Therefore, it focuses not on developing a system, hardware or software, but on modelling their *life-cycle processes*.

# 4 Definition of Usability in International Standards

ISO/IEC 9126-1 (ISO/IEC 25000, respectively) represents the Software Engineering (SE) perspective on usability. In SE, usability is defined as being 'the capability of the software product to be *understood, learned, used* and *attractive* to the user, when used under specified conditions'.

ISO 9241-11 represents the Human Computer Interaction (HCI) perspective on usability that is defined as being 'the extent to which a product can be used by specified users to achieve specified goals with *effectiveness, efficiency* and *satisfaction* in a specified context of use'.

The differences in defining the usability can be explained by the focus that each community has. While SE is concerned with providing high-quality intermediate or final *software products* that conform to specified requirements, HCI is concerned with developing usable *interactive systems*. Therefore, in SE usability is just one component of software product quality, while in HCI reaching a high level of usability is the ultimate goal of the system development. Another difference is that SE focuses on *software product* development and evaluation, while

HCI focuses on *system* (interaction between software, hardware and users) development and evaluation.

To include the latter perspective, ISO/IEC 9126-1 (ISO/IEC 25000) added a new concept, namely, *quality in use*, which is defined as being 'the capability of the software product to enable specified users to achieve specified goals with effectiveness, productivity, safety and satisfaction in specified contexts of use'. In this definition, the attribute safety is added and efficiency is named productivity.

According to these definitions, usability is not an intrinsic quality of a product, but its measured level depends on many factors, which are generically described as the *context of use*. The context of use may include the users and their goals, the tasks, the equipment and the environment. Both ISO 13407 and ISO 18529 use the definition of usability given in ISO 9241-11.

Table 2 summarizes the definitions of usability adopted by each standard. Regardless of which definition is used, assessing the level of usability achieved by an information technology or information system requires careful planning of the measurement. Usability evaluation represents the methodology used for planning and conducting usability measurement. In Sect. 5, we present different approaches to usability evaluation as provided by the international standards.

**Table 2.** Definitions of usability in international standards

| Standard | Definition of usability |
|---|---|
| ISO/IEC 9126-1 (ISO/IEC 25000) | **Usability** is the capability of the software product to be *understood*, *learned*, *used* and *attractive* to the user, when used under specified conditions. |
| | **Quality in use** is the capability of the software product to enable specified users to achieve specified goals with *effectiveness*, *productivity*, *safety* and *satisfaction* in specified contexts of use. |
| ISO 9241-11 | **Usability** is the extent to which a product can be used by specified users to achieve specified goals with *effectiveness*, *efficiency* and *satisfaction* in a specified context of use. |

# 5 Usability Evaluation Approaches in International Standards

Here we compare the approaches to UE provided by different standards and examine the level of detail of the guidelines. There are four standards that address UE of information technology and interactive systems. These standards are: ISO/IEC 14598-1, ISO 9241-11, ISO 13407 and ISO 18529. Table 3 presents the approaches to UE provided by the four standards.

By comparing the four approaches, the following observations can be made:

ISO/IEC 14598-1 provides a general process of software product quality evaluation. The phases and activities of the process are well defined. The guidance allows identification of inputs and outputs of each activity. The evaluation is based on the quality model specified in the first phase of the process. The evaluation process can be employed for any intermediate or final product throughout its life-cycle.

ISO 9241-11 distinguishes between evaluation of a product during design and evaluation of a system during its use, but the evaluation process is not discussed in detail.

ISO 13407 addresses mainly evaluation of design, and also the long-term monitoring of the system in use in the context of human-centred design process. The guidance provided is a framework that identifies different situations and objectives that usability evaluation can address.

ISO 18529 describes the evaluation of the design against requirements as an iterative sub-process within the general human-centred design process. The evaluation is carried out in all phases of the human-centred design process from requirements to use. The standard provides guidance with regard to the activities to be performed in different stages of the evaluation process. However, the standard does not detail how these activities have to be conducted.

**Table 3.** Evaluation approaches in ISO/IEC 14598-1, ISO 9241-11, ISO 13407 and ISO 18529

| Standard | Evaluation approach |
|---|---|
| ISO/IEC 14598-1 (ISO/ IEC 25000) | Four phases evaluation process, applicable throughout the software product life-cycle<br>1. Quality requirements definition<br>2. Specify the evaluation<br>3. Plan the evaluation<br>4. Execute the evaluation |
| ISO 9241-11 | Distinction between specification and evaluation of usability during design and during use of system:<br>1. During design: usability input to a quality plan.<br>2. During use: evaluate how changes in components of context of use affect efficiency, effectiveness and/or satisfaction of the user |
| ISO 13407 | –Three phases prior to evaluation (human-centred design approach)<br>1. Identification of the context of use and its components represents a basis for evaluation.<br>2. Specification of user and organizational requirements should be done in terms that permit subsequent testing and should be confirmed or updated during the life of the project. (Reference to ISO/IEC 14598-1 for specifying software)<br>3. Produce design solutions<br>4. Evaluate designs against requirements<br>–Identifies and addresses three goals of evaluation (providing feedback to improve the design, assess whether the objectives have been met and monitor long-term use of the product).<br>–Discusses evaluation plan and different evaluation situations |
| ISO 18529 | –Distinction between formative evaluation (identification of problems) and summative evaluation (assessment of whether objectives are met).<br>–Discusses the following evaluation activities:<br>1. Specify context of evaluation<br>2. Evaluate for requirements<br>3. Evaluate to improve design<br>4. Evaluate against system requirements<br>5. Evaluate against required practice<br>6. Evaluate in use. |

The standard that provides the most extensive guidance on how to proceed with the quality evaluation of information technology is ISO/IEC 14598-1. We summarize in Table 4 the phases, activities and outputs of the UE process as derived from the general model of quality evaluation given in ISO/IEC 14598-1. Accordingly, the UE process usability consists of four phases: (1) quality requirements definition, (2) specify the evaluation, (3) plan the evaluation and (4) execute the evaluation.

**Table 4.** Process model for usability evaluation (derived from ISO/IEC 14598-1)

| Phase | Activity | Output/documents |
|---|---|---|
| 1. Define usability requirements | 1.1 Establish purpose of evaluation | Purpose of evaluation document |
| | 1.2 Identify type of product | Specification of product and context of use |
| | 1.3 Specify usability model | Usability characteristics, sub-characteristics, attributes |
| 2. Specify the evaluation | 2.1 Select metrics for each attribute | Metrics |
| | 2.2 Establish rating levels for each metric | Rating levels |
| | 2.3 Establish assessment criteria | –Assessment criteria<br>–Procedure to summarize evaluation results |
| 3. Plan the evaluation | 3.1 Produce evaluation plan | Specification of evaluation method, schedule and evaluator actions |
| 4. Execute the evaluation | 4.1 Take measures | Measured values for each metric |
| | 4.2 Compare with criteria | Rated level for each metric |
| | 4.3 Assess results | –Statement of usability<br>–Managerial decision (acceptance or rejection of product) |

In the first phase, quality requirements definition, the context of use and the usability attributes are identified. In the second phase, suitable metrics for each attribute are identified. Moreover, rating levels for the metrics as well as assessment criteria are defined. In the third phase, an evaluation plan is produced in order to describe the evaluation method to be used, the schedule of the evaluation and the evaluator actions. The evaluation phase consists of a series of activities such as *measurement*, *rating* and *assessment* of the usability attributes. *Measurement* means applying usability or quality in use metrics to the system or component under evaluation. For conducting this activity, a usability evaluation method is defined in order to properly collect, analyse and summarize the measurement data. The *rating* means that the measured value is mapped to a rating level, a priori established. Finally, the *assessment* requires applying assessment criteria to the system or component under analysis for determining the acceptance of the system in terms of usability.

The other standards, ISO 9241-11, ISO 13407 and ISO 18529, do not address in detail the steps of UE. ISO 9241-11 focuses on specifying the context of use. ISO 13407 highlights the phases needed for UE and mentions the use of appropriate evaluation methods (ISO 13407). ISO 18529 provides general guidelines applicable to different evaluation purposes.

# 6 A Framework for UE of IS

The comparative review of the international standards has yielded that these standards complement each other as follows. First, ISO/IEC 9126-1 and ISO/IEC 14598-1 focus on software products, while the other standards take into account also the hardware and interactive system as a whole. Moreover, ISO/IEC 9126-1 and ISO/IEC 14598-1 are addressed to the stakeholders responsible with all phases in software product development life-cycle, including maintenance. The other standards are not addressed to maintainers. ISO 18529 focuses on modelling the life-cycle process, and not on software, hardware or interactive system. In addition to these differences and relationships observed by analysing the scopes of the standards, other differences between the standards regard the way they define usability and approach usability evaluation (Tables 2 and 3, respectively).

Regarding the approach to usability evaluation recommended by a standard, we observed that the standard that provides the most extensive guidance on how to proceed with the evaluation is ISO/IEC 14598-1. This standard provides the phases and activities required in the process of quality evaluation of a software product, but the guidelines can be extended to usability evaluation of information systems (Table 4).

Taking into account also the guidelines provided by the other standards, we propose a framework for UE of IS. The framework lists the principal activities in the UE process (Table 5), as derived from the guidelines provided by all standards (Tables 3 and 4). The framework also provides references to the standards that mention and/or guide the activities.

**Table 5.** Activities in UE process

| Activities | Standards |
|---|---|
| 1. Distinguish between system under development and system in use | ISO 9241-11, ISO 18529 |
| 2. Specify purpose of evaluation and evaluation target (users, technology or system and phase in product/system development life-cycle) | ISO/IEC 9126-1, ISO/IEC 14598-1, ISO 9241-11, ISO 13407 and ISO 18529 |
| 3. Specify context of use of the information system | ISO 9241-11, ISO 13407 and ISO 18529 |
| 4. Specify usability and quality in use characteristics, sub-characteristics, attributes | ISO/IEC 9126-1, ISO/IEC 14598-1 |
| 5. Select or create validated metrics to be used in measurement of the system usability attributes | ISO/IEC 14598-1, ISO 9241-11 |
| 6. Specify rating levels for each metric | ISO/IEC 14598-1 |
| 7. Specify assessment criteria | ISO/IEC 14598-1 |
| 8. Select and specify an appropriate usability evaluation method | ISO 13407, ISO 18529, ISO/IEC 14598-1 |
| 9. Measure usability attributes | ISO/IEC 14598-1, ISO 9241-11 |
| 10. Map measured values to rating levels | ISO/IEC 14598-1, ISO 9241-11 |
| 11. Assess result | ISO/IEC 14598-1, ISO 9241-11 |

Activities 1, 2, 3 and 4 belong to the Define usability requirements phase. Activities 5, 6 and 7 represent the Specify evaluation phase. Activity 8 represents the Plan evaluation phase. Activities 9, 10 and 11 belong to the Execute evaluation phase.

Table 5 points out that at activity 2 the target of the evaluation has to be specified and that all five standards mention or provide guidelines for this activity. However, the extent to which the standards guide the evaluation from each of these perspectives (i.e., users, technology, systems and phase in life-cycle) differs as follows.

ISO/IEC 9126-1 focuses on software product evaluation, but addresses the evaluation from all three perspectives (users, technology and system). It focuses on providing a detailed model of usability and quality in use characteristics and sub-characteristics. ISO/IEC 14598-1 focuses on a general evaluation process and activities that can be applied to evaluate attributes that are relevant to users, technology and system. ISO 9241-11 and ISO 13407 focus on interactive system evaluation. They especially guide the specification of the context of use. In addition, ISO 13407 and ISO 18529 discuss the involvement of the user during the development life-cycle process. ISO 18529 does not address the user or technology evaluation, but lists the activities required in the system evaluation in the context of human-centred design approach (Table 3).

Table 6 summarizes the aspects for which guidelines are provided in each standard with respect to user, technology or system.

**Table 6.** Guidance on usability evaluation with respect to user, technology or system

| | User | Technology (software product) | System |
|---|---|---|---|
| ISO/IEC 9126-1 | –User requirements –User satisfaction | –Usability attributes | –Quality in use attributes |
| ISO/IEC 14598-1 | –Activities for UE of attributes relevant to user | –Activities for UE of attributes relevant to technology | –Activities for UE of attributes relevant to system |
| ISO 9241-11 | –Context of use (identification of users) | –Context of use (identification of equipment and tasks) | –Context of use (identification of users, equipment, tasks and environment) –Activities for UE |
| ISO 13407 | –User involvement in design process, including evaluation –User requirements specification | –Activities for UE | –Context of use (users, tasks, environment) –Activities for UE |
| ISO 18529 | –Focus on user throughout the system development life-cycle process, including system strategy and evaluation | – | –Activities in the evaluation process during system development life-cycle process |

Table 7 provides an assessment of the level of detail at which each standard addresses the evaluation process at different phases of systems' life-cycle. The difference between 'extensive guidance' and 'guidance at some detail' is that the former includes guidelines on how to perform different activities in the evaluation process, while the latter limits to enumerating the activities and distinguishing between different evaluation situations. ISO/IEC 9126-1 provides a model of usability and quality in use characteristics that can be used in any phase of life-cycle. However, it does not address the overall UE process and, therefore, we did not include it in the table.

**Table 7.** Guidance on usability evaluation during the system life-cycle

|  | Requirements | Design | Implementation | Use | Maintenance |
|---|---|---|---|---|---|
| ISO/IEC 14598-1 | +++ | +++ | +++ | +++ | + |
| ISO 9241-11 | +++ | ++ | ++ | ++ | – |
| ISO 13407 | ++ | ++ | – | ++ | – |
| ISO 18529 | ++ | ++ | ++ | ++ | – |
| +++: extensive guidance; ++: guidance at some detail; +: mentioning the situation; –: no guidance |||||| 

# 7 Conclusion

In this paper, we analysed comparatively five international standards that address the definition and evaluation of usability of information technology (software) and interactive systems: ISO/IEC 9126-1, ISO/IEC 14598-1, ISO 9241-11, ISO 13407 and ISO 18529. The purpose of the study was to investigate the extent to which the standards provide guidance for planning and conducting usability evaluation of information systems.

We first analysed the standards to uncover relationships and differences between the guidelines. The standards provide different approaches on defining and evaluating usability (Tables 2 and 3, respectively) and provide different levels of detail and coverage of the aspects considered (Tables 1, 6 and 7). Based on the standards' approaches to usability evaluation, we provided a framework for usability evaluation of information systems that highlights the main activities of usability evaluation process (Table 5). We also discussed the extent to which the guidelines for conducting usability evaluation take into account the user, technology and system (Table 6), and different phases in system life-cycle (Table 7).

The analysis of the standards showed that the guidelines complement each other as follows. ISO/IEC 9126-1 and ISO/IEC 14598-1 focus on software products, while the other standards address also the hardware and interactive system as a whole. Moreover, ISO/IEC 9126-1 and ISO/IEC 14598-1 are addressed to the stakeholders responsible with all phases in software product development life-cycle, including maintenance. The other standards are not addressed to maintainers. ISO 18529 focus on modelling the life-cycle process, and not on software, hardware or interactive system. Regarding the usability evaluation approaches provided by the standards, ISO/IEC 14598-1 provides the most detailed guidelines to usability evaluation process in almost all phases of product and system life-cycle (Tables 3, 4 and 7), but does not discuss in detail the identification of context of use of the product/system. ISO 9241-11 focuses on describing the context of use (Table 6), but does not discuss in detail the phases, activities, inputs and outputs required in the usability evaluation process. ISO 13407 and ISO 18529 focus on highlighting the importance of user involvement throughout the system development life-cycle process in the context of human-centred design approach, and limit themselves to enumerating the activities of this process, but do not discuss them in detail. ISO/IEC 9126-1 provides extensive models of usability and quality in use.

**Acknowledgements** I gratefully acknowledge the contribution of Professor Barbro Back and the financial support of Tekes (grant number: 40435/05) and the Academy of Finland (grant number: 104639).

# References

Avison, D. E. and Fitzgerald, G. (2003) *Information Systems Development: Methodologies, Techniques and Tools*, 3rd Edition, McGraw-Hill, London.

Dix, A., Finlay, J., Abowd, G., and Beale, R. (1998) *Human Computer Interaction*, 2nd Edition, Prentice Hall, Englewood Cliffs, NJ.

Hornbæk, K. (2006) Current practice in measuring usability: Challenges to usability studies and research. *Int. J. Hum-Comput Stud.* 64 (2), 79–102.

ISO 9241-11 (1998) Ergonomic requirements for office work with visual display terminals. Part 11: Guidance on usability.

ISO 13407 (1999) Human-centred design processes for interactive systems.

ISO/IEC 14598-1 (1999) Information Technology – Software product evaluation – Part 1: General overview.

ISO/IEC 9126-1 (2000) Information Technology – Software product quality – Part 1: Quality model.

ISO/IEC 25000 (2005) Software Engineering – Software product quality requirements and evaluation (SQuaRE) – Guide to SQuaRE.

ISO 18529 (2000) Ergonomics – Ergonomics of human-system interaction – Human-centred lifecycle process descriptions.

Ivory, M. Y. and Hearst, M. A. (2001) The state of the art in automating usability evaluation of user interfaces. *ACM Comput. Surv.* 33 (4), 470–516.

Jokela, T., Iivari, N., Matero, J., and Karukka, M. (2003) The standard of user-centered design and the standard definition of usability: analyzing ISO 13407 against ISO 9241-11. In *Proc. of the Latin American Conference on Human-Computer interaction* (Rio de Janeiro, Brazil, August 17–20, 2003), CLIHC'03, vol. 46. ACM Press, New York, NY, 53–60.

Nielsen, J. (1993) *Usability Engineering*, Morgan Kaufmann, Los Altos, CA.

Seffah, A., Donyaee, M., Kline, R. B., and Padda, H. K. (2006) Usability measurement and metrics: A consolidated model. *Softw. Qual. Control* 14 (2), 159–178.

# User Involvement in the Design and Appropriation of a Mobile Clinical Information System: Reflections on Organisational Learning

Liz Burley[1], Helana Scheepers[2] and Libby Owen[3]

[1]Faculty of ICT, Swinburne University of Technology, lburley@ict.swin.edu.au

[2]Caulfield School of IT, HMonash University, elana.Scheepers@infotech.monash.edu.au

[3]Metropolitan Ambulance Service, Libby.Owen@mas.vic.gov.au

**Abstract** User participation during systems development has been linked to the success of IS and to the elicitation of improved user requirements. The focus of most of the research on user participation is on the systems development process and does not consider the role of the user after the system has been implemented. This chapter explores user participation in the development, implementation and use of a Mobile Clinical Information System within the Metropolitan Ambulance Service, Melbourne, Australia. The chapter draws the following three conclusions. User involvement should be established during the systems development of the new IS, and also needs to be followed up during the implementation and use of the system. Various levels of user involvement can be utilised during the life cycle of the IS. Effective user involvement during the use of the system relies on fast and reactive responses to change requests by users.

## 1 Introduction

There has been extensive research investigating the effect of user participation in the design of information systems on the overall success of the system. However the results have been far from clearcut (Cavaye, 1995; Hirschheim, 1983). Some have suggested this is due to the widely differing views on what user participation actually means, ranging from minimal user involvement simply as a signatory for decisions through to extensive involvement as equal partners in the decision-making process during the design and implementation of the information system (Howcroft and Wilson, 2003; Mumford, 1981). In spite of the equivocal results of the research to date, most organisations intuitively recognise the importance of involving end users in the design of interactive information systems. However few actually practice it (Poltrock and Grudin, 1994). This may be due to environmental

C. Barry et al. (eds.), *Information Systems Development: Challenges in Practice, Theory, and Education, Vol.1*, doi: 10.1007/978-0-387-68772-8_12,
© Springer Science+Business Media, LLC 2009

factors such as having difficulty obtaining access to the end user, having to work with intermediaries or a reluctance by the organisation to fund time-consuming workshops (Webb, 1996). Some researchers have argued that user-centred design may not be feasible due to a heterogeneous end-user community (Webb, 1996).

Most of the research in the area of participatory design focuses on the design and development of new information systems. Very few studies have attempted to address the role of the user during maintenance (after the system has been implemented). Carroll (2004) highlights the need to expand the role of the user as co-designer in the latter part of the systems development life cycle and even after implementation. The research question for this chapter is: How can user involvement be utilised during the life cycle of the development of an IS?

We explored this question in the case of mobile clinical technology implementation in the Metropolitan Ambulance Service, Melbourne, Australia. We found that in this case user involvement was utilised during the design, implementation and use of the IS. The culture of user participation was established during the design of the mobile system and was actively followed by user involvement during the implementation. After the implementation of the mobile clinical IS user involvement has been encouraged through fast, reactive responses to requests for changes from users. We make the following conclusions. User involvement should be established during the design of the IS and also needs to be followed up during the implementation and use of the system. Various levels of user involvement can be utilised during the life cycle of the information systems. Effective user involvement during the use of the system relies on fast and reactive responses to change requests by users.

The rest of the chapter is structured as follows: Section 2 reviews the literature on user participation in design and user participation in the design of healthcare information systems. This is followed by Sect. 3, including a description of the case study. In Sect. 5 we highlight some comments from paramedics about the design, implementation and use of the IS. We conclude with implications of our findings for user involvement during the design, implementation and use of information systems.

## 2 User Participation in Design

There has been extensive research from the mid-1970s onwards investigating the effect of user participation in the design of information systems on the overall success of the system. However the results have been far from clearcut (Cavaye, 1995; Hirschheim, 1983). One view of user participation is described by Mumford (1981) as handing over the responsibility of the design of an IS over to the user who will use the system (Mumford, 1981). Researchers arguing for user participation suggest it can alleviate some of the risks associated with implementing an IS. Introducing a new IS into an organisation can have political implications as it invariably introduces change into that organisation. User participation can highlight impending industrial relations issues early, allowing these to be resolved prior to the system being released. Any grievances can be aired prior to full-scale development (Howcroft and Wilson, 2003). Researchers questioning user participation have suggested that it is not applicable to all information systems projects. User-centred design principles are most often applied where there is a specified user community (Webb, 1996). *Some have argued that it may actually be undesirable in that it may limit the creativity process* (Webb, 1996).

Heinbokel et al. (1996) conducted a study of 29 commercial software development companies to determine the advantages and disadvantages of user-centred design. They explored two aspects of user-centred design – *user participation* and *user orientation*. In their study, *user participation* was defined as having a user representative on the development team and *user orientation* was a cognitive-emotional concept referring to a positive attitude of the development team member towards users. The results of their study found that user participation and user orientation were negatively related to team effectiveness and the quality of the resulting system. High user participation resulted in 'low overall success, few innovations, less flexibility, low team effectiveness and low changeability' (Heinbokel et al., 1996). In conclusion they emphasised that they were not recommending that user-centred design be abandoned but that there should be acknowledgement of the difficulty of putting user-centred design into practice and urged more research into the key problem areas and how they may be overcome.

The two prominent methodologies of user involvement are the Scandinavian Participatory Design approaches and the North American Joint Application Design. Both emphasise the positive effect of continuous user involvement in the design process on the overall quality of the outcome (Carmel et al., 1993). Scandinavian approaches have at their core, the notion of democracy in the workplace and the right of individual workers to have effective participation in workplace decisions often through trade union representation (Kuhn and Muller, 1993). One of the early Scandinavian studies was the Florence project which had the objective of enabling 'nurses to gain control over the computer systems applied in their work' (p. 282, Bjerknes and Bratteteig, 1987). Scandinavian approaches have heavily influenced the way IS researchers talk about user participation in systems development (Howcroft and Wilson, 2003). However it has been suggested that although there is a difference in the way IS researchers talk about user participation in systems development, in practice the development of systems is very similar across geographical boundaries (King, 1998).

Some have argued that user participation may not be possible in some industrial environments, for example, developing nations (Avgerou and Land, 1992). The idea that user participation in system design is not possible in developing nations has been disputed by Korpela et al. (1998). They conducted a 7-year study in Nigeria, involving the cooperative system design of their Primary Health Care system. A key finding was that user participation is a must in developing countries (Korpela et al., 1998).

In a survey of software practitioners conducted in US and Australia it was found that the key to project success was '(1) Having a sponsor throughout the project, (2) users who make adequate time for requirements gathering, (3) a high level of customer/user participation in the development process, and (4) agreement on requirements between customer/users and the development team' (Procaccino et al., 2005).

In their taxonomy of Participatory Design, Kuhn and Muller (1993) map examples of participatory design practice against two visual dimensions – 'time during the development cycle' and 'who participates with whom in what?' The time dimension represents whether the participatory design practice occurs early or late in the development cycle, and the other dimension refers to whether the developers participate in the user's world or the user directly participates in the designer's world (Kuhn and Muller, 1993). As noted by Carroll (2004) conventional approaches to user participation in design focus on the early stages of the development life cycle. This can be expanded to include users as co-designers late in the development life cycle and also even after the implementation. The model developed by Carroll (2004) makes a distinction between the *technology as designed* during the development process and the *technology in use* that is affected by changes as requested by the user.

User participation can take many forms. Mumford (1983) (as quoted by Avison and Fitzgerald (2003)) identifies three types of user participation: consultative participation, representative consultation and consensus participation. Consultative participation is the lowest form of participation in which the design of the system is the responsibility of the systems designers. The systems designers ensure that the users are consulted about requirements and changes to the IS. Representative participation is a higher level of user participation and describes a situation where the users and the designers are on equal footing in the design of the system. Consensus participation is the highest form of participation. This form of participation is termed user-driven design and involves all users in the design of the system. The negative aspect of this type of user participation is that it is very difficult to make a decision due to the large number of users that are taking part in this decision.

Establishing user involvement as part of systems development is a complex process due to a number of characteristics (Clement and van den Besselaar, 1993). First, participation is a highly complex process that involves technology and multiple levels of the organisation. Second, participation is highly dependent on the organisational context. The review of a large number of participatory design projects has highlighted (Clement and van den Besselaar, 1993) the need for a sponsor or a group of sponsors that understand the organisation and work practices to initiate participatory design. Furthermore, to engage users in participatory design requires a focus on immediate needs of the users. However, when participation has been adopted a large number of techniques are available that can be utilised (for example: mock-ups, theatre for work impact (Kuhn and Muller, 1993)).

User participation in systems design and implementation can have positive results on the system acceptance and overall success, but not always. Gallivan and Keil (2005) argue that this is because previous studies in user participation have underemphasised the quality of the communication between the user and the developer (Gallivan and Keil, 2005).

In summary, the research into user involvement has identified some contradicting results. User involvement, however, has intuitively been viewed by systems developers as a key factor in the success of the development and implementation of information systems. Most of the work of the research in user participation focuses on the design process to deliver an IS for implementation. However, current research points out that user participation should also be utilised after the implementation to ensure that users adopt the technology and derive value from the technology. User involvement during the implementation and use of the system has not been studied in detail.

# 3 Research Method

Case study research lends itself to the exploration of new areas of research (Eisenhardt, 1989) such as mobile computing. The research strategy allows for in-depth description of the relationships in context (Benbasat et al., 1987; Galliers, 1993). The case research strategy was chosen here owing to the novelty of mobile technology applications within organisations and to examine individual use contexts in depth (Yin, 1994).

**Table 1.** Interview details

| | | |
|---|---|---|
| | Formal interviews | 43 |
| Number of interviews | Informal interactions | 5 VACIS training sessions |
| | | 7 meetings with MAS staff |
| | Information systems group | 3 |
| Range of interviewees | Management | 2 |
| | Clinical support Officers | 2 |
| | Paramedics (before implementation) | (12) [12] = 24 (Pilot group) |
| | [after implementation interviews] | (10) [ 2] = 12 (Main group) |

Forty-three ½-h to 1-h interviews were conducted over a 12-month period from late November 2005 through to early December 2006 (see Table 1). These were interviews with the information systems group – the CIO of the MAS, the technical project manager and systems analyst of VACIS (Victorian Ambulance Clinical Information System). There were interviews with management – one with the subject matter expert for data for the VACIS system who was also manager of the clinical support officers at the time and two with clinical support officers. There were also interviews with ten paramedics from the pilot group and two team leaders from the pilot group and another ten paramedics from the main group obtaining their views prior to using the VACIS system and then after they had been using VACIS for at least 3 months. The interviews were semi-structured and the participants were free to discuss the main issues/advantages of the mobile computing initiative from their perspective. Each participant signed a consent form giving permission to be interviewed and to have the interview audio-taped. The interview was then transcribed and the transcript was sent back to the participant for review.

The interview script was based on a similar study done in another healthcare organisation and centred on the staff member's perceptions of VACIS – importance, ease of use, management support, advantages and disadvantages of use and the implementation process. The management interviews were conducted mainly in December 2005. The Pilot group paramedic interviews prior to using VACIS began late November 2005. The next round of interviews for obtaining paramedic perceptions of VACIS after using it for around 3 months began mid-February 2006. The main group interviews began in July 2006. MAS also provided release notes for each of the 25 releases over the 12-month period, and these were classified into categories of change (see Table 2).

## 3.1 Mobile Computing Application: VACIS

The VACIS system records the clinical treatment of the patient, and it is also an information tool containing Clinical Practice Guidelines, eMIMS drug reference, Clinical procedure animation and maps. It resides on a Panasonic Toughbook tablet PC in a magnesium alloy case with spill-resistant keyboard. It had to be able to withstand the rigours of day-to-day use by paramedics and was tested to US military standards. The battery has a 3–3.5 h life and can be recharged in the ambulance. Also spare batteries are available at the hospitals if required. It uses a digitised screen with a digitised stylus. Major hospitals have 802.11 wireless networked printers, and each ambulance is equipped with a Canon IP90 printer which uses Bluetooth software to print the case sheet from the toughbook within a 5-m range. The toughbook can be used as a standard laptop with keyboard or can have the top swivelled into a tablet. Having access to a keyboard and mouse was very important to some of the paramedics, whereas others were quite happy to use the pen and tablet. The VACIS system is very intuitive and reliable, and the paramedics have been happy with the usability and reliability of the system overall. The MAS management and the Information Management group were keenly aware of the importance of acknowledging the needs of the paramedics when designing the VACIS system. They conducted extensive consultation with the paramedics and ran several focus groups working through the requirements for the VACIS system from the paramedics' perspective. As noted by the emergency operations manager: 'VACIS is designed by paramedics for paramedics'. [Emergency Operations Manager, February 2006, Line 243]

## 4 Analysis of the Case

This section describes the role of user involvement demonstrated in the case study in a complex implementation process. It highlights the history of the implementation process, the activities that took place during the design, implementation and use of the system. The diagram describes (see Fig. 1) the implementation process that has been followed at MAS. The first implementation of VACIS, from the paramedics' perspective, did not involve extensive user involvement and could not be easily adapted to user requirements. The first implementation of VACIS is not discussed in detail as very little user involvement was perceived by the paramedics as the following comment highlights:

*VACIS [implementation] 1 was announced at a media conference .... and no one had seen it till on that day..... Well no one except those [who] were implementing it, and it arrived on the first ambulance a year later. [Team Leader Paramedic 1, Interview 21, Lines 31–38]*

The design for the second implementation of VACIS was performed with extensive user involvement. A post implementation review was conducted after the first implementation and a list of lessons learned was developed. The requirements for the second implementation were derived from the requirements of the first implementation combined with the lessons learned. One interviewee described the process of requirements specification for the second implementation as follows:

*There was a post implementation review on VACIS [implementation] 1, so lessons learned [was developed]. We did have our original requirements which the original builders of VACIS [implementation] 1 used to build .. which didn't meet the requirements at all. So what [person X] and I did is we took the original requirements. We didn't redo the analysis phase at all. We took the original requirements we took the lessons learned and we did ... a gap analysis between the two .. given the complaints ... that we had with VACIS [implementation] 1 and so forth. And had user groups meetings and ... user group forum which is all for paramedics and basically came up with the initial requirements. [Interview 3, Lines 60–67]*

The user involvement activities that were utilised were: infield trials by users for hardware and the VACIS system, focus groups and User acceptance testing (UAT). The importance of user involvement in the form of focus groups for the design of VACIS for the second implementation is evident in the following quote from an interviewee:

*There's a hard way and easy way, they chose the hard way , which is the best way to do it.. they got together people who loved VACIS [implementation] 1 and people who couldn't drive it to save themselves, and put them all into a room.. so they made sure that whatever they came up with for VACIS [implementation] 2 would be able to be used by people who were completely computer illiterate basically.. but it had great advantage of flexibility for people who could use a computer,  to make it more user friendly for both sort of user groups. [Team Leader Paramedic 1, Interview 21, Lines 24–30]*

The trial for the hardware was described as follows:

*We went to tender [for the mobile device]. Seven companies were in the running for it. We narrowed that down to three. One was clearly ahead of the other two but it was almost double the price of the other tablets. But we put those in the field and got the paramedics to choose what hardware they felt ...that was going to do the best job for them as the endusers. [Emergency Operations Manager, Lines 159–163]*

A member of the information systems group described their reaction to the in-field trial of VACIS as follows:

*It went into production,...Prior to that there was an infield trial which ran for, I think almost two months. But basically they were using that in a live environment. What they were doing is using VACIS and printing the case sheet and the printed case sheets went into the Finance system. So what they weren't doing is transferring the information so that wasn't really part of the scope of the infield trial. It was very useful. Just really I think to give people comfort that it's working and ... hardly any application issues came out of it. It was mainly requests for changes to the clinical data, which was fantastic. [Interview 3, Lines 173–181]*

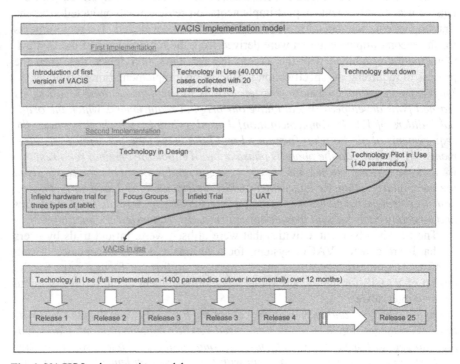

**Fig. 1.** VACIS Implementation model

A quality development team was formed to develop VACIS for the second implementation, and the development was performed by the organisation. The result of this inhouse development was that the software was more flexible and could be adapted to the local conditions. The following quotes highlight this:

- *The most important [aspects of the interaction with the IS Group] would be the quality of the staff that they have recruited for the project and the support that they have given the project. [Emergency Ops Manager, Lines 161–162]*
- *They chose to write the code from scratch themselves, which meant that it was more flexible and would actually be using words that are common in the Australian vernacular, and so they got a lot of brownie points .. and for just*

*investing the time to try and release something ... which was robust and had been well tested, and they sold it like that from the get-go for VACIS [implementation] 2. [Team Leader Paramedic 1, Interview 21, Lines 31–38]*

VACIS was rolled out gradually across the MAS branches in the metropolitan area of Melbourne starting in the Northern Suburbs. MAS were keenly aware of the possible anxiety that some paramedics may feel towards VACIS so they had an in-depth training session for every paramedic. Each paramedic attended a 4-h training session which was conducted by senior paramedics. The training classes were limited to fifteen paramedics per session. Another senior paramedic was also present to assist the paramedics as they worked through the sample case step by step. The training was from a paramedics perspective and very practical – walking through how to enter a case onto the VACIS tablet. Following the training session a senior paramedic was rostered to go on the first shift with the newly trained paramedics to help them use VACIS for the first time out in the field. This proved invaluable to the paramedics and was very much appreciated.

*I have been impressed actually with what they are doing. The fact that we had someone, one of the trainers, prepared to spend basically a whole shift with us,... if we need it on our first day out. That didn't happen with the original one. We all struggled ourselves basically with that one.  [Paramedic 2, Interview 6, Lines 186–190]*

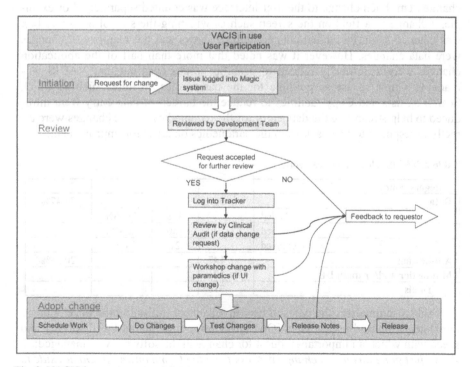

**Fig. 2.** VACIS in use – user participation

VACIS has been adapted extensively during the last 12 months through an active process of change requests. One paramedic explains the process as follows: *Every new program has to be refined and put in place and improvements made incrementally. So hopefully we are getting towards that with this [VACIS]....... Experience has shown what works and what doesn't. The feedback is letting them make those changes. [Paramedic , Interview 43, Lines 57–59 and 83–84]*

Figure 2 illustrates the formal process has been followed to gather change requests and to react to them. (Note: The magic system is used to log all change requests within MAS, whereas the Tracker system is used internally by the IS group to track changes from initiation through to release). An evaluation of the change requests that have been received and implemented during the releases highlights a number of categories:

- Application changes to the user interface, back end processes and business rules
- Data changes for example adding a medication to the list of medications available
- Middle Tier, Corporate Database changes

Table 2 gives an outline of the types of changes that have been requested and implemented through releases. There were 25 releases of the VACIS system over the 12-month period involving 716 individual changes. Each change to a data item was counted separately as was each change to the User Interface. For example, the addition of a medication to the medication list was counted as an individual change item. Each change to the user interface was counted separately. For example, a change to a field on the screen such as widening the size of a display box was counted as an individual change item. It shows that the majority of changes were data changes. However it was noted that more than half of the application changes were specifically related to usability issues ensuring that VACIS was made as simple to use as possible for the paramedics. Features such as Quick Search on lists and Copy facilities to reduce the burden of data entry were introduced to help streamline the data entry for the paramedics. These changes were directly in response to feedback from the paramedics on areas for improvement.

**Table 2.** VACIS release notes categories

| Category counts | | | | |
|---|---|---|---|---|
| Data | 569 | | | 79.47% |
| Added | | 418 | 73.46% | |
| Modified | | 130 | 22.85% | |
| Removed | | 21 | 3.69% | |
| Application | 147 | | | 20.53% |
| Middle tier and/or main DB | 0 | | | |
| Totals | 716 | | | |

Table 3 summarises the types of user involvement utilised in the development, implementation and use at MAS. One interviewee highlighted the flexibility and speed with which an important request for change in the software was managed: *We've just gone through a change process from the Commonwealth Games side to put in a new field, you know, a new billing field to relate to the Commonwealth games competitors.. who a number of them are being paid for by the State Government so.. these guys, the VACIS people said 'oh no we can write that in for you', update everybody the next time they synch. It's very easy.* *[Team Leader Paramedic 1, Interview 21, Lines 130–134]*

User participation was very important as highlighted by the following comment: *Having the paramedics having a voice in the design, the build, the hardware, everything right through and them having the ability to give us feedback and for us to make those changes.* *[Emergency Operations Manager, Lines 539–541]*

**Table 3.** Types of user participation

| Stage | Type of user participation | Value/focus |
|---|---|---|
| Technology in design | Infield Hardware trial | Feedback on usability of mobile device |
|  | Focus group | Joint application design |
|  | Infield trial | Feedback on usability of VACIS application |
|  | User acceptance testing | Feedback on accuracy of VACIS application |
| Technology in implementation/rollout | Training sessions run by 'expert' users | Training done from enduser perspective |
|  | Mentoring | Building confidence in use of system. Expert users and end users work side by side on their first shift using the VACIS system |
| Technology in use | Change requests | Feedback on areas for improvement |
|  | Post Implementation review | Feedback on areas for improvement |

# 5 Discussion

The case study describes a number of areas of user involvement. User involvement has been linked to improved user satisfaction with a system. In the case of MAS the paramedics did not perceive the first implementation of VACIS as catering for their needs. It is important to notice that paramedics as a general rule are not very computer literate and like most healthcare organisations were not enthusiastic about adopting such a new technology. To alleviate the lack of fit with the work of paramedics extensive user involvement was employed. A representative group of users was identified to take part in the focus groups and correspond to the technique such as Joint Application Design. The users consisted of paramedics who believed that the technology will be to the advantage of MAS, those who were vehemently opposed to the technology and trade union members. Further techniques that were used to obtain feedback on the usability of VACIS and the accuracy of the system were infield trials and user acceptance testing. Infield trials are similar to techniques such as mock-ups in which the user uses the system in a real-world situation. In summary it can be concluded that the user involvement that was utilised during the design phase would correspond to the category of representative participation (Mumford, 1983). Key factors in the success of the user involvement in this phase are a diverse group of users that formed part of the focus group and the identification of key paramedics to take part in the design process.

During the technology implementation two types of user involvement were used: training sessions by 'expert' users and mentoring. The training session was run by 'expert' users who were themselves paramedics and could therefore associate with the paramedics that were trained. The mentoring also provided a valuable support to the paramedics who could easily be overwhelmed by the introduction of information technology. The users in this phase were in control of the rollout with extensive support from the IT department. The user involvement in this phase can be classified as consensus participation (Mumford, 1983).

The user involvement during the use of the system was scaled down to the report of requests for change by paramedics. The important aspect that was highlighted by the case was that it was important to have a fast response time to requests for changes. Again, such techniques as workshops were used to determine the effect of a change of for example the user interface. Workshops are similar to joint application design sessions. The organisation ensured that the paramedics were kept informed of the changes through publication of release notes which summarised the changes. These were published on the electronic portal, through bulletins and via emails to the branch team managers. The change requests were frequent and acted upon quickly. The type of user participation during the use phase can be classified as consultative participation as most of the decisions were made by the design team.

The case study highlights the importance of continuing the user involvement not just during the design but also during the implementation and the use of the IS. The user participation ebbed and flowed over the life cycle of the VACIS system. Figure 3 highlights the user involvement that was used over the life of the VACIS system. The importance of the user involvement for this system is that paramedics perceived the system as designed for paramedics by paramedics.

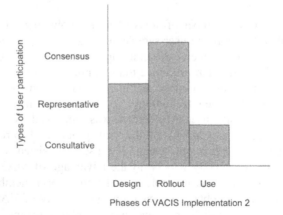

**Fig. 3.** User participation over VACIS life cycle

One outcome of the careful management of the design, implementation and use of VACIS is the potential for the organisation to improve their process of managing change. The following comments highlight this potential:

- *It will be interesting to see how they manage change in the future. Because I think this has been a really really good process they've gone through and they've done it really well.... with VACIS. Quite in stark contrast to the way they did it the first time. And even the way they have done other things........ there is a number of things they've managed really really poorly in trying to change the service. They're almost notorious for it. Within..... the culture of Ambulance.... people expect change to go badly. This has gone really well. The support that has been there. The training that has been there has been really positive and hopefully.... it will....at an organisational level....change how they implement change. [Paramedic 7, Interview 22, Lines 314–322]*
- *We've been asked to talk to other projects about what we have done and how we've done it, within MAS. So I think MAS has recognised that what we have done in our training and support has had a big impact with the rollout and the success of it. So what we've been doing hasn't been as good as it could have been, so let's keep making it better and this is one way of making it better. Hopefully we can build on this. [Emergency Ops Manager, Lines 471–476]*

# 6 Conclusion

The chapter has reviewed the user involvement literature and focused on the utilisation of user involvement during the design, implementation and use of the VACIS system. An analysis of the comments made by paramedics was done and documentation relating to the change requests have been analysed.

The chapter draws the following three conclusions. User involvement should be established during the systems development of the new IS, and also needs to be followed up during the implementation and use of the system. Various levels of user involvement can be utilised during the life cycle of the IS. Effective user involvement during the use of the system relies on fast and reactive responses to change requests by users.

The study has the following limitations. First, we have focused only on the user involvement of a single system. Second, the case incorporates influences that pertain to healthcare professionals.

# References

Avgerou, C., Land, F. (1992). Examining the appropriateness of Information technology. In B. Bhatnagar and M. Odedra (Eds.), *Social Implications of Computers in Developing Countries* (pp. 26–41). Proceedings, Tata McGraw-Hill, New Delhi.

Avison, D., Fitzgerald, G. (2003). *Information Systems Development: Methodologies, Techniques and Tools*, 3rd edition, McGraw Hill Education (UK) Limited, Spain.

Benbasat, I., Goldstein, D., Mead, M. (1987). The case research strategy in studies of information systems. *MIS Quarterly, 11*(3), 368–386.

Bjerknes, G., Bratteteig, T (1987). Florence in Wonderland – System development with nurses. In: G. Bjerknes, P. Ehn and M. Kyng (Eds.), *Computer and Democracy – A Scandinavian Challenge*. Gower Brookfield, Vermont.

Carmel, E., Whitaker, R., George, J. (1993). PD and joint application design: a transatlantic comparison. *Communications of the ACM, 36,* 40–48.

Carroll, J. (2004). *Completing Design in Use: Closing the Appropriation Cycle*. ECIS 2004, June 14–16, Turku, Finland.

Cavaye, A. (1995). User participation in system development revisited. *Information and Management, 28,* 311–323.

Clement, A., van den Besselaar, P. (1993). A retrospective look at PD projects. *Communications of the ACM, 36*(4), 29–37.

Eisenhardt, K. (1989). Building theories from case study research. *Academy of Management Review, 14*(4).

Galliers, R. (1993). Choosing Information systems research approaches. In *Information Systems Research: Issues, Methods and Practical Guidelines* (pp. 144–162): Blackwell Scientific, Oxford.

Gallivan, M., Keil, M. (2005). The user-developer communication process: A critical case study. *Information Systems Journal, 13*(1), 37–68.

Heinbokel, T., Sonnentag, S., Frese, M., Stolte, W., Brodbeck, F. (1996). Don't underestimate the problems of user centredness in software development projects there are many! *Behaviour and Information Technology, 15*(4), 226–236.

Hirschheim, R. (1983). Assessing participative systems design: Some conclusions from an exploratory study. *Information and Management, 6,* 317–327.

Howcroft, D., Wilson, M. (2003). Participation: 'Bounded Freedom' or hidden constraints on user involvement. *New Technology, Work and Employment, 18*(1), 2–19.

King, J. (1998). Commentary on "Research on Information Systems Development in Scandinavia – Unity in Plurality." *Scandinavian Journal of Information Systems, 10*(1 and 2), 205–208.

Korpela, M., Soriyan, H., Olufokunbi, K., Onayade, A., Davies-Adetugbo, A., Adesanmi, D. (1998). Community participation in Health Informatics in Africa: An experiment in Tripartite partnership in Ile-Ife, Nigeria. *Computer Supported Cooperative Work, 7*(304), 339–358.

Kuhn, S., Muller, M. (1993). Participatory design. *Communications of the ACM, 36*(6), 24–28.

Mumford, E. (1981). Participative systems design: Structure and method. *Systems, Objectives, Solutions, 1,* 5–19.

Mumford, E. (1983). *Designing Participatively*: Manchester Business School, Manchester.

Poltrock, S. E., Grudin, J. (1994). Organisational obstacles to interface design and development: Two participant-observer studies. *ACM Transactions on CHI, 1,* 52–80.

Procaccino, J., Verner, J., Darter, M., Amadio, W. (2005). Towards predicting software development success from the perspective of practitioners: An exploratory Bayesian model. *Journal of Information Technology, 20*(3), 187–200.

Webb, B. (1996). The role of users in interactive systems design: when computers are theatre, do we want the audience to write the script? *Behaviour and Information Technology, 15*(2), 76–83.

Yin, R. K. (1994). *Case Study Research – Design and Methods*, 2nd edition, Sage, Thousand Oaks, CA.

# A Practical Example for Model-Driven Web Requirements

**M.J. Escalona[1], C.L. Parra[2], F.M. Martín[3], J. Nieto[4], A. Llergo[5] and F. Pérez[6]**

[1]Department of Computer Languages and Systems, University of Seville, mjescalona@us.es

[2]Hopitales Universitarios Virgen del Rocio, Sevilla, carlos.parra.sspa@juntadeandalucia.es

[3]Servicio Andaluz de Salud, Sevilla, franciscom.martin.sspa@juntadeandalucia.es

[4]Hopitales Universitarios Virgen del Rocio, Sevilla, jaime.nieto.sspa@juntadeandalucia.es

[5]Servicio Andaluz de Salud, Sevilla, antonio.llergo.sspa@juntadeandalucia.es

[6]Servicio Andaluz de Salud, Sevilla, francisco.perez.torres@juntadeandalucia.es

**Abstract**  The number of approaches for Web environments has grown very fast in the last years: HDM, OOHDM, and WSDM were among the first, and now a large number can be found in the literature. With the definition of MDA (Model-Driven Architecture) and the acceptance of MDE (Model-Driven Engineering) techniques in this environment, some groups are working in the use of metamodels and transformations to make their approaches more powerful. UWE (UML-Based Web Engineering) or OOWS (Object-Oriented Web Solutions) are only some examples. However, there are few real experiences with Web Engineering in the enterprise environment, and very few real applications of metamodels and MDE techniques. In this chapter the practical experience of a Web Engineering approach, NDT, in a big project developed in Andalusia is presented. Besides, it shows the usability of metamodels in real environments.

## 1 Introduction

In the last years, Web Engineering (Deshpande et al., 2002) has been studied by several important research groups. With the first approach for Hypermedia Systems, HDM (Garzotto et al., 1993), research groups started to propose, develop, and analyze different techniques, models, and procedures in order to offer a suitable methodological environment for the new Software Engineering area.

As a recent development, several groups are basing their approaches on the Model-Driven Engineering (MDE) (Schmidt, 2006) and in the paradigm defined by the OMG with MDA (Model-Driven Architecture) (OMG, 2003). Recent literatures

C. Barry et al. (eds.), *Information Systems Development: Challenges in Practice, Theory, and Education, Vol.1*, doi: 10.1007/978-0-387-68772-8_13,
© Springer Science+Business Media, LLC 2009

offer suitable examples of MDE applications in the Web Engineering. They analyze their advantages and their powerful possibilities. However, very few practical
applications can be found. Previous comparative studies (Retschitzegger and
Schwinger, 2000) (Koch, 1999) (Escalona and Koch, 2004) show that Web Engineering is being ardently studied by the research community, but all of them conclude that it is not applied enough on the enterprise environment. The same is
happening with MDE.

This chapter presents a real experience with Web Engineering and MDE. It
starts by analyzing the situation of MDE in the Web Engineering environment,
and it analyzes briefly its advantages and consequences. In Sect. 3, NDT (Navigational Development Techniques) (Escalona, 2004) is presented. NDT is an MDE
approach for Web environments that has been used in different real projects in
Spain. NDT is mainly focused on the requirements and analysis phases; for this
reason, this chapter presents the practical experience in this area. Although NDT is
being applied in several real projects, and several studies about practical experienced have been published (Escalona, 2004) (Escalona et al., 2006), this chapter
presents the application of NDT in Diraya project. Diraya was selected for its special characteristics. This is a very ambitious project to manage health information
in any hospital in Andalusia. As presented in Sect. 4 Diraya is a complex system
with a high group of developers and users; thus, it was an important challenge for
our approach. Besides, it requires special aspects: the use of HL7 (http://www.hl7.
org), the use of a power tool for a large number of developers, etc. that offers an
important experience and feedback for our research work. Section 5 shows the real
advantages of using MDE and Web Engineering in a project like Diraya. It analyzes how metamodels can offer a powerful environment to fuse approaches, standards or, even, to use different tools based on metamodels. Finally, conclusions
and future works are presented.

## 2 Related Works

Nowadays, MDE and MDA are frequently used. In the Web Engineering environment it is not different. This chapter is mainly focused on the requirements
phase; for this reason, we are going to focus on approaches based on metamodels
and MDE for Web requirements. However, it is necessary to point out that every
day, more Web Engineering research groups are working in MDE environment.

One of the most recent works is (Valderas et al., 2006). This study presents an
approach to transform a Web requirements model to a set of prototypes. They propose a requirements treatment based on the task metaphor. Valderas et al. offer an
extension of this approach to deal with the specific characteristics of Web requirements. After that, they present a way to derive the navigational model of OOWS
(Fons et al., 2003). Firstly, they propose to define requirements like tasks; these
tasks are translated into an AGG Graph. Using Graphs transformations, analysis
models are obtained. The approach is supported with a tool that is available. This

work is very interesting because they offer a suitable solution for transformation supported by a tool. However, its transformations are not based in OMG tendencies. This shows that they are not compatible with other similar approaches.

In (Escalona and Koch, 2006) the power of metamodel is presented. In comparative studies about Web approaches, a general conclusion is that similar concepts are used or represented with a different number of models, techniques, or artifacts. Thus, for instance, navigational classes are presented with different elements in UWE (Koch, 2001), OOHDM (Rossi, 1996), or WebML (Ceri et al., 2000). Escalona and Koch show in this chapter how a metamodel can represent a concept independent of its representation or notation; only concepts are important. They present a metamodel for Web requirements, named WebRe, that represents requirements models of W2000 (Baresi et al., 2001), NDT, OOHDM, and UWE. Koch et al. (2006) continue their work using QVT to get analysis models from this metamodel. These works are interesting because they are completely based on UML and QVT, standards defined by OMG. However, the results too theoretic.

Fernández and Monzón (2000) present the possibilities of working with metamodels and tools. Thus, they present how a requirements metamodel can be easily defined in IRqA (Integral Requisite Analyzer). IRqA is a commercial tool that lets define metamodels for requirements. In this sense, this study presents the power of tools that support metamodels because they are suitable for any approach defined using metamodels. This work is very practical in fact, but it is not an approach for Web. They do not offer specific artifacts to deal with Web environment; they just offer an approach for classical requirements treatment.

However, although these works are specific for requirements, other classical approaches are working in the MDE environment. For instance in (Schauerhuber et al., 2006) (Moreno et al., 2006), some metamodels for WebML can be found. They present how metamodels can represent classical concepts independent of the artifact used to represent them.

## 3 NDT (Navigational Development Techniques)

NDT is a methodological approach to deal with requirements in Web Environments. NDT was proposed in order to support the requirements engineering and the analysis phase of Web Systems, and it is based on the MDE paradigm.

Several comparative studies, e.g., that analyzed in (Escalona and Koch, 2004), have proved that one of the less treated phases in Web Engineering is the requirements phase. Most of approaches in Web Engineering are focused on the analysis and design phases. They usually propose to use classical requirements techniques, like use cases, in order to capture and define requirements in Web.

Although use cases is a suitable technique to deal with requirements and it is usually very easy to be understood by the user, frequently they are very ambiguous (Insfrán et al., 2002; Vilain et al., 2000). For this reason, since 2006, several research groups are working in specific requirements treatment for the Web environment. For instance, OOHDM has proposed the UID (User Interaction Diagrams) (Vilain et al., 2000), a specific diagram to deal with interaction requirements.

Another conclusion from comparatives studies is that, in Web Engineering, different aspects of software are treated in a separate way. This idea is followed in the analysis and design phases for several approaches, e.g., OOHDM, UWE, WebML, and OOH (Cachero, 2003). This idea of concept separation can be moved to the requirements phase in order to get the advantage of concept separation. Thus, UWE deals separately with information requirements, functional requirements, etc. W2000 defines different use cases for functional and navigational requirements.

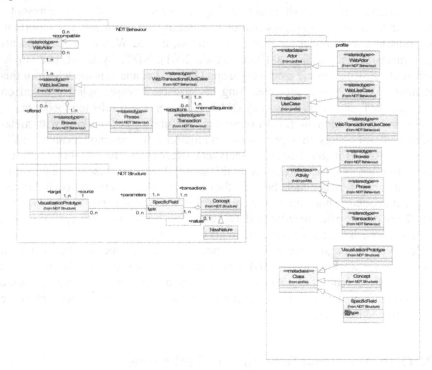

**Fig. 1.** NDT requirements metamodel

Finally, a fact detected by the comparative studies is that, sometimes, requirements are defined in a very ambiguous way, and it is very difficult for the analysis to translate the knowledge from the requirements definition to the analysis models.

With these ideas, NDT was proposed. Thus, it proposes an MDE approach in order to offer a suitable environment to capture, define, analyze, and validate Web requirements. The life cycle of NDT starts with requirements engineering. Its artifacts are described with a metamodel for requirements that extends the metamodel of UML and follows the structure of WebRe (Escalona and Koch, 2006) metamodel. In Fig. 1 the metamodel of NDT is presented. This metamodel can be defined using a UML profile, which is also presented in Fig. 1. In the requirements level, NDT divides requirements into four different kinds, which are all presented on the metamodel: **storage information requirements**, represented by Concept,

NewNature, and SpecificField metaclasses. They capture the information that the system has to manage. **Actors' requirements**, represented by the WebActor metaclass. A web system can change depending on the user who interacts with it. **Functional requirements**, represented by WebTransactionalUseCase and Transaction metaclasses. They capture information about the functionality that the system has to offer. **Interaction requirements**, represented by Phrases, Browse, and VisualizationPrototype metaclasses that compile the structure of the interaction with the system.

Thus, NDT follows the idea of concept separation. Each of these artifacts is treated with a specific technique. In order to describe each kind of requirements, NDT proposes the use of patterns. A pattern is a table with specific fields for each kind of requirements. Each pattern is a practical vision of each concept in the metamodel. For instance, in Table 1 the specific pattern to describe an actor is presented. This pattern was derived from our practical experience in Diraya project. Although not presented in the metamodel in Fig. 1, each row in the pattern is an attribute of the WebActor metaclass in the metamodel. Thus, patterns are really an easy interface to present the metamodel to the development team. Following the MDA notation, the requirements level of NDT represents the CIM (Computation Independent Model) level of this MDA approach.

**Table 1.** An example of NDT patterns

| ACT-01 | Health expert |
|---|---|
| Associated | OBJ-01. Manage information about specialists that work with Diraya |
| Description | This actor represents any person who interacts with Diraya system. It represents doctors, nurses, janitor, etc. |
| Comments | This actor assumes the functionality common for any actor in Diraya |

The life cycle of NDT continues with the analysis phase. However, in this phase, NDT does not propose any analysis metamodel. As concluded in several comparative studies, there are too many analysis approaches for Web Engineering. For this reason, NDT uses the UWE analysis metamodel (Kraus and Koch, 2003). The selection of UWE is because UWE is completely based on UML, and also, UML profiles are defined. Thus, in this phase, a content model, a navigational model, and an abstract interface model are generated. UWE analysis models represent the PIM level of NDT. Between the CIM and the PIM metamodels, NDT defines a set of relations and transformations using QVT. Thus, NDT solves some problems detected:

It offers specific techniques for each kind of Web requirements.

It proposes the use of an MDE environment in order to make easier the translation between requirements and analysis.

It proposes the use of patterns to deal with requirements. Patterns are very easy to be understood by the user, but they also represent metamodel artifact in a structured way that is very useful for the development team.

It follows the separation concept paradigm proposed by several research groups for the design and the analysis phase. Thus, it can assume the advantage of this paradigm.

Besides, NDT is not only a theoretical approach. It has been applied in several real projects as presented in (Escalona et al., 2006). This study analyzed real experiences of NDT and how they are influenced in the approach. Nowadays, it is applied by several public organizations like Culture Andalusian Government (http://www.juntadeandalucia.es/cultura/) and Andalusian Health Service (http://www.juntadeandalucia.es/servicioandaluzdesalud), as the requirements methodology for their software projects. Also, some private companies are using it (e.g., everis and Telvent) in several projects.

## 4 An Example: Diraya Project

Diraya Project is a very ambitious project developed by the Andalusian Health Service (SAS in Spanish). SAS is the government organization in Andalusia that manages hospitals, health centers, and other health public systems. In order to manage the information of patients and health centers, SAS developed Diraya System. Some years ago, the Diraya project was used to manage the primary health attendance in Andalusia. This first module was called Primary Diraya. However, now, it is extended to the specialized health centers as Specialized Diraya.

Specialized Diraya is a Web system to manage all the information about patients who visit any hospital in Andalusia, irrespective of whether they visit the hospital with a prior appointment or as a case of urgency. Specialized Diraya will be installed in 34 hospitals in Andalusia, and it will be used by more than 62,000 final users composed of doctors, nurses, etc.

The project started some months ago, and it is developed by six big software companies in Andalusia: Telvent, Indra, everis, Tecnova, Accenture, and Isoft. They are working together in order to get the best results. They are experts in health systems, and they are using their previous knowledge during the development process. Specialized Diraya development is divided into two phases. The first one was presented in June 2007 and it was installed in one hospital in order to value it. The analysis phase has just been completed.

Specialized Diraya development is based on Métrica (2007), a methodology proposed by the Spanish government for public software projects. Métrica is a very complex and very extensive approach that was used on UML models for modeling systems. NDT is also based on UML; thus, Métrica and NDT are compatible. NDT offers a normalization of Métrica for Web System. For this reason, it was the platform used in the requirements and the analysis phase.

The group of analysts is composed of 13 people from the different companies, and they are working together in order to get a consistent product. The complete development team includes people from companies, analysts, designers, software experts in SAS, etc. It is composed of more than 40 people.

The magnitude of Diraya is a very interesting example. The large number of final users, analysts, designers, etc., the huge number of requirements, and the vast number of different roles in the development offer a complex and an interesting real example of our research results.

# 5 The Practical Experience

For 6 months approximately, the group of Specialized Diraya was working in the requirements and the analysis phase. In order to use NDT as a methodological environment in these phases, the group had to follow some guidelines.

The first one was to define a suitable architecture for the system. Diraya is a very big project. For this reason, it was decided to divide it into different modules. Thus, six modules interconnecting each other were defined. The division into six modules follows a practical decision. Each company is expert in one area. The system was divided into these areas and each company developed one of them.

Another decision very important for the project was the selection of a tool. In Sect. 5.1 the selection is presented. In the study of available tools, the use of metamodels was an important advantage for the team.

A guideline proposed by SAS is the use of a standard, HL7, for representing the communication of the system. In Sect. 5.2 the power of metamodels for fusing approaches like NDT and HL7 is presented. Finally, in Sect. 5.3, the advantages of using MDE in Diraya are offered.

## 5.1 The Power of Metamodels for Tools

Another important decision in the project was the tool. With more than 13 people working in the analysis phase and a large number of requirements, a tool had to be used. To begin with, the first selection was NDT-Tool (Escalona et al., 2003). NDT-Tool covers the complete life cycle of NDT. It was developed by the University of Seville and it is free. The first version of NDT-Tool was developed in Visual Basic. Now, a new version developed in J2EE is being developed in collaboration with two companies, everis and Telvent. When it was tested by Diraya group, the old version was not suitable for a group of analysts that are working in different offices and at the same time. The new version in J2EE via internet was a good choice, but it was too young for the project.

For this reason, SAS and the University of Seville were worked in order to find a suitable tool for Specialized Diraya. After looking at and comparing different possibilities, Enterprise Architecture (http://www.sparxsystems.com/) was the selection. Enterprise Architecture was selected for several reasons. It supports UML, and it offers the possibility of extending the initial definition of UML with its extension mechanisms. NDT requirements metamodel and also UWE analysis model are defined with a UML profile, as presented in Sect. 3. For this reason, it was very easy to adapt the tool for the group. With Enterprise Architecture profile option, the profile of NDT was defined, and companies used them to define requirements and analysis artifacts. Besides, Enterprise Architecture was not a very expensive tool and its interface is very suitable for working. The last point for this selection was the possibility of defining documents normalized according to NDT, UWE, and SAS preconditions in Enterprise Architecture. In Fig. 2 the interface of Enterprise used in Diraya is presented.

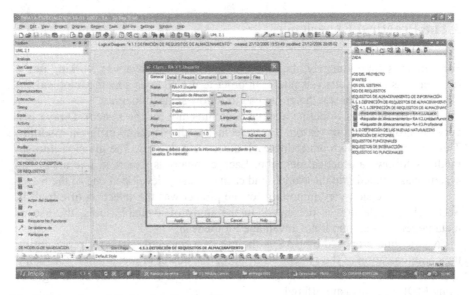

**Fig. 2.** Enterprise architecture interface for Diraya

On the left, profiles for each phases of NDT are defined (requirements, conceptual model, and navigational model). In the right an index for NDT results in each phase is presented.

With this environment, companies can work with NDT metamodels without any special knowledge about metamodels. Besides, Enterprise Architecture offers a tool to define transformation between models using MDA and, now, we are trying to implement NDT transformation in order to get the derivation of CIM to PIM model automatically.

However, the power of metamodels for using tools offers a bigger number of tools for using an approach. In our experience other possibilities were offered to the companies. Thus, for the second phase of Diraya, a double use of tool is being adapted. IRqA (http://www.irqaonline.com/) is a tool especially for the requirements treatment. It is also based on UML and it offers the possibility of defining metamodels and UML profiles. IRqA offers a better interface for users. Although the phase of requirements will be dealt with IRqA, the rest of the life cycle, even the analysis, will be treated with Enterprise Architecture.

Nowadays, we are working in the generation from IRqA models to the Enterprise Architecture models using the QVT relations of NDT.

Thus, thanks to the definition of metamodel, Diraya users has three possibilities: NDT-Tool, Enterprise Architecture, and the fusion between IRqA and Enterprise Architecture.

In conclusion, if an approach works with UML profiles, its artifacts can be easily defined in tools that work with UML and offer its extensions possibilities. Nowadays, other tools are adapted to NDT. The idea is to offer a different number of possibilities. Thus, they could select the best for their companies and their environment.

## 5.2 The Power of Metamodels for Merging Approaches

Another important lesson learned is the power of metamodel for merging approaches. NDT is a methodology that works only in the requirements phase and the analysis. When NDT was proposed, we noticed the importance of making it compatible with other works and approaches. As it was introduced, comparative studies concluded that there were too many models and techniques that dealt with the same concepts in Web Engineering. For this reason, NDT uses UWE metamodels for analysis.

However, although metamodel can be very useful to make compatible different software engineering approaches, in Diraya project we detected that they are also very useful in order to fuse approaches of different environments.

In medical environments, a standard, named HL7, was defined in order to get a standard communication system in medical software system. In Diraya project an important requirement was to follow this standard.

Fortunately, HL7 is defined using also a set of metamodels. It offers a metamodel for use case and interaction metamodel, information model, message design and data type, and vocabulary. HL7 metamodel must be used in the design phase, and it is necessary to translate user requirements into its metamodel artifacts.

In order to make the use of NDT useful for SAS requirements, we studied HL7 and NDT metamodels. Thus, some correspondences between analysis and design concepts were defined.

## 5.3 The Advantages of MDE

Although in the first phase of Diraya a practical tool to translate requirements into analysis models was not offered, because the time of this phase was too hard and tools could not be prepared, MDE was still applied.

As it was presented, NDT transformations are defined with QVT. In NDT-Tool, these transformations were translated into Java algorithms. Thus, the step from requirements to analysis is automatic. These algorithms were offered to analysts and they applied them manually. Although this process is not the most orthodox, in the enterprise environment the time of development is one of the most important elements, and they could not wait for the preparation of Enterprise Architecture.

Obviously, for analysts, the manual application of MDE was not easy, but the result was very important for the project. The capture and definition of requirements in Diraya took more than 3 months. During this phase, the results were:

- More than 200 storage information requirements
- Sixty-seven actors defined

- More than 250 functional requirements
- More than 210 interaction requirements

Despite this large number and the manual application of MDE transformation, the generation of the analysis models just took 1 week. This is despite the fact that the coordination group estimated more than 2 months at the beginning of the project when the use of MDE was not included.

This reduction of time was an important advantage detected and pointed out by the companies and SAS.

Besides, during the MDE generation, the consistency between requirements definition and analysis model is assured. MDE keeps the consistency between models, and it assures that requirements and analysis models represent the same. Thus, it was very interesting to detect the high number of failures and mistakes during the transformation. When analysts generated the analysis models from the requirements, they detected that, sometimes, the analysis model that they had in mind was not the same as that represented by their requirements definition.

The consistency that MDE offers, stops the snow ball effect. At the beginning of the life cycle, the correction of mistakes is simple, but in each posterior phase, the correction is more expensive. The cost of changes grows like a snow ball. Thus, the correction of the requirements definition in Diraya just takes 3 days. However, it would be more expensive if they were detected in a posterior phase, for instance, in the implementation phase.


# 6 Conclusions and Future Works

The rapid advance in the Web Engineering research and approaches presented in the last years offers suitable environments to work in Web development for companies and real projects. The advantages included with the application of MDE have improved these environments. However, these environments are not really applied in practical experience. In Web Engineering, and in Model-Driven Web Engineering, there is an important gap between theory and practice.

In the literature, studies have presented the advantages of applying Web Engineering in Web projects, the reduction of time of MDE, the consistency between model when MDE is used, the power of metamodels, etc. However, very few practical experiences in real projects, with real development teams are presented. This chapter offers a different vision of Web Engineering. It shows a practical experience with Web Engineering in a real project. The study has presented NDT, a methodological approach to deal with requirements in web systems based on MDE, and a big project developed in Andalusia, Specialized Diraya.

The research has offered a practical and a real vision about the application of NDT to Diraya. It has presented how metamodels are optimal to fuse approaches and offer a group of suitable tools for the development team. Besides, it presents how MDE can reduce the time of development and detect inconsistence and mistake in early phases, although in our case MDE was applied manually.

Obviously, tools offered by Diraya are not the best ones. At present, we are looking at implementing QVT transformations in order to offer the possibility of automatic generation. In Enterprise Architecture, a language for MDA applications is offered, but it is not based on QVT and it is not sufficiently documented, so we are finding a lot of problems. In any case, we think that it is very important to count with practical approaches like the presented one. They offer an important feedback for research results. For us, the most important learned lessons were:

- Metamodels are a powerful tool for methodological environment. However, development team is not usually an expert in metamodels. For this reason, it is necessary to offer a suitable interface to work with these metamodels. In the case of NDT, it proposes to use patterns. They are very useful to work with the team and also with the final users.
- Metamodels are powerful, but they must be compatible. For instance, for the fusion between NDT and HL7, if both are defined using a UML profile, it would be easier to detect the common artifacts.
- MDE and Web Engineering are necessary because Web systems have special characteristics that must be treated in a special way. However, they are useless in the enterprise environment if they are not supported by a tool. For companies, the development team is an important variable, and if they have to spend a lot of time in documentation, modeling, or transformations, they will never use research approaches.

Commercial tools are supporting the definition of metamodels and profiles. However, they are starting to work with MDE transformations. The research community needs powerful tools to implement transformations. For this reason, one of our future works is researching in tools that have offered these possibilities, like SmartQVT (http://sourceforge.net/projects/smartqvt) or Moment (Queralt et al., 2006), and measuring if they are useful for the enterprise environment.

# References

Baresi, L., Garzotto, F., Paolini, P. (2001). Extending UML for Modeling Web Applications. Proc. HICSS 2001, pp. 1285–1294.

Cachero, C. (2003). Una extensión a los métodos OO para el modelado y generación automática de interfaces hipermediales. PhD Thesis. Universidad de Alicante, Alicante, España.

Ceri, S., Fraternali, P., Bongio, A. (2000). Web Modelling Language (WebML): A Modelling Language for Designing Web Sites. Conference WWW9/Computer Networks (33) pp. 137–157.

Deshpande, Y., Marugesan, S., Ginige, A., Hanse, S., Schawabe, D., Gaedke, M., White, B. (2002). Web Engineering. Journal of Web Engineering, 1(1), 3–17.

Escalona, M.J. (2004). Modelos y técnicas para la especificación y el análisis de la Navegación en Sistemas Software. Ph. European Thesis. University of Seville, Spain.

Escalona, M.J., Koch, N. (2004). Requirements Engineering for Web Applications: A Comparative Study. Journal of Web Engineering, 2(3), 193–212.

Escalona, M.J., Koch, N. (2006). Metamodelling the Requirements of Web Systems. Proc WebIST 2006, pp. 310–317, Setúbal, Portugal, April 2006. ISBN: 978-972-8865-46-7.

Escalona, M.J, Mejías, M., Torres, J., Reina, A.M. (2003). NDT-Tool: A Tool Case to Deal with Requirements in Web Information Systems. Proc ICWE 2003, LNCS 2722, pp. 212–213.

Escalona, M.J., Gutierrez, J.J., Villadiego, D., León, A., Torres, A.H. (2006). Practical Experience in Web Engineering. Proc ISD 2006, Budapest, Hungary.

Fernández, J.L., Monzón, A.A. (2000). Metamodel and a Tool for Software Requirements Management. Reliable Software Technologies. Ada-Europe, Germany.

Fons, J., Pelechano, V., Albert, M., Pastor, O. (2003). Development of web applications from web enhanced conceptual schemas, ER'03, Springer, LNCS Vol. 2813.

Garzotto, F., Schwabe, D., Paolini, P. (1993). HDM-A Model Based Approach to Hypermedia Application Design. ACM Transactions Information Systems, 11(1), 1–26.

Insfrán, E., Pastor, O., Wieringa, R. (2002). Requirements Engineering-Based Conceptual Modelling. Requirements Engineering Journal, 7(1).

Koch, N. (1999). A Comparative Study of Methods for Hypermedia Development. Technical Report 9905. Ludwig-Maximilian-University, Munich, Germany.

Koch, N. (2001). Software Engineering for Adaptative Hypermedia Applications. Ph. Thesis, FAST Reihe Softwaretechnik, Vol(12), Uni-Druck Publishing Company, Germany.

Koch, N., Zhang, G., Escalona, M.J. (2006). Model Transformations from Requirements to Web System Design. Proc ICWE 2006, pp. 281–288.

Kraus, A., Koch, N.A. (2003). Metamodel for UWE. Technical Report 0301, Ludwig-Maximilians-Universität München.

Métrica v3. (2007). Ministerio de Administraciones Públicas. http://www.map.es

Moreno, N., Fraternalli, P., Vallecillo, A.A. (2006). UML 2.0 Profile for WebML Modeling. II International Workshop on Model-Driven Web Engineering. Palo Alto, CA.

OMG. (2003). MDA Guide, http://www.omg.org/docs/omg/03-06-01.pdf. Version 1.0.1.

Queralt, P., Hoyos, L., Boronat, A., Carsí, J.A., Ramos, I. (2006). Un motor de transformación de modelos con soporte para el lenguaje QVT relations. III Taller sobre Desarrollo de Software Dirigido por Modelos. MDA y Aplicaciones (DSDM'06). España.

Retschitzegger, W., Schwinger, W. (2000). Towards Modeling of Data Web Applications – A Requirements Perspective. Proc AMCIS 2000, Vol. 1, pp. 149–155.

Rossi, G. (1996). An Object Oriented Method for Designing Hipermedia Applications. Ph.D. Thesis, Departamento de Informática, PUC-Rio, Brazil.

Schauerhuber, A., Wimmer, M., Kapsammer, E. (2006). Bridging existing Web Modeling Languages to MDE: A Metamodel for WebML. II International Workshop on Model-Driven Web Engineering. Palo Alto, CA.

Schmidt, D.C. (2006). Model-Driven Engineering. IEEE Computer, 39(2), 41–47.

Valderas, P., Pelechano, V., Pastor, O. (2006). A Transformational Approach to Produce Web Application Prototypes from a Web Requirements Model. International Journal of Web Engineering and Technology (IJWET) (1476-1289).

Vilain, P., Schwabe, D., Sieckenius, C. (2000). A Diagrammatic Tool for Representing User Interaction in UML. Lecture Notes in Computer Science. UML'2000. York, England 2002.

# A Model for Users' Action Prediction Based on Locality Profiles

Tarmo Robal and Ahto Kalja

Department of Computer Engineering, Tallinn University of Technology, Estonia
tarmo@pld.ttu.ee, ahto@cs.ioc.ee

**Abstract**  In this chapter we propose a model for predicting users' next page requests. The model is based on the recognition and mining of navigational paths and patterns users typically follow. A special access log system is employed and techniques of web mining are used. Experimental results with developed prediction model are presented.

## 1 Introduction

The Internet provides us with an enormous source of information and has become a part of our everyday lives. Users are browsing the web pages of a site while they are searching for information. Their behaviour depends on many factors, such as visual experience and site attractiveness, logicality of navigation organization (especially on large sites), placement of objects, colour schema and page loading time (Bernard 2001; Geissler et al. 2001; Bernard and Chaparro 2000; Lee 1999), and also the information presented. User-friendly sites that provide up-to-date information and are concerned about their users, gain visitors easily, as users prefer to know their location on the site and what else could be found for their interest, rather than feel lost in the hyperspace. Hence, we need to observe the actions of users, their preferences and base our websites on that knowledge. To provide such aforementioned conveniences, we need users' action prediction and recommender systems.

In this chapter we discuss a model for predicting users' actions. We propose a model for the locality profiles mining and for the prediction calculation, which is a part of a recommender engine being developed. In brief, the task is to extract frequently accessed sequences of page views and based on that construct relevant locality profiles to be used in the prediction process.

The research is based on the access data of the website of the Department of Computer Engineering (DCE) at Tallinn University of Technology, which is a dynamic website run by the web systems kernel developed at our lab. The site consists of 118 pages either in English or Estonian and has an average access rate:

250 sessions daily, averaging 1.9 operations in sessions and 4.3 operations in sessions consisting of more than one page request. The access log has been collected over 4 years and was about 189.5 MB in raw data size, consisting of more than 269,782 sessions at the time of the analyses. In addition to providing information to general public, the DCE website serves as an experimental environment for research and development.

The chapter is organized as follows. In Sect. 2, we discuss web mining and adaptive websites with an emphasis on the aspects important in this chapter. Sect. 3 provides an overview of capturing web usage data and the used access log system. In Sect. 4 we consider the locality model with profiles extraction, present the prediction model, system architecture and experimental results for the proposed models.

## 2 Web Mining and Adaptive Websites

### 2.1 Web Mining

Each page request visitors perform on a website produces information about them and their needs. Collecting this information and analysing it permits us to reason about the users and the site itself. The process in general is called web mining. Srivastava et al. define it as the application of data mining techniques to extract knowledge from web data, where at least one of structure (hyperlink) or usage (web log) data are used in the mining process (with or without other types of web data) (Srivastava et al. 2002). The definition does not rule out any other types of web data to be used. Perkowitz and Etzioni define web mining as the use of data mining techniques to automatically discover and extract information from web documents and services (Perkowitz and Etzioni 2001). Researchers of the field divide web mining into three categories (Kosala and Blockeel 2000): (a) web content mining, (b) structure mining, and (c) usage mining. Some authors also highlight a fourth category called user profile mining (Li and Zhong 2006). Srivastava and colleagues have studied research projects and also the products in the field and have outlined the major application areas as follows: web personalization, system improvement, site modification (website attractiveness in terms of content and structure), business intelligence (discovery of marketing trends) and usage characterization (users' interaction with the browser interface and navigational strategies taken) (Srivastava et al. 2000).

Hereby, we will concentrate on web usage and structure mining to construct users' locality profiles over navigational paths and produce predictions for website tactical adaptation.

## 2.2 Adaptive Websites and Recommendation Systems

To provide users with enhanced web experience, adaptive websites are applied. Perkowitz and Etzioni define adaptive websites as sites that automatically improve their organization and presentation by learning from visitor access patterns (Perkowitz and Etzioni 2001). These adaptations can be either tactical or strategic.

Tactical adaptations are triggered in real time and do not need the approval of a webmaster as they do not interfere the structure of the site whilst completing it with additional information, e.g. providing references to other pages a user might be interested in, highlighting or raising certain hyperlinks to draw more attention on them and thus make them easily located by users (Bernard 2001). Strategic adaptations on the other hand can have a serious impact on the site's structure through proposed modifications. Therefore, they need to be done offline and approved beforehand.

The ability to track down users' actions has made it possible to construct and develop systems to provide users with dynamically discovered recommendations. This is becoming a popular practice, especially in e-commerce and marketing. Evidently, such systems are a step towards the intelligent web and the basis for adaptive websites. The aim of any recommender system is to assist users in information retrieval by providing pages or page-sets they otherwise might not find during their web session. The recommendations are usually shown to a user applying tactical adaptation.

Herein we have limited our discussion down to the prediction model only, which is aimed on providing basis for tactical adaptations.

# 3 Data Capturing for Predictions

## 3.1 Data Collection Methods

The implementation of adaptive websites largely depends on the data collected about the usage of the websites as well as how it is processed in further. Here, implicit data collection methods, which are hidden and thus transparent to the end-users and can be fully automated, are practical to apply, as then and only then we are able to construct users' navigational behaviour afterwards. The implicit techniques make it possible to monitor accessed pages, time spent on a particular page, navigational paths followed, discover usage patterns and user profiles.

The implicit data capturing techniques generally involve data collection from server, proxy or client level using either web server logs, web browsers modified for data capturing or special log systems, which utilize session-based IDs and cookies (Srivastava et al. 2000). Web server logs chronicle all the operations on a server and do not produce log data for particular analyses. Evidently, these logs do not contain all the needed information, though they include a lot of detailed information about every element accessed on the web server. For instance, it contains records for every single object accessed on a web server (e.g. dots and lines as elements of graphic design). Moreover, Davison has proven that HTTP traffic logs appear to be flawed (Davison 1999). Many authors outline that when dealing with server-side data collection from a web server or some other general system alike, which is not specially designed for producing log from web visits, there are some major difficulties due to data incompleteness (Mobasher et al. 2000; Srivastava et al. 2000). One of the many problems with web server log files is that they do not allow to identify visitor sessions (Kimball and Margy 2002). Web server logs contain client IP addresses, which cannot be reliably used as Internet Service Providers (ISP) tend to have a pool of proxy servers, and a user might be assigned a different IP for every request, which leads a user session to have more than one address. This could be overcome with getting the users to identify themselves, but it is a common truth that users prefer to maintain strict anonymity on the web and are against of any tracking of their web visits and other such characteristics. Hence, we have to find a concession between the users' privacy and the need for usage data collection for application and user experience improvement.

As web server logs occurred not to be suitable, we decided to implement a special log system as an additional module to the dynamic web systems kernel developed at DCE and used by many websites at the university.

## 3.2 The Access Log System

The access log system was developed in 2003 based on the log system introduced in 2002 and elaborated as an extension to the dynamic web systems kernel. The major improvement towards access log system was the ability to capture distinct and recurring user sessions (Robal et al. 2006) making use of embedded session IDs and cookies. Thus, this improvement made a relevant step towards making users' actions prediction possible. The data stored by the log system are as follows:

- Page requested by the user together with a timestamp
- IP and host of domain, where the request was made from
- Browser and operating system used to view the page
- Query method and full query string
- Site referrer, if available
- Client identifier (session-based ID)
- Operations performed during a session
- Page load time with a reference to server load during the page composition
- Previous visit identifier (session-based ID) and time (if available)
- Screen resolution used for viewing the requested page

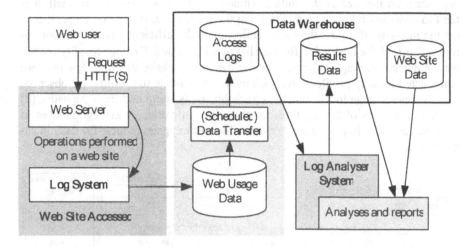

**Fig. 1** Data collection and pre-processing using the log system and analyser

The aim of the log system is to capture a precise snapshot of the web system at the moment it was accessed. It is initialized with every page request made (Fig. 1); with the first request a new session is opened and a previous session cookie is searched for. In case the latter is found, a reference to a prior visit is made. The system contains crawlers/robots detection rules based on general information available about robots, experiences of (Tan and Kumar 2002) and our own practice to filter out the real site users. As robots gather and index the content of the site for free, blocking them is not a solution as it incorporates the risk of losing potential visitors. The data pre-processing is performed by the log analyser system.

# 4 Predicting Users' Actions

## 4.1 The Locality Model

Having collected a fair amount of log data, profiles of site usage can be extracted applying the locality model. The model is based on the belief that if a large number of users frequently access a set of pages, then these pages must be related. The locality itself is defined by the user's nearest activity history within the site, where the order in which the pages are accessed is also important. During a web session, a user is moving from one locality to another, which can be represented by the $w$ latest operations (requests for pages). This model is applicable as people tend to repeat themselves over visits; thus, there exist probable and less probable paths users follow while surfing the web and searching for information.

The locality profiles $L$ are constructed based on the users' navigational paths. The process is described in Fig. 2. The efficiency of the locality model is heavily dependent on the size of the sliding window $w$. If the window is too small, it is hard to construct relevant predictions. On the other hand, if $w$ is too large, it covers the majority, if not all the users' actions, and the efficiency could be compromised. To find the best value for the sliding window $w \in W$ of our locality model, we conducted an empirical study for the dynamic website of DCE. For that, we constructed locality profiles $L$ for various $w$. To evaluate the results, we observed (1) cover percentage for the number of combinations computed from the paths, (2) average frequency of finding these combinations in paths, (3) average number of possible localities in path, and (4) availability of next page request for each locality profile.

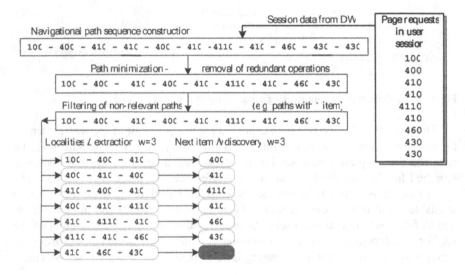

**Fig. 2** Extraction of locality profiles and next items from navigational paths (example: $w = 3$)

**Table 1** Results of empirical window size $w$ study

| Properties observed | Studied window size $w$ | | | |
| --- | --- | --- | --- | --- |
| | 2 | 3 | 4 | 5 |
| (1) Combination coverage (%) | 31.2 | 35.5 | 20.7 | 12.6 |
| (2) Combination frequency | 1.1 | 1.0 | 1.0 | 1.0 |
| (3) No. of localities in path | 6.3 | 6.6 | 6.5 | 5.9 |
| (4) Availability of next page request (%) | 76.6 | 77.4 | 74.1 | 76.3 |

The results (Table 1) of the experiment revealed that for the website under study, the locality profile with window size $w = 3$ performed the best, according to the properties observed (higher values assure better performance for $w$). With $w = 3$, the availability of next request was also the highest. This is very important, as the prediction model depends on the next item referred by the locality. We also noticed that the suitable size of $w$ seems to be in correlation with the absolute menu depth of the website being studied (in case of DCE it is 3), which is a subject of another study. However, for model construction and experiments, we decided to observe both window sizes, i.e. $w = 2$ and $w = 3$.

## 4.2 The Prediction Model

Our prediction model for the recommendation engine is based on the locality model described in the previous section. The model is dynamic and depends on the access log data. As the amount of data in the log grows, the prediction model should be trained again by repeating the locality profiles extraction process. The frequency of training the model mainly depends on the site's access rate. Obviously, for sites with average access rate, monthly calculations would be sufficient enough to cover the changes of access trends, though an automatic model update after a preset amount of new accesses is also an option to keep the model up to date.

For constructing the prediction model the access log data are processed and locality profiles extracted from navigational paths. A navigational path is based on user session and defined as a sequence of accessed pages $s=\langle p_i, p_{i+1},...p_n\rangle$, where $p_i \in P$ and $P$ is the set of all pages. Thus, we are searching for localities $L$ of size $w$, such as $L = p_j, p_{j+1},...p_m$, where $p_j \neq p_{j+1} \neq ... \neq p_m$, $p_j$ is a requested page ID. For each $s_t \in S$ we apply a function $L=CalculateLocality(s_t,w)$ to extract the localities and a function $N=FindNextItem(s_t,w)$ to discover the pages users have accessed in further, while occupying the locality $L$. The function $FindNextItem$ returns the element $p_{j+1}$, if available. For the empirical study of window size $w$, the same process was performed and the attribute "next page request" was found applying the function $FindNextItem$.

The web access log contains raw website usage data for every page request made. Evidently, these data need to be cleaned from noise and filtered before they can be used. Preliminary data cleaning and classification was performed by the log analyser, during which website crawler robot records were identified and marked, user sessions collected and annotated, and other operations performed. After that we derived 269,782 navigational paths from the log as sequences of requests, which were further filtered. Firstly, the paths were minimized by removing duplicate neighbouring items (e.g. the result of accidental double clicking), as they only represent the same action performed by the user and do not carry any value at this point for us; also it would have no sense to predict a page the user is already on. Secondly, paths with only one operation were removed, leaving after these two steps a total of 87,953 paths to be processed in further. To these paths, we applied localities and next item extraction algorithms, implemented by the functions *CalculateLocality* and *FindNextItem*. After the extraction process, each locality profile had a set of users' further requests (here onwards we call them next items) while occupying the locality, equipped with rank and probability values. For ranking, an inverse time-weighting algorithm (Middleton et al. 2001) was applied (1), and the probability value for each next item was calculated (2). The results of the paths processing into localities and corresponding next items were stored into a repository. The process itself is described in Fig. 2.

$$\text{Rank} = p\sum_{i=1}^{n} \frac{\text{Interest value}(i)}{\text{Age}(i)} \qquad (1)$$

In the formula (1), Age*(i)* represents the time period into past (e.g. days, weeks, months), Interest value*(i)* the number of hits for a page during Age*(i)*, $p$ is a probability value between 0 and 1 and can be predefined, i.e. by a webmaster for adjustment purposes. In our experiments (Sect. 4.4) we applied $p = 1$ for the simplicity. As can be seen, only the nearest past will play a crucial role in ranking. We applied the period of one month for Age*(i)*.

$$p = \sum_{i=1}^{n} \frac{\text{Next item access rate}(i)}{\text{Locality access rate}(i)} \qquad (2)$$

Hence, the task is to discover sequences of pages that are frequently requested together and are common for many users, where the order of items is important; group users with similar browsing patterns and discover the requests for pages they have performed while occupying certain locality. These further requests are then mapped to locality profiles and used for actions prediction jointly with calculated ranking and probability values.

## 4.3 System Overview and Architecture

The amount of information available over the Internet is enormous – even the quantum of information on an average website is fairly large for users to maintain easy navigation by remembering everything. This problem can be revealed by providing recommendations based on locality profiles mined from web logs. The general rationale behind the approach is that users implicitly use a concept model based on their own knowledge of the domain or topic searched, even though mostly they do not know how to represent it (Li and Zhong 2006). However, monitoring users' actions and collecting them into access logs, we are able to construct such models post factum by employing detection algorithms to produce locality profiles. These profiles are site dependent and describe typical actions of users on that particular website. Herewith, we use those locality profiles for users' next page request prediction. The mining of locality profiles and detection of next items has been discussed in the previous sections. The overall implementation of the system is described in Fig. 3.

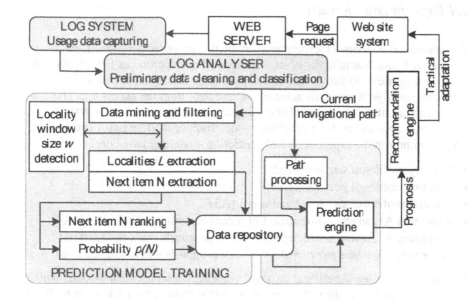

**Fig. 3.** Prediction model implementation

The processed access log data are stored in a data repository. We used the MySQL DBMS for data storing. The repository contains all the locality profiles derived from the navigational paths, their characteristics (e.g. length), corresponding next items with calculated ranking and probability values.

The prognosis for the current user is generated by analysing the latest actions of that user online and comparing it to the locality profiles and next items in the repository. The prediction engine extracts from the current users nearest action history a locality profile $L$ of size $w$ and performs matching over the repository to the pages other users have requested, while operating in this particular locality profile. For predicting, it is necessary that a user has made at least $q=min(w)$ requests. Otherwise, no prognosis is computed. Typically there are multiple predictions possible, with varying confidence. For the prediction calculation, next item ranking and existence probability are used together to form the prediction confidence. The system may choose to make no prediction at all, for instance if no matching locality profile is found. The computation is done online and needs to have a short response time, otherwise the prognosis is said to be failed, to avoid any extra delays in page loading.

The model is applicable for dynamic as well as for static web pages, as its training only depends on the collected log data. However, on the assumption of tactical adaptations, we are considering dynamic web pages here.

## 4.4 Experimental Results

We conducted a series of experiments with the proposed prediction model, to evaluate it in practice in terms of its efficiency. The experiments fall into the following categories: (a) active use of the prediction model on a real website, (b) empirical study with randomly selected sample data from the access log. The predictions in the studies were calculated using different algorithms as to evaluate the algorithmic approaches for prediction model training and engine development. The algorithms in the experiments had prediction modelling based on:

- Locality profiles of size $w = 2$ (A1)
- Locality profiles of size $w = 3$ (A2)
- Locality profiles of size $w = 2$ and $w = 3$ (A3)
- Algorithm A1, where an ordered set of three prognosis was calculated (A4)
- Algorithm A2, where an ordered set of three prognosis was calculated (A5)
- Algorithm A3, where an ordered set of four prognosis was calculated (A6)

For the active use experiment on a real website, we set up a test module, which worked in parallel with the website management system of the DCE website. With every page request, the latest action history of a user was taken from the session cookie and sent to the prediction engine. The engine returned the prognosis for the algorithmic implementations. These results with the users' next action and timestamp were stored into a database for further analyses. At the time of the analyses 2,251 predictions were made during a 15-day period. In 79% of the cases locality profiles of $w = \{2,3\}$ were found; thus, 21% of the localities remained in size $w = 2$. This is normal since the localities were extracted from the session data as soon as the current user had made sufficiently enough page requests, in this case $q = 2$ requests.

All the six aforementioned algorithms were also exploited in an empirical study with randomly selected sample sessions from the access log used for the model training. As the experiments were aimed on locality profile size $w = 3$ (see Sect. 4.1), sample data were restricted to sessions having at least four operations in it. Experiments were performed with 29,311 (V10) and 147,883 (V50) sessions selected randomly.

The error rate analysis (Fig. 4) showed that the locality profile with size $w = 2$ performed better in terms of prognosis made. The profile size $w = 3$ performs fairly good, if redundant operations are discarded (Fig. 4b). In this case, the majority of redundant operations consisted of series of page requests to a page where a user was already on; thus, there was no progress in information seek. The prediction engine is to be trained to handle such cases in the future. However, this analysis only depicts that a prediction was made regardless of its accuracy.

The prediction accuracy analysis (Fig. 5) revealed that the model performed better than just using blunt probability for the next page request. Algorithms A4 and A5 performed better than A1 and A2, as they contained more predicted elements in the return set with combined rules. Algorithm A3 did not provide expected results.

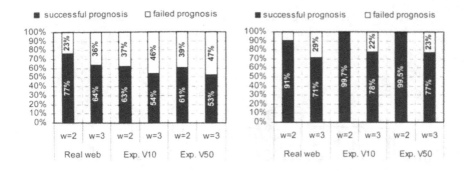

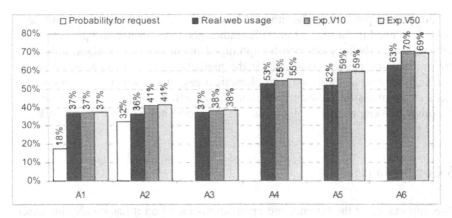

**Fig. 4** Error rate analysis: **(a)** over all operations, **(b)** after removing redundant operations

**Fig. 5** Prediction accuracy analysis

Evidently, the bigger the prediction result set is in terms of containing the next item user accesses, the more accurate it can become. However, users choose only one of the predicted items, if at all. Thus, the bigger the result set is, the vaguer the prediction becomes. This is the cost of accuracy. For instance, the difference between the result set of algorithms A2 and A5 is approximately 20% in favour of A5. The experiments showed that predictions based on locality model, which follows the paths users take, perform better than based on average probability calculated for possible next items. Clearly, the locality model is appropriate and usable herein.

We also analysed the average confidence applied by the engine while computing predictions. As can be seen (Fig. 6), the average confidence for real web and empirical study experiments is greater than the average probability over the possible combinations for next items. Evidently, the model has operated as expected.

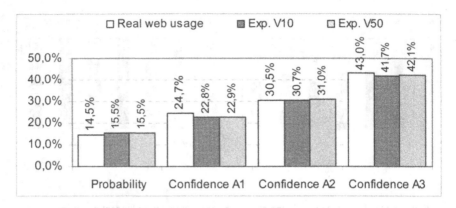

**Fig. 6** Prediction confidence analysis

For precise prediction, algorithms A1 and A2 and their derivates A3–A6 need to be developed in further. A2 provides rather good confidence and prediction accuracy, but we believe this can be optimized in further. These algorithms were preliminary and mainly presented for the prediction model evaluation purposes. The analyses revealed also some problematic areas, one of which is that the model lacks of prognosis for redundant operations. We will continue the development of the prediction engine and its algorithms, as the model has been proven to work.

## 5 Conclusions

The importance of the Internet and applications based on it has rapidly increased in our lives during the recent years. The enormous amount of information available over the World Wide Web has produced the need to build adaptive websites, which would easily adapt and help users to find the information they are seeking.

In this chapter we have developed a model for user's page requests prognosis, which is based on the locality model. The latter is defined by the user's nearest action history. It has been proven and also the experimental results here showed that users follow certain paths while visiting websites. During the research, we studied the appropriate window size for our locality model using web data mining and found the size of the locality window to be correlated to the absolute menu depth of that particular website. For capturing website access data, a special log system was used together with a log analysing system, from which the navigational paths were mined. Possible paths were modelled as locality profiles, and items accessed while occupying that locality were discovered and ranked for the prediction model. This model was then used for forecasting the user's next page requests applying a prediction engine. The experiments revealed the model to perform better than just trying to guess the next page by applying probability. The prediction engine was based on the proposed model and is integral part of a recommendation engine allowing features of tactical adaptation to be added to websites to improve the cognitive experience users get while visiting a site. As the work progresses, these features will also be available on the website of our department.

In terms of the future plans, we are targeting to supplement the prediction model, which currently enables to foretell only web pages requests, with website ontology to make it possible to anticipate the informational needs of users as well.

**Acknowledgments** We appreciate the support of Estonian Information Technology Foundation, Doctoral School in ICT (Measure 1.1 Estonian NDP), and the ETF grant no. 5766.

# References

Bernard, M. L. (2001) User expectations for the location of web objects. In: *Proc. of CHI '01 Conference: Human Factors in Computing Systems*, pp. 171–172.

Bernard, M. L. and Chaparro, B. S. (2000) Searching within websites: A comparison of three types of sitemap menu structures. In: *Proc. of The Human Factors and Ergonomics Society 44th Annual Meeting in San Diego*, pp. 441–444. (PDF format) http://psychology. wichita.edu/hci/projects/sitemap.pdf.

Davison, B. (1999) Web traffic logs: An imperfect resource for evaluation. In: *Proc. of 9th Annual Conference of the Internet Society (INET '99)*. San Jose, CA.

Geissler, G., Zinkhan, G. and Watson, R. (2001) Web home page complexity and communication effectiveness. Journal of the Association for Information Systems, 2(2), 1–48.

Kimball, R. and Margy, R. (2002) *The data warehouse toolkit: the complete guide to dimensional modelling*. Wiley, New York.

Kosala, R. and Blockeel, H. (2000) Web mining research: A survey. ACM SIGKDD Explorations, 2(1), 1–15.

Lee, A.T. (1999) Web usability: A review of the research. ACM SIGCHI Bulletin, 31(1), 38–40.

Li, Y. and Zhong, N (2006) Mining ontology for automatically acquiring web user information needs. IEEE Transactions on Knowledge and Data Engineering, 18(4), 554–568.

Middleton, S., De Roure, D. and Shadbolt, N. (2001) Capturing knowledge of user preferences: Ontologies in recommender systems. In: *Proc. of the 1st Int. Conference on Knowledge Capture*, ACM Press, New York, pp. 100–107.

Mobasher, B., Cooley, R. and Srivastava, J. (2000) Automatic personalization based on web usage mining. Communications of the ACM, 43(8), 142–151.

Perkowitz, M. and Etzioni, O. (2001) Adaptive web sites: Concept and case study. *Artificial Intelligence*, 118(1–2), 245–275.

Robal, T., Kalja, A. and Põld, J. (2006) Analysing the web log to determine the efficiency of web systems. In: *Proc. of the 7th International Baltic Conference on Databases and Information Systems DB&IS'2006*. Technika, Vilnius, pp. 264–275.

Srivastava, J., Cooley R., Deshpande M. and Tan P.N. (2000) Web usage mining: Discovery and applications of usage patterns from web data. ACM SIGKDD Explorations, 1(2), 12–23.

Srivastava, J., Desikan, P. and Kumar, V. (2002) Web mining: Accomplishments and future directions. In: *Proc. US Nat'l Science Foundation Workshop on Next-Generation Data Mining (NGDM)*. Nat'l Science Foundation.

Tan, P-N. and Kumar, V. (2002) Discovery of web robot sessions based on their navigational patterns. Data Mining and Knowledge Discovery, 6(1), 9–35.

# A Survey of the Web/Hypermedia Development Process in Croatia

Dijana Plantak Vukovac[1] and Bozidar Klicek[2]

[1]Department of Information Systems Development, Faculty of Organization and Informatics, University of Zagreb, Varazdin, dijana.plantak@foi.hr

[2]Department of Information Systems Development, Faculty of Organization and Informatics, University of Zagreb, Varazdin, bozidar.klicek@foi.hr

**Abstract**  Academic literature suggests that the design of web-based systems differs from the development of information systems on account of the significant differences in their characteristics. Accordingly, to cover many aspects of web/hypermedia system design, new development methods have been proposed. In order to explore web/hypermedia design and development practice, and also the usage of those specific methods, studies have been conducted in many developed countries. However, no study has previously been conducted in Croatia or in any transitional country. This chapter provides the findings of an exploratory survey conducted to profile Croatian web designers/developers, to explore the characteristics of their projects and to identify the development process and the activities and methods used in the development of web/hypermedia systems.

## 1 Introduction

Many authors emphasize that web development is different from software and/or information system development. This premise is based on the hypermedia features of web-based systems where different types of media are connected by hyperlinks which allow users to navigate through an information space along various paths. Hypermedia features, even in their 'primitive, low-level [...] implementation' on the web platform (Lang and Fitzgerald 2005), are the key attributes that distinguish web-based systems from information systems. These are:

- The aesthetic and cognitive aspects of web/hypermedia systems (Nanard and Nanard 1995)
- Security and privacy aspects of web-based systems (Murugesan and Ginige 2005)
- The non-linearity of the documents that can lead to complex structures which are hard to maintain as the application size grows (Koch 1999; Murugesan and Ginige 2005)

C. Barry et al. (eds.), *Information Systems Development: Challenges in Practice, Theory, and Education, Vol.1*, doi: 10.1007/978-0-387-68772-8_15,

- Continuous change in information content, web technologies and standards used (Murugesan and Ginige 2005)
- Shorter life cycles of web-based systems (Baskerville and Pries-Heje 2004)
- The need for a development team consisting of people with different professional backgrounds and skills (Koch 1999; Murugesan and Ginige 2005)
- Different users/customers of the web site with different information needs and computer literacy (Kyaw and Boldyreff 1998; Murugesan and Ginige 2005)

Regarding all these issues, a field of web engineering has emerged to provide 'scientific, engineering, and management principles and systematic approaches to successfully develop, deploy, and maintain high-quality Web systems' (Ginige and Murugesan 2001). Under its umbrella, over 50 methodologies, methods, techniques and models for web/hypermedia design have been proposed. They cover different phases of the web/hypermedia system life cycle and provide different levels of specification of a particular phase. Many of them focus on a detailed description of the design phases, while other phases, if described, are covered only in a few sentences.

Consequently, comparing web/hypermedia development methods is not an easy task. Koch (1999) presented three comparisons of eleven of these methods. One of the comparisons identifies phases in the development process of the methods explored, based on the life cycle proposed by the Unified Process. The phases identified are *Requirements Capture, Analysis, Design, Implementation* and *Testing*. The *Design* phase comprises *Conceptual Design, Navigational Design* and *Presentational Design*. Similarly, Kyaw and Boldyreff (1998) identified the hypermedia development stages that differ from the stages in software engineering: *Feasibility Study and Requirement Analysis, Conceptual Design, Navigational Design, User Interface Design, Conversion and Implementation, and Testing and Maintenance.*

Although a great deal of effort has been made to establish specialized web/hypermedia development methods, and a great number of academic papers have been written to unveil them, little research has been done to explore the use of these methods in practice. However, the findings of studies already conducted (Barry and Lang 2001; Lang 2003; Venable and Lim 2001) have shown that very few designers have used a web/hypermedia-specific method, while the majority have never even heard of such methods.

It has also been noted that little scientific research has taken place on the usage of proprietary methods for information systems development in Eastern European countries. Only one study on the use of structural and object-oriented development methodologies has been conducted, also in Croatia (Muzar 2005). This study revealed that only 36% of computer professionals used one of the methodologies. It also showed that the structural methodologies were best valued by developers in production-orientated organizations (manufacturing, industry, business services, etc.).

The present study was conducted to explore whether Croatian web designers/developers are acquainted with specialized web/hypermedia methods and whether there is any relation between the development phases proposed by these

methods and the development process that designers actually practice in their everyday work. The ultimate goal was to gain a broader view of web/hypermedia systems development in Croatia.

## 2 Research Methodology

The working title of the study was 'Research of web and multimedia systems development characteristics' due to the common terminology used in Croatia. The
research objectives were to determine the Croatian web designers/developers profile, the characteristics of web/hypermedia projects, and those of the development
process, with a focus on the phases and activities involved.

The study was based on Lang's (2003) work which is recognized as the most
comprehensive, recent study of hypermedia systems development. The research
method used for our study was a web survey, and Lang's web questionnaire was
broadened to identify phases and activities in the development process, as well as
attitudes about web trends. At the end of the questionnaire, a blank field was provided to enable respondents to give comments on the survey subject.

In order to gather a representative population sample, a list of companies of interest had to be compiled. This process required a great deal of effort because no
suitably detailed business register was available and the data were compiled and
filtered from five different web registers (business search engines) with different
data formats. Companies included in the initial list satisfied the following criteria:

- The company is registered in a court register and is indexed in at least one of
  the five online business registers.
- The company develops web and multimedia systems within the broader list of
  primary business activities: web site development, web application/system development, software and/or information system development, multimedia system development, graphic and visual design, marketing, branding, advertising,
  telecommunications, web hosting.
- The company has its own web site with a portfolio and company information
  including e-mail address (or contact form).

The final population sample comprised 418 companies to whom a cover letter
(e-mail) was sent including a description of the research, a link to the web survey
and authorization data. To reduce the likelihood of non-response error, a summary
of the survey findings was promised to all participants who finished the survey.

After 31 days and two reminders about the ongoing survey, responses were received from 169 participants, or an overall response rate of 40.4%.

Out of the 169 responses received, 68 surveys were insufficiently completed.
Thus, usable responses were gathered from 101 participants. This means that
based on the true size of the relevant population (418 sample size – 8 undelivered
e-mails + 16 additional participants from 10 companies = 426 respondents), the
response rate was 23.7%.

## 3 Findings

### 3.1 Profile of Web Designers/Developers

At the beginning of the web questionnaire, demographic data were gathered which could not be obtained from secondary sources. These data revealed that the average web designer/developer is male (87.1% of respondents), of a younger age (mean = 32.8, median = 32). He works in a small company with up to ten employees (80.2% of respondents) which is consistent with the structure of IT companies in Croatia (86% of enterprises in Croatia are small enterprises according to the Croatian Chamber of Economy's report (Croatian Chamber of Economy 2004)).

The majority of respondents have an advanced or very advanced level of knowledge in the professional disciplines that contribute to web/hypermedia systems development, except for film production (55.4% respondents have basic or no knowledge in that discipline). As expected, the level of knowledge of respondents in film production was found to be correlated to the number of web-based systems with rich multimedia content that respondents had developed ($p < 0.01$, $r_s = 0.42$). Also, almost half of the respondents indicated that their company was outsourcing audio/video producers (49.4% of 79 respondents) and specialists in animations (45.4% of 75 respondents).

On average, respondents have 7 years of experience in developing different types of web/hypermedia systems (mean = 7.1, median = 7). In terms of the number of projects that respondents have been working on, they indicated between 2 and 500 projects. To reduce the impact of extreme values, 5% trimmed mean and median were calculated (5% trimmed mean = 51.6, median = 32.5), giving about 5–7 projects per year per respondent. Interestingly, almost half of the respondents who reported 100 or more projects that they had been working on noted their function in the company (project manager, director, owner) instead of their professional discipline or design role (graphic designer, web designer, web programmer, developer, multimedia programmer, etc.).

### 3.2 Characteristics of Web Projects

To identify the types and features of web/hypermedia systems developed in Croatia in the past 2 years, two questions were asked. Responses indicate that *brochureware* web sites and Content Management Systems (CMS) were developed most often (more than 15 projects within 2 years in 28.7 and 21.9% of cases, respectively). Some respondents had also developed more complex systems, but less often (up to five projects in 2 years): web portals/web directories, electronic catalogues, transactional business applications, CD-ROM/DVD applications, as well as the two systems already mentioned. However, the vast majority of respondents have never developed e-learning applications (74.7%), news and other information services (61.3%), or complex cross-referenced documentation (63.4%). A few respondents included feed aggregators, web services, blog systems, touch screen applications and interactive maps as web/hypermedia systems developed in the last 2 years.

The features that characterize the most commonly developed web/hypermedia systems include database-driven web sites, dynamically generated web pages and frequent, significant changes to content. However, many respondents did not develop systems with support for multiple delivery devices and web 2.0 applications (44.1 and 43.0%, respectively) in the last 2 years. Three respondents added that their web/hypermedia systems were optimized for search engines.

The measure for system complexity was expressed by the number of screens/online pages (Lang 2003). Almost half of the respondents indicated that they mostly developed small web/hypermedia systems (up to 50 online pages/screens), while 38.4% of respondents developed large-scale systems. This result is quite different from Lang's findings (Lang 2003) where two-thirds of the systems were over 50 pages/screens in size. This difference can be explained by the bias generated by the desire to gain a broader picture of web/hypermedia development practice in Croatia, not just the practice of experienced developers. Interestingly, some of the respondents did not know or could not estimate the average size of their web/hypermedia systems. Vora (1998) identified a similar problem in his research due to the ambiguity of a survey question.

The size of the project teams was easier to identify. The team size ranged from 1 to 14 persons. The average Croatian web team has three designers/developers (mean = 3.3, median = 3) which is consistent with the findings of other studies (Lang 2003; Vora 1998; Zhou and Stålhane 2004). Small teams with up to four designers/developers exist in almost 80% of companies.

General project management principles state that key elements of successful project management are a good balance among time, costs and team resources allocated to deliver a quality system (Friedlein 2001). These principles also apply to web project management. Time and cost control of Croatian web projects was explored in two questions. Participants had to indicate the actual and planned project duration and the cost of their most recently completed project of 'non-trivial complexity'. The project duration in weeks was indicated by 71.7% of 92 respondents, while the project cost was acknowledged by only 38.4% of 86 participants who responded to the questions (other answers were 'Don't know' or 'Not planned/ recorded').

Since extreme values were gathered both for project time and cost, 5% trimmed mean and median were used as measures of central tendency. It was found that the average planned delivery time was 8 weeks (5% trimmed mean = 7.8, median = 5.5), while the actual project duration was 11 weeks (5% trimmed mean = 11, median = 6) or two and a half months, so a '3 × 3' profile (three designers deliver the project in about 3 months) can be found in web-based systems design in Croatia. The planned and actual times of recently completed projects were provided by 72 participants. Comparing these data, it was found that 60.6% of projects exceeded the planned schedule, 21.2% of projects were delivered on time and 18.2% of projects finished earlier than planned. This finding is consistent with other study findings that show that the majority of projects fall behind schedule

(Ginige and Murugesan 2001; Lang and Fitzgerald 2005).

Considering the planned and actual project costs, the analysis shows that these costs are much lower in Croatia than in Ireland. The average planned cost ranges from about EUR 2,000 to EUR 5,400 (median and 5% trimmed mean, respectively), while the range of average actual costs is slightly higher (median ≈ EUR 2,120, 5% trimmed mean ≈ EUR 5,800). These low amounts reflect the current state of the economy in Croatia. However, project costs are far better managed than project schedules, with one-third of projects being delivered within the agreed costs and one-third of projects experiencing cost over-runs.

To identify whether web projects showed discipline through the use of documentation, participants were asked to indicate the written requirements specification by number of requirements and/or the number of pages, as well as the usage of documented procedures or guidelines for web/hypermedia development. Out of 94 respondents, 51.1% reported written requirements specifications for the most recently completed project.

Only a minority of companies use documented procedures or guidelines for web/hypermedia development, with only 37.2% of 94 respondents giving an affirmative answer in this respect. Although a low percentage of documentation use is identified in this research, Croatian designers/developers are nevertheless aware of its importance. They believe that project plans and working methods are essential and need to be explicitly documented (94.7 and 59.4% of respondents, respectively, hold these opinions). Also, a statistically significant correlation was found between the opinion on the need for documented procedures and the view that an ad hoc hypermedia development approach generally results in systems of poor quality ($p < 0.01$, $r_s = 0.33$). So, the question is why are the development deliverables not documented if the respondents are aware of the benefits. The answer might lie in a large percentage of respondents (36.1%) who believe that an ad hoc approach does not produce low-quality systems, while many respondents have a neutral opinion in this respect (20.6%). This leaves only 39.2% of respondents who believe that an ad hoc approach is not appropriate, in contrast to 68.6% of Irish respondents who hold this view (Lang 2003). Even when respondents who mainly develop *brochureware* web sites were omitted from the test, which left 77 respondents, the percentage changed by only ±2%.

The respondents also stated that a lack of adequate design documentation represents a minor to moderate problem in web/hypermedia development practice. The most significant problem concerning web project management is communication with customers, on account of their volatile and changing requirements. Vague requirements are also found to be a significant problem in other studies (Baskerville and Pries-Heje 2004; Lang and Fitzgerald 2005). Other problems are preparing accurate time and cost estimates, and also controlling project scope and feature creep. Web time development pressure to keep up with all the requirements in shorter cycle time presents a minor to moderate problem for more than half of the respondents. On the other hand, most respondents indicated that designing a user interface or the lack of guidance in the use of design methods and techniques does not pose a problem at all (see Table 1).

**Table 1** Range of problems in web/hypermedia systems development practice

| | N | Don't know (%) | No problem (%) | Minor to moderate problem (%) | Major to the greatest problem (%) |
|---|---|---|---|---|---|
| Volatile and changing requirements | 94 | 1.1 | 1.1 | 28.7 | 69.2 |
| Preparing accurate time and cost estimates | 94 | 1.1 | 11.7 | 48.9 | 38.3 |
| Controlling project scope and feature creep | 94 | 7.5 | 10.6 | 55.3 | 26.6 |
| Induction and training of staff in the use of design methods and techniques | 94 | 3.2 | 12.8 | 62.8 | 21.3 |
| Lack of adequate design documentation | 94 | 10.6 | 18.1 | 54.3 | 17.0 |
| Coping with accelerated timescales of the web environment ('web time') | 94 | 10.6 | 22.3 | 57.5 | 9.6 |
| Managing communication between team members | 95 | 1.1 | 31.6 | 61.1 | 6.3 |
| Controlling and coordinating project tasks | 95 | 2.1 | 26.3 | 66.3 | 5.3 |
| Lack of guidance in the use of design methods and techniques | 94 | 12.8 | 37.2 | 47.9 | 2.1 |
| Designing the user interface | 94 | 1.1 | 54.3 | 42.6 | 2.1 |

## 3.3 Development Process

A common attitude of researchers (Lowe and Hall 1999; Koch 1999; Kyaw and Boldyreff 1998; Murugesan and Ginige 2005) is that web/hypermedia development practice is a chaotic, ad hoc, *quick and dirty* activity that needs a 'disciplined development process and a sound methodology' (Murugesan and Ginige 2005). Findings of one study (Rosson et al. 2005), although slightly biased toward informal web developers, and particularly Lang's findings (Lang 2003) contradict this point of view. The current research also upholds the latter view: about 85% of respondents indicate that their organization uses a web/hypermedia development process that has clear tasks and/or phases (see Table 2).

**Table 2** Organization's web/hypermedia development process

| | |
|---|---|
| There is no clear process and this is not considered a problem | 6.9% |
| There is no clear process and this is considered a problem | 7.9% |
| Clear phases and/or activities, though the process used is not explicitly documented | 62.4% |
| Clear phases and/or activities, according to an explicitly documented process | 22.8% |

To further explore the web/hypermedia development process in practice, participants were asked in open-ended questions to describe the phases and/or activities of their organization's development process. Fifty-one respondents (50.5%) provided a more or less detailed description of the development process in their organization, including answers from two participants who indicated in the previous question that there were no clear processes in their organizations. This can be explained by the participants' difficulty in understanding the term, which was also recognized in later answers, 'because in the language of everyday practice these terms ['approach', 'method', 'technique'] overlap to the point of almost being interchangeable' (Lang and Fitzgerald 2006).

After analyzing and classifying all the responses, in which many were ambiguous and hard to classify, several phases and activities were identified in the development process in practice. Phases can vary according to the purpose and complexity of the future web-based system and the contract with the client. Many respondents indicated the need for feedback from clients after every phase, which suggests that the development process is iterative and incremental. An iterative and incremental process was also recognized in the findings of Zhou and Stålhane (2004). The development process in practice is as follows:

- *Requirements Capture and Analysis*: During an initial meeting with the client, important issues of the future web-based system are identified: purpose, goals, information needs, content and potential users of the web site. Then the web team analyses the business processes, defines the required functionality and chooses the web technology and development tools. Other activities that might be included in this phase are an analysis of the client's organization brand, and an analysis of competitors' web sites and marketing research. The deliverables of the phase are project documentation or a development plan with time estimates.
- *Initial Proposal*: This comprises the building of a rough concept of web site graphic and navigation design. Mock-ups and storyboards are delivered on paper or in graphic editing software which are then presented to the client. After approval, the content for the web site is collected.
- *Design Phase*: In this phase, three activities can be distinguished

  o *Conceptual Design:* Includes the design of the information architecture of the application. During this stage, the structure of the database is planned and different diagrams are built
  o *Navigational Design*: Includes the construction of models with different navigational paths
  o *User Interface Design*: Several templates of user interface are sketched and authored in HTML/CSS. In this stage, different multimedia elements are edited and optimized

- *Development or Programming Phase* (*Implementation*): Activities in this phase are

  o Database construction, programming module development and/or CMS design or upgrade

o System integration
o Content loading

- *Testing and Implementation of Subprojects*: Different types of testing are carried out, as well as the implementation of smaller subprojects. The web-based system is also upgraded on the basis of user evaluation.
- *Launching* – a 'soft' launch of a beta version is performed before client approval and final release.
- *Education and User Documentation*: Depending on the system complexity and contract with the client, education is performed to introduce the client or maintenance team to the system functions. User and technical documentation is also provided.
- *Release*: A 'hard' launch is performed and the web-based system goes online for a wide audience. Other activities included in this phase are site promotion and search engine optimization.
- *Maintenance*: The final phase comprises maintenance of the system and enhancements.

Comparing this development process in practice with the development phases of specialized web/hypermedia design methods, significant similarities have been identified. Although the development process in practice is not as formalized as that of the design methods, it consists of all the phases identified in the web/hypermedia design methods and also includes web project management activities. The main difference is found in the terminology used for the phases in practice and literature. *Implementation* is the term that literature describes as application building, but Croatian developers denote that phase as the *Development or Programming Phase* and broadly use the term 'implementation' to denote the launching phase. Another difference identified is the loose border between the *Requirements Capture* and *Analysis* phases in practice, so they are represented in one phase.

To identify whether the web/hypermedia development process in practice is supported by any methods, closed multiple-choice questions were introduced. More than half the participants, or 52.5% out of 101 respondents, indicated that they use in-house or hybrid methods. Only 5.9% of respondents use proprietary methodology, while 26.7% of respondents do not know or 14.9% of them do not use any methods.

To further explore the use of different methods and approaches in web/hypermedia systems design, a list was introduced based on the categories proposed by Lang (2003). Participants were asked to indicate the extent of their use in their organization's development process. Not surprisingly, the majority of respondents often or all the time use approaches that focus on the use of tools and development environments, e.g. *PHP, Java, Flash, ASP, J2EE* (70.3% of 91 respondents). The other two top response categories were object-oriented development methods and approaches, e.g. *OOA&D, UML and MSF* (25.3% of 87 respondents) as well as rapid or agile development methods and approaches, e.g. *RAD, Extreme Programming* (19.5% of 87 respondents). The majority of respondents do not know or do not use any method (with the exception of approaches that focus on the use of tools and development environments), and the top three categories were specialized web/hypermedia development methods, traditional 'legacy' software development methods and approaches, and incremental or evolutionary methods and approaches.

Surprisingly, 12 respondents (13.5%) indicated that they use specialized web/hypermedia development methods, such as RMM, OOHDM, WSDM or WebML, to some extent. This is a high percentage compared with the findings of two other studies (Lang 2003; Venable and Lim 2001) which identified 4 and 2 respondents, respectively, who used some of those methods. As far as the authors of this study are aware, none of the web/hypermedia development methods has been introduced by Croatian universities yet, so we believe that this high percentage represents a bias produced by the fact that these methods were the first on the list of the given method categories and also due to the respondents' tendency to provide positive rather than negative answers.

## 3.4 Attitudes to Web/Hypermedia Systems Development

In the study, attitudes to web/hypermedia systems development were also explored. More than half of the respondents, when developing a web site, take into consideration user needs and usability standards, not only the client's requirements if they are contrary to good web design guidelines. The majority of respondents believe that usability and accessibility standards increase the quality of the web site and make maintenance an easier task. Visual presentation is not the most important issue of web design. However, respondents are not well acquainted with the new ways of using web platforms, such as Web 2.0. This somehow contradicts the respondents' attitude to the internet as the most useful informal knowledge source (97.9% respondents made this claim), as they apparently do not use all its learning opportunities.

Another very useful knowledge source is observing or consulting experienced colleagues, reading books, periodicals and magazines, and consulting external specialists. The majority of respondents are neutral about the usefulness of organizational policies and procedures, with a slight tendency towards a positive attitude, but the vast majority do not use this source of knowledge. Attending training programmes is a useful formal source of knowledge, but few respondents take advantage of training programmes. Roughly an equal percentage of respondents consider formal education (secondary or tertiary) both useful and not useful. Possible reasons for the negative attitude are the inconsistent and outdated curriculum, and the rapid advances in web technologies, or, as one respondent commented, 'Web-based system development is too dynamic for a set of scholarly rules and methods. Even acknowledged methods and approaches become out of date in one or 2 years or until the next Microsoft update. So, depending on the project, we almost always develop our own tools and procedures for complex systems'.

# 4 Conclusion

This chapter has outlined the web/hypermedia development process of Croatian web designers/developers and supports the findings of other studies (Barry and Lang 2001; Lang 2003; Rosson et al. 2005) that the development process is not as undisciplined as it is considered to be. Moreover, the study shows that the development process comprises phases and activities identified in specialized web/hypermedia design methods, even if their usage in practice is very low, although it is higher than in other studies (Lang 2003; Venable and Lim 2001).

Given that this study was based on the already acknowledged study by Lang (2003), similar findings are evident. A Croatian web team consists of three designers/developers who develop web/hypermedia systems through clear phases and/or activities during which they experience the same problems as the Irish web teams. However, slight differences have been identified in project management practice and in development attitudes:

- The majority of Irish respondents develop more complex systems than Croatian respondents, so the actual project duration is longer.
- More Croatian respondents believe that the ad hoc approach does not produce low-quality systems and, hence, the majority do not use documented procedures for web/hypermedia development (in contrast to the Irish respondents). There is a lower percentage of written requirement specifications than is the case with the Irish respondents.

These differences should be considered from the following points of view:

- Since the purpose of this study was to gain a broader insight of web/hypermedia development practice in Croatia, the study did not exclude inexperienced developers who mainly develop simple web sites.
- There is a time span of 4 years between the two studies, so the practice and development attitudes might have been found to differ more if the studies had been conducted at approximately the same time.

As the web is evolutive by nature, and as more complex web solutions are introduced, there is a need to deal with problems identified in web/hypermedia development practice in several areas:

- Further qualitative scientific research is needed to explore the rationale for using specialized web/hypermedia design methods in practice and to provide flexible design tool support.
- A revision of graduate programmes is essential in order to provide practical coverage of issues identified in web/hypermedia development practice.
- More web project management workshops should be organized to help practitioners deal with problematic aspects of development, especially in requirements management, work planning and documentation.
- The popularization of scientific findings in IT magazines and newspapers is advisable to introduce current and future customers to the complexity of web/hypermedia development and to sensitize them in this respect, which could help bridge the communication gap between them and web professionals.

**Acknowledgements**    Our thanks go to Michael Lang, National University of Ireland, Galway, for a copy of his questionnaire and insightful comments about research methodology, and to Danijel Radosevic, Faculty of Organization and Informatics, Varazdin, for the programming modules of the web survey. Finally, we would like to extend special thanks to all participants in the study.

# References

Barry, C. and Lang, M. (2001) A survey of multimedia and web development techniques and methodology usage. *IEEE Multimedia*, 8(3), 52–60.

Baskerville, R. and Pries-Heje, J. (2004) Short cycle time systems development. *Information Systems Journal*, 14(3): 237–264.

Croatian Chamber of Economy, Information System and Statistics Department (2004) *Croatian ICT Sector*. Zagreb, July. http://www2.hgk.hr/en/depts/IT/hrv_ict_sektor.pdf.

Friedlein, A. (2001) *Web Project Management: Delivering Successful Commercial Web Sites*. Morgan Kaufmann Publishers, Imprint of Elsevier, San Francisco, USA.

Ginige, A. and Murugesan, S. (2001) Web engineering: An introduction. *IEEE Multimedia*, 8(1): 14–18.

Lang, M. (2003) Summary Report on Hypermedia Systems Design in Ireland. *Department of Accountancy and Finance, National University of Ireland*, Galway.

Lang, M. and Fitzgerald, B. (2005) Hypermedia systems development practice: A survey. *IEEE Software*, 20(2), 68–75.

Lang, M. and Fitzgerald, B. (2006) New branches, old roots: A study of methods and techniques in web/hypermedia systems design. *Information Systems Management*, 23(3), 62–74.

Lowe, D. and Hall, W. (1999) *Hypermedia and the Web: An Engineering Approach*. Wiley, England.

Koch, N. (1999) A Comparative Study of Methods for Hypermedia Development. Technical Report 9905. *Ludwig-Maximilians-Universität München*. November.

Kyaw, P. and Boldyreff, C. (1998) *A Survey of Hypermedia Design Methods in the Context of World Wide Web Design*. http://citeseer.ist.psu.edu/kyaw98survey.html

Murugesan, S. and Ginige, A. (2005) Web engineering: Introduction and perspectives. In: Suh, W. (Ed.), *Web Engineering: Principles and Techniques*, 1–30. Idea Group Publishing.

Muzar, R. (2005) Research about the use of structural and object-oriented methodologies for the development of Information Systems in the Republic of Croatia. In: *Proceedings 16th Intl Conf on Information and Intelligent Systems*, September, 21–23, Varazdin, Croatia, 321–329.

Nanard, J. and Nanard, M. (1995) Hypertext design environments and the hypertext design Process. *Communications of the ACM*, 38(8): 49–56.

Rosson, M.B., Ballin, J., Rode, J. and Toward, B. (2005) 'Designing for the Web' revisited: A survey of informal and experienced web developers. *Lecture Notes in Computer Science*, 3579, 522–532.

Venable, J.R. and Lim, F.C.B. (2001) Development activities and methodology usage by Australian web site consultants. In: *4th Western Australian Workshop on Information Systems Research*, WAWISR

Vora, P. (1998) Designing for the Web: A Survey. *ACM interactions*, 5(3), 13–30.

Zhou, J. and Stålhane, T. (2004) Web-based system development: Status in the Norwegian IT Organizations. *Lecture Notes in Computer Science*, 3009, 363–377.

# Requirements Engineering During Complex ISD: A Sensemaking Approach

**Päivi Ovaska[1] and Larry Stapleton[2]**

[1]South Carelia Polytechnic, Finland, paivi.ovaska@scp.fi

[2]Waterford Institute of Technology, Ireland, larrys@eircom.net

**Abstract**  This chapter describes the study that extends the previous research of social and organizational requirements engineering. The study suggests that requirement shaping during an ISD project can be described as a highly iterative sensemaking process of incongruence, filtering, negotiating and shifting. We studied two large e-commerce platform development projects by applying grounded theory and observed that attitudes and expectations about systems development among project participants filtered the understanding of IS requirements; negotiating between project participants resolved the issues caused by filtering and shifts in these attitudes and expectations facilitated changes in the understanding of requirements. This sensemaking process was highly iterative continuing the whole project lifetime and produced an IS product that exceeded the customer's needs and expectations. We approached the subject with a theory of sensemaking and claim to provide a new interpretation of how technology is collectively constructed in organizations.

## 1 Introduction

Studies of large IS projects show that they fail at an unacceptably high rate (Lyytinen and Robey 1999). Even if an IS project is completed in time, it produces a final system, which is of heterogeneous quality and often exceeds its budget (Lyytinen and Hirschheim 1987; Keil et al. 1995). Many of the problems encountered during ISD are attributable to shortcomings in the IS product's requirements. The problems reported in earlier research on requirement engineering typically involve the following issues: insufficient user involvement as well as ambiguous, changing and incomplete requirements (Pohl 1994; Jarke et al. 1999; Kotonya and Sommerville 1998).

Intensive research on software tools, modelling methods and processes for performing requirement elicitation has not yet delivered tools or techniques that could guarantee success in ISD projects. Traditional requirement engineering (RE)

C. Barry et al. (eds.), *Information Systems Development: Challenges in Practice, Theory, and Education, Vol.1*, doi: 10.1007/978-0-387-68772-8_16,

approaches offer poor understanding of how to specify and manage requirements for large evolving systems, how the requirements are understood and what kind of problems exist in commercial practice (Bubenko 1995). Recent research directed at the social and organizational processes in requirement elicitation sees it as an emergent political process (Bergman et al. 2002) constructed through conflicting interests and agendas, resource constraints and political influences. Alternatively, it is seen as a socio-cognitive problem-solving process (Orlikowski and Gash 1994; Davidson 2002). This socio-cognitive problem-solving process is characterized by differences and repeated shifts in assumptions and expectations of technology, which disrupt the project participants' understanding of requirements.

ISD in general can also be seen as a process of sensemaking (Waterman 1990) in which people 'structure the unknown'. This theory is a promising departure for ISD because it enables researchers to treat humans as active bodies interacting with others in the shaping and re-shaping of their world as they make sense of organizational realities. The goal of this research was to study how a theory of sensemaking informs requirements discovery practices in distributed ISD projects. We studied, using a grounded theory approach, two large-scale e-commerce ISD projects within a large telecom operator. Already, in the beginning of the study we observed that the requirements did not stabilize during the projects but instead kept changing, causing problems and delays for the project. This led us to study how the IS requirements were shaped and structured during the projects, using sensemaking theory as a lens to the data.

The rest of the chapter is structured as follows. Section 2 describes distribution, requirement elicitation and sensemaking process in the literature and terminology. It also sets out two propositions for the study. Section 3 presents the case organization and research methods used in the study. Section 4 outlines briefly key findings of this study. Section 5 discusses the findings and offers theory arising from the findings. Finally, we make conclusions and propose future research.

# 2 Literature review

This section briefly sets out the important literature which informs the key elements of this study. It starts by reviewing modern ISD contexts, then explores requirements elicitation and finally briefly outlines sensemaking as a theory for ISD. The section ends with two key propositions for consideration in this chapter.

## 2.1 ISD as a Distributed Activity

ISD is a complex process involving teams that may be large and cross functional with representatives from varying organizational functions (Kraut and Streeter 1995) and in multiple locations. The coordination required to successfully manage large-scale ISD is significant. The breadth of stakeholders in ISD offers diversity in experience, knowledge and perspectives. However, this diversity can often result in diminished interaction, lack of commitment and the inability to arrive at agreed decisions (Gruenfeld et al. 1996).

Findings show that rapid short-term projects consisting of three developers are presently commonplace, with customization of 'off the shelf' packages also common (Fitzgerald 1998). A significant amount of development now occurs in the form of the customization of commercial packages rather than the creation of bespoke systems. Added to this, customers now request a development team be present on site. In today's competitive labour market, the creation of a virtual team with only some members on site is frequently the adopted solution (Cramton and Webber 2003). This type of development involves smaller project teams, shorter time scales for completion of each customization, close and constant contact with users and the use of virtual teams.

Coordination in a distributed development environment is particularly challenging. Multi-site organizations use many mechanisms, such as plans, processes, interface specifications and software architecture, to coordinate their work. These mechanisms can be vulnerable to unexpected events, which require complex communication to coordinate activities (Hersleb and Grinter 1999). As the size and complexity of IS increases, the need for supporting informal communications increases dramatically but can be difficult to incorporate (Kraut and Streeter 1995).

## 2.2 The Requirement Elicitation Problem

Requirements engineering (RE) as a field originated in software engineering (SE). It was born of the early observation that regardless of how good the specification techniques for software are, they do not help if the developers do not know which problem to solve. In this view, requirement elicitation deals with *detecting* and *representing* requirements (Pohl 1994). In SE requirements engineering is usually seen as a set of techniques for requirements elicitation, documentation and management. The process is described by Pohl's three dimensions of RE (Pohl 1994) in which requirement specifications are developed through a process that leads from vague ideas, presented in textual languages and without consideration to agreed viewpoints, into a desired end state where there is a common agreement on a set of relatively formalized requirements that serve as a blueprint for information systems design and implementation (Pohl 1994). This *systematic process* is considered to ensure that system requirements are complete and consistent (Kotonya and Sommerville 1998).

In the information systems (IS) field, requirements are seen as a more *socially constructed phenomenon*. The classical view of Davis (1982) already saw that the effective inclusion of end users and other stakeholders was vital to this process. A third view assumes that requirements are defined in a *political process* arguing that requirement elicitation is a political process that includes selecting whose goals are addressed and whose are not (Keen 1981; Markus 1983; Boehm and Ross 1989; Bergman et al. 2002).

## 2.3 Sensemaking

People 'structure the unknown' (Waterman 1990, p. 41) and researchers interested in sensemaking concern themselves with how and why people create these constructions and what the affects of these structures are. This theory is a promising departure for ISD because it enables researchers to treat humans as active bodies shaping and re-shaping their world, and making sense of that same world inter-subjectively. This goes to the heart of the ISD process as those pioneers of participative systems development and design, Ehn, Mathieson, Dahlbom, Checkland, Mumford and so many others, envisioned ISD. Simultaneously, it recognizes that humans act and enact, and provides a trajectory which addresses some of the criticisms of the overly discourse-based view of ISD which has emerged around participative approaches.

It is stressed in sensemaking literature that professional problem solvers such as systems engineers and managers cannot derive adequate solutions to complex, socially located problems through observation and analysis alone, as is typified in the dominant approaches to ISD (Fitzgerald 2000). Solutions can only be found (and re-found) by open and active experimentation. As people's interaction and learning proceeds the very basis for an analytic solution changes. Analysis and interaction are thus seen as two modes of organizational problem solving which supplement each other (Boland 1985). In equivocal situations, such as those which prevail in requirements discovery, this problem-solving mode is more potent than comprehensive data analysis (Weick 1995).

In sensemaking a stimulus (new technology, work practices, etc.) raises a series of questions, which must be explicated and understood. These questions result in actions which change the environment, resulting in new stimuli and so the cycle begins again. People involved in sensemaking activities must interact with others in order to make sense of organizational realities. Furthermore, there is evidence that indicates that these groups of sensemakers need sensemaking support personnel to facilitate this process (Weick 1995; Stapleton 1999, 2002). This cooperative sensemaking indicates the *inter-subjective* nature of technology deployment activities (Boland and Day 1989). Inter-subjectivity implies a high level of trust between participants in the process. Indeed, research based upon these types of activities emphasize the building of deep friendships and common understanding. Trust can only be built through what might be termed socio-political processes through which negotiations proceed and agendas become clear. People learn to hear and respect each other's views. Consequently, we find in the recent IS literature researchers of sensemaking using political thinkers such as Habermas in order to explore how individuals and communities come to understand what the information systems mean to them (c.f. Janson and Cecez-Kecmanovic 2005).

It is clear that modern ISD involves complex knowledge work. In recent literature associated with knowledge work and the creation of advanced information
systems researchers have used sensemaking in order to the dynamics of knowl-
edge-sharing and human interaction in the development of an online trading system (Choo and Johnston 2004), as well as in an attempt technology adoption more
generally (Seligman 2006). During sensemaking, the convergence upon solutions
implies a cyclic process during which questions we are trying to answer are pro-
gressively reviewed and understood. Sensemaking theorists argue that when the
question is adequately understood the required solutions should be obvious
(Weick 1995). This aspect of sensemaking was incorporated into Soft systems
Methodology (SSM) by (Checkland 1999). This cyclic process of sensemaking is
illustrated in Fig. 1. Whilst sensemaking is directed from question formulation to
action through to the stimuli which are produced by the action it is important to
note that sensemaking also involves retrospection. Retrospection (or reflection) is
a process by which we come to understand how we got to where we are now and
is also used to make sense of complex realities, including the unfolding nature of
the sensemaking cycle itself. In sensemaking sense is imputed retrospectively and
we construct ourselves in retrospection and reflection (Weick 1995).

stimuli

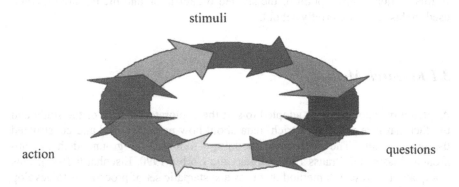

action                                                                questions

**Fig. 1.** Sensemaking cycles (from (Stapleton 2002)

Except for a few notable papers, sensemaking theory has received little attention from IS research in general and ISD research in particular. However, recent
work has demonstrated the power of sensemaking theory in understanding human
interactions during technology-mediated activities in complex communities. However, it is clear that ISD researchers need to focus upon building theories of social
and political action in this context. Recent research clearly demonstrates that complex social and political interactions during technology-mediated activities are not
uncommon and are demonstrably linked to the information technologies in use.
Whilst, for example, Janson and Cecez-Kecmanovic (2005) show how we urgently
need to develop theories of social and political interaction in information technology-mediated relationships in e-commerce, how these technologies come to be

developed and deployed still receives little attention in this context. This chapter therefore seeks to address this theoretical gap. As few studies are available which have gathered rich data on these phenomena, a grounded research strategy was deemed appropriate. With grounded studies it is not usual to set out research questions according to the classical research approach. Instead, guiding propositions are set out to direct the study. In this context the two primary propositions for this study were:

*P1*: In a case study of complex, distributed information systems development evidence can be identified of sensemaking processes amongst ISD participants

*P2*: If proposition one is shown to be true (i.e. evidence is found), the evidence within the case will indicate that sensemaking activities lead to more effective ISD outcomes

## 3 Research Methods

In this section a description of the studied organization and the research method used in this study are briefly set out.

### 3.1 Research Method

A qualitative approach was adopted to suit the exploratory nature of the study and the fact that it required very 'rich' data about how people shaped and constructed the requirements. The research methodology followed the grounded theory approach (Glaser and Strauss 1967; Strauss and Corbin 1990; Eisenhardt 1989). This is a qualitative research method that uses a systematic set of procedures to develop an inductively derived theory about a phenomenon. It can be used to study organizations, groups, and individuals (Glaser and Strauss 1967; Strauss and Corbin 1990). A requirement of the grounded theory is that the researchers demonstrate theoretical sensitivity (Glaser and Strauss 1967). Theoretical sensitivity comes from familiarity with the literature, and from professional or personal experience (Strauss and Corbin 1990). The qualitative data analysis was performed in three phases: open coding, axial coding and selective coding (Strauss and Corbin 1990).

The study gathered data from extensive documentation available from the case study projects using a theoretical sampling strategy. Based on the analysis of the documentation we decided to complement the written project material with focused interviews among project participants. Glaser and Strauss (1967) call this a dynamic process of data collection where the sample is extended and focused according to emerging needs as theoretical sampling.

## 3.2 Case Organization

This study was carried out in a software development department of an international ICT company. The software development department was an internal partner for the company's business units. The development of applications and services was assigned to an in-house software development unit (Internal Development Unit, later referred as IDU) or outsourced companies. The use of IDU for development of new services was mandated by the company's top management. IDU had approximately 150 employees that had formerly focused on R&D work in the company. During the past few years it had tried to improve its software skills and processes in order to make its development more effective and also to prove its capability to other business units. All the business units of the company did not agree with IDU's processes and did not trust in its software development capability. Their attitudes towards IDU competencies in software development were quite suspicious, mainly because of IDU's history as an R&D department. Quite often business units preferred outsourcing instead of developing in-house.

The projects, called here the 'DS project' and the 'EC project', respectively, developed mobile services for both the global and domestic telecommunication markets. A major goal of both projects was the renewal of old platform architecture to allow the services to be better and easier modifiable, maintainable and scalable.

The DS project developed a directory service platform for international markets. The project was partitioned into two subprojects to facilitate easier management. Partitioning was carried out on the basis of the architecture and technology: one subsystem had a highly distributed, component-based architecture (Server) and the other was a centralized subsystem (Client), which handled authentication, authorization and user interfaces. The functionality of the services required subsystems to communicate only through an extensible and configurable interface.

The goal of the EC project was to develop an Electronic Commerce mobile service platform. The system was intended to enable organizers or their sponsors to promote their products in all kinds of events, such as ice hockey and football games. The system was composed of two subsystems: the platform in which the services are run (Platform subsystem) and the toolbox (Tool subsystem). The Tool subsystem allowed adding, configuring and simulating of services to run in a Windows PC and with a service platform in a UNIX environment.

The actual systems development projects took place in IDU during the year 2001, and they were planned and organized according to a traditional waterfall model with distinct requirement elicitation, analysis, software design, implementation and testing phases.

# 4 Findings

During the projects, differences in attitudes and expectations were a source of disruption in ISD. Differences in participants' attitudes and expectations redirected their attention away from the information and led them to reinterpret the final product requirements.

For example, it was evident from both the documentation and the interview data from the DS project that participants varied a lot in their understanding of the architecture of the system. Indeed, every designer and developer saw the architecture of the system and its component dependencies quite differently. There were as many interpretations as there were component designers and developers. Interestingly, in each design interpretation the respective designer placed their particular component in the centre of the design model.

In the later phases of development, it was evident that the lack of common understanding of the architecture caused a lot of coordination problems in the Client subproject. The Client subsystem was tightly coupled with the Server subsystem, which significantly complicated the development of the Client subsystem even further. A change implemented in the information structure of the Server could have a major influence on the functionality of the Client.

The interface specification between the Client and Server was sketched parallel to the other Server subproject design specifications, which meant that the interface specification was far too late to be useful to the Client project design team. The design of the Server subsystem should have been ready before the Client and not vice versa. This brought about serious difficulties for the Client module designers and especially for those developing modules near the subsystem interface. The relevant module functionality depended on the structure of the information in the interface and the designers were not aware of that until quite late in the project. The specification of the interface was delayed, and it was evident that a lot of work had been a waste of time causing significant schedule overruns on the project.

It was also clear that differences in attitudes and expectations were not directly related to the system, but they were more concerned with organizational politics related to business value and ISD strategy and approach. Different assumptions about system development capabilities and resource allocation significantly added to ISD complexity.

For example, the EC project team organized three requirement workshops which were essentially brainstorming meetings. The primary agenda item during these meetings was the system and its features. The workshop records revealed that meeting discussions were very difficult, as the Business Unit (BU) preferred technical conversations, whereas the Internal Development Unit (IDU) preferred to discuss the project from a business and end user point of view. It was evident that BU and IDU saw the role of the development unit from different perspectives: BU viewed IDU as a technical resource and IDU considered themselves more as a business partner. These disagreements got deeper during the negotiations between BU managers and IDU managers, when it was revealed that the IDU strategy was not to offer consulting services, but software solutions. The company's top managers wanted IDU consulting services in order to get the Electronic Commerce Platform service ready as soon as possible. These pressures resulted in the BU managers adjusting the goal of the project to focus upon enhancing the current Electronic commerce platform with additional services and use IDU as the system developer. The aim of this new project was reformulated as: 'to make a new, enhanced version of the current Electronic commerce platform'. The enhancements were: 'a possibility to establish WAP, SMS and web services' and 'Content Administrator features that make service establishment easier (currently it is made with Oracle procedures)' (Project Setup Letter 1.0, Feb 2, 2001). As a consequence of all this, the role of the IDU was clarified and reframed as the system developer.

## 4.1 Classifying Differences in Attitudes and Expectations

During the analysis, we observed four categories of attitudes and expectations that affected the understanding of requirements between various project participants. The identified categories can be summarized as:

- Business value of system development, i.e. the attitudes and expectations about the relationship between business and system development.
- System development strategy, i.e. the attitudes and expectations about the suitable system development life cycle model and processes.
- System development capability, i.e. the assumptions and expectations about competencies in different areas of system development, such as user interfaces and databases.
- System development resource allocation, i.e. the assumptions and expectations about scheduling, budgeting, and priorities of systems development projects in time-to-market pressures.

## 4.2 Shifting from Waterfall to Cyclic ISD

Another important finding as regards requirements capture was that, as the EC progressed, the whole development moved from waterfall-style development towards interactive conversations with the customer. The designer of the Tool subsystem and the user interface designer made a prototype of the user interfaces and discussed with customers asking further exploratory questions and based on these questions made a new prototype. In this way, they made over twenty user interface prototypes and iterations of system requirements. Figure 2 presents a sample iteration of this process taken from the user interface documentation. As we can see from the figure, designers in the project devised one initial solution (First Solution space) for the two user interface layouts of the Service simulation tool (Tool subsystem) and showed it to the customer. This was followed by a conversation with the customer. They discussed how this service creation process should be shown to the administrator, and this in turn raised new problems (Problem space). The problem was how the service administrator should be informed of the service simulation progress. To resolve these problems further designs were made. The designers decided to show the progress in the form of a table beneath the user interface layouts. This produced new user interface sketches (Second Solution space), which formed the starting point for a new cycle.

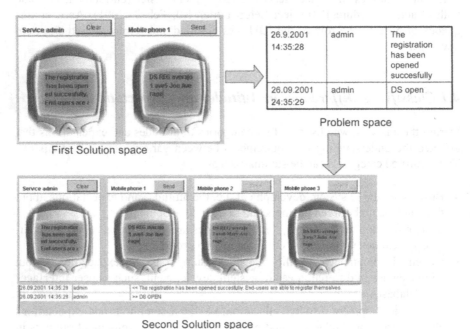

**Fig. 2** Sample iteration

## 4.3 Managing Requirements Discovery in the Tool Subsystem

Finally, it is important to present findings as regards the management of requirements discovery itself. We will review requirements discovery in the Tool subsystem in order to illustrate how things unfolded. The EC project formally used an approach set out within the IDU's overall ISD methodology. This methodology incorporated a strict requirements capture and closure process in which requirements were signed off early on in ISD, and only after a formal requirements review process would changes be countenanced. The process resulted in few change requests. During this time it also became evident that the Tool subsystem of the

project would not be delivered according to the requirements as originally specified and that updating the requirements specification was not a good way to manage this process, due to the high level of changes the team were encountering. This
in turn led to the emergence of an iterative design and development approach
through which people could physically see what requirements meant in technology
terms, work with those features which emerged, discussing them at length with
designers and developers involved in the effort. This new ISD process emerged,
based around a growing understanding of the system through prototyping and
working with the prototype design and development team. It, in turn, brought to
the surface a raft of change requests, but these requests were not managed at all
through the original formal requirements review procedure. These major changes
in the ISD process were a direct result of the active engagement with each other of
IDU and BU representatives as they tried to understand each other's perspectives
and what the emerging technology meant in terms of those perspectives. The
documentary and interview evidence strongly suggest that this process not only
worked very well, but was crucial to the delivery (albeit late) of a high-quality
system as well.

## 5 Discussion

Firstly, there was clearly evidence for positive sensemaking processes during the
re-negotiation of the overall projects and during the shift from waterfall to iterative prototyping. There was also negative evidence of sensemaking problems, especially during the design process during which the lack of interaction between
and within design and development teams led to narrow interpretations of the system and, in particular, the interfaces between system components. It is therefore
possible to initially characterize two dimensions of sensemaking here:

1. 'Socio-political' sensemaking (making sense of roles and ownership)
2. 'Technical' sensemaking (making sense of complex designs and interfaces and
   what they mean for the sensemaker)

It was also evident that in order to address technical decisions socio-political
sensemaking had to occur first. The social element of the sensemaking process involved working out who owned what, how the groups were to interact with each
other and how this was to be shaped by (and ultimately shape) the ISD process itself.

In the Tool subsystem this was seen in the way in which requirements discovery was managed and how that process changed and emerged, as the participants
discovered together a way of developing the technology simultaneously with developing an understanding of the new technology and what it meant for them. It
involved a series of iterative, sensemaking processes stimulated by each new prototype and the possibilities it raised. This stimulus then raised questions which had
to be explored inter-subjectively in order to understand what the key dimensions
of those questions were and what was appropriate action (technology redesign

etc.) in this context. Action also occurred in re-engineering the ISD process itself as the group reflected upon what they were learning in terms of managing requirements. The group thus moved from a formal, normative, timephased approach to requirements discovery to a sensemaking approach. As the sensemaking activities emerged and intensified, the key issues began to become clear and were addressed within the prototype solution. People began to understand what the Tool subsystem 'meant' for them and could create this meaning both in the technology and in their interaction with each other. The evidence suggests that this process of reshaping ISD was due to contingencies which arose during ISD.

On the political front, the projects participants were only able to resolve differences in assumptions and expectations through intensive negotiations. The more effective the negotiations, the better the feature associated with those negotiations worked. In these negotiations the projects participants' attitudes and expectations towards systems development shifted more and more towards attempts to build a mutual understanding of the situation. The negotiation process thus facilitated new interpretations of the requirements. The main forces in the new interpretation of the requirements were shifting attitudes and expectations concerning the systems development strategy and process, and systems development capability.

It is possible to identify a process of sensemaking that had important effects on how the projects participants emphasized the attitudes and expectations in different phases of the project. This overall sensemaking process had four main dimensions which can be associated with the phases on the sensemaking cycle (provided in parentheses below):

1. Making sense of incongruence where attitudes or expectations differed among the stakeholders, causing conflicts and misunderstanding (stimulation to question phase)
2. Negotiating that tried to resolve the incongruence between stakeholders. Whilst incongruence happened when understanding, attitudes or expectations differed among the stakeholders, negotiating helped build common understanding of attitudes and expectations across the team (question to action phase)
3. Filtering that occurred when a stakeholder of the development process left something out of the scope because of his/her understanding, attitudes, expectations or experiences (action to stimulation phase)
4. Shifting that took place when the understanding of a frame changed. After a frame shift, the parties involved got an understanding of a frame that was more aligned with and suitable for the current situation than before the shift (stimulation to question phase)

In the opening part of this study two propositions were set out:

*P1*: Evidence will be found of sensemaking processes in a case study of complex, distributed information systems development.

*P2*: If proposition one is shown to be true, there will be evidence within the case which suggests that sensemaking activities lead to more effective ISD outcomes.

Both propositions were supported by the case data. However, it was clear that the sensemaking processes emerged spontaneously from the dynamics of ISD, rather than as a result of well-informed ISD structures or guidelines as to how a sensemaking ISD process might be organized. Indeed, it was clear that the ISD approach as planned broke down and had to be significantly modified in order that key sensemaking processes is supported. The extent to which this was formally managed was entirely unclear and seemed to emerge as part of the dynamics of social and political interaction.

This suggests significant opportunity for research which can set out how best to develop systems using sensemaking approaches. There was strong evidence that sensemaking occurred along socio-political lines. This in turn suggests that STS approaches should be revisited given their emphasis upon social and political dynamics within ISD. Certainly, evidence gathered here strongly supports the contingent approach advocated in both Multiview and Multiview2 (Avison and Wood-Harper 1991; Avison et al. 1998). On the other hand major STS approaches have not generally emphasized sensemaking in any direct way, with the exception of SSM. In the case of SSM, Checkland (1999) argues that his approach is fundamentally based upon sensemaking principles and it is clear that, in terms of questioning and problem exploration, SSM is a powerful tool for developing this phase of the sensemaking cycle. However, close examination of SSM reveals little specific support for distributed ISD, or for identifying who should be interacting when. Neither does SSM provide clear guidelines for the full sensemaking cycle as set out in Stapleton (1999) or the importance of retrospection recently demonstrated as important theoretically for any understanding of technology adoption activities (Seligman 2006). Indeed, the relationship between action and stimulus, which raises the possibility of reshaping the ISD process itself, is not given much attention by Checkland.

# 6 Conclusions

Systems development practitioners and researchers are becoming aware of the messy nature of requirement engineering and ISD in general. In this chapter, we traced the requirement shaping and construction process in two projects of a large telecommunication company with a single, interpretive case study. We observed that attitudes and expectations among participants as regards systems development had a severe impact on requirements understanding. Requirements were understood through an iterative, inter-subjective sensemaking process involving incongruence, filtering, negotiating and shifting.

The results of our study contribute to existing requirements research in an important way. This study makes a substantive contribution to the understanding of the requirements engineering process and systems development in general.

Current approaches still largely assume that projects proceed with distinct phases in a more or less waterfall fashion, and the system is developed from an understanding of the idea into a final system, which satisfies the originally stated requirements. Instead, our study implies that the requirement shaping is an iterative sensemaking process in which filtering, negotiating and shifting of different attitudes and expectations about systems development change and increase the participants' interpretation and understanding of requirements during the project. This implies a close relationship between creating inter-subjective meanings and the development of successful technology. Given that this study is limited to one case a great deal more work is needed in order to determine primary dimensions of sensemaking in ISD and how these might best be supported under different conditions. Future research is needed to explore more generally socio-political processes within ISD in order to further validate or otherwise these findings.

# References

Avison, D.E., Wood-Harper, A.T. 1991, Conclusions from action research: The Multiview experience, in Jackson, M. C. et al. (eds.). *Systems Thinking in Europe*, Plenum Press, New York.

Avison, D. E., Wood-Harper, A. T., Vidgen, R. T., Wood, J. R. G. 1998, A further exploration into information systems development: The evolution of Multiview2, *Information Technology and People*, 11(2), 124–139.

Bergman, M., King, J. L., Lyytinen, K. 2002, Large scale requirements analysis revisited: the need for understanding the political ecology of requirements engineering, *Requirements Engineering*, 7(3), 152–171.

Boehm, B. W., Ross, R. 1989, Theory-W software project management: principles and examples, *IEEE Transactions on Software Engineering*, 15, 902–916.

Boland, R. 1985, Phenomenology: A preferred approach to research on information systems, in Mumford, E., Hirschheim, R. A., Fitzgerald, G., Wood-Harper, A. T. (eds), *Research Methods in Information Systems*, Elsevier: Holland.

Boland, R., Day, W. 1989, The experience of systems design: A hermeneutic of organisational action, *Scandinavian Journal of Management*, 5(2), 87–104.

Bubenko, J. A. 1995, Challenges in requirements engineering, *Second IEEE International Symposium in Requirements Engineering*, March 27–29, York, England.

Checkland, P. 1999, *Soft Systems Methodology: A 30-Year Retrospective*, Wiley, Chichester.

Choo, C. W., Johnston, R. 2004, Innovation in the knowing organization: A case study of an e-commerce initiative, *Journal of Knowledge Management*, 8(6), 77–92.

Cramton C. D., Webber S. S. 2003, Relationships among geographic dispersion, team processes, and effectiveness in software development work teams, *Journal of Business Research*, 58, 758–765.

Davidson, E. J. 2002, Technology frames and framing: A socio-cognitive investigation of requirement determination, *MIS Quarterly*, 26(4), 329–357.

Eisenhardt, K. M. 1989, Building theories from case study research, *Academy of Management Review*, 14(4), 532–550.

Fitzgerald, B. 1998, An empirical investigation into the adoption of systems development methodologies, *Information and Management*, 34(6):317–328.

Fitzgerald, B. 2000, System development methodologies: A problem of tenses, *Information Technology and People*, 13, 174–185.

Glaser, B., Strauss, A. L. 1967, *The Discovery of Grounded Theory*: Strategies for Qualitative Research, Chicago, Adline.

Gruenfeld, D. H., Mannix, E. A., Williams, K. Y., Neale, M. A. 1996, Group composition and decision making: How member familiarity and information distribution affect process and performance, *Organizational Behavior and Human Decision Processes* 67(1), 1–15.

Hersleb, J., Grinter, R. 1999, Splitting the organization and integrating the code: Conway's law revisited, *Proceeding of International Conference in Software Engineering, ICSE '99*.

Janson, M., Cecez-Kecmanovic, D. 2005, Making sense of e-commerce as social action, *Information Technology and People*, 18(4), 311–242.

Jarke, M., Rolland, C., Sutcliffe, A., Dömges, R. 1999, *The Nature of Requirements Engineering*, Shaker, Aachen.

Keen, P. G. W. 1981, Information systems and organizational change, *Communications of the ACM* 24, 24–33.

Keil, M., Mixon, R., Saarinen, T., Tuunainen, V. 1995, Understanding runaway information technology projects: Results from an international research program based on escalation theory, *Journal of Management Information Systems* 11(3), 65–85.

Kotonya, G., Sommerville, I. 1998, *Requirements Engineering – Processes and Techniques*, Wiley, Chichester.

Kraut, R., Streeter, L. 1995, Coordination in software development, *Communications of the ACM*, 38(3).

Lyytinen, K., Hirschheim, R. 1987, Information systems failures: A survey and classification of the empirical literature, *Oxford Surveys in Information Technology* (4), 257–309.

Lyytinen, K., Robey, D. 1999, Learning failure in information system development, *Information Systems Journal*, 9(2), 85–101.

Markus, M. L. 1983, Power, politics and MIS implementation, *Communications of the ACM*, 26, 430–444.

Orlikowski, W. J., Gash, D. C. 1994, Technological frames: Making sense of information technology in organizations, *ACM Transactions on Information Systems*, 12(2), 174–207.

Pohl, K. 1994. Three dimensions of requirements engineering: Framework and its application, *Information Systems*, 19(3), 243–258.

Seligman, L. 2006, Sensemaking throughout adoption and the innovation-decision process, *European Journal of Innovation Management*, 9(1), 108–120.

Stapleton, L. 1999, Information systems development as interlocking spirals of sensemaking, in: Zupancic, J., Wojtkowski, W., Wojtkowski, W. S. (eds.), *Evolution and Challenges in Systems Development*, Plenum, New York, pp. 389–404.

Stapleton, L. 2002, *Information Systems Development: An Empirical Study of Irish Manufacturing Firms*, Ph.D. Thesis, Dept. of B.I.S., University College, Cork.

Strauss, A., Corbin, J. 1990, *Basics of Qualitative Research: Grounded Theory Procedures and Applications*, Sage, Newbury Park, CA.

Waterman, R. 1990, *Adhocracy: The Power to Change*, Whittle Direct Books, Knoxville, TN.

Weick, K. 1995, *Sensemaking in Organisations*, Sage Publications, Newbury Park, CA.

# Understanding the Problems of Requirements Elicitation Process: A Human Perspective

**Dace Apshvalka[1], Dace Donina[2] and Marite Kirikova[3]**

[1]Department of System Theory and Design, Riga Technical University,
Dace.Apshvalka@gmail.com

[2]Department of System Theory and Design, Riga Technical University,
dacelim@yahoo.co.uk

[3]Department of System Theory and Design, Riga Technical University,
Marite.Kirikova@cs.rtu.lv

**Abstract** Issues about requirements elicitation have been an ongoing problem area since the very earliest days of computing. However, incorrect requirements, misunderstood requirements, and many other requirement problems are still present in systems development projects. The purpose of this chapter is to look at the causes of problems in requirement elicitation process. We will look at these problems from the human perspective, trying to understand the role of human cognitive, emotional, motivational, and social processes. Our goal is to understand the aspects which should be taken into consideration when choosing requirement elicitation approaches and methods.

## 1 Introduction

Rapid development of information and communication technologies and new information storage and exchange possibilities have made knowledge, the most valuable asset, and collaboration skills, the best tool for the success of a modern business and daily life activities (Davenport and Prusak, 1998; Nonaka and Takeuchi, 1995).

Knowledge and knowledge processes have always been an important subject of research among scientists belonging to different research branches. Processes where value can only be created through the fulfillment of particular knowledge requirements of the process participants are called knowledge-intensive processes (Richter-von Hagen et al., 2005). Based on this definition, we can say that information systems development (ISD) process is also a knowledge-intensive process. In the ISD process, many participants are involved, and the success of the ISD process and the quality of the achieved result are highly dependent on the knowl-

C. Barry et al. (eds.), *Information Systems Development: Challenges in Practice, Theory, and Education, Vol.1*, doi: 10.1007/978-0-387-68772-8_17,
© Springer Science+Business Media, LLC 2009

edge of many different participants and the productivity of their collaboration. ISD process consists of many sub-processes, and each of them is more or less a knowledge-intensive process. However, one of the most knowledge-intensive sub-processes in ISD is requirement elicitation. It involves many different stakeholders, with different interests, expectations, and domain knowledge, which should be aligned, distilled, and incorporated into requirement specification. All their relevant knowledge, experience, and expectations about the future information system are crucial for the success of the whole ISD process and the final system.

Issues regarding requirement elicitation, analyzing, documenting, and communicating have been an ongoing problem area since the very earliest days of computing. However, incorrect requirements, misunderstood requirements, and many other requirement problems are still present in systems development projects (Avison and Fitzgerald, 2006). Avison and Fitzgerald (2006) suggest that maybe it is impossible to solve the requirement problems as they are still present after thousands of years (since the first project of mankind) of attempts to solve these problems. Nevertheless, many approaches, techniques, and methodologies have been and are being developed to minimize errors and misunderstandings in requirement process.

The purpose of this chapter is not to make a contribution to the requirement elicitation methods or techniques, but to look at the causes of problems in requirement elicitation process. We will look at these problems from the human perspective, trying to understand the role of human cognitive, emotional, motivational, and social processes which cause misunderstandings, incompletely expressed information, misinterpretation, and other threats for the success of requirement elicitation process. Our goal is to understand what aspects influence the knowledge and behavior of different stakeholders involved in the requirement elicitation process, and how they influence each other's conceptual systems. This understanding can help us to interpret the usability of different existing requirement elicitation methods and techniques.

We start our discussion in Sect. 2 with a brief look at the requirement elicitation process and problems. In Sect. 3, we focus on the theory of human knowledge and aspects influencing human knowledge. In Sect. 4, we discuss the requirements which are important for the success of requirement elicitation process.

# 2 Requirement Elicitation Process

Requirements are regarded as the most important and crucial part of the systems development process, and they are often the most misunderstood development issue (Avison and Fitzgerald, 2006). Requirements are everything that the set of relevant stakeholders want from a system. A requirements engineer needs to identify relevant sources of requirements, elicit requirements from identified sources, analyze and document elicited requirements, communicating requirements (Avison and Fitzgerald, 2006).

Requirement elicitation is a process of capturing all relevant requirements from identified sources – documents, systems, stakeholders, and others. In this chapter, we focus on the process of requirement elicitation from the identified stakeholders. By stakeholders, we understand any person who will be affected by the developed system directly or indirectly. Such persons are, for example, customers, end users, domain experts, senior or line management, and others.

Capturing requirements from stakeholders is a knowledge-intensive process because the value of the process can only be created from the knowledge of process participants. The success of requirement elicitation process depends on the success of communication, collaboration, and understanding among different stakeholders and between stakeholders and requirements engineer.

Communication is about sending and receiving information. Collaboration is actively working together to deliver a work product or to make a decision (Cockburn and Highsmith, 2001). Understanding is alignment of conceptual systems (Davidson et al., 2003).

Requirements engineering literature identifies several problems in the requirement elicitation process (Avison and Fitzgerald, 2006, pp. 101–104; Sommerville, 2004, p. 146). In this chapter, we will focus our attention on the problems caused by insufficient communication between the process participants. Some of these problems are as follows:

- *Missing requirements* – stakeholders do not mention all requirements because they do not know what they want and they do not know the possible options what a new system could offer, or they forget to tell about some requirements, or the requirements engineer forgets to ask some specific questions.
- *Reluctant participation* – stakeholders are not interested to participate sufficiently in the requirement elicitation process.
- *Misperception* – requirements engineer incorrectly captures requirements. Onc of the reasons for misperception is that stakeholders express requirements in their terms and with implicit knowledge of their own work. The requirements engineer, without experience in the stakeholders' domain, may misunderstand these requirements.
- *Disagreement* – stakeholders disagree about some requirements.

Different approaches and methods are developed to support requirement elicitation and to deal with possible problems in the requirement elicitation process. Some of the approaches are as follows (Hoffer et al., 2004):

- Traditional approaches, such as interviews, Nominal Group Technique, observation, analyzing procedures and documents.
- Contemporary approaches, such as Joint Application Design, group support systems, CASE tools, prototypes.
- Agile approaches, such as continual user involvement, Agile Usage-Centered Design, Planning Game.

However, none of these approaches can fully avoid misunderstandings and other problems in a requirement elicitation process. Our assumption is that these

problems are caused because of the human-centered nature of requirement elicitation process. Most of the processes in the ISD life cycle can be more or less automated and formalized. But effective requirement elicitation from stakeholders
requires face-to-face communication with stakeholders to avoid misunderstandings
(Li et al., 2005). However, face-to-face communication is not a panacea for avoidance of misunderstandings. In some situations, it can lead to even more misunderstandings than written or more formal ways of communication. Sutcliffe (2002)
writes that natural language is prone to misinterpretation, and therefore requirement analysis has been a frequent cause of system failure.

Human communication and the alignment of different conceptual systems involve cognitive and social processes which are still not fully understood even by
cognitive and social scientists (Sun, 2006) and little studied in the Requirements
engineering field.

## 3 Inside the Human Mind

Requirement analysis can be seen as discovery-based learning where we start with
an obscure understanding of the problem domain and what is required for the new
system. It is a cognitive process of understanding problems and communicating
with people (Sutcliffe, 2002).

Our assumption is similar to one of Sutcliffe (2002) that given the fact that requirement elicitation is much about interpersonal communication, collaboration
and personal cognition, understanding how these processes work and affect each
other can help us to understand the causes of the problems in requirement elicitation process. This understanding can help us to interpret the usability of different
existing requirement elicitation methods and techniques.

As described in Sect. 2, requirement elicitation is a knowledge-intensive process. It means that the main resource of the requirement elicitation process is
knowledge, and the success of the process result is based on the fulfillment of the
knowledge requirements of the process participants. To understand the knowledge-intensive requirement elicitation process, we need to understand the concept
of knowledge.

There are many definitions of knowledge. The variety of the definitions depend on the knowledge definer's perspective on knowledge (e.g., philosophical,
managerial, engineering) and the objective why it has been necessary to define the
knowledge.

One of the most popular knowledge definitions in the managerial and business
domain is given by Davenport and Prusak, who state that knowledge is "*a fluid
mix of framed experience, values, contextual information, and expert insight that
provides a framework for evaluation and incorporating new experiences and information. It originates and is applied in the minds of knowers (..) Knowledge exists within people, part and parcel of human complexity and unpredictability*"
(Davenport and Prusak, 1998, p. 5).

This definition states that knowledge is something personal and resides in human minds. Therefore the next concept we need to understand is the concept of human mind or the "room" of human knowledge.

The traditional model of human mind is expressed by three basic human mental processes: *cognition, emotion*, and *motivation*. The original source of this structure comes from Plato who was arguing for a tripartite structure of the human soul (Davidson et al., 2003). Plato created these three concepts and put them in partial opposition to each other. While this doctrine has had many critics, it profoundly still affected modern psychology where cognition is often seen as an antagonist to emotion (Davidson et al., 2003). However, a recent tendency in psychology as well as in other disciplines (e.g., computer science) has been to study the interaction between cognition, emotion, and motivation (Meredith et al., 2000; Sloman, 2001; Picard, 1997).

Meredith et al. (2000), based on the traditional view of mind mentioned earlier, represent human knowledge as residing in a three-dimensional space, where cognition, emotion, and motivation are three dimensions of knowledge space. The three dimensions affect each other and are closely interwoven. Each process pervades the other to a great extent. The same external stimulus results in responses from all three processes. None of the three exists in a vacuum without the other two. Since knowledge is at least cognitively based, it is impossible to know something without having an affect and conative (motivational) reaction to it, these reactions adding to and becoming a part of knowledge (Meredith et al., 2000).

Affective science research shows that human affective states have a powerful influence on the way people perceive, interpret, represent, and categorize information and the way they formulate attitudes and judgments. Emotions bias cognitive processing during judgment and inference. For example, happiness allows unusual associations and improves creative problem solving (Isen et al., 1987).

The last several years have witnessed a burst of interest in the role of emotions in cognitive processes, such as decision making. Researchers have shown that even the affect that is unrelated to the decision at hand can have a significant impact on judgment and choice, but emotional deficits can degrade the quality of decision making. Traditional decision making theory paid little attention to emotion. Decision making was viewed as a cognitive process where decision makers dispassionately choose actions that maximized the "utility" of potential consequences of their decisions (Davidson et al., 2003).

It is regarded that there are two basic kinds of affective influence on decision making: *expected emotions* and *immediate emotions*. Expected emotions consist of predictions about the emotional consequences of decision outcomes. They influence a person to select actions that maximize positive emotions and minimize negative emotions. Immediate emotions are experienced at the time of decision making. Theories of decision making, if they incorporate emotions at all, typically assume that expected emotions are the only emotions that matter. People are assumed to choose options that they expect will maximize positive emotions. However, not only expected emotions influence decision-making process, but also immediate emotions influence decisions by altering the decision maker's perceptions of probabilities or outcomes or by altering the quality and quantity of processing decision-relevant signs (Davidson et al., 2003). The interrelationship between decision making, immediate, and expected emotions is illustrated in Fig. 1.

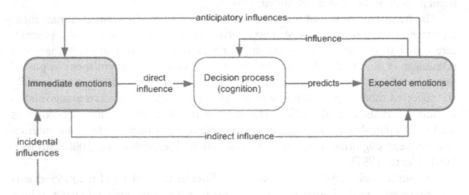

**Fig. 1.** The interrelationship between decision making, immediate, and expected emotions (adapted from Davidson et al., 2003, p. 621)

Figure 2 represents human mental processes described in this section. It shows that knowledge is embedded in the human cognition, emotion, and motivation space and formulates a person's judgments and attitudes. Knowledge (previous knowledge or experiences together with judgments and attitudes) influences the way a person processes information. Although information processing is also a cognitive process, the figure displays it as a separate process (outside the process of cognition which forms one of the dimensions in the knowledge space) to outline the information-processing processes. Information processing influences decision making, as information is an important resource for making decisions. Decision making is influenced also by other knowledge dimensions – motivation and emotion. During the decision-making process, a person's emotion and motivation are influenced, and knowledge structures are changed as well.

(Note that Fig. 2 is just a representation of the concepts described here. It is not a detailed process or a conceptual model.)

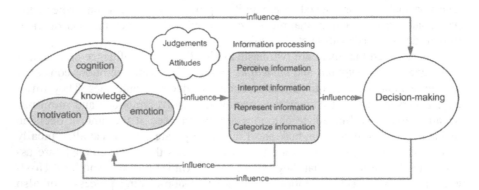

**Fig. 2.** Representation of human mental processes

Cognitive scientists tend to focus on the behavior of single individuals thinking and perceiving on their own. Although a significant amount of work has been done in cognitive science in studying individual cognition, the sociocultural processes and their relation to cognition have never been a focus of cognitive science (Sun, 2006). However, humans are social beings. It means that humans are influenced by other humans, besides influencing other humans. Dynamic relationships are formed among different individuals, and these relationships initiate changes in an individual's inner states, personality facets, and knowledge. Cockburn and Highsmith (2001) note that what can be seen from the brainstorming and joint problem-solving sessions is that people working together with good communication and interaction can operate at higher levels than when they use their individual talents only.

# 4 Requirements for Successful Requirements Elicitation Process

What can we learn from the theory of human knowledge and mental processes in the context of requirement elicitation? As requirement elicitation is a knowledge-intensive process which involves different "knowledge holders," it is necessary to understand how knowledge processes work in the human mind. When we understand these processes, we will be able to adjust them in the right way to make the best use of the knowledge intensiveness in the requirement elicitation process.

As discussed in the previous section, human knowledge is embedded into cognitive, emotional, and motivational processes, and all these processes influence human information processing and decision making (see Fig. 2). Therefore, the requirements engineer should choose methods and approaches, which support positive environment for the three mental processes in the stakeholders' minds, to help, support, and initiate stakeholders' knowledge sharing and creation. Appropriately supported cognitive processes, positive emotional environment, and sufficient level of stakeholders' motivation are crucial for the successful requirement elicitation process.

In this section we will discuss how to avoid problems mentioned in Sect. 2: missing requirements, reluctant participation, misperception, and disagreement.

## 4.1 Supporting Cognitive Processes

As stated previously, one of the requirement elicitation problems is that stakeholders do not know what they want and what they know. Therefore, the right knowledge should be triggered from outside the stakeholders' minds by introducing them with possible options the new system could offer and by asking them about their knowledge domain and expertise.

Studies of mind and knowledge show that complex structures of human mind and human knowledge make it difficult and sometimes even impossible for the knowledge owner to express and explain (to make explicit) particular "piece" of his/her knowledge (Polanyi, 1964; Ortner, 2002). Very often, even the owner of the original knowledge does not know its real and/or complete meaning. Polanyi (1964, p. 252) writes: "*I can say nothing precisely. (...) I do not focally know what I mean, and though I could explore my meaning up to a point, I believe that my words (descriptive words) must mean more than I shall ever know, if they are to mean anything at all (..) We can know more than we can tell.*"

Requirements engineer should take this aspect into account when planning, organizing, and leading requirement elicitation process. Requirements engineer is responsible for initiating stakeholders (the knowers of requirements) to tell as much as possible/necessary. How can we help stakeholders to realize what they know and how can we help them to express what they know? Ortner (2002) writes that information acts like a command or a trigger that prompts the selection of a specific pattern in the mind. These impulses from outside are essential for "actuating" knowledge or for arranging specific combinations of knowledge material into a specific structure and starting specific knowledge processes. It means that knowledge is *context* and outside *impulse* dependent. To elicit the right requirements from stakeholders, it is necessary to provide them with the right context and the right impulses.

Interview is one of the most common methods which support the knowledge triggering from stakeholders. Interviews are good for getting an overall understanding of what stakeholders do, how they might interact with the system, and the difficulties that they face with the current system (Sommerville, 2004). On the other hand, interviews also help stakeholders to get at least a basic understanding about aspects of their knowledge and working processes, in which the requirements engineer is interested in, and about what kind of subjects they need to think about to give their valuable contribution into the development of the new system.

Other methods of knowledge triggering are, for example, scenarios and prototyping. People find it easier to relate to real-life examples than to abstract descriptions as often used in interviews. Imagination of the possible interaction of the new system is a powerful way of triggering expression of specific requirements from stakeholders.

## 4.2 Supporting Emotional and Motivational Processes

As discussed in the previous section and represented in Figs. 1 and 2, affect or emotion (these terms are often used as synonyms) has a powerful influence on a person's cognitive processes. Requirement elicitation involves many cognitive processes, such as information perception, interpretation, representation, and decision making. Since a person's emotional state has a powerful influence on these processes, the requirements engineer must not ignore this important aspect. Besides that, emotion has an influence on a person's motivation as well (see Fig. 2).

Reluctant participation is one of the frequent problems in the requirement elicitation process (see Sect. 2). Therefore, every recommendation about the factors influencing person's motivation should be considered by the requirements engineer. However, requirement literature tells little about the role of stakeholders' emotions during the requirement elicitation process. (Although the emotional state of the requirements engineer is also important, we do not discuss it, assuming that he, as a professional, manages his emotion in the best way.)

The requirements engineer needs to be attentive to recognize stakeholders' emotional states to avoid possible threats. Such threat may be, for example, undesirable *expected emotions* (see Fig. 1) for the new system. Such emotions may occur, for example, when stakeholders imagine or realize that the new system will burden their habitual work processes, or make the working conditions less enjoyable, or provoke the firing of some employees as some work processes will be automated. Such expected emotions during the requirement elicitation process affect stakeholders' decision making and knowledge sharing in a negative way. Therefore requirements engineer needs to work as a motivator and psychologist to predict, detect, and avoid unwilling emotions and to arouse motivating emotions, such as happiness, hope, inspiration, openness, and the like.

## 4.3 Supporting Knowledge Exchange

Another challenging aspect that the requirements engineer should consider is the social nature of humans. Much deeper and detailed research should be done to understand how individuals influence each other's cognitive processes, as well as each other's emotion and motivation. In this chapter, we will mention a rather general assumption based on Knowledge Management literature review (Nonaka and Takeuchi, 1995; Davenport and Prusak, 1998) that social communication and group knowledge creation are a continual process of the conversion between tacit and explicit knowledge (Nonaka and Takeuchi, 1995). Tacit knowledge is personal, context-specific, and therefore hard to formalize and communicate. Explicit knowledge is also called "codified" knowledge and is transmittable in formal, systematic language.

Nonaka and Takeuchi (1995) introduce knowledge conversion model which consists of four knowledge conversion processes.

- Tacit-to-tacit knowledge conversion is called *socialization*. It is a process of sharing experiences and creating shared mental models. To successfully share mental models, it is necessary to have at least some shared experience.
- Tacit-to-explicit knowledge conversion is called *externalization*. It is a process of concept creation. It is triggered by dialog or collective reflection.
- Explicit-to-tacit knowledge conversion is called *internalization*. It is a process of embodying explicit knowledge into tacit knowledge – understanding the explicit knowledge. It helps if the knowledge is documented, because documentation helps individuals to internalize what they experienced.

- Explicit-to-explicit knowledge conversion is called *combination*. It is a process of systemizing concepts into a knowledge system. Reconfiguration of existing information through sorting, adding, combining, and categorizing of explicit knowledge can lead to new knowledge.

As requirement elicitation is a knowledge-intensive process and its success depends on the effectiveness of knowledge sharing and creation among process participants, it requires to be a continual process of conversion between tacit and explicit knowledge supporting all four knowledge conversion processes (Kirikova, 2004) described earlier. And as such, the requirement elicitation process requires using both formal and informal methods.

During the *socialization* process, participants (stakeholders and requirements engineer) learn to understand each other, learn about each other's needs, expectations, and wishes. The acquired knowledge becomes explicit conceptual knowledge through the *externalization* process. Acquired conceptual knowledge becomes a guideline for creating systemic knowledge through *combining* different concepts expressed by different participants. Systemic knowledge (for example a diagram or a system's prototype) through the process of *internalization* creates new or changed understandings and expectations and often triggers a new cycle of knowledge creation.

In a knowledge creation process through continual knowledge conversion, improvement of mutual understanding among participants and requirement (expressed concept) refinement occurs. Knowledge creation cycle ends when the requirements engineer is satisfied with acquired systemized stakeholders' requirements (see Fig. 3).

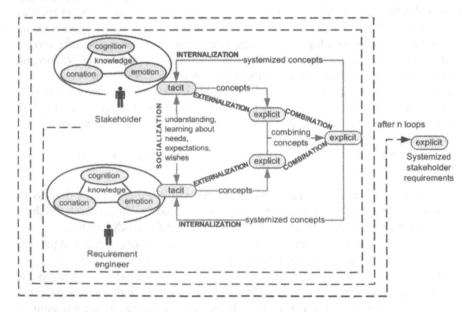

**Fig. 3.** Requirement elicitation as a cyclic knowledge conversion process

During the cyclic knowledge or requirement creation process, each partici-pant's mental models are changed, too, as learning is an important sub-process of knowledge creation. And each participant's knowledge space (namely, cognition, emotion, motivation) is persistently affected, too. Continual knowledge conver-sion process cycle is necessary to avoid such requirement elicitation problems as misperception and disagreement. The requirement engineer needs to use both for-mal and informal methods to ensure that all participants' conceptual systems are aligned. This means that mutual understanding and agreement regarding system requirements are achieved, as well as informally externalized requirements are correctly "translated" into formal requirement specification.

## 5 Conclusions

Requirement elicitation is a knowledge-intensive process, and because knowledge is embedded in humans, the requirement engineer needs to understand aspects affecting human knowledge. Modern requirements engineering approaches and methods tend to concentrate on user aspects. Such approach is, for example, User-Centered Requirements Engineering (Sutcliffe, 2002), and such methods are, for example, Continual User Involvement, Agile Usage-Centered Design, and the Planning Game (Hoffer et al., 2004). However, based on the literature review, we conclude that little attention has been paid to the processes occurring in the stake-holders' minds and issues of how these processes affect success of requirement elicitation process.

As requirement elicitation is a knowledge-intensive process, its success depends on communication, collaboration, and understanding among process participants. The main problems caused by insufficient and unsuccessful communication are missing requirements, reluctant participation, misperception, and disagreement.

An individual's cognition, emotion, and motivation affect each other and form a three-dimensional space where the individual's knowledge is embedded. Besides that, humans are social beings; therefore, individual's knowledge is affected not only by his/her inner states but also by other individuals. Consequently, the re-quirements engineer should use approaches and methods which positively affect all three dimensions of requirement stakeholder' knowledge space, as well as sup-port social communication and group knowledge creation. Such methods require being both formal and informal. And the requirement engineer needs to be both analytical and intuitive to be able to understand and support stakeholders' cogni-tive, emotional, and motivational processes, as well as produce formal require-ment specification document.

To support understanding, agreement, and successful knowledge exchange among process participants, a continual process of the conversion between tacit and explicit knowledge is required (see Sect. 4). Therefore, successful requirement elicitation method should support all four knowledge conversion processes: sociali-zation, externalization, combination, and internalization. Successful knowledge conversion within a requirement elicitation process will ensure highly intensive knowledge exchange among process participants. That will improve mutual understanding and agreement regarding system requirements because of continual externalization/expression of individual knowledge and internalization/understanding of other participants' knowledge which helps to align different conceptual systems as well as express one's existing knowledge and come to know ideas. Successful knowledge conversion also ensures that informally externalized/expressed requirements are correctly "translated" into formal requirement specification document. This requires using more formal and traditional knowledge combination approaches.

The main contribution of this chapter is to justify the importance of human aspects and necessity for combination of informal and formal approaches in requirement elicitation process. There are at least two important directions for the further research. The first is a need for better understanding of human mind and different aspects which affect human knowledge, communication, and collaboration. Such an understanding will help to predict and avoid possible causes of problems which occur in requirement elicitation and other knowledge-intensive collaboration processes.

The second area for further research is comprehensive study and analysis of existing requirement elicitation methods to evaluate how well each of them supports process participants' cognitive, emotional, and motivational processes, as well as four knowledge conversion processes: socialization, externalization, combination, and internalization.

# References

Avison, D. E., Fitzgerald, G. (2006). *Information Systems Development: Methodologies, Techniques, and Tools*, 4th Rev. edition, McGraw-Hill College, New York.

Cockburn, A., Highsmith, J. (2001). Agile Software Development: The People Factor. *IEEE Computer*, 34, 11, 131–133.

Davenport, T. H., Prusak L. (1998). *Working Knowledge*, Harvard Business School Press, Boston, MA.

Davidson, R. J., Goldsmith, H., Scherer, K. R. (Eds.) (2003). *Handbook of the Affective Sciences*, Oxford University Press, New York and Oxford.

Hoffer, J. A., George, J. F., Valacich, J. S. (2004). *Modern Systems Analysis and Design*, 4th edition, Prentice-Hall, Englewood Cliffs, NJ.

Isen, A. M., Daubman, K. A., Nowicki, G. P. (1987). Positive affect facilitates creative problem solving. *Journal of Personality and Social Psychology*, 52, 1122–1131.

Kirikova, M. (2004). Interplay of tacit and explicit knowledge in Requirements Engineering. In H. Fujita and V. Gruhn (Eds.), *New Trends in Software Methodologies, Tools and Techniques: Proceedings of the Third SoMet_W04*, IOS, pp. 77–86.

Li, K., Dewar, R. G., Pooley, R. J. (2005). Computer-assisted and customer-oriented requirements elicitation. In Proceedings of the *13th IEEE International Conference on Requirements Engineering* (RE'05), pp. 479–480.

Meredith, R., May, D., Piorun, J. (2000). Looking at Knowledge in Three Dimensions: An Holistic Approach to DSS Through Knowledge Management. Monashh DSS Lab Publication, http://dsslab.sims.monash.edu.au

Nonaka, I., Takeuchi, H. (1995). *The Knowledge-Creating Company*, Oxford University Press, New York.

Ortner, J. (2002). Knowledge in an electronic world? In D. Karagiannis and U. Reimer (Eds.), *Practical Aspects of Knowledge Management, 4th International Conference*, Vienna, Austria, December 2002, Proceedings, pp. 281–300.

Picard, R. W. (1997). *Affective Computing*, The MIT Press, Cambridge, MA.

Polanyi, M. (1964). *Personal Knowledge: Towards a Post-critical Philosophy*, Harper & Row, Evanston, New York.

Richter-von Hagen, C., Ratz, D., Povalej, R. (2005). Towards self-organizing knowledge intensive processes. *Journal of Universal Knowledge Management*, 2, 148–169.

Sloman, A. (2001). Beyond shallow models of emotion. *Cognitive Processing*, 2(1), 178–198.

Sommerville, I. (2004). *Software Engineering*, 7th edition, Pearson/Addison-Wesley, New York.

Sun, R. (Ed.) (2006). *Cognition and Multi-Agent Interaction*, Cambridge University Press, New York.

Sutcliffe, A. (2002). *User-Centred Requirements Engineering Theory and Practice*, Springer, Berlin.

# Contextual Inquiry and Requirements Shaping

Peter M. Bednar[1,2] and Christine Welch[3]

[1]School of Computing, University of Portsmouth, & Lund University, Department of Informatics, peter.bednar@port.ac.uk

[2]Department of Informatics, Lund University, peter.bednar@ics.lu.se

[3]Department of Strategy and Business Systems, University of Portsmouth, christine.welch@port.ac.uk

**Abstract**  A primary purpose of traditional systems analysis is seen as 'capture' or 'elicitation' of user requirements, in order to produce specifications as a basis for information systems design. Such a view presupposes that user requirements are pre-existing, and that the particular 'users' concerned know what they are, and can therefore articulate them. We argue that these assumptions cannot be taken for granted. If a system is to be created which is useful to particular individuals, we suggest they need to take ownership and control of the analysis themselves. By exploring their own experiences, aspirations and sense-making processes in the context of their problem space, they enable richer and more comprehensive understandings to emerge. A creative process of requirements shaping is then promoted. Our focus, therefore, moves away from problem description by an external analyst, towards contextual inquiry, which supports creative thinking and problem redefinition by those individuals most affected. We discuss contextual inquiry and requirements shaping to facilitate exploration of multiple, simultaneous and dynamic roles of the same autonomous individuals, separately and collectively. Their purpose is to enable emergence of reflective, shifting perspectives, leading to deepened understandings of problem experiences. It is then possible for resolutions to be created that address experiences, rather than descriptions, of problems.

## 1 Introduction

As information systems (IS) are now fundamental to the activities of people in organizations, both in business and other walks of life, the ways in which they are planned and created is a subject worthy of a careful consideration. The theme of this study is systems analysis and its role in supporting requirements shaping. This forms a basis for design of systems which are useful to the particular individuals who engage with them in their work or everyday lives. A primary purpose of traditional systems analysis may be seen as 'capture' or 'elicitation' of user requirements,

C. Barry et al. (eds.), *Information Systems Development: Challenges in Practice, Theory, and Education, Vol.1*, doi: 10.1007/978-0-387-68772-8_18,

to produce a specification upon which IS design may be based (Avison and Fitzgerald, 2005). Such a view presupposes that user requiremetns are pre-existing. It suggests that the particular 'users' concerned ultimately know what their requirements are, and can therefore be helped to articulate them by an expert analyst or requirements engineer. We argue that none of these assumptions can be taken for granted. Instead, the assumptions guiding the ideas presented in this chapter are related to a move from the general to the specific (from the standardized to the unique). People engaged in the activities of organizational life, continually create and apply 'knowledge' relevant to their work. It is important to consider different ways in which a person 'knows' something. Some 'knowledge' is explicit and it is possible for one person to attempt to communicate it to another, e.g. I might give someone directions from the car park to a particular building. Other things are known at a less accessible level, e.g. I know how to drive a car, but I could not tell another person exactly how to do it – I could only demonstrate my skill. There are still further aspects of our knowing which are not accessible even to ourselves – things we are not aware that we know, which only become accessible through experience or perhaps by experiment (Nonaka, 1991; Polyani, 1966). If an expert analyst simply asks a person to describe the requirements of her job, this may reveal those aspects of which the person is explicitly aware. Observation and questioning can reveal some of her implicit knowledge of the way she performs certain tasks but a description which is at best imperfect is likely to result. At their best, traditional methods for requirements analysis enable people to transform their implicit knowledge into explicit knowledge, in order to produce a 'useful' description of requirements for a system. If it is possible to use methods which go beyond this, to enable individuals to explore multiple experiences of dynamic roles, and tease out a range of shifting, reflective perspectives (requirements shaping), then they may go further. In seeking to explore experience, rather than to describe a problem space, tacit as well as implicit knowledge may be supported to emerge. When designed systems are not perceived as useful this may result from lack of analysis, or less-than-comprehensive analysis. No analysis aimed at mere description of a problem space is likely to form a basis for creation of systems that will fully satisfy their users. One aim of analysis is to uncover what is not known. This in itself cannot suffice, however, without opportunities to reflect and evaluate what emerges. Individuals need opportunities to explore multiple, simultaneous and dynamic roles, and consequent differing perspectives, in their experiences of a problem space (Bednar, 2007; Minati, 2006). This is an active process of 'knowledge' (re)creation, and not a discovery of something existing. Problems which arise in organizational life tend to be complex. Many different dimensions impact on one another and are difficult to disentangle when seeking for a resolution. Those engaged in analysis can become discouraged in the face of complexity and to wish to find ways to simplify problem spaces. As Ciborra (2002) points out, there is a tendency for IS developers to ignore the role of human choice behind exploitation of technical artifacts, and to use common methods to tackle technical and human dimensions of a design space. We propose to 'complexify' analytical approaches. It is recognized in cybernetics that every distinct dimension of a complex system needs to be controlled in a way which is appropriate to its characteristics (Ashby's law of requisite variety). It is easy to see that a car with brakes but no steering wheel would be difficult to drive – direction and speed each needing appropriate controls (Ashby, 1964). By analogy, every dimension of a complex problem space needs to be addressed with an appropriate analytical approach. This does not necessarily mean that we need a multiplicity of tools and techniques, but we do need to exercise our human ingenuity to reflect and adapt methods available to us in order to address complex problem spaces (Ciborra, 2002). We need to engage in what Bateson (1972) calls 'second order' reflection in relation to professional IS development practice. We believe that it is possible to analyse, design and implement information systems to support organizational needs and processes. In order to achieve this vision, it is necessary to pursue development of methods for analysis as part of IS development. Fundamental to these ideas is a belief that the particular individuals involved in a problem situation requiring resolution should own and control the process of inquiry (Friis, 1991). Only then can design of systems perceived by them to be useful become possible. The contribution of this study is to explore the idea of requirements shaping through contextual inquiry. We also briefly introduce a methodology for such inquiries, the Strategic Systemic Thinking Framework (Bednar, 2000).

## 2 Requirements Shaping

Researchers and practitioners are faced with a growth not only of new technologies and resulting new communication media, but also with an unprecedented surfacing of hybrid cultures and communities of practice (Klein, 2004). This has an impact on our understandings of the interrelated processes occurring in IS development in practice. The multiple perspectives within this field are creating new and interesting challenges. One particular area which poses such a challenge is systems analysis. Human behaviour and interaction, communication processes and individual and collective sense-making approaches all provide legitimate concerns for analysis. However, in practice, attention is often confined to technological concerns and descriptions of task-based activities (e.g. socio-technical design). The acquisition of new IT systems or capabilities by an organization is necessarily preceded by, and intertwined with, a set of activities in which the organization develops an understanding of its current state, its goals, and the possible costs and benefits relating to this innovation. We refer to this process as 'Requirements Shaping'. In software engineering, the term 'requirements capture' is used (Sommerville, 2004) to describe creation and modification of documents for use in contractual negotiations related to design and delivery of ICT (requirements specifications). Such practices of 'requirements capture' are not our primary focus. The term 'requirements analysis' may incorporate all the activities we hope to denote when we use the term 'requirement shaping'. For example, analysis using the Soft Systems Methodology (Checkland, 1999) begins from the assumption that there is a 'problem situation' rather than a known problem to be solved, and inquires into both the situation and possible actions within that situation. However, 'requirements analysis' may also imply that some 'requirements' are pre-existing and, hence, available to be 'found' or 'elicited'. In coining the term 'requirements shaping' we seek to avoid this narrow interpretation of requirements analysis. Analysis using participatory approaches, e.g. ETHICS (Mumford, 1995) or SSM (Checkland, 1999), does not always support requirements shaping effectively, due to problems of decontextualization. Efforts to explore a problem space must focus on questions of emergence (De Zeeuw, 2007; Bednar, 2007). Ways in which a problem is defined and redefined when perspectives shift will influence conceptualization and ultimately any proposed solutions. In our view, contextual inquiry forms an agenda for analysis in which individual perspectives can emerge and play a role in a creative process of requirements shaping (see Table 1).

**Table 1.** Nature of inquiry

|  | Decontextualized | Contextualized |
|---|---|---|
| Overview | External analyst supports users in carrying out their problem definition | External analyst supports actors in becoming analysts themselves |
| Characteristics | Danger that solutions will be sought to problems described (pre-defined), not necessarily problems experienced by users | Possibility for actors to take ownership of the analysis. Solutions sought based on problems as experienced by actors |

Research into the success of IS/IT projects (e.g. Caldeira and Ward, 2003) illustrates the importance of problem ownership in relation to IS/IT projects in business organizations. In this research, senior managers in a range of businesses were asked about their perceptions of realized benefits from IT projects. Greatest satisfaction was expressed in those firms where IS competence was regarded as an integral part of managing a business. In those firms where IT was seen as a separate function, owned and controlled by IT professionals, and servicing the business, satisfaction with the outcome of projects was considerably reduced. If organizations are to be enabled to develop their IS 'capability', collaborative approaches to IS development are indispensable. We view IS development as one special case of intentional, beneficial change in a human activity system (see Checkland, 1999). Writing specifically in the field of software engineering, Sommerville (2004) asserts:

*"... human, social and organizational factors are often critical in determining whether or not a system successfully meets its objectives. Unfortunately, predicting their effects on systems is very difficult for engineers who have little experience of social or cultural studies ... .if the designers of a system do not understand that different parts of an organization may actually have conflicting objectives, then any organization-wide system that is developed will inevitably have some dissatisfied users."* p. 35

# 3 Contextual Analysis

The pervasive nature of IS in organizational life has led to a blurring of traditional boundaries between system development practice and organizational or business development. We also note that many smaller organizations are unlikely to have access to services of professional system analysts, management consultants or requirement engineers. They may often depend for advice upon the organization responsible for the supply and implementation of technical systems, often limited to delivery of a combined hard- and software 'solution'. Such an arrangement puts the whole burden of responsibility of system analysis, system planning and requirements analysis on the client organization itself. However, the impact of implementing new technologies on organizational development could be quite significant. Hence, a high standard of systems analysis, uncovering needs and expectations which members of the organization have from the proposed system, is crucial. Evidence exists to suggest that an effective inquiry into the fit between an IS process and a business process in a specific organization could make or break the business (Fincham, 2002; Markus and Robey, 2004). We should not underestimate the importance of organizational analysis, to make sense of possible business process enhancements that could be supported by new technologies (Child, 1984). Furthermore, the increasing importance of IS implementation practices for the political and social arenas that constitute organizations must be considered. If these inquiries are confined to a superficial examination of goals, tasks and decisions, the results may be very unsatisfactory. Inquiry into opinions and sense-making processes, relating to a multitude of issues in the organizational arena forming the context of IS development, can be seen as crucial to successful IS development practice (Walsham, 1993). Accelerating pace and complexity of activities in a global economy have, in recent decades, led to a growth in pressure for faster exploitation of new information and communication technologies (ICTs). Such pressures put new demands on organizational and business processes for the planning and acquisition of information technologies. The coming of the Internet, and the growth in international networks, both technological and organizational, have brought with them new demands for technologies to support organizational business activities, from managing client relationships to strategic planning, decision making and management of 'knowledge'. As ICTs become more and more advanced and pervasive in organizational life, their successful implementation becomes even more crucial to the survival of the organization. In several methodologies (for instance, SSADM and DSDM inter alia) systems analysis is depicted as an early stage in the process of developing an information system (see, e.g. Sommerville, 2004). However, when considering systems analysis, a question arises – who it is intended to benefit? One perspective suggests it is the professional analyst herself, contemplating the task of designing an information system for someone else. This puts the analyst into a central role in the process of development. A further question then arises as to the purpose of analysis. If its aim is to enhance understanding of the problem space, who is supposed to create a better understanding, and of what? An information system may be defined as one whose purpose is to support individual people in their efforts to inform themselves or others in relation to their affairs. We wish to look differently at the supposed audience for IS analysis methods, and their place in the overall progress of development. Experience suggests that expert-dominated (and/or man-agement-imposed) solutions to information problems may not always be 'bought into' by the users, because they may find that the systems produced are not rele-vant to support them in their professional activities. This has led researchers to be-lieve that it may be worthwhile to involve the users themselves in co-creation of systems. Client-led design (Stowell and West, 1995; Friis, 1991), or participatory techniques, such as the ETHICS methodology (Mumford, 1995), have resulted. However, in a client-led or participatory approach, focus is often placed on a communication gap. It is assumed that users do not necessarily know their own re-quirements well enough to communicate them effectively to an analyst/developer. Techniques to bridge this perceived gap are seen to be needed – to enable the us-ers to articulate their needs and the developers to appreciate fully what the re-quirements are so that a useful system may be produced (i.e. both functionalist and neo-humanist approaches). While efforts to overcome the communication gap are important to take further, this view still fails to address sufficiently the contextu-ally dependent dimensions of complexity. It is not simply that the users are unable to articulate their pre-existing requirements, and therefore need a developed lan-guage and tools. First, they must be able to create an understanding of what those requirements might be, in relation to a problem space which represents their ex-perience of working life. It is not a process of requirements capture or require-ments specification, but one of requirements shaping for creation of understand-ing. Support for this creative process is vital to any vision of useful systems. We suggest a collaborative approach to development in which analytical efforts con-tinue throughout the process. Those individuals who will use the systems to be designed must own and control the analysis, supported by professional facilitators, in order to be able to explore their understandings of their experiences. A need to focus on the individual was recognized as long ago as the 1960s, when Langefors started to develop the 'infological equation' (Langefors, 1966). This served to highlight the significance of interpretations made by unique individuals within specific organizational contexts. During the early 1980s, some researchers (e.g. Olerup, 1982) focused on organizational contingencies and contexts. Others (e.g. Sandstrom, 1985; Flensburg, 1986; Mumford, 1983; Hirschheim and Klein, 1994) paid attention to interpretations in local contexts of individuals and groups. In work on continuous development and prototyping, contextual analysis was related to individuals, groups and teams (Agner Sigbo and Ingman, 1992; Friis, 1991). Team learning in participative design was introduced by Hagerfors (1994). Some researchers focus on business managers as 'users' (e.g. Carlsson, 1993). Others relate to national and political contexts (e.g. Baark, 1986). Ciborra, who also recognized the difficulty to address individual uniqueness in relation to complexity, turned to Heidegger for inspiration (e.g. Ciborra, 2001). Contemporary approaches to contextual analysis (e.g. Bednar, 2000) aim to apply specially adapted methods to study how people construct understanding and meaning, and how information needs and information use, are created by individuals within this process. The concept of contextual dependency is of interest because it supports a focus of inquiry on unique individuals, and their beliefs, thoughts and actions, in specific situations and contexts. This kind of inquiry is intended to provide support to individuals in a contextually dependent creation of necessary knowledge. This in turn enables successful communication, analysis and, eventually, IS development to occur. A contextual approach to analysis is intended to focus on a user-oriented perspective. Put simply, an inquiry might focus on what Organization A wants to achieve with its information and communication system. However, inquiry based on contextual analysis, asks instead what the individual users want to achieve, and what roles and specific purposes their activities in organizational contexts might have. What makes their unique situation recognizable? What specific role do they give to information within the organization's business? The inquiry therefore focuses on user assumptions and needs within the space of an open information system (an 'organization'). This takes a bottom-up perspective on information and communication systems, i.e. systems that are shaped with the intention to serve specific organizational actors and their needs. Contextual inquiry, which tries to take contextual dependencies into consideration when systems are to be designed, is a response escalation in complexity in organizational life.

# 4 Contextual Inquiry

Contextual inquiry is an exploration into the nature of open systems thinking and how systemic identities are maintained and generated within a specific context. Analysis involves a professional analyst's activities and specific use of methodologies, rhetoric and strategies to construct local arguments and findings. By the end of an initial study, an analyst might become familiar with some of the major strategies currently available (within a targeted organization) for further inquiries into contextual dependencies. The nature of 'inquiry' is problematic. What are the boundaries of a particular inquiry? What are the characteristics of that inquiry? In order to facilitate requirements shaping, we need to approach boundary setting carefully. Support for this may be found for instance in work by Ciborra. Writing of the process of developing large scale infrastructures, he said:

*'The message emanating from this… can be captured in a nutshell by stating that the complex process of 'wiring the corporation' cannot be understood let alone managed by applying approaches that were effective for mechanical organizations and assembly line type of technologies and processes'* (Ciborra and Hanseth, 2000, p. 2).

Not only do we not always know the answers to our inquiries, but very often the problems themselves need to be reframed before we can know what questions to ask. The boundaries of a problem space require consideration and critical reflection since observation varies with the stance of the observer. Any particular observer has both the duty and the privilege to make judgements regarding the boundaries of the problem space according to her own perspectives (Ulrich, 2001; Maturana and Varela, 1980). In contextual inquiry, we are concerned with a double hermeneutic cycle since we attempt to make sense of a problem space populated by people who are themselves autonomous sense-making agents. A discussion of this phenomenon may be found in Klein (2004).The first cycle is that found in all processes of human inquiry, including those of the natural sciences, where personal sense making is harnessed to interpret phenomena. The second cycle arises when personal sense making is engaged to interpret social phenomena. Here, subjects of the inquiry include other human beings, who are themselves autonomous sense-making agents. There is a need to consider their sense-making processes as part of the inquiry, which adds a further level of complexity to the investigation. Consider the word 'artifact' as it relates to IS. As pointed out by Saur (1993), information systems consist of a great deal more than simply artifacts:

*'Economic task, organizational, human relations/labour process and technical perspectives are all involved'* (Saur, 1993, p. 10).

The term is problematic to the questions we would wish people to ask in their requirements shaping. Human individuals communicate with intention (see Habermas, 1984). Communication and intention is context-dependent and interpretation of context continually changes over time. This influences sense-making and communication efforts (see Wittgenstein's later work and his discussion of language games). Constant change of interpretation, and consequently of perceived meaning, (i.e. information) was highlighted by Langefors (1966) in the infological equation. We are concerned with phenomenology and hermeneutics – human consciousness. Husserl (1954) considered that structured organizing human consciousness cannot be explained in terms of generalizations learned from experience, but are presumed by experience. Thus they form the basis of an individual's 'life-world'. Gadamer (1987) developed this concept of life-world to point out individuals' submergence in the constantly changing context of their experiences. Individuals are embedded within their historical culture through the interdependence of language and context which cannot be transcended. According to Gadamer we interpret our world through language which is at the same time a part of our life-world. From a perspective of hermeneutic dialectic sense making is an act of creation not just interpretation. There is a continual exchange/interchange between an individual's pre-understanding and experience. A dialectic emerges in such interactions because each individual is concurrently interacting with others (Hermeneutic Dialectics). At the level of scene-setting we agree with Berger and Luckman (1966) that individuals construct their own views of reality by interpretation of experience. Going beyond this we emphasize the importance of boundary setting through critical reflection to include the need to consider the second hermeneutic cycle. One vehicle for contextual analysis is the Strategic Systemic Thinking framework (Bednar, 2000). Actors participating in this, in support of requirement shaping, develop individual narratives which are then classified and categorized. Actors also develop their sense making about those narratives through language games (see Wittgenstein, 1958). The language game is the process which shapes a clustering exercise, by which actors categorize their narratives.

As a result, participants create an understanding of similarities and differences between narrative clusters. A language of categories is created through language games. The intention is to create some foundation for a common language (see Habermas, 1984), built up through interaction in the form of language games. A living language is interpreted; meaning it is not part of the language itself.

Contextual inquiry using the SST framework can be undertaken as follows:

1. Through language games, clusters of narratives are developed.
2. Every narrative is discussed by every actor.
3. Every narrative is compared and elaborated upon in relation to previously discussed narratives.
4. Both the discussion and its content include the level of abstraction.
5. Understanding is developed through negotiation and interaction, language is also developed through interaction.

Language and meaning making constantly change through negotiation in a double hermeneutic circle. Contextual inquiry becomes a voyage of discovery and creation of new understandings. This supports breaking away from prejudice and brings about a shift in the dominant paradigm within which sense making takes place. Kuhn recognized that perception of progress is almost inevitable as those espousing a 'winning' paradigm will not encourage further interest or attention to the work of defeated rivals.

*"Why should progress also be the apparently universal concomitant of scientific revolutions? Once again, there is much to be learned by asking what else the result of a revolution could be. Revolutions close with a total victory for one of the two opposing camps. Will that group ever say that the result of its victory has been something less than progress? That would be rather like admitting that they had been wrong and their opponents right. To them, at least, the outcome of revolution must be progress, and they are in an excellent position to make certain that future members of their community will see past history in the same way."* (Kuhn, 1996, p. 166)

Returns to earlier paradigms are possible, but are likely to be patchy (e.g. The Flat Earth Society denying modern ideas of geography, or the Seventh Day Adventist Church objecting to the Theory of Evolution) or derived from a longer-term view in which further evidence is available to confront the prevailing paradigm. We do not suggest that contextual inquiry will inevitably lead to 'good decisions'. The purpose in undertaking contextual inquiry is to provide a richer information base upon which decisions could be made for better or worse.

# 5 Conclusions

This study focuses on a process of requirement shaping through contextual inquiry, carried out by the organizational actors themselves. The scope of such inquiry does not just focus on data and processes, but on a phenomenon of processes that is human interaction. Analysts conducting contextual inquiry into requirements shaping also have an opportunity to recognize individual emergence through a hermeneutic dialectic. The concept of a 'network of actors' is relevant for us to consider. If an information system is seen as an artifact, consisting of linked elements (including people) making up a greater whole, then complexity is ironed out, as the individuals become invisible to the inquirer. However, if an information system is seen as a network of human actors, interacting and communicating using available means (including technological artifacts), then complexity is recognized through the individual sense-making processes of each actor. The 'system' is something which emerges from interactions among individuals. An essential feature of contextual inquiry is framing of problem spaces (see Orlikowski, 1994) and boundary critique (Ulrich, 2001). These are responsibilities of individual analysts, i.e. owners of problem spaces. Boundaries change through many dimensions of experience of the nature of problem spaces. In this chapter, requirements shaping is distinguished from other related concepts, such as requirements elicitation or specification. Arguments are presented in favour of requirements shaping and its relevance for effective systems analysis. Finally, a case is made that it is important for individuals involved in a problem space to take ownership and control of their own analysis, with support from an external analyst.

# References

Agner Sigbo G., Ingman S. (1992). Sjalvstyre och flexibilitet drivkrafter vid kontinuerlig systemutveckling. Uppsala: Arbetsmiljofonden & NUTEK, Ord & Form AB.

Ashby, R. (1964). An Introduction to Cybernetics. Methuen: London.

Avison, D. E., Fitzgerald, G. (2005). Information Systems Development: Methodologies, Techniques and Tools, McGraw-Hill: Maidenhead, 2nd edition.

Baark, E. (1986). The Context of National Information Systems in Developing Countries: India and China in a Comparative Perspective. Research Policy Institute, Lund University.

Bateson, G. (1972). Steps to an Ecology of Mind. Ballantine: New York.

Bednar, P. M. (2000). A contextual integration of individual and organizational learning perspectives as part of IS analysis. Informing Science, 3 (3).

Bednar, P. M. (2007). Individual emergence in contextual analysis. Special Issue on Individual Emergence, Systemica (Journal of the Dutch Systems Group), 14 (1–6) 23–38.

Berger, P. L., Luckman, T. (1966). The Social Construction of Reality: A Treatise in the Sociology of Knowledge. Anchor Books: Garden City, NY.

Caldeira, M. M., Ward, J. M. (2003). Using Resource-based Theory to interpret the successful adoption and use of information systems and technology in manufacturing SMEs. European Journal of Information Systems, 12, 127–141.

Carlsson, S. (1993). A Longitudinal Study of User Developed Decision Support Systems. Department of Informatics, Lund University, Lund.

Checkland, P. (1999). Systems Thinking, Systems Practice: A 30-Year Retrospective. Wiley: Chichester.

Child, J. (1984). Organization: A Guide to Problems and Practice. Paul Chapman: London.

Ciborra, C. U. (2002). The Labyrinths of Information. Oxford University Press: Oxford.

Ciborra, C. U., Hanseth, O. (2000). Introduction: From control to drift. In C. Ciborra et al. (editors), From Control to Drift: The Dynamics of Corporate Information Infrastructures. Oxford University Press: Oxford.

De Zeeuw, G. (2007). Foreword to Special Issue on Individual Emergence, *Systemica (Journal of the Dutch Systems Group)*, 14 (1–6) ix–xi.

Fincham, R. (2002). Narratives of success and failure in systems development, British Journal of Management, 13, 1–14 (British Academy of Management)

Flensburg, P. (1986). Personlig databehandling – introduktion, konsekvenser, mojligheter. Chartwell-Bratt and Studentlitteratur; Lund.

Friis, S. (1991). User Controlled Information Systems Development – Problems and Possibilities Towards Local Design Shops. Lund University Publications.

Gadamer, H. G. (1987). The problem of historical consciousness (J. F. Close, Trans.). In P. Rabinow and W. M. Sullivan (editors), Interpretive Social Science: A Second Look, pp 82–140. University of California Press: Berkeley. (Reprinted from La probleme de la conscience historique. Louvain: Institut Superieur de Philosoophie, Universite Catholique do Louvain, 1963).

Habermas, J. (1984). The Theory of Communicative Action, Vol. 1: Reason and the Rationalization of Society. (T. McCarthy, Trans.) Beacon Press: Boston.

Hagerfors, A. (1994). Co-learning in Participative Systems Design. Department of Informatics, Lund University, Lund.

Hirschheim, R., Klein, H. K. (1994). Realizing emancipatory principles in information systems development: The case for ETHICS. *MIS Quarterly*.

Husserl, E. (1954). The Crisis of European Sciences. Northwestern University Press: Evanston, IL.

Klein, H. K. (2004). Seeking the new and the critical in critical realism: déjà vu. Information and Organization, 14, 123–144.

Kling, R. (1999). What is social Informatics and Why Does it Matter? D-Lib Magazine, 5 (1), http://www.dlib.org/. Accessed 17 November 2006.

Kuhn, T. S. (1996). The Structure of Scientific Revolutions. University of Chicago Press: Chicago, IL, 3rd edition.

Langefors, B. (1966). Theoretical Analysis of Information Systems. Studentlitteratur, Lund.

Markus, M. L., Robey, D. (2004). Why stuff happens: Explaining the unintended consequences of using IT. In K. V. Anderson and M. T. Vendelø (editors), The Past and Future of Information Systems. Elsevier: Oxford.

Maturana, H., Varela, F. (1980). Autopoeisis and Cognition. D. Reidel Publishing: Dordrecht.

Minati, G. (2006). Multiple systems, collective beings, and the dynamic usage of models. The Systemist, 28 (2), 200–212.

Mumford, E. (1983). Designing Human Systems for New Technology: The ETHICS Method. Manchester Business School.

Mumford, E. (1995). Effective Systems Design and Requirements Analysis: The ETHICS approach. Macmillan Press: Basingstoke.

Nonaka, I. (1991). The Knowledge-Creating Company. Harvard Business Review: pp 96–104.

Olerup, A. (1982). A Contextual Framework for computerized Information Systems, Nyt Nordisk Forlag Arnold Busk: Copenhagen.

Orlikowski, W. J. (1994). Technological frames: Making sense of information technology in organizations. ACM Transactions on Information Systems, 12 (2) 174–207.

Polyani, M. (1966). The Tacit Dimension. Routledge & Kegan Paul: London.

Sandstrom, G. (1985). Towards Transparent Data Bases – How to Interpret and Act on Expressions Mediated by Computerized Information Systems. Chartwell-Bratt & Studentlitteratur.

Saur, C. (1993). Why Systems Fail. Alfred Waller: Henley-on-Thames.

Sommerville, I. (2004). Software Engineering. Addison Wesley: Reading, MA, 7th edition.

Stowell, F. A., West, D. (1995). Client-Led Design: A Systemic Approach to Information System Definition. McGraw-Hill: Maidenhead.

Ulrich, W. (2001). Critically systemic discourse: A discursive approach to reflective practice in ISD, Parts 1 and 3. The Journal of Information Technology Theory and Application (JITTA), 3 (3), 55–106.

Walsham, G. (1993). Interpreting Information Systems in Organizations. Wiley: Chichester.

Wittgenstein, L. (1958). Philosophical Investigations. Basil Blackwell: Oxford.

# Building a Process Performance Model for Business Activity Monitoring

Claire Costello and Owen Molloy

Department of Information Technology, National University of Ireland, Galway
{c.costello | owen.molloy}@nuigalway.ie

**Abstract**  A formal business process model serves as a common understanding of how business tasks are carried out to achieve end goals. The business process life cycle is managed using Business Process Management tools and methodologies. Business Activity Monitoring provides (near) real-time visibility into process execution notifying relevant personnel of process exceptions. Business process modelling captures business and execution semantics, but lacks any foundation for process analysis. This chapter will outline a model for process performance management for use in the monitoring phase of the process life cycle and how this model is leveraged within the iWISE architecture. iWISE provides a single view of business processes spanning disparate systems and departments.

## 1 Introduction and Motivations

Traditionally, reporting and Business Intelligence systems rely on the details of workflow logs and separate, standalone modules to support process reporting. Mendling and Neumann (2005) provide a comparison of current process modelling languages with respect to common modelling aspects. WfMC's XML Process Description Language (XPDL) emerges as the only language of fifteen candidate languages that supports the gathering of statistical data useful for simulation analysis of business processes. There is a need to integrate the development and definition of a process with associated past and expected performance measures. This chapter presents a process model that combines event and other process performance information to allow (near) real-time process monitoring and alert generation.

The remainder of this study is organized as follows. Sect. 2 describes the background for this research and provides a context for Business Process Management (BPM) and Business Activity Monitoring (BAM). Process modelling and definition languages are also summarized along with a review of some related process monitoring research. Section 4 and Section 5 present the model used as part of this work, whilst Sect. 6 presents the iWISE architecture which uses this model.

C. Barry et al. (eds.), *Information Systems Development: Challenges in Practice, Theory, and Education, Vol.1*, doi: 10.1007/978-0-387-68772-8_19,
© Springer Science+Business Media, LLC 2009

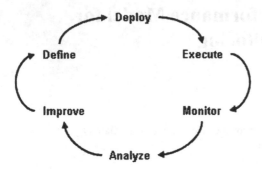

**Fig. 1.** Typical phases of the process life cycle

## 2 Background

Business Process Management can be defined as 'supporting business processes using methods, techniques and software to design, enact, control and analyse operational processes involving humans, organizations, applications, documents and other sources of information' (van der Aalst et al., 2003). A BPM system (BPMS) is an integrated software platform that allows for full management of the process life cycle. Managing process performance is paramount to business effectiveness. Melchert et al. (2004) view Process Performance Management (PPM) as a method for 'collecting and reconciling all operational data related to a certain business process' to identify areas for process improvement. Neely (2004) defines a performance measure as a metric used to quantify the efficiency and/or effectiveness of an action. The terms 'metric' and 'key performance indicator' (KPI) are also used when discussing process performance.

### 2.1 Business Process Life Cycle Management

A business process has many phases and constitutes what is widely accepted as the *process life cycle* (zur Muehlen and Rosemann, 2004; van der Aalst et al., 2003). The life cycle is depicted in Fig. 1 as a closed loop of activities. A process model is captured during the *define* phase. Once modelled, a process model is transformed into an executable model ready for *deployment* on process execution architectures. Once deployed, a process is ready to be *executed*. As a process instance is executing, a *monitoring* module will track its execution against predefined metrics and generate exceptions if necessary. The *analysis* phase may use complex statistical techniques to analyse process execution data and metrics to identify any unwanted trends in the process. Using this information, *improvements* can be made which lead back to the define phase where the cycle begins once more. This closed loop for process management is similar to the Define, Manage, Analyse, Improve and Control (DMAIC) model of the Six Sigma approach to process improvement (Smith, 1993).

## 2.2 Process Modelling and Definition Languages

The current set of standards for process management complement the process life cycle depicted in Fig. 1 Process modelling languages (PMLs) specify a notation and include the Unified Modelling Language (UML), Business Process Modelling Notation (BPMN) and Business Process Definition Metamodel (BPDM). Process execution or definition languages (PELs/PDLs) are specifications which contain semantics understood by process execution engines. Prominent process execution languages include Business Process Execution Language (BPEL), Business Process Modelling Language (BPML) and the XML Process Definition Language. The Event-driven Process Chain (EPC) modelling notation contains symbols for functions, events and control flow points. An EPC model does not have a corresponding machine representation.

Rather than separate the process modelling and monitoring phases using different underlying models, this research builds a process model inclusive of fields for metric calculations, in particular, cycle time performance measures. Further enhancements will include the specification of business parameters defined at the process definition phase. The use of a single model will also enable portability of process definitions between various software modules regardless of what phase in the life cycle they apply to.

## 2.3 Business Activity Monitoring

Business activity monitoring (BAM) is a term coined by The Gartner Group. BAM seeks to 'provide real-time access to critical business performance indicators to improve the speed and effectiveness of business operations. Unlike traditional real-time monitoring, BAM draws its information from multiple application systems and other internal and external (inter-enterprise) sources, enabling a broader and richer view of business activities' (McCoy, 2002).

The key term in this definition is *real time*. BI approaches take a historical perspective providing information retrospective to the time when important events may have occurred. In contrast, BAM is event-driven and provides quick-time visibility by capturing events from operational IT infrastructure. *Decision latency* is the length of time between the point when an important event occurs during operations processing and when a decision should be made to correct any anomalous behaviour. To decrease decision latency and therefore increase responsiveness to changing conditions, organizations need BAM software that will provide real-time visibility into their key operations. A BAM system must be able to detect enterprise events, integrate event and contextual information on-the-fly and provide intuitive interfaces for rules and metrics (Nesamoney, 2004).

## 3 Related Research

Thomas et al. (2005) describe a loosely coupled architecture overlaid upon a business process expressed in a PEL such as BPEL. The architecture is agent-based and uses the Web Ontology Language (OWL) for describing performance criteria for business processes and individual activities, but does not show how to model the metric itself or how the parameters of a metric are mapped from operational business data.

A Web service-based intelligent Decision Support System called the 'Solution Manager Service' is described in McGregor et al. (2006). The contribution here focuses on the ability to monitor Web service executions which is important given that many process modelling and definition languages are based on Web services.

Haller and Oren (2006) describe an 'intermediate ontology' that will act as a common mapping mechanism between the various internal and external process formats used by business systems. However, the *measurement aspect* of a process is omitted by this ontology and other workflow and process modelling and definition languages (Mendling and Neumann, 2005; Thomas et al., 2005).

McGregor (2002) suggests an amendment to the WfMC reference model that incorporates business performance monitoring information for use with the Balanced Scorecard (BSC) approach to business performance management.

Although the works mentioned here outline various frameworks for process performance monitoring and management, they do not detail a process model that explicitly contains the elements for aiding process monitoring activities in (near) real time. In addition, since a process model is captured at the define phase (see Fig. 1), then a user should also be able to express important business parameter thresholds or control limits such as target cycle time or expected utilization level. The proposition of this research is that performance metrics and relevant metric thresholds should be incorporated into the process model.

## 4 Modelling Process Performance Information

The process model developed uses XML as its internal representation. The major elements of the model are discussed in this section. The section also details an ontology representation of the concepts required to capture process performance information.

### 4.1 Model

At a diagram level, a model contains processes. The XML Schema for a model is shown in Fig. 2a. Important information relating to a model includes a unique modelID, name and description. An additional boolean attribute, called root, denotes a model that is the root of a model hierarchy. This attribute is necessary for efficient retrieval and reconstruction of multi-level models during both the

process capture and monitoring stages. Links between processes are expressed using transition elements. This research does not concern itself with controlling
process executions, but instead aims to model and analyse as-is processes which
may execute across many different systems. For this reason, complex control
structures such as those described in van der Aalst (2003) are not represented here.

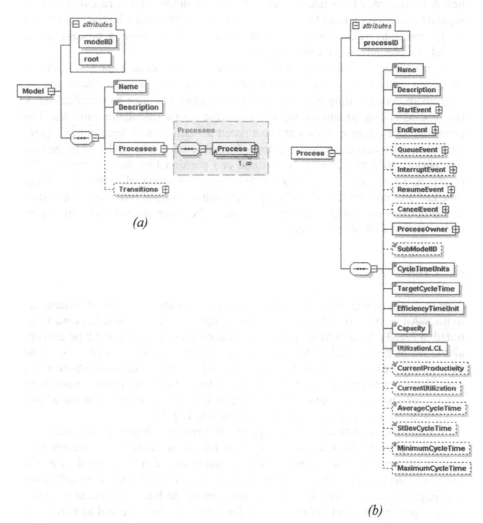

Fig. 2. Model XML Schema (a) and Process XML Schema (b)

## 4.2 Process

A process represents a business activity. The XML Schema for a process is shown
in Fig. 2b. Along with general attributes such as a unique processID, name and

description, a process is also associated with multiple event definitions. A process must contain at least a start and end event which help to identify the total processing time for a process. Each event is defined by an EventType element which is described in more detail in Sect. 4.3. A process owner must also be specified. A process owner has typical attributes such as name, email address and mobile number. A process may be defined by another level of detail. This is captured using a separate model (associated by subModelID) and is considered a level deeper in the model hierarchy. There is a one-to-one relationship between a process and a model to represent a sub-model of a process.

Some elements relate to cycle time statistics for a process. Time granularity is expressed using CycleTimeUnits, whilst TargetCycleTime is a constant for the expected processing time of a task. Both these elements must be specified when the process is defined and are inputs to runtime metric calculation modules. The remaining cycle time elements are calculated at runtime and represent an aggregate view of process execution over time. Valuable information relating to the current performance of a process is captured and preserved by these elements. Elements Capacity and EfficiencyTimeUnit must be specified at process design time and are required for calculating process utilization and productivity statistics as a process is executing. These elements described here are not included as part of any current PDL specification.

## 4.3 Event

A process containing event definitions represents an abstract view of system activities. All events are defined according to the EventType XML Schema illustrated in Fig. 3a. Similar to the model and process elements, an event type element also contains general fields for eventID, name and description. A process can be in various states such as queued, started or finished. The model supports an event classification scheme that includes six event types to model process execution: queue, start, interrupt, resume, cancel and end. Each event definition is linked to a process definition using the appropriate element in Fig. 3b.

Events have significance; they happen for a reason. Therefore, an XMLSchema element is provided to describe the expected format of business information relevant in the context of an event. This information can also be referred to as the *business object*, and its XML Schema structure is supplied during event definition. It is important to note that there is no restriction on the business content encapsulated as part of an event definition; if information can be observed as part of an event that occurs in the IT infrastructure, then it may also be defined as part of an event making it available during process analysis. In this way, business data can be linked to particular process instances through event definitions.

Events are related to each other through the process they are defined with (referred to as *event relativity*). Therefore, an event correlation technique is required such that all events related to each other are grouped together for process analysis. This is achieved using the XMLPathExpression element in Fig. 3a which specifies an XPath value from the XML Schema supplied with the event definition. At runtime, this XPath value is evaluated, based on the XML document packaged as part of the enterprise event. This value must be capable of uniquely identifying event instances for a given process definition. The same value must be present across all event definitions for each process defined within a particular model. For example, for an Order Fulfilment process model, an Order Number could be used to match start and end events for each process within the model.

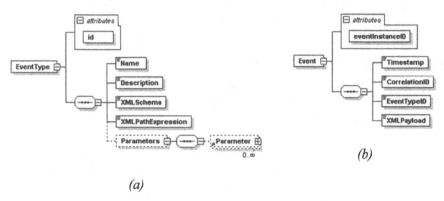

*(a)*

*(b)*

**Fig. 3.** EventType XML Schema (a) and runtime Event XML Schema (b)

Given the structure of an event definition in Fig. 3a, an event at runtime follows the structure of Fig. 3b. The eventInstanceID is assigned by the source system or listener software. The Timestamp element is the time when an event occurred as recorded by the source system. The EventTypeID relates the event to its appropriate EventType definition. The XMLPayload element is an XML document containing the business information defined by the XML Schema supplied during event definition. The CorrelationID is the value of the XMLPathExpression specified at process design time.

The recursive nature of models and processes allows a model hierarchy to be constructed. Events defined for one process must be reused at the sub-model level. In this way, a process and its associated event definitions can be seen as an aggregation of all processes and events defined at the sub-model level. Using this balancing approach, metrics for high-level processes can be derived using lower-level process and event definitions.

The model developed here links events, processes and business information to provide a comprehensive process description that includes metric thresholds and measurements. With the exception of XPDL which provides a limited set of elements for simulation activities, current process modelling standards do not provide any fields for performance metrics or measurement definitions; this is the contribution of this work.

## 5 Defining Rules for Activity Monitoring

A business rule engine (BRE) is a software component that will execute business rules against a set of facts from a given scenario. A BRE consists of a knowledge base (or rules base), a working memory of facts and an inference engine.

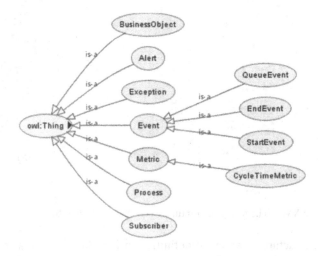

**Fig. 4.** Defining concepts for a process metric ontology

## *5.1 An Ontology for Performance Management*

Lera et al. (2006) state that it is 'impossible to make a complete ontology that embraces all existing metrics' and that the scope of the ontology will depend on the domain of interest. The model discussed earlier has a corresponding ontology representation. This ontology was developed using OWL (W3C, 2004). A straightforward mapping of the major components of the event-based model presented in the previous sections leads to the ontology in Fig. 4. This will serve as a basis for writing rules to test the current state of a process with respect to its performance thresholds.

## *5.2 SWRL for Process Exceptions*

SWRL (Horrocks et al., 2004), a W3C member submission, is a Semantic Web Rule Language combining OWL (W3C, 2004) and RuleML (RuleML, 2000). SWRL facilitates rule authoring using ontology concepts as part of rule predicates. In addition to OWL axioms, a knowledge base can now include Horn-like rules written using a logical implication between an antecedent (body) and consequent (head). Since SWRL is based on the RuleML, it inherits the RuleML rule structure.

Using the knowledge concepts discussed previously, the SWRL rule specification is used to compose IF-THEN rules to specify when exceptions arise in processes. For example, a rule might be constructed to test the value of a metric for process utilization against a pre-defined lower control limit (UtilizationLCL element in Fig. 2b). The rule given later raises an exception where a process performance metric has dropped below an acceptable lower limit. The rule is an IF-THEN rule which is true only when all predicates in the IF portion are true. Each predicate is joined using logical AND, also known as conjunction. A variable is denoted using the '?' symbol, for example, ?x and ?y are variables and are given sample values here.

**Rule definition (abstract syntax):**

**Sample Rule (with values):**

Process(?x)   ∧

IF there is a process ?x, e.g., 'analyse sample' *and*

hasBusinessObject(?x, ?b)   ∧

A process ?x 'analyse sample' has an associated business object ?b, e.g. with value 'specimen.345', *and*

hasPerformanceMetric(?x, ?y)   ∧

A process ?x 'analyse sample' has a performance metric ?y, e.g., 'utilization' *and*

hasMetricValue(?y, ?a)   ∧

A performance metric ?y 'utilization' has a particular value ?a, e.g., '85' *and*

hasLowerControlLimit(?y, ?z)   ∧

A performance metric ?y 'utilization' has a pre-defined lower limit value ?z, e.g., '92' *and*

swrlb:lessThan(?a, ?z)

The actual metric value ?a of '85' is *less than* the pre-defined lower limit value ?z of '92'

→   hasException(?x, ?b)

THEN process ?x 'analyse sample' with business object ?b 'specimen.345' is in an exception state.

From Fig. 4, the OWL classes BusinessObject, Process, Metric and Exception are used in the SWRL rule definition given here. Through definition of OWL properties, a process ?x has a business object ?b and performance metric ?y. In the sample rule, it may not be fully necessary to track the business object that has given rise to the exception, but for the sake of (near) real-time processing, current business data may be necessary for alerting purposes. The rule given here also uses the SWRL built-in lessThan. The SWRL specification includes a set of built-in predicates (SWRLB), named the 'SWRL built-ins', which includes predicates for comparisons, mathematical operations and string handling methods to name a few.

## 6 iWISE Architecture

The iWISE software facilitates management of the business process life cycle
(Costello et al., 2006). Once a process is captured and deployed, raw event
streams are correlated with relevant processes to provide monitoring software with
appropriate metrics. iWISE is a common event infrastructure that uses the event-
based process model described in Sect. 4. The iWISE software addresses each of
the phases outlined in Fig. 1 with the exception of the *execute* phase. Process execution is handled by the systems already in place within an organization. Such systems may include ERP systems or more process-oriented systems such as process
execution engines. The iWISE system does not seek to replace these systems but
leverage the system events triggered and business data created or manipulated.

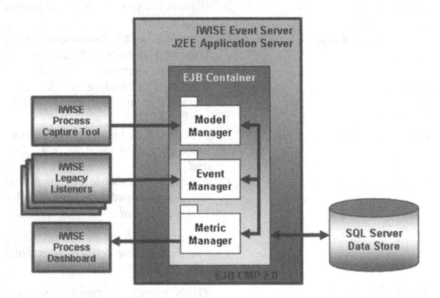

**Fig. 5.** iWISE architecture containing the iWISE Event Server as the core

The iWISE architecture is illustrated in Fig. 5. Process models are captured using the *iWISE Process Capture Tool* (PCT) which is a Microsoft Visio-based
standalone application. The PCT allows users to construct a process map and define events and metric thresholds linked to a process. The *iWISE Legacy Listener*
components are configured to detect events in IT systems. Once detected, the
events are constructed using the format in Fig. 3b and sent to the iWISE Event
Server where they are parsed and stored.

The *iWISE Event Server* is the central component responsible for managing
models, event streams and metric calculations using the three software packages
shown in Fig. 5: the Model Manager, Event Manager and Metric Manager. The
Model Manager receives process models from the iWISE PCT and compiles them
for further processing. The Event Manager component receives enterprise events

from Listeners defined in the format as specified during process capture. When raw events arrive, they are parsed and associated with the correct process. As events are processed, the Metric Manager component generates alerts based on a pre-defined set of rules. It also generates metrics on-the-fly to provide an up-to-date process view for the iWISE Process Dashboard. The *iWISE Process Dashboard* is a Microsoft portal application that provides a timely snapshot of process performance.

## 6.1 Generating Process Alerts

The iWISE Event Server Metric Manager (see Fig. 5) component detects process execution anomalies in (near) real time and structures these exceptions for further processing by Microsoft Notification Services (MSNS). Before alerts can be generated, rules must be defined, based on the model described in Sect. 4. The rules are specified using SWRL based on the ontology concepts defined in Sect. 5. The Protégé Ontology Editor is used to create both the ontology and SWRL rules to form the knowledge base required for analysing process runtime exceptions. Once specified, the rules are loaded into the Event Server for access at runtime. At runtime, a Java stateless session bean is invoked at every time interval (set in configuration properties before application deployment) to calculate various process measurements. For example, using the rule given in Sect. 5, the current process utilization level can be calculated and compared against a minimum acceptable value defined during the process design phase. The details of the process and metric are supplied to the *Bossam reasoner* (Jang and Sohn, 2004), where the SWRL rules are used to reason if the metric supplied, and therefore the process, are outside normal limits of execution. In the case of process utilization, if the current level is below a minimum level, then that process is out of bounds. When a process metric is in such an exception state, the monitoring software will supply the exception information to an SQL Server database. MSNS will detect the information and generate a notification and alert if there are any subscribers defined for the process and metric in question. The iWISE Process Dashboard contains a process alerts subscription management page to allow users to subscribe to pre-defined alerts for processes deployed within the Event Server.

## 7 Conclusions

iWISE supports process exception alerting by executing business rules against thresholds using semantic techniques. This research addresses the major functionality of a BAM system as outlined in Nesamoney (2004). Most important is the process-aware nature of the iWISE framework and underlying model that incorporates a performance aspect into its structure. Current work is focussing on the extension of the event model to cater for business parameter definitions not related to cycle time to allow calculation of Six Sigma type metrics on a constant basis. Further discussion can be found in Costello et al. (2005). The use of business rules to monitor process performance is novel compared with the retrospective nature of BI techniques.

# References

Costello, C., Molloy, O., Duggan, J., and Lyons, G. (2005). Using Event-Based Process Modelling to Support Six Sigma Quality. In *Sixteenth International Workshop on Database and Expert Systems Applications (DEXA)*, Copenhagen, Demark, 22–26 August.

Costello, C., Fleming, W., Molloy, O., Duggan, J., and Lyons, G. (2006). iWISE: A Framework for Providing Distributed Process Visibility Using an Event-Based Process Modelling Approach. In *Eighth International Conference on Enterprise Information Systems (ICEIS)*, Paphos, Cyprus, 23–27 May.

Haller, A. and Oren, E. (2006). A Process Ontology to Represent Semantics of Different Process and Choreography Meta-Models, http://www.m3pe.org/deliverables/process-ontology.pdf.

Horrocks, I., Patel-Schneider, P. F., Boley, H., Tabet, S., Grosof, B., and Dean, M. (2004). SWRL: A Semantic Web Rule Language Combining OWL and RuleML, http://www.w3.org/Submission/SWRL/.

Jang, M. and Sohn, J.-C. (2004). Bossam: An Extended Rule Engine for OWL Inferencing. In *Rules and Rule Markup Languages for the Semantic Web. Third International Workshop, RuleML 2004*, Hiroshima, Japan, 8 November.

Lera, I., Juiz, C., and Puigjaner, R. (2006). Performance-related Ontologies for Ubiquitous Intelligence Based on Semantic Web Applications. In *AINA '06: Proceedings of 20th International Conference on Advanced Information Networking and Applications*, Vienna, Austria, 18–20 April.

McCoy, D. (2002). Business Activity Monitoring: Calm Before the Storm, http://www.gartner.com.

McGregor, C. (2002). The Impact of Business Performance Monitoring on WfMC Standards. In *WfMC Workflow Handbook 2002*, Vol. (Ed., L. Fischer), Future Strategies: Lighthouse Point.

McGregor, C., Schiefer, J., and Muehlen, M. z. (2006). A Shareable Web Service Based Intelligent Decision Support System for On-Demand Business Process Management, *International Journal of Business Process Integration and Management*, 1 (3).

Melchert, F., Winter, R., and Klesse, M. (2004). Aligning Process Automation and Business Intelligence to Support Corporate Performance Management. In *Tenth Americas Conference on Information Systems*, New York, NY, August 5–8.

Mendling, J. and Neumann, G. (2005). A Comparison of XML Interchange Formats for Business Process Modelling, In *WfMC Workflow Handbook 2005*, Vol. 185–198.

Neely, A. (2004). Performance Measurement System Design: A Literature Review and Research Aagenda, *International Journal of Operations and Production Management*, 25 (12), 1228–1263.

Nesamoney, D. (2004). BAM: Event-Driven Business Intelligence for the Real-Time Enterprise, *DM Review*, 14 (3), 38–40.

RuleML (2000). The Rule Markup Initiative (RuleML), WWW, http://www.ruleml.org/.

Smith, B. (1993). Making War on Defects: Six-Sigma Design, *IEEE Spectrum*, Vol. 43–47.

Thomas, M., Redmond, R., Yoon, V., and Singh, R. (2005). A Semantic Approach to Monitor Business Process, *Communications of the ACM*, 48 (12), 55–59.

van der Aalst, W. M. P. (2003). Workflow Patterns, *Distributed and Parallel Databases*, 13 (7), 5–51.

van der Aalst, W. M. P., ter Hofstede, A. H. M., and Weske, M. (2003). Business Process Management: A Survey. In *Proceedings 1st International Conference on Business Process Management*, Eindhoven, The Netherlands, 26–27 June.

W3C (2004). OWL Web Ontology Language Overview, http://www.w3.org/TR/2004/REC-owl-features-20040210/.

zur Muehlen, M. and Rosemann, M. (2004). Multi-Paradigm Process Management. In *CAiSE'04 Workshops – Fifth Workshop on Business Process Modeling, Development and Support (BPMDS 2004)*, (Eds., J. Grundspenkis and M. Kirikova), Riga, Latvia, 7–8 June.

# Service-Oriented Foundation and Analysis Patterns for Conceptual Modelling of Information Systems

Remigijus Gustas and Prima Gustiene

Department of Information Systems, Karlstad University
Remigijus.Gustas@kau.se, Prima.Gustiene@kau.se

**Abstract**  Everyday companies are inventing new configurations of service architectures, which prescribe and motivate information system design. Information system architectures are intrinsically complex engineering products that can be defined on different levels of abstraction and represented by using various dimensions. Designers are building them fragment by fragment, but when the design is complete, typically the business and technical components do not fit each other. The attempt to maintain the relevance of each specification fragment across disparate dimensions is very expensive and time consuming. The notion of service is not used explicitly in traditional information system engineering methods, which cover just a part of required modelling notations that are currently emerging under the service-oriented analysis and design approaches. The most fascinating idea about the service concept is that it applies equally well to organisational as well as technical components, which can be viewed as service requestors and service providers. The primary goal of service-oriented architecture is to align the business process models with the information system design in order to make both organisational and technical system parts more effective. One of the reasons why the traditional methods do not provide effective support for engineering of information systems is that service architectures are difficult to visualise and comprehend for business experts who determine the organisational strategies. The main goal of this chapter is to present a new service-oriented foundation and the associated analysis patterns for computation neutral information system modelling. A service concept integrates various information system dimensions of static and dynamic aspects into one modelling notation.

## 1 Introduction

The primary goal of Service-oriented Architecture (SOA) is to align the business design with the information technology (IT) innovations in order to make both organisational and technical system parts more effective. SOA (High et al., 2005) starts from the premise that all businesses and IT solutions can be expressed by graphical representations of Enterprise Architecture (EA). The term EA (Lankhorst et al., 2005) has been used for many years within information system (IS) engineering community. EA refers to various types of graphical representations that define how business, data, technology and software application structures are perceived from different points of view. The Zachman framework (Zachman, 1996) can be considered as a comprehensive guide of documents that comprise the enterprise architecture. It is defined by using various types of diagrams such as the 'why', 'what', 'who', 'where', 'when' and 'how'. There is one fundamental challenge facing the EA engineering process. To obtain value from diagrams that are populating various cells of the Zachman Framework, they must be integrated. Semantic incompleteness, ambiguity, discontinuity, redundancy and inconsistency of specifications are very difficult to identify in the traditional modelling approaches. This situation results in wasting huge financial resources for engineering of architectures, which have no significant impact.

Companies are using IT innovations for decades, but at the moment system analysis and design methods that support business experts with appropriate understanding of service architectures (Erl, 2005) are quite weak. Only in sub-domains such as business modelling, software engineering and database design can we find quite established conceptual modelling languages. For instance, database design languages are centred on modelling of the static aspects, which represent business data (the 'what' dimension). In contrary, the Business Process Modelling Notation (BPMN) (BPMN Working Group, 2004) is restricted to a business process modelling (the 'how' dimension), which excludes the static aspects. Unified Modelling Language (UML) (Booch et al., 1999) is de facto industry standard, which can be partially used for business process modelling as well as software design. It offers various diagram types for dealing with the 'what', 'who', 'where', 'when' and 'how' dimensions and therefore can be used for representation of services. Unfortunately, UML has some inherent weaknesses as far as the semantic integrity between the static and behavioural aspects is concerned. Semantics of individual diagram types are clear enough, but integrated semantics among models is missing. It makes difficult to analyse and to develop one holistic representation of IS architecture.

Many industries are successfully using architecture drawings for making a transition from strategy to implementation. Lack of an integrated method for modelling of service architectures is the cornerstone of frustration in the area of information systems. The traditional methods are dividing the technical system representations into three major parts that are known as data architecture, application architecture and technology architecture. Although there is a great power in separation of the different views for design of a technical system part, there is a deep fallacy in such orientation in the early system analysis stages. The fundamental problem is that conventional information system development methods are not taking into account some important semantic interdependency types between the static and dynamic models, which are crucial for gluing the strategic, organisational and technical descriptions into one computation independent (Gustas and Gustiene, 2004) and integrated representation. Such tradition tends to draw attention away from the strategic business process modelling aspects and concentrates on the implementation dependent issues (Finkelstein, 2004). Therefore, it is not readily accessible and understandable for business consultants and managers. Integrated service architecture should be established before any implementation specific decisions are taking place.

Interdependencies among models and perspectives that specify IS cannot be analysed in isolation. There is always an overlapping in different perspectives to some degree, because they are defining the same artefact. Likewise, there are intersecting elements, which are represented in different dimensions. For instance, the concept of operation in UML is represented in a class diagram (the 'what' dimension), activity diagram (the 'how'), sequence diagram (the 'where') and state-transition diagram (the 'when' dimension). Furthermore, the atomic operations are typically aggregated into the higher granularity operations that are represented as the elements of a use case diagram (the 'who' dimension). At the highest level of abstraction, some use case functionality can be interpreted as a goal that belongs to the 'why' dimension (Singh, 2002; de Moor, 2005). During the architecture engineering process, there are typically many users, designers and business experts involved. It is very difficult for these stakeholders to get a holistic understanding of IS architecture from the overlapping specifications that are defined on different levels (Gustas and Gustiene, 2002). To understand the advantages and disadvantages, the business experts should maintain a holistic representation of IS architecture, where all dimensions are integrated and analysed together. It is not reasonable to duplicate the same concept many times in different diagrams just because such separation is required from a technical design point of view.

## 2 Ontology of Enterprise System

One of the most general ontological definitions of a system is provided by Bunge (1979). This definition served as a basis in defining such notions as an organisation (Dietz, 2001) and enterprise ontology (Dietz, 2006). A starting point of our ontological definition of an enterprise system is quite similar. It is a composition of the organisational and technical components, which are viewed as various types of enterprise actors. Actors are subsystems that are represented by individuals, organisations and their divisions or roles, which denote groups of people. Technical actors are subsystems such as machines, software and hardware components, etc. Any two actors can be linked by inheritance, composition, classification or interaction dependencies, which are represented graphically in Fig. 1.

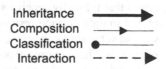

**Fig. 1.** Actor dependencies

Inheritance dependency between actors is used for sharing the static and dynamic similarities. More specific actors inherit the composition and interaction dependencies from more general actors. Dependencies represent additional intrinsic actor interoperation features and structural properties that are prescribed by an enterprise system. It should be noted that in object-oriented approaches, inheritance link is defined just for attributes and operations (Blaha and Rumbaugh, 2005).

Composition is a conceptual dependency used to relate a whole to other concepts that are viewed as parts. It is a stricter semantic relation (Storey, 1993) as compared to a composition that is defined in the object-oriented approaches. Composition is characterised by the following properties: (a) a part cannot simultaneously belong to more than one whole of the same concept, (b) if it does belong to more than one whole, then it must be a whole that is an instance of another concept, (c) a part and a whole are created at the same time. Once a part is created, it is terminated at the same time the whole is terminated.

Classification link between two actors is used to define their instances. For example, Apollo is an instance of a Swedish travel agency. In conceptual modelling, an instance can be viewed as an element of a set that is defined by a concept it belongs to. Sometimes classification dependency is referred to as instantiation, which is reverse of classification. In object-oriented approaches it represents a link between an object and a class. In the same way as an object can be manipulated by operations, an actor has interaction privileges and responsibilities that are defined by the interaction dependencies.

Interaction dependencies are used to conceptualise services between various enterprise system actors. Since actors are implemented as organisational and technical system components, they can use each other according to prescribed patterns to achieve their goals. Two interaction dependencies into opposite directions between a service requester and service provider define a typical action workflow loop (Denning and Medina-Mora, 1995). This idea is illustrated graphically in Fig. 2.

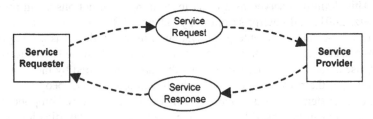

**Fig. 2.** Service as an interaction loop

Service providers are actors that typically receive service requests, over which they have no direct control and initiate service responses that are sent to service requesters. Services are dynamic subsystems, because outputs depend not only on inputs, but on service states as well. The dynamic aspect of service can be characterised by using pre-condition and post-condition states. States define constraints on service objects and restrict service responses to the present and future inputs. Requests, responses and states are crucial to understand the semantic aspects of services. Pre-condition states are important for determining a service output flow and a post-condition state. A system can be defined as a set of interacting loosely connected components, which are able to perform specific services on request. Examples of actor dependencies are represented in Fig. 3.

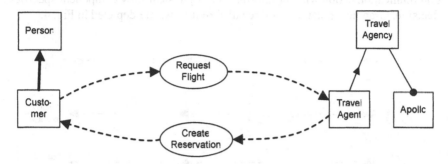

**Fig. 3.** Examples of semantic dependencies between actors

Service requests and service responses are understood as communication actions (Dietz, 2001). Actions are performed by actors and will be represented by ellipse. Interaction link between two actors indicates that one actor depends on another by a specific action. Actors are represented by square boxes.

The effect of every communication action is twofold. There are two orthogonal aspects of a communication action: intersubjective and objective. Orthogonality guarantees that modifying the effect produced by an objective part of an enterprise system neither creates nor propagates side effects to intersubjective part and vice versa. Cohesion of the intersubjective and objective aspects of communication action result into a more complex abstraction that allows representing static and behavioural perspectives using one modelling notation. An advantage of such new principle resides in its modelling power and inference rules (Gustas, 2005), which allow semantic consistency control of static and dynamic aspects. Traditional information system modelling notations do not combine the static and dynamic aspects together, but they represent them in totally different types of diagrams.

# 3 The Intersubjective Aspect of Communication Action

Intersubjective aspect of an action indicates that one actor depends on another actor. It is represented by the interaction dependency (·····▶) notation. The meaning of interaction arrow is similar to a strategic dependency link that was introduced by i* (Yu and Mylopoulos, 1994) approach. Intersubjective aspect is typically distinguished by identifying a physical, information or a decision flow between two actors involved. Actions are carried out by actors, who are called agents. In this case, the interaction dependency can be viewed as a communication channel for transferring an information or physical flow from agent to recipient. Typically, an agent is sending a flow to a recipient in order to achieve his goal (Gustas and

Gustiene, 2004). The achievement of goal will depend on a service provider, which should deliver a service flow into the opposite direction.

Flows are concepts that are represented by rectangles. Solid boxes are used for representation of physical flows, and light boxes represent information flows. A communication action without information or physical flow component specifies a decision. Graphical notations of three different flows are depicted in Fig. 4.

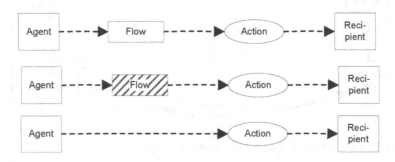

**Fig. 4.** Notation of information, physical and decision flows

A communication action has also an objective aspect. It typically represents object creation, termination or a state change effects (Hull et al., 2003) in an enterprise system. Without the ability to represent noteworthy changes, designers would have difficulties to understand the rationale and effect of every action. If effects are not identifiable, then the action cannot be considered as purposeful. Object world changes are specified for every communication action by using a transition dependency link (→).

Fundamentally three kinds of changes are possible during any transition: an action is either terminating or creating an object, or it can perform termination and creation at the same time. A creation is denoted by an outgoing transition arrow to a post-condition class. Graphical notation of the creation action is represented in Fig. 5.

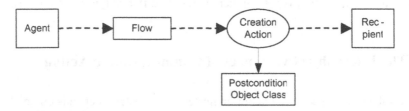

**Fig. 5.** Graphical representation of the creation action

A termination action is represented by a transition dependency directed from a pre-condition object class. Before an object is terminated, it must be created. Since a future state makes no sense for a termination event, it is not included in a specification of action. Pre-condition class in a termination action can be understood as final in an object's life time. The graphical notation of a termination action is represented in Fig. 6.

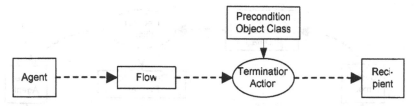

**Fig. 6.** Graphical representation of the termination action

Reclassification of object can be defined in terms of communication action that is terminating an object in one class and creating it at the same time in another class. Sometimes, objects are passing several classes, and then they are removed. Graphical notation of the reclassification action is presented in Fig. 7.

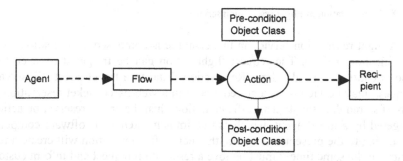

**Fig. 7.** Graphical representation of the reclassification action

Pre-condition and post-condition classes typically define constraints on objects, which restrict sending and receiving of communication flows between technical or business components. Reclassification action in a computerised system can be implemented either as a sequence of one or more object creation and termination (or read and update) operations. Request and response flows together with created and terminated object classes are crucial to understand the semantic aspects of services. A pre-condition object state and the input flow should be sufficient for determining a service output flow and a post-condition object state.

Information flows are reminiscent of arrows in dataflow diagrams (Hoffer et al., 2004), because they represent moving data between actors, which may be interpreted as data sources and sinks. If a system has no computer support, then information flows may be understood as moving documents and post-condition classes can be viewed as archived data at rest. Classes can be viewed as database files or data stores in the computerised system. It should be noted that the presented notation is used for service architecture modelling, which does not prescribe any sort of implementation details. It follows the basic conceptualisation principle (van Griethuisen, 1982) by representing only computation independent aspects. An example of a typical action workflow loop is presented in Fig. 8.

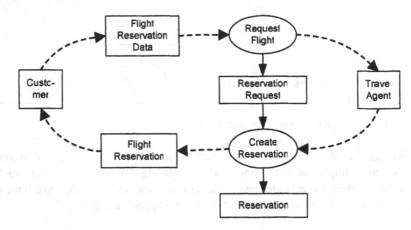

**Fig. 8.** Representation of Flight reservation service

A flight reservation service in this example is composed of a creation and reclassification actions. The request flight action can be triggered by a customer who is entitled to send 'Flight Reservation Data' to a travel agent. 'Reservation Request' may be viewed as a stored record in a web-based ticket reservation system. If stored data satisfy a specific condition, then the create reservation action is triggered by a travel agent, which can be implemented as a software component. According to the presented diagram, the reclassification action will create a reservation; at the same time it must remove a reservation request and inform customer by sending 'Flight Reservation' flow.

Composition of different types of communication actions results in the diagrams, which define a continuous or finite lifecycle for one or more objects. A lifecycle of an object is typically represented by an initial, intermediate and final class. A creation event corresponds to a starting point and removal action – to the end point in an object's lifecycle. The most critical issue in modelling of the interaction details is semantic integrity of the static and dynamic aspects. It is not sufficient to represent what type of objects are created and terminated. For instance, reservation request and reservation data in our example may correspond to a database view, or they may be implemented as independent classes of objects. Enterprise ontology models must clearly represent the semantic details of attribute values that must be either removed or preserved in any creation, termination and reclassification action. Various kinds of class and attribute links in semantic models are typically defined by using cardinality constraints.

# 4 The Objective Aspect of Communication Action

The usefulness of a great number of semantic relations (Snoeck et al., 1999; Storey, 1993) in system analysis and design is an open problem. Another problem is that the principles of interplay (Gustas, 2005) between the static and dynamic dependencies are not clear. This is the reason why the semantic integrity control is very difficult in information system development methodologies. As a consequence, the semantic quality of system specifications is often compromised. In the service-oriented approach, any concept can play a role as an actor, a flow, a class, an attribute, an instance or a relationship. The same concept may have different interpretations, which depend on the specified dependency links to other concepts. Any two actors are required to be connected by the interaction dependency, which is fully defined by using the intersubjective and objective aspect of communication action. Any concept to be viewed as a class must be provided by the attribute dependency links. Attributes of the pre-condition object class in any action define types of instances to be removed and attributes of the post-condition object class represent types of instances to be created. This is illustrated in Fig. 9.

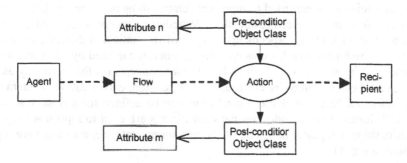

**Fig. 9.** Representation of the semantic difference between two classes

Attribute dependencies define an important semantic difference between two concepts. Lack of the noteworthy difference between a pre-condition and post-condition class indicates that specification is incomplete or communication action is not purposeful. These two sets of attributes represent types of affected values in the reclassification, creation or removal action. Therefore, an action defines what needs to be done, but it does not show how the transition is implemented. Pre-condition and post-condition classes in every action specify the permissible ways in which changes may occur. In the conventional information system modelling approaches, changes are represented by using state-transition links in a finite state machine (Harel and Rumpe, 2004).

The attribute dependencies stem from the traditional data models. Semantics of static dependencies in object-oriented approaches are defined by multiplicities. They represent a minimum and maximum number of objects in one class that can be associated to objects in another class. We use only static associations without semantic holes (just mandatory constraint) from at least one side of association.

A graphical notation of the attribute dependencies and their cardinalities is represented in Fig. 10.

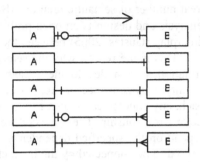

**Fig. 10.** Graphical notation of the attribute dependencies

This graphical notation corresponds to a classical way for representing associations (Hoffer et al., 2004) between two entities. One significant difference of this notation from the traditional approaches is that the association ends are nameless. Dependencies are never used to represent relationships or mappings between two sets of objects in two opposite directions. Whether a concept is regarded as a class, attribute or relationship depends upon types of the static and dynamic dependencies they are related to other concepts. Every noun is captured by a box and a verb is captured by an ellipse. Additionally, any two concepts (in the same way as any two actors) can be linked by inheritance, composition, classification or interaction dependencies. States or Boolean conditions can be defined for a class or an actor as well. Interaction dependencies between classes are used to represent the static relationships. Graphical notations of the remaining static dependencies are represented in Fig. 11.

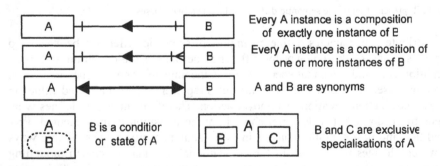

**Fig. 11.** Graphical notation of the static dependencies

Similar attributes are inherited by more specific classes according to the inheritance link (⟶). Inheritance arrow denotes a specialisation and generalisation. It always points out to a more general concept. We may distinguish between complete or incomplete as well as total and partial inheritance situations (Hoffer et al., 2004). All these cases can be expressed by using the exclusive specialisation and mutual inheritance link. Mutual inheritance dependency ($\longleftrightarrow$) can be used for representing classes that are viewed as synonyms. It is defined as follows:

A $\longleftrightarrow$ B if and only if A $\longrightarrow$ B and B $\longrightarrow$ A.

Composition of classes can be defined in the same way as composition of actors. We distinguish among the single-valued and multi-valued composition. In general, the whole and a part are required to be created and terminated at the same time. In a multi-valued case of composition, a new part can be created for an already exiting whole and sometimes a part can be terminated without removing a whole. Nevertheless, if the last part is terminated, then the whole is terminated at the same time. A part cannot simultaneously belong to more than one whole of the aggregate concept. If it does belong to more than one whole, then it must be a whole that is instantiated by another class. A transition action (including creation and termination) on the whole propagates to its parts and vice versa. Interaction between independently created actors propagates just to a whole. Independently created are concepts whose objects are not composed of each other. Various combinations of static and dynamic dependencies are illustrated in Fig. 12.

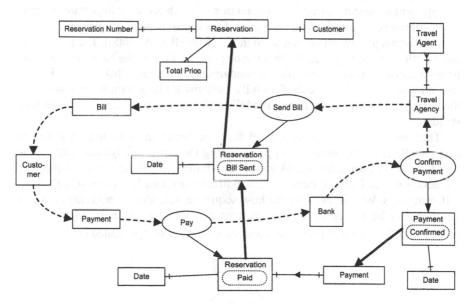

**Fig. 12.** Example of the static and dynamic dependencies in one interaction loop

This interaction sequence consists of three creation actions. The first action requires a reservation object, which must be created in a previous interaction loop (see the flight reservation service). Send Bill action is supposed to create a Reservation [Bill Sent] object that is a specialisation of an already-created Reservation object (see the post-condition class). Existence of this object depends on the attribute dependency link that represents specific constraints for association links with other objects (see Customer, Total Price, etc.). Once a Reservation [Bill Sent] object is created by a Travel Agency, the Pay action can be triggered by a Customer. It is supposed to create Reservation [Paid] object, which is a composition of exactly one Payment (propagation to part) If so, the Bank is obliged to Confirm Payment by associating it with the state Confirmed.

# 5 System Analysis Patterns

Expressive power of the static and dynamic dependencies must be sufficient for defining the main workflow patterns such as: sequence, selection (choice and merge), synchronisation (split and join) and iteration. Semantics of a service can be defined by using one or more interaction loops. As it was demonstrated, every interaction loop is composed of creation, termination or reclassification actions. By matching the interaction dependencies from agents to recipients, one can explore opportunities that are available to actors. The static dependencies define complementary semantic details of interactions, which are very important for reasoning about service architecture patterns. An extensive and very general description of various pattern details can be found at (Russell et al., 2006). The pattern research efforts were triggered for two major reasons. Firstly, the basic patterns can be used for demonstrating interplay of fundamental constructs that are used in system analysis and design process. Secondly, patterns are important for evaluation of the expressive power of semantic modelling languages and service architecture standards.

The number of basic patterns used for representation of system ontology is quite small. They are constructed by combining the static and dynamic dependencies together. Understanding and visual recognition of the fundamental patterns are necessary for building more specific pattern variations by composing them in different ways. We will demonstrate how sequence, selection, synchronisation and iteration can be expressed. Remaining patterns are just variations of the basic ones. First of all, we will explain a sequence pattern. It is represented in Fig. 13.

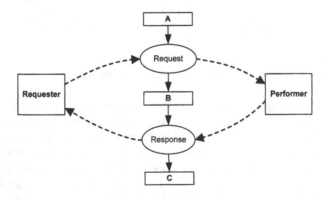

**Fig. 13.** Sequence

The sequence pattern can be defined by using composition of two or more re-classification actions. Since creation and termination action is a special case of re-classification, it can be used instead of a reclassification action. For instance, in the previous example (see Fig. 12) three creation actions were used to express the interaction sequence. Every action is responsible for removal of the attribute object links that are associated with the pre-condition class and for creation of the post-condition class attribute object links. It cannot be responsible for any changes of object links of more general classes or for object links of the attributes. Creation, reclassification and removal of objects in more general classes and in the attributes that are viewed as classes with their own attributes should proceed in an earlier sequence. For instance, For the Send Bill action to be triggered, a Reservation object is required to be created in advance by another service.

Compositional attribute objects must be created, reclassified or terminated by the same action, because a part and a whole have identical lifecycle. That is the reason why an action propagates according to the class composition links from a whole to a part and vice versa. Propagation of actions is a useful property, because it allows modelling synchronisation in a natural way. This feature is illustrated graphically in Fig. 14.

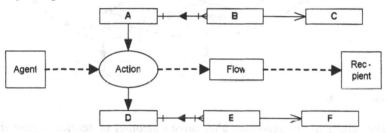

**Fig. 14.** Synchronisation

This pattern illustrates that an action is responsible for removal of object A and all its parts B. It is also used for creation of object D together with all necessary parts E. Note: parts and wholes are created and terminated together with their specified attribute links (see attributes C and F). For instance, the Pay action (see Fig. 12) prescribes creation of Payment and Reservation [Paid] objects together with the intrinsic link to a Date object.

Iteration is a special case of sequence, where a post-condition class of the response action plays the role of a pre-condition class for the service request. Iteration pattern is represented graphically in Fig. 15.

Iteration pattern with a missing pre-condition class for request and post-condition class for response would express a special case of a search pattern, where a found object (B) is created and then consumed in a response action, which is presented for requester.

Selection pattern can be expressed by using composition of two different sequences between the same two actors. Selection pattern is represented graphically in Fig. 16.

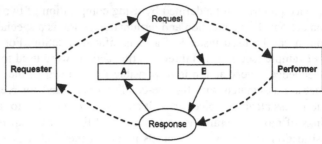

**Fig. 15.** Iteration

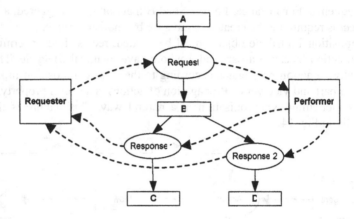

**Fig. 16.** Selection

The selection represents two alternative outcomes of service request that are selected by performer. Typically, only one type of response is desirable by requester. For instance, if Person (requester) applies (action) for a job by sending application (flow) to company (performer), then it may employ (response 1) or reject an application (response 2). The apply action should create an Application object, which is composed of an Applicant. In the case of employ action, Applicant object should be reclassified to Employee. Otherwise, the reject action should terminate Application object.

A search pattern can be defined by using a composition of sequence and iteration patterns. Search pattern is represented graphically in Fig. 17.

A post-condition of request action can be represented by using an exclusive specialisation of two classes of objects (D and E), where depending on failure or success one of the objects will always be created. In case of a failure an object (D) is terminated by performer (response 1), and search pattern can be again reiterated by requester. In case of a success, a requested object is found (class E) and then reclassified by displaying it to a requester.

Various combinations of the static and dynamic dependencies are capable to express the main workflow control patterns. This is a unique feature of our approach. Typically, just dynamic models such as variations of Petri-nets (Russell et al., 2006) or Business process diagrams (BPMN Working Group, 2004) that are

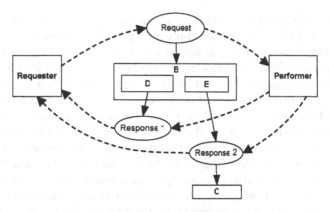

**Fig. 17.** Search

isolated from their static aspects are used in the pattern research. Separation of the static and dynamic details in pattern modelling creates fundamental difficulties for two major reasons. Since the static details must somehow be compensated by using dynamic constructs, the number of the basic patterns is becoming bigger than it is really necessary. Sometimes, their tiny differences are difficult to understand and visually recognise by business experts. If static aspects are not taken into account, then patterns will become more complicated to use for business process change evolution.

# 6 Concluding Remarks and Outlook

The changes of service architecture need to be constantly captured, visualised and agreed upon. They are critical to align the business design with IT system architecture design in order to make both organisational and technical system parts more effective. Just as complex buildings require explicit representations of their architectures, so does an entire organisational network, enterprise system or service. Various static and dynamic diagrams that describe service architectures cannot be analysed in isolation. The presented integrated foundation for modelling the intersubjective and objective perspectives of an enterprise system is necessary to facilitate reasoning and understanding of service compositions across organisational and technical boundaries. It integrates various dimensions of service-oriented architecture into one unified modelling notation. The presented patterns and dependencies are rooted in the basic building constructs of the traditional approaches.

One of the difficulties with the traditional IS analysis and design methods is that they rest on the perspectives of designer and builder. Therefore, IS specifications are difficult to comprehend for business experts, who determine the organisational strategies. The traditional methods cover just a part of required modelling notations that are currently emerging under the service-oriented analysis and design approaches (Zimmerman, 2004). The notion of service is not used explicitly in UML, which is based on the object-oriented paradigm. Moreover, to the best of our knowledge, there is no clear agreement on how the service-oriented and object-oriented modelling principles can be combined together. Integration principles among different perspectives are missing in the traditional IS development methodologies. The presented foundation for defining conceptual representations of service architectures can be used for systematic analysis of the overall enterprise system changes and boundary shifts. The given definition of a communication action provides a comprehensible interplay among the basic elements of five enterprise architecture dimensions: the 'what', 'who', 'where', 'when' and 'how'.

Expressive power of the static and dynamic dependencies was evaluated by defining the main workflow patterns. It was demonstrated that they are sufficient for defining such basic patterns as sequence, selection, synchronisation, iteration and search. Typically, just dynamic models are used in pattern research. If the static aspects are not taken into account, then the patterns will become more complicated to use for business process change evolution. They are also more difficult to understand and visually recognise by business experts. By using the service-oriented approach, the ontology of enterprise system can be represented on different levels of abstraction and it can be bridged to various perspectives. Therefore, service architecture specifications can be used as a basis for reasoning about semantic completeness, consistency and continuity of information system design. Identification of incompleteness, overspecification or underspecification is difficult by using the contemporary IS models.

The presented graphical approach opens a totally new way of enterprise system engineering from services that span across the organisational and technical system boundaries. The most fascinating idea about service concept is that it applies equally well to organisational as well as technical components. It has a capacity to integrate the static and dynamic aspects in one modelling notation. Redesign of well-established architectures can be performed by replacing enterprise service performers with more competitive business or technical components. Self-describing nature of interaction loops and particularly the ability to define new configurations of service architectures provide significant competitive advantages, because adopting a new service-oriented paradigm has the potential to reduce information system development complexity and to lower enterprise architecture maintenance costs. A new way of modelling provides improved integrity of service architectures across different perspectives and along various dimensions.

# References

Blaha, M. and Rumbaugh, J. (2005). *Object-Oriented Modelling and Design with UML*, Pearson, London.
Booch, G., Rumbaugh, J., and Jacobsson, I. (1999). *The Unified Modelling Language User Guide*, Addison Wesley Longman, Reading, MA.

BPMN Working Group (2004). Business Process Modeling Notation. Retrieved June 09, 2005, from http://www.bpmn.org.

Bunge, M. A. (1979). *Treatise on Basic Philosophy, vol. 4, A World of Systems*, Reidel Publishing Company, Dordrecht, the Netherlands.

Denning, P. J. and Medina-Mora, R. (1995). Completing the Loops, *Interfaces, vol. 25*, pp. 42–57.

Dietz, J. L. G. (2001). DEMO: Towards a Discipline of Organisation Engineering, *European Journal of Operational Research (128)*, Elsevier, Amsterdam, pp. 351–363.

Dietz, J. L. G. (2006). *Enterprise Ontology: Theory and Methodology*, Springer, Berlin.

Erl, T. (2005). *Service-Oriented Architecture: Concepts, Technology, and Design*, Pearson Prentice Hall, Crawfordsville, IN.

Finkelstein, C. (2004). Enterprise Integration Using Enterprise Architecture. In H. Linger et al. (Eds.), *Constructing the Infrastructure for the Knowledge Economy*, Kluwer/Plenum, the Netherlands/New York.

van Griethuisen, J. J. (1982). Concepts and Terminology for the Conceptual Schema and Information Base, Report ISO TC97/SC5/WG5, No 695.

Gustas, R. (2005). Inference Rules of Semantic Dependencies in the Enterprise Modelling. In H. Fujita and M. Mejri (Eds.), *New Trends in Software Methodologies, Tools and Techniques*, IOS Press, Amsterdam, pp. 235–251.

Gustas, R. and Gustiene, P. (2002). Extending Lyee Methodology Using the Enterprise Modelling Approach, *Frontiers in Artificial Intelligence and applications*, IOS Press, Amsterdam, pp. 273–288.

Gustas, R. and Gustiene, P. (2004). Towards the Enterprise Engineering Approach for Information System Modelling across Organisational and Technical Boundaries, *Enterprise Information Systems V*, Kluwer, Netherlands, pp. 204–215.

Harel, D. and Rumpe, B. (2004). Meaningful Modeling: What's the Semantics of 'Semantics'? IEEE Computer, October, pp. 64–72.

High, R., Kinder, S., and Graham, S. (2005). IBM's SOA Foundation, IBM Corporation, version 1.0. Retrieved November 02, 2005, from http://download.boulder.ibm.com/ ibmdl/pub/software/dw/webservices/ws soa whitepaper.pdf.

Hoffer, J. A., George, J. F., and Valacich J. S. (2004). *Modern System Analysis and Design*, Pearson Prentice Hall, NJ.

Hull, R., Christophides, V., and Su, J. (2003). E-services: A look Behind the Curtain, *ACM PODS*, San Diego, CA.

Lankhorst, M. et al. (2005). Enterprise *Architecture at Work*, Springer, Berlin.

de Moor, A. (2005). Patterns for the Pragmatic Web, *Proceedings of the 13th International Conference on Conceptual Structures*, Kassel, Germany, LNAI, Springer, Berlin, pp. 1–18.

Russell, N., Hofstede, A. H. M., Aalst W. M. P., and Mulyar, N. (2006). *BPM Center Report* BPM-06-22, BPMcenter.org.

Singh, M. P. (2002). The Pragmatic Web, *IEEE Internet Computing*, May–June, pp. 45.

Snoeck, M., Dedene, G., Verhelst, M., and Depuydt, A. M. (1999). *Object-Oriented Enterprise Modelling with MERODE*, Leuven University Press, Leuven, Belgium.

Storey, V. C. (1993). Understanding Semantic Relationships, *VLDB Journal*, F. Marianski (Ed.), *vol. 2*, pp. 455–487.

Yu, E. and Mylopoulos, J. (1994). From E-R to 'A-R' – Modelling Strategic Actor Relationships for Business Process Reengineering, *Proceedings of 13th International Conference on the Entity – Relationship Approach*, Manchester, UK.

Zachman, J. A. (1996). Enterprise Architecture: The Issue of the Century, *Database Programming and Design Magazine*.

Zimmerman, O., Krogdahl, P., and Gee, C. (2004). Elements of Service-Oriented Analysis and Design. Retrieved June 9, 2005, from http://www128.ibm.com/developerworks/library/ws-soad1/.

# Specifying Collaborative System Requirements in Terms of Platforms and Services

Igor T. Hawryszkiewycz

Faculty of Information Technology, University of Technology, Sydney, igorh@it.uts.edu.au

**Abstract** Increasing collaboration in business processes has resulted in increased demand for information systems that support collaboration in business processes. Many system development methodologies, however, are oriented towards defining processes that are fixed both in their process steps and process functions. Collaborative systems, however, are more uncertain in nature and collaborative processes usually evolve to accomplish the goal. Hence requirements cannot be specified to the same level of detail. Collaborative processes are often user driven and requirements must accommodate such users by providing a flexible platform of services that can be configured by users to fit their work practices. This paper introduces the concept of collaboration level as a way to specify collaborative platforms of services and ways to implement such platforms.

## 1 Introduction

Trends to collaborative systems in domains such as health (Tan et al., 2006) require emphasis to be placed on user analysis when building such systems. Furthermore, such user analysis must take place early in requirements analysis (Zhang et al., 2002). Furthermore, it is increasingly recognized that new approaches in requirements engineering are needed (Jiang et al., 2005; Padula, 2004) to cater for the wide range of processes now found in practice. For example, in predefined processes the emphasis is on tasks and flows of information between tasks. Analysis here looks at the detailed structures and process flows. Modeling concepts to describe such processes include data flows, entities, relationships, or objects depending on the methodology used. Collaborative processes, on the other hand, place more emphasis on social relationships needed in collaboration and services to maintain them. This is because of the project complexity and volatility found in most such processes. Such volatility exists because collaborative systems place more emphasis on roles of people, their responsibilities, and the way they communicate.

The elicitation process in the requirements analysis for collaborative processes must, therefore, increasingly emphasize social issues and the relationships between stakeholders. Furthermore, the developed systems must be increasingly user driven and hence it is necessary to analyze user capabilities to provide support systems consistent with these capabilities. As a result, the emphasis is not on supporting a predefined process but to give users the ability to adapt technology to the process. The implication here is that the specification must specify an adaptable platform and user oriented services that can be combined to support collaborative processes on that platform.

Few methods now exist for this purpose. The paper introduces the concept of a collaboration level that can be used to identify broad requirements of such platforms and provides adaptable services and describes a systematic approach for gathering social requirements. This platform is sometimes called the Cyberinfrastructure (Zimmerman and Nardi, 2006). This paper addresses ways to define requirements for such platforms by introducing the concept of collaborative levels to specify such platforms and defines ways to analyze community environments to determine the levels needed for a particular application.

## 2 The Requirements Analysis Method

The kind of requirements analysis needed is illustrated by a typical process. A typical process may be preparing a submission in response to a client request, making a budget to meet the request, and organize the needed resources. The specification must determine the support platforms needed in each of the three activities and ways to coordinate the activities.

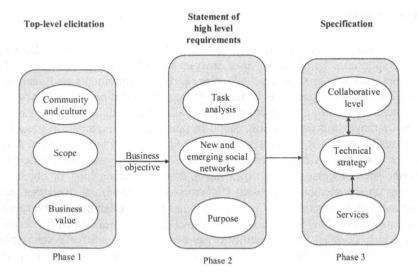

**Fig. 1.** Proposed approach

In more complex systems such as emergency systems (Jacobs et al., 1998), activities may be more complex including situation assessment and determining courses of action. These again must provide group support for each activity and coordinate these activities. In such cases there is considerable uncertainty on the exact communications that will be followed as process evolution is usually user driven and depends on intermediate outcomes as the process evolves. Again what are needed are platforms of services that can be adapted to the emerging situation.

The requirements analysis method described here is illustrated in Fig. 1. Phase 1, top-level elicitation, focuses on analyzing the social environment, the community and culture within it what the expected business value is, and the scope of the project. Phase 2 is a more detailed statement of community activities and phase 3 is the technical specification.

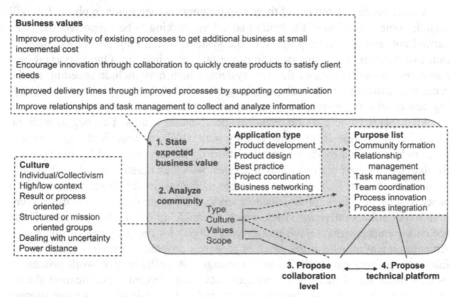

**Fig. 2.** Design parameters in phases 1 and 2

The process is shown in more detail in Fig. 2 following from earlier descriptions (Hawryszkiewycz, 2006a,b). It begins by identifying the expected business value including the general application type as shown in Fig. 2. It also defines the scope. The scope defines the social or organizational boundaries of the project. The scope is based on determining the structure of personal relationships and groups within the system. It must define the structures of teams, the whole organization, and size of organization—does it cover the entire organization, or part of the process, or part of the organization? Examples include:

- Small local team—usually working on one or more artifacts or with limited external relationships.
- Organization wide team—usually involves a number of functional units working to a wider organizational goal.

It then follows with step 2 to analyze the community. The kinds of community issues raised include:

- Open or closed community—usually independent people sharing knowledge or exchanging information.
- Team and organizational structure—Hierarchical, mission oriented, open.
- Culture—social, generally based on Hofstede's measure.
- Social networking—how do people communicate and use services?
- Community values—explicit definition of what business value is expected of the new system.
- Networking across organizations—The kind of relationships across organizational boundaries, as for example, supply chains.

A more precise statement of these requirements is then made in phase 2. It will include some definition of the kind of social networking to be supported, the tasks carried out, and the broad purpose of the system, which may be, for example, to improve client relationships or to improve task coordination. One important outcome here is the purpose of the new system, which may include speeding up the process, maintaining relationships, raising effectiveness of carrying out tasks, adding new capability, or supporting some particular task.

After this is completed the technical specification begins. This begins with the idea of collaboration level (Hawryszkiewycz, 2006b) to specify the general services to be provided by the technical platform. The services must be more powerful than those found in predefined processes, which as illustrated in Fig. 3 usually require services for the exchange of simple messages. In collaborative user driven processes, higher level communication services are often oriented towards a combination of collaborative activities, which are made up of simple messages. These are called engagements (Hawryszkiewycz, 2006a) for the purposes of this paper. An engagement may be to get ideas, or prepare a proposal, or review the proposal. Each engagement can include many messages. A collaborative work process is usually made up of many such engagements. Requirements specification should thus specify the technical platform that provides the kinds of services to support the engagements.

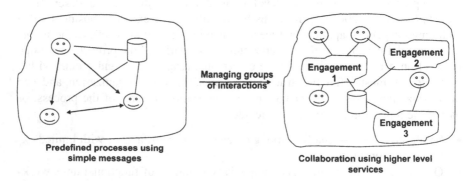

**Fig. 3.** Identifying patterns for collaboration in context

The requirements outcome is then used to specify a platform of services. We first define a collaboration level that defines the general level of collaborative activity and then the services required to maintain the collaborative level. Users will be required to choose services at execution time depending on the situation at the time. Such choice will often take place within the social and cultural environment of the organization, and requirements must be guided by the social relationships within the enterprise. We next define the collaboration levels and then ways to use these to design the technical platform.

## 3 Defining Collaboration Levels

This paper takes a strategic business approach and proposes a set collaboration levels (Hawryszkiewycz, 2006a,b) shown in Fig. 4.

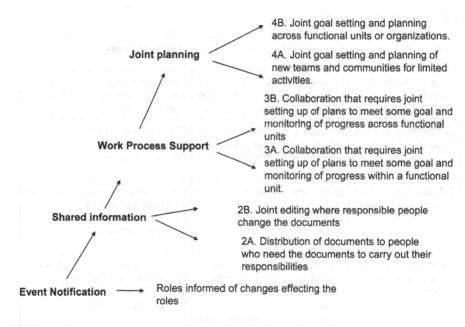

**Fig. 4.** Collaboration levels

The levels are

- Event notification, where roles are informed of any changes that affect the roles with the goal of raising awareness across an organization.
- Shared information (level 2A), where documents are distributed between responsible roles. At the higher level (2B) the participants collaborate to jointly develop the artifacts.

- Work process support (3), which often defines monitoring levels of activity and sends reminders to collaborators. Such collaboration can be within organizational units (3A) or between them (3B).
- Joint planning and goal setting (4), where people jointly decide how they will work together. This includes joint planning including support for emerging communities (4A) and across functional units (4B).

Often collaboration starts with simply notifying people of changes that can impact their work. Then document sharing is added to ensure that people are provided with information needed to carry out their responsibilities. Subsequent levels are more complex as they require more intense interaction to coordinate activities. Work process support, requires a precise definition of the way a collaborative process takes place. It includes the definition of responsibilities of identified roles. For example, the process may define a way to propose a response to a customer request. The specific rules may define the expertise needed to define a solution,

**Table 1.** Levels of Collaboration

| Level | Characteristics of collaboration levels | Where applicable |
|---|---|---|
| Collaboration level 1 Event Notification | Informing people about events related to their roles. Presenting the functional situation globally. | Maintaining awareness of activities across the organization. Reducing repetitive work. |
| Collaboration level 2A Document Sharing | Sharing explicit information. Presenting to roles responsible for functional units. Obtaining comments on information. | Capturing best practices. Complaint handling. Promotional marketing. |
| Collaboration level 2B Document preparation | Jointly preparing an artifact. | Loosely structured groups contributing to the same artifact. Developing documents jointly. Order configuration. |
| Collaboration level 3A Local work process support | Explicit definition of work activities and responsibilities. Definition of relationships between tasks. Group meetings to resolve issues. | Projects requiring task coordination. New product development. Continuous innovation. Developing proposals. |
| Collaboration level 3B Organizational process support | Joint work across organizational boundaries. | Response to tenders of people involved in a task. Product strategy development. |
| Collaboration level 4 Joint planning | Developing shared plans. Devise coordination strategies between functional units. Develop and agree on work processes. | Organizational strategy and mission. Strategy development. |

the risk assessment, budgetary evaluation, legal aspects, and so on. Joint work is an extension of level 3 by providing ways to carry out synchronously thus reducing completion time. Defining the processes to be followed also requires collaboration and agreement on the ways people will work to achieve organizational goals. This process must be clearly defined and clearly understood and followed. Joint planning requires involved units together plan and agree on their work processes. This level often requires support for asynchronous work as goal setting often includes resolving many imprecisely defined alternatives. Table 1 describes the characteristics of these levels including their applicability. The detailed dimensions are then used in requirements specification. They are out of the scope of this paper to describe in detail but include:

- *Structure*: The relationships between collaborative objects.
- *Knowledge*: About collaborative objects.
- *Governance*: Responsibilities within the system.
- *Social process*: Ways that people network and communicate.
- *Relationship building*: Between objects.
- *Negotiation*: Negotiation about ways to meet client requirements.
  *Reflection*: On previous outcomes.

## 4 Selecting the collaboration level

A number of guidelines can now be proposed based on the examination of earlier applications and using fundamental theories.

- Capturing best practices, resulting in savings in completing tasks, testing vehicles for emission in the case of Artail. Here the emphasis is on recording practices, collecting comments on them, and observing their usage—Generally level 1 where users post their practices for others to try and comment on.
- New product development that stresses the need for technology to support coordination. The emphasis here is on bring experts together to use their knowledge to improve products and services—Generally level 3 as it requires considerable coordination especially in larger projects.
- New business development that stresses the need to support emerging strategic communities—A mix of levels 3 and 4.
- Process improvement as exemplified in responses to client requests to consulting organizations. The emphasis again is not only on collecting information but also on improving processes by adopting standard costing and report structures.
- Provision of high level personalized services such as health services (Tan et al., 2006; Zhang et al., 2002) which require adaptation to health workers especially responding to new inputs.

274    Igor T. Hawryszkiewycz

Empirical evidence of the kind described above suggests the kind of guideline shown in Fig. 5.

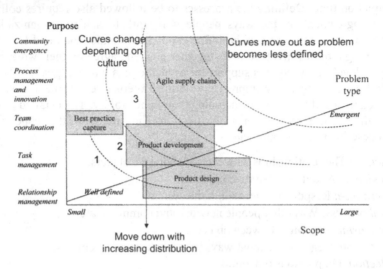

**Fig. 5.** Guidelines for specifying collaboration levels

The collaboration level may be different for different parts of the system. As an example in Fig. 6 is typical of social network structures found in many organizations.

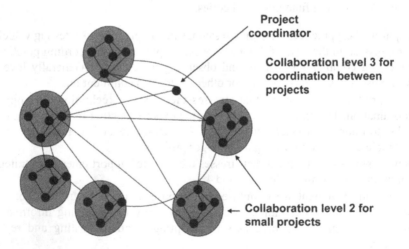

**Fig. 6.** A structure of collaborating groups

Here there are a number of specialist groups, which are coordinated to a given goal. Each specialist group is contributing to a part of the overall process and works closely as a group. The group usually develops an artifact that is part of a larger project. There is a coordination group that ensures the artifacts developed by the local groups all converge to a common goal. In this case the scope is of two parts. One is support for the local groups, which is usually sufficient as level 2. The coordination requires collaboration level 3 in order to coordinate the different groups.

## 4.1 An Example

We now illustrate with the application of the method to business networking. Figure 7 shows a top-level diagram of a model of business network formation. The main activities are

- identifying an opportunity,
- finding business partners, and
- negotiating contract.

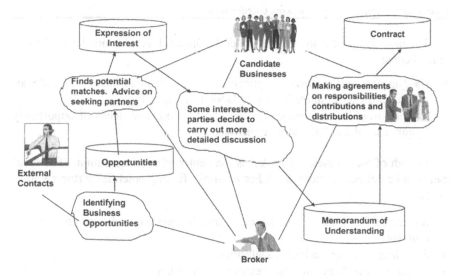

**Fig. 7.** A lightweight conceptual application model

At this stage the collaborative levels and goals are also specified. For example, the high level collaborative requirement may be level 1 where level 2 must be supported in making claims and level 3 is needed in assessing claims. Goals can also be specified. For example,

Typical documentation following priority setting takes the following form.

---

*Organizational cultural assumption:*

The network is mission oriented with emphasis on building relationships with well-defined purpose. Businesses are individual in nature but require close collaboration once they become part of a network.

*Scope with some justification:*

The proposal centers on supporting brokers by enhancing relationships with their client businesses to help them developing responses to opportunities. There are groups associated with networks whereas the entire network is coordinated through the network sponsors.

*Proposed improvements in direct business benefits:*

The direct business benefits will be increased business through the development of partnerships.

Purpose—state the benefit.

Relationship management—establish communication between brokers and businesses.

Task management—not addressed here.

Team coordination—provide ways for small businesses to work together.

Process management—support network coordination.

---

The next step here is to describe the collaboration level in more detail. Choices made here are

- *Finding potential partners*: Requires knowledge of small businesses and ways to contact them. Requires level 1 collaborative capability.
- *Keeping track of opportunities*: Seek clarifications and needs of opportunity. Requires level 2 collaborative capability.

In both of these cases, the broker is the center of communication. The levels can then be defined in more detail For example, finding potential partners will include:

- *Structure*: The links between brokers and businesses, and contacts and government.
- *Knowledge*: About business capabilities.
- *Social process*: Ways that businesses work together.
- *Relationship building*: Between objects.
- *Negotiation*: Negotiation about ways to meet client requirements.
- *Reflection*: Records of earlier business networks.
- *Support*: Internet technologies for maintaining contacts.
- *Collaborative database*: Contact information.

High level use cases can now be defined require some feedback on the kind of interactions that take place and which of these are to be computer mediated.

# 5 Selecting the technical platform

We now briefly describe ways to specify the technical strategy. Generally, light-weight technical strategies as follows are suggested.

- Lightweight exchange primarily concerns exchange of messages between loosely connected individuals. It usually supports an environment where people stay in touch and share their responsibility but have no particular goal to achieve some outcome.
- Lightweight coordination now includes the need to proceed to some outcome, although the outcome is decided as the process proceeds. Hence we now require ways to set up tasks, create new tasks, and assign responsibilities for them.
- Work coordination where the goal is more specific and usually requires the setting up of a plan and monitoring progress. The plan can be easily changed although the goal usually remains the same.
- Process management, where goals are now precisely defined and processes strictly followed.

The idea of lightweight exchange and collaboration was introduced by Whittaker to illustrate the kinds of technologies needed to establish and maintain productive relationships. Typical technologies focus on exchanging messages and maintaining a space usually a portal to keep common information. Lightweight collaboration goes further where the communication exchange leads to some expected result. Usually there is a program board is a centralized collection of tasks with progress reports regularly posted on the boards. They also include services for discussion and agreements on future courses of action through an issues board. In addition, roles with clearly defined responsibilities must be defined and assigned to the tasks.

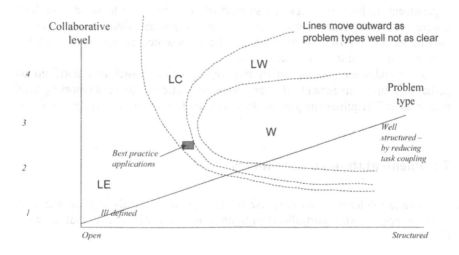

**Fig. 8.** Specifying technical strategies

Figure 8 provides some guidelines for the selection of a technical strategy. Generally, higher collaborative levels and increasingly structured processes require higher level technical strategies.

## 6 Specifying Generic Engagements

Typical engagements identified in earlier work are as follows:

*e-portfolio*—Supports working on an artifact by a number of people. It supports a collection of artifacts developed by a number of people. Different responsibilities are assigned in the e-portfolio. Examples include education with teacher and student responsibilities. Strategic documents with planning and expert responsibilities or paper preparation with author and reviewer responsibilities. The parameters of this engagement will be document names, roles, and role responsibilities for each document.

*Workflow instance*—To arrange work actions associated with an activity. Here a workflow is defined in terms of events, which are assigned to roles. A completion event initiated by one role can result in an initiation event for some other role. The process can change dynamically by adding new events dynamically.

There are other engagements not illustrated here that include *group management* or *team formation* or *program and issues boards*. There are a number of advantages of using such higher level concepts in collaborative systems. One is to provide a social construct that can be easily understood. Another is that engagements as particularly suitable as a way of integrating processes. It provides such a basis ranging from predefined processes to emerging processes that include supporting mobility in the workforce. It can be used as the basis for supporting communication beyond the simple exchange of messages to supporting more goal oriented communication that integrates a number of messages into the one engagement. It, however, sees that support must be provided to manage such engagements and suggests agents as suitable for this purpose. Conceptually it can be viewed as a composite object that can be represented in terms of modeling concepts such as entities or relationships.

Low collaboration levels usually require engagements such as e-portfolio and perhaps group management. Higher levels, in particular those supporting work processes, will require engagements such as team formation or workflow instance.

## 7 Implementation and Summary

One simple implementation is to use workspaces that directly support the meta-model concepts. An e-portfolio is presented by one workspace as that shown in Fig. 9.

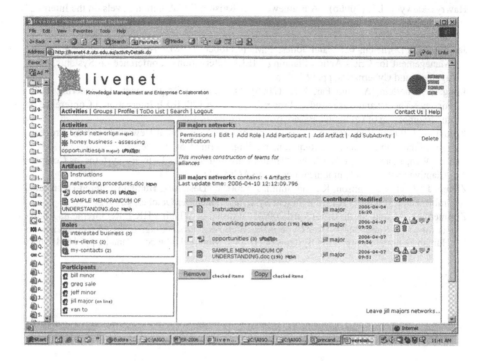

**Fig. 9.** Implementation of a broker interface

The workspace provides the customization needed to implement the services. Thus any roles, documents, and work-items can all be added to the workspace and can be accessed through the workspace. For example, in this case the roles are repairer and assessor as shown in Fig. 7. It also includes a discussion forum for clarifications and support for instant messaging. Similar mappings can be made to other technologies but the flexibility provided by workspaces tends to give it some advantage.

This paper addressed the need for raising the collaborative capability of organizations by providing platforms of services that support collaborative business processes. It defined a way to identify the collaborative requirements, which are needed to develop such capability. The paper defined a structured way for defining collaboration in terms of a number of levels and a way to specify a technical strategy to realize a required level.

# References

Hawryszkiewycz, I.T. (2006a): "Engagements as a Unifying Concept for Process Integration," Proceedings of the 14th International Conference on Information Systems.

Hawryszkiewycz, I.T. (2006b): "A Framework for Raising Collaboration Levels on the Internet," 7th International Conference on Electronic Commerce and Web Technologies, Krakow, Poland, pp. 82–91.

Jacobs, J.L., Dorneich, C.P., and Jones, P.M. (October, 1998): "Activity Representation and Management for Crisis Action Planning," IEEE International Conference on Systems, Management and Cybernatics, pp. 961–966.

Jiang, L., Eberlein, A., and Far, B.H. (2005): "Combining Requirements Engineering Techniques—Theory and Case Study," Proceedings of the 12th IEEE International Conference on the Engineering of Computer-Based Systems (ECBS 05).

Padula, A. (2004): "Requirements Engineering Process Selection at Hewlett-Packard," Proceedings of the 12th International Requirements Engineering Conference.

Tan, J., Wen, J., and Awad, N. (2006): "Health Care and Services Delivery Systems  as Complex Adaptive Systems," Communications of the ACM, 48(5), 37–44.

Zhang, J., Patel, V., Johnson, K., and Smith, J. (2002): "Designing Human Centered Distributed Information Systems," IEEE Intelligent Systems, September/October, 42–47.

Zimmerman, A., and Nardi, B.A. (April 2006): "Whither of Whether HICI: Requirements Analysis for Multi-Sited, Multi-User Cyberinfrastructures," Proceedings of ACM Conference on Human Factors in Computing Systems (CHI '06), Montréal, Québec, Canada, pp. 1601–1606.

# An Improved Partitioning Method for Distributed Object-Oriented Systems

Hamish T. Barney and Graham C. Low

University of New South Wales, School of Information Systems, Technology and Management, {hamish| g.low}@student.unsw.edu.au

**Abstract** The design of distributed systems involves the partitioning of the system into components or partitions and the allocation of these components to physical nodes. Techniques have been proposed for both the partitioning and allocation process. However, these techniques suffer from a number of limitations. For instance, object replication has the potential to greatly improve the performance of an object oriented distributed system but can be difficult to use effectively and existing techniques offer limited support for developing and harnessing object replication. An improved technique for partitioning of object-oriented distributed systems is proposed which incorporates support for static object replication, improved concurrency identification and class similarity. It builds on existing techniques from the field of distributed systems. The technique developed is demonstrated and tested on an example system. The new technique is compared with existing partitioning techniques in order to demonstrate both the validity and superiority of the new technique.

## 1 Introduction

The design of a distributed system involves decomposing the system into components that are allocated to physical nodes. The process of breaking the system down into components is called partitioning. Partitioning has the major goals of minimizing inter-process communication, exploiting potential concurrency, and limiting the size of processes (Shatz, 1993). There are a variety of partitioning techniques including those described by Low and Rasmussen (2000), Chang and Tseng (1995), Savonnet et al. (1999), and Huang and Chang (2000). A review of these techniques in Section 2 indicates that each has limitations, which impact the effectiveness of the partitioning decision. Support for replication, which offers many advantages for distributed systems including local object invocation, potential for reduced network traffic, higher availability, and elimination of the delays that network latency imposes, is one notable omission. The benefits of replication must be considered against the overhead of keeping replicas consistent (Chen and Suda, 1997).

C. Barry et al. (eds.), *Information Systems Development: Challenges in Practice, Theory, and Education, Vol.1*, doi: 10.1007/978-0-387-68772-8_22,
© Springer Science+Business Media, LLC 2009

This paper compares existing partitioning techniques (Section 2) before presenting an improved technique (Section 3) based on Low and Rasmussen (2000). This improved technique incorporates support for static replication, improved concurrency identification, and class similarity. The use of the modified technique is illustrated using an example system (Section 4). The solution is used to compare the modified technique with existing object-oriented partitioning techniques.

# 2 Literature Review

Partitioning is the process of dividing the system into a set of logical modules that are assigned to processors in a system. This process has three major goals: minimizing inter-process communication, exploiting potential concurrency, and limiting the size of processes (Shatz, 1993). These three goals conflict, for example, creating a single partition would eliminate all inter-process communication but this arrangement would violate the other two goals of the partitioning process. A viable partitioning technique must, therefore, balance these three competing goals. Existing solutions to the partitioning problem will be examined.

## 2.1 Discussion of Techniques

Chang and Tseng (1995) proposed a partitioning strategy that attempts to minimize the volume of communication between nodes and the cost of method invocation in the given class hierarchy whilst utilizing all nodes in the network. Initially, each object/class in the system is placed in a separate partition. The two partitions with the highest association, estimated communication cost, and code similarity are merged to form a single partition. Partitions are merged until the number of partitions matches the number of processors in the system. They tested the algorithm experimentally and confirmed its effectiveness.

Low and Rasmussen (2000) also proposed a technique for partitioning and allocation. Objects/classes are assigned to partitions based on the estimated level of communication and the potential for concurrency between the object/classes. The proposed partition sizes are checked to ensure they are within acceptable limits. Partitions are then allocated to processors based on estimated communication costs between partitions and the processing load on each of the nodes in the distributed system.

The estimated level of communication between each object/class is determined from sequence diagrams or event model diagrams and their accompanying trace tables. These authors suggest various metrics for determining the estimated level of communication between object/classes, the most detailed being counting of the number of messages sent and weighting these messages based on the size of the arguments sent with the message.

Sequence diagrams are used to identify objects/classes that may operate concurrently. Object/classes are assumed to be able to operate concurrently if there is no path of control between them. The level of concurrency possible between other objects/classes is decided by further analysis taking factors such as asynchronous communication into consideration.

The sizes of the resultant executable partition processes are estimated by using an appropriate size metric like lines of code. Weightings are assigned to these measures to allow conversion into executable image size.

Savonnet et al. (1999) propose a distributed design methodology that encompasses both partitioning (or 'fragmentation' using their terminology) and allocation. Their methodology is designed for use with object oriented databases but is nevertheless worth considering within the context of object-oriented distributed systems.

A user of Savonnet et al.'s methodology would first create a class dependency graph, where each node represents an object and each edge represents a relationship between two objects traversed during the operation of the system. The edges are then weighted based on the estimated frequency of communication between the two objects. To estimate the weight of each edge they suggest using decapsulation, which uses a petri-net simulation of the program to derive an estimate of the magnitude of the communication between classes.

The graph of classes is then broken into partition trees—containing relatively independent groups of strongly related classes—which are used to "produce autonomous and self-contained database fragments".

Huang and Chang (2000) suggest a fourth partitioning methodology based on a technique called "Function Class Decomposition". Function Class Decomposition (Chang et al., 2001) uses a combination of object oriented and structural modelling techniques to model a system in a top-down manner that takes into account a module's functionality while maximizing cohesion and minimizing coupling between modules. They recommend using the resultant class groupings as the partitions.

## 2.2 Comparison of Techniques

The Low and Rasmussen (2000), Chang and Tseng (1995), Savonnet et al. (1999), and Huang and Chang (2000) techniques are compared below. Any apparent deficiencies not addressed in these techniques are also discussed.

### 2.2.1 Class similarity

Chang and Tseng's technique explicitly deals "with the cost of invoked method execution on the class hierarchy" and minimizing the size of the processes associated with each partition. They do this by incorporating object/class similarity in their metric for partitioning.

While Low and Rasmussen's technique considers the size of the resultant processes, it does not incorporate the object/class similarity concerns addressed by Chang and Tseng as a method of limiting size.

Neither Savonnet et al.'s nor Huang and Chang's technique considers class similarity or partition size explicitly. In both techniques, classes are assigned to partitions without explicit reference to their position in the class hierarchy or the size of the executable produced by the partitioning process.

### 2.2.2 Concurrency identification

Low and Rasmussen's, and to a lesser extent, Huang and Chang's, and Savonnet et al.'s techniques provide concurrency identification while Chang and Tseng's algorithm does not. Some types of concurrency will, however, go unidentified regardless of which technique is applied.

Chang and Tseng's, Huang and Chang's, and Savonnet et al.'s partitioning techniques do not facilitate the exploitation of asynchronous communication. If two classes communicate frequently, but asynchronously, then a performance advantage could be gained by placing the two classes into separate partitions and allocating the two partitions to separate nodes to facilitate improved concurrency.

Some objects/classes are highly co-dependent. Such co-dependant objects/classes will, in response to every event, invoke methods of the object/class on which they are dependent. A gain in concurrency is unlikely if these two objects/classes are allocated to separate partitions. Huang and Chang's and Low and Rasmussen's techniques explicitly address this concern. In the former case classes that are highly interdependent are assigned to the same partition while in the latter case the concurrency algorithm will indicate no possible concurrency.

However, not all objects/classes are totally reliant on one another. They only call the methods of another object/class in response to a sub-set of potential events. These objects/classes offer a degree of potential concurrency. None of the techniques implicitly or explicitly addresses this concern.

### 2.2.3 Replication concerns

None of the techniques considered explicitly consider replication. For instance, placing an object that rarely changes state or that can afford to have low replica consistency in the same partition as another object that frequently changes state will limit the possibility of replicating that partition. If a partition containing an object/class that changes state frequently is replicated the cost of keeping those replicas consistent will mean a decrease in performance that far outweighs the benefits of replicating that partition (Coulouris et al., 2005). Therefore, placing two objects that change state with differing frequencies in the same partition will limit the potential for replication.

### 2.2.4 Partition coherency and low inter-partition coupling

The technique proposed by Huang and Chang produces a partitioning arrangement where there is high cohesion within partitions and low inter-partition coupling. This is, however, a means to solving the partitioning problem rather than an end. The goals of the partitioning process (Shatz, 1993) imply dividing the system into partitions that have high internal cohesion and loose inter-partition coupling.

The other three techniques indirectly address this issue by using estimated communication volumes, concurrency considerations, and/or class similarity.

# 3 Proposed Partitioning Technique

Low and Rasmussen's partitioning technique (2000) is used as a basis for the proposed technique due to its better support for concurrency identification. Three modifications are incorporated: additional concurrency identification, replication, and class similarity support. The proposed technique is meant to give its users better information in order that they can choose the best partitioning arrangement.

A summary of the proposed modified technique is outlined below. The modifications to the Low and Rasmussen's technique are shown in italics.

1) *Communication determination:*
   The estimated level of communication between each object/class is determined from sequence diagrams or event model diagrams and their accompanying trace tables. These values are recorded in a matrix where each cell represents the expected communication, in either direction, between a pair of objects/classes in the system.

2) *Concurrency identification:*
   The following steps should be taken to identify potential concurrency:

- Using the sequence or event diagrams, build a matrix where the rows represent objects/classes and columns represent the objects/classes that require services from this object/class. An "X" is shown where this is the case. In addition, set the diagonal entries in the matrix to "-" since concurrency between instances of the same object/class are not relevant to the partitioning process.
- Find the transitive closure of the matrix using Floyd–Warshall's (Floyd, 1962) algorithm or equivalent.
- The matrix and corresponding object/class model now represent the inter-object/class dependencies that prevent concurrency between objects. Set all non-"X" symbols to "A" as these object/classes do not collaborate.
- "B" grade concurrency is assigned to the matrix cell where there is asynchronous communications between object/classes represented by that matrix row and that matrix column. This requires an examination of all event model diagrams where those objects/classes interact.

- Concurrency is possible if object/class A shares B with object/class C. If A and C can operate concurrently, this means that B may provide a service to C while A is doing something else. This is labeled "C" grade concurrency between A and B.
- *Limited concurrency is also possible if in every event that involves object/class A, A does not always invoke a method on object/class B, then this is labeled "D" grade concurrency.*
- Finalize the concurrency matrix by taking the lowest level of concurrency possible between two classes.

3) *Similarity identification:*

It is suggested that the best way to incorporate object/class similarity concerns is to produce a matrix showing the estimated level of similarity between each object/class.

*Chang and Tseng (1995) suggest using the proportion of methods shared between two partitions as a guide to whether they should be merged. If the size of the methods varies substantially, a better metric might be the number of shared lines of code. It is acknowledged that the number of lines of code in each method may not be known at the time of partitioning. It is suggested that in this case other size metrics may be used such as object points. This would enable developers to perform the partitioning before the development of an application is complete.*

*It is possible to merge the two metrics, the proportion of shared methods and the number of shared lines of code, so that the twin goals of minimizing the "cost of invoked method execution on the object/class hierarchy" (Chang and Tseng 1995) and minimizing the size of processes (Shatz, 1993) are met effectively. Giving:*

$$s(p_{x,y}, m_{x,y}, a) = [p_{x,y}\, a] + [m_{x,y}\,(1 - a)] \qquad (1)$$

| | |
|---|---|
| $x$ and $y$ | The two partitions whose similarity is to be compared. |
| $s$ | A function that provides an estimate of the similarity between two partitions. |
| $p_{x,y}$ | The number of methods shared by x and y divided by the total number of unique methods x and y implement. |
| $m_{x,y}$ | The size (lines of code or other measure) of the shared methods between object/classes x and y divided by the total size of the whole project. |
| $A$ | Parameter, weighting the importance of the two inputs $p$ and $m$. The value of this parameter must be between one and zero. A value closer to 1 implies that the size ($m$) shared code is more important while a value closer to 0 indicates that the number of methods ($p$) is considered more important. |

*Equation 1 encompasses both the size and the number of shared methods, the two simple metrics previously discussed. The parameter, a, allows the user of this equation to weight the factor he/she feels to be more important.*

*Equation 1 is used to create an object/class similarity matrix where each cell represents the calculated similarity between a pair of objects/classes in the system.*

4) *Assign object/classes to partitions*

- Examine the concurrency matrix:
    a. Allocate objects/classes that show "A" level concurrency to separate partitions. Objects/classes that show no potential for concurrency (i.e. an "X") are allocated to the same partition; and
    b. Consider allocating objects/classes that show "B", "C," *or "D"* level concurrency to separate partitions.
- *Examine the object/class similarity and communications matrices to determine if objects/classes allocated to separate partitions may be better allocated to the same partition.*
- *Examine each partition to ensure that replication concerns are satisfied. It is suggested that the objects are examined to further understand the frequency with which they change and, therefore, their replica consistency requirements. It is necessary to identify objects that change frequently and require high replica consistency. Once identified, objects with these requirements should only be placed in partitions with other objects that have similar requirements.*

# 4 Example Application

A worked example is used to illustrate the modified partitioning technique. The example is based on an implementation of a ticket booking system and has been designed to highlight the different aspects of the proposed and surveyed methods. The system and its operation are described and partitioned using the modified technique. The partitioning arrangement is compared to the results from using the other techniques (Chang and Tseng, 1995; Huang and Chang; 2000, Low and Rasmussen, 2000; Savonnet et al., 1999).

## 4.1 Description of Example System

Frustrated by the disparate booking systems of the various airlines and cruise ship companies, a group of 50 travel agents, have convinced the transport operators that they need a centralized booking system. The airlines and cruise companies, convinced of the cost savings centralized booking system would entail and agree to participate.

Travel Agents help customers find flights or cruises that suit their travel plans. They search for flights or cruises that will take a customer where he/she wants to go on the dates that the customer requests. When a customer has chosen a flight, the Travel Agent will try to book the tickets. If a customer decides that he/she no longer wishes to take the flight or cruise the travel agent can cancel it.

Each airline has decided that it will offer a frequent flyer bonus points program. Customers who have flown with an airline will gain bonus points that the customer can later reclaim on flights with that airline. The cruise companies have decided that a similar frequent cruiser program would not benefit them and prefer to offer their customers slightly cheaper prices on their cruises instead.

The use case descriptions are described below.

- *New customer:* The new customer case allows a travel agent to enter the details of new customers into the ticketing system. Customer's details such as name and address are required in order to send the customer the tickets he/she purchases. The customer object is used as a reference when tracking the number of frequent flyer points the customer has saved. When a new customer is entered into the system, he/she is also given the opportunity to join one or more of the airlines' frequent flyer programs. It is expected that approximately 100 new customers will be entered into the system per day each joining on average two of the three frequent flyer programs.

- *Search:* When a customer wishes to go somewhere he/she must first search for flights or cruises that are suitable. The flight or cruise must depart from the customer's desired location, arrive where the customer wants to go, and on the dates he/she desires. This process is somewhat simplified; the system will only find routes that go directly between two locations. In addition, tickets of the appropriate sort must still be available on the plane or boat. It is expected that each customer will make on average three searches before finding an appropriate ticket as he/she searches for suitable dates or decides between alternative destinations. There will be approximately 9,000 searches conducted per day. The customer must choose the origin and destination for his/her journey. It is assumed that, on average, there will be three routes that match the customer's criteria. For each of those routes it is assumed that two flights or cruises will operate within the date range the customer desires. The travel agent will then query each of the transports that match the customer's criteria and test if there are seats remaining and whether they match the customer's desired departure dates. In order to test whether there are tickets remaining, the Transport object must first get a list of the stopovers that lie between the customer's origin and destination. The Transport then checks the availability of tickets on the journey legs on which the customer is interested in traveling. Approximately 100 Ticket objects are expected to be queried during each such search. The tally of sold tickets is then compared to the number of tickets available for that leg of the journey. If there are still tickets available then a value of true is returned.

- *Book Ticket:* Once a customer has decided on which flight or cruise he/she will take in order to get to the destination, the travel agent will book it. In order to book the ticket the Transport object for that flight is contacted to see if there are still sufficient tickets from the desired origin to the desired destination. The Transport object, in an identical procedure to that given above for the search event, polls the ticket objects to ascertain the number of free seats over the journey leg of interest. If there are enough seats, a new Ticket object will be returned, which the Travel Agent completes with the customer's details. Customers are expected to make approximately 3000 bookings per day. Each of those bookings is estimated to be for an average of two tickets.

- *Cancel Ticket:* Sometimes a customer decides he/she doesn't actually want to take the flight or cruise. In this case, the customer can go to the travel agent and cancel the ticket. This will occur 100 times per day on average.
- *Update frequent flyer points:* Each of the three airlines runs their own frequent flyer points program as a service to its customers. Each customer who is a member of a particular airline's frequent flyer program has an account that stores his/her frequent flyer points and a history of flights with that airline. These accounts are updated on a daily basis by the airlines by awarding points to customers that have flown with the airline on that day. Each airline operates an average of 14 flights per day with an average of 150 tickets sold for each.

## 4.2 Applying the Proposed Method

Table 1 shows the proposed technique's concurrency identification, estimated communication cost, and class similarity matrices for this system. The parameter value of 0.5 was used in the class similarity calculations. The standard cost table (Low and Rasmussen, 2000) has been used to estimate the cost of communication between objects/classes.

## 4.3 Comparison of results

The variation in the results of the different techniques can be explained in terms of the particular focus of that technique. Examples of partitioning arrangements suggested by the various techniques are examined which illustrate the differences between the partitioning techniques and how the modified technique improves upon the previous techniques with respect to object/class similarity, concurrency identification, and replication concerns.

### 4.3.1 Concurrency analysis

Travel Agent and Flight objects/classes are likely to be placed into the same partition in Chang and Tseng's (1995) and Savonnet et al.'s (1999) techniques due to the estimated volume of communication between these two objects/classes. Their techniques do not conduct any form of concurrency analysis and may waste potential concurrency by assigning objects/classes that communicate frequently to the same partition that could otherwise operate concurrently. Low and Rasmussen's

**Table 1.** Object/Classes comparison matrix showing the triple communication, concurrency, and class similarity levels

| | Port | Airport | Flight | Cruise | Ticket | Route | Airline | Bonus Account | Customer |
|---|---|---|---|---|---|---|---|---|---|
| Travel | 75600 | 248400 | 14803440 | 510560 | 20600 | 5670000 | 0 | 0 | 121600 |
| Agent | D | D | B | B | B | C | D | D | D |
| | 0 | 0 | 0 | 0 | 0 | 0 | 0 | 0 | 0 |
| Port | - | 0 | 0 | 0 | 0 | 0 | 0 | 0 | 0 |
| | | A | A | A | A | A | A | A | A |
| | | 0.0216 | 0 | 0 | 0 | 0 | 0 | 0 | 0 |
| Airport | | - | 0 | 0 | 0 | 0 | 0 | 0 | 0 |
| | | | A | A | A | A | A | A | A |
| | | | 0 | 0 | 0 | 0 | 0 | 0 | 0 |
| Flight | | | - | 0 | 63792000 | 842280 | 9420 | 0 | 0 |
| | | | | A | D | X | B | A | A |
| | | | | 0.3654 | 0 | 0 | 0 | 0 | 0 |
| Cruise | | | | - | 2208000 | 29440 | 0 | 0 | 0 |
| | | | | | D | X | A | A | A |
| | | | | | 0 | 0 | 0 | 0 | 0 |
| Ticket | | | | | - | 49500 | 36000 | 0 | 40500 |
| | | | | | | D | A | A | D |
| | | | | | | 0 | 0 | 0 | 0 |
| Route | | | | | | - | 0 | 0 | 0 |
| | | | | | | | A | A | A |
| | | | | | | | 0 | 0 | 0 |
| Airline | | | | | | | - | 1400 | 2000 |
| | | | | | | | | B | D |
| | | | | | | | | 0 | 0 |
| Bonus Account | | | | | | | | - | 27000 |
| | | | | | | | | | X |
| | | | | | | | | | 0 |

For example, the matrix cell at the intersection between Travel Agent and Port shows the estimated values of the various variables:

- 75600—communication volume
- D—concurrency level
- 0—class-similarity.

*Note*: The proposed object/class similarity metric with a parameter value of 0.1 was used to calculate class similarity.

(2000) technique and the modified technique both identify potential "B' level concurrency between Travel Agent and Flight and as such would suggest allocating these objects/classes to separate partitions. In the case of the Airline and Flight objects/classes, Huang and Chang's (2000) technique would suggest allocating both objects/classes to the same partition since they constitute a coherent piece of functionality and the technique does not incorporate any concurrency analysis. In contrast, both Low and Rasmussen's (2000) technique and the proposed technique suggest allocating these two objects/classes to separate partitions on the basis of potential "B" level concurrency. As Low and Rasmussen's (2000) technique for concurrency analysis finds no potential concurrency between the Travel Agent and

Airport objects/classes and the estimated level of communications between the two objects/classes is high, the two objects/classes would be assigned to the same partition. However, the modified technique takes the concurrency analysis a step further. It finds that there is indeed possible "D" level concurrency between the two objects/classes because not all the methods of the Travel Agent object/class rely on calling methods of the Airport object/class (and vice versa). If someone was seeking to maximize concurrency there is the possibility that they could assign the two objects to separate partitions.

### 4.3.2 Replication concerns

Using Chang and Tseng's (1995) or Savonnet et al.'s (1999) technique instances of the Flight, Cruise and Ticket objects/classes will almost certainly be placed in the same partition. The Flight and Cruise objects/classes communicate frequently with the Ticket objects/classes. Using Chang and Tseng's (1995) technique they are even more likely to be allocated to a single partition because the estimated level of communication is very high coupled with the degree of similarity identified between the Flight and Cruise objects/classes and this increases the chances of co-locating these objects/classes.

Similarly, using Huang and Chang's (2000) partitioning technique the Ticket, Flight and Cruise objects/classes will, in all probability, be allocated to the same partition. Together these classes implement a cohesive block of functionality and, as such, would be allocated to a single partition.

Low and Rasmussen's technique identifies no opportunity for concurrency between the Ticket and Flight or the Ticket and Cruise objects/classes. The Ticket object/class also communicates extensively with both the Flight and the Cruise objects/classes. On the basis of this analysis, the Flight and Cruise objects/classes' strong interaction with the Ticket object/class suggests that all three objects/classes be assigned to a single partition.

The modified technique recommends not assigning objects/classes with differing consistency requirements and different propensities to change to the one partition. In this case the Flight and Cruise objects/classes will change infrequently whereas the Ticket object/class will change frequently. In this case, the Flight and Cruise objects/classes should be placed in a separate partition from the Ticket objects/classes. Instances of the Flight and Cruise objects/classes are candidates for replication because they do not change state after they have been created. The state of the Ticket object/class changes frequently. Placing these three objects/classes in the same partition means we are not free to decide if it is advantageous for the Flight and Cruise object/class to be replicated at allocation time.

### 4.3.3 Class similarity

In Chang and Tseng's (1995) technique, the greatest level of similarity is found between the Cruise and Flight objects/classes because they inherit the most methods from their super-class relative to the methods that they overload or implement themselves. The similarity their technique finds between the Port and Airport objects/classes is quite low. On that basis, Cruise and Flight are more likely to be allocated to a single partition than Port and Airport.

Savonnet et al.'s (1999), Huang and Chang's (2000), and Low and Rasmussen's (2000) techniques do not incorporate class similarity concerns explicitly. For this reason the class similarities between the Cruise and Flight objects/classes and between the Port and Airport classes would play no explicit role in determining in which partition they should be placed.

In the modified technique, class similarity (as a function of both estimated size and functions inherited) is taken into account along with potential for concurrency and communication between the objects/classes (Table 1). The similarity between the Port and Airport objects/classes is relatively low. This, combined with the A level concurrency and no direct communications between these two objects/ classes, suggests allocating them to separate partitions.

Using the modified technique to analyze the relationship between Flight and Cruise objects the conclusion is less clear-cut. The potential for concurrency between the two objects/classes is high (A level concurrency) and there is no direct communication between them (see Table 1). This would suggest allocating them to separate partitions. However consideration of class similarity suggests allocating them to the same partition.

## 5 Conclusion

The modified technique has been demonstrated to better meet Shatz's (1993) goals for the partitioning process by addressing the following:

- The modified technique extends the concurrency identification process suggested by Low and Rasmussen (2000) to identify "D" grade concurrency. The example system demonstrates the success of this extended concurrency identification process. The potential concurrency between Travel Agent and Airport, not identified by the Low and Rasmussen's (2000) concurrency identification process, was uncovered. The other techniques (i.e. Chang and Tseng, 1995; Huang and Chang, 2000; Savonnet et al., 1999) do not explicitly consider concurrency. As such the potential for concurrency between objects/classes is reduced.
- The modified technique incorporates object replication concerns by suggesting strategies for identifying objects/classes that will hinder replication if they are placed in the same partition. This facet of the technique can be seen in the example where it is suggested that Ticket be placed in a separate partition from Flight and Cruise in order to maximize the replication potential of the Flight and Cruise objects/classes. None of the other techniques reviewed (i.e. Chang and Tseng, 1995; Huang and Chang 2000; Low and Rasmussen, 2000;

Savonnet et al., 1999) incorporate replication and as such the partitioning arrangement they produce may be sub-optimal.

- The modified technique also incorporates a class similarity metric aiding in the identification of ways to reduce the size of suggested partitions extending the partition size metric suggested by Low and Rasmussen (2000). The suggested class similarity metric incorporates shared methods and class size rather than just the number of shared methods as suggested by Chang and Tseng (1995). The success of this class similarity metric is demonstrated in the illustrative example. A significant similarity between the Cruise and Flight objects/classes was found while the Port and Airport objects/classes were found not to have a significant enough level of similarity to be placed in a single partition. Savonnet et al.'s (1999) and Huang and Chang's (2000) techniques do not incorporate class similarity explicitly. Neither of these techniques offer the user a systematic way of minimizing the size of the suggested partitioning arrangement.

Application of the modified partitioning technique with an associated allocation technique, such as that proposed by Rasmussen and Low (2000) or Barney and Low (2006), will enable analysts to be more effective in designing distributed applications.

# References

Barney, H. T. and Low, G. C. (2006) Harnessing Replication in Object Allocation. In Camel, A. (Ed.) XVI. International Conference on Computer and Information Science and Engineering. Venice, pp. 129–134.

Chang, C. K., Cleland-Huang, J., Hua, S., and Kuntzmann-Combelles, A. (2001) Function-Class Decomposition: A Hybrid Software Engineering Method. IEEE Computer 34, 87–93.

Chang, W. T. and Tseng, C. C. (1995) Clustering Approach to Grouping Objects in Message-Passing Systems. Journal of Object Orientated Programming 7, 42–43 and 46–50.

Chen, L. T. and Suda, T. (1997) Designing Mobile Computing Systems Using Distributed Objects. IEEE Communications Magazine 35, 62–70.

Coulouris, G., Dollimore, J., and Kindberg, T. (2005) Distributed Systems: Concepts and Design, Addison-Wesley, Reading, MA.

Floyd, R. W. (1962) Algorithm 97 (Shortest Path). Communications of the ACM 5, 345.

Huang, J. L. and Chang, C. K. (2000) Supporting the Partitioning of Distributed Systems with Function-Class Decomposition. The 24th Annual International Computer Software and Applications Conference (COMPSAC 2000), pp. 351–356.

Low, G. C. and Rasmussen, G. (2000) Partitioning and Allocation of Objects in Distributed Application Development. Journal of Research and Practice on Information Technology, 32, 75–106.

Savonnet, M., Terasse, M.-N., and Yetongnon, K. (1999) FRAGTIQUE: An OO Distribution Design Methodology. 6th International Conference on Advanced Systems for Advanced Applications, pp. 283–290.

Shatz, S. M. (1993) Development of Distributed Software: Concepts and Tools, Macmillan, New York.

# Towards Multifractal Approach in IS Development

Marite Kirikova

Riga Technical University, Department of Systems Theory and Design,
marite.kirikova@cs.rtu.lv

**Abstract**  Since today's enterprises must constantly adapt to rapidly changing external environment, it is necessary to be able to deal with variation and changing conditions in information systems (IS) development. This may be achieved by the use of multifractal IS development methodologies. Fractal approaches to some extent have already been tested in adaptive enterprise development, adaptive manufacturing systems development, and software development. This suggests that multifractal IS development, on the one hand, is appropriate, because the information system should properly reflect the business enterprise (in this case a fractal one) and, on the other hand, it is possible, because some elements of it have already been implemented. Development of multifractal IS aims at managing relative completeness by relative simplicity that has to be discovered in different subsystems that influence the development of the information system. This, in essence, implies the need of thorough analysis an understanding of business structures and processes to discover patterns useful for the identification of fractal features. Currently, only some guidelines for development of multifractal IS are derived from reported experiences of fractal systems development and the use of fractal approaches in other domains.

## 1 Introduction

Usually information systems (IS) development is understood as a particular project that starts at a particular date and ends with the delivery of the computer system that meets requirements stated by customers and designers. After the delivery, the system enters the maintenance phase, which finishes with the replacement of the existing system with a new radically different system. In the rapidly changing environment of today, however, the system is under continuous changes during the maintenance period. Those changes may affect different aspects of the system, including data structures, functional procedures, access rights, etc. Thus, one can say that the IS continues to be developed after basic software has been designed and implemented according to the user requirements and project agreements. This

C. Barry et al. (eds.), *Information Systems Development: Challenges in Practice, Theory, and Education, Vol.1*, doi: 10.1007/978-0-387-68772-8_23,
© Springer Science+Business Media, LLC 2009

continuous development, on the one hand, is natural, because the IS is closely related to the processes in the human mind and outer world, which open new understanding of things and new ways of performing organizational activities. On the other hand, it is a cumbersome task for systems developers to follow those changes swiftly and correctly. From the IS viewpoint, the emergence of new requirements may look rather chaotic and unpredictable, inducing the threat that the outer "chaos" will diffuse in systems development and maintenance activities to such extent that their management will become an almost irresolvable problem.

Software engineering tries to solve the software changeability problem by introducing more intelligent complex adaptive software that can participate in its own installation and customization and adapting to new circumstances (Gabriel et al., 2006). In IS development, a similar paradigm could be appropriate. However, in IS case, it is necessary to take into consideration not only software performance but also processes performed by human beings. Therefore, it is necessary to deal with various internal and environmental factors from the viewpoint of different types of systems: social, economical, informational, computational, etc. The paper suggests multifractal IS development approach for handling the problem of IS development in turbulent environment. The essence of the approach is considering information system as a multifractal system in all stages of its development and maintenance.

The paper is structured as follows. In Sect. 2, the main components of IS potentially exposing fractal nature and relationships between those components are analyzed. In Sect. 3, related work on fractal systems relevant to IS development is considered. In Sect. 4, some practical aspects of IS development are discussed in a light of multifractal paradigm. Section 5 proposes some guidelines for multifractal IS development. Section 6 consists of brief conclusions.

## 2 Fractal Nature of IS Components

"Fractality" has been introduced as a watchword for a new way of thinking about the collective behavior of many basic and interacting units. Fractality, thus, is the study of the behavior of macroscopic units that are endowed with the potential to evolve in time. Their interactions lead to coherent collective phenomena, so-called emergent properties that can be described only at higher levels than those of the individual units. Fractal theory is based on relationships, emergence, patterns, and iterations (Fryer, 2004). It is used to describe structure and processes of flexible, adaptive, and evolving systems. Fractal theory is applied in biomedicine, fractal geometry, mathematics, statistical analysis, signal analysis, image analysis (Klonowski, 2000), manufacturing (Tharumarajah et al., 1998), product design (Chiva-Gomez, 2004), enterprise development (Ryu and Jung, 2003; Ramanathan, 2005; Hongzhao et al., 2005), software development (Gabriel and Goldman, 2006), and other areas. This suggests that this theory most probably is applicable also in the domain of IS development.

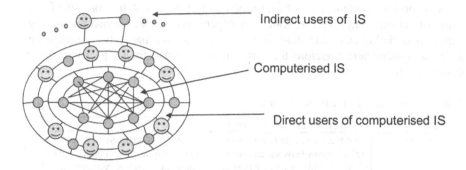

**Fig. 1.** A simplified view on information systems components

The main peculiarity of IS is interplay of many different natural and artificial systems that influence each other in various modes and at different levels of scale (Fig. 1). The computerized subsystem of the IS may consist of different related software and hardware systems that support various organizational processes and individual requests. This computerized IS may be directly or indirectly used by other components of the IS, namely, certain human beings and certain components of other computerized IS (Sprice and Kirikova, 2005). Each of the components at all three levels (the level of computerized IS, the level of direct users, and the level of indirect users) can be randomly related to all other components of the system. An important point here is the fact that IS as such may be regarded as *naturally* adaptive and evolving system. However, a computerized IS interacts during different phases of its lifecycle with a special category of users, namely, developers and maintainers, who can *artificially* change the natural evolution of the system.

The use of fractal paradigm in IS development offers an opportunity to regard IS as a multilevel composition of relatively small and simple components or fractal entities, where the composition exhibits self similarity, implying recursion, pattern-inside-the-pattern (Tharumarajah et al., 1998). An essential feature of fractal systems development is the possibility to structure fractals bottom-up, where higher level fractals assume only those responsibilities that cannot be fulfilled by lower order fractals. Fractals function as a coherent whole through a process of participation and coordination among fractals with the purpose of fulfilling the goals of the fractal system.

The purpose of fractal design is to achieve a high degree of flexibility to react and adapt quickly to environmental changes using decentralized and autonomous organizational units (Canavesio and Martinez, 2007). In case of IS, those units are composed of humans and computers, which are processing knowledge, information and data, each of which can change information processing functionality and behavior according to particular internal goals and constraints, and/or environmental influences.

In Table 1, several properties of fractal systems are listed and their applicability to the IS domain is illustrated (Fryer and Ruis, 2006). It has to be noted here that to be considered as fractal, the system should not manifest all of these properties.

A most common canonical list of the properties of fractal systems consists of self-similarity at different levels of scale, self organization, goal-orientation, and dynamics and vitality (Ryu and Jung, 2003). Table 1 shows that IS has properties of a fractal system, and therefore there is a reason to use fractal paradigm in IS development.

**Table 1.** Properties of IS as a fractal systems

| Property | Manifestation of the property in IS domain |
|---|---|
| Emergence | IS depends on user requirements, organizational structure of enterprise, relationships between enterprise partners, suppliers, and clients. All of them are influenced by external environment, therefore requirements change in apparently random rather than planned way, which in turn introduces the same type of changes in the IS. |
| Coevolution | All components of IS represented in Fig. 1 are systems themselves and can form different higher level systems, which exist in their own environment and are parts of that environment. When the environment changes, the systems evolve to achieve the best fit, but because they are part of their environment, when they change, they change the environment. Consider, e.g., changes in the software introduced by user request that require a different type of data entry, which, in turn, creates new patterns of interaction between users. |
| Suboptimality | IS does not have to be perfect in its performance to be useful for the organization. Actually it never is, because of the nature of requirements that never are perfect (it may slightly differ with embedded IS and safety critical systems). |
| Requisite variety | The more alternative tasks and more exceptions IS can handle, the wider service it can offer to the enterprise. |
| Connectivity | The very existence of IS is needed because of information it can provide. The components of IS are connected by physical or virtual information channels. The IS cannot exist without these channels. |
| Simple rules | With passing of time we can see how very complex structures and processes (e.g. centralized databases, ERP systems) are gradually replaced by simpler, more loosely coupled alternatives, e.g., data warehouses, distributed databases, service oriented architectures, etc.). |
| Self-organization | In IS self-organization may manifest at different levels of abstraction; at one level, there can be self-organizing software agents and, at another level of abstraction, there can be data base manager, who reorganizes database with purpose to handle new data requests. From the user point of view, the data base administrator, whose work usually is not seen by the user, is also part of the self organizing system that does the things without direct involvement of the user. |
| Self-similarity | Self-similarity may be interpreted as similarity between goals of organizational IS in a wider sense and computerized part of the IS in a narrower sense. |
| Goal-orientation | Different components of IS may have different goals, e.g., a marketing information subsystem and an accounting information subsystem; still, all these goals are coordinated to achieve the strategic goals of the enterprise. |
| Dynamics and vitality | Since a human being is a component of IS, which is dynamic and vital, the dynamics and vitality propagate to other IS components. On the other hand, intellectual software agents can be dynamic and vital, too. |

Thus, taking into consideration the fact that IS consists of widely different components, which are systems that can form various other systems, a multifractal system paradigm (Klonowski, 2000) is a proper metaphor for IS development. A multifractal system has global and also different local fractal dimensions, and, hence, global and local differences in complexity. Multifractals most likely are produced by two or more processes in enterprises where one and the same IS serves several organizational processes.

# 3 Related Work

Since the late twentieth century, fractal approach has become more and more popular not only in such areas as medicine or biology, but also in enterprise development, manufacturing, and software development. Probably the most cited work in this research field is Warneke's (1993) book on a fractal company. Different authors address fractal approach in various contexts, each of which adds to the understanding of potential applicability of this approach in IS development.

## 3.1 Fractal Paradigm vs. Other Systems Paradigms

Ryu and Jung (2003) discuss the difference between hierarchical organization and fractal-based organization in terms of structure, entity relationships, task processing, unit function, adaptability, and flexibility. They show that hierarchical organization is structured hierarchically only once, at a specific point of time; it has an administrative higher unit and passive lover units; it performs tasks according to specified objectives; each hierarchy's unit has its own functions according to its position and role; hierarchical organization is suitable for stable environment; it is inflexible. Fractal-based organization is subject to constant change (dynamically restructured); it has coordinative higher fractal and active lower fractals, it performs tasks through goal formation process; every fractal has the same functions, but its roles can be dynamically changed; fractal-based organization is suitable for turbulent environment; it is flexible.

Tharumarajah et al. (1998) compare bionic manufacturing, fractal factory, and holonic manufacturing. All three organizational structures are conglomerates of distributed and autonomous units, which operate as a set of cooperating entities. However the authors show that fractal structure is the only one that bases its adaptation on goals. Because of this feature the fractal paradigm is superior to holonic and bionic ones in the context of IS development. The authors also emphasize a bottom up design approach in fractal factory in contrast to a top-down one in other two conglomerates.

## 3.2 Fractal Enterprise

Taking into consideration the fact that IS has to reflect different organizational issues adequately, it is important to focus on properties of fractal enterprises that are to be supported by IS. Fractal enterprises are quite broadly discussed in different research fields (Ryu and Jung, 2003; Ramanathan, Hongzhao et al. 2005, Canavesio and Martinez, 2007). Although research and solution approaches slightly differ, almost all of them consider the enterprise from *agent perspective*, directly or indirectly refer to particular *basic processes/functions*, and highlight *project orientation* of fractal enterprises.

Because of the self-organization property of a fractal system, each fractal entity can be considered as an agent. Agents may have similar functional structure (Ryu and Jung, 2003; Hongzhao et al., 2005) and have particular cooperation relationships (Canavesio and Martinez, 2007), information flows, and feedbacks, as well as participate in overall fractal workflow (Ryu and Jung, 2003; Hongzhao et al., 2005).

The basic processes are addressed via functions of agents and/or via functions of fractal workflow. The following basic process/function taxonomies are addressed by different approaches to fractal enterprises:

- Sensing, observing, analyzing, resolving, organizing, reporting, actuating, – the main related functionalities of each fractal entity in fractal-based organization (Ryu and Jung, 2003)
- Sensing, requirements definition and planning, execution, delivery, responding, – the main constituents of transaction loops in adaptive complex enterprise (Ramanathan, 2005)
- Monitoring, analyzing, reporting, planning, executing, – the main functions of a fractal management unit in project-oriented fractal company (Canavesio and Martinez, 2007)
- Goal dissociation, partner selection, business coordination, tasks execution, schedule-progress monitoring, – the main functions of fractal workflow in fractal Web-based extended enterprise (Hongzhao et al., 2005)

All above-mentioned taxonomies are quite general and do not address specific organizational processes. In IS development context, the specifics of organizational processes are extremely important, therefore those general taxonomies have to be cross-referenced by business specific frameworks, such as business process handbooks (Klein and Petti, 2006) or detailed business process reference frameworks.

Several papers recommend project-oriented approach to business process identification and definition in fractal enterprises. Hongzhao et al. (2005) suggest Web-based project bidding. Canavesio and Martinez (2007) propose to put in the center of a fractal company a project manager, which can play means or ends manager role. The client–server relationship is established between a project manager that plays ends manager role and another actor that plays a means manager role. The delegation-to-do relationship is established between two project managers that are playing ends manager roles at different levels of abstraction.

## 3.3 Information Flows and Information Stores

There are the following four main information flows to be considered in fractal systems (Ryu and Jung, 2003; Tharumarajah et al., 1998):

- Information flows inside the fractal entity
- Information flows between the same level fractals
- Information flows between different level fractals
- Information flows between fractal entities and external environment

Information flows between external environment and fractal entities are used for assessment of change against specific levels of work environment such as cultural, strategic, socio-informal, financial, informational, and technological (Sihn, 1995; Tharumarajah et al., 1998).

Koutsakas et al. (2002) discuss the notion of information supply chains as the means for information organization in fractal systems.

Each fractal entity has its own knowledge base (Canavesio and Martinez, 2007). Additionally, Hongzhao et al. (2005) suggest availability of the following information resources for each fractal entity: enterprise database, experts database, products database, manufacturing resources database, cooperation case database; as well as availability of decision support tools, specific search engines, knowledge acquiring tools, cooperative manufacturing systems, and other tools.

## 3.4 Fractal Systems Development Approaches

Currently, there is no approach, which would suggest the fractal approach for the development of IS as interpreted in Fig. 1 (Sect. 2). However, there are the following attempts to use fractal approach for the development of different subsystems of IS:

Fractal approach in requirements definition (Beers, 2003), which distinguishes between relatively stable and volatile customer requirements

Fractal components model for software development (Bruneton et al., 2004), where a fractal component is formed out of two parts: a controller and content. The content of a component is composed of subcomponents, which are under the control of the controller of the enclosing component

- Fractal paradigm in intelligent software construction (Gabriel et al., 2006)

Fractal approach in data (Koike and Yoshihara, 1993; Lewison, 1994) and memory (McNutt, 2000) management

Fractal framework for dynamic application protocol adaptation (Lufei and Shi, 2006)

Bussler (2007) critically discusses the fractal nature of Web services and service-oriented architectures. The main message of the author is that fractal service-oriented architectures, being useful at the conceptual level, are not equally applicable during execution, and that it is necessary to separate service-oriented architecture concepts from implementation technology.

## 3.5 Indirectly Related Work

Research on patterns (Bubenko et al., 2001) when in association with other issues of IS development could provide useful background for analysis of fractals in enterprise and IS development.

Object-oriented systems development methods provide means for modeling aggregation, abstraction, inheritance, communications of objects and classes, and relating classes to objects.

Aspect-oriented systems development (Baniassad et al., 2006) deals with relevant concerns to be reflected in different software classes and objects. These concerns may appear to be useful in detection of fractal patterns not only in software architectures in particular (Bruneton et al., 2004), but also in IS architectures in general.

## 4 Fractals in IS Development Practice

Author's research in fractal aspects of IS was inspired by technical university's IS development project. When analyzing the needs of the university, it became obvious that similar (fractal) IS components are needed at the university level, at the departmental level, at the group level of, and even at the level of individual professors. Analysis of commercially available software packages revealed that currently none of them support the development of IS that are capable to meet the above-mentioned similarity.

Another important issue pointing at multifractal approach was the need to support "evolving" granularity of information. For instance, when a professor's CV is considered, information about the project may be requested very differently (all projects, scientific projects, and industrial projects separately; projects, where a person was a manager, an expert, or a researcher, to be given separately; and other similar combinations). The question arose how many combinations of one and the same information are to be kept in the database and whether procedures for project classification are necessary. The answer was that the information retrieval should be organized so that the final version of CV could be formed automatically, where there is a proper automatic procedure, or manually, where the procedure does not exist yet. If the system checks the manual procedures, gradually the decision may be made to provide an automatic generation means for particular information granule (or fractal).

One more issue suggesting research on fractal IS development is considerable similarity between project management systems designed for research funding organizations (Van Grootel, 2006; Leyesdorff and Meyer, 2003). They expose quite strong conceptual relationship between university, industry and government, on the one hand, and an ambition of each funding institution (except the university) to control all projects developed by national researchers, on the other hand.

Fractal approach is not uncommon in IS development. Many data warehouses support fractal, e.g., snowflake type data structures (Levene, 2003). Development and use of several CASE tools is based on particular, quite simple, basic meta-models (Tenteris et al., 1996; Tolvanen, 2006). Analysis of business model completeness for IS development suggested fractal enterprise models as superior to other modeling techniques (Kirikova, 1999). Therefore, consideration of IS as a multifractal system in all developmental stages could provide new, probably simpler means for IS requirements and architecture definition, as well as could support easier implementation and maintenance of computerized part of IS.

## 5 Some Guidelines for Fractal IS Development

Development of multifractal IS aims at managing relative completeness by relative simplicity that has to be discovered in different subsystems that influence the development of IS. This, in essence, implies the need for thorough analysis and understanding of business structures and processes to discover patterns useful for fractal identification. In view of the experience of fractal systems development discussed in previous sections, the following guidelines for development of multifractal IS emerge:

1. The fractals of IS should correspond to the fractals in its environment, therefore fractal properties of the IS environment should be analyzed in terms of common and individual properties of business units, feedback mechanisms, and mental models exposed by requirement holders. The guideline is based on the role of human issues discussed in Sect. 2 and properties of fractal enterprises described in Subsect. 3.2.

2. A bottom up approach may be used in identification and design of IS fractals. The guideline is based on comparison of different types of conglomerates of distributed and autonomous units (Sect. 3).

3. Once the potential fractal structure at some dimension is discovered, the knowledge, information, and data feed forward and feed back links must be identified so that lower level fractals could be nourished by information emerging in larger granularity fractals, and larger fractals would receive all information needed for the overall management of the business system. In other words, forward and backward knowledge chains in the fractal IS should be

introduced to ensure knowledge and information circulation in the system. The guideline is based on related work discussed in Subsects. 3.2 and 3.3.

4. In IS design, process the following principles relevant in adaptive complex systems (Chiva-Gomez, 2004) should be applied:

   - Maximize the relationships between enterprise members and the outside
   - Foster relationships between areas of people within the design process
   - Maximize the information flow
   - Promote heterogeneous participation and its balance in design decision making.

   The guideline supports the need to assess changes against the work environment as discussed in Subsect. 3.3.

5. At a conceptual level, introduce IS routines that can identify the need for restructuring the system in terms of procedural/service subsystems, data structures, and communication patterns. The guideline is introduced to solve practical problems discussed in Sect. 4 and takes into consideration service-oriented architecture properties, discussed in Subsect. 3.4.

The guidelines stated above are theoretical and should be tested and modified in attempt to develop a multifractal IS development methodology, which could be tested on real-life and artificially designed IS development examples.

# 6 Conclusions

As today's business must continuously adapt to external conditions in accelerated time frames, it is necessary to embrace variation and changing conditions in IS development (Ramanathan, 2005). One of the promising ways how to achieve it, is the use of multifractal IS development methodologies. The use of fractal approach to some extent has already been tested in adaptive enterprise development, software development, and adaptive manufacturing systems development. This suggests that development of multifractal IS development methodology is reasonable and feasible. Multifractal IS could properly reflect the highly dynamic business enterprise and provide necessary information for enterprise operation and management. Currently, only some guidelines for development of multifractal IS are derived from reported experiences of fractal IS component development and use of fractal approaches in other domains, and from problems discovered within the existing IS. Further research is needed to prove these guidelines as practically useful and to formulate multifractal IS development methodologies.

**Acknowledgments**  The research work reflected in the article is supported by the Ministry of Science and Education of Republic of Latvia and Riga Technical University, Project No. R7199.

# References

Baniassad, E. et al. (2006) Discovering early aspects, *IEEE Software*, January/February, pp. 61–69.

Beers, T.W. (2003) Fractal framework: finding sub-themes and implementing sub-frameworks, *Proceedings of IEEE International Conference on Information Reuse and Integration*, pp. 580–583.

Bruneton, E., Coupaye, T. and Stefani, J.B. (2004) The Fractal Component Model. Specification, The ObjectWeb Consortium.

Bubenko, J.A. jr, Persson, A. and Stirna, J. (2001) *User Guide of the Knowledge Management Approach Using Enterprise Knowledge Patterns,* deliverable D3, IST Programme project "Hypermedia and Pattern Based Knowledge Management for Smart Organisations", project no. IST-2000-28401, Dept. of Computer and Systems Sciences, Royal Institute of Technology, Stockholm, Sweden.

Bussler, Ch. (2007) The fractal nature of Web services, *IEEE Computer*, March, pp. 93–95.

Canavesio, M.M. and Martinez, E. (2007) Enterprise modeling of a project-oriented fractal company for SMEs networking, *Computers in Industry*, doi: 10.1016/j.compind.2007.02.-05., available online at http:// www.sciencedirect.com, accessed July 30, 2007.

Chiva-Gomez, R. (2004) Repercussions on complex adaptive systems on product design management. In *Technovation* 24, pp. 707–711.

Fryer, P. and Ruis, J. (2006) What are fractal systems: A brief description of complex adaptive and emerging systems, available at http://www.fractal.org, accessed April 14, 2007.

Gabriel, R.P. and Goldman, R (2006). Conscientious Software, *Proceedings of OOPSLA'06*, pp. 433–450, ACM 1-59593-348-4/06/0010.

Hongzhao, D., Dongxu, L., Yanwei, Z. and Chen, Y. (2005) A novel approach of networked manufacturing collaboration: fractal web based enterprise. *International Journal on Advanced Manufacturing Technology*, No. 26, pp. 1436–1442.

Kirikova, M. (1999) Towards completeness of business models. *Information Modelling and Knowledge Bases X*, H. Jaakola et al. (Eds.), IOS Press, Amsterdam, Netherlands, 1999, pp. 42–54.

Klonowski, Wl. (2000) Signal and image analysis using chaos theory and fractal geometry, available at http://www.fractal.org, accessed April 14, 2007.

Klein, M. and Petti, Cl. (2006) A handbook-based methodology for redesigning business processes, *Knowledge and Process Management*, Vol. 13, No. 2, pp. 108–119.

Koike, H. and Yoshihara, H. (1993) Fractal approaches for visualizing huge hierarchies. *Proceedings of the IEEE Symposium on Visual languages*, pp. 55–60.

Koutsakas, F., Hatzaras, P., Vontas, A. and Koumpis, A. (2002) Implementing information supply chains: the IST Adrenalin project. *Logistics Information Management*, Vol. 15, Issue 4, pp. 320–326.

Levene, M. and Loizou, G. (2003) Why is the snowflake schema a good data warehouse design? *Information Systems*, 28 (3). pp. 225–240.

Leydesdorff, L. and Meyer, M. (2003) The triple helix of university-industry-government relations, *Sociometrics*, Vol. 58, No. 2, pp. 191–203.

Lewison, L. (1994) Fractal databases – new horizons in database management, available at http:// www.iie.org, accessed July 30, 2007.

Lufei, H. and Shi, W. Fractal (2006) A mobile code-based framework for dynamic application protocol adaptation. *Journal of Parallel and Distributed Computing*, Vol. 66, Issue 7, pp. 887–906.

McNutt, Br. (2000) *The Fractal Structure of Data Reference: Application to the Memory Hierarchy (Advances in Database Systems)*, Springer.

Ramanathan, Y. (2005) Fractal architecture for the adaptive complex enterprise. *Communications of ACM*, May, Vol.48, No. 5, pp. 51–67.

Ryu, K. and Jung, M. (2003), Fractal approach to managing intelligent enterprises. *Creating Knowledge Based Organisations*, J.N.D. Gupta and S.K. Sharma (Eds.), Idea Group Publishers, pp. 312–348.

Sihn, W. (1995), Re-engineeringthrough fractal structures. *Proceedings of IFIPWG5.7 Working Conference Reengineering the Enterprise*, Ireland, pp. 21–30.

Sprice, R., and Kirikova, M. (2005) Feasibility study: New knowledge demands in turbulent business world. *Advances in Information Systems Development: Bridging the Gap Between Academia and Industry* Vol. 2, A.G. Nilsson, R. Gustas, W. Wojtkowski, W.G. Wojtkowski, S. Wrycza, J. Zupancic (Eds.), Springer, Berlin, 2006, pp. 131–142,

Tenteris, J., Vilums, E. and Zulis, V. (1996). Development and optimization of large system by GRADE, available at http://www.gradetools.com, accessed April 15, 2007.

Tharumarajah, A., Wells, A.J. and Nemes, L. (1998) Comparison of emerging manufacturing concepts. *Systems, Man and Cybernetics*, October, Vol. 1, pp. 325–331.

Tolvanen, J.-P. (2006) Creating domain-specific modeling language for an exixting framework, available at http://www.metacase.com, accessed April 15, 2007.

Van Grootel, G. and Poort, J. (2006) IWETO, a research in information clearing house. *Proceedings of the 4th International Conference on Politics and Information Systems, Technologies and Applications*: PISTA'06, 2pp.

Warneke, H.J. (1993) *The Fractal Company*, Springer Verlag, Berlin.

# Modeling of Product Software Businesses: Investigation into Industry Product and Channel Typologies

Sjaak Brinkkemper, Ivo van Soest and Slinger Jansen

Institute of Information and Computer Sciences, Utrecht University, The Netherlands
{S.Brinkkemper, I.Soest, S.Jansen}@cs.uu.nl

**Abstract**  The product software industry lacks a method for describing their products and business models on a high abstraction level. The lack of good methods to model a software product makes it harder to evaluate a business model especially for people with less knowledge of software architectures and more knowledge about the business side of creating software. This chapter presents a model consisting of two diagrams the product context diagram (PCD), which describes the context in which a software product operates and the software supply network (SSN) diagram, which describes the different parties involved in the delivery and deployment of a software product or service. Furthermore, this chapter presents a typology for both diagrams. The proposed diagrams are simple and easy to create therefore providing a quick insight to the core of a business model, creating the diagrams supports the process of evaluating the business model.

## 1 Introduction

The software industry is a relative young industry that is still developing at a high pace (OECD, 2000/2001). It is therefore surprising that there is little research being conducted in the area of business models for software products. The product software industry accounts for substantial economic activity all over the world (OECD, 2000/2001). In 2001, the total market of the product software industry was estimated to be 196 billion USD, which is just 9% of the overall ICT spending of 2.1 trillion USD worldwide. "The product software sector is among the most rapidly growing sectors in OECD countries, with strong increases in added value, employment and R&D investments" (OECD, 2001). Xu and Brinkkemper (2005) developed the following definition of product software:

"A software product is defined as a packaged configuration of software components or a software-based service, with auxiliary materials, which is released for and traded in a specific market."

C. Barry et al. (eds.), *Information Systems Development: Challenges in Practice, Theory, and Education, Vol.1*, doi: 10.1007/978-0-387-68772-8_24,
© Springer Science+Business Media, LLC 2009

Product software differs from other types of software in the following two ways:

• One copy is sold multiple times whereas tailor-made software is sold only once.
• The product sold is the software itself in contrast with embedded software where the software comes on a device that is sold as one product.

The software business is a special industry where it costs about the same to make one copy or one million copies of a software product (Cusumano, 2004). Investing in a software product can result in substantial productivity gain and strategic advantage (Brynjolfsson, 1993), much like in the movie, music, and medicine production industries.

## 1.1 Business and Product Modeling

The starting point of this research is the fact that there is a need within the product software industry to discuss their product options and marketing on a strategic level. For instance, the choice to sell the product directly to customers or only through resellers is a main issue at board level or the decision to change from a proprietary product DBMS to a standard DBMS from another vendor. The software industry has developed several methods and models to describe their products on a very technical level. Some examples of these established methods are ARIS (Scheer, 2000) and the Unified Process (Jacobson et al., 1999). These models are excellent in describing a product on detailed level but lack the ability to describe a software product to people with less knowledge of software architectures and more knowledge about the business side of creating software.

In the past, software companies developed their software completely in house, where today most software companies develop their software around and on top of generic software components supplied by other software companies. This evolution has led to a change in the software industry. Software companies are transforming from mainly self-oriented to firms that are part of a network of other software companies (Farbey and Finkelstein, 2001). Being part of a network also creates dependencies between the companies in a network. These dependencies are becoming more important but the software industry lacks a method to identify and visualize the networks behind a software product.

Weill and Vitale (2001) developed an e-business model schematic that is a graphical representation highlighting important elements that comprise an e-business model. Although e-business is related to product software, the schematic of Weill and Vitale lacks specific features to model the supply chain of a product software company. Nevertheless, parts of their schematic are closely related to our research.

Jansen and Rijsemus (2005) showed that platform providers in a software supply network determine the speed of development, not only for their own products, but also for those of third parties. Furthermore, Jansen et al. (2007) describe software supply network models for a company that provides "printing" machines for software products, enabling retail stores to always have the latest version of a product available and create product CDs, manuals, and boxes on demand. These works have a strong focus on the software and product development process, instead of business models, however.

In this chapter, we propose an integrated business model that defines and evaluates a software product. The proposed model must be considered as an addition to the existing modeling techniques. Were other techniques like BPMN, DFD, UML, etc have technical and process approaches our proposed model focuses on the business and (inter) organizational aspects of a software product.

This model consists of two diagrams, being the Product Context Diagram (PCD) and the Software Supply Network (SSN) diagram. We show several example models and present validation through an extensive case study.

## 1.2 Research Method

As stated earlier, there is hardly any research in the field of business modeling for product software companies. Therefore, this research can be qualified as design research. Vaishnavi and Kuechler (2004/2006) formulated the following description for design research related to Information Systems: "Design research involves the analysis of the use and performance of designed artifacts to understand, explain and very frequently to improve on the behavior of aspects of Information Systems."

The design cycle consists of five process steps: (a) problem awareness, (b) suggestion, (c) development, (d) evaluation, and (e) conclusion. This research project was carried out according to the design cycle. The starting point of this research was the question whether there is a need for an uniform business modeling method for a product software company. The research problem therefore is defined as: How to define and evaluate a set of models that describes the business model of a product software company?

To develop a functional model, a literature study has been conducted to find related research and models. With the knowledge gathered from literature study during the suggestion step, it was possible to develop the proposed model. To evaluate the model, several case studies have been carried out according to the case study methods of Yin (2003). These case studies resulted in models for a number of software products. The product software companies evaluated the created model by determining whether the model reflects their actual situation. After the evaluation, it was possible to assess whether the proposed model was able to describe the real world situation. Furthermore, it was possible to generate product and channel typologies and propose suggestions for further research.

In the following section, the two diagrams that were proposed earlier are presented. In Sect. 3, we present one case study for which the diagrams are applied. In Sect. 4, we present a product and channel typology on the basis of the generic patterns found in the case studies. Finally, in Sect. 5, we discuss our conclusions and future work.

## 2 Business Modeling Approach

The term business model is a relatively vague term in scientific literature. Oster-walder et al. (2005) reviewed the literature of this subject and also discussed the origin of the term business model. The first occurrence of the term was in a scientific article from 1957. The term became mainstream at the end of the 1990s. On the basis of a lengthy literature study, Osterwalder et al. (2005) defined the term business model as:

"A business model is a conceptual tool that contains a set of elements and their relationships and allows expressing the business logic of a specific firm. It is a description of the value a company offers to one or several segments of customers and of the architecture of the firm and its network of partners for creating, marketing, and delivering this value and relationship capital, to generate profitable and sustainable revenue streams."

This definition is closely related to our perception of a business model for a software product, except for the fact that our model only looks at the product, the network of direct suppliers, and the financial consequences. It does not address issues related to marketing and staffing as they can be treated as derivatives of the aforementioned.

As described earlier, our proposed business model for a software product covers two aspects, being technical and organizational. On the basis of the literature found about business models and software products, the decision was made to cover these aspects by making two diagrams namely the Product Context Diagram and the Software Supply Network diagram. In the next two paragraphs, we describe both diagram types.

### 2.1 Product Context Diagram

The product context diagram (PCD) describes the context in which a software product operates. The PCD consists of other software products, which are required for the main software product. Besides software products, the product context diagram also shows how the different software products communicate with each other. The diagram also indicates whether the product of interest (PoI) is the product for which the business model is to be made, and the PoI indicates whether it is a stand-alone application or one that communicates with other software products via a medium, such as for client-server and Internet applications. If the software product is not a stand-alone application, the diagram is extended with at least two extra columns. One column indicates the medium through which the two software

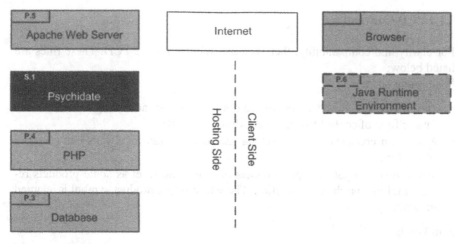

**Fig. 1.** Example PCD

products communicate, and the second column indicates the software products needed on the other side of the medium. Figure 1 shows an example of a PCD.

The PCD is a layered diagram in the sense that it stacks different software products on each other. The way of stacking is determined by the flow of information through the different software products. The PCD differentiates four components (Table 1):

**Table 1.** PCD components

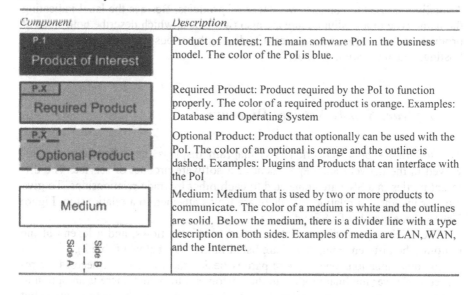

| Component | Description |
| --- | --- |
| Product of Interest | Product of Interest: The main software PoI in the business model. The color of the PoI is blue. |
| Required Product | Required Product: Product required by the PoI to function properly. The color of a required product is orange. Examples: Database and Operating System |
| Optional Product | Optional Product: Product that optionally can be used with the PoI. The color of an optional is orange and the outline is dashed. Examples: Plugins and Products that can interface with the PoI |
| Medium | Medium: Medium that is used by two or more products to communicate. The color of a medium is white and the outlines are solid. Below the medium, there is a divider line with a type description on both sides. Examples of media are LAN, WAN, and the Internet. |

### 2.1.1 PCD Conventions

For clarity and comparability, there is a set of rules for the PCD. These rules are listed below:
Positioning

- The products in the PCD are stacked on each other, according to the flow of data or flow of control through the different products.
- A medium connects two product stacks, so a medium is always between two product stacks
- It is allowed to put multiple products on the same level as some products require multiple products to function. The width of the product symbol is adapted accordingly.

Numbering

- The labels and numbering in the left corner of a product are the same as in the software supply network. More information on the software supply network is given in paragraph 2.3.
- In cases where the product is obviously available, such as an Internet browser, the product is modeled without a label in the left corner. These products are necessary for the main product to function but the relation between the supplier of these products and the end-user is not relevant for the Software Supply Network and they do not have a P.* indicator in the left corner. (Please see the browser product in Fig. 1).

A medium is used to connect two stacks of products. Besides the label indicating the name/type of a medium, there are also two labels, which describe both sides of product stacks. Common examples of side combinations are client-server, client-hosting, and application-database.

## 2.2 Software Supply Network Diagram

The software supply network (SSN) diagram displays the different parties involved in the delivery and deployment of a software product or service. The different parties in a SSN are connected to each other by trade relationships. To give a better insight in a relationship, there are flows attached to a relationship. Figure 2 shows an example of a SSN diagram.

The SSN diagram differentiates parties, relations, flows, and a legend at the bottom. The different components are listed in the table below (Table 2).

In some situations one or more parties beside the CoI are not necessarily required to deliver the final product to the customers, for which there is an option to make a party optional. Optional parties are represented with the same symbols but they have dashed outlines.

A connector line displays the trade relationship between two parties. Two parties can only have one direct connector line. Connector lines do not have arrow ends to indicate the direction of a relationship. To provide insight and direction of a relationship, there are flows that can be connected to a connector line, and the direction of the arrow indicates the direction of al flow. Just like the different parties, a relationship and the related flows can be optional. These relationships are also displayed by dashed lines.

In some cases, there is a choice between two or more products. For example in the case a customer purchases a product, which needs a DataBase Management System (DBMS). Suppose the supplier of the PoI supports two or more different DBMSs but the product only requires one. For these cases, there is the OR operator. When the customer has a relation with the OR operator, the OR operator has two optional relations with the suppliers of the DBMSs. Fig. 1 shows an example of the use of an OR operator for the direct and indirect relationship between the vendor and customer.

An SSN diagram is always accompanied by a legend consisting of all the flows in the model and a short description of each flow. The flows should be listed per flow type. Fig. 2 shows an example of a SSN legend.

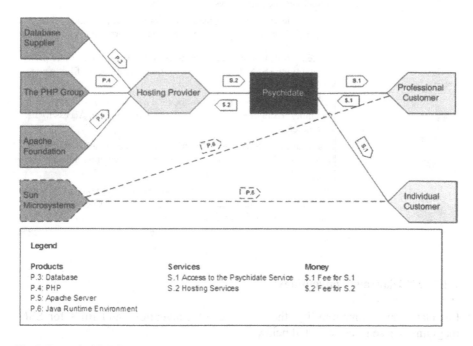

**Fig. 2.** Example SSN diagram

**Table 2.** SSN components

| Component | Description |
|---|---|
| Company of Interest | Company of Interest (CoI): Company delivering the main PoI in the business model. The color of the CoI is blue. |
| Customer | Customer: Individual or organization that has acquired the PoI. The color of the customer is yellow. |
| Supplier | Supplier: Company that direct or indirect supplies a crucial or required part or service. The color of a supplier is orange. Examples: Suppliers of Operating Systems, Database Management Systems, Plugins, etc. |
| Intermediary | Intermediary: Company acting as an intermediary between two or more parties in the SSN. The color of an intermediary is green. Examples are Distributors, Resellers, and Hosting providers. |
| _____ | Trade relationship: A relation that connects two parties in the SSN containing one more flows. |
| P.1 | Product Flow: Software or hardware product that is obtained from a supplier. Examples: DBMS, OS, libraries, servers, etc. |
| C.1 | Content Flow: Content that is transferred between two or more parties within the SSN. Examples: XML files, symbol data files, game level files, etc. |
| S.1 | Service Flow: Service related to the PoI, which can be obtained from a supplier. Examples: Support, Training, Consultancy, Access to a system, etc. |
| €.1 | Financial Flow: Financial transaction between two parties within the SSN. Examples: License Fees, Service Fees, Payments, Subscription Fees. |
| OR | OR operator: Operator to enable a choice between two or more trade relationships and the related flows. The color of an OR operator is black; the color of the text label is white. |

## 2.2.1 SSN Diagram Conventions

For clarity and comparability, there is a set of conventions and rules for SSN diagrams. These rules are listed below:

Positioning of parties and flows

- The CoI is placed in the middle of the diagram.
- Suppliers are placed at the left side of the diagram.
- The customer is placed at the right side of the diagram.
- Flows going to the right (toward the customer) are placed above of a relation.

- Flows going to the left (from the customer) are placed below a relation.

Scoping

- The SSN diagram only shows parties and flows have a direct relation with the PoI. The following types of parties are not in the scope of the SSN diagram:
- Suppliers of basic office-related materials required for running a company (office rental, furniture, computers, etc).
- Suppliers of development environments (Visual Studio, Borland Delphi, etc). An exception is when the development environment also delivers a platform/engine, which is required for the PoI to function. In this case, the development environment can be part of the SSN, but preferably the engine name is indicated instead of the development environment.
- Suppliers of packaging materials for the PoI.

Numbering

- Using an uniform numbering for the flows makes it easier to interpret a SSN diagram. Therefore, there is a set of rules for the numbering
- The PoI uses the number 1.
- Different kinds of flows that are connected to the same relation and are related to each other use the same flow number. So if for example P.1 is the main product that is sold by the CoI then there should also be a financial flow for the sold products, which is therefore labeled €.1.
- Multiple financial flows should stay separate as far as possible and may not be combined to one flow. In some cases, the PoI requires an installation service (S.2) to function properly.
- If a flow is past on by a party without making major changes, the flow keeps its flow number. For example P.2 of supplier X is bought by the customer via a intermediary Y, P.2 will first be connected to the relation between supplier X and intermediary Y, But P.2 will also be connected to the relation between intermediary Y and the customer.
- Flow numbers do not need to be numbered consecutively. As described earlier, clarity is improved by giving related flows the same number. This can result in the fact that the sequence of numbers for a flow type is disturbed. For example, a diagram can have three products flows P.1, P.2, and P.3, where P.1 and P.3 need to be bought; P.2 is distributed at no cost. Because of the fact that P.1 and P.3 need to be bought there will also be an €.1 and €.3 but there will be no €.2.

## 2.3 Consistency Between the PCD and the SSN Diagram

PCD and SSN diagrams are closely related due to the fact that all product flows mentioned in the SSN diagram must also be in the PCD. The purpose of PCD is to give a better technical insight in the way different software products cooperate with each other. This relation is formalized by using the same numbering in the PCD and SSN diagram, a product flow mentioned in the SSN for example P.1 should also be mentioned in one of the product stacks in the PCD.

There can be products in the PCD that are not in the SSN. These products are necessary for the main product to function but the relation between the supplier of these products and the end-user is not relevant for the Software Supply Network. Because of the fact that these products are not in the Software Supply Network they do not have a P.* indicator in the left corner. An example of this is a web browser, a product considered to be a standard available for most operating systems. The customer does not have to make an arrangement with a supplier, which is irrelevant for the supplier in the Software Supply Network.

# 3 Case Studies

In total, eight case studies at product software companies in the Netherlands were conducted. In this paragraph, we will show the results of one case study.

To ensure validity and reliability, a case study approach was developed. The case study method is based on the steps suggested by Soy (1997), which are based on the literature of well-known case study researchers Simons, Stakes, and Yin. Yin (2003) formulated the following four kinds of validity threats that could influence the research quality when using case studies:

- Construct validity: Each case study was conducted in the same way following the case study protocol.
- Internal validity: The results of the first interview were checked with the interviewee and a second employee in two separate sessions.
- External validity: The cases studies are representative for the product software market in the Netherlands because each company is active in a different domain and each company has a different number of customers.
- Reliability: Repeating the case studies will generate the same results except for the situation in which the company has decided to change their business model.

## 3.1 PhraseWorld

PhraseWorld is a Web-application which main functionality is to help the visitor translate phrases from one language into another, by showing pretranslated phrases that are quite similar to or an exact match of the user's input. The content (phrases) of PhraseWorld is generated by the visitors itself. By involving the users in the process of updating the content, the Website is kept dynamic and up to date. Furthermore, it enables the visitors to contribute to the quality of the service.

A community feel makes the visitors feel involved with the Website and induces them to keep visiting.

PhraseWorld earns money in several ways, and the most important are advertisements on the website, lead generation for related products such as language courses and dictionaries, and the sale of digital phrasebooks (PDF) based on the content of PhraseWorld. The PhraseWorld is offered as a Web application and must be accessed via a webbrowser. PhraseWorld is built on the so-called LAMP (Linux, Apache, Mysql, PHP) platform. Fig. 3 presents the Product Context Diagram of PhraseWorld.

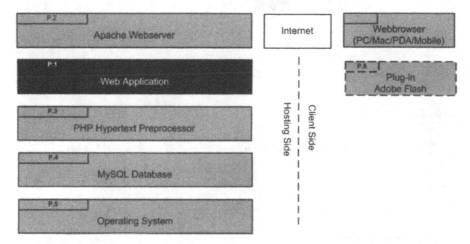

**Fig. 3.** PCD PhraseWorld

PhraseWorld must be accessed with a Webbrowser via the Internet. Request from the browser are answered by the Apache Webserver (P.2), which sends the request to the PhraseWorld Web Application (P.1). The PhraseWorld Web Application (P.1) uses the PHP scripting Language (P.3) to answer the requests. Furthermore, it uses the MySQL Database (P.4) to store the data related to PhraseWorld. The components on the server side run on a Linux Operating System (P.5).

Fig. 4 shows the Software Supply Network of PhraseWorld. PhraseWorld has three types of customers: users, advertisers, and bookshops. The user obtains the phrases directly from PhraseWorld. In the case that the user purchases a digital phrasebook from PhraseWorld, the intermediary Payment Service Provider is also involved in the transaction because they facilitate the payment.

The Advertiser has two options two advertise on PhraseWorld direct or via an intermediary Online marketing partner.

PhraseWorld also integrates the comparison-function of the Woordenboek.EU into the PhraseWorld application. Via this integration PhraseWorld generates leads for bookshops and language-courses.

PhraseWorld has three suppliers which all supply services. The Reviewer and Content supplier help creating the phrase data. The ISP supplies the hosting platform consisting of three software products, PHP scripting language (P.4) from the

PHP Group, MySQL DBMS (P.7) from MySQL AB, and the Apache Webserver (P.3) from the Apache Foundation.

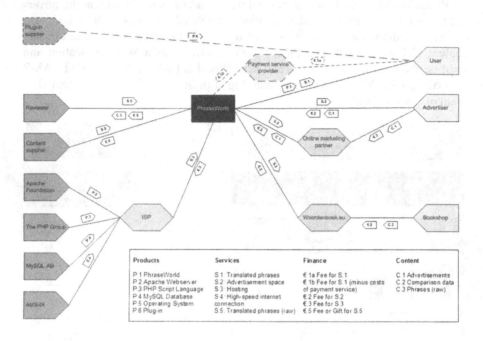

**Fig. 4.** SSN PhraseWorld

# 4 Typology of Generic Patterns

After conducting the case studies, we studied similarities between the different cases for each of the two diagrams. The similarities led to a typology of generic patterns for both the PCD and SSN diagrams.

## 4.1 Typology of Product Contexts

The PCD evolved during the case studies. Before the case studies, there where two types of PCD diagrams namely an one-column diagram for a stand-alone software product, and a three-column diagram for a client server software product. Some of the products in the case studies indicated the need for a diagram with five columns. Sorting the cases by the number of columns created a categorization: stand-alone (one-column), client-server/webservice (three columns), and enterprise software (five or more columns).

After categorizing the product by their number of columns in the PCD diagram, it was interesting to see what kind of products were in each category, and if there are similarities between the products in a category.

### 4.1.1 Stand-Alone Product

A stand-alone software product has quite a small PCD diagram, which consists of one column with 1–4 stacked products. The relative small size of the PCD diagram of a stand-alone product does not indicated that product itself is technical less complex compared with two other product types. The PoI can contain very advanced algorithms and logic. Fig. 5 shows an example of the PCD diagram of a stand-alone software product.

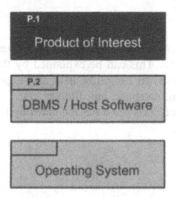

**Fig. 5.** PCD Example of stand-alone software product

The PoI only needs limited number of other software products to function. Besides an operating system (OS), a stand-alone software product some times needs one or two other software products such as for example a DBMS or a Host Software Package. In some cases, there are optional products in the PCD for example software products, which can interface with the PoI or that use the PoI as a host such as plugins.

### 4.1.2 Client–Server

A client–server software product has a PCD diagram with three columns. The right column consists of the PoI client, the middle column only consists of a medium (Internet, LAN, WAN, etc) the left column consist of the PoI and the required components. Fig. 6 presents an example of the PCD diagram of a Client–server.

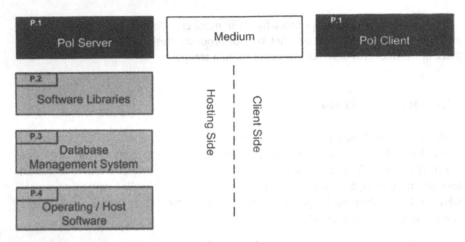

**Fig. 6.** PCD example of a client–server software product

Besides the three columns the PCD for a client–server software product often has more software components in the PoI column. This can be explained by the fact that these types of software products are used to centralize data and logic, which often require software such as application, database, and file servers. The client side mostly consists of one component, which is some times extended by for example a plug-in or host component.

### 4.1.3 Web Service

The Web service software product is related to the client–server software product. The main difference is the fact that a Web service does not have a PoI Client on the right side of the diagram. In the Web service product, the PoI client is replaced by a standard web browser. In some cases the right side of the diagram is extended with a plug-in or optional software product. Fig. 3. PCD PhraseWorld shows an example of such an extension.

### 4.1.4 Enterprise Software

An enterprise software product consists of five or more columns. An enterprise software product can be considered as an extension of client–server/Web service software. An enterprise software product can be accessed through a medium. The component that accesses the enterprise software is not always directly controlled by a human such as the client/Web browser. An enterprise software product is often part of a larger system such as an ERP system (Fig. 7).

The reason behind the use of two or more extra columns is mainly because enterprise software products require more resources, which are supplied by multiple physical servers systems, each performing a specific task which in most cases

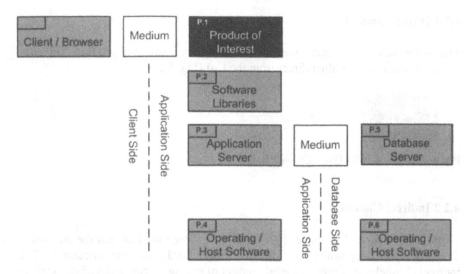

**Fig. 7.** PCD example of an Enterprise software product

requires different operating systems on each physical server. A common example of this situation is an application server running on a Linux OS and a database server (MS SQL/Oracle) on Windows OS. The use of more columns often results in more software components to facilitate the communication between the different components.

## 4.2 Typology of Software Supply Networks

The SSN diagrams did not show a clear distinction between different types of software products when we considered the complete diagram. If we separate the SSN diagram into two parts namely the supply part (left of the CoI) and the delivery part (right of the CoI), we do find similarities and the delivery part. The delivery part describes the sale and delivery of a software product to the customer and is often referred to as the distribution channel. In the case studies the following examples were found:

A. Direct Channel
B. Indirect Channel
1. Reseller
2. Agent + Reseller
3. Value Added Partner/Reseller
C. Direct/Indirect Channel Combinations
1. Direct + Reseller
2. Direct + Value Added Partner/Reseller

### 4.2.1 Direct Channel

This is the most simple and common way of selling a software product. The customer purchases the product direct from the CoI (Fig. 8).

**Fig. 8.** Example of a SSN Direct Channel design

### 4.2.2 Indirect Channel

As the name states, there is no direct relation between the CoI and the customer. The delivery of the product goes via one or more third parties/intermediaries. The indirect channel is a commonly used method of selling software especially shrink-wrapped software. The product stays the same through out the process, the financial flows changes because the reseller takes its margin from the retail price (Fig. 9).

**Fig. 9.** Example of an Indirect Channel SSN Agent + Reseller design

### 4.2.3 Value Added Reseller/Partner

In this design, a reseller creates a new product (combination) by combining the software of the CoI with a product from another supplier before selling it to the customer. The difference between a Value Added Reseller and a Value Added Partner lies in the fact that a reseller adds a product where a partner adds a service to the PoI (Fig. 10).

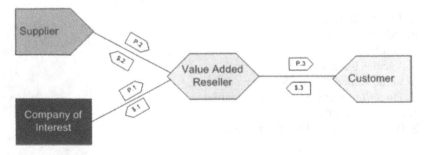

**Fig. 10.** Example of a SSN Value Added Reseller/Partner Design

### 4.2.4 Direct/Indirect Channel Combinations

It is also possible to combine two of the above-mentioned designs. The most common two combinations are:

Direct and Reseller combination, this is a combination of the Direct and Reseller design. The main reason for selecting this design is the opportunity to sell more products with the help of the reseller.

Direct and Value Added Reseller/Partner combination, Fig. 11 shows an example of the Direct and Value Added Reseller/Partner Design. In this design, two different products are sold namely the PoI (P.1) and the combination product (P.2) of the PoI (P.1) and a second product (P.3). This design is often used because combining and reselling products is not the field of expertise of the CoI.

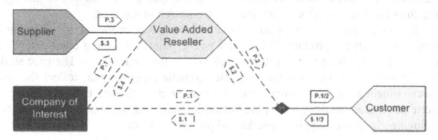

**Fig. 11.** Example of a SSN Direct + Value Added Reseller/Partner design

## 5 Discussion and Conclusions

The main research question of this article was formulated as: How to define and evaluate a set of models that describes the business model of a product software company? The research questions were answered in several steps resulting in a business model consisting of the PCD and SSN diagrams.

Since its inception, the PCD and SSN diagrams have been used to model approximately 40 businesses. The eight case studies for this research were evaluated by means of expert validation by company representatives. Furthermore, a study was conducted into the gaming industry in the Netherlands, which resulted in five models for gaming companies. The other models were created during two consecutive years of a course in ICT entrepreneurship at Utrecht University. In this course, external evaluators read and assessed business models of IT startups.

The PCD and SSN Diagrams proved to be simple to apply and create, providing a quick insight into the core of a business model. Furthermore, the creation of the diagrams supports the process of evaluating business models. During this process opportunities and threats can be discovered, which can result in alternative business models.

Because of the relatively simple structure of PCD and SSN diagrams, they can be used to communicate business models to persons without in-depth IT knowledge.

The PCD gives insight in the deployment architecture and operational environment of a software product. The SSN diagram also determines the internal organization design. The decision between a direct or indirect channel approach, for example, has a large influence on the organization design. A direct channel approach requires expertise within the CoI on areas such as marketing, sales, etc. By making use of an indirect channel approach, this expertise is shifted from the CoI to a reseller or another third party. The product and channel typologies help to analyze the alternative business models to make the right decisions when choosing between two business models.

As a company grows, its PCD and SSN diagrams tend to change. The diagrams can be used to illustrate and evaluate a developing product and business model of a software company through time. Such diagrams can elegantly demonstrate how product software vendors develop and change their strategies throughout their lifetime. We hope to conduct more research in this area.

In this chapter, an integrated business model was proposed to define and evaluate a software product. This model was evaluated by doing eight extensive case studies into the product software industry in the Netherlands. The case studies showed that it was possible to create valuable diagrams that reflect the real world situation for eight companies. The case studies showed that there are generic patterns in the diagrams of the business model and were used to develop typologies of software supply networks and product contexts.


# 6 Further Research

During the research we encountered various options for further research. As described, one of the results of this research is a formal method for creating the diagrams. This formalization is limited to the design conventions and rules presented in this chapter. The method can be taken a step further by formalizing the data related to the objects of a diagram. In the current diagrams, the data related to an object is limited to basic information, such as name and price of a product this can be extended with all kinds of other information such as license type, requirements, programming language, etc. This information can be used for detailed analysis on subjects like license structures and dependencies within the SSN. At the moment, the diagrams are modeled with Microsoft Visio Stencils. The current modeling method can further be described to create a tool that ensures consistent use of the concepts and modeling techniques.

An important part of a business model is financial analysis. In our research, we also studied financial consequences by analyzing the financial flows within the SSN diagram. Results from these analyses were limited, but this subject still remains interesting for further research.

Because of several constraints, the number of case studies in this research was limited. More case studies will result in a better understanding and wider classification of business models within the product software industry.

**Acknowledgments**    The authors thank the companies that participated in this research. Without their help this research would not have been possible. We also thank the students of the Informatics Business course at the Utrecht University. The students provided us with cases and valuable feedback. Furthermore, we thank the students of the Junior College Utrecht for their research into the gaming industry in the Netherlands.

# References

Brynjolfsson, E. (1993) The productivity paradox of information technology. Communication of the ACM, 36(12):66–77.

Cusumano, M.A. (2004) The Business of Software. Free Press.

Farbey, B. and Finkelstein, A. (2001) "Software Acquisition: a business strategy analysis" Proc. Requirements Engineering (RE01).

Jansen, S., Brinkkemper, S., Finkelstein A. (2007). Providing transparency in the business of software: a modeling technique for software supply networks. Submitted for publication

Jansen, S. and Rijsemus, W. (2006). Balancing Total Cost of Ownership and Cost of Maintenance Within a Software Supply Network, Proceedings of the IEEE International Conference on Software Maintenance, Philadelphia, Sept. 2006, pp. 1–2.

OECD (2000). The software sector: Growth, structure and policy issues. OECD Report DSTI/ICCP/IE(2000)8/REV2.

OECD (2001). Highlights of the OECD information technology outlook 2002. OECD Report.

Osterwalder, A., Pigneur, Y., Tucci, C.L. (2005). Clarifying Business Models: Origins, Present, and Future of the Concept. Communications of AIS, Volume 15, Article 40

Scheer, A. (2000), ARIS – Business Process Modeling, 3rd ed. Berlin: Springer.

Soy, S.K. (1997). The Case Study as a Research Method published online at http://fiat.gslis.utexas.edu/~ssoy/usesusers/l391d1b.htm, retrieved at 6th of March, 2007.

Vaishnavi, V. and Kuechler, W. (2004/2006). "Design Research in Information Systems" February 20, 2004, last updated January 18, 2005. URL: http://www.isworld.org/Researchdesign/drisISworld.htm

Weill, P. and Vitale, M.R. (2001). Place to space: Migrating to eBusiness Models, Harvard Business School Press, Boston.

Xu, L. and Brinkkemper, S. (2005). Concepts of Product Software: Paving the Road for Urgently Needed Research, In: Proceedings of 1st International Workshop on Philosophical Foundations of Information Systems Engineering (PHISE'05). Orlando Belo, Johann Eder, Oscar Pastor and Joao Falcao eCunha (Eds.), FEUP edicoes, Porto, 2005.

Yin, R.K. (2003) Case study research – design and methods, 3rd ed. SAGE Publications. Thousand Oaks, CA.

# IS4DEV: IS Development and Development Issues

John Traxler

Applied Innovative Digital Technologies Research Group, School of Computing and IT, University of Wolverhampton, John.Traxler@wlv.ac.uk

## 1 Introduction

Individual members of the ISD community have been interested in development issues for some time, and some are members of the longstanding ICT4D collective (http://www.ict4d.org.uk) organised by Prof Tim Unwin of Royal Holloway College and the World Economic Forum. This year for the first time, in Galway, the ISD community have the opportunity to engage more formally with development issues, in the shape of an 'IS in Developing Nations' track.

In recent years, outside the immediate ISD community, there has been increased interaction and synergy between various academic, research and development communities; between the e-learning and ICT communities (for example, Online Educa in spawning the e-Learning Africa conference series, CAL'07's running an ICT4DEV stream in Dublin); the global corporates (for example, Dr. Michelle Selinger's role in Cisco, the work of Bill and Melinda Gates Foundation), and governments, NGOs, and the donor community (for example DfID's now-defunct Imfundo initiative, (http://www.dfid.gov.uk/research/imfundo.asp) ) to tackle development issues. This has been driven and symbolised by the Millennium Development Goals and the prominence of development issues at recent G8 summits.

In part, this interaction is due to the improving power, cost and diversity of globally available technologies (particularly personal wireless, mobile and portable devices, and wireless connectivity) and their global commercial exploitation and due in the growing recognition of the potential power of combining ICT and education to address problems of extreme poverty and deprivation, especially in sub Saharan Africa.

Historically, this kind of interaction has often led to small innovative bilateral projects with few roots into their target or host communities and with no realistic or clearly articulated mission in terms of equity, sustainability, scaling-up and capacity building and beset by weaknesses in local governance, commerce, maintenance, capacity and infrastructure. The World Bank through its InfoDev organisation has recently reviewed its ICT-for-Development projects and documented these and similar difficulties (Batchelor et al., 2003), and these perceptions have

C. Barry et al. (eds.), *Information Systems Development: Challenges in Practice, Theory, and Education, Vol.1*, doi: 10.1007/978-0-387-68772-8_25,
© Springer Science+Business Media, LLC 2009

led to some players in the development and donor communities adopting a more strategic and policy-focussed agenda, sometimes called 'sector-wide planning' (in which they implicitly relinquish their capacity to monitor and evaluate projects they fund), and a more systemic and holistic viewpoint that many in the IS community would recognise.

This chapter gives some discussion of core issues and a brief case study to provide a context for other contributors to the ISD track.


# 2 Theories of Development

This account of the theoretical foundations of development draws heavily on the recent work of Gudrun Wicander, one of the ISD community (Sundén and Wicander, 2006), and is intended to provide a general overview for other subsequent ISD contributions. A comprehensive review of background literature relevant specifically to mobile phones in a development context will be published shortly by Jonathan Donner of Microsoft Research India in Bangalore (Donner, 2007); DfID has published a useful guide to the economic aspects of mobiles phones in rural contexts (Souter et al., 2005) and the World Bank has recognised and reviewed the critical role of ICT in development efforts around the world (World Bank, 2006). The International Telecommunication Union (ITU, http://www.itu.int/net/ITU-D/index.aspx) is the leading United Nations agency for information and communication technologies and as a global focal point for governments and the private sector, addresses development as one of its three core sectors by research, publication and regulation. A forthcoming book by Tim Unwin (Unwin, 2007) provides an overview of the many different technologies that are referred to by those working in the field of ICT4D, usually a more inclusive definition of ICT technologies than is the norm in more 'developed' countries.

In seeking to theorise her fieldwork in rural Zambia, Wicander draws on four different theoretical perspectives, namely

- Development theories
- Diffusion of innovations
- Information systems theories
- Sustainability theories


## 2.1 Development Theories

Wicander begins her account of development theories by exploring the concepts of development, a politicised vocabulary characterised by a succession of dichotomies, initially underdeveloped/developed then developing/developed, followed by non-industrialised/industrialised, traditional/modern, poor/rich and most recently south/north. Elsewhere, we have argued (Traxler et al., 2007) that in these simple dichotomies conceal more complexities, for example aspects of ICT attitudes, ownership, access and use, and digital disadvantage and division, than they reveal and more inclusive and permeable perspective looking at policy, infrastructure, resource distribution and organisational issues might suggest that rural communities, ethnic minorities and the urban dispossessed, whatever their location, have much in common whether north or south. We have also argued that possibly newer forms of ICT, for example podcasting, wikis, blogs, handheld computers and mobile phones, have the potential to 'disrupt' and trouble conventional ideas about development and the extent to which metropolitan areas of Europe, North America and the Pacific Rim can act as transferable models for ICT development and deployment elsewhere.

Wicander does in any case cite other development categorisations that cut across these dichotomies, for example the political one of First World, Second World, Third World (all widely understood, albeit based on constructs of the 1950/1960s Cold War) and now Fourth World. She also introduces some concepts, 'development', related to technology and contrasted with underdevelopment, 'modernisation', related to industrialisation and contrasted with traditional, and 'globalisation', related to digitization and contrasted with localisation. This brief account of her work does not so much define or explain any of the concepts, though perhaps their meanings are fairly clear, so much as illustrate the complexity of perspectives and terminology.

Wicander goes onto identify the main development theories themselves; the modernisation paradigm, a type of convergence or 'catching up', copying what was perceived as a linear progress from the First World onto the Third World but sometimes subverted, especially by ICT, by the notion of 'leap-frogging'; the dependency paradigm, based on the notion of capitalism causing a core/periphery division that can be tackled with 'appropriate' technologies; the multiplicity paradigm, based on the possibility of 'bottom-up' and 'alternative' developments each appropriate to different regions and the post-development paradigm, based on 'grass-roots' participative approaches and the recognition that development may be a purely Western construct entailing 'modernity, science, reason, technology, westernisation, consumption, nation-state, globalisation and development'. The role of technology including ICT can be problematised as 'technology-as-problem' vs. 'technology-as-solution' and invoked as 'appropriate' technology and 'alternative' technology. The development theories perspective should teach us in the ISD community to be very cautious and circumspect about valuations and perceptions of progress and improvement and about the role of IS systems and other ICT technologies.

## 2.2 Diffusion of Innovations

Many people, especially those involved in technology or commerce, are familiar with Rogers' ideas of the diffusion of innovations (Rogers, 1962; Rogers and

Scott, 1997). In the context of ICT in the south, these depend on viewing 'development' as the potential progress of an 'innovation'.

One of the contributions of these theories is to try and account for successful diffusion in terms of the attributes of the innovation (For example, does it offer a relative advantage? Is it compatible with existing systems? Is it observable? Is it 'trialable'? Is it complex?); in terms of the attributes of the media through which awareness of the innovation travels (are they formal and informal? Do they address attitudes as well as knowledge? Are there opinion-formers?) and in terms of the attributes of the group that might adopt the innovation (Are there innovators in the group? Are there spare resources? Do group members value innovation and change? Is decision-making consensus- or command-driven?). Diffusion theories have been criticised as based largely on an evidence base of successful innovations, rather than failed, innovations and as having a Western bias in terms of culture – Rogers himself recognises the validity of these criticisms. Diffusion theories have, nevertheless, often been applied and exploited in the development and marketing of IT systems but interestingly – in the light of our case study - grew out of work with Iowa farmers in the 1940s. They have been used as the basis for identifying optimal tactics to change public opinion and government attitudes (Gilman, 1991). These tactics may include incentives, publicity, legislation, pilots and experimentation but crucially each is only effective at specific points in the progress of diffusion and these specific points are also specific to the innovation and the society.

These concerns are all very relevant to our case study, involving the adoption of a Web-based information system by small farmers in Kenya. Interestingly, the more development-focussed partners (and their colleagues in the field working on parallel projects) are very aware of Rogers' work whereas the technical partners are less so. The system under development, the 'innovation', could certainly be critiqued in terms of Rogers' criteria and would lead to very productive debate, about amongst other things how the system and its boundary are defined, how different stakeholders would see the boundary issue and how cultural issues would impacts on those definitions. (Incidentally, Rogers himself draws attention to the cultural bias in his work, though Wicander overlooks this.)

The diffusion of innovations perspective should teach us in the ISD community to be very conscious of local values, local resources, local affordances if a 'development' or 'innovation' is to be a valued and successful change.

## 2.3 Information Systems Theories

These theories referred here are probably familiar to the ISD community and revolve around the key concepts of information and information systems, and information and communications technology (ICT). One significant point is that the latter are often taken in a development context to include TV, radio, audiocassettes, satellites and now also mobile phones and other personal wireless and mobile technologies. Another point is that in Anglophone sub Saharan Africa, the

English education system is often revered and the English legal, administrative and organisational legacy is often still apparent. This can mean that African IS education and training, when it happens, can be rooted in practices that participative, agile, global IS development has left behind. The African context certainly means that training, education and practice do not necessarily use the latest software and hardware tools or costly proprietary methods, or are not necessarily familiar with issues such as business process re-engineering, especially in public sector projects. Wicander rehearses the historical phases of IS development – this is significant, though she does not make this point, because where there recognised IS development methodologies are being followed, they may come from a previous historical phase of IS development.

Wicander discusses the eras of IS, identifying three phases, and characterises these in terms of different perspectives on the people/technology dichotomy; on views about techniques and technological process and on the shift from technology-as-solution to technology-as-enabler. Such an account is clearly embedded deep within a Western intellectual framework, and hence transplanting must always be problematic. Wicander also draws attention to the geography (as well as the history) of IS; the apparent split between an US (and positivistic empirical) tradition and an European (and pluralistic and interpretative) tradition is something that might be significant outside Western IS cultures. The information systems perspective encourages a systemic analysis of the development challenges associated with information but identifies unfamiliar political, legal, economic and socio-cultural factors in its influencing environment and unfamiliar markets, organisations and groups in its institutional environment.

If we look back at the innovations diffusion perspective, it is possible to argue 'systems' and 'innovations' are synonymous and that the difficulty of defining an appropriate boundary is common to both and has similar implications in the context of both perspectives.

Also, the information systems perspective should teach us in the ISD community to be very cautious about the role of any 'soft' (organisational, culture, social, procedural, organisational) components of systems, about the available portfolio of technologies and about the tacit or unrecognised (western) epistemology that underpins IS as an academic and professional activity.

## 2.4 Sustainability Theories

These come from an environmental and ecological background and have connotations of 'sustainable development'. Today the phrase has a technological perspective and a socio-economic perspective as well as the original ecological-environmental one. All prioritise movement and improvement that can be upheld. To focus on the technology perspective, Wicander cites one author's criteria or conditions for sustainable technologies as being:

- Adequate demand, the technology is required and yields productivity or safety gains
- Appropriateness of the technology to the environment
- Availability of local technological capacity

In summarising other authors, she says of sustainable development that, "improvements achieved by the technology are sustained and are enjoyed *over time*......the technology itself is *usable* and *useful* ...... possible changes in an organisation or in environment [or group] are *intended, manageable, far-reaching* and *humane*......further improvements are possible to conduct *smoothly* ...... the technology should be able to be used without dependence on *external assistance*...... dependence on *imported hardware* should be restricted". These are all significant issues in our case study and resonate with the author's experience elsewhere in sub Saharan Africa.

Dealing with the complexity of sustainable development, Wicander identifies strands including the systems approach (i.e., the work of Peter Checkland so familiar to IS practitioners and researchers) that recognises the emergent i.e. unexpected properties of systems; the expert view, which seems to revisit the role of the consultant and the rhetoric of capacity-building; and the capital concept, the old concept of Marxist analysis but partitioned (and interlinked) into human capital, natural capital, physical capital, social capital and financial capital and required, over time for sustainable development, to increase.

The sustainability theories perspective should teach us in the ISD community to be conscious of the wider social and historic context of our work but also to question the extent to which the 'softer' IS approaches are shot through with tacit cultural assumptions that the 'harder' IS approaches had ignored.

## 2.5 Convergence Across Four Perspectives

Finally, it is constructive to look for any convergence in these four perspectives and for their significance to IS in development contexts. Certainly at a superficial level, there seems to be considerable resonance and relevance.

However, to return to practicalities, we should remind ourselves (Traxler, 2006) that in much of sub Saharan Africa, physical infrastructure is characterised by:

- Poor roads and postal services
- Poor landline phone networks
- Poor mains electricity
- Little or no Internet bandwidth outside major cities; often just internet cafes or hotels in a few large cities
- Very few modern PCs or peripherals in the any of the public sector, and little or no user expertise, especially in smaller towns and rural areas

These characteristics are often balanced by

- Lively and energetic mobile phone networks
- The potential for solar power
- A regulatory and licensing system in a state of flux
- High levels of mobile phone ownership, acceptance and usage

There are of course major differences across sub Saharan Africa, say between South Africa and Ethiopia but, nevertheless, these remarks are a basis for understanding the context. This rapidly changing infrastructure and the associated governmental and commercial activity in sub Saharan is very effectively documented by Balancing Act (http://www.balancingact-africa.com) and a number of NGOs, for example, OneWorld (http://www.oneworld.org), Digital Links International (www.digital-links.org) and Fahamu (http://www.fahamu.org ), work to monitor and exploit ICT for the poor in sub Saharan Africa

## 3 A Case Study

The case study illustrates IS work in a development context. It is necessarily brief since the project is relatively young. It is also largely non-technical; it inevitably fails to capture the reality of working in situations where, not only is the physical infrastructure (roads, mains electricity, computers, buildings) is challenging or poorly established but civil society (management, bureaucracy, governance, voluntary sector, commerce, education, markets) is often equally weak. The case study possibly poses more questions than it answers!

Our example is drawn from Kenya where the author is now working with a Swiss NGO, BioVision-Foundation, alongside a Swiss content development and delivery company specialising in informal e-learning, Avallain AG (http://www.avallain.com), and local consultants, agronomists and technologists, Cellulant (http://www.cellulant.com), to develop and deploy an IS designed to support sustainable agriculture. BioVision-Foundation functions as an intermediary between research institutes in Europe and Africa and local communities and farmer groups in Kenya, ensuring that benefits of science reach the people most in need of them. BioVision aims to facilitate and support participatory development and dissemination of ecological and sustainable management with simple, local and relevant methods and technologies that are available. It aims to address community-driven needs in an integrated approach and places an emphasis on food security (sustainable and organic farming, preservation of vegetables, etc., marketing of produce, farm planning, etc), poverty alleviation (through income generation with environmentally sustainable methods), human and animal health and reduction of environmental degradation (with coexistence of people, animal and nature in a high biodiversity). In some ways, this project is an example of the high hopes held out by ICT for specifically *rural* or *agricultural* development.

The core of the system being developed is a substantial multi-media Web-based database, the infonet-BioVision, which has been developed with the help of Avallain. Structural ideas (that is, the layout and database dimension, linking content, and multimedia functions) were developed collaboratively and then implemented by Avallain. This will provide information and answer questions and will provide treatments on human health, animal health, plant health and environmental health and the threats to all these posed by pests (such as armyworm, stemborer), diseases, epidemics (such as mosaic virus, RVF – Rift Valley Fever) and perhaps market conditions and commercial information (though these latter are driven by local demand rather than built into the original project specification).

The system provides information on animal health (including how to keep animals, etc.) and environmental health (the whole hygiene, latrine, soil and water management, purification, how to build a well, how to get safe drinking water, water storage, etc.) and in short, the 150 important things people need to know in human, plant, animal and environmental health to improve the life of rural communities – the information which they cannot get currently, all in one place, with images and descriptions, with text that is local relevant and not in a scientific language? This will not only be disseminated electronically but also serve as a resource pool where the relevant information for printing out information or dissemination in different ways.

Infonet-BioVision is a highly visual and highly cross-referenced Web application. The content is stored in a database and viewed and modified via browser. Currently, Internet Explorer (tested from v6.0, works also on v5.0), Firefox from v1.0 and Netscape from v6.0 are supported. The application is compatible with Windows, Macintosh and Linux. The client is implemented in HTML and JavaScript. Java servlets are used to generate the client code. Java version 1.5 and a servlet container are necessary. For the servlet container, Avallain recommend Tomcat or Resin. Java 1.5 is working on Windows, MacOSX 10.4 and Linux. A relational database is used as a backend. At the moment Avallain have implemented MySQL v4.1.14. This runs on platforms including Windows, MacOSX and different Unix versions, and it should be possible to use other relational databases within acceptable change effort. Avallain have invested considerable effort in compressing image size in anticipation of bandwidth problems and are also developing an offline version. A test version of the internet-platform has been set up at http://www.infonet-biovision.org, and the system will be launched in the first week of October 2007 at the International Centre for Insect Physiology and Ecology (ICIPE), (http://www.icipe.org), Duduville ('dudu' is Swahili for 'insect') on the outskirts of Nairobi.

The content is been developed as a collaborative process involving local farmer groups in Kenya and research scientists in Switzerland and Africa in order to combine 'developed world' scientific rigour and procedures with local knowledge and folk approaches. English is used throughout but with local terminology (for example, in Swahili or one of the local tribal languages such as Kikuyu) but nevertheless it is likely that farmers are not highly literate and certainly most will not be computer-literate.

It is hoped that once the system goes live in the field that the technology will continue this collaborative methodology by using some Web2.0 methods to capture continued farmer contribution. The target audience is small-scale farmers and rural communities. The field trials have already started in order to explore various delivery mechanisms and specifically bridging the 'last mile' metaphorically between the end of electricity and broadband connectivity in as medium-sized town and farmers in their fields and settlements. The trials sites are:

- Kinangop Plateau, a farmers collective based in a relatively remote, high and arid area an hour's drive from Naivasha, the nearest town, with internet access in community centre
- Wangige, a peri-urban farmer group outside Nairobi, with internet access in internet café
- Kilifi with internet access through an access point provided as part of the UNDP Millennium District programme

The trial sites were chosen to cover some differences in Web-access, farmer organisation and agricultural practice; understanding how to contextualise and generalise from such a small sample will form part of the analysis. This is currently being explored using the critical incidents technique (CIT), a tool for exploration/planning, for evaluation of projects and other empowerment/animation activities (Hettlage and Steinlin, 2006). As part of this, responses, reactions and feedback will be elicited using semi-structured face-to-face interviews and focus groups, identifying a base-line and then looking for change. Incidentally, earlier attempts to use PCs supported by a satellite network and based in post offices in large towns failed when field work revealed the state of dereliction of the PCs; an indicator of both of the state of the infrastructure and also of the frequent discrepancies between its apparent condition as portrayed from Nairobi and its actual condition out in the country.

The project team are talking to mobile phone technologists, Cellulant, in the hope that there are GSM or GPRS messaging technologies that can help bridge that 'last mile' (and may add some extra richness and resilience to the system) and hope too to talk to 'extensionists', the locally-based Ministry of Agriculture officials tasked with supporting farmers, for their help too. These are all potential components – and stakeholders – in the BioVision IS. But then so are several NGOs and GOs: UNDP and the Kenya Agriculture Research Institute (KARI) are both keen to help.

The project is attempting to combine the participative approaches of much current development work in sub Saharan Africa with the user-involvement of much current IS development. In the face of cultural barriers, those about the authority of Western science and those about the authority of technical experts, this is not easy and is made harder by the barriers to contact and communications presented by the infrastructure.

Interestingly, BioVision has attempted to theorise their 'problem-space' diagrammatically. This helps us understand the significance of the various infrastructural and perhaps environmental factors at work in this particular IS but might be generalisable in similar situations. However, it ignores the cultural and organisational dimensions.

Infonet-Biovision is, in one sense, an archetypical modern IS, a multi-media, multi-user, Web-based content-manageable database-driven information system; in another sense, if the system boundary is relaxed to include the human, social, scientific, organisational and infrastructural components, the system is unlike anything most IS professionals, developers and researchers are familiar with.

# 4 Conclusion

In a broader sense, the project raises issues or questions probably common to many IS projects in sub Saharan Africa and elsewhere in the South, these include:

i. Knowing when to build IS capacity and when to implement directly, and knowing how the domain (e.g. governance, management, organisation, communications or technology) makes a difference
ii. Knowing what to try to change and what to try to preserve when working with local, official or traditional systems (e.g. local hierarchies, entrenched bureaucracies, business processes, local IS methodologies and training)
iii. Choosing between equity and example as project priorities; the issues of transferability and generality; scaling up or throwing away
iv. Striking a balance between short-term outcomes and benefits on the one hand and sustainability and maintainability on the other; defining realistic and achievable exit strategies
v. Understanding the role and validity of sampling, pilots, trials, case studies; the merits of 'hard' cases vs. 'easy' cases; getting meaningful and appropriate user-involvement in the IS development process
vi. Understanding that reducing one 'digital divide' may create or increase others (e.g. peri-urban areas vs. remote rural areas, high-bandwidth vs. low-bandwidth); how IS analysis and design may have to have a very broad range of options before moving to IS implementation
vii. Knowing where to draw the IS system boundary: tight around the technology or loose around diverse and disparate subsystems
viii. Striking a balance between IS development, implementation and delivery on the one hand and lobbying, disseminating and networking on the other; and also a balance between informal and local practice and attempts at influencing policy at a higher level
ix. Defining effective and appropriate IS evaluation and monitoring procedures; uncovering 'soft outcomes and distance travelled' in unfamiliar cultures (Wagner et al., 2005; Dewson et al., 2002)

This piece has attempted to draw together three different inputs, a case study in progress, a review of literature and sources and some practical insights. We can hope that ISD2007 marks a point at which the skills and expertise of the IS development community of the IS-rich become more accessible and engaged in the development process with the IS-poor.

**Acknowledgements**  I am indebted to Gudrun Wicander for conversations and her thesis, to Ursula Suter and Ignatz Heinz of Avallain AG and Monique Hunziker of BioVision for reviewing the case study. The analysis, opinions and mistakes are all, however, entirely mine.

# References

Batchelor, S., Evangelista, S., Hearn, S., Peirce, M., Sugden, S. & Webb, M. (2003) ICT for Development: Contributing to the Millennium Development Goals: Lessons Learned from Seventeen infoDev Projects. Washington: InfoDev

Dewson, S., Eccles, J., Tackey, N. D. & Jackson, A. (2002) Measuring Soft Outcomes and Distance Travelled: A Review of Current Practice. London: Institute for Employment Studies for DfEE

Donner, J. (2007) Research Approaches to Mobile Use in the Developing World: A Review of the Literature. Bangalore: Microsoft Research India

Gilman, R. (1991) Reclaiming Politics – The times are changing, and our approach to politics may need to change as well. In Context (Fall/Winter), 10.

Hettlage, R. & Marc Steinlin, M. (2006) The Critical Incident Technique in Knowledge Management-Related Contexts. Zurich: IngeniousPeoplesKnowledge. Available online at http://www.i-p-k.ch/files/CriticalIncidentTechnique_in_KM.pdf

Rogers, E. M. (1962) Diffusion of Innovations. New York: Free Press.

Rogers, E. M. & Scott, K. L. (1997). The Diffusion of Innovations Model and Outreach from the National Network of Libraries of Medicine to Native American Communities., 2001(10/12/01). http://nnlm.gov/pnr/eval/rogers.html

Souter, D., Garforth, C., Jain, R., Mascarenhas, O., McKemey, K. & Scott, N. (2005) The Economic Impact of Telecommunications on Rural Livelihoods and Poverty Reduction: a study of rural communities in India (Gujarat), Mozambique and Tanzania. London: DfID

Sundén, S. & Wicander, G. (2006) Information and Communication Technology Applied for Developing Countries in a Rural Context – Towards a Framework for Analysng Factors Influencing Sustainable Use. Karlstad University Studies 2006:69, Karlstad, Sweden.

Traxler, J. (2006) Educational Management Information Systems: An Example For Developing Countries In Proceedings of ISD2006, Budapest, September 2006

Traxler, J. (2007) Managed Mobile Messaging and Information for Education, Proceedings of IST-Africa, Maputo, Mozambique, May 2007

Unwin, T. (2007) ICT4D Information and Communication Technology for Development. Cambridge: Cambridge

Wagner, D.A., Day, B., James, T., Kozma, R.B., Miller, J., & Unwin, T. (2005) The Impact of ICTs in Education for Development: a Monitoring and Evaluation Handbook, Washington DC: infoDev

World Bank (2006) Information and Communications for Development: Global Trends and Policies. Washington: World Bank.

# An Exploration of the Critical Success Factors for the Sustainability of Rural ICT Projects – The Dwesa Case Study

Caroline Pade, Brenda Mallinson and David Sewry

Rhodes University, Department of Information Systems
g01p1472@campus.ru.ac.za, b.mallinson@ru.ac.za, d.sewry@ru.ac.za

**Abstract** Rural development can be enhanced and supported by information and communication technology (ICT), the use of which is highlighted by the emerging importance of information and knowledge as key strategic resources for social and economic development. The use of ICT presents a number of constraints which threaten the sustainability of rural ICT projects. Sustainability is key to the effectiveness of a rural ICT project. The categories of sustainability reveal critical success factors that need to be considered in the implementation and management of rural ICT projects. An exploration of the Dwesa project reveals the extent and effect of the application of these critical success factors of sustainability.

## 1 Introduction

Information and communication technologies (ICT) can make a significant contribution to the rural development process, given the growing information and knowledge society. Rural ICT projects, however, are confronted with constraints which threaten sustainability. The sustainability of an ICT project is essential for a long-term positive impact in rural communities. The aim of this research study is to highlight the concept of sustainability, and identify a trend in the factors that contribute towards ICT project sustainability in rural areas, with an exploration of the Dwesa project.

Literature on rural development and sustainable ICT is examined. Subsequently, the derived critical success factors of rural ICT project sustainability are summarized, followed by an exploration of these factors in the Dwesa ICT project. The conclusion summarises the findings and identifies the need to formulate an approach to rural ICT project management that is sensitive to the critical factors that promote rural ICT project sustainability.

C. Barry et al. (eds.), *Information Systems Development: Challenges in Practice, Theory, and Education, Vol.1*, doi: 10.1007/978-0-387-68772-8_26,
© Springer Science+Business Media, LLC 2009

## 2 The Significance of Sustainable ICT in Rural Development

Rural development is a significant focus for developing countries as the poverty that exists in the world today is predominantly rural (Mwabu and Thorbecke 2001). Rural areas hold substantial human and natural potential which must be harnessed to contribute effectively to development. Information and knowledge are key strategic resources in the rural development process as they provide rural people with the ability to expand their choices through knowing what works best in their communities, hence contributing to development, competitiveness and productivity (Canadian International Development Agency 2003). Access to information and knowledge can be enhanced by ICT, which effectively connects and facilitates information flows between rural communities and more developed regions (Heeks 1999; Pade et al. 2006a). Although some rural ICT projects have been successful with major project goals being attained, the challenges associated with ICT use has resulted in projects that either *totally fail* (the project has ended up not being implemented) or *partially fail* (major goals have not been attained, hence sustainability failure) (Heeks 2002).

The success of an ICT project to enable rural development relies on its ability to be sustainable. Sustainability can be defined as, "Development that meets the needs of the present generation without compromising the ability of future generations to meet their own needs" (NetTel 2005). It can be viewed either as the sustainability of ongoing rural ICT access, independent of specific technologies or projects; and/or the sustainability of rural development results through ICT-enabled development (for example, education, health, empowerment) (TeleCommons Development Group (TDG) 2000). The concept of sustainability in most research is closely related to the *financial* sustainability (cost recovery) of the project. However, it also considers other facets such as rootedness in local communities, cultural and political acceptance, and value to rural individuals (Keniston 2005). Pade et al. (2006b) identify the categories of sustainability that need to be applied in rural ICT projects:  *Social and Cultural, Institutional, Economic/Financial, Political, and Technological* sustainability. It is important that the needs, demands and driving forces of these categories are in harmony and integrated to achieve the overall sustainability of the project (Pade et al. 2006b; Hietanen 2002). The significance of the development of sustainability implies that ICT project implementation needs to be receptive to critical factors that promote the sustainability of the ICT project in rural areas.

## 3 The Dwesa Case Study

Dwesa is a rural area situated within the former Transkei, along the Wild Coast of the Eastern Cape Province of South Africa. It forms part of the Dwesa–Cwebe area which comprises the protected area (nature reserve) and extended frontline (Palmer et al. 2002). The Dwesa–Cwebe area has become involved in a development initiative as the nature reserve and wild coast that they share are a chief asset for the communities (tourism) (Palmer et al. 2002). The vision for development for Dwesa–Cwebe has been to take advantage of their rich natural asset through tourism. The land's ownership has recently been restored to the community.

The Dwesa ICT project consists of a collaboration of research projects between the Telkom Centres of Excellence (COE) at Rhodes University and the University of Fort Hare. The aim of the project is to develop an open source/standard e-commerce/telecommunications platform to deploy within rural and semi-rural areas in South Africa. The ICT project therefore endeavours to promote e-commerce in tourism (through the nature reserve, a chief community asset) and other rural development activities. The project commenced in November 2005 and provides an opportunity to observe the critical success factors applied to promote sustainability. The researchers in the project consist of postgraduate students experiencing an ICT project in context for the first time. Their different research sub-projects support the overall goal of the Dwesa ICT project. This research investigates the Dwesa project at its early stages of development. The project is currently still active within a pilot stage. The Dwesa ICT project team chose to initially implement the project within the Mpume community of Dwesa, at Mpume Primary-Junior Secondary School.

## 4 Research Methodology

The overall research investigation examined the project management techniques applied in the Dwesa rural ICT project. An exploration of the critical success factors of sustainability formed a part of the overall research investigation. A case study qualitative research methodology has been adopted to assess the ICT project in a *real-life* rural environment (Yin 2003). Data were collected from November 2005 to September 2006. The main instruments used as sources of evidence include:

- **Interviews:** These were conducted in September 2006. Members of the project team were interviewed as they are familiar with the progressive life and practices of the project. The Dwesa community directly involved in the project (two project champions, the School Headmaster, and two community members) were also interviewed separately to explore their different perspectives on the uses and challenges of ICT, and the project's approach to promoting sustainability.
- **Participant Observation:** The researcher was exposed directly to the operations associated with the project through participatory-observation from early development to intermediate operation (from November 2005 to September 2006). The role of observer was ultimately participant, although participation was limited to assisting and sharing in delegated project tasks. Participant observation did not necessarily interfere with the general operation of the project.
- **Documentation:** Project funding proposals, project progress reports, the community training register, and published background research of the Dwesa area by Palmer et al. (2002) were made available to the researcher.

The data collected were analysed to extract relevant themes and their incidence or frequencies. The approach adopted was content analysis which uses a special application of systematic observation to examine the data collected for key themes (Welman and Kruger 2002).

## 5 The Critical Success Factors for Sustainability

The categories of sustainability relevant to an ICT project rely on factors that are critical for the development of ICTs in a rural community. A range of previous project case studies from development organisation literature reveal the *lessons learned* and *good practice* for the success or sustainability of rural ICT projects. An analysis of these related lessons disclose critical success factors (CSFs) that need to be applied to support the effectiveness of the rural ICT project process. The importance of some CSFs depends on the objectives of the particular project. Nevertheless, most of these factors, to an extent, play a significant role in promoting sustainability across a variety of projects. The CSFs of rural ICT project sustainability are summarised below, followed by an exploration of their application in the Dwesa case study:

1. **Simple and Clear Project Objectives:** Clear and simple project objectives sensitive to the community's needs and limitations need to be determined for specific phases of implementation, hence setting out a solid realistic plan of small achievable steps and project deliverables that can be clearly communicated and accountable to stakeholders (Batchelor and Norrish 2002; Bridges 2006a; IDRC 2004; Standish reports in Schwalbe 2006; Talyarkhan 2004; UNDP et al. 2001).
2. **Approaching the Project in a Holistic Way:** The project should not focus unduly on its immediate and narrow concerns, but keep in mind the specific needs of the rural community at large, in relation to the capability and sustainability of the technology for an enduring impact. Most of the CSFs of sustainability are based on applying this holistic approach (Batchelor and Sugden 2003; Schwalbe 2006; UNDP et al. 2001).
3. **Using ICT to Enhance Existing Rural Development Activities:** ICT projects need to be anchored to local organisational and existing rural development activities so as to be part of wider development plans and processes, hence providing a more immediate and identifiable development benefit (Batchelor and Sugden 2003; Ferguson and Ballantyne 2002).
4. **Cultivating an Influential Project Champion:** ICT champions essentially inspire, drive, create awareness, and encourage the targeted community to use ICT, thereby facilitating the introduction of ICTs as smoothly as possible (Batchelor and Sugden 2003; IDRC 2004; Schwalbe 2006; TDG 2000; UNDP 2001)
5. **Incorporating Socially Excluded Groups:** ICT projects should incorporate social cultural factors (for example, gender awareness) into policy formulation, planning, implementation and the evaluation of projects for effective participation of social groups (Bridges 2006a; Ferguson and Ballantyne 2002; Talyarkhan 2004; TDG 2000; UNDP 2001).

6. **Awareness of Specific ICT Policy Influencing the Project:** Research is required on the policy environment, to understand the issues arising across the country and regions which affect rural ICT implementation and sustainability, both directly and indirectly, so as to take measures to enhance or mitigate the effects of policy (Batchelor and Norrish 2002; Bridges 2006b; Ferguson and Ballantyne 2002; Stoll 2003; Talyarkhan 2004; TDG 2000).

7. **An Understanding of the Local Political Context:** The introduction of ICTs to a community can be perceived as a threat to local authority, such as government officials and traditional village leaders, which can considerably influence rural community buy-in. Steps need to be taken to mitigate the political effects on the project, and hence adapt in the political environment as needed (Bridges 2006a; Ferguson and Ballantyne 2002; TDG 2000; UNDP 2001).

8. **Participation of Community Target Groups in the Project Process:** Participation aims to create the conditions in a project required to speed up and make appropriate the purpose of ICTs in the rural context, based on the expectations of the community. Aspects include selecting target groups to participate, introducing the goals and benefits of the project, identifying the limitations and risks in the community, performing a needs assessment and local content development, and providing continuous communication and feedback (Batchelor and Sugden 2003; Mphahlele and Maepa 2003; Talyarkhan 2004; TDG 2000; UNDP 2001).

9. **Focusing on Local/Demand Driven Needs:** ICTs need to focus on being demand driven and not supply driven, in accordance with the assessed needs for information and services (Batchelor and Sugden 2003; Bridges 2006a; Conradie et al. 2003; Keniston and Kumar 2003; Jacobs and Herselman 2005; TDG 2000; UNDP 2001, UNDP et al. 2001).

10. **Building on Local Information and Knowledge Systems:** Taking into consideration the local context associated with sharing knowledge created from social interactions between people ensures that information can be substantially understood, adopted and integrated into the daily lives of rural people (Batchelor and Sugden 2003; Bridges 2006b; Talyarkhan 2004; UNDP 2001).

11. **Appropriate Training and Capacity Building:** Appropriate training that is sensitive to the community ICT skill gaps should be practiced. Training should importantly consist of content development, technical support, and business and development activity support. A train to train approach needs to be applied for widespread community training (Batchelor and Sugden 2003; Bridges 2006a, 2006b; Conradie et al. 2003; Ferguson and Ballantyne 2002; IDRC 2004; Jacobs and Herselman 2005; Stoll 2003; Talyarkhan 2004; TDG 2000; UNDP 2001; UNDP et al. 2001).

12. **Facilitating Local Content Development:** The community needs to engage in local content development that is sensitive to the rural livelihood environment, so as to become producers of locally relevant, understandable, meaningful and applicable information and knowledge (Batchelor and Sugden 2003; Bridges 2006b; Keniston and Kumar 2003; Stoll 2003; Talyarkhan 2004; TDG 2000; The World Bank 2003; UNDP et al. 2001).

13. **Motivation and Incentive for ICT Job Placement in the Community:** Local ICT project training and capacity building should ensure that the skills acquired respond to the job market need, assist trainees with job placements in the telecentre, and equip them with proactive skills for finding jobs (Bridges 2006a, 2006b; Dymond and Oestman 2004; Ferguson and Ballantyne 2002; Mphahlele and Maepa 2003; The World Bank 2003).

14. **Focus on Economic Self-Sustainability – Entrepreneurship:** Entrepreneurship and creativity (economic sustainability) need to be fostered in rural areas, as the economic environment in which they operate eventually determines the extent and frequency of ICT use in the long term (Bridges 2006a, 2006b; Ferguson and Ballantyne 2002; Keniston and Kumar 2003; Mphahlele and Maepa 2003; UNDP et al. 2001; The World Bank 2003).

15. **Encouraged Local Ownership:** Ownership plays a significant role in setting the foundation for local buy-in and is crucial for relevance, effectiveness, efficiency and impact. It translates into a willingness to invest effort and resources in the ICT project (Bridges 2006a; CIDA 2003; Ferguson and Ballantyne 2002; Mphahlele and Maepa 2003).

16. **Building Local Partnerships:** The essence of partnership is that different actors have special competencies and capacities based on their particular mandates that can contribute to rural ICT project sustainability in the form of finance and/or non-financial support (promoting services, raising awareness, and technological infrastructure) (Batchelor and Sugden 2003; Bridges 2006a; Ferguson and Ballantyne 2002; IDRC 2004; Mphahlele and Maepa 2003; Stoll 2003; TDG 2000; Talyarkhan 2004; The World Bank 2003; UNDP et al. 2001; UNDP 2001).

17. **Choosing Appropriate Technology:** Mechanisms aimed at selecting the right technology for rural environments need to be incorporated. For instance, an infrastructure audit should be undertaken to determine existing and required infrastructure, etc. (Batchelor and Sugden 2003; Bridges 2006a, 2006b; Dymond and Oestman 2004; Ferguson and Ballantyne 2002; IDRC 2004; Talyarkhan 2004; TDG 2000; The World Bank 2003).

18. **Building on Existing Public Facilities:** Ideally, a community should support the project through providing a building that is rent and maintenance free. Preferred requirements of a building to house the ICTs include electricity, a telephone connection (if no wireless technology), security, and an appropriate location (visible and accessible) (Jacobs and Herselman 2005; Mphahlele and Maepa, 2003; The World Bank 2003).

19. **Ongoing Monitoring and Evaluation of the Project:** Continuous monitoring and evaluation keep the project on track and reveal the impact on the rural community. Evaluation aims to enable stakeholders to understand the change that has occurred in the community as a result of the project, identify and understand mistakes and shortcomings of the project, improve on past experience, and influence project policy formulation (Batchelor and Sugden 2003; Bridges 2006a; Dymond and Oestman 2004; Jacobs and Herselman 2005; Talyarkhan 2004; TDG 2000; UNDP 2001).

## 5.1 CSFs Applied to the Dwesa Case Study

*Simple and Clear Project Objectives (1):* The Dwesa project was not planned sufficiently and the development of simple and clear objectives that can be communicated to the project team and community still needs to be improved. Meetings were held occasionally with the community to discuss the project's progress, but were avoided at times because the project team assumed it was too formal, and would pressurize or intimidate community stakeholders. Decisions were at times ad hoc and unplanned. The sub-projects were also not sufficiently integrated to support the main project goal, with limited planned delegation, monitoring and accountability of deliverables, possibly due to the absence of a project manager.

*Approaching the Project in a Holistic Way (2):* There is slight evidence (Table 1) that the Dwesa project aims to approach the project holistically. Focusing on Mpume School initially would eventually reveal other rural development activities, as the school acts as a centre for community meetings on development. As ICT acts as an enabler in rural development, project stakeholders (Mpume teachers) can work together through partnerships, also setting the groundwork for community members who have been trained in ICT.

*Using ICT to Enhance Existing Rural Development Activities (3):* Mpume School was chosen as an initial target in the Dwesa ICT project as it is an existing influential organisation in the local community. The project team assumed that focusing on the school initially as a base for the ICT project's impact, will eventually reveal other rural development activities, as the school acts as a centre for community development meetings.

*Cultivating an Influential Project Champion (4):* Initially, two project champions who would drive the project in the community were selected: Mr. Jabe (Deputy Headmaster of Mpume) and Mrs. Gxarisa (teacher at Mpume). They were involved in planning and decisions regarding the implementation of the project in the community, and motivating community involvement. They both have good ties in the community, and were able to link the project team with other local schools, and community members involved in commercial activities such as the production and selling of indigenous craft. The Dwesa project team maintained communication with the project champions so as to be informed about the local progress of the project.

*Incorporating Socially Excluded Groups (5):* A vital component of the Dwesa project was community participation, especially involving social groups such as the youth and women in project meetings. In addition, a female project champion was chosen, who played a significant role in promoting the confidence of rural women, particularly elderly craft women to become involved in the project. The champions have also encouraged the enthusiastic youth to become actively involved.

*Awareness of specific ICT Policy Influencing the Project (6):* The Dwesa project team is aware of the influence of the ICT policy environment, particularly considering it is a Telkom (Telecommunications Company) funded project. For instance, the project did not necessarily apply for certain licences (WiMAX) individually, as the licences fell under Telkom. Furthermore, the research students are aware of the ICT policy environment, given their field of research and educational knowledge on ICT policy.

*An Understanding of the Local Political Context (7):* The Dwesa project team attempted to understand the political environment through background research on the Dwesa area, and the assistance of project champions. Furthermore, the Dwesa Development Board that manages the Trust (political body) was initially approached to create awareness of the ICT project, so as to promote community buy-in. However, the project team chose to avoid involvement in local politics and left it to the champions to be accountable to their political environment. A community meeting led by the Chief of Mpume was also held to introduce the ICT project, therefore motivating the community to participate in the project. In effect, participation and buy-in from local political leaders required a constant flow of communication to generate awareness which allowed the project to be less vulnerable to any significant political shifts when they occur.

*Participation of Community Target Groups in the Project Process (8):* The main community target in the Dwesa ICT project for the participation process has been the teachers, who would eventually train the community. Community target groups have not necessarily been identified at the current stage of the project. Nevertheless, local entrepreneurs involved in crafts have been targeted and an attempt has been made to elicit their requirements. Community meetings have also been held occasionally to introduce the goals of the project, and understand the needs and limitations of the community. The project champions continually communicate project issues between the community and project team through phone calls and email.

*Focusing on Local/Demand Driven Needs (9):* It is imperative that the Dwesa ICT project implementation meets the local needs of the community. Since the community lacks an understanding of ICTs capabilities, it is difficult for them to articulate their technology needs in relation to their rural development goals. The teachers at Mpume School have been trained to train and introduce community members to ICT, so as to stimulate demand and user requirements for ICT services in the community. Furthermore, one of the researchers is embarking on an approach to elicit requirements, especially from local entrepreneurs (craftsman and shop owners) who may take advantage of the technology.

*Building on Local Information and Knowledge Systems (10):* A research subproject in the Dwesa ICT project focuses on the development of knowledge networks in the ICT project through analysing the local knowledge system. This will assist in the development of locally relevant content.

*Appropriate Training and Capacity Building (11):* The project team attempted to understand the skill gap in the community by occasionally interviewing the teachers at Mpume School. This enabled the project to provide sufficient and ongoing training (refresher courses) for the community to take effective advantage of ICT. The project team selected the teachers at Mpume and the local youth as key gatekeepers in the community to be trained so as to be able train other community members. At this stage, the community has been trained in how to use Open Office, Internet and email, Wikipedia, and the installation and network connection of computers.

Training in the project process needs to be associated with an appropriate training structure to apply to the rural community, such that training can be effective and widespread. No training structure was designed for the project team, nor were the teachers assisted in designing an appropriate structure to train the community. Training in the Dwesa project was therefore done in a sporadic and ad hoc manner.

*Facilitating Local Content Development (12):* The project champions and teachers at Dwesa have been trained to produce their own content (for example, to assist with education/lesson planning) with the ICT resources available. As more community members are trained, they are encouraged to produce their own content to support their rural livelihood activities.

Language compatibility is also important in local content development. The Open Source Edubuntu platform used in the Dwesa project has the option of being used in English, Xhosa, or Zulu. This allows some community members constrained by language to use the ICT. Other aspects to still consider include communication habits, cultural norms, literacy, appropriate taxonomies, and intellectual property rights.

*Motivation and Incentive for ICT Job Placement in the Community (13):* The Dwesa ICT project has not necessarily employed any community members to run the ICT services provided. It currently operates on a volunteer basis with the project champions in charge of the provision of ICT services. The project champions are, however, planning to provide an incentive for the youth to assist in community training, through eventually charging for training.

*Focus on Economic Self-sustainability – Entrepreneurship (14):* At the early experimental stages of the Dwesa rural ICT project, ICT services were provided free of charge to build up awareness and confidence in use. However, it is imperative that the community does not become entirely dependent on donor funding, as the project may not be sustainable in the long run once donor funding discontinues. The Dwesa project team has encouraged the community to raise money for a printer, which has resulted in planning how to charge for computer literacy training. As the community pays for the services provided, they should become aware of the costs of providing services, such as maintenance of equipment and purchasing paper or toner, so that they become more willing to support the ICT services provided.

*Encouraged Local Ownership (15):* Local ownership has been significantly encouraged in the Dwesa project, through the level of responsibility and involvement of project champions and community members in making some decisions about the project. Furthermore, training and capacity building has equipped community representatives to effectively drive the project. The aim of the project is to build a system of accountability within the community. The type of ownership assumed by local stakeholders at different stages of the project needs to be redefined accordingly, as the ownership of the project is dynamic and embedded in the social context. As the ICT project expands to more communities and schools, the ownership assumed by the initial location, Mpume, will change as resources are shared over the network.

*Building Local Partnerships (16):* The Dwesa project has a partnership with their major donor Telkom, the national telecommunications organisation in South Africa. Telkom provides funding for the Dwesa ICT project, and liaises with the universities to assist in the purchase or use of required telecommunications infrastructure. However, there is no evidence in the Dwesa ICT project of planning to build *local* partnership in the Dwesa community. The Dwesa project team has indicated that it plans to research and create more partnerships to complement the rural ICT project. Once partners have been selected to participate, the goals of the project and their defined roles and responsibilities need to be clearly communicated through a *Memorandum of Understanding*. Similar documents were drafted in the initial proposal of the project for funding.

*Choosing Appropriate Technology (17):* The Dwesa project team conducted a feasibility study in the initial stages of the project to determine appropriate applications and compatible locations for the ICT project. Schools were mainly targeted for implementation. Therefore, the computer applications chosen are appropriate for educational environments in developing countries. These include the Edubuntu Open Source platform (an open source Linux-based operating system designed for school environments (http://www.edubuntu.org)), the Gutenberg project (a collection of free online books) and Wikipedia (a free content encyclopaedia of information).

A WiMAX (Worldwide Interoperability for Microwave Access) Terminal has been implemented in Dwesa. It is considered to be appropriate communication technology for rural environments and will eventually host a potential fixed telephony service among different communities in Dwesa. In addition, a VSAT (Very Small Aperture Terminal) has been installed at Mpume School, which has provided access to the Internet.

Refurbished computers were also used to keep costs low. The first computers provided were all new, but the project has recently received a donation of computers (in good condition) from an Australian University.

*Building on Existing Public Facilities (18):* Mpume School was selected as an initial base for the ICT project during the feasibility study. The school acts as a central location for community meetings, and is located along the main road in Dwesa. The Headmaster and teachers have allocated a classroom (with sufficient electricity) for community training and access to ICT services. The classroom originally did not have burglar bars, which posed a security threat. Community funds were therefore raised to install the burglar bars, before the project team was willing to provide the school with more computers and hardware. This also promotes ownership and accountability in the community. The computers are, however, affected by an occasional discontinuous flow of electricity which was identified at a later stage of the project.

*Ongoing Monitoring and Evaluation of the Project (19):* The practice of monitoring and evaluation is weak in the Dwesa ICT project. The occasional field visits were relied upon for updates on the progress of the project. However, there was no plan or designed assessment tool to monitor and evaluate the progress of the project towards achieving its goals. Project team meetings were held to discuss the project's progress, but these were not held on a regular basis which sometimes hindered the progressive development of the project. Regular reports were also compiled and loaded onto a Wiki to show project progress. However, these reports were informal with no defined template for guidance.

No evaluation has necessarily been conducted for the Dwesa ICT project. Furthermore, no exiting strategy exists to guide post implementation monitoring and evaluation.

# 6 Classification of the Critical Success Factors

The CSFs identified support one or more of the different categories or types of sustainability as shown in Table 1. Table 1 also provides a summary of the extent of the presence ("strong", "slight", "weak", "none") of the CSFs in the Dwesa ICT project.

**Table 1.** Classification of the critical success factors into the categories of rural ICT project sustainability

| Categories of sustainability / CSFs | Social and cultural | Institutional | Economic/financial | Political | Technological | Presence |
|---|---|---|---|---|---|---|
| 1. Simple and clear project objectives | * | * | * | * | * | Weak |
| 2. Approaching the project in a holistic way | * | * | * | * | * | Slight |
| 3. Using ICT to enhance existing rural development activities | * | * | * | | | Slight |
| 4. Cultivating an enthusiastic influential project champion | * | * | * | * | * | Strong |
| 5. Incorporating socially excluded groups | * | | | | | Slight |
| 6 Incorporating/awareness of specific ICT policy influencing the project | | | * | * | | Slight |
| 7. A good understanding of the local political context | | | | * | | Strong |
| 8. Significant participation of community target groups in the project process | * | * | | * | | Slight |
| 9. Focusing on local/demand driven needs | * | * | | | | Slight |
| 10. Building on local information and knowledge systems | * | | | | | Weak |
| 11. Appropriate training and capacity building | | * | | | | Slight |
| 12. Facilitating local content development | * | * | | | | Weak |
| 13. Existing motivation and incentive for ICT job placement in the community | * | * | * | | | Weak |
| 14. Focus on economic self-sustainability - business development (entrepreneurship) | | | * | | | Slight |
| 15. Encouraged local ownership | | * | | | | Slight |
| 16. Building local partnerships | * | * | * | | | Slight |
| 17. Choosing the appropriate or right technology | * | | | * | * | Strong |
| 18. Building on existing public facilities | * | | | | | Strong |
| 19. Ongoing monitoring and evaluation of the project | * | * | * | * | * | Weak |

*Critical success factors associated with specific categories of sustainability

# 7 Conclusion

Information and knowledge are key strategic resources which can be effectively applied through ICTs that *enable* rural development. However, the constraints to rural ICT use result in projects that fail at different levels particularly with respect to sustainability. Sustainability is key to the effectiveness of a rural ICT project. The categories of sustainability reveal critical success factors that need to be considered in an ICT project. An exploration of the Dwesa rural ICT project presents the application of the CSFs of sustainability. The practice and application of particular CSFs in the Dwesa case still needs to be improved to promote the sustainability of the project. Nevertheless, given some factors that have been adopted, there are successful aspects of the project, and this has equipped and provided researchers with the experience and reality of rural ICT projects. The CSFs show that the effective implementation of rural ICT projects relies heavily on the consideration of human/user (community-oriented) factors related to social, political, cultural and economic influences. The factors that need to be considered and characteristics of such projects differ significantly from the approach to development of ICT projects in more developed countries or regions. Consequently, an approach towards ICT project management that is sensitive to rural requirements and the critical factors that promote ICT project sustainability needs to be formulated.

# References

Batchelor, S. and Norrish, P. (2002) Sustainable Information Communication Technologies (ICT): Sustainability. *Sustainable Initiatives*. http://www.sustainableicts.org/Sustainable.htm [28/10/2005].

Batchelor, S. and Sugden, S. (2003) An Analysis of InfoDev Case Studies: Lessons Learnt. *The Information for Development Program: Promoting ICT for Social and Economic Development*. http://www.sustainableicts.org/infodev/infodevreport.pdf [22/01/2006].

Bridges (2006a) 12 Habits of Highly Effective ICT-Enabled Development Initiatives. *Bridges.Org*. http://www.bridges.org/12_habits [04/04/2006].

Bridges (2006b) Real Access/Real Impact criteria. http://www.bridges.org/Real_Access. *Bridges.Org* [04/04/2006].

Canadian International Development Agency (CIDA) (2003). CIDA's Strategy on Knowledge for Development through Information and Communication Technologies. http://www.acdi-cida.gc.ca/INET/IMAGES.NSF/vLUImages/pdf/$file/ICT.pdf [14/03/2005].

Conradie, D. P., Morris, C. and Jacobs, S. J. (2003) Using Information and Communication Technologies (ICTs) for Deep Rural Development in South Africa. *Communicatio.* 29(1and2), 199–217.

Dymond, A. and Oestman, S. (2004) *A Rural ICT Toolkit for Africa.* The World Bank, InfoDev (Washington DC).

Ferguson, J. and Ballantyne, P. (2002) Sustaining ICT-Enabled Development: Practice Makes Perfect? *Report from a workshop, The Hague, 22nd–23rd May 2002, No. 9.* http://www.ftpiicd.org/files/research/reports/report9.pdf [28/10/2005].

Heeks, R. (1999) Information and Communication Technologies, Poverty and Development. *Development Informatics, Working Paper Series,* Paper No. 5. http://www.sed.manchester. ac.uk/idpm/publications/wp/di/di_wp05.pdf [05/03/2004].

Heeks, R. (2002) Failure, Success and Improvisation of Information Systems Projects in Developing Countries. *Development Informatics, Working Paper Series, Paper No. 11* http://www.sed.manchester.ac.uk/idpm/publications/wp/di/di_wp11.pdf [25/05/2005].

Hietanen, O. (2002) Indicators of Sustainable Development. *Futura.* 21(2), 6–7.

International Development Research Centre (IDRC) (2004) Networking Institutions of Learning – SchoolNet: *Information and Communication Technologies for Development in Africa, vol. 3, 2003.* Jointly published by IDRC (Ottawa) and the Council for the Development of Social Science Research in Africa (CODESRIA) (Dakar).

Jacobs, S. J. and Herselman, M. E. (2005) An ICT-Hub Model for Rural Communities. *International Journal of Education and Development using ICT.* 1(3), 57–93.

Keniston, K. (2005) *Notes on Sustainability.* Massachusetts Institute of Technology (MIT). http://web.mit.edu/~kken/Public/PAPERS/on_sustainability.html [11/05/2005].

Keniston, K. and Kumar, D. (2003) *The Four Digital Divides.* Sage Publishers (Delhi, India).

Mphahlele, M. E. K. and Maepa, M. E. (2003) Critical Success Factors in Telecentre Sustainability: a Case Study of Six Telecentres in the Limpopo Province. *Communicatio.* 29(1and2), 218–232.

Mwabu, G. and Thorbecke, E. (2001) Rural Development, Economic Growth and Poverty Reduction in Sub-Saharan Africa. *Journal of African Economies.* 13(1), i16–i65.

NetTel (2005) Macro Environment and Telecommunications. http://cbdd.wsu.edu/kewlcontent/ cdoutput/TR501/page59.htm [Accessed: 14/03/2005].

Pade, C., Mallinson, B. and Sewry, D. (2006a) An Investigation of Sustainable ICT Projects in Rural Development. *Second Sangonet Conference on ICTs for Civil Society.* Johannesburg, South Africa, March 2006.

Padc, C., Mallinson, B. and Sewry, D. (2006b) An Exploration of the Categories Associated with ICT Project Sustainability in Rural Areas of Developing Countries: A Case Study of the Dwesa Project. *Conference of the South African Institute of Computer Scientists and Information Technologists (SAICSIT).* Gordon's Bay, South Africa, October 2006.

Palmer, R., Timmermans, H. and Fay, D. (2002) *From Conflict to Negotiation: Nature-based Development on South Africa's Wild Coast.* Human Sciences Research Council (Pretoria).

Schwalbe, K. (2006) *Information Technology Project Management (4e).* Thomson Course Technology (Boston, Massachusetts).

Stoll, K. (2003) Somos@Telecentres: The Story So Far and Lessons Learnt? *ICT for Development, Development Gateway.* http://topics.developmentgateway.org/ict/sdm/preview-Document.do~activeDocumentId=442785?activeDocumentId=442785 [14/02/2006].

Talyarkhan, S. (2004) Connecting the First Mile: a Framework for Best Practice in ICT projects for Knowledge Sharing in Development. *Intermediate Technology Development Group (ITDG).* http://www.itdg.org/docs/icts/ict_best_practice_framework.pdf [19/05/2005].

TeleCommons Development Group (TDG) (2000) Rural Access to Information and Communication Technologies (ICTs): The Challenge of Africa. *Prepared for African Connection Initiative of the African Connection Secretariat. Department for International Development (DFID)* http://www.unbotswana.org.bw/undp/docs/bhdr2002/rural%20access%20to%20ICT%20the %20challenge%20of%20Africa.pdf [18/03/2006].

The World Bank (2003) *ICT for Development Contributing to the Millennium Development Goals: Lessons learnt from Seventeen InfoDev Projects.* The World Bank (Washington DC). http://www.infodev.org/files/835_file_Case_Studies.pdf [21/07/2005].

United Nations Development Programme (UNDP) (2001) Essentials: Information Communication Technology for Development. *Synthesis of Lessons Learnt, Evaluation Office No. 5, September 2001.* United Nations Development Program (New York). http://www.undp.org/ eo/documents/essentials_5.PDF [2/08/2005].

United Nations Development Programme (UNDP), Accenture and Markle Foundation (2001) *Creating a Development Dynamic: Final Report of the Digital Opportunity Initiative.* United Nations Development Program (New York).

Welman, J. C. and Kruger S. J. (2002) *Research Methodology (2e).* Oxford University Press (Cape Town).

Yin, R. K. (2003) *Case Study Research: Design and Methods (3e).* Sage Publications (Thousand Oaks).

# An Analysis of IT-Enabled Change in a Public Organization in Tanzania

Edephonce N. Nfuka and Lazar Rusu

Department of Computer and System Sciences Stockholm University/Royal Institute of Technology, Sweden, {nfuka ! lrusu}@dsv.su.se

**Abstract**  The implementation of information technology (IT) is always associated with a series of complex organizational change issues. In developing countries, these issues are even more complex because the IT infrastructure, technology and governance are still poorer and information systems development and associated resources are less established. Therefore in our research paper we have analyzed the IT-enabled change in Tanzania Revenue Authority, a public organization in Tanzania by applying Ward and Elvin framework. Using this framework, we have analyzed the changes from almost paper to computerized-based business operations and how such changes affected the performance of the organization. The results indicate that, although there is some problems related to the maturity of technology deployment in the country and scarcity of resources, the IT-enabled change (that takes into account both technology and organizational issues) is likely to meet the organizational change objectives. Based upon the results arrived from use of the Ward and Elvin framework, we have summarized six main success factors that are worth noting for replication to other similar IT-enabled changes or research programs including the ones focusing to developing countries. It includes involvement and commitment of senior/top management; engagement of the key stakeholders; alignment of IT and business; identifying and developing necessary skills, competence and motivation; institutionalization of the change process; and incorporation of the learning process for adjustment and future intervention. Finally in conclusion, we could notice that the alignment of IT with business is the backbone of any meaningful IT-enabled change process and is illustrated by use of a benefit dependency network schema.

## 1 Introduction

Information technology (IT) has been regarded as the enabler in achieving business efficiency and cost-effectiveness. It has changed the way organizations conduct their businesses by connecting involved parties instantaneously (Davenport 2000). Despite its rapid growth and benefits, it was revealed that its implementation is not simply a technological matter. Instead, it often drives changes in management systems and culture, which can result in a number of issues including power shifts, resistance, and system difficulty, and eventually to the failure of its realization (Markus and Pfeffer 1983). A successful IT-enabled change therefore requires a structured management.

Since 1950s, there have been studies for IT-enabled change and the area has grown rapidly and received a lot of attention (Robey and Boudreau 1999). Despite such studies many organizations still have difficulty in taking advantage of IT (Kling and Lamb 2000), one of the reasons being the conflicting results of relationship between technology and organizational change (Markus and Robey 1988) such as preoccupation with the economic value of IT and neglecting the human and organizational aspects of IT-enabled change (Coghlan and McDonagh 2001).

With such limitations, several studies have called the need for a well-addressed mixed level of analysis considering the strategic change on the three dimensions of content, context, and process (Pettigrew and Whipp 1991). These are adopted to match the particular nature of the social–economic dynamic process of interaction amongst technology, organization, and environment in IT-enabled change (Markus and Robey 1988), and approach developed by the IS/IT community to enable IT-based systems to be implemented successfully (Earl 1992). One of the results of these attempts is Ward and Elvin framework that essentially is a set of principles to understand and describe conceptual issues and the actual problems that occur in four streams of the intervention, i.e. context, business content, IT content, and outcome.

The goal of this study is to analyze IT-enabled change in Tanzania Revenue Authority (TRA), a public organization in Tanzania that has undergone a significant number of changes to enable efficient revenue collection. The analysis is based on Ward and Elvin framework, the emphasis being on coming up with major success factors for IT-enabled change, taking into account inadequate IT infrastructure and relatively less developed capacity for IS development, implementation and integration in such developing country (Tanburn and Singh 2001).

The methodology employed is qualitative (Sapsford and Jupp 2006). It included interviewing relevant people and collecting data related to current (second period) and past (first period) corporate (business, organizational, and IT) plans, implementations, interventions, and outcomes within a period of 2 months. The main source was various TRA documents, operating applications, Web site, and interviews. We also did related literature to identify the framework and necessary organization data, taking into account technical and organizational issues.

In subsequent sections, we provide an overview of the Ward and Elvin framework followed by a synopsis of the case study and its analysis. Finally, we discuss the main success factors and conclude.

## 2 The Framework for Managing IT-Enabled Change

The framework for managing IT-enabled change (Ward and Elvin 1999) is based on the premise that IT alone delivers few benefits. The benefits mainly arise from changes made in processes, practices, and structures that IT enables to pursue the end not the means. The framework was conceived as the effort to recognize and put together issues affecting the outcome of IT-enabled change initiatives to increase the potential for success in changing contexts. The development of the framework has as well recognized that IT has a key role in enabling business change (Davenport and Short 1990; Venkatraman 1991; Teng et al. 1994). It provides a dynamic environment in which an organization can achieve its stated ends to satisfy its socio-economic purpose in a constantly changing situation.

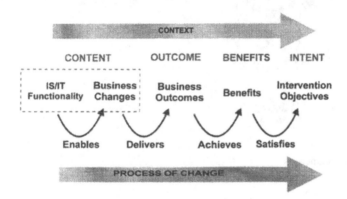

**Fig. 1.** Satisfying the intent (Ward and Elvin 1999)

A need for change arises when the actual state of an organization is seen to be problematic. Several interventions in terms of actions are taken thereafter to reach actual outcome. Such interventions provide the content of change that delivers an outcome that satisfies the intent. This is achieved by the process of change that in turn achieves benefits that are perceived to satisfy the intent objectives (Fig. 1).

Although many requirements for change derive from the organizational context, three sources of intent can be identified as a starting point based on what is known at the outset of the intervention; context driven where reason for starting is clear; outcome driven where objectives are clear; or content driven where what has to change is clear. With the framework you can also apply learning and control throughout the intervention lifecycle thus likeliness to meet the intended intent. As we will see later, the framework is used to analyze IT-enabled change in our case, through factors that affect the outcome at each of its seven (1–7) stages (Fig. 2).

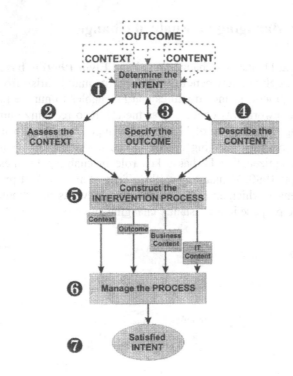

**Fig. 2.** Ward and Elvin framework

## 3 The Analysis of a Case Study

In this section, we provide an overview of TRA covering the drivers for change and the situation before, during and after the change from both business and IT perspective. All these findings are then analyzed and discussed using the Ward and Elvin framework.

### 3.1 Overview of the Case Study

TRA is a semiautonomous agency of the Government of Tanzania responsible for the administration of the Central Government revenues. It was established in 1995 and its main functions include assessing, collecting, and accounting for all Central Government Revenue.

### 3.1.1 Situation Before the Change

On its establishment, TRA had an inadequate infrastructure and was divided in three main departments: Sales Tax and Inland Revenue, Income Tax, and Customs and Exercise. The main problem with them was that every department used none or isolated semicomputerized system to accomplish its task. Generally, most of the transactions or communication within and outside the organization required the use of paper. Due to this and organizational structure by then, TRA had inefficiencies services delivery due to inaccuracies, delays, bureaucracies, and duplication of efforts in and across the departments (Kitillya 2006).

### 3.1.2 Drivers for Change

The government of Tanzania depends on the tax collected and therefore embarked in a major tax administration program in 1995. It had a vision to have a revenue authority that can provide services in a transparent manner, speed, flexibility, ease of interaction, and certainty to improve the revenue collection efficiency and cost-effectiveness without increasing tax rates (Ruparel 2006).

### 3.1.3 Process and Situation After the Change

Due to the major problems that TRA was facing and the new vision of the organization to become a Modern Tax Administration (DRP, 2007), TRA established first corporate plan. This plan lasted from 1998 to 2003, mainly on rehabilitation but also managed to establish: Automated SYstem for CUstoms Data (ASYCUDA) that handled customs related tax, computerized Taxpayer Identification Number (TIN), with which every taxpayer was registered to get a unique number to handle all tax related payments; VAT Information Processing System (VIPS), in which VAT taxpayers were registered, trader declarations processed and penalties and interest calculated; Central Motor Vehicle Registration System (CMVRS) with which new and existing vehicles were registered; Integrated Financial Information System that simplified management of logistics and financial transactions. Also as an effort to get rid of the isolated tax related systems, started to develop Integrated Income Tax System (ITAX) for integrated Tax operations (Sophia and Wakati 2005).

While the first corporate plan had not finished yet, TRA conducted a midterm review focusing on its overall performance. Many separate reviews from different sources were also produced. All of them recommended that TRA had to proceed in a second corporate plan with which a massive input of computerized systems in each and across the department(s) would transform the organization in a Modern Tax Administration (DRP, 2007). Having some experience from the first corporate and IT strategy plans and the mistakes that were made and challenges encountered, TRA prepared the new plan not only with the employees' participation but also with other stakeholders from government, development partners, business community, and TRA board of directors. This was a realistic attempt to design and implement a successful plan that would give TRA the ability to fulfill its main goals (Kitillya, 2006).

The second corporate plan started from 2003/2004 to 2007/2008 and together with its aligned IT strategy, among others, focused on the development, integration, and implementation of various information systems (IS) and supportive infrastructure that simplified the internal processes and cost-effective service delivery (Sophia and Wakati 2005). This can be separated in two major categories; IS and supportive infrastructure. IS included mainly two major systems: Upgrading and integrating the Automated System for all Customs Data Management (ASYCUDA++) that together with associated infrastructure enabled TRA to link its various custom centers in major airports, harbors, and inland borders stations; ITAX that was integrated with TIN and VIPS enhanced, and accelerated implementation of TRA zone centers in the country. Other were supportive IS like HR management, e-payments via bank systems, and the Web site.

Supportive IT Infrastructure included extension of communication infrastructure, IS department to support corporate systems, and equipments and software for staff productivity. Also different training programs were done not only on IT-related applications but also on change management and other business-related aspects.

Other implemented issues included institutionalized Tax Modernization Program Unit (TMP) to manage the change organization-wide, Large Taxpayers Department to deal with all tax issues for large tax payers, and a new scheme of benefits and services to match relevant market rate and changes made (Kitillya 2006).

## 3.2 Analysis Based on a Ward and Elvin Framework

As discussed earlier, we use Ward and Elvin framework to analyze our case using a number of factors that affect the outcome at each of its seven (1–7) stages (Fig. 2) in two major periods: first corporate plan (1997/1998–2002/2003) and second corporate plan (2003/2004–2007/2008). Given the fact that there were differences in approach and the potential to learn from both, we assess them throughout independently.

### 3.2.1 Determine the Intent (1)

Given the fact that the origin of the intent influences the process by which the intervention is carried out throughout, we look at the nature of the IT-enabled change in TRA to determine the nature of the intent. Looking at the primary drivers for change it leads us to outcome-based intent. The intervention then focuses on identifying the content of the change that will deliver the outcome (Fig. 3). The whole range of the success factors at this stage are analyzed (Table 1) and subsequent stages outcome (3), assess context (2), describe content (4), construct intervention process (5), manage process (6), and satisfied intent (7) (Fig. 2).

**Table 1** Determine the intent: success factors

| Case in two periods | 1st P | 2nd P |
| --- | --- | --- |
| Involve senior management who make explicit drivers for change | + | ++ |
| Definition of the problem/opportunity based on current dissatisfaction | + | ++ |
| Engagement of key-actors – beneficiaries of the changes | – | ++ |
| Stakeholders interests identification – supportive, negative, and hostile | – | ++ |
| Establishment of a management structure (stages 2–4) | – | ++ |

Keys ++, the factor was understood and dealt with successfully

+, the factor was recognized and dealt with adequately

0, not observed in the case

–, the factor was not dealt with effectively leading to project problems

1st P, first corporate/IS plans (1997/1998–2002/2003)

2nd P, second Corporate /IS Plans (2003/2004-2007/2008)

*This coding is used throughout in Tables 1–7*

## 3.2.2 Specify the Outcome (3)

The purpose of this stage is to assess the particular benefits which were to be obtained when the intent objectives are achieved. The relevant success factors including involvement of the key stakeholders are analyzed (Table 2). Also TRA benefits dependency network schema (Fig. 3), which identifies benefits implied by the intervention objectives and the main changes needed to achieve them are constructed in line with the process of change (Fig. 2) and TRA collected-data. This stage and the schema in specific are important and useful as creates alignment of IS/IT functionalities against business changes, benefits, and objectives in the organization (Fig. 3).

**Table 2.** Specify the outcome: success factors

| Case in two periods, see Table 1 for keys used | 1st P | 2nd P |
| --- | --- | --- |
| Use workshop to reconcile viewpoints and share collective knowledge | – | ++ |
| Identify benefits due to intervention goals and changes to achieve them | + | ++ |
| Involve all the key stakeholders, especially the owners of the problem and the actors who have to deliver the solution | – | ++ |
| Ensure all benefits are measurable, each owned by its beneficiary | + | ++ |
| Produce documentation, in form of a benefits dependency network | – | + |

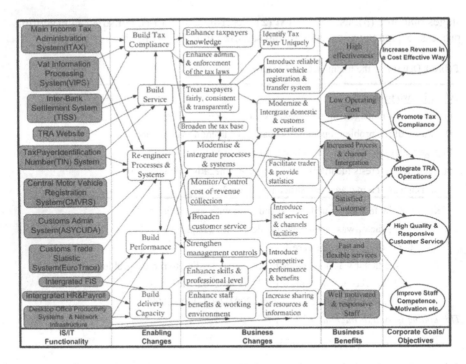

**Fig. 3.** Benefit dependency network, TRA IT-enabled change

### 3.2.3 Assess the Context (2)

The purpose for this stage is to assess the organizational and business context within which the intervention objectives (Fig. 3) have been set, and also to assess the identified and addressed issues that affect the organization's ability to achieve them. Issues include readiness of the organization to respond to the changes (Table 3).

**Table 3.** Assess the context: success factors

| Case in two periods, see Table 1 for keys used | 1st P | 2nd P |
|---|---|---|
| Ensure intended outcome, objectives, and benefits are appropriate | – | ++ |
| Understand the organization's capability to carry out the intervention and identify areas where knowledge or skills need to be developed | – | + |
| Involve key stakeholders in a structured/open debate to elicit the factors and assess specific relationships to intervention and likely impact | – | ++ |
| Allocate responsibility for action to the owners/stakeholders | + | ++ |

### 3.2.4 Describe the Content (4)

In this stage we assess the intervention process; IT and business content to see how they were defined, developed, and then made to happen (Fig. 3 and Table 4).

**Table 4.** Describe the content: success factors

| Case in two periods, see Table 1 for keys used | 1st P | 2nd P |
|---|---|---|
| Understand scope of changes and relationships to satisfy the objectives | – | ++ |
| Focus on requirements not designs or solutions | – | + |
| Maintain a tolerance for ambiguity and a degree of uncertainty | 0 | 0 |
| Facilitate collaboration between business managers and IT specialists | + | ++ |

### 3.2.5 Construct the Intervention Process (5)

This is the stage where intervention process (Fig. 3) is analyzed. This is done by observing current shortfalls in the state of knowledge in any part of the intervention. It requires consistency and the approach is based on the work of Venkatraman (1991), from which the change analysis heptagon elements might have influenced intervention and are assessed accordingly (Table 5).

**Table 5.** Construct the intervention process: success factors

| Case in two periods, see Table 1 for keys used | 1st P | 2nd P |
|---|---|---|
| Pooling and structuring the knowledge of stakeholders | – | ++ |
| Explicit consideration of all known risks and uncertainty | – | + |
| Setting up management, structures, and roles tailored to change needs | + | ++ |
| Setting up management, structures, and roles for change coordination | – | ++ |
| Documentation/publication of the benefits plan and the key decisions | + | ++ |
| Production of interventions strategy and its communication channels | – | + |
| Handling changes affecting business processes, internal/related parties | - | ++ |
| Describing the key aspects of the IS/IT in the change | + | ++ |
| Changing in attitude and behavior to deliver the benefits | - | + |

### 3.2.6 Manage the Process (6)

The purpose here is to assess the activities of the intervention (Fig. 3). This involves seeing how they were monitored and the flexibility for adjustment so that the intervention converges on an outcome that satisfies the intent, while recognizing that the actual outcome may differ somewhat from the outset (Table 6).

**Table 6.** Manage the process: success factors

| Case in two periods, see Table 1 for keys used | 1st P | 2nd P |
|---|---|---|
| Monitor project continually to ensure the process and control regimes | – | ++ |
| Take early action to remove uncertainties/gap in knowledge | – | + |
| Make explicit the interdependencies of the business and IT | + | ++ |
| Ensure process is focused on delivering benefits that satisfy the intent | + | ++ |
| Ensure that allocated roles and responsibilities are fulfilled | + | ++ |

### 3.2.7 Satisfied Intent (7)

The goal of the interventions is to satisfy the objectives established. In this stage, we therefore review the degree to which the objectives set were met. Considering importance of alignment of IT and business goals in the IT-enabled change, results are presented below based on the five TRA corporate goals (Fig. 3).

*Increase revenue collection in a cost-effective way*
TRA increased revenue collection since IT-enabled changes were introduced. During first period, its revenue collection, for example, in 2002 was US$1,145m which is 165% increase compared to US$404m collected in 1995. Also more increase is observed in second period, for example, in year 2005 collected US$1,679m. Such increase (Fig. 4), is an indication on how this objective was met, among others, due to increased compliance and efficiency in collection and management of the revenues through the use of automated systems like ITAX and ASYCUDA (Fig. 3).

Average exchange over these years: ~1000TZs to 1US$

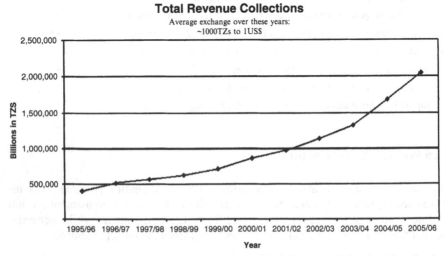

**Fig. 4.** Revenue collection trends (http://www.tra.go.tz/Total_Revenue_Collection_Chart.htm)

*Integrate TRA operations*
The integration and automation of the three TRA's main departments as well as development and integration of associated information systems; ITAX, TIN, VIPS, and ASYCUDA (Fig. 3), provided efficient and cost-effective way of managing and monitoring the tax payers.

*High quality and responsive customer service*
Customer satisfaction has increased through a number of developments including Web site that enables customers to conveniently access various information and documents such as tax information, forms, and reports (TRA 2007). Similarly has enabled taxpayers' e-payments through banking institutions using Inter-Bank Settlement System (TISS). Also the use of all Revenue Information Systems in place increased the quality and responsiveness to serve the customers (Fig.3).

*Promote tax compliance*
Tax compliance has increased among tax-payers due to the implementation of the equitable, consistent, and transparent IS that improve easy access to tax information and services as well as the introduction of a Large Taxpayers Department that enabled integration of VAT and Income Tax operations (Fig. 3).

*Improve staff competence, motivation, integrity and accountability*
TRA improved skills and level of professionalism during the change including change management, customer care, total tax person for integrated operations, and specific training on new processes and procedures (Kitillya, 2006). Also TRA upgraded level of staff benefits and working environment that among others improved staff motivation (Table 5). Additionally introduced HR IS that strengthened and allowed easy way to serve, control, and manage the staff (Fig. 3).

Also the purpose at this stage is to understand the particular contextual and process management factors that influence the organization's ability to succeed for further improvement or any other change initiatives (Table 7).

Table 7. Satisfied intent: success factors

| Case in two periods, see Table 1 for keys used | 1st P | 2nd P |
|---|---|---|
| Plan to hold review meetings after implementation of the changes | ++ | 0 |
| Involve stakeholders and ensure they prepare views before the meetings | ++ | 0 |
| Focus on the achievement of the intervention's objectives | ++ | 0 |
| Learn for future interventions rather than attribute blame | ++ | 0 |

### 3.2.8 Problems Encountered and Solutions

The organization also encountered numerous problems, mostly in first period (Table 1–6). This was from organizational, technological, culture to behavior (Venkatraman 1991; Orlikowiski and Barley 2001). It included staff resistance that was resolved by change management programs; staff turnover that was resolved by a new schemes with competitive remunerations; inadequate/timely fund and organization wide coordination that were resolved by modernization program unit the changes organization wide ; and inadequate national IT infrastructure that though expensive, TRA developed its own telecommunication infrastructure that links TRA offices across the country (Kitillya 2006, Sophia and Wakati 2005).

### 3.2.9 Major Success Factors

Use of Ward and Elvin framework to analyze IT-enabled change in TRA brought forward success factors in each stage (Table 1–7). We hereby categorize and discuss the most critical ones that are worth replicating to other similar IT-enabled change or research programs, including the ones focusing to developing countries.

*Involvement and commitment of senior/top management*
IT-enabled change involves IT and business change that cut across the organization. The involvement of top management in the nurturing of such changes and commitment to its development is an important aspect that can make the intervention succeed or fail (Kling and Lamb 1999). Furthermore in specific case of developing countries where IT is relatively new with traditional culture-oriented behaviours, a drive from top is required to bring the rest on board. In our case, overall involvement of the senior management was an important aspect as can be seen in second period where even board members were involved and therefore much better results (Table 1).

*Engagement of the key stakeholders*
Implementing an IT-enabled change requires an understanding of the drivers for change. Whether they originate in the context of the business, particular performance improvement, business/IT content problems/opportunities, or a combination of them, it is critical to determine the degree of dissatisfaction with the current situation as perceived and agreed by the key stakeholders. This helps to determine broader view of the need and approach to the change, but also gain commitment of these stakeholders during the construction and management of intervention process (Table 1–2) ensuring that intended outcome, objectives, and benefits are appropriate to the intervention (Fig. 2, Table 1–3 and 5). This is even more crucial for IT-enabled change that involves integration across the departments, processes, and external parties, like in this case. In our case, it was seen that in the second period there are more involvement of stakeholders and this led to better intervention and results.

*Alignment of IT and business*
Successful IT-enabled changes require alignment of IT and business. When effectively linked with improvements to business processes, advances in IT enables change to do business better and more competitively than before (Pearlson and Saunders 2006). It is an enabler of business transformation, a process that requires challenging the old assumptions and shed the old rules that made the business

under perform in the first place (Hammer 1990). This way in our case it was important to assess the current dissatisfaction (Table 1) and scope of change (Table 4), identify benefits implied by the intervention objectives, business changes, and IS/IT functionalities needed to achieve them (Fig. 3 and 4). All these indicate that for alignment to work should focus on requirements first and not solutions, which then at the later stage allow implementation of ICT Systems that are "Business-led" rather than "Technology driven" ensuring the business and IT contents are aligned. The assessment in our case indicates that in the second period more attention were paid to these factors thus achieving more alignment between them. This is the major factor in the change and its importance is also supported by various research works (Henderson and Venkatraman 1993; Luftman 1996, 2000; Papp 2001).

*Identifying and developing necessary skills, competence, and motivation*
IT-enabled change process also require skilled, competent, and motivated workforce (Venkatraman 1991). Therefore understanding the organization's capability to carry out the intervention and identifying areas where knowledge or skills are lacking need to be developed (Table 3) as well as changing in attitude and attractive incentives (Table 5) are essential. In assessing these concerns, we have seen that some of them were encountered especially in first period, thus slowing down the change process. However, after addressing those in the second period accelerated the change (Table 3 and 5) and therefore its importance in the change process.

*Institutionalization of the change process*
IT-enabled change process needs to be managed for enabling changes in the work practices, business processes, and structures of an organization (Kling and Tillquist 2000). Given such variety of aspects and its effect in an organization, to reach the intervention goals need to institutionalize tasks involved (Levinson 1988). In fact many IT-enabled projects have not realized, or delayed realizing their benefit because the change process did not recognize the institutionalization phase (Benjamin and Levinson 1993). In our case, we have seen that institutionalization was very important and this is seen in the second period results where it was instituted. It allowed setting up of management structures, communication channels, and responsibilities for coordination of the change process (Table 5). Similarly, control and monitoring was made to be continual thus ensuring that benefits are measured (Table 2) and process and control regimes remain fit for the purpose (Table 6).

*Incorporation of the learning process for adjustment and future intervention*
Even if it is possible to envisage an outcome that will satisfy the intent (Fig. 1 and 3), there is no guarantee that the specified content will deliver the outcome over the time. Consequently, the process of change needs to be adaptable to cope with evolving context and incorporate periods of learning to overcome shortfalls in the state of the organization's knowledge. In our case, it is a success story as in second period goals were achieved (Table 1–6), this being the result of what was learnt and incorporated from the first period (Table 7).

# 4 Conclusions

In this study, we analyzed IT-enabled change in a public organization in Tanzania, TRA, using Ward and Elvin framework. The framework provided the mechanism to measure an IT-enabled change intervention. Its approach on benchmarking successful factors and flexibility built around it showed that it is quite useful even for a developing country like Tanzania, where IT infrastructure and related resources are scarce and information systems development less established.

The analysis of the IT-enabled change and the respective implementation indicates that use of IT has a great potential in the process and is a key enabler to productivity growth. However, it was also seen that there are important issues including organizational structure, culture, and reengineering of the processes that need close attention. This is also indicated in the problems encountered during the change that included cultural issues like resistance to change, organizational issues like institutionalization of change process and dependency on external funding, and external context issues like inadequate national wide IT infrastructure.

The framework in conjunction with the case indeed helped in pointing out important successful factors worth replicating especially in the developing countries where IT infrastructure and associated culture is still on the infant stages. The success factors were observed to include involvement and commitment of senior/top management; engagement of the key stakeholders; alignment of IT and business; identifying and developing necessary skills; competence and motivation; institutionalization of the change process; and incorporation of the learning process for adjustment and future intervention. Specifically, we have noted that the alignment of IT and business is the backbone of any meaningful IT-enabled change process in an organization and we illustrated it with the benefit dependency network (Fig. 3).

# 5 Recommendation for Further Research

This study has used the Ward and Elvin framework to analyze IT-enabled change from perspective of the entire organization. It will be interesting to do further studies on each of the major information systems where the change process can catch more specific business changes, benefits, and objectives. Specific systems could be Integrated Income Tax System (ITAX) and Automated SYstem for CUstoms DAta (ASYCUDA). This way, among others, more success factors can be identified and added to the pool of identified success factors and further used for similar purpose.

# References

Benjamin, R.I. and Levinson, E. (1993), A Framework for Managing IT-Enabled Change. Sloan Management, Review, summer 1993.

Coghlan, D. and McDonagh, J. (2001), Research and Practice in IT-Related Change: The Case for Clinical Inquiry. Research in Organizational Change and Development, pp. 195–211. Elsevier Science Ltd.

Davenport, J.H. and Short, J.E. (1990), The New Industrial Engineering: IT and Business Process Redesign. Sloan Management Review, summer, pp. 11—27.

Davenport, T.H. (2000), Mission Critical: Realizing the Promise of Enterprise Systems. Harvard Business School Press, Boston, Massachusetts.

Department of Research and Policy (DRP). (2007), The New Corporate Plan 2003/04–2007/08, http://www.tra.go.tz/current.htm last visited 12th April 2007.

Earl, M.J. (1992), Putting IT in Its Place: a Polemic for the Nineties. Journal of Information Technology, 7 (2), 100–108.

Hammer M. (1990), Reengineering Work: Don't Automate, Obliterate. Havard Business Review, (July–August 1990), p. 4.

Henderson, J.C. and Venkatraman, N. (1999), Strategic Alignment: Leveraging IT for Transforming Organizations. IBM Systems Journal, 38(2/3), 472–484.

Kling, R. and Lamb, R. (2000), IT and Organizational Change in Digital Economies: a Socio-Technical Approach. ACM SIGCAS Computers and Society, 29(3), 17–25.

Kling R. and Tillquist J. (2000), Conceiving IT-Enabled Organizational Change, scholarworks.iu.edu

Kitillya H. (2006), C, Aspects of Administrative Reforms TRA Experience, by Commissioner General, Workshop on Issues in Revenue Administration, Tax Compliance, and Combating Corruption, CapeTown, South Africa.

Levinson E. (1988), The Line Manager and Systems induced Organizational Change, in: Success Factors for Change from a Manufacturing Point of View. Dearborn, Michigan: Society of Manufacturing Engineers.

Luftman, N.J. (1996), Competing in the Information Age – Strategic Alignment in Practice. Oxford Press.

Luftman, N.J. (2000), Assessing Business – IT Alignment Maturity, Communication of AIS, Volume 4, Article 14.

Markus, M.L. and Pfeffer, J. (1983), Power and the Design and Implementation of Accounting and Control Systems. Accounting, Organizations and Society, 8, (2–3), 205–218.

Markus, M.L. and Robey, D. (1988), Information Technology and Organizational Change: Causal Structure in Theory and Research. Management Science, 34, (5), 583–598.

Orlikowiski, W.J. and Barley, S.R. (2001), Technology and Institutions: What Can Research on Information Technology and Research on Organizations Learn from Each Other? MIS Quarterly, 25, 145–165.

Papp, R. (2001), Strategic Information Technology: Opportunities for Competitive Advantage, Idea Group Publishing.

Pearlson E. and Saunders S. (2006), Managing and Using Information Systems, A Strategic Approach (3rd edn). John Wiley and Sons.

Pettigrew, A. and Whipp, R. (1991), Managing Change for Competitive Success. Blackwell Business, Oxford.

Robey, D. and Boudreau, M.C. (1999), Accounting for the Contradictory Organizational Consequences of Information Technology: Theoretical Directions and Methodological Implications. Information Systems Research, 10 (2), 167–185.

Ruparel R. (2006), Project Appraisal Document for Tax Modernization Project in Tanzania, World Bank, Volume 1, Report No. 36221–TA, available at http://www-wds.worldbank.org/, last visited April, 12, 2007.

Tanburn J. and Singh A.D. (2001), ICTs and Enterprises in Developing Countries: Hype or Opportunity? Series on Innovation and Sustainability in Business Support Services, Seed working paper, No. 17, ILO.

Teng, J.T.C., Grover, V. and Fieldler, K.D. (1994), Redesigning Business Processes Using IT. Long Range Planning, 27 (1), 95–106.

TRA. (2007), Tanzania Revenue Authority (TRA) Website, http://www.tra.go.tz , last visited 13th April 2007.

Sapsford, R. and Jupp, V. (2006), Data Collection and Analysis (2nd edn). Sage Publications, (DCA).

Sophia and Wakati K. (2005), TRA ICT Strategy, Tanzania Revenue Authority.

Venkatraman, N. (1991), IT Induced Business Reconfiguration. In: Corporation of the 1990s, Scott Morton, M.S. (ed.), pp. 122–158. Oxford University Press, Oxford.

Ward J. and Elvin R. (1999), A New Framework for Managing IT-Enabled Business Change. Information Systems Journal, 9 (3), 197–221.

# Virtual Communities and eMunicipalities as Innovations

Malgorzata Pankowska

University of Economics, Information Systems, pank@ae.katowice.pl

**Abstract**  The chapter covers explanations of innovations for public administration and analysis of virtual communities and eMunicipalities as innovations. The objectives and results received from survey of municipalities' Web sites are presented to enable concluding.

## 1 Introduction

The implementation of information and communication technologies (ICTs) accelerates the transformation of governmental institutions and their methods of operations. The use of ICTs in governments opens up many possibilities for improving services to citizens and businesses, for increasing efficiency and reforming traditional paper processes.

European Union agencies are particularly interested in supporting the creation of innovative Europe. Innovation is understood as comprising the renewal and enlargement of a range of products and services and their associated markets; the establishment of new methods of design, production, supply and distribution; the introduction of changes in management, work organization, and working conditions and skills of the workforce. It covers technological, non-technological and organizational innovations (Decision No 1639/2006). The main problem of the chapter is to explain innovations in public administration at the municipality level and reveal the ways of their development.

## 2 eGovernment as an Innovative Challenge

eGovernment is defined as the use of ICTs in public administrations combined with organizational change and new skills to improve public services and democratic processes and strengthen support to public policies. It improves the development and implementation of public policies and helps the public sector to cope with the conflicting demands of delivering more and better services with fewer resources. Public administration agencies are looking for innovative solutions enabling them citizen-oriented strategy realization. eGovernment is not an objective per se, it has to be seen more as means in organizing public governance for better

C. Barry et al. (eds.), *Information Systems Development: Challenges in Practice, Theory, and Education, Vol.1*, doi: 10.1007/978-0-387-68772-8_28,
© Springer Science+Business Media, LLC 2009

serving citizens and enterprises (Traunmuller and Wimmer 2004). eGovernment concerns the whole scope of administrative actions and the connected political processes, because ICT is an enabling force that will enhance effectiveness, quality and efficiency of public actions as well as its legitimacy. The vision that emerged places eGovernment at the core of public management modernization to increase public value. The creation of public value encompasses the various democratic, social, economic, environmental and administrative roles of governments. The particular examples of the roles cover the provision of public administration services, implementation and evaluation of policies and regulations, the guarantee of democratic political processes (Centeno et al. 2004).

In eGovernment, two complementary perspectives are of equal importance, i.e. cooperation and knowledge. Support of computer-mediated cooperation in a comprehensive sense means sophisticated tools. Multiple media for the contacts become a must. The meeting activities as such may be performed online and via video techniques and improved by tools using multimedia. Prospects for knowledge management in eGovernment are remarkable from the point of demand: nearly all administrative tasks are informational in nature, decision making is a public task, and for any agency its particular domain knowledge is an asset of key importance. The aim of eGovernment is to enhance public participation in decision making. Worldwide varieties of eGovernment Web sites have been set up, providing services and information at different levels (Cordoba 2006).

This practice-based experience paper is to present a certain strategy to create innovative public administration. Generally, innovation is usually related to the first idea of using a new technology. A technical innovation is defined as the first commercial application or production of a new process or product, and innovation is defined as a change of decision rules to fit with the surrounding requirements (Pedersen and Pedersen 2006). Administrative innovation includes changes that affect the policies, allocation of resources and other factors associated with the social structure of the organization. Innovation in many organizations is not a luxury, but a critical means of keeping up with changing circumstances and opportunities. Innovations are made in the context of institutional embeddings. That is, the object of innovation does not stand alone, but is set within an economy, within cultural and business practices. The circumstances determine the unique development of innovation. The true value of innovation hinges on the ability of an organization to exploit tacit knowledge from both internal and external sources to improve organizational and competitive performance. According to B. Roberts innovation is an invention plus its exploitation (Gaynor 2002) and at least one must be brilliant, modern and unique. Innovation is a practice of creation, conversion and commercialization of services and products. Innovative practices rely very much on existing knowledge networks in communities and on how such networks are converted to allow for knowledge management in new and meaningful ways (Justesen 2004). Innovation is the specific tool of entrepreneurship by which entrepreneurs exploit change as an opportunity for a different business or service. Innovation has to address market needs, and requires entrepreneurship as a change of state, a dynamic process, a unique event (Zhao 2006). Entrepreneurship involves capturing ideas, converting them into products and services and then building a venture to take the product to market and to community. The key elements of innovations' development include risk-taking, proactivity and innovation. Innovation is a proposed theory or design concept that synthesizes extant knowledge and techniques to provide a theoretical basis for a new concept. Innovation has many facets and is multidimensional. Innovation can be radical or incremental. Radical innovations refer to pathbreaking, discontinuous, revolutionary, original, pioneering, basic or major activities. Incremental innovations are small improvements made to enhance and extend the established processes, products and services. The creativity in innovations adds value to the individual and to the community and is based upon perceiving and capturing opportunities. Open source software, open contents, open standards are opportunities, demanding risk-taking to receive benefits. An opportunity utilization is a change of state, exploitation of change as an opportunity for a different business or service.

According to Gulbrandsen (2004), innovations and innovativeness as concepts are relative: they are judged on the basis of current knowledge, only a certain result is regarded as novel one. This is probably particular to science: the innovation literature often underscores the fact that an innovation only needs to be new to the adopting firm. The scientific innovativeness is not only a personal quality, but a phenomenon that develops in the interaction of the field of science, peers and individuals. Also culture and institutional arrangements for science and society's knowledge requirements provide for constructing and sustaining a system that makes innovativeness possible. Unambiguous or universal criteria for innovations do not exist since they are socially constructed in varying social contexts. Similar opinions are delivered by Sundbo and Fuglsang (2006). They argue that innovation can be seen as a special case of development, which is relevant to some firms and organizations. Innovation could be defined as the successful introduction and development of new products or processes that can be clearly isolated and identified and which have a certain degree of radicalism and novelty. The innovation process should be as a process as such, it should have the character of a specific, novelty-oriented project. Innovation is more than change. It is a change in the direction that is unfamiliar in the setting (Alter 2004). Innovations in eGovernment start from:

- Technology: New technology or better use of existing technology makes it possible to change administrative process at governmental offices.
- Information: Intention to use different information or provide, process and store information in a new way leads to innovative use of IT.
- Participants: Providing new IT leads to new possibilities for decision making and for doing work differently.

## 3 Assumptions and Method of Research

In Poland, the following Acts adapted by the Parliament were extremely important for eGovernment development:

- The Act on Computerisation of the Operations of Certain Entities Performing Public Tasks of 17th February 2005. The Act sets up programmes for all the sectors of public administration and establishes a common interoperability framework for ICT systems in the Polish public sector.
- The eGovernment Action Plan for 2005–2006 of 26th October 2004, aimed at implementing the eGovernment objectives of the Poland Information Society strategy.
- New Law on Public Procurement of 29th January 2004, enabling the development of eProcurement systems for Polish public administrations and allowing the use of electronic auctions for contracts up to €60000.
- ePoland – The Strategy on the Development of the Information Society in Poland for the years 2004–2006 adopted by the Cabinet on 13th January 2004.
- The launch of the Public Information Bulletin (PIB) (official electronic journal on public information) in accordance with the Act on Access to Public Information of 6th September 2001.

These legal acts constitute fundamentals for Web sites development for public administration. The right of access to public information constitutes a major component of the democratic standard of open government or openness of public authorities. Cyberspace represents a place in which people can communicate to exchange views and to develop socio-economic and political initiatives. This practice-based experience elaboration results from the research covering the analysis of the contents of Web sites developed for municipalities in Poland. Such comparative analyses are realized to evaluate the development of eBusiness strategy. This research focuses on eGovernment concepts implementation in practice for communities. Generally, municipality is understood as an urban political unit having its own local government. According to the Parliamentary Act on the Official Public Administration Division of 28 June 1998 there are 2,489 municipalities in Poland, including 333 towns and 2,156 villages. This report covers comparative analysis of the contents of 150 Web sites of randomly selected villages and towns. The observations are reported in the separate chapter.

## 4 Web Sites Analysis

The analysis was conducted from two points of view:

- eMunicipality as innovation to ensure initiatives' development and eGovernment strategy realization
- Virtual communities as innovations to ensure eDemocracy and eParticipation development

eMunicipality covers a number of mechanisms which convert the paper procedures of a traditional municipal office into electronic processes, with the goal to create paperless office, to increase productivity and performance of municipalities. Its objective is to introduce transparency and accountability leading to better eGovernment within municipalities. Citizens need knowledge for solving a problem or making a decision. A knowledge service is a service for solving a problem.

The important characteristic of knowledge service different from that of data service is the level of knowledge. A data service assumes the same level of knowledge between the provider and the recipient, but knowledge service assumes the different knowledge levels between the provider and the client (Lee and Neff 2004). The question is what knowledge in eMunicipality is transferred among municipal authorities and citizens. In public administration top down flow of knowledge covers rules, regulations and orders. Bottom up transfer can include comments, suggestions, ideas, initiatives, critiques and proposals. To evaluate eMunicipalities development in Polish communities, the following criteria have been accepted:

• Community office organizational structure
• Access to knowledge from governmental sources (i.e. Parliament, Ministries, central agencies) to ensure top down public administration knowledge dissemination
• Specification of legal acts compulsory for citizens
• Access to law interpretation portals and Web sites
• Access to training materials on public administration procedures
• Opportunity to download forms of documents concerning issues dealt with at the office
• Access to Citizen Service Office
• Specification of procedures of behaviour in emergency cases, alert mechanisms
• Access to emergency assistance support systems
• Access to databases containing tenders and proposals specifications within eProcurement system

eProcurement makes it possible to capture accurate and timely information on every purchase. The first and the most obvious are the savings that come from automating the process. The second focus area for efficiency savings is more structural than procedural, and comes from shifting the selection and ordering process back to the employees' desktop, eliminating the multiple purchasing middlemen now involved in everyday indirect goods procurement.

Since the late 1990s there was much energy around virtual communities. They are a self-defined electronic networks of interactive communication organized around a shared interest or purpose, although sometimes communication becomes the goal in itself (Hildreth 2004). Within the virtual community relationships are the key aspects. They determine the motivation and the legitimating of the members, which in turn determine their identity and mutual trust. H. Rheingold described virtual communities as cultural aggregations that emerge when enough people, who exchange comments and ideas through the mediation of computer bulletin boards and networks, meet in cyberspace (Thompson, 2004). Virtual communities may help citizens to revitalize democracy by enabling massive participation in the political processes, but also they may cheat them into buying attractively packaged substitutes of democratic discourses. Virtual communities provide an exiting platform for knowledge sharing and relationship building as well as for public participation, which is a growing part of spatial and environmental planning (Lesser and Fontaine 2004). Knowledge is exchanged in a network of practice through mutual engagement in practice, through asynchronous, text-based computer-mediated communication and through the participation open to anyone with a desire to interact. Cyberspace is the total interconnectedness of human beings through computers and telecommunication without regard to their geographical location. Common goal is factor of social capital. It is a resource that comes from relation between people that makes lives more productive and easier. Social capital is not only created from groups of people living in very close proximity, such as in neighborhood. It might be created between people belonging to the same church or group of people who are alumni of a particular university. Those groups of people can be said to constitute communities. Virtual communities are built through conversations of members exchanging information and social support. These conversations, through their exchange, are owned jointly by the community and generate social capital. There are virtual communities for nearly every interest that comes to mind, from medical afflictions (e.g. breast cancer, Parkinson's Disease, Down's Syndrome) to hobbies (e.g. coin collecting, wine, saltwater aquariums) and professions (e.g. nursing, law, finance).

The main purpose of environmental decision making and thus the main purpose of public participation is to achieve protection, conservation and wise management of the socio-economic and natural environment. The level at which the public is involved varies with the relevant legislation, and the attitude of the other stakeholders. For interactive, collaborative decision making between citizens and politicians, two key elements are required. First, citizens must be prepared to become knowledgeable about current issues and to express opinions (particularly on new initiatives) to bring clarity to the decision making process of elected representatives. Secondly, the state must be prepared to provide timely, comprehensive information as well as channels of communication through which the citizens can express their opinions and engage in debate. eParticipation means the ICT supporting joint activities in municipality governance processes (Miia et al. 2006). To evaluate eParticipation development in Polish communities the following criteria have been accepted:

- Presentation of the community mission, vision and strategy
- Presentation of community history (i.e. people, buildings, calendar of events)
- Access to information from non-governmental sources to create relations and knowledge exchanges
- Access to land use plans, to land information system and to geographic information system for citizens and business organizations
- Availability of search engines, FAQs on the Web sites
- Providing public opinion questionnaires on the Web sites for citizens, tourists
- Providing links to commercial and business units, their advertisements, through the Web sites
- Presentation of the special activities within the community for the physically and mentally impaired, for the unemployed and the homeless on the Web sites
- Presentation of the special activities of benevolent institutions and charity houses on the Web sites

- Access through the community Web site to chat rooms, forums, blogs of citizens, politicians and communities' officers
- Presenting the information on contests, competitions for citizens and guests
- Providing eNews containing citizens' comments, questions and suggestions on the community and its Web site development

eDemocracy encourages radical decentralization in which every municipal unit, so citizens and business units, is involved in the innovation process of using the Internet for joint governance within a community. Computer-aided democracy covers the access to politically relevant information (teleconsulting), the availability of pluralistic discussion places (electronic conferences, newsgroups and forums), and the possibility for all to intervene in decision making (eVoting, televoting). Therefore, eDemocracy means that citizens will not only use technology to inform themselves about current events, but will also use it as a voting tool in both their national and local elections or administration and as a means for active participation (Biasiotii and Nannucci 2004, Lambropoulos 2006). However, to be involved in eDemocracy people must be educated. There is a need to promote awareness of the responsibilities that are incumbent on each individual in a democratic society, in particular within the local community, for an elected representative, local administrator, public servant and ordinary citizen. In this research to evaluate eDemocracy development in Polish communities, the following criteria have been accepted:

- Rules and regulations for community, resolutions, meetings' protocols, projects for community, private properties declarations of main officials in municipality
- Information on municipal elections, addresses of polling stations and information on opening hours
- Links to political parties Web sites
- Journals published by municipality office or citizens

## 5 Analysis' Results

Analysis of the content of 150 Web sites for communities resulted in some important comments:

- Resolution of the Act on Access to Public Information of 6th June 2001 caused rapid development of municipalities' Public Information Bulletin (PIB) and Web sites. They are linked, although developed separately. 98% of municipalities included in this research have implemented PIB. This electronic journal, according to the requirements included in the Act on Access to Public Information, contains information important for citizens on municipality authorities, organization of municipality offices, electronic forms of documents, administrative procedures mandatory for citizens and for local businesses, declaration of private properties owned by municipality authorities, community legal regulations and rules, information on procurements for municipality, invitations for tenders and auctions, municipality budgets and land planning.

- Generally, municipalities' Web sites and PIBs ensure achievement of eGovernment strategic goals. They enable transfer of top down administrative information and access to governmental sources of public information, as well as to portals for law interpretation and public administration knowledge dissemination. The citizens have the opportunities to learn about legal acts mandatory for them, to recognize office procedures. They can download forms of documents. They have the possibility to utilize multichannel communication with Citizen Service Office, where an official can use stationary telephone, mobile, emails. However, citizens still mostly prefer face-to-face contacts. The administrative processes are not yet fully automated because of the lack of common implementation of electronic signature.
- The PIBs usually ensure investors and business units access to databases of tenders considering jobs for public institutions.
- Municipalities' authorities reveal spatial plans on the Web sites or in PIBs. Obtaining maps including buildings, roads and data on media deliveries and on environment protection from GISs is possible. Municipalities' Web sites cover links to many non-governmental institutions, e.g. charity houses or to private business companies, e.g. restaurants, hotels, but municipalities are not interested in the development of advertisements for them. Municipalities' Web sites contain information on help for the unemployed and the homeless as well as for others that need social security.
- Information included in municipalities' Web sites is addressed to different info market segments, i.e. citizens, tourists, investors, sponsors, business units and non-profit organizations. Citizens have the opportunity of two-way communication with central institutions, i.e. State Archive, Central Office of Geodesy and Cartography, European Information, Environmental Protection Inspection, the Institute of National Remembrance, Supreme Chamber of Control, Supreme Administrative Court, National Bank of Poland, President of the Republic of Poland, Supreme Court of the Republic of Poland, Social Insurance, etc.
- However, involvement of citizens in public debates and discussions is not sufficiently well developed. Municipalities' Web sites do not sufficiently well utilize Internet as a medium to involve citizens and sponsors to act for community. Contests, competitions, festivals, fairs, joint actions and projects are not well promoted and advertised in Internet, however they are a real source of citizens' involvement in network of inter-community social relations.
- eParticipation tools, i.e. fun games, blogs, video interviews, chats, forums, interface agents are still not sufficiently well used to engage citizens in discussions, exchanging views, and in the creation of social relations. Citizens are very rarely involved in ePublication, only 10% of the analysed municipalities published eNews.
- Internet is still mostly used as a one-way communication channel to inform citizens or to withdraw information from citizens, e.g. questionnaires. There is no visible feedback and lack of common interchange of information between authorities and citizens. In November 2006 in Poland, municipal elections have been very weakly supported by the Internet. Political candidates preferred TV,

radio and billboard campaigns as well as direct meetings. On the Web sites of communities there are no links to any political parties.

- Citizens still underestimate the role of eNews, which has been termed "ordinary people journalism". The municipality members may have the ability to write their own articles on local events, people or public comments to their films and photos. eNews, municipal Internet TV and radio could integrate citizens within a virtual community. However, it is a long-time process of further development. Municipal agencies should understand that virtual communities sponsored by them could help them to create their image.

## 6 Conclusions

eGovernment initiatives enable receiving the following benefits:

- eMunicipality is the opportunity to regulate public administration processes, to visualize and simplify them and to realize them online. Administrative tasks and processes are legally formulated, publicly accessible and realized the same way in different municipalities.
- Virtual communities are true innovations and the source of innovativeness. eNews, forums, blogs, emails, chats, webinars, webcastings encourage to knowledge creation, externalization, dissemination and reusing.

Virtual community at municipal Web site is an innovation developed by citizens and for citizens to disseminate knowledge on public administration laws and procedures. In this way people have the opportunity to emphasize the local community problems and to be involved in local governance of the town. In virtual communities people are creative when they feel motivated primarily by the interest, enjoyment, satisfaction and the challenge of the work itself – not by external pressures. Generally, the idea of virtual community is not new and a lot have been written on it, however, the each particular form of virtual community is unique and innovative. Each case covers other people. The different ideas and contents are delivered by them to the Web sites in form of textual information, audio and video presentations, films and photos. Individuals do not have to develop everything they need on their own, they can benefit from innovations developed by others and freely shared within the user community. Virtual community is an innovation because as innovation it typically implies a focus on outside orientations, originality, emergent strategies and freedom, while the rest of municipal office is better served by an orientation towards the opposite. Virtual community could integrate citizens around their common issues as well as exceptional, local events. In virtual community, blogs, journals, films and presentations are for citizens who play the main roles as well as the municipal officials.

# References

Alter, S. (2004) IT Innovation Through a Work Systems Lens. In: Fitzgerald, B., Wynn, E. (Eds.) *IT Innovation for Adaptability and Competitiveness*. Kluwer Academic Publishers, pp. 43–64.

Biasiotii, M. A., Nannucci, R. (2004) Learning to Become an E-citizen: The European and Italian Policies. In: Wimmer, M.A. (Ed.) *Knowledge Management in Electronic Government*. Springer, Berlin, pp. 253–264.

Centeno, C., van Bavel, R., Burgelman, J.C. (2004) eGovernment in the EU in the Next Decade: the Vision and Key Challenges, Based on the Workshop Held in Seville. In: *eGovernment in the EU in 2010: Key Policy and Research Challenges*. European Commission, Directorate General Joint Research Centre, EUR 21376, Brussels.

Cordoba, J. (2006) Communities and Evaluation of e-Government Services. In: Coakes, E., Clarke, S. (Eds.) *Encyclopedia of Communities of Practice in Information and Knowledge Management*. Idea Group Reference, Hershey, pp.32–35.

Decision No 1639/2006/EC of the European Parliament and of the Council of 24 October 2006 Establishing a Competitiveness and Innovation Framework Programme, http://eur-lex.europa.eu/ LexUriServ/site/en/oj/2006/l_31020061109en00150040.pdf

Gaynor, G.H. (2002) *Innovation by Design*. Amacom, American Management Association, NY.

Gulbrandsen, M. (2004) Acord or Discord? Tensions and Creativity in Research. In: Hemlin, S., Allwood, C.M., Martin, B.R. (Eds.) *Creative Knowledge Environments*: *The Influences on Creativity in Research and Innovation*. Edward Elgar, Cheltenham, UK.

Hildreth P.M. (2004) *Going Virtual: Distributed Communities of Practice*. Idea Group, Hershey.

Justesen S. (2004) Innoversity in Communities of Practice. In: Hildreth, P., Kimble, Ch., (Eds.) *Knowledge Networks, Innovation Through Communities of Practice*. Idea Group Publishing, pp. 79–95.

Lambropoulos, N. (2006) Human Resources and Knowledge Management Based on e-Democracy. In: Dasgupta, S. (Ed.) *Encyclopedia of Virtual Communities and Technologies*. Idea Group Publishing, Hershey, pp. 238–243.

Lee, L.L., Neff, M. (2004) How Information Technologies Can Help Build and Sustain an Organization's CoP: Spanning the Socio-technical Divide? In: Hildreth, P., Kimble, Ch. (Eds.) *Knowledge Networks, Innovation Through Communities of Practice*. Idea Group Publishing, Hershey, pp. 165–183.

Lesser, E.L., Fontaine, M.A. (2004) Overcoming Knowledge Barriers with Communities of Practice: Lessons Learned Through Practical Experience. In: Hildreth, P., Kimble, Ch. (Eds.) *Knowledge Networks, Innovation Through Communities of Practice*. IGP, Hershey, pp. 14–23.

Miia, K., Outi, C-P., Blomqvist, K. (2006) Virtual Communities and Local Youth E-Democracy. In: Dasgupta, S. (Ed.) *Encyclopedia of Virtual Communities and Technologies*, Idea Group Publishing, Hershey, pp. 487–493.

Pedersen S.M., Pedersen J.L. (2006) Innovation and Diffusion of Site-Specific Crop Management, In: Sundbo J., Gallina A., Serin G., Davis J. (Eds.) *Contemporary Management of Innovation*. Palgrave Macmillan, Houndmills, pp. 110–123.

Sundbo, J., Fuglsang, L. (2006) Strategic Reflexity as a Framework for Understanding Development in Modern Firms. In: Sundbo, J., Gallina, A., Serin, G., Davis, J. (Eds.) *Contemporary Management of Innovation*. Palgrave Macmillan, Houndmills, pp. 147–164.

Thompson, H. (2004) Web-Based Services Meeting the Diverse Needs of Regional and Rural Australia, In: Marshall, S., Taylor, W., Yu, X. (Eds.) *Using Community Informatics to Transform Regions*. Idea Group Publishing, Hershey, pp. 132–146.

Traunmuller, R., and Wimmer, M. (2004) E-Government – a Roadmap for Progress. In: Mendes, M.J., Suomi, R., Passos, C. (Eds), *Digital Communities in a Networked Society, e-Commerce, e-Business and e-Government*. IFIP Kluwer Academic Publishers, Boston, pp. 3–12.

Zhao, F. (2006) *Entrepreneurship and Innovations in E-Business: An Integrative Perspective*. Idea Group Publishing, Hershey.

# Open Source Public Sector Business Intelligence Systems

Jörg Becker, Björn Niehaves, Felix Müller-Wienbergen and Martin Matzner

European Research Center for Information Systems (ERCIS), University of Muenster,
{becker | bjoern.niehaves | felix.mueller-wienbergen | martin.matzner @ercis.uni-muenster.de

**Abstract**  Although business intelligence (BI) solutions have been a long-standing topic of major interest in private sector, public administrations (PA), however, took only first steps towards strategic management. While PA are obliged to implement new public management (NPM) approaches, such as new accounting systems or an output-oriented management, to collect management-relevant data, there is little support regarding how to employ these new structures in terms of BI. Here, balanced scorecards (BSC) can provide a valuable conceptual basis. This chapter presents a design science-oriented case study on BI design and organisational implementation in a medium-sized local PA facing core problems of such an approach. A case study analysis identifies generalisable issues.

## 1 Introduction

The concepts of new public management (NPM) and electronic government (eGovernment) contribute to public administration (PA) modernising efforts. NPM targets the improvement of quality, efficiency and effectiveness of PA processes resorting to private sector management techniques. Electronic government accounts for the exploitation of information technology (Schedler and Proeller 2003; Scherlis and Eisenberg 2003). While organisation-external eGovernment services, involving citizens or businesses, have been intensively discussed (Cox and Ghoneim 1998; Tung and Rieck 2006), the internal use of IT (Ang et al. 2001), for instance, for management support, is less analysed though being evenly important. The major feature of NPM is the dominance of output orientation in public administrations' decisions. For example, in Germany that leads PA to substitute established "financial reporting under the cash basis of accounting" concepts by product-oriented budgeting and double-entry accounting, which basically aim at providing data and improving the environment for an output-oriented management. On the other hand, the beneficial perspective, how to actually use these data and how to in fact implement and benefit from output-oriented strategic management (Schedler and Proeller 2003), is underemphasised in PA practice with a strategy deficit being the consequence.

An instrument explicitly outlining this strategic perspective and being widely accepted in the private sector is the balanced scorecard (BSC) approach (Kaplan and Norton 1996a, 2000; Olve et al. 1999). Hence, BSC aims at balancing performance measurement between strategy and operations, taking into account various types of measures, and including different stakeholder perspectives (Kaplan and Norton 1996b). At present, BSC is the most known and applied performance measurement concept in practice (Günther and Grüning 2002).

The operative implementation of BSC is faced with specific problems. The need for domain-specific adaptations is often underestimated (Rocheleau and Wu 2002). Particular characteristics of public organisations are habitually not fully appreciated (Alt 2004). A heterogeneous IS environment regularly leads to problems in systems interoperability (Becker et al. 2004) and, thus, in (automatically) collecting BSC-relevant data. Due to public administrations' financial condition low-cost solutions are preferred. Technological know-how deficits and a latent change resistance (Schedler and Proeller 2003; Thom and Ritz 2004) suggest a technologically evolutionary, rather than a revolutionary approach.

Hence, the research question we seek to address within this chapter is how to solve major (managerial and technical) design and implementation problems that a BSC-based business intelligence approach in public administrations faces? The line of argumentation addresses the following sub-questions:

- What is a BSC-based approach to business intelligence and what are domain-specific problems in the public sector? (Sect. 2)
- What are the characteristics of open source software (OSS) and how is it applied in public administration? (Sect. 3)
- Regarding a design science approach, how may Web technology and OSS approach resolve major problems of BSC implementation in PA? (Sect. 4)
- What is the value added by integrating BSC and project management software? (Sect. 4)
- Which aspects of the design science case study can potentially be generalised and support further design-oriented strategic BI projects in PA? (Sect. 5)

Addressing this research objective, the methods chosen are that of conceptual and empirical research, the latter primarily in terms of conducting and analysing a BSC-based BI implementation case study in a medium-sized German PA. We consider the chapter to contribute to and to be part of design science research in IS (Hevner et al. 2004; March and Smith 1995). We will therefore provide a brief summarising assessment of this research, complying with the guidelines for evaluating design science in IS research (cf. Hevner et al. 2004), within the concluding section.

# 2 Business Intelligence in Public Administrations

Business intelligence (BI) is of top relevance in practice (Gfaller 2006). Nevertheless, it is also an approach with a fine tradition. Cleland and King defined the task of assuring the timely availability of credible external information on competitors, environmental systems in the marketplace, and political, economic, legal, social and technological systems affecting an organisation's competitive posture as the purpose of a competitive business intelligence system (Cleland and King 1975). The organisation-internal perspective corresponds with related ideas such as management information systems (MIS), executive information systems (EIS) and management support systems (MSS) as well as with the contemporary core idea of BI coined by Howard Dresner in 1989. It is about aligning corporate actors and processes with an enterprise's purpose and objectives on the basis of a complete view of an organisation (Scott 2006). However, by and by BI became an umbrella term adopted by IT companies for successfully promoting a various set of analysis tools. Here, BI has to be understood as the analytical process which transforms fragmented corporate and competitive knowledge into action-oriented knowledge about capabilities, positions, operations, and objectives of internal and external actors and processes within the scope of consideration (Grothe and Gentsch 2000).

When BI approaches are applied for performance measurement (Brignall and Modell 2000) and strategic management in PA (for an example case study see Poister 2005; for a theoretical framework see Skok 1989), the need for domain-specific adaptations is often underestimated (Alt 2004). From a managerial perspective, such specifics of the public sector include, among others:

- *Complexity of political decision processes.* Recent research on the relationship between politics and administration (Nalbandian 2006) has proven the specific conditions of decision-making processes in public organisations (Heikkila and Isett 2004) which necessitate an effective domain-specific adaptation of BI concepts (for a critical perspective see Holmes et al. 2006).
- *Complexity of BI addressees.* The addressee of BI is not only the management (e.g. majors or public managers), but also major stakeholder groups, such as citizens, parties or parliaments acting in the public sector decision-making process.
- *Old vs. New Public Management).* Over the last about 15 years, the public sector has been object to various reform approaches (Dwivedi and Henderson 1990; Pollitt and Bouckaert 2005). Managerial thinking, as reflected in the term new public management, seems to be today's paradigm. However, managerial issues have been largely addressed before. As a result, today's BI solutions have to deal with legacies, for instance, distributed strategic competencies and fragmented planning capacities.

Balanced scorecard is a well-established performance measurement and strategic management instrument which aims at balancing strategy and operations (Kaplan 2001). This includes various types of measures, e.g. qualitative and quantitative, and a variety of stakeholder perspectives (Kaplan et al. 1996a, 1996b, 2000).

It has been developed as a response to the discovery that, for instance, there exist significant deficits in actually aligning the business strategy and business operations, that classical financial measures often run too short when it comes to strategic management decisions, or that controlling and reporting systems are often perceived as too complex but insufficient when it comes to ad hoc requests (Kaplan et al. 1996b). BSC has been applied in public sector (e.g. Johnsen 1999). BSC implementation process comprises several phases, each of them rendered by a specific task and concern (Fig. 1. outlines a schematic and archetypal BSC implementation procedure which takes into account the most common process features).

Major advantages of BSC as BI concept in PA are that (1) it can be embedded into a complex political decision-making environment (see above) as it primarily seeks to create management transparency, to stimulate an informed argumentative decision process, and as it can (simply) be regarded as a container for actual political decisions. (2) BSC is flexible towards addressees (output) as well as stakeholder groups (input), while both points ought to be discussed as the initial step of BSC implementation (see again). (3) BSC can be regarded as a BI approach on a strategic management level, that well complement with current NPM concepts.

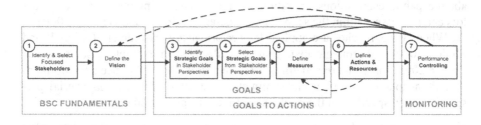

**Fig. 1.** Schematic balanced scorecard implementation process

# 3 Open Source Software in Public Administrations

The "open source software" (OSS) concept comprises a particular licensing, distribution and development model. OSS literature and practice also relate to this concept as "free and open source software" (Fitzgerald 2006). This variation stresses the idea of freedom as the very core of OSS transcending the mere disclosure of source code. Here, freedom is related to in a fourfold manner: OSS is unrestricted in use, the analysis of its functionality, its distribution and its adaptation (Free Software Foundation 2004). The specified freedom is granted by releasing OSS under certain licences approved by the open source initiative (OSI) (Carbone and Stoddard 2001).

The open source development process reveals certain particularities. OSS development lacks central control. Software is developed by a community of independent programmers frequently globally distributed (Michlmayr et al. 2005).

Although this collective typically does not resemble the mythical image of a group of highly talented developers dedicating their services to an idealistic idea (Michlmayr et al. 2005; Schach et al. 2002), open source communities still comprise heterogeneous groups of individuals often motivated by incentives different from monetary gain (Ghosh et al. 2004).

However, recently the OSS phenomenon evolves from its original roots into a more mainstream and commercial viable form. Opposed to software developed from "an itch worth scratching" (Raymond 1999) by a classical open source community there are more and more OSS development projects motivated and organised in a more professional manner (Fitzgerald 2006). Corporate try to leverage free community manpower or the OSS brand by engaging. To safeguard their interests these firms systematically employ developers for participating or taking in leading roles in OSS projects. This leads to an OSS portfolio shifting from mainly back-office infrastructure to more visible front-office applications (Fitzgerald 2006).

A trend to a professional harnessing of the OSS phenomenon may also be observed in the area of PA. The open source observatory encourages the spread and use of OSS best practices in European PA. Furthermore, a guideline for partnering with free software developers has been published by the European Commission (Ghosh et al. 2004). A multitude of OSS-related activities is initialised by a German OSS competence centre which, relating to its mission, resembles the European open source observatory (Marquardt 2004). Aside from these initiatives encouraging the use of OSS in PA, literature and practice already provide us with first practical examples of successfully implemented free software applications in the public sector (see for instance Becker et al. 2005).

# 4 Open Source BSC Software for Public Administration: A Design Science Case Study

IT-support in BSC implementation and maintenance has become an obligatory, in that valuable, part of almost every BSC project (Günther and Grüning 2002). Such systems allow for an efficient documentation and versioning of an enterprise BSC and foster its development process by providing graphical means to illuminate a scorecard structure. Furthermore, they offer a technical infrastructure supporting scorecard communication among all organisational entities of an enterprise. The provision of means for real-time monitoring of key performance indicators is also one of a BSC software tool's main advantages. Contemporary tools integrate data from operative systems or data warehouses for keeping objective compliance under surveillance and thus foster a real-time exception handling and irregularity escalation.

However, technically implementing BSC software tools in public organisations is confronted with severe problems. While a domain-specifically adapted BSC approach provides a valuable conceptual basis for business intelligence in

PA, major problems arise when it comes to an operative technical implementation. The application of BSC software tools has to accomplish some domain-specific requirements. Budgetary restrictions, as omnipresent as in the majority of PA (Pollitt et al. 2005), necessitate low-cost solutions. Technological know-how deficits and a latent change resistance (Schedler and Proeller 2003; Thom and Ritz 2004) suggest a technologically evolutionary, rather than a revolutionary approach. A heterogeneous IS environment regularly leads to problems in systems interoperability (Becker et al. 2004). Both PA processes lacking a sufficient support by IS and the application of proprietary stand-alone software solutions (Becker et al. 2005) impede self-controlled provision of data for BSC measurement. Furthermore, the technical environment in which PA-specific BSC tools have to be implemented is currently subject to a substantial shift. Due to recent changes related to software standards and attitude towards OSS in the PA sector, it is hard to predict how the software environment will evolve for this domain in the long run (Ghosh et al. 2004; Statskontoret 2003; Wheeler 2005). Aside from technological instability, unsteadiness in the conceptual adjustment of BSC to the PA domain also imposes some specific requirements on its technical implementation. The design of such a system will probably take course in a trial and error process of assimilations. The utilisation of Web technologies, developing software on the basis and under the licence model of OSS, and integrating BSC and project management adequately addresses these PA-specific particularities (see Table 1).

To test these hypotheses' and theories' feasibility we applied them in a case study in a medium-sized German PA in 2005. Our research relates to design theory by contemplating on principles of how to design IS in the context of a specific domain (Gregor 2006). Design science research is taking into account the implementation and application phases of research processes. It emphasizes the link of problem understanding (theory building and justification) and problem solution (design and evaluation). The presented case study is thus not to be regarded as an extensive proof of theory, but as an initial step towards analysing its feasibility.

The environmental conditions for this project resemble the situation described in Sect. 1. The PA faced the challenge of adopting the BSC concept to its own domain specifics to pave the way for output-oriented strategic management. A BSC software tool should support the entire implementation process as sketched in Sect. 2. However, due to budget limitations, utilising a commercial tool for this purpose was not feasible and therefore applying OSS became the favoured solution. A preceding evaluation revealed that there was no open source BSC software at that point of time. Therefore, a new OSS development project (BASIS – BAlanced Scorecard based Information System) was initialised. It was benefited from basing the project on existing OSS solutions (PHP, MySQL, Apache Web server, smarty template engine, PHPeclipse) and reusing the framework of an available open source application (dotProject) for realising a modular software architecture.

BASIS provides a wide range of functions presented by a clear user interface. As explicitly demanded by the PA and consistent with the propositions stated above, the tool comprises a tight integration of BSC and project management functionality. The overall compliance with the defined BSC objectives is illustrated on a cockpit-screen (see Fig. 2) serving as an entry point to the system. Besides

**Table 1.** Public administration-specific BSC software tool implementation

| Concept | Addressed issue |
|---|---|
| Web technology | *Financial restrictions*<br>• Most of the components necessary for setting up a Web IS are free of charge.. Often the infrastructure is already in place.<br>• The centralised architecture of Web IS limits administration and maintenance tasks to the Web server side. The installation of a Web-based software tool does not impose any further requirements on the client systems.<br><br>*Latent change resistance*<br>• Implementing a system which easily integrates with users' existing working environment fosters acceptance.<br>• As users can operate a Web-based BSC software tool by using well-known concepts like navigation via back and forth navigation keys and setting bookmarks, convincing them of supporting the BSC idea and inducing commitment for the new strategic initiative becomes easier.<br><br>*Changing IS infrastructure*<br>• By applying Web technologies, applications become independent of the underlying software. The necessary software infrastructure for Web applications being a Web server and a browser exists for almost every operating system. Thus, a PA investing money in Web technology-based applications stays flexible in future decisions related to changes in its software environment. |
| Open source software | *Financial restrictions*<br>• In the very core of the OSS concept is that it may be employed free of charge. Thus, the initial investment in an OSS solution is limited to the necessary IT infrastructure. This fact carries weight especially for systems serving a huge number of users as licence fees often are regulated by this factor.<br>• The internet offers a source for free documentation and assistance for solving installation and maintenance issues. However, a sufficient degree of technical know-how within PA is necessary to revert to OSS.<br>• Due to further cost advantages in maintenance, OSS is regularly found to outperform proprietary solutions concerning total cost of ownership (Wheeler 2005).<br><br>*Ongoing adaptation process*<br>• Due to a prompt and independent peer review practice within OSS communities, altered needs or identified bugs are instantaneously converted into new releases (Michlmayr et al. 2005). |
| BSC and project management integration | *Heterogeneous IS infrastructure*<br>• Actions defined to accomplish BSC objectives often show features characteristic for projects. They have a specific objective to be accomplished under certain temporal and resource restrictions (for the definition of a project see Kerzner 2003; PMI 2004). Thus, supporting the execution of the specified BSC actions via a project management software tool offers the ability to automatically obtain BSC relevant data. However, information on whether a project is on time and budget do not entirely substitute the original BSC measures but provide a fruitful source for additional strategic monitoring.<br><br>*Latent change resistance*<br>• Assigning projects to organisational objectives explicates the contribution every employee participating in a project makes to the fulfilment of the overall vision. Operative work becomes directly linked to strategic targets preventing the BSC from being misunderstood as out of touch with reality. |

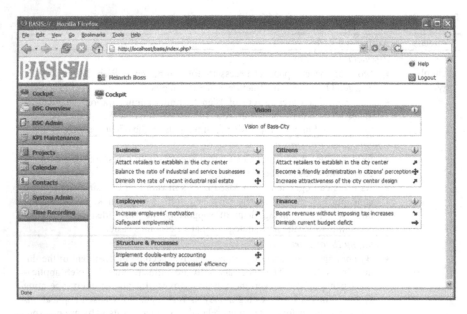

**Fig. 2.** BASIS cockpit

system and BSC administration functions, time recording, storage and maintenance of both contacts and events, the administration and monitoring of projects
comprises a further corner stone of BASIS. Here, key performance indicators
(KPI) function as a central construct. The progress of tasks as well as the adherence to budget and time restrictions is supervised and evaluated by the system. On
this basis, a variety of KPI are derived pointing out possible negative effects on
the attainment of BSC goals.

Both the specification of a BSC adhering the particularities of PA and the development of a conformable OSS BSC and project management tool took 8
months in total. In this regard, falling back on existing OSS solutions and related
assisting resources on the internet considerably saved time. At present, the developed BSC and the supporting tool are successfully used in every-day business of
the PA. Although the developed Web system does not act as an all-embracing BI
solution it serves as a practical starting point to gradually evolve IT infrastructure
for backing PA on its move to market- and output-oriented management.

# 5 Case Study Analysis and Results

According to Lee (1989), we will add a brief case study analysis to address the
questions of repeatability and generalisability of the case study (results). Here, we
will refer to four core questions in case study research:

- *What is the initial setting in the organisation (case study data) and in how far is it bound to specific situational and historical circumstances?* A core issue in the case study setting was the need for strategic BI resulting from severe societal, legal and information-technological changes. Constraints for designing the desired system were mainly interoperability problems in a heterogeneous system environment (about 40 different IS), budgetary restrictions and a latent resistance to (technological) change. The situation is not expected to alter significantly within a 5-year horizon; merely efforts to harmonize system landscape have been undertaken.

- *Which (design) conclusions are drawn from the case study data and in how far are these conclusions bound to specific situational and historical circumstances?* The main design decisions consist of pursuing the BSC concept, an OSS approach, an integration of project management functionalities and a Web technology implementation. Here, especially the BSC concept can be understood as an initial approach to strategic management and business intelligence for PA (Alt 2004). It is expected that, over time, other management functionalities can provide valuable extensions to this single-concept approach. Anyhow, still BSC is expected to be the major conceptual basis for strategic BI efforts in the organisation within a 5-year horizon. The OSS approach, even if being considered as better-quality solution, will still have to practically prove its positive network effects.

- *In how far do other settings show similar features and, thus, in how far is the case study setting generalisable?* Especially medium-sized European PA share major features with the described setting. Not only that services and processes that these organisations have to provide are existentially similar by law, they also have major problems in common, for instance, budgetary restrictions, heterogeneous systems environments (Becker et al. 2004) or latent change resistance (Schedler and Proeller 2003; Thom and Ritz 2004). Individual differences do evidently exist. However, especially their BI maturity can be expected similar as, for instance, legal changes in accounting systems will affect most PA within the same time horizon. Other BSC case studies provide similar insights, even though there might be country-specific adaptations.

- *Are the (design) conclusions made in the case study setting transferable to other organisational settings?* Especially the integration of BSC and project management had major advantages in the particular setting (see Sect. 4). Firstly, project management software support was explicitly demanded by several employees. Secondly, the given PA had restricted resources available for the project so that a feasible and practicable alternative to a huge IS integration was found. However, other BSC implementation projects chose dissimilar paths (Scherer 2002).

As a consequence, the case study setting can be – regarding its strategic BI maturity – considered as typical medium-sized European PA. Major features affecting the design decisions will be apparent in most organisations of this kind within a 5-year time horizon. However, major differences in resource availability and financial support may affect design decisions, for instance, the OSS approach or an integration of project management functionalities.

## 6 Conclusions and Future Research

There exists a high demand for strategic management and business intelligence solutions in PA. Here, BSC – adapted to the specific domain of PA – has proven to be a valuable approach enacting strategy and vision in daily operations. At this juncture, several key success factors were identified for the domain of PA:

- A strong involvement of employees and stakeholder representatives is crucial to the BSC project success. Defining the corporate vision (phase 2) is often the first step towards manifesting strategic thinking in PA.
- A combination of BSC-based strategic BI and project management can contribute to solving the data problem, avoid additional work, increase acceptance.
- OSS is in most cases low-cost and a valuable alternative to proprietary software products, also for business intelligence systems in PA.
- Applying Web technologies for PA information systems has proven to be a low-cost, but effective solution which is accompanied by a relatively high user acceptance also due to its recognition effect.

At this juncture, a brief paper self-assessment seeks to bring further clarity to presenting our research findings and follows Hevner et al.'s guidelines (Hevner et al. 2004) for design science research evaluation (see Table 2).

To provide evidence supporting the concept feasibility, a case study implementation was conducted. Following the case study implementation, further evaluation is necessary (see, for instance, Gupta and Jana 2003). For further future research, an analysis of OSS capability for other application areas in the field of eGovernment is to be conducted. Furthermore, OSS applications, such as the presented BASIS, should be made open to the public to facilitate a discussion of advantages, disadvantages and application experiences. In addition, PA research is inherently bound to country or regional specifics (if not explicit comparative research). To name a few, the administrative system, the organisational culture or the legal framework are major circumstantial factors which may vary deeply. Though research has shown that the case study data and the design decisions are generalisable to European PA to a great extent (see Sect. 5), future research is necessary on how far these findings can be applied to US or Asian PA.

**Table 2.** Design science research assessment

| Guideline | Addressed in the paper |
|---|---|
| Epistemological positioning | • *Linguistic interpretivism.* Assuming that a real world exists, the perceptions of it are influenced by the subject. The reason for such subjective perceptions of reality is assumed to be language differences, as languages not only provide representative means, but also form perceptions. An aim is to create a language community relating to the issue of interest (Becker and Niehaves 2006; Kamlah and Lorenzen 1973). |
| Addressing a relevant problem | • A strategy gap exists in many PA. While some NPM approaches address the issue of strategic management, a full exploitation of available information technology is rarely to be found in public administration practice.<br>• While BSC acts as a strategic management concept, the need for its domain-specific adaptations is often underestimated.<br>• A heterogeneous information systems environment regularly leads to problems in systems interoperability and collecting BSC-relevant data.<br>• Budgetary restrictions, as omnipresent as in the majority of public administrations, favour low-cost solutions. |
| Making a research contribution | • A research contribution was made in terms of the design, case study implementation and post-implementation analysis of an integrated BSC and project management software. This domain-specific approach seeks to extend existing strategic management approaches in the public sector. |
| Choosing an adequate research method | • Conceptual and theoretical-argumentative method as well as empirical case study implementation was chosen as research method. |
| Addressing the question of research rigour | • It was sought to rigorously apply the conceptual and theoretical-argumentative method by remaining a high clarity of argumentation. Furthermore, empirical data collection within the case study was conducted rigorously against the background of the underlying linguistic interpretivist epistemology. |
| Designing an artefact | • BASIS software as design artefact; an implementation of a BSC-based business intelligence system in public administrations. |
| Research evaluation | • The first steps of research evaluation, implementing and evaluating the BASIS software in a medium-sized German public administration in terms of a design science case study, yet indicated its feasibility. However, further evaluation is necessary. |

# References

Alt, J. M. (2004) Balanced Government – Die Eignung der Balanced Scorecard als Organisationsentwicklungsprozess in der Öffentichen Verwaltung. In: A.G. Scherer and J.M. Alt (Eds.) Balanced Scorecard in Verwaltung und Non-Profit-Organisationen. Schäffer-Poeschel, Stuttgart, pp. 43–72.

Ang, C.-L., Davies, M. A. and Finlay, P. N. (2001) An Empirical Model of IT Usage in the Malaysian Public Sector. *Journal of Strategic Information Systems* 10, 159–174.

Becker, J. and Niehaves, B. (2006) Epistemological Perspectives on IS Research – A Framework for Analysing and Systematising Epistemological Assumptions. *Information Systems Journal* 16.

Becker, J., Algermissen, L., Delfmann, P., Falk, T. and Niehaves, B. (2004) Reorganizing Public Administrations – How to manage Process Oriented eGovernment Projects. *Proceedings of the Eigthth Pacific Asia Conference on Information Systems (PACIS'04)*, Shanghai, Peoples Republic of China.

Becker, J., Algermissen, L., Delfmann, P., Falk, T. and Niehaves, B. (2005) Identifikation von Best Practices durch Geschäftsprozessmodellierung in öffentlichen Verwaltungen. HMD 41, 86–96.

Brignall, S. and Modell, S. (2000) An Institutional Perspective on Performance Measurement and Management in the "New Public Sector". *Management Accounting Research* 11, 281–306.

Carbone, G. and Stoddard, D. (2001) *Open Source Enterprise Solutions. Developing an E-Business Strategy.* John Wiley, New York.

Cleland, D. I. and King, W. R. (1975) Competitive Business Intelligence Systems. *Business Horizons* 18, 19–28.

Cox, B. and Ghoneim, S. (1998) Strategic Use of EDI in the Public Sector: the HMSO Case Study. *Journal of Strategic Information Systems* 7, 37–51.

Dwivedi, O. P. and Henderson, K. M. (1990) Public Administration in World Perspective, Ames, Iowa.

Fitzgerald, B. (2006) The Transformation of Open Source Software. *MIS Quarterly* 30, 587–898.

Free Software Foundation. (2004) *The Free Software Definition.*

Gfaller, H. (2006) Liegt BI nicht mehr im Trend? Downloaded from http://www.zdnet.de/itmanager/print_this.htm?pid=39142895-11000015c on 2007-07-31.

Ghosh, R. A., Glott, R., Robles, G. and Schmitz, P.-E. (2004) *Guideline for Public Administrations on Partnering with Free Software Developers.* European Commission, Brussels.

Gregor, S. (2006) The Nature of Theory in Information Systems. *MIS Quarterly* 30, 611–642.

Grothe, M. and Gentsch, P. (2000) *Business Intelligence: Aus Informationen Wettbewerbsvorteile gewinnen.* Addison-Wesley, Munich et al.

Günther, T. and Grüning, M. (2002) Performance Measurement-System im praktischen Einsatz. *Controlling* 14, 5–13.

Gupta, M. P. and Jana, D. (2003) E-government Evaluation: A Framework and Case Study. *Government Information Quarterly* 20, 365–387.

Heikkila, T. and Isett, K. R. (2004) Modeling Operational Decision Making in Public Organizations. *American Review of Public Administration* 34, 3–19.

Hevner, A. R., March, T. S., Park, J. and Ram, S. (2004) Design Science in Information Systems Research. *MIS Quarterly* 28, 75–105.

Holmes, J. S., Gutiérrez de Piñeres, S. A. and Kiel, L. D. (2006) Reforming Government Agencies Internationally: Is There a Role for the Balanced Scorecard? *International Journal of Public Administration* 29, 1125–1145.

Johnsen, A. (1999) Implementation Mode and Local Government Performance Measurement: A Norwegian Experience. *Financial Accountability & Management* 15, 41–66.

Kamlah, W. and Lorenzen, P. (1973) *Logical Propaedeutic. Pre-School of Reasonable Discourse*, 1st Edition. University Press of America, Lanham/MD.

Kaplan, R. S. (2001) Transforming the Balanced Scorecard from Performance Measurement to Strategic Management: Part I. *Accounting Horizons* 15, 87–106.

Kaplan, R. S. and Norton, D. P. (1996a) *The Balanced Scorecard: Translating Strategy into Action.* Harvard Business School Press, Boston, MA.

Kaplan, R. S. and Norton, D. P. (1996b) Using the BSC as a Strategic Management System. *Harvard Business Review* 74, 75–85.

Kaplan, R. S. and Norton, D. P. (2000) *The Balanced Scorecard: Measures that Drive Performance.* Harvard Business School Press, Boston, MA.

Kerzner, H. (2003) *Project Management: a Systems Approach to Planning, Scheduling, and Controlling*, 8th Edition. Hoboken.

Lee, A. S. (1989) A Scientific Methodology for MIS Case Studies. *MIS Quarterly* 13, 33–52.

March, T. S. and Smith, G. (1995) Design and Natural Science Research on Information Technology. *Decision Support Systems* 15, 251–266.

Marquardt, C. (2004) Open-Source-Software-Strategie der deutschen Verwaltung. HMD – Praxis der Wirtschaftsinformatik, 58–61.

Michlmayr, M., Hunt, F. and Probert, D. (2005) Quality Practices and Problems in Free Software Projects, in Marco Scotto and Giancarlo Succi (Eds.). *Proceedings of 1st International Conference on Open Source Systems (OSS'05)*, Genova, Italy, 24–28.

Nalbandian, J. (2006) Politics and Administration in Local Government. *International Journal of Public Administration* 29, 1049–1063.

Olve, N. G., Roy, J. and Wetter, M. (1999) *Performance Drivers: a Practical Guide to Using the Balanced Scorecard*. Wiley, Chichester.

PMI. (2004) *A Guide to the Project Management Body of Knowledge*, 3rd Edition. Newton Square, USA.

Poister, T. H. (2005) Strategic Planning and Management in State Departments of Transportation. *International Journal of Public Administration* 28, 1035–1056.

Pollitt, C. and Bouckaert, G. (2005) *Public Management Reform. A Comparative Analysis*. Oxford University Press, New York.

Raymond, E. S. (1999) *The Cathedral and the Bazaar*. O'Reilly, Sebastopol, CA.

Rocheleau, B. and Wu, L. (2002) Public Versus Private Information Systems: Do They Differ in Important Ways? A Review and Empirical Test. *American Review of Public Administration* 32, 379–397.

Schach, S., Jin, B. and Wright, D. (2002) Maintainability of the Linuy Kernel, in J. Feller, Brian Fitzgerald, S. Hissam and K. Lakhani (Eds.). *Proceedings of the Second Workshop on Open Source Software Engineering*, Orlando, FL.

Schedler, K. and Proeller, I. (2003) *New Public Management*. UTB, Bern et al.

Scherer, A. G. (2002) Besonderheiten der strategischen Steuerung in Öffentlichen Institutionen und der Beitrag der Balanced Scorecard, in A.G. Scherer and J.M. Alt (Eds.). *Balanced Scorecard in Verwaltung und Non-Profit-Organisationen*. Schäffer-Poeschel, Stuttgart, pp. 3–26.

Scherlis, W. L. and Eisenberg, J. (2003) IT Research, Innovation, and e-Government. *Communications of the ACM* 46, 67–68.

Scott, E. (2006) Q&A: BI Visionary Howard Dresner, Downloaded from http://www.intelligententerprise.com/showArticle.jhtml?articleID=181501967 on 2007-07-31.

Skok, J. E. (1989) Toward a Definition of Strategic Management for the Public Sector. *American Review of Public Administration* 19, 133–147.

Statskontoret. (2003) *Swedish Agency for Public Management: Free and Open Source Software - A Feasibility Study*.

Thom, N. and Ritz, A. (2004) *Public Management*. Gabler, Wiesbaden, Germany.

Tung, L. L. and Rieck, O. (2006) Adoption of Electronic Government Services Among Business Organizations in Singapore. *Journal of Strategic Information Systems* 14, 417–440.

Wheeler, D. A. (2005) Why Open Source Software/Free Software (OSS/FS, FLOSS, or FOSS)? Look at the Numbers! Downloaded from http://www.dwheeler.com/oss_fs_why.html on 2007-07-31.

# Sourcing Decisions of Software Applications Hosting: What Influence has e-Government Services?

Björn Johansson[1] and Ulf Melin[2]

[1] Copenhagen Business School, Center for Applied ICT, bj.caict@cbs.dk

[2] Linköping University, Department of Management and Engineering, ulf.melin@liu.se

**Abstract**  There are a lot of reasons reported for why organisations start a sourcing decision. This chapter discusses this theme based on two questions: Does the need and/or wish to increase e-Government services influence the start of a sourcing decision process aiming at reorganising hosting of software applications and if it does, how does it influence the start of such a decision-making process? The point of departure, besides a literature review, is a sourcing decision-making process in a Swedish municipality. When analysing the sourcing decision, five suggested propositions developed from the factors, control, core competence, capability, cost, and strategy, are used. It is concluded that municipalities in Sweden has to prepare for being more of an e-Government organisation, which means that more of the services the municipalities' employees has done before citizens will do by themselves. This demands that to be able to offer future e-Government services municipalities need to have control over software applications. From this study it is suggested that centralisation of hosting can be seen as decentralisation of work tasks from an e-Government perspective.

## 1 Introduction

There are a lot of reasons reported for why sourcing decisions are made (Dibbern et al. 2004). Sourcing in this chapter is a generic term for outsourcing, insourcing, external service provision, and so on. Sourcing decisions are decisions made in organisations whether to buy or produce services that they need. This chapter suggests and discusses five propositions developed from the five factors, control, core competence, capability, cost, and strategy, often reported as influential in a sourcing decision process aiming at reorganising hosting in organisations (Johansson 2004). Hosting in this chapter is defined as localisation. It can be said that irrespective of what products or services organisations they need have two distinct options, to buy or to produce. This distinction is discussed in, for instance, transaction cost theory as a distinction between market and hierarchy (Williamson 1985) and by Kishore et al. Rao (2004) as market governance and hierarchical governance, and can be compared to a decision whether organisations should handle hosting of software applications external or internal. It could also be compared to if hosting should be more or less centralised, respectively, decentralised.

From the five propositions the focus is on the connection to delivering e-Government services. The question is how the start of a sourcing decision-making process, when deciding on how to host software applications in the future, is influenced from the need to increase e-Government services. The chapter uses a sourcing decision-making process in a Swedish municipality to discuss this. The question to a high extent depends on what e-Government stands for. The definition we adopt is "e-Government is the use of technology to enhance the access to and delivery of government services to benefit citizens, business partners and employees" (Silcock 2001 p. 88). Evolution of e-Government is described in different ways, and several stage models have been presented, for example by Layne and Lee (2001). From the definition of e-Government it could be said that e-Government is about how organisation uses its information and communication technologies (ICTs) resources with the aim of reducing its internal workload and at the same time letting the customer (citizen) to the organisation help themselves. E-Government is thereby strongly related to hosting, though customers use software applications and receive services from software hosted by the organisation they interact with. This means that the users of the software could be seen as external by the organisation that delivers the possibility to use the software. In that way this can be related to, for instance, outsourcing or the usage of external service provision. A commonly quoted reason when organisations decide on adopting or non-adopting external service provision is control (Jurison 1998). This can be described as an organisation that investigate and think about using an external service provider for the hosting often is doubtful about doing so because of the perceived risk of loosing control. Control in this case can be compared to questions about security and protection. And how an organisation secure and protect its ICT resources can to a great extent be related to hosting of the resources. Based on this discussion, the chapter deals with the following research questions: (1) Does the need and/or wish to increase e-Government services influence the start of a sourcing decision process aiming at reorganising hosting of software applications and (2) if it does, how do decision-makers thought of e-Government influence the start of such a decision-making process?

The chapter is organised in the following way. Section 2 describes five propositions developed from reported reasons in the literature of why organisations start a sourcing decision process. Section 3 introduces the research design and the case followed by a description of the sourcing decision-making process conducted in the municipality. Section 4 delivers an analysis and discussion about why the sourcing decision-making process in the municipality started. The final section summarises the chapter, gives some conclusions that can be drawn from the study together with some issues for further studies.

## 2 Why Do Organisations Start a Sourcing Decision Process?

The need to increase **control** is often one reason suggested for why sourcing decision processes starts. Control could be either to control the cost of using software applications, or to control the actual usage of the software applications. The latter could be described as a need to control what, when, and how the software application is used, so that the software application support the business processes in the organisation. Control can be compared to governance. Weill and Ross (2004) describe ICT governance as decision rights regarding ICT management and they define ICT governance as "specifying the decision rights and accountability framework to encourage desirable behaviour in the use of ICT" (2004 p. 8).

Governance, in this context, is about controlling what happens in the organisations and especially how organisations make the best use of ICT. It could be compared to centralisation as well as decentralization, and it can be suggested that to increase control (from a specific decision-makers point of view) centralisation of resources are made. It can also be said that the lack of control to a great extent can be traced back to decentralisation of ICT. However, as Simon (1960, 1997) and Markus (1984) say, centralisation or decentralisation is not a question for organisations whether they should centralise or decentralise. Instead it is a question of how far they should go with the decentralisation or centralisation. This means that for organisations' that need to improve control, centralisation is one way to do that. It can be proposed that the most centralised hosting option is outsourcing. This means that organisations that want to control their software applications outsource to a greater extent than other organisations does. However, it also means that there is a need to have control over software applications before outsource. This discussion can be summarised as: organisations need to increase control over usage of software applications because they have decentralised hosting to a great extent. To increase control and thereby governance outsourcing is a feasible sourcing option. However, to be able to have a successful outsourcing the organisation need to have a certain degree of control, and the first step in outsourcing can therefore be said is to do an internal restructuring. Control then refers to both cost control, control over the usage, control over what software applications that are used as well as control over versions of software applications. What can be concluded is that evolution of ICT has made this possible to have, without making increased level of control to become a hindrance for the organisation's development. From this discussion the following proposition can be formulated:

**Proposition 1:** A sourcing decision process starts because organisations need to improve their control/governance of the software applications used in the organisation.

Another reason often suggested for why sourcing decision processes starts is influences from stakeholders stipulating that the organisation should focus on its **core competence**. However, this depends to a great extent on how core competence is defined. Axelsson and Wynstra define core competence as: "the most critical and most distinctive resources a company controls and which are the hardest for others to copy when they are in a number of processes connected to the relevant strategic goals which the company pursues" (Axelsson and Wynstra 2002

p. 72). Kakabadse and Kakabadse (2002) say that one key driver for using external service provision is a desire to focus on core competences. Dewire (2001) says that an organisation should adopt external service provision if ICT is not a core competence. Aalders (2001) proposes that ICT outsourcing makes it possible to focus on core competence as well as increase control of the cost and quality of ICT. Besides that it gives the buying organisation access to skilled personnel and ICT competence. This latest statement can be compared with another commonly quoted reason for ICT outsourcing, which is that ICT outsourcing increases flexibility in handling personnel and offers increased competence regarding ICT.

Despite the discussion above it can be said that the start of hosting decisions is influenced by a desire to focus on core competence. It can be described as influencing the start of a sourcing decision because decision-makers see this as a way of focusing on the organisation's core competence. From this discussion the following proposition can be formulated.

**Proposition 2:** The decision-makers' view of hosting as part or not part of the organisation's core competence influences the start of a sourcing decision process with the aim of focusing on core competence in the organisation.

The need to increase **capability** and especial capability received by usage of software application influence the final decision in a sourcing decision-making process to great extent (Johansson 2004). If Whether capability also influences the start of the process is dependent on whether decision-makers see it as possible to increase the organisations capability gained from software applications usage or not, and if a change in hosting is needed. It is also dependent on the decision-makers thoughts about how different sourcing options impacts and influences the possibility to increase capability, which indicate that if decision-makers are not satisfied with received capability from software application they start a sourcing decision-making process.

From the capability perspective, another reason for why organisations start a sourcing decision can be suggested and that is that decision-makers see internal ICT departments as unresponsive to organisational needs (McLellan et al. 1998). Organisations want a flexible ICT organisation and the sourcing decision process is started with the aim of investigating how different sourcing options increases flexibility. A change in the structure of the organisation and the usage of external service provision is seen as a way of reaching this. A commonly quoted reason for ICT outsourcing is that ICT outsourcing provides increased flexibility to cope with changes in technology and in the business environment. Paradoxically, the traditional ICT outsourcing agreement is based on long-term contracts that rather tend to inhibit than facilitate change (Shepherd 1999). The aim of the sourcing decision process can be said to investigate if external service provision is a way for organisations to take advantage of the rapidly changing opportunities in ICT (Currie and Seltsikas 2000; Turban et al. 2001), and if it can assist organisations with ICT skills, especially in the development and software maintenance areas (Kern et al. 2001). According to Mata et al. (1995), organisation of resources is closely related to competitive advantage, and it can be proposed that having competitive advantage is having capability. Based on this discussion the following proposition is formulated.

**Proposition 3:** The start of a sourcing decision process on hosting of software applications is influenced by a need to increase organisational capability through its usage of software applications.

One of the most described reasons for outsourcing is that organizations thereby reduce **costs** (Cronk and Sharp 1995). But, as Lacity and Hirschheim (1993) say outsourcing has not fulfilled the cost saving as expected. From this it could be asked how the cost perspective influences the start. A related factor to cost is capability, since if there were no cost limitations, organisations could have the capability they wanted. But this is not the case and therefore it can be implied that a reason for starting a sourcing decision process could be that the organisation needs to decrease costs. The reason is that a lot of resources are spent on maintenance of ICT and software applications in organisations (Brandt et al. 1998). One of the most reported reasons for why organisations make a restructuring is that they want to decrease costs (McLellan et al. 1998). Leffler (1987) argues that in most enterprises the cost for maintenance of ICT amounts to 50–80% of the ICT budget. Bearingpoint (2004) suggests that 57% of organisations ICT budget goes to support and maintenance, and it can be said that to decrease cost of ICT, savings on hosting would be fruitful. From this it could be suggested that one reason for starting a sourcing decision is that the organisation needs to decrease its costs of hosting, since hosting is a work task that spend a lot of resources and thereby costs a lot of money in organisations. This indicates that cost probably has the clearest connection to the final choice of solution and also the closest connection to a clear assessment of the outcome of a sourcing decision. In other words, this means that the option that has the lowest cost is the one that is finally chosen. Based on this the following proposition is formulated.

**Proposition 4:** The start of a sourcing decision process on hosting of software applications is influenced by a need to decrease the costs involved in the hosting part of software applications.

An organisation's **strategy** can also be suggested as a starting point of a hosting decision. It could be clearly stated in the strategy that hosting of software applications is not something the organisation should do. If that not is the case, it could be clearly said that the organisation should not deal with questions regarding ICT resources. But, these clearly stated strategies are probably rare. However, in most organisations there exists some kind of strategy, which could be expressed in a written document or just existing in the head of some decision-maker. In any case, it can be said that strategy probably plays an important role when it comes to why organisations start a sourcing decision. This can be described as strategic architecture. According to Hamel and Prahalad (1994) strategic architecture is the link between the now and the future. It could help decision-makers to structure the organisation so that it starts to build the competencies that are needed in the future. Relating this to hosting decisions, it could be that hosting decisions is initiated from a decision-maker's thoughts about the future and could be seen as an approach for developing future opportunities.

However, this probably depends not only on the size and structure of the organisation but also on what role does hosting play in the organisation. This could be compared to a discussion about emergent strategy (Mintzberg and Quinn 1996).

If the hosting structure is a result from an emergent strategy (the structure emerged from a set of different decisions), this probably demands a reorganisation and a reason to reformulate the organisation's strategy. From that point, the start of a sourcing decision-making process could be seen as departure from a change in strategy. From this discussion the following proposition can be formulated.

**Proposition 5:** An organisation's strategy acts as the main influence on why a sourcing decision process is started.

This chapter has so far discussed why organisations start a sourcing decision process. From that discussion, theoretically grounded propositions have been presented. The next section presents a case study of a sourcing decision process.

# 3 The Municipality Sourcing Decision Case

## 3.1 Case Study Introduction and Research Design

This section reports from a retrospective case study of a decision-making process done in a Swedish municipality. In 2002, the municipality, a local government, started to investigate how they should organise its hosting of software applications. The case study of this process consists of 11 semi-structured, tape recorded, and transcribed interviews. The interviews were made in January 2005, just after the decision-making process was finalised. The material under investigation also consists of documented materials in the form of minutes, reports from investigations made by the participants in the decision-making process, and an external consultancy report. A qualitative content analysis (Krippendorff 2004) was made based on the multiple data sources; typical of case studies (Stake 1994). The propositions presented in the section above have been used to structure the analysis and should be seen as a point of departure for the analysis. The propositions have been used as a theoretical lens (Walsham 1995) when analyzing empirical data. The motivation for the use of the pre-defined propositions when analyzing empirical data also follows the arguments proposed by Walsham (1995) – to take account of previous knowledge and studies. Of course there is also a well known danger in doing this – the fact that we risk to see only what the propositions focus.

According to Pettigrew (1973), it is important to describe and understand the history of the organisation if a decision-making process and the reasons for starting the process should be described in an appropriate way. The history of the municipality can be described by its ideology, which is to strive for a great extent of decentralisation. The municipality administrative unit consists of 11 different offices. Six of these offices are organised into one group, the municipal executive office. The other five are self-organised offices. They are supposed to be supervised by the municipal executive office. The ideology of the municipality focuses on decentralisation to a great extent which means that the offices have a far-reaching decision authority. The effects of this ideology are clearly shown in how the municipality has organised its hosting of software applications. Each office has developed its own organisation of software applications and hosting of their software applications at the same time as the municipal executive office should have the overall responsibility for the municipality's general ICT infrastructure. To il-lustrate the effect of this decentralisation, it can be mentioned that a great diversity of software is used in the municipality. There are nine different office products, 11 different database systems, 16 different operative systems, 5 different e-mail soft-ware, and 66 different software applications that are identified as critical for the municipality. In addition to those 66 software applications, there are an unidenti-fied number of software applications. The diversity and the huge amount of soft-ware applications could be seen as one reason for the decision-making process. As described by the chief executive officer (CEO) in the municipal executive office "the welter of the municipality's software applications and ICT has to be con-trolled". This could probably be seen as the starting point of the decision-making process regarding deciding on hosting of software applications.

## 3.2 The Sourcing Decision-making Process

The process started in March 2002. A standing committee, consisting of the five municipal commissioners and the CEO of the municipal executive office, gave the municipal executive office the task to investigate the common ICT infrastructure in the municipality. The reason was the expansion of ICT used in the municipality. The directions were to review the municipality's general ICT infrastructure. The investigation should define the municipal executive office's responsibilities of de-velopment, maintenance, and hosting of the municipality's general ICT infrastruc-ture. It should also describe the need for competence development and how this should be arranged. This directive meant that the municipal executive office en-gaged an external consultant for the investigation. The consultant interviewed em-ployees on different offices, including some employees with responsibilities for the different office's software applications. The consultant stated that the organi-sation was distinguished, to a great extent, by decentralisation, and there were no established long-term plans for how software applications should be developed.

In December 2002, the municipal executive board gave the commission to the municipal executive office, in cooperation with involved offices, to investigate the possibility to coordinate hosting of software applications to the planned data cen-tre. The next step in this decision-making process and the step that probably had most impact on the decision's outcome was the employment of the new chief information officer (CIO). The CIO began to work in this matter in 2003 and im-mediately organised the decision-making process as a project. The CIO then pre-sented a report to the municipal executive board, in October 2004, in which the result of the project was described. The report describes that the decision is neces-sary to position the Municipality for its future development, and that there is a choice between two different options. The options were to "continue with the ICT infrastructure that historically has been built up at the different offices with a very low grade of coordination" or "to coordinate the ICT function and telephony for better usage of existing resources making the municipality prepared to meet future challenges and possibilities to increased effectiveness".

The basic data for the decision-making was a report from the project work, a register over investments necessary from 2005 to 2007 and a compilation of costs for hosting after the reorganisation. The municipal executive board decided on the option aimed at restructuring and coordinating hosting of software applications in the municipality. Since this decision demands going beyond the decided budget, it needed to be decided upon in the municipal council. This was granted in November 2004, and the decision was to coordinate operation of software applications in a new data centre. The decision by the municipal council was unanimous.

## 3.3 Why the Decision-making Process Started?

The reason for why the decision-making process aimed at restructuring hosting of software applications started in the municipality can be described in three ways. First, the municipality needed to increase the control over software application costs. The costs for software applications have probably increased considerably. The reason for using the word "probably" is that the municipality does not know how much its software applications costs. Each of the offices has, according to the CEO, a good grasp of its own costs in each office. But, when it comes to the overall control of costs the control is weak. Cost control is emphasised as one area that must be improved. Weak cost control is also given as one reason why outsourcing was not seen as a possible alternative at this stage. The reason reported for that was that it was not possible to evaluate a cost proposal from an external provider since the municipality did not know what the costs for delivering the same services internal was. The attempt to coordinate and to increase control was described as aiming to give the possibility of having an external partner to compete with the internal data centre in the future.

Second, security was raised as an important factor for starting the process. In the decentralised structure the hosting of a lot of critical software applications was dependent on only one person. This was an effect of the decentralisation and the municipality's decision-makers only saw one way to solve this and that was to centralise hosting. The other security concern was that some of the offices did not have suitable premises for their servers. Both cost and security reasons could be described as a wish to increase control and could therefore be seen as an attempt to increase governance of software applications in the municipality.

Third, the necessity to increase e-Government services to its citizens. According to the municipality's CIO, the municipality has to prepare itself for being more of an e-Government in the future. To do that he see it as necessary to increase interoperability between software applications. The way to do this according to him is to coordinate the municipality's hosting of software applications.

To increase control can therefore be seen as the reason for the initial directive from the standing committee in March 2002 which was to investigate the municipality's general ICT infrastructure. This investigation was done by a consultant and he gave some advice that a total investigation should be carried out aiming at centralising all hosting to a central data centre. Case study interviews with representatives in the decision-making process indicated that the outcome of the process was already decided on before it started. They also say that they were not involved in the first investigation made by the consultant despite the fact that the investigation involved their work to a great extent. The consultant's report has one very interesting point that reflects the results of the entire decision-making process. He states that the development of broadband connections in the municipality put forward the question of a coordinated hosting of the entire collection of the municipality's servers. This goes back to the start of the investigation and the question of power and politics (Pettigrew 1973) in the decision-making process. In this study, it has become clear that there is a group of five persons who, on a more or regular basis, meet every week. This group consists of CIOs from different offices and the CEO of the municipality. They have no formal decision authority but they do have the possibility to discuss and propose what should be done.

It could be argued that one reason for the municipality to start the sourcing decision was that it had decentralised too far at least from the entire organisation's perspective. The municipality had built up a structure in each department leading to increased complexity in the hosting and maintenance work of its software applications.

## 4 Analyses and Discussion

The structure of software applications and ICT in the municipality is overgrown and straggling. On one hand, it is *well controlled*, though each office controls its own resources. On the other hand, from an overall perspective, there is *weak control*. The municipal executive office that is supposed to have the overall control and who also should coordinate generally used software applications and ICT in the municipality has a hard time doing this. That ICT resources are not well controlled in the municipality is shown by, for instance, the statements by the municipality's CIO who says nobody can clearly inform how many different systems are there. The CIO says that the number of different software applications used is in the range of 300–400. The structure of hosting follows the decentralisation ideology of the municipality.

*Increasing control and governance* (cf. Proposition 1) can be seen as reasons for the initial directive from the standing office. The initial directive in March 2002 was, as described in Sect. 3, to investigate the municipality's general ICT infrastructure. From the consultancy report, it is quite clear that he investigated more than the original directive stated as it was not stated that the different offices' ICT infrastructure should be investigated. This increase in scope resulted in that the consultant also advised to do a total investigation aiming at *centralising hosting* into a central data centre. In the report, it is stated that the development of broadband connections in the regime of the municipality put forward the question of coordinating hosting of the entire collection of the municipality's servers. This was a major reason for the start of the decision-making process regarding hosting. The reason is that the municipality by providing its citizen with a broadband connection, they had in mind that the citizen would do more of the communication with the municipality through this broadband. It can also be said that the municipality by investing in broadband connection has to provide that investment with meaningful usage. From this discussion it can be concluded that *one reason for the municipality to start the sourcing decision was that the organisation had decentralised too far* and that the decentralised hosting structure was not seen as suitable for the municipality when it gave the possibility to citizens in the municipality to what could be seen as e-Government. However, as Simon (1960, 1997) and Markus (1984) describe it, decentralisation is not a question the organisation has to decide on if it should do or not. Instead *it is a question of how far the decentralisation should go*. In the municipality the decentralisation of software applications has gone too far, at least, when one looks at it from the entire organisation's perspective. Each department has its own structure of software applications. This means that hosting and maintenance of software applications have increased in complexity which makes it harder to control. To control software applications is important if a municipality should aim at increasing its e-Government services.

Relating the empirical data to the propositions (in Sect. 2) and the questions asked in the introduction of the paper, it can be concluded that the control proposition (Proposition 1), the capability proposition (Proposition 3), and the cost propositions (Proposition 4) are supported. These are factors that the data have raised. It can also be concluded that the core competence proposition (Proposition 2) as well as the strategy proposition (Proposition 5) also are supported. The strategy of the municipality is to decentralise and this means that the different offices should concentrate on what they do best, in other words their core competence. The decision of centralisation hosting could be seen as going in the other direction. But, this depends on the perspective of the future, and it can be argued that *if the strategy is to provide citizens with e-Government services then the centralising hosting strategy aims at decentralising work tasks further*. This means that the start of the sourcing decision-making process could be seen as both focusing on core competence, which is to deliver e-Government services to its citizens, as well as initiated by the municipality's decentralisation strategy.

## 5 Conclusions and Further Studies

The strategy of the municipality can be seen as aiming at decentralisation as much as possible. In spite of this, it started a sourcing decision process regarding hosting of its software applications, which from the very beginning aimed at deciding on a solution that centralised the hosting to a great extent, a decision contradicting the strategy. An important question is why the decision-makers in the municipality did so. Comparing with Hamel and Prahalad's (1994) discussion about strategic architecture it can be suggested that the decision was made with the objective of making it possible to decentralise even further. This can be explained if one looks at the new users and the new usage of the municipality's software applications. The municipality has far-reaching decentralisation and continued decentralisation by letting the citizens themselves produce the services they need is seen as beneficial. The next step for the municipality is to decentralise (outsource) certain tasks to the citizens and thereby become an e-Government. To be able to do that, the decision-makers has seen it as necessary to restructure the hosting of software applications, which means that they have suggested centralisation of hosting as a way of further decentralise usage of software applications. The need and/or wish to increase e-Government services and decision-makers thought of e-Government influences the start of a sourcing decision process aiming at reorganising hosting of software applications.

From this it can be concluded that there is a potential need for municipalities in Sweden to prepare for its future usage of software applications which means that citizens by themselves will do more and more of the services the municipalities' employees has done before. This demands that municipalities have to prepare to have a higher share and number of services provided by e-Government in the future. The change from a common local government to an e-Government could be seen as a factor that makes organisations start a sourcing decision process regarding hosting of software applications.

This study opens up for a number of further studies. To complement this study further, longitudinal and detailed studies of how the suggested propositions influence organisations when they strive for being an e-Government, delivering e-services, would be interesting. The propositions could also act as input to further quantitative variance studies. From a practical point of view it would be interesting to see in what way decision-makers' different assumptions about centralisation vs. decentralisation of hosting impact e-Government in the future. One limitation of the present study is that the case study is not put in the profound light of e-Government literature. The present study has a more exploratory purpose and focus the discussion of the e-Government phenomenon primary from a sourcing perspective. However, it is possible in the future to refer more to the ongoing theoretical work in the field of e-Government, relate the propositions to stage models, etc.

# References

Aalders, R. (2001) *The IT outsourcing guide*. Wiley, New York; Chichester.

Axelsson, B. and Wynstra, F. (2002) *Buying business services*. Wiley, Chichester.

Bearingpoint (2004) IT-benchmark 2003/2004. White paper from BearingPoint, Inc.

Brandt, P., Carlsson, R. and Nilsson, A. G. (1998) *Välja och förvalta standardsystem*. Studentlitteratur, Lund.

Cronk, J. and Sharp, J. (1995) A framework for deciding what to outsource in information technology. *Journal of Information Technology* (Routledge, Ltd.) 10 (4), 259–268.

Currie, W. L. and Seltsikas, P. (2000) Evaluating the application service provider (ASP) business model. Executive Publication Series CSIS2000/004, Centre for Strategic Information Systems, Department of Information Systems & Computing, Brunel University, UK.,

Dewire, D. T. (2001) ASPs: Applications for rent. In *Proceedings of the seventh Americas Conference on Information Systems*, pp. 2275–2282.

Dibbern, J., Goles, T., Hirschheim, R. and Jayatilaka, B. (2004) Information systems outsourcing: A survey and analysis of the literature. *The DATA BASE for Advances in Information Systems* 35 (4), 6–102.

Hamel, G. and Prahalad, C. K. (1994) *Competing for the future*. Harvard Business School Press, Boston, MA.

Johansson, B. (2004) *Deciding on using application service provision in SMEs*. Linköping University, Linköping.

Jurison, J. (1998) A risk-return model for information technology outsourcing decisions. In *Strategic sourcing of information systems: Perspectives and practices* (Willcocks, L. P. and Lacity, M. C., Eds), pp. 187–204. Wiley, Chichester, England.

Kakabadse, A. and Kakabadse, N. (2002) Application service providers (ASPs): New impetus for transformational change. *Knowledge and Process Management* 9 (4), 205–218.

Kern, T., Lacity, M. C., Willcocks, L., Zuiderwijk, R. and Teunissen, W. (2001) ASP market space report 2001. Mastering the customers' expectations. GMG report.

Kishore, R., Agrawal, M. and Rao, H. R. (2004) Determinants of sourcing during technology growth and maturity: An empirical study of e-commerce sourcing. *Journal of Management Information Systems* 21 (3), 47–82.

Krippendorff, K. (2004) *Content analysis: An introduction to its methodology*. Sage.

Lacity, M. and Hirschheim, R. (1993) *Information systems outsourcing: Myths, metaphors, and reality*. John Wiley and Sons, New York, NY.

Layne, K. and Lee, J. (2001) Developing fully functional e-government: A four stage model. *Government Information Quarterly* 18 (2), 122–136.

Leffler, J. (1987) Systemförvaltning. Delrapport nr 2: Organisation och styrning. Stockholm.

Markus, M. L. (1984) *Systems in organizations: Bugs + features*. Ballinger, Cambridge, MA.

Mata, F. J., Fuerst, W. L. and Barney, J. B. (1995) Information technology and sustained competitive advantage: A resource-based analysis. *MIS Quarterly* 19 (4), 487–505.

Mclellan, K., Marcolin, B. L. and Beamish, P. W. (1998) Financial and strategic motivations behind is outsourcing. In *Strategic sourcing of information systems: Perspectives and practices* (Willcocks, L. P. and Lacity, M. C., Eds), pp. 187–204. Wiley, Chichester.

Mintzberg, H. and Quinn, J. B. (1996) *The strategy process: Concepts, contexts and cases*. Prentice-Hall, Upper Saddle River, NJ.

Pettigrew, A. M. (1973) *The politics of organizational decision-making*. Routledge, London.

Shepherd, A. (1999) Outsourcing it in a changing world. *European Management Journal* 17 (1), 64–84.

Silcock, R. (2001) What is e-government? *Parliamentary Affairs* 54 (1), 88–101.

Simon, H. A. (1960) *The new science of management decision*. Harper, New York.

Simon, H. A. (1997) *Administrative behavior: A study of decision-making processes in administrative organisations*. Free Press, New York; London.

Stake, R. E. (1994) Case studies. In *Handbook of qualitative research* (Denzin, N. K. and Lincoln, Y. S., Eds), pp. 236–247. Sage, Thousand Oaks, CA.

Turban, E., Mclean, E. R. and Wetherbe, J. C. (2001) *Information technology for management: Making connections for strategic advantage*. Wiley, New York.

Walsham, G. (1995) Interpretive case studies in is research: Nature and method. *European Journal of Information Systems* 4, 74–81.

Weill, P. and Ross, J. W. (2004) *IT governance: How top performers manage IT decision rights for superior results*. Harvard Business School Press, Boston, MA.

Williamson, O. E. (1985) *The economic institutions of capitalism: Firms, markets, relational contracting*. Free Press, New York.

# A Case Study of Systems Development in Custom IS Organizational Culture

Päivi Ovaska

Faculty of Technology, South Carelia University of Applied Sciences, Finland,
paivi.ovaska@scp.fi

**Abstract**  This chapter presents a study of how the custom IS organizational culture influences ISD practices in organizations developing tailored information systems. We studied four organizations by applying grounded theory and using organizational culture perspective as a lens to the data. The study provides example that illustrate the importance of partnership with customer in the perpetuation of a custom information systems work community. It presents a community of practice that embodies the beliefs in customer satisfaction, growth from global markets, and project work along with values of business domain knowledge, customer closeness, and doing things right. This study shows how these beliefs and values are manifested in systems development practices and artifacts. Findings show evidence of traditional and customer driven practices aiming to gain a trusted partnership position among customers. The study also reveals the change process going on in those organizations competing in the global markets. This change manifests itself in more product-driven practices aiming to develop more repeatable solutions for multiple customers. The possible consequences of this change process are discussed in this chapter.

## 1 Introduction

There has been strong indication of productivity problems since the mid-1980s associated with ISD projects. These productivity problems include slipping schedules and cost overruns (Boehm 1987; Brooks 1995), and low systems quality with increased maintenance costs (Boehm 1987). In the 1980s, many researchers went so far as to speak of a "software crisis" or a "system crisis" (Brooks 1995). The problems forced information systems (IS) and software engineering (SE) communities to direct their efforts primarily towards improvement of software quality and productivity (Keil and Robey 2001; Glass 1994). In spite of this effort problems associated with the software crisis continue unabated. Both IS development and use are full of difficulties and recurrent problems, and most causes of these are social (Lyytinen 1987).

Intensive research on software tools, modeling methods and processes for systems development has not yet delivered tools or techniques that could guarantee

C. Barry et al. (eds.), *Information Systems Development: Challenges in Practice, Theory, and Education, Vol.1*, doi: 10.1007/978-0-387-68772-8_31,
© Springer Science+Business Media, LLC 2009

success in ISD projects. As against this, there remains a lack of research investigations which are grounded in empirical studies of software development in the organizational context. Also, the importance of understanding organizational culture has been brought up by Avison and Myers (1995). This study is part of the larger study to investigate the linkage between organizational context and ISD practices.

This chapter contributes to the literature on software and systems development by examining how custom IS organizational culture influences on systems development practices in tailored software developing organizations. According to our study, the beliefs in customer satisfaction and growth from global markets along with values of business domain knowledge, customer closeness, project work, and doing thing right influence the ISD process significantly.

This chapter is organized as follows. The next section discusses of what constitutes the custom IS organizational culture by giving a short review on related literature. Furthermore, the research methodology of this study is described. In the third section, we present findings of our case study. The fourth section discusses the findings. Finally, a summary of this study along paths for future work are outlined.

# 2 Literature Review

This section briefly sets out the important literature which informs the key elements of this study. It starts by reviewing the custom information system, then explores the community of practice, and finally briefly outlines the organizational culture as a theory for ISD. The section finishes with the review of organizational cultural perspective and IS research.

## 2.1 Custom Information Systems

Custom information systems (IS) are those made either by an organization's internal IS staff or by direct subcontract to a software firm (such as Andersen Consulting or Computer Associates). Custom IS are made-to-order systems and are typically built for specific users. This definition of custom IS also includes most government work (Carmel and Sawyer 1998). For example, US Department of Defense (DoD) software development (the focus of much attention by software engineering researchers) is typically custom development. The degree of customization varies within this kind of IS. Some IS are totally constructed from scratch while others, like ERP (Enterprise Resource Planning) systems, are more software products that are tailored to customer needs (Carmel and Bird 1997).

## 2.2 Community of Practice

A community of practice (COP) is a group of people who share similar goals, interests, beliefs, and value systems in a common domain of recurring activity or work (Brown and Duguid 1991; Wenger 1998). Typically, such groups do not overlap with company-assigned teams or task forces. Because they grow out of human sociability and efforts to meet job requirements (especially those not anticipated and supported by the formal organization and formal training for work), a COP is typically not an authorized group nor a role identified on an organization chart. People in COPs may perform the same job (technical representatives) or collaborate on a shared task (software developers) or work together on a product (engineers, marketers, and manufacturing specialists). They are colleagues, bound together by their common responsibility to get a certain type of "real work" done. There are typically many communities of practice within a single company, and most people belong to more than one of them.

The notion of "practice" is critical in COP, pointing out that the group concentrates on learning that emerges only though working, or actually practicing one's craft. COPs supplement the book and classroom learning of many trade and professional workers. To learn how one does in this area (like developing custom IS systems), that goes beyond the official "canonical" training for that activity implies that a key part of learning how to work is learning how to communicate and share information within the community of practice. In this sense, learning is about work, and work is about learning, and both are social (Wenger 1998).

## 2.3 Organizational Culture

Much like social cultures have beliefs and values manifested in norms that form behavioral expectations, organizations have cultures that form and give its members guidelines for the way of developing information systems (Martin 2002; Schein 1992).

Trice and Byer (1993) provide a method of studying an organization's social processes. Organizational culture can also be looked at as a system with inputs, processes, and outputs. Inputs include feedback from, e.g., society, professions, laws, customers, contracts, and competitors. The process is based on our assumptions, values, and norms, e.g., our values on money, time, facilities, space, and people. Outputs or effects of our culture are, e.g., organizational behaviors, practices, technologies, strategies, image, products, and services.

Organizational culture helps individuals and groups deal with uncertainties and ambiguities while offering some degree of order in social life. The substances of such cultures are formed from ideologies, the implicit sets of taken-for-granted beliefs, values, and norms. Members express the substance of their cultures through the use of cultural forms in organizations, acceptable ways of expressing and affirming their beliefs, values, and norms. Organizational cultures, like other cultures, evolve as groups of people struggle together to make sense of and cope with their worlds (Trice and Byer 1993). It is through the interaction between ideologies and cultural forms that cultures maintain their existence. Cultural forms facilitate how people make sense of their world. The reality of the world people cope with becomes socially constructed (Berger and Luckmann 1966). Most organizational culture researchers view work culture as this kind of consensus-making system

(Ott 1989; Schein 1992; Trice and Byer 1993). However, some researchers view organizational culture as an emergent process (Martin 2002; Smircich 1983).

Researchers have defined organizational culture in myriad ways (Martin, 2002). We use the following organizational culture definition as the background of this study: "Culture is the pattern of shared beliefs and values that give members of an institution meaning and provide them with the rules for behaviour in their organization".

In this study, the organizational culture is viewed as a phenomenon manifested in an organization's work practices, norms, and artifacts. We analyze the connection between content themes and cultural manifestations in the custom IS community of practice by using the Martin's framework (Martin 2002). Table 1 lists typical cultural manifestations found in organizational culture studies.

**Table 1.** Descriptions of organizational cultural manifestations (Martin 2002)

| Category | Examples |
| --- | --- |
| Cultural artifacts | Rituals, organizational stories, jargon, humor, physical arrangements (architecture, dress codes, etc.) |
| Formal practices | Organizational structure, task and technology, rules and procedures, and financial controls |
| Informal practices | Norms and social rules (not written down) |
| Content themes | Cognitive (beliefs or tacit assumptions) or attitudinal (values) that underlie interpretations of cultural manifestations |

According to this framework, the substance of a culture is its ideology—shared, interrelated sets of emotional beliefs, values, and norms that bind people together and help them to make sense of their world (Trice and Beyer 1993). While generally closely interrelated with behavior, beliefs, values, and norms are unique concepts as defined below (Trice and Beyer 1993).

- Beliefs—Express cause and effect relations (i.e. behaviors lead to outcomes).
- Values—Express preferences for certain behaviors or for certain outcomes.
- Norms—Express which behaviors are expected by others and are culturally acceptable ways to attain outcomes.

There exist many other approaches to organizational culture, which differs greatly in relation to how this complex concept culture is defined (Smirchich 1983)

## 2.4 Organizational Culture Perspective and IS Research

Studies have revealed a multitude of ways organizational culture affects organizational change efforts. Some studies highlight that compatibility between change effort and culture is a very important criterion for success. These studies have defined compatible culture types for different kinds of change efforts, e.g. a "group culture type" is a major facilitator of diffusion of telecommuting (Harrington and Ruppel 1999), "adhocracy" and "group" culture types are suitable for TQM (Total Quality Management) (Dellana and Hauser 1999), mature TQM organizations have proactive and collaborative cultures (Fok et al. 2001), and "adhocracy" and "hierarchy" culture types are correlated with early adoption of intranets (Ruppel and Harrington 2001).

However, other studies have shown problems in the implementation efforts to be caused by a mismatch between a unique organizational culture and an implementation effort. The studies show that an IS implementation was resisted because the organization was presumed to have different organizational culture than it actually did (Pliskin et al. 1993), an enterprise resource planning packages implementation problems were caused by a mismatch with the values of the organizational culture (Krumbholtz and Maiden 2001) and differences between the cultures of implementers and adopters caused difficulties in an IS implementation (Robey and Rodriquez-Diaz 1989).

Finally, studies on culture highlight that different meanings can be attached to same change efforts in different contexts. Accounting was vested with different meanings in different cultures (Dent 1991), and planned change was interpreted in different ways in different subcultures (DiBella 1996). Culture has been a focus of analysis in studies on organizational change related to the development, implementation, or use of IS in organizations. Researchers have theorized the application of a cultural perspective to understand IT implementation and use (e.g. Avison and Myers 1995; Cooper 1994; Robey and Azevedo 1994). Pliskin et al. (1993) suggest that important characteristics of the unique culture of the organization should be considered prior to implementing new technologies.

# 3 Research Methods

This section briefly sets out a short description of the target organizations and describes the research methodology.

## 3.1 Target organizations

Following Glaser and Strauss' (1967) technique of theoretical sampling, the four organizations were selected for their similarities as well as their differences in the following way:

- *Alfa* is an internationally operating big software company in Scandinavia. The department participated in this study develops information systems for forest industry customers.
- *Beta* is a small company that develops custom information systems in the agriculture business domain. It is owned by its customers and operates mainly in the domestic markets in Finland.

- *Gamma* is an internationally operating medium sized company in Finland. It develops custom IS for forest industry customers.
- *Epsilon* is a medium sized company that develops custom IS for information logistics customer. The customer owns the company. The company operates mostly in Finland but also has a couple of ongoing projects with the company's subsidiaries in other European countries.

## 3.2 Research Methodology

This study is part of the empirical study of systems development contexts and their relationship to ISD practices. We interviewed totally six custom IS developing organizations in which four of them were selected to this particular study. The ultimate target of the whole research was to increase the understanding of the relationships between organizational context and ISD work. Based on these research objectives this part of the study concentrated on organization culture and its influence on systems development. The research question was formulated as follows:

Q1: How custom IS organizational culture influences systems development practices?

The data for this qualitative study was collected using theme-based interviews, company's web pages, and annual reports. There were three themes present in interviews: systems development projects, methods and practices, effects of company and its business environment on systems development practices, and networking and cooperation. We interviewed totally 26 employees from these four organizations representing different organizational status. The interviews were made between October and December 2006 and five interviewers visited these organizations. Interviews lasted from 30 minutes to 3 hours. Interviews were transcript as text and analyzed using grounded theory (Glaser and Strauss 1967, Strauss and Corbin 1990).

Grounded theory is a qualitative research method that uses a systematic set of procedures to develop an inductively derived theory about a phenomenon. It can be used to study organizations, groups, and individuals (Glaser and Strauss 1967, Strauss and Corbin 1990). The basic idea of the grounded-theory-based data analysis resides in finding conceptual categories and abstractions related to the research goal from data, and combining these categories meaningfully to provide theoretical insight into the phenomenon in question. A requirement of grounded theory is that the researchers demonstrate theoretical sensitivity (Glaser and Strauss 1967). Theoretical sensitivity comes from familiarity with the literature, and from professional or personal experience (Strauss and Corbin 1990). Qualitative data analysis was performed in three phases: open coding, axial coding, and selective coding (Strauss and Corbin 1990).

The analysis started with open coding phase in which the seed categories (Strauss and Corbin 1990) from Martin's framework presented in Sect. 2.2 were used. The open coding phase was followed by axial coding phase that proceeded almost parallel with previous phase. In the open coding phase we interpreted organizations website descriptions as well as physical manifestation of the culture such as dress norms, workplace furnishing, and atmosphere. The analysis ended with selective coding phase where the core categories and their relationships were formed. The following table (Table 2) lists the found beliefs and value categories along with examples from data.

**Table 2.** Categories of beliefs and values with examples from data

| Categories | Concepts | Examples from data |
|---|---|---|
| Beliefs | Customer satisfaction | "The principle of our company is customer satisfaction. We develop everything customer wants. We also have another principle that is once we have developed a feature for the customer it can also be used by other customers. Finally, we have a situation that when a customer wants something it is probably already developed" |
| | Growth from global markets | "At this moment, our growth is in the international markets and we there are a different organization from others. We are not an ordinary IT firm, because we concentrate on the know-how of business. But the price is still the most important factor among our customers…" |
| | Project work | "The more difficult the project is the more leadership is needed from project managers. If it does not work with project people, then you just have to instruct as to what to do; you must try to motivate them in a positive way to work hard." |
| Values | Customer closeness | "It is always like this: the customer has been put on the pedestal and we have tried to do everything the customer wants. Sometime we have tried to change this by trying to get more distance, but always we have turned back. Customer closeness is perhaps the most important factor in the competition." |
| | Business domain knowledge | "Our strength is that we are experts in business domain. So our areas of expertise should be in forest industry domain. Information technology knowledge is the area that every software organization must know; it is like basic knowledge." |
| | Doing things right | "We do not have a standard way of developing systems. If we could have this some day in the future it would give some kind of routine to this work and certainly it would cause better quality of the final system. This standard can be quite simple, for example, just standardizing the development process. In the beginning it may take some more time and delay projects, but it is the only way to increase the quality. At the same time it influences the motivation of employees. The motivation in the projects mostly comes from the feeling that it is going in the right way." |

# 4 Findings

## 4.1 Beliefs and Values

During the analysis, we observed six categories of beliefs and values which seemed to influence mostly on the ISD practices in the case organizations. These categories can be summarized as:

1. *Belief in customer satisfaction:* customer satisfaction forms the core motivator of custom IS software developers.
2. *Belief in growth from global markets*: belief that business growth is in international markets, not in domestic markets.
3. *Belief in project work*: ISD work is done in projects and project organization is quite formal with project managers who lead the project.
4. *Value of customer closeness*: customer satisfaction is gained by doing everything the customer wants.
5. *Value of business domain knowledge*: business domain knowledge seemed to be more important than technical skills in developing custom IS systems. The domain expertise is highly valued and the organizations hire employees who have a degree in a particular business area.
6. *Value of doing things right*: this seems to be a very important motivator for software developers.

## 4.2 ISD Work Practices

Above introduced beliefs and values seemed to influence much on the case study organizations' systems development work practices. The following categories of work practices could be observed in the case organization:

### 4.2.1 Formal Practices

1. *Project planning and management*: Organizations have formal instructions or a model for project planning and management. It is based on distinct phases of requirements gathering, design implementation, testing, and maintenance.
2. *Documentation and coding standards*: Related to the above mentioned project planning and management model, the instructions or model includes the documentation standards and coding standards.

### 4.2.2 Informal Practices

1. *Process driven*: The ISD process with customer is seen more importantly than the final information system. Besides, the process is determined by customer

and mostly follows a waterfall style of development (distinct phases of development following each other in a waterfall fashion) because the customer knows it best.

2. *Customer driven*: The belief of customer closeness leads to customer driven practices. This means that development process in projects depends on the customer.

3. *Requirements driven*: The value of business domain knowledge lead to the requirements driven ISD process.

4. *Distributed project teams*: The belief in project work and globalization influences distributed project teams, where the members of the team are in different locations.

## 4.3 Artifacts

According to Martin's framework (Martin 2002), artifacts are the outcomes of the ISD work. The following artifacts could be observed during the analysis:

1. *Trusted partner*: Close partnership with customer is the most important outcome of the ISD projects, even more important than the actual information system. Also, the ability to help the customer organizations in its business processes is very important.

2. *Repeatable solutions:* In those organizations starting or willing to develop custom IS solutions for the global markets, the change from developing pure custom IS solutions to develop global repeatable solutions was evident. It is more a software product that can be re-used or 'repeated' meeting the needs of more than one customer.

## 5 Discussion

According to our study, the custom IS industry's ways to success is by achieving a trusted partner position among their customers by possessing good business domain knowledge, project work skills, and motivated personnel. This trusted partner position seemed to be more important than the developed information system. Custom IS organizational success is tied, in large part, to the business understanding, project work skills, and customer closeness. In custom IS organizations, domain expertise is highly valued and their focus is on hiring employees who have a degree in a particular business area. This was the situation in most of our case study companies. For example, in company Alfa, most of the project personnel had a degree in software engineering, but in the other companies approximately half of the employees had a degree other than software engineering, such as agriculture, logistics, and forest industry. All the organizations that participated in this study appreciated the work of the project people working together and having specified a project manager within this project. According to this study, all the other roles, such as designer, tester, etc. were not always clear. In most of the organizations, the project manager has a clear leadership role within the project. For example, in company Gamma, the only person assigned to the project permanently was the project manager, all the other roles were assigned on a need basis. Project teams seemed to be more like "ad-hoc" work groups working together only during the project. In some organizations, these custom IS teams were quite big and multi-located distributed teams. In this kind of environment, it is natural that project planning and management becomes very important. All the interviewed companies had a company-specific project model to advice project managers in their work. When the success factor for project managers is good leadership, the main motivator for software developers working in the custom IS projects is doing things right. This value of doing things right along with process driven practices has lead the custom IS companies in the study to develop documentation and coding standards to aid software developers in their work.

As shown in the findings, customer IS developers have a process view of development. By process view of development we mean belief in the importance of process, not the final system. Besides, in most of these organizations that participated in the study the development work was driven by customers. According to interviewers this was a reason why their development process was more or less a traditional waterfall model with separate requirement capture, design implementation, testing, and maintenance phases. They said that customers are used to this kind of model and it is the only model customers know.

The analysis of the data revealed the change process going on in these organizations competing or willing to compete in the global markets. According to the interviews, competition is hard in international markets and the only way to compete is too seek cost reductions in relation to their normal way of developing information systems. In this kind of situation, some companies seek cost reductions by outsourcing their development work. Organizations that participated in this study did not believe that they were ready for outsourcing and turned their development efforts to seek and develop repeatable solutions for their global customers. This means a turn to the more software product oriented way to develop information systems.

This kind of change from pure custom IS development to more product oriented development needs evidently some kind of change in their systems development practices. Perhaps the organizations had to change their practices from customer driven to more product focused practices. A product focus means that the dominant goal of the software development effort is to develop a product and the process is secondary. While for custom IS development the project management and planning is very important in the product oriented software development, the release management and planning (Sawyer 2000) forms the most important activity. That is, the software evolves through a planned set of releases.

Organizations changing their practices to more product oriented ones also face changes in their organization culture related to systems development. We can speculate that the value of customer closeness changes mostly. These companies also need different kinds of knowledge in software development, especially knowledge of software products and release management. It is also clear that one cannot be so close with a customer when developing software products because the requirements of the system must be wide angled. Especially, the development process cannot be customer specific in this kind of situation.

# 6 Summary

In this chapter, we have illustrated how the organizational cultural beliefs and values influence systems development practices in four custom IS software organizations. We applied grounded theory and used organizational culture perspective as a lens to the data. Our study suggests cultural beliefs in customer satisfaction, growth from global markets, and project work along with values of business domain knowledge, customer closeness, and doing things right. These beliefs and values influence remarkably the custom IS development practices. Findings show evidence of traditional and customer driven practices aiming to gain a trusted partnership position among customers.

The study also reveals the change process going on in those organizations competing in the global markets. This change manifests itself in more product-driven practices aiming to develop more repeatable solutions for customers. This kind of change from pure custom IS development to more product oriented development evidently needs change both in their organizational culture and systems development practices. The challenge to these organizations is in keeping the customer satisfied in a situation where they cannot be close to one single customer and do everything that customer wants.

# References

Avison D.E, Myers M.D (1995) Information systems and anthropology: an anthropological perspective on IT and organizational culture, Information Technology & People, 8(3): 43–56.

Berger P.L., Luckmann T. (1966) *The Social Construction of Reality: A Treatise in the Sociology of Knowledge,* Garden City, New York: Anchor Books.

Boehm, B. (1987) Improving Software Productivity, IEEE Computer, 20(8): 43–58.

Brooks, F. P. J. (1995) *The Mythical Man-Month - 20th Anniversary Edition,* Boston, Addison-Wesley.

Brown J.S, Duguid P. (1991) Organizational Learning and Communities-of-Practice: Toward a Unified View of Working, Learning and Innovation, Organization Science, 2(1): 40–57.

Carmel E. and Bird B. (1997) Small is beautiful: a study of packaged software development teams, The Information Society 13(1), 125–142.

Carmel E. and  Sawyer S. (1998) Packaged software development teams: what makes them different? Information Technology&People 11(1), 7–19.

Cooper R.B. (1994) The inertial impact of culture on IT implementation, Information Management, 27, 17–31.

Dellana, S.A. and Hauser, R.D. (1999) Toward defining the quality culture. Engineering Management Journal, 11(2), 11–15.

Dent J.F. (1991) Accounting and organizational cultures: a field study of the emergence of a new organizational reality. Accounting, Organizations and Society, 16 (8), 705–732.

DiBella, A.J. (1996) Culture and planned change in an international organization: a multi-level predicament. The International Journal of Organizational Analysis, 4 (4), 352–372.

Fok, L.Y, Fok, W.M. and Hartman, S.J. (2001) Exploring the relationship between total quality management and information systems development, Information & Management. 38(6), 355–371.

Glaser, B., A. L. Strauss (1967*)* The Discovery of Grounded Theory: Strategies for Qualitative Research, Chicago, Adline.

Glass, R. (1994) The Software Research Crisis, IEEE Software, 11(6), 42–47.

Harrington, S. and Ruppel, C.P (1999) Practical and value compatibility: their roles in the adoption, diffusion, and success of telecommuting, Proceedings of the 20th international conference on Information Systems, p. 103–112, December 12–15, Charlotte, North Carolina, United States.

Keil, M., Robey, D. (1999) Turning around troubled software projects: An exploratory study of the deescalation of commitment to failing courses of action, Journal of Management Information Systems, 15(4), 63–88.

Krumbholz, M. and Maiden, N. (2001) The implementation of enterprise resource planning packages in different organisational and national cultures, Information Systems 26(3), 185–204.

Lyytinen K. (1987) Different perspectives on information systems: problems and solutions, ACM computing surveys 19(1), 5–46.

Martin J. (2002) Organizational Culture: Mapping the Terrain, Thousands Oaks: Sage Publications.

Ott J. (1989) The Organizational Culture Perspective, Pasific Grove, Ca: Brooks/Cole.

Pliskin N., Romm T., Lee A.S. and Weber Y. (1993) Presumed versus Actual Organizational Culture: Managerial Implications for Implementation of Information Systems, The Computer Journal 36(2), 143–152.

Robey D. and Azevedo A. (1994) Cultural Analysis of the Organizational Consequences of Information Technology, Accounting Management and Information Technology, 4(1), 23–37.

Robey, D. and Rodriquez-Diaz (1989) The organizational and cultural context of systems implementation: case experience from Latin America, Information and Management,17, 229–239.

Ruppel C.P. and Harrington, S. (2001) Sharing knowledge through intranets: a study of organizational culture and intranet implementation, IEEE Transactions on Professional Communication, 44 (1), 37–52.

Sawyer S. (2000) Packaged software: implications of the differences from custom approaches to software development, European Journal of Information Systems 9: 47–58.

Schein, E.H. (1992) Organizational Culture and Leadership, San Francisco: Jossy-Bass

Smirchich L. (1983) Concepts of Culture and Organizational Analysis, Administrative Science Quarterly, 28, 339–358.

Strauss, A., Corbin, J. (1990) Basics of Qualitative Research: Grounded Theory Procedures and Applications, Sage Publications, Newbury Park, CA.

Trice, H.M, Beyer, J.M. (1993) The Cultures of Work Organizations, Englewood Cliffs, NJ:Prentice Hall.

Wenger E. (1998) Communities of Practice: Learning, Meaning and Identity, Cambridge, Massachusetts: Cambridge University Press.

# Building a Dolmen: An ISD Approach to the Management of Innovation

Gabriel J. Costello[1], Kieran Conboy[2], Brian Donnellan[3] and Colm Rochford[4]

[1] Galway-Mayo Institute of Technology, gabrielj.costello@gmit.ie

[2] National University of Ireland, Galway, {kieran.conboy; brian.donnellan}@nuigalway.ie

[3] National University of Ireland, Galway, brian.donnellan@nuigalway.ie

[4] APC-MGE, Castlebar, Ireland, colm.rochford@apcc.com

**Abstract**  This chapter addresses a "challenge in practice" by describing the initial stage of an information systems development (ISD) project to support the management of innovation within a subsidiary of APC-MGE. To begin with, a review is presented of relevant literature on the management of innovation and on ISD. The background of the case study is outlined and the advantages of a dialogical action research approach to ISD are discussed. Then the development of a conceptual model using the organizational analysis approach of Multiview2 is described. The work proposes to make a contribution in a number of areas. Firstly, it provides empirical evidence of the role of innovation in an organizational transformation and the challenge of designing an information system to support this objective. Secondly, it presents an example of using dialogical action research, recently introduced to the MIS discipline by Mårtensson and Lee, to develop an information system. Future work will involve tracking the implementation of the concept in order to evaluate its impact on the organization.

## 1 Introduction

The aim of this chapter is to report on the initial stage of an information systems development (ISD) project to support the management of innovation. The work is presented in the context of a case study of APC-MGE, formerly a subsidiary of American Power Conversion (APC), which has recently been acquired by Schneider Electric. The subsidiary is located in Ireland's Border, Midland, and Western (BMW) region. This region is designated by the European Union (EU) as Objective 1: a less well developed area that qualifies for additional structural funds under the EU state aid scheme. The national context is Ireland, which in recent decades has leapfrogged from a traditional agrarian economy to a deliberately created information economy (Trauth 2000). The original impetus was fuelled by foreign direct in-

C. Barry et al. (eds.), *Information Systems Development: Challenges in Practice, Theory, and Education, Vol.1*, doi: 10.1007/978-0-387-68772-8_32,
© Springer Science+Business Media, LLC 2009

vestment (FDI) from North American multi-national corporations (MNCs) setting up offshore manufacturing facilities to avail tax incentives, a young educated workforce, and proximity to their growing number of European customers. However, this initially successful model is increasingly being threatened by the low cost economies of Eastern Europe, India, and China. Ireland is now entering a new era which, according to Porter (2003), requires a transition to an innovation economy.

This chapter proposes to answer the following research question: How can ISD support the management of innovation in this context? The approach is that of a dialogical action research, recently proposed to the MIS community by Mårtensson and Lee (2004), that involved "reflective one-on-one dialogs" between the Plant Manager of the corporate subsidiary and the IS researcher. The research proposes to make a contribution to practice by examining the role of IS in supporting the development of an innovative supply chain organization. The chapter now proceeds as follows. Firstly, a literature review is provided on innovation management and ISD. The background and context of the case study is then presented. Next, the research approach is outlined and the scope of the research question and data collection are described. Following this, the initial ISD concept is illustrated and implications for practice and research are discussed. Finally, the conclusions of the study are presented and suggestions are made for future work.

# 2 Literature Review

This section will provide a short review of the main body of literature and theoretical frameworks in which this work is based: namely management of innovation and ISD.

## 2.1 Management of Innovation

One of the main challenges for an organization that is committed to innovation is the creation and management of an innovative culture. This task is also being spoken of as the challenge of generating an organizational "climate" with the increasing evidence of its positive link to innovation effectiveness (Leavy 2005). According to Zien and Buckler (2004) successful companies create a culture where everyone participates in innovation and where it is seen as the fundamental way to provide value to customers. Herzberg's (2003) seminal work on motivation found that people are "motivated by interesting work, challenge, and increasing responsibility." Good management and working conditions will help ensure that they do not become dissatisfied but will meet their deep-seated need for growth and achievement.

Tidd et al. (2005, p. 138) propose that innovation must not be seen as a lottery but as a continuous improvement process and point out that, based on recent research on innovation successes and failures, a number of models have been developed to help assess innovation management performance. In order to provide some initial reference point for innovation management, they have developed an assessment tool and audit framework. Such self-assessment tools have been widely used in the area of total quality management (TQM) in order to benchmark an enterprise against best in class, for example, the Malcolm Baldrige National Quality Award. The framework proposes five dimensions under which innovation management are to be assessed and profiled: strategy, process, organization, linkages, and learning (Tidd et al. 2005, p. 568). These dimensions will be discussed further when the IS development is described in Sect. 5. Some related themes from the innovation literature associated with these dimensions are presented in Table 1.

**Table 1.** Themes from the innovation literature

| Attribute | Characteristic and Reference |
|---|---|
| Identity | Treasure identity as an innovative company (Zien and Buckler 2004). |
| Employment | Hire people with a range of abilities, interests, and backgrounds and involve peers heavily in the selection process (Leavy 2005). |
| Responsibilities | Remove control while retaining accountability (Herzberg 2003). |
| Creativity | $C = K \times I \times E$: Creativity requires Knowledge, Imagination, and Evaluation (Basadur 2006). Look outside the box (Nemeth 2004). |
| R&D | Not all the smart people work here (Chesbrough 2003). R&D is everyone's business and problems are "golden eggs" (Basadur 2004). |
| Suggestions Schemes | Look for simple focused solutions (Tushman and O'Reilly 2004) to real problems (Drucker 2003). Use to develop motivation, job satisfaction and teamwork: not make money (Basadur 2004). |
| Learning | Give people room to grow, try things out and learn from mistakes (Leavy 2005). 7–3 formula: expect to make wrong decisions 3 times out of 10 (Tushman and O'Reilly 2004). |
| Management | Place people and ideas at the heart of management philosophy (Leavy 2005). Managers are "symphony conductors" not army generals and strategy flows from bottom up (Tushman and O'Reilly 2004). People do not resist change: they resist being changed (Herzberg 2003). |
| Motivation | People are "motivated by interesting work, challenge, and increasing responsibility" (Herzberg 2003). A-rated motivations and B-rated capabilities are better than vice-versa (Katz 2004). |

We will now proceed to examine the ISD literature in the light of our research objective: to investigate how ISD can facilitate the management of innovation.

## 2.2 Information Systems Development

Throughout the early years of computing from the 1940s to 1960s, ISD was a highly *ad hoc* and unstructured activity (Colter 1982; Ward 1992) with formal methods only being introduced in the following decades as systems technology became more advanced, complex, and difficult to develop. These methods were quite successful in so far as they provided a structured means of documenting and implementing technical specifications and functionality. However, while the fulfillment of technical requirements is indeed important, the development environment faced by organizations is much different from that of the 1960s and 1970s, where such a narrow focus on technical engineering is no longer appropriate. Firstly, and significantly for this study, the fast changing nature of the business environment is identified as one of the main reasons why traditional ISD methods are obsolete and there is a need "for new and radical approaches to ISD" (Avison and Fitzgerald 2003). In this environment the traditional, large-scale, long-timeframe, multiple-phased, formalized approaches are being challenged by the "faster metabolism" (Baskerville and Pries-Heje 2004) of modern organizations, the pressure to finish development "yesterday" (Overmyer 2000), and other traits which reflect the reality of contemporary business. Secondly, many researchers contend that the "context" is of fundamental importance to the development process and that the uniqueness of each situation requires both awareness and detailed understanding (Boehm 1981; Brooks 1987; Glass 1991). These authors were critical of the technical rationality that emerged from information engineering methodologies, and were of the opinion that over emphasis on computer-based artifacts resulted in a neglect of the social and contextual aspects of ISD. In particular, much research focuses on the inability of ISD methods to handle people factors (Avison and Fitzgerald 2003).Two contextual areas are emphasized: the technological context, both internal and external in which the ISD is taking place, and the organization culture which has a significant influence on how the ISD can be approached.

There is a general consensus among the ISD community that older methods have ignored the issues discussed above. Most methods are still founded on concepts that originated over 30 years ago, and there is a distinct need to "update the tenses" (Fitzgerald 2000). There are, however, some initiatives which are exceptions to this general rule. The emergence of "lightweight" or "agile" family of methods (Fowler and Highsmith 2001; Beck 1999; Schwaber and Beedle 2002) are based on short iterations, minimal processes, and constant developer interaction, all of which address some of the issues plaguing ISD. Fitzgerald et al. (2002) propose the concept of "method-in-action" which differentiates between the generic text-book method and the uniquely enacted context-based method that is actually implemented in practice. They argue that successful implementation depends more on the social and technological "contextual factors" than on the method that is used. This concept also raises connotations relating to innovation which is of particular relevance in this study. In contrast to the rather negative approach of problem-solving your way out of an unwanted situation (see Yourdon 1997 for terms associated with ISD such as "fire-fighting" and "death-march"), the method-in-action concept views change as an opportunity to creatively "form a new context".

Another significant influence on the ISD field has been the Multiview methodology which has been in development since 1985, a time when the area of ISD methodologies was described as a jungle (sic) (Avison and Fitzgerald 2003).The initial methodology was refined based on feedback from a number of action research projects that criticized its implicit adherence to a waterfall structure, resulting in what is now known as Multiview2, which Avison and Fitzgerald propose is more usefully seen as "a metaphor which is interpreted and developed in a particular situation" rather than being a detailed and prescriptive set of actions. There was also a realization that the ISD world had changed significantly since the mid-1980s due to developments in ICT, organizational forms, and business processes. Figure 1 illustrates the Multiview2 framework as consisting of four parts that are mediated through the ISD process itself: organizational analysis, socio-technical analysis and design, technical design and construction, and information modeling (acting as a "bridge between the other three, communicating and enacting the outcomes in terms of each other").

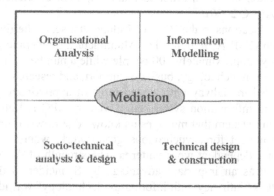

**Fig. 1.** The Multiview2 framework adapted from Avison and Fitzgerald (2003).

In the context of this chapter, the most significant quadrant is "organizational analysis" which is focused on identifying the reasons why the organization requires the IS and understanding the business and social context. The aim of this process is to obtain "an appreciation of the purposeful activity that the information system is to support". It is also important to realize that the authors of Multiview2 insist that the methodology continues to evolve and expect additional iterations based on feedback from "further action research and in-depth case studies" (Avison et al. 1998). Having presented an overview of the literature, the chapter will now provide a description of the context: the case study company in which the ISD is situated is followed by the research approach that is being taken in the study.

# 3 Case Study

The case study is based in APC, Ireland, a subsidiary of the American Power Conversion (APC) Corporation. The Corporation entered a major period of transition in the first quarter of 2007 with completion of its acquisition by Schneider Electric and the formation of a new division: APC-MGE. As the main part of this study was developed before the acquisition, this section will focus on providing a background to the APC context in which the work was carried out. APC designs, manufactures, and markets back-up products and services that protect hardware and data from power disturbances. The explosive growth of the Internet has resulted in the company broadening its product offerings from uninterruptible power supplies (UPS) to the high-end InfraStruXure™ architecture in order to meet the critical availability requirements of internet service providers (ISP) and datacenters. However, recent financial reports have stressed that the company needs to implement significant improvements in manufacturing and the supply chain. According to these reports, the company must work to develop a "lean, customer-centric, ambidextrous organization" in order to reach "optimal efficiencies in our processes" (Results APCC 2006).

APC has two locations in the West of Ireland that serve the European, Middle East, and African (EMEA) regions. The Manufacturing Operations site, based in Castlebar, employs approximately 100 people while a number of functions including sales, information technology, business support, and research and development (R&D) are situated in Galway with a workforce of approximately 300. The primary management information system employed by APC is Lotus Notes, a collaborative software system that manages its knowledge flows. It provides a tightly controlled environment for asynchronous group work, where collaborators can have different or independent work patterns. The strength of the MIS function in APC was viewed as an important advantage by Schneider in their acquisition analysis and APC's "intimacy with information technology" was identified as central to the creation of synergies with Schneider's power solutions subsidiary MGE.

# 4 Research Design

The conclusions by Benbasat and Zmud (1999) concerning the lack of relevance in IS research was, to put it mildly, a criticism of the discipline. Consequently, the initial approach to the case study was closely related to the following recommendation in their chapter:

> IS researchers should look to practice to identify research topics and look to the IS literature only after a commitment has been made to a specific topic.

However, we believe that the linear nature of their recommendation does not sufficiently accommodate the dynamics of a real-world corporate environment so we have adopted a more iterative approach, going from practice to literature in a continuous cycle. Initially, the work followed Yin's (1994) description of a case study as an "empirical enquiry that investigates a contemporary phenomenon within its real-life context" and where a "how or why question is being asked about a contemporary set of events over which the investigator has little or no control". The preliminary research aim was to consider the human and technological factors involved in the management of innovation. To this end the following research question was posed based on discussions with APC management and informed by the preliminary literature review.

RQ: How can ISD support the management of innovations in this context?

This chapter focuses on the initial stage of the design of an information system, during the period from January to April 2007, using the Multiview 2 framework that is aligned with the Schneider Electric corporate objectives (Schneider Electric 2005).

## 4.1 Ethnographic study—January to December 2006

The research design was initially formulated to take an inductive approach and followed the recommendation of Benbasat and Zmud outlined above. The rationale was that, first of all, there was a need to spend time in the organization, observing and listening, in order to get a feel for the situation. Data collection methods during this phase involved: maintaining a log book, reviewing documents and information systems, records, interviews, observations (direct and participant), artifacts, and surveys in order to develop a database and body of evidence (Yin 1994). A total of 29 unstructured or open interviews were undertaken that involved approximately 60 hours of interview time and 24 days spent in the company sites.

The interviews were conducted across a wide area of the organization that included: Senior Managers with global, EMEA, and site responsibilities, Middle-Managers, Team Leaders, Engineers, and a number of people in general planning roles. In order not to disconcert interviewees at the early stage of the research, it was decided not to use a recording system. However permission was obtained to take notes. To confirm that the researcher had correctly understood the social world in which the research was carried out and that the data were correctly reported, a technique known as "respondent validation" or "member validation" was employed. This involved returning a typed version of the notes to the interviewee for comments and agreement, with the aim of ensuring that they were an accurate representation of the meeting (Kelly and Murnane 2005).

## 4.2 Dialogical Action Research—January 2007 to April 2007

Recently, Mårtensson and Lee (2004) have suggested and described a new form of action research called dialogical AR. Here is a brief description of their approach:

*In dialogical action research, the scientific researcher does not "speak science" or otherwise attempt to teach scientific theory to the real-world practitioner, but instead attempts to speak the language of the practitioner and accepts him as the expert on his organization and its problems.*

The main contact point during Phase 1 was the Plant Manager of the Castlebar location which involved approximately 11 direct meetings with an estimated 17 hours of interaction. He is leading the "Innovation Management" project which will run throughout 2007 with two main objectives:

- Establish a culture/climate of innovation in APC Castlebar.
- Capture, Manage, and Diffuse the Innovations across the wider APC-MGE and Schneider Corporation.

There was an agreement in January 2007 to move forward using dialogical Action Research with meetings every two weeks in Castlebar. In their paper Mårtensson and Lee propose that "reflective dialogs outside the organization can help the manager to reflect on, learn from, and remedy managerial problems in the organization." In particular, the discipline of having to take regular timeout in a "time-pressured" manufacturing environment was a major incentive for the Plant Manager to agree to this approach. However, the realities of the situation have resulted in a further adaptation of Mårtensson and Lee's methodology: the research "timeout" consists of finding a quiet place in the building and away from the office. The Plant Manager also considered the framework advantageous since it allowed him to retain control and responsibility for all decisions, implementations, and communications. However, there are a number of practical risks to this type of longitudinal research in a dynamic changing corporate environment, such as the realities of reorganizations and relocations, which are not pointed out by Mårtensson and Lee.

# 5 Building a Dolmen Using Multiview2

## 5.1 Preliminary Model Development

This section presents the development of a model to address the requirement to manage innovation in the APC-MGE supply chain subsidiary described in Sect. 3. The model emerged from a number of sources: the innovation management literature; the ISD literature with its emphasis on the primacy of contextual factors; the debates on relevance and alignment in the IS literature, and the dialogical action research interactions that took place within a three-month period early in 2007. An innovation assessment, carried out in 2006 using the questionnaire proposed by Tidd et al. (2005), had identified that the subsidiary was a Type 2 firm where they "know they need to change but are unsure about how to bring this about." The Plant Manager recognized that there had been significant innovative activity, especially during a Lean Transformation project, but there was now need for a structured approach to innovation management. In the taxonomy of Tidd et al., this would involve moving initially to a Type firm 3 and finally to Type 4: where a firm sees itself as having the capability to generate and absorb innovation. In order to accomplish this, an MIS would be required to capture and manage the innovations together with a related goal to enable the diffusion of these innovations across the wider Corporation. A preliminary objective was to plan the "2007 Innovation Project" with an associated information system to support the venture. It was decided to use the five dimensions proposed by Tidd et al. as a starting point: strategy, process, organization, linkages, and learning. In terms of the ISD, the Mutiview2 approach was seen to be the most appropriate as the quadrant in Fig. 1 entitled "organizational analysis" is focused on identifying the reasons why the organization requires the IS and understanding the business and social context. A sixth dimension IS/IT was also included that follows the advice to "keep technology present" in the organizational analysis (Avison et al. 1998, p. 131).

## 5.2 Reification – Developing a Metaphor

A stakeholder analysis was carried out to include the main stakeholders and users of the proposed innovation MIS (Avison and Fitzgerald 2003, p. 277) and they were identified as: APC-MGE Castlebar personnel, APC-MGE Castlebar management team, APC-MGE Castlebar supply chain partners, APC-MGE Ireland management team, APC-MGE/Schneider peers, and APC-MGE/Schneider executive decision makers. Finally, the Schneider Annual Report of 2005 was reviewed to check that the innovation project was aligned with the corporate objectives. It was considered that the NEW[7] Schneider Operating Priorities 2005–2008's third objective "Make people passionate about what they do" was significantly aligned to this project and would be now adopted as the project mission statement. A new dimension "environmental performance," was added based on the alignment analysis (Schneider Electric 2005). Another important aspect that emerged was the challenge of communicating the project objectives to the two main audiences: employees in the Castlebar location and the APC-MGE Ireland Management forum. After a number of iterations, and in order to facilitate communication, the model underwent a process of "reification" which resulted in the innovation "Dolmen" that is shown in Fig. 2. Kelly (2005) has suggested that "reification" can contribute to opening "new frontiers" in IS theorization but it must be acknowledged that the concept is the subject of controversial debates in the academic literature which are outside the scope of this chapter. However, it is used here solely as a literary device to describe the development of a metaphor for the management of innovation in this context.

This conceptualization aimed to take a number of factors into account:

- Cultural context: the "Dolmen" analogy is familiar in the West of Ireland and it gives the message of putting in place a system that will endure. A "Dolmen" (from the Breton for "stone table") is an ancient monument, found in many areas of Europe, consisting of two or more upright large stones that support a horizontal capstone.

- The concept seeks to impart the message that the innovation "culture/climate" is supported by a number of critical dimensions.
- Some dimensions are more important than others, e.g. strategy and processes being critical.
- Some attributes closely depended on each other, e.g. strategy and organization.

It was also considered significant that developing the "Dolmen" was aligned with Mintzberg's idea of "strategy as craft" and consistent with his identification of the multiple facets of strategy (Mintzberg 1987).

**Abbreviations**
C = Innovation Culture/Climate
O = Organisation
S = Strategy
$L_k$ = Links
$L_r$ = Learning
$I_{st}$ = Information Systems/ Technology
$E_p$ = Environmental Performance
$P_{sb}$= Supply Chain /Business processes

**Fig. 2.** A representation of the innovation "Dolmen."

This section has described the initial stages of the development of an information system to support innovation management that is cognizant of the organizational, business, and social contextual factors in the APC-MGE subsidiary. Furthermore, an important initial requirement was to ensure that the idea could be communicated to gain the support of the stakeholders which is critical to the success of an innovation project. The approach is aligned with the primacy given in Mutliview2 to organizational analysis (O) and the vision that this "O" perspective is typified by "shared understanding and organizational learning." The chapter will now proceed to discuss the implications arising from the "challenge in practice" outlined in this case.

## 6 Discussion

The previous sections of this chapter have provided an overview of the literature from which this study emerged, the context of the case study, the research approach employed, and the initial ISD model constructed from the organizational analysis of the contextual factors. The chapter will now proceed to propose some implications of the study for both practice and research.

## 6.1 Significance of Work and Implications for Practice

Innovation management is now seen as an important source of competitive advantage for enterprises and MNC subsidiaries located in Ireland's changing economy. The study is located in the Operations function of an MNC at a time when the future of supply chain management (SCM) in Ireland is being questioned. It is argued that the evolution of the APC Ireland supply chain is an important case in this context and "commonalities" can provide lessons for other MNCs in the region. Furthermore, the main objective of the study is to examine the role of IS in supporting the innovation agenda. The work has built on a previous innovation audit that identified areas requiring development, and which provided a reference point to begin the transformation to an innovative organization through development of strategy and roadmaps. In addition, the development of the "Dolmen" concept is in line with use of a "Pentathlon" analogy by Goffin and Mitchell (2005) in their recent work on innovation management.

## 6.2 Implications for Research and Limitation of the Study

This longitudinal study proposes to address a gap in the literature that indicates the need to examine the role of IS in supporting the management of innovation in the context of an MNC subsidiary. The study seeks to build on previous work such as Kelly (2004), which has sought to "understand the potential of ICT to facilitate innovative forms of organizing". In terms of the continuing evolution of Multiview2, the study has provided empirical evidence of engaging in "concept modeling" before the "information modeling" phase shown in Fig. 2 which could contribute to further refining the framework. The use of the "Dolmen" analogy follows Avison and Fitzgerald's argument that the framework can "more usefully be seen as a metaphor which is interpreted and developed in a particular situation" and provides an industry based study to examine this contention. In addition, the case study provides empirical evidence of utilizing dialogical action research recently proposed to the MIS community by Mårtensson and Lee (2004) in the context of an ISD which is regarded as a core topic in the discipline. The study is limited in that it provides a progress report on the development of the preliminary ISD model to capture the contextual factors of this particular case. The model now needs to be examined further to see if the conceptual framework does help to effect an innovative transformation of the organization and has the capability to communicate the vision to the main stakeholders.

# 7 Conclusions

This chapter has addressed the theme of a "challenge in practice" for the IS community by describing the initial stage of an ISD to support the management of innovation in the APC-MGE Irish subsidiary. To begin with, a brief overview was presented of the main literature on which the study was based. The background of the case study was outlined and the advantages of a dialogical action research approach to ISD were discussed. Then the development of a conceptual model, an innovation "Dolmen", utilizing the organizational analysis quadrant of Multiview2 was described. Future work will involve tracking the implementation to provide evidence of its impact and contribution.

# References

Avison, D. E. and Fitzgerald, G. (2003) Information systems development: methodologies, techniques and tools. McGraw-Hill, London.

Avison, D. E., Wood-Harper, A. T., Vidgen, R. T., and Wood, J. R. G. (1998) A further exploration into information systems development: the evolution of Multiview2, *Information Technology & People* 11 (2), 124–139.

Basadur, M. (2004) Managing Creativity: A Japanese Model, In *The Human Side of Managing Technological Innovation: A Collection of Readings* (Katz, R., Ed), Oxford University Press.

Basadur, M. (2006) The Creativity Equation $C = K \times I \times E$ (available on-line at http://www.basadur.com/profile/creativity_eq.htm).

Baskerville, R. and Pries-Heje, J. (2004) Short cycle time systems development. *Information Systems Journal* 14 (3), 237–264.

Beck, K. (1999) Embracing change with extreme programming. *IEEE Computer* 32 (10), 70–77.

Benbasat, I. and Zmud, R. W. (1999) Empirical research in information systems: The practice of relevance. *MIS Quarterly* 23 (1), 3–16.

Boehm, B. (1981) Software Engineering Economics, Prentice Hall, Englewood Cliffs, NJ.

Brooks, F. (1987) No silver bullet: essence and accidents of software engineering. *IEEE Computer* 20 (4), 10–19.

Chesbrough, H. W. (2003) Open innovation: the new imperative for creating and profiting from technology, Harvard Business School, Boston.

Colter, M. (1982) Evolution of the Structured Methodologies. In *Advanced Systems Development Feasibility Techniques* (Al, C. E., Ed), pp. 73–96, Wiley & Sons, New York.

Drucker, P. (2003) The Discipline of Innovation. In *Harvard Business Review on The Innovative Enterprise*, Harvard Business School Press.

Fitzgerald, B. (2000) Systems development methodologies: The problem of tenses. *Information Technology & People* 13 (3), 13–22.

Fitzgerald, B., Russo, N., and Stolterman, E. (2002) *Information Systems Development: Method-in-Action*. McGraw-Hill, Berkshire.

Fowler, M. and Highsmith, J. (2001) The agile manifesto. *Software Development* 9 (8), 28–32.

Glass, R. (1991) *Software Conflict: Essays on the Art and Science of Software Engineering*. Yourdon Press, Prentice Hall, Englewood Cliffs, NJ.

Goffin, K. and Mitchell, R. (2005) *Innovation Management: Strategy and Implementation Using the Pentathlon Framework*. Palgrave Macmillan, Houndmills, Basingstoke.

Herzberg, F. (2003) The best of HBR 1968; one more time: how do you motivate employees? *Harvard Business Review*, 87–96.

Katz, R. (2004) The Motivation of Professionals. In *The Human Side of Managing Technological Innovation: A Collection of Readings* (Katz, R., Ed), Oxford University Press, Oxford.

Kelly, S. (2004) *ICT and Social/Organisational Change: A Praxiological Perspective on Groupware Innovation*. Ph.D. Thesis, University of Cambridge.

Kelly, S. (2005) New frontiers in the theorization of ICT-mediated interaction? Exploring the implications of a situated learning epistemology. *Proc International Conference on Information Systems*, December 11–14: Las Vegas, NV.

Kelly, S. and Murnane, S. (2005) Academic performance evaluation and the organisation of knowledge in the research-intensive university. *The Irish Journal of Management*, Selected papers from the 2005 Irish Academy of Management Conference, pp. 95–109. Blackhall, Dublin.

Leavy, B. (2005) A leader's guide to creating an innovation culture. *Strategy & Leadership* 33 (4), 38–45.

Mårtensson, P. and Lee, A. S. (2004) Dialogical action research at omega corporation. *MIS Quarterly* 28 (3), 507–536.

Mintzberg, H. (1987) Crafting strategy. *Harvard Business Review* 65(4), 66–75(July/August).

Nemeth, C. J. (2004) Managing innovation: When less is more. In *The Human Side of Managing Technological Innovation: A Collection of Readings* (Katz, R., Ed), Oxford University Press.

Overmyer, S. (2000) What's different about requirements engineering for web sites? *Requirements Engineering Journal* 5 (1), 62–65.

Porter, M. (2003) Irish Competitiveness: Entering a New Economic Era. IMI Top Management Briefing, Dublin, Ireland, 9 October 2003 (available online through www.isc.hbs.edu).

Results APCC (2006) American Power Conversion Reports First Quarter 2006 Financial Results (available on-line through http://www.apcc.com/, accessed June 2006).

Schneider Electric (2005) Schneider Electric 2005 Annual Report (available online through http://www.schneider-electric.com/wps/portal/corp/).

Schwaber, K. and Beedle, M. (2002) *Agile Software Development with Scrum*. Prentice-Hall, Englewood Cliffs, NJ.

Tidd, J., Bessant, J., and Pavitt, K. (2005) *Managing Innovation : Integrating Technological, Market and Organizational Change*. John Wiley & Sons, Chichester.

Trauth, E. M. (2000) *The Culture of an Information Economy: Influences and Impacts in the Republic of Ireland*. Kluwer Academic Publishers, Norwell, MA.

Tushman, M. L. and O'Reilly, C. (2004) The Ambidextrous Organization: Managing Evolutionary and Revolutionary Change. In *Managing Strategic Innovation and Change: A Collection of Readings* (Tushman, M. L. and Anderson, P., Eds), Oxford University Press, Oxford.

Ward, P. (1992) The evolution of structured analysis: Part II—Maturity and its problems. *American Programmer* 5 (4), 18–29.

Yin, R. K. (1994) *Case Study Research: Design and Methods*. Sage Publications, London.

Yourdon, E. (1997) *Death March*. Prentice Hall, Upper Saddle River, NJ.

Zien, K. A. and Buckler, S. A. (2004) Dreams to Market: Crafting a culture of innovation. In *The Human Side of Managing Technological Innovation: A Collection of Readings* (Katz, R., Ed), Oxford University Press, Oxford.

# The Role of Improvisation and Politics in ISD Practice

Karlheinz Kautz, Hans-Kristian Jørgensen, Casper Pedersen, Michael Sinnet and Sameen Rab

Department of Informatics, Copenhagen Business School, Howitzvej 60, DK-2000 Frederiksberg, Denmark, karl.kautz@cbs.dk, {hajo03ab, cape03ac, misi03ab, sara03ad}@student.cbs.dk

**Abstract**   The research described in this chapter investigates the role of improvisation and politics in information systems development (ISD) practice. It takes its starting point in a case study in which a large Danish software vendor is handed over an IT system from a large international software corporation. As part of an ISD project the system in question was to be ported to a new technical platform as well as documented for further development. We provide a rich description of the socio-technical interplay that takes place during the project by following human and non-human actors, and by analyzing the impact this interplay has on improvised decisions and actions in the project. Using Actor Network Theory (ANT) and a theory of improvised action, we map out translations that contribute to the development of unstable actor-networks and in many cases take part in triggering improvised actions. As it turns out, several of the improvised actions lead to further improvisations, which—once again—affect and shape the socio-technical interplay in the case study. Our work confirms that ISD projects face a lot of its challenges because they are driven by political motivation against better judgment. It verifies and extends prior research on the opportunistic and improvised nature of ISD and also sheds some light on the—problematic—role of external consultants.

## 1 Introduction

The aim of this chapter is to contribute to a better understanding of information systems development (ISD) in practice. Since its beginning ISD has struggled with unfinished projects, resource problems, erroneous systems, and systems with lacking functionality. Numerous attempts to solve these problems by introducing technical remedies have only lead to limited success. ISD is traditionally recognized as a technical process and dominated by normative techno-centric and engineering approaches. Recent research has, however, recognized that ISD is not just a rational, methodical, and controlled process, but more what some would call

C. Barry et al. (eds.), *Information Systems Development: Challenges in Practice, Theory, and Education, Vol.1*, doi: 10.1007/978-0-387-68772-8_33,
© Springer Science+Business Media, LLC 2009

an adaptive (Highsmith 2000), amethodical (Truex et al. 2000), agile (Cockburn 2002), emergent (Madsen et al. 2006), or improvised process (Bansler and Havn 2003, 2004) in which politics has long been recognized as a vital influence (see e.g., Markus 1983; Andersen et al. 1986).

However, ISD practice is still poorly understood as a social activity. Research in the field is largely ahistorical, acontextual, and aprocessual, which has lead to a fragmented understanding and limited advances in practice. There is a need for a sustainable understanding based on extensive, empirical field work (Kautz 2004).

With this chapter we want to contribute to this body of knowledge. The research described in this chapter investigates, in particular, the role of improvisation and politics in ISD practice. It is based on a case study of an ISD project in a large Danish software company. We provide a rich description of the socio-technical interplay that takes place during the project by following human and non-human actors and by analyzing the impact this interplay has had on improvised decisions and actions in the project.

For this purpose we are applying Actor Network Theory (ANT; Callon 1986, 1991; Latour 1987, 1992, 2005; Law 1988, 1992), which has been applied in IS research before (see e.g., Aanestad 2003; Mitev 1996; McMaster et al. 1997; Quattrone and Hopper, 2006 to name just a few) and a theory of improvised action (Ciborra 1999) as theoretical perspectives and we demonstrate the benefits and appropriateness of these—individual and combined—perspectives to get a deeper understanding of ISD.

This chapter is structured as follows. The next section outlines the ANT as our research approach and Sect. 3 introduces a theory of improvisation as our theoretical background. Sect. 4 contains the case description and analysis subdivided into the four chronological phases of the project. Based on our analysis we end the chapter with a discussion and some reflections on improvisation, politics, and ANT in Sect. 5.

# 2 Using ANT as Research Approach

The research reported in this chapter investigates an ISD project that has involved a number of persons, organizations, and non-human actors who have had different relations to the project. The mapping of these relations is of significant importance to understand the involvement of different actors in the project, because a separation of different concepts is only meaningful when they are seen in relation to other concepts (Jensen 2003). The actor "developer," for instance, only gains significance by virtue of the difference to "project manager" and because of its difference to "user."

ANT is a social theory which focuses on the actors' relations that establish the coherence in a network (Latour 2005). We agree with Walsham (1997) that ANT is both a theory and a research methodology. It looks at stable networks and concentrates on changes of existing relations and the establishment of new ones. These changes of relations are identified through the narrative that ANT tells—a narrative told by the actors (Latour 2005) which makes it the appropriate background for our research.

**Table 1.** Key ANT concepts

| ANT concepts | Our understanding of the concepts |
| --- | --- |
| Actor or actant | Both human beings and non-human actors (persons, systems, documents). Corresponds to a network which is stable, predictable, and appear as a "black box." |
| Actor-network | Heterogeneous collection of relations including people, organizations, and technology. |
| Translation | The establishment of a relation between actors who were not connected before. When an actor mediates another actor into a network or when the actors in the network create a new actor. |
| Enrolment | A part of a translation when an actor seeks to influence another actor to act in a particular manner. |
| Inscription | A transformation of substances into inscriptions, e.g., when interests are inscribed into written material. |
| Delegate | An actor who represents interests of other actors. |

ANT assumes no a priori distinction between human and non-human actors—to emphasize this, both are called *actants*—and sees them as active makers of actor-networks. When we utilize ANT it is important to make the distinction between the concepts network and actor. Jensen (2003) explains that an actor is a network that has become stable, predictable, and appears as a *black box*. At times one considers a department in a company as an actor—at other times the whole company is seen as constituting an actor. This depends on how the network is put together, which leads to the concept of *translation*. Latour (2005) describes translation as "a relation that does not transport causality but induces two mediators into coexisting." This coexisting seeks to align interests working toward the achievement of a common goal; for example, when a software vendor develops a system on the basis of the requirements of a customer, a relation is established between two actors who previously had different goals. To achieve this relation it is often required to *enroll* the actors to establish shared interests and characteristics (Jensen 2003). In this way the actors can be disciplined and forced to act in a particular manner.

ANT can overall be utilized as a conceptual framework that allows the mapping of relations in an actor-network (Jensen 2003). To ensure that we do not loose sight of the perspective of associations, we use a number of concepts—translations, inscriptions, enrolment—and we consider ANT to be a salient basis for our analysis of the investigated ISD project by providing a structured way to describe the relations and dependencies of different actors. Our understanding of the key ANT concepts is inspired by Walsham (1997) and Abrahall et al. (2006) and is summarized in Table 1.

The empirical basis for our research is built by eight recorded and transcribed interviews with developers and managers involved in the project. They were conducted within a two-month period in 2006. Put together as quite a complex and at times dramatic narrative (Fincham 2002), this qualitative data leads us to an interpretive research and analysis method characterized by direct quotes and visual representations of actors, networks, and events.

To create an overview of the case we use a graphical time line inspired and earlier used to depict ISD projects by Dittrich and Lindeberg (2003) and by Madsen et al. (2006). The timeline illustrates actors entering and leaving the project together with important events shaping the project and often provoking translations. It is aimed at giving a general idea of the case study representing a puzzle assembled by many different pieces during the data collection. As a result, we have been able to divide the case study into four phases. Following Abrahall et al. (2006) we also depict the identified and analyzed ANTs in a graphical form.

# 3 A Theory of Improvisation in ISD

As a theoretical lens, Ciborra's (1999) work helped us to define and characterize improvisations as the main driver of the development process in the case study. Ciborra (1999) defines improvisation as a situation where "thinking and action emerge simultaneously and on the spur of the moment." Despite the clarity of the definition, improvisation is hard to typecast. Ciborra (1999) puts up three different surroundings in which improvisation within organizations may occur:

Improvisation in emergencies
Improvisation in work organizations
Improvisation on markets.

Ciborra (1999) cites Nachmanovitch (1990) and puts forward that "improvisation is simultaneously rational and unpredictable; planned and emergent; purposeful and blurred; effective and irreflexive; perfectly discernible after the fact, but spontaneous in its manifestation." He argues that any improvised action is carried out in accordance with a vision about its result on reality. There are two motives for an improvised action:

The *In-order-to motive*—Actors act according to a project's rational artifacts like plans, goals and means; these are the immediate controls of the action and its official justification.

The *Because-of motive*—Actors act according to their experience and personal interests; these tacit motives represent the actual intention with the act.

The moment of vision or in Ciborra's words "Der Augenblick" is often decisive for an improvisation which frequently occurs when new actants originate or get involved in networks. We will, therefore, focus on Der Augenblick by looking at the motives and identify the situation, prior to and after, to understand the course of the investigated project.

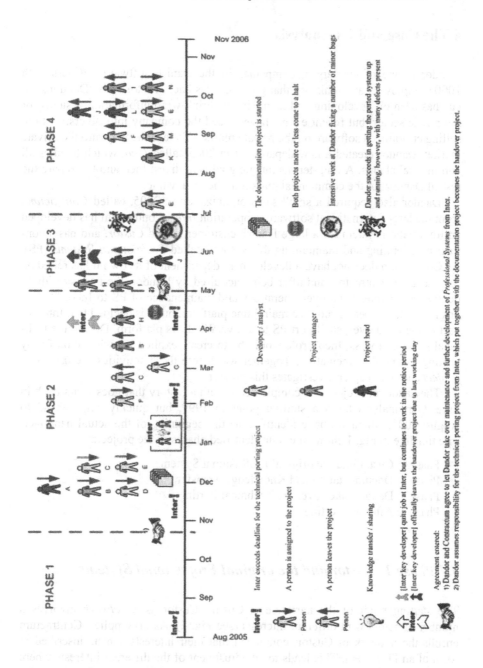

**Fig. 1.** The timeline of the handover project.

## 4 The Case and Its Analysis

Dandor is one of the largest companies in the Danish software business with 1000+ employees and a history that goes decades back. Historically, Dandor's focus has been on developing and maintaining shrink-wrap information systems for the public sector, but recent events have forced the company into diversification: selling customized software on the private market. To lead the way into the private market, Dandor created a new department in 2005 called *Ineo*, which handles all commercial clients. A long-term strategic goal is to divest Ineo and to prepare the rest of Dandor for the commercial market in the meanwhile.

Dandor also acquired a small sales organization in 2005, called *Contractum*, from the large international software cooperation *Inter*. Contractum has developed an information system for a large Danish customer, called *Custor*, and has a contract on operating and maintaining this system, called *Professional Systems* (PS). As Contractum does not have a development department of its own it has relied on Inter as a subcontractor, and after being acquired by Dandor, the new subsidiary decides to let Inter hand over operations and maintenance of PS to Ineo. PS was originally developed to run on a mainframe platform, but it is decided that Inter, as part of the hand over, shall port PS to a Java/Windows platform. During the technical porting process, Ineo's role would be to create explicit knowledge on PS by writing formal documentation. Together we denote these activities the *handover project* and our chapter investigates this project.

The handover project is a complex case with a history that goes years back in time. Our analysis takes a starting point in 1999, but quickly skips ahead to August 2005, which we have identified as the beginning of the actual handover. The timeline in Fig. 1 shows the four identified phases of the project:

Phase 1: Custor and the original Professional Systems
Phase 2: Documentation and Knowledge Transfer
Phase 3: Dandor takes over the Technical Porting
Phase 4: After the Porting

### *4.1 Phase 1: Custor and the original Professional Systems*

The starting point of the narrative is Custor. Custor as a *network* involves a number of actors with different interests (see Fig. 2). As IT-supplier, Contractum enrolls the network of Custor, convinced that their interests can be inscribed in form of an IT-system. This leads to an adjustment of the different interests where Contractum seeks to cut off the immediate opponents of IT. In 1999, Custor decides to let Contractum develop the IT-system PS, which demonstrates Contractum's success in persuading Custor.

The same year the contract is entered and the initial development is started—a large Danish vendor buys Contractum. This event results in a remarkable change and translates Contractum into a new actor with new interests. Even though the buyer has a professional background, this is not evident from the development process and documentation standard of PS as a Dandor project manager comments: "I was actually surprised that a department in such a big corporation could function without any use of methods or standards and just developed the system using the quick and dirty principles [...]"

In 2002, Custor starts using PS and that year it also initiates an operating agreement with Dandor. In 2004, Inter buys the large Danish vendor and as a result of this trade Contractum becomes a part of Inter. It seems that Contractum has no place in Inter's future plans as the small company is resold to Dandor already in 2005. Contractum as an actor clearly does not get a chance to be a part of the network of Inter. Acquiring Contractum appears to be a purely political decision and it plays a significant role in Dandor's adjustments towards the private market. Phase 1 ends with the event that marks the change to phase 2: Ineo as part of Dandor agrees to take over the maintenance of PS from Inter. As Dandor's operating department already has its own independent agreement with Custor, it is important to highlight the difference of Ineo's agreement with Contractum as its IT-supplier and Contractum as the contract owner and supplier to Custor.

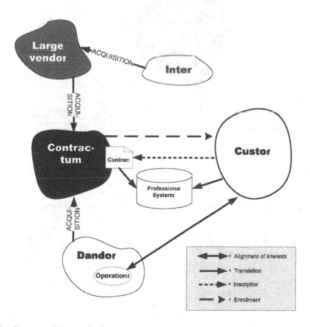

**Fig. 2.** Actor Network diagram—phase 1.

## 4.2 Phase 2: Documentation and Knowledge Transfer

In October 2005, Ineo accepts to take over the further development and maintenance of PS and thus translates Custor into its actor-network—a decision that is a
matter of opinion: "[...] [Dandor] says to the customer, that we are able to take
over the project. This statement is based on miserable foundation, I think." as a
project manager puts it.

The network between Dandor (including Ineo and Operations) and Custor is
based on the wish to port PS to another technical platform (see Fig. 3). Inter, the
current supplier of PS, bears the responsibility of porting PS. Although the actors
agree upon the porting project, they all have quite different interests and intentions
regarding the project. These interests are important when considering the stability
of the established actor-network. *Custor*—the customer— has intentions of making PS future-proof without compromising the stability of the system. They cooperate with an actor-network of IT vendors which have an interest in improving the
IT-infrastructure of Custor.

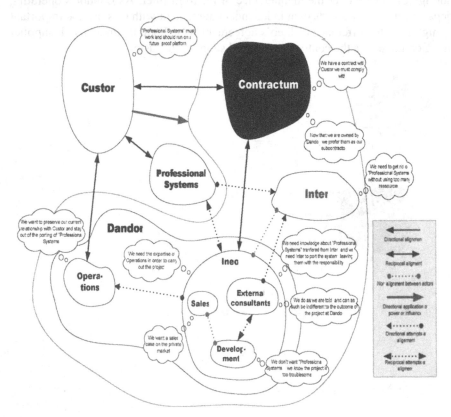

**Fig. 3.** Actor Network diagram—phase 2.

*Dandor* as a "black box" is not of further interest. Therefore, the company is divided into a number of organizational units. *Ineo*—the main character in this narrative—is in fact an unstable actor-network consisting of:

*Sales*, which establishes the agreement with Custor and wants to do well on the commercial market.

*Development*, which is responsible for the handover project from the Dandor perspective. They are not interested in the given assignment. This leads to a conflict of interests with Sales as this missing alignment causes the actor-network of Ineo to be unstable.

*External consultants* are the solution to the missing qualifications in Ineo. The consultants, who make up half of the project group, function as an integrated part of Ineo, but do not have the same interest in the long-term success of the company compared with the permanent employees.

The decision to hire external consultants can be described as an improvisational in-order-to action that causes transformation of the actor-network in Ineo and is justified by the project's need for qualified personnel. But the underlying because-of motives are quite different. Being in a new market Dandor and Ineo want to be seen as professionals at solving assignments for commercial customers—which is why they decide to buy the service of external consultants. However, in the improvisational moment, Ineo has not fully considered the consequences of the use of external consultants. The fact that external consultants only are available for a limited period of time turns out to be a problem later in the project, as the knowledge they acquire is not made explicit.

Contractum holds the Custor contract. As Contractum does not have a development department, they have come to an agreement with Inter who assumes responsibility of porting PS. Although Inter wants to get rid of PS as quickly as possible, they accept and require their key developer of PS to do the technical porting and share his knowledge.

These different interests in the project indicate that there are several actors in the network who are not aligned. Especially, the missing alignment between Sales and Development gives the handover project an unstable foundation.

In December 2005, the documentation project is launched. The project's main purpose is to gather as much information as possible to maintain and develop PS in the future. Ineo puts a project manager, a method expert, and two external developers working onsite at Inter on the project. Despite high expectations, the assignment given to the developers is not quite concrete and it is hard for them to gain the necessary knowledge in the period they spend at Inter. One developer said: "[…] we just sat and twiddled our thumbs—to be honest."

The two developers do not get the chance to participate in the required activities as deeply as they are supposed to. They also question the appropriateness of the documentation method, but try to document their gained knowledge by following the required standard. However, they are not very successful. This failed attempt of knowledge sharing was by some respondents described as politically motivated: Dandor not wanting to get too involved in the project! In February 2006, Inter fails in another attempt to port PS, another deadline is crossed and several project participants are worried about the success of the project. Several unsatisfactory elements in the project lead to the removal of Ineo's current project manager. This is an internal political move toward the Sales department who made the initial agreement. The enrollment of Sales causes another improvisational action—the sales department puts the head of sales in the position as project manager.

Looking at the in-order-to-motive behind this improvisational action, it appears that the project from a professional point of view can not be without a project manager. The because-of-motive is, however, political, as the sales department does not want to close the project, but wants to force Development to find a qualified project manager on a permanent basis. The new project manager lacks the required qualifications in project leadership; thus, he lets the project members manage their work on their own, but he handles the contact with the customer well and solves the problems that occurred regarding the contract.

As a new actor in the network the head of sales gets involved in an essential moment in the project: the key developer at Inter resigns his position. This worries Dandor as the main knowledge is possessed by this person. The resignation leads to a cessation of the technical porting project and a deadline is again crossed. Dandor attends several meetings with other actors, where it is decided that the responsibility of the technical porting now lies at Dandor. This leads to phase 3.

### 4.3 Phase 3: Dandor takes over the Technical Porting

As Inter is not successful in porting PS and Dandor gets assigned the further responsibility of maintenance, the head of sales decides to improvise and take over the technical porting (see Fig. 4). Dandor takes over the technical porting in-order-to be successful where Inter has failed, but the actual motives are that Ineo is eager to get a successful case in the private market. Unfortunately, it turns out that Ineo has not got the necessary resources and is again forced to hire external consultants. "[…] It is not a deliberate transfer […] there is a considerate underestimate of the possible problems […] on both suppliers' and customers' side. No doubt about that!" as a project manager explains.

As another improvisation, a new external project manager is hired. The reason for this improvisation is apparently to get the project running, but the because-of motives are that she comes directly from Custor and that the prior project manager has not got the required competencies. By hiring this external project manager Ineo hopes to benefit from the consultant's former relationship with the customer.

Ineo tries to further enroll Inter by inscribing an agreement on the use of resources for knowledge transfer for a month-long period after project closure. Unfortunately, the key developer at Inter has decided to leave the company which obliterates the alignment of interests between Inter and Ineo, and Ineo is left with a critical need for knowledge. During May 2006, there is intense co-operation between Ineo and Inter where much time is used to understand and document PS before the developer's departure.

In the beginning of May 2006, the differentiation between the technical porting, originally Inter's responsibility, and the document project, Ineo's responsibility, ceases to exist, as the two projects merge into the *handover project*. Difficulties arise as Ineo lacks resources with database knowledge, but due to time constraints this problem is postponed as the knowledge transfer has to finish before the key developer at Inter leaves. The project participants at Ineo insist that Inter originally was responsible for the porting and thus responsible for the time limitation and criticize the system's documentation as obscure. Even so, both parts agree that PS is a complex system requiring extra competencies and time.

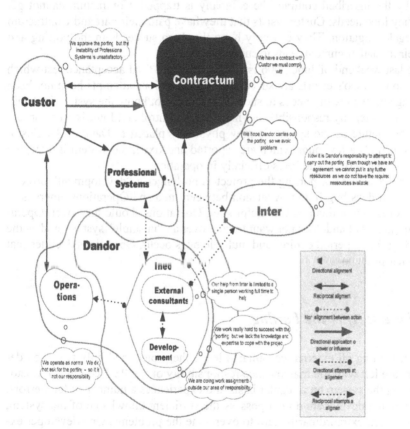

**Fig. 4.** Actor Network diagram—phase 3.

Management issues also appear, according to the project manager saying that management "are engaged when face-to-face, but after meetings Custor is a small customer again." This indicates that the project, as it is run under Ineo, is isolated from the rest of Dandor. Inter also questions the interest of Dandor's management in the project as most of the responsible management has been absent, but appreciates that Dandor at least sent its technical personnel to participate in the knowledge transfer.

In the meantime, Custor has started using the system and has set aside time for a weekend test which is postponed several times. This creates frustration and results in Custor halting funds. Custor's major concern is that PS is unstable, as the different parts of the system are not interacting without errors. To sustain the daily operation, solutions to reported problems are on request frequently improvised. As one developer said: "Custor is often on the phone: 'this does not work and that does not work.' [...] make it work [..] without a thorough analysis of the problem, just make it work."

Custor wants the working system they have paid for and as Contractum is bound by the inscribed contract the company is trapped. Contractum cannot get the money Ineo needs; Custor insists that they have paid their part and Contractum has a legal obligation. They can only hope that Ineo succeeds in the porting and that their mutual alignment leads to success.

The last weekend of June 2006 is agreed to be the final acceptance test which has to show if Ineo's efforts are successful. Four previous attempts have not been satisfying and Ineo really needs to succeed but does not know the system in detail. Contractum is legally responsible, but has limited control and Inter is more or less out of the picture as the system is now physically placed at Dandor. As Custor tests PS, it finds a few bugs which are reported and fixed, the system is accepted and the porting is over, and PS is officially in operation.

After the successful porting the project is no longer a "development" project, but Ineo still does bug fixing. A tension between Ineo and Operations emerges as Ineo believes that at this point in the project, Operations should take over. Operations on the other hand does not want to take over an "unstable" system, and as the agreed bug fixing period expires and multiple bugs occur, Operations declines that this is their problem.

## 4.4 Phase 4: After the Porting

After the porting all external consultants leave the project and only two Ineo developers are left with the maintenance responsibility of the PS (see Fig. 5). Custor starts using the system on a regular basis and experiences a number of fatal errors. The remaining developers do not possess the sufficient knowledge of the system, thus they work extraordinarily hard to overcome the problems. One developer expresses his feelings as "[...] It was awful being left in the lurch like that."

The project manager returns after some weeks and puts in an extra effort to help these developers. But some confusion concerning responsibilities starts to appear between Ineo and the collaborating actors Contractum, Inter and in particular Operations, as their original maintenance assignment has become a regular task for Ineo. Ineo management through their head of projects calls representatives from all parties to a meeting and succeeds to clarify the responsibilities.

The project manager decides to leave when her contract expires. This translates a new project manager into Ineo's network in August 2006. This project manager undertakes the task of enrolling all Custor management, the preceding failed attempt of knowledge transfer described by the Dandor manager as "A lot of errors occurred because of the failed knowledge transfer from the external consultants to our internal employee," and forces Ineo to rehire the key external consultant to transfer the necessary knowledge to a new developer at Ineo. This stabilizes the PS and improves the knowledge about the system in Ineo.

As the new project manager is still considered a trainee, Ineo hires an additional new and experienced project manager in October 2006 as a complementary project manager to deal with Custor. This proves to be a good decision as the Dandor manager confirms, "[The new project manager] has a great influence on the cooperation between the different suppliers or at least all stakeholders— including both internal and external relationships with Contractum and towards the customer."

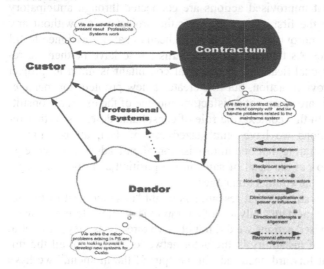

**Fig. 5.** Actor Network diagram—phase 4.

Even though the system has been challenging for Ineo it is relatively stable today. After a successful enrolment of each relevant actor, the network taking care of the system also appears to be stable—with Inter out of the picture and Dandor representing a black box that strives to fulfill its agreements with Custor.

## 5 Reflections on Improvisation, Politics, and ANT

Our narrative describes a project characterized by frequent replacement of actors, unclear assignments of responsibilities, and unfortunate outcomes. Using ANT as a theoretical lens, we have come to an understanding of the interplay between the actors in the process. Due to conflicts of interest the overall actor-network is unstable from the beginning, but politics motivated by the desire to acquire a large customer drives forward the process; in the words of a developer "[...] But it is due to some political reasons, I think. One will probably find them with a little digging. They want Custor as a customer to get other assignments through the door [...]."

Our case study shows how unstable networks and non-aligned interests of actors lead to improvised actions. By hiring external consultants, Ineo solves the problem of a lack of human resources through improvisation, but this leads to another problem: The knowledge gained by the consultants must be transferred to the permanent staff. This is solved by letting the consultants write formalized documentation, but as this codification and externalization turns out to be inadequate, permanent staff is added to the project in order to transfer knowledge through personalization and socialization instead (Hansen et al. 1999; Nonaka and Takeuchi 1995).

It also illustrates that improvised actions are connected through anticipatory feedback. By removing the first project manager the project is left without any management, and in an improvised turn of events a head of sales is assigned to fill the project manager role. As the head of sales turns out to have neither the required time nor proper qualifications, an external consultant is hired as project manager in a new improvised action, but this creates a new problem for management: formalized reports are again not satisfactory and one of the external consultants has to be re-hired. In this context, the role of consultants deserves further research. The improvisations we have emphasized can, in fact, all be chained together in pairs demonstrating that one improvisation often leads to another, e.g., the improvised action to put the head of sales in the position as project manager leads to employment of a new project manager.

While Ciborra (1999) stresses that researchers might "miss the heat of the action" when doing a "post mortem analysis" of an improvisation, we found it meaningful to analyze improvised actions we did not observe directly as they turn out to be an important source of instability in the actor-networks. While not all the improvisations we brought forward occurred "in the spur of the moment," we have been able to characterize them all in terms of Ciborra's concepts, and by putting ourselves in Der Augenblick we have been able to better understand the reasons behind improvised decisions.

The handover project proved more challenging for Ineo than anyone had expected. The project was initiated against the recommendations of several preliminary analyses resulting in a number of complicated technical issues which had to be resolved. Such issues are, however, not uncommon for software companies, and the ANT analysis shows that it was on the political level the "real" problems existed. By describing the interplay between people, organizations, and non-human actors, this chapter reveals a process of politics, emergencies, and lack of co-operation. The complex interplay described has lead to several improvised actions. Our research shows that one improvisation often leads to another, as is the case when Dandor takes over the technical porting from Inter at the culmination of our narrative. While Inter's because-of motives are simply to get rid of the project, Dandor wants to demonstrate to itself, to its customers, and to the external environment that it can handle the situation.

The nature of ANT has allowed us to create a rich description of a complex process in terms of the actors—and to a high extent in their own words—without at the same time having to analyze and criticize every event. However, due to ANT being more of a broad theory and less a specific, well defined research method, our understanding and definitions of the ANT terms can be challenged. There is a great variation in how much we use these terms during the narrative, and while this might have lead to a slightly inconsistent analysis, it has been important for us to follow the actors through the unfolding narrative.

We have put great emphasis on visualizing the evolution of the actor-networks during the phases through graphical illustrations. Some of these illustrations are so complicated that they might be difficult to understand. Still—after all they depict a very messy process—we consider the visualizations a valuable companion of the textual ANT analysis.

In conclusion, our research confirms and extends prior research on the emergent, opportunistic, and improvised nature of ISD (Bansler and Havn 2003, 2004; Madsen et al. 2006; Truex et al. 2000;) and shows the appropriateness of ANT and the theory of improvised action (Ciborra 1999) for such studies and understanding.

# References

Aanestad, M. (2003) The Camera as an Actor: Design-in-use of Telemedicine Infrastructure in Surgery. Computer Supported Cooperative Work 12, 1–20.

Andersen, N. E., Kensing, F., Lassen, M., Lundin, J., Mathiassen, L., Munk-Madsen, A., and Sørgaard, P. (1986) *Professional Systems Development, Experience, Ideas and Action* (in Danish). Teknisk Forlag, Copenhagen.

Abrahall, R., Cecez-Kecmanovic, D., and Kautz, K. (2006) Understanding Strategic ISD Projects in Practice—An ANT Account of Success and Failure. *Proceedings of 15th International Conference on Information Systems Developments, Methods & Tools—Theory & Practice*, Budapest, Hungary.

Bansler, J. and Havn, E. (2003) Improvisation in Action: Making Sense of IS Development in Organizations. *Proceedings of the International Workshop on Action in Language, Organisations and Information Systems (ALOIS 2003)*, pp. 51–63.

Bansler, J. and Havn, E. (2004) Improvisation in information systems development. *Information Systems Research: Relevant Theory and Informed Practice*, Proceedings of IFIP TC8/WG8.2 20th Year Retrospective, Manchester, July 15–27, 2004, Kluwer Academic Publishers Group, pp. 631–646.

Callon, M. (1986) Some Elements of a Sociology of Translation: Domestication of the Scallops and the Fisherman of St. Brieuc Bay. In: Law , J. (Ed.) *Power, Action and Belief: A New Sociology of Knowledge?* Routledge, London.

Callon, M. (1991) Techno-economic Network and Irreversibility. In: Law, J. (Ed.), *A Sociology of Monsters. Essays on Power, Technology and Domination*. Routledge, London, pp. 132–164.

Ciborra, C. (1999) Notes on improvisation and time in organizations. Accounting, Management & Information Technologies 9, 77–94.

Cockburn, A. (2002). *Agile Software Development*. Addison Wesley/Pearson Education, New York.

Dittrich, Y. and Lindeberg, O. (2003) How use-oriented development can take place. Information and Software Technology 46, 603–617.

Fincham, R. (2002) Narratives of success and failure in systems development. British Journal of Management 13, 1–14.

Hansen, M. T., Nohria, N., and Tierney, T. (1999) What is your strategy for managing knowledge. Harvard Business Review March–April, 106–116.

Highsmith, J. (2000). *Adaptive Software Development: A Collaborative Approach to Managing Complex Systems*. Dorset House, New York.

Jensen, T. (2003) Actor Network Theory—A Sociology of common knowledge, cargo vessels and scallops (in Danish). *Papers in Organization*, No 48, Online: http://ep.lib.cbs.dk/paper/ISBN/x656378343.

Kautz, K. (2004) The Enactment of Methodology—The Case of Developing a MultiMedia Information System. *Proceedings of the International Conference on Information Systems*, Washington, DC, USA, December 12–15.

Latour, B. (1987). *Science in Action: How to Follow Scientists and Engineers through Society*. Cambridge, Harvard University Press.

Latour, B. (1991). Technology is Society Made Durable. In: Law, J. (Ed.), *A Sociology of Monsters. Essays on Power, Technology and Domination*. Routlegde, London, pp 103–131.

Latour, B. (2005) *Reassembling the Social: An Introduction to Actor-Network-Theory*. Oxford University Press.

Law, J. (1988) The Anatomy of Socio-Technical Struggle: The Design of the TSR2. In: Elliot, B. (Ed.), *Technology and Social Processes*, Edinburgh University Press.

Law, J. (1992) Notes on the Theory of the Actor-Network: Ordering, Strategy and Heterogeneity. Systems Practice 5 (4), 379–393.

Madsen, S., Kautz, K., and Vidgen R. (2006) A framework for understanding how a unique and local IS development method emerges in practice. European Journal of Information Systems 15 (2), 225–238.

Markus, M.L. (1983). Power, politics, and MIS implementation. CACM 26 (6), 430–444.

McMaster, T., Vidgen, R. T., and Wastell, D. G. (1997) Technology Transfer—Diffusion or Translation, In: T. McMaster, E. Mumford, E. B. Swanson, B. Warboys, and D. Wastell (Eds.), *Facilitating Technology Transfer Through Partnership: Learning from Practice and Research*. Chapman and Hall, London, pp. 64–75.

Mitev, N.N. (1996) More than a failure? The computerized reservation systems at French Railways. Information Technology and People 9 (4), 8–19.

Nachmanovitch, S. (1990) *Free play-improvisation in life and art*. Putnam, New York.

Nonaka, I. and Takeuchi, H. (1995) *The knowledge creating company*. Oxford University Press, Oxford.

Quattrone, P., and Hopper, T. (2006) What is IT? SAP, accounting, and the visibility in a multinational organization. Information and Organization 16, 212–250.

Walsham, G. (1997). Actor-network theory and IS research: current status and future prospects, *Proceedings of the IFIP TC8 WG 8.2 International Conference on Information Systems and Qualitative Research*, pp. 466–480.

Truex, D., Baskerville, R., and Travis, J. (2000) Amethodical Systems Development: The Deferred Meaning of Systems Development Methods. Accounting, Management & Information Technologies 10, 53–79.

# Designing Job Descriptions for Software Development

Jack Downey

University of Limerick, Lero, the Irish Software Engineering Research Centre
jack.downey@ul.ie

**Abstract**   This chapter presents an approach to creating job descriptions for roles within software development project teams. An artifact-centric skill framework has been created, which suggests a way that companies can create meaningful job descriptions based on the artifacts persons work on and the people they cooperates with. This chapter will describe the framework, before presenting real-world example job descriptions and their equivalent artifact-centric variants.

## 1 Introduction

According to Shapero (1985), "the most important management decision in the conduct of professional activities is hiring" (p. 1). Although it might be pre-mature to describe software development as a professional activity (Ford and Gibbs 1996), attracting and retaining good software developers is well worth while. As DeMarco and Lister (1999) assert, the best software people outperform the worst by a factor of 10.

Although "it is impossible to turn hiring into a science" (Fernandez-Araoz 1999, p. 109), there are recognized stages to the process, one of which is the creation of job descriptions. Unfortunately, there "can never be a 'standard' job description because the tasks and responsibilities vary" from company to company (Casteleyn 1996, p. 3). This is very much the case in the software domain. Yet it should be possible to create an adequate job description by carrying out job analysis (Hackman and Oldham 1980). There are several techniques available to do this (Casteleyn 1996): observing someone carrying out the job, interviewing the person who has the job, interviewing that person's immediate manager, or identifying the purpose of the job and deciding what activities are required to achieve this purpose.

Most of these are possible only if the goal is to describe an existing role. However, it should be remembered that people are not interchangeable and what one person does may reflect the skill set of an individual practitioner and may not apply to someone else in, ostensibly, the same role. Also, if the job being described

C. Barry et al. (eds.), *Information Systems Development: Challenges in Practice, Theory, and Education, Vol.1*, doi: 10.1007/978-0-387-68772-8_34,
© Springer Science+Business Media, LLC 2009

is for a position that is not already filled, developing a description becomes even more difficult.

It seems that job descriptions should be of more concern to human resource managers than to software developers. However, human resource people are not usually able to specify the technical content of software positions and require input from the software managers.

It might be for this reason that job advertisements in the software industry tend to emphasize technologies rather than knowledge, skills, and abilities (Litecky et al. 2004). For instance, the following is an advertisement for a systems architect, taken from a recruitment web-site:

*"As part of a small tightly knit team, using cutting edge technology you will Design/Architect, Implement and Deploy Internet based software solutions, from the ground up, using .net, windows forms, xml & c#.*
*You should be able to implement OO based solutions and have good problem solving skills, along with excellent interpersonal skills and the ambition and energy to assist a small start up company become a global leader in their sector!*
*You will be an EC Citizen, already living in Ireland, with native level fluency in English and educated to 3rd level in IT.*
*Consistent performers can expect stock options in the company.*

*Skills & Experience required:*
*You should have strong software development experience with a minimum of 2 years using:*
- *.net*
- *c#*
- *xml*
- *VB*
- *windows forms*
- *web based development"*

Given the vagueness of the advertisement itself, it is unlikely that the company has much experience in recruiting staff. The main feature of the advertisement is its list of technologies, but it is not clear what the successful candidate is expected to do with those technologies. For instance, the job title is for a systems architect. However, the job description suggests that the company wants a programmer, not an architect. Also, mention that it is "a small start up company" suggests that the role will be a lot more extensive than that presented here. Potential interviewees would be wise to probe what requirements and feasibility processes are in place. They should also inquire about who creates the documentation and training artifacts. It also seems likely that this company does not have an independent test group or a dedicated customer support organization.

It should be possible to provide a better description than this. Research has been done on the skills required in this sector, but the tendency has been to group all the roles under one heading. For instance, the British Office for National Statistics places team leaders, systems architects, software developers, and testers under the same heading—standard occupational classification code 2132 (Office for National Statistics 2000). Similarly, Irish studies (that make use of the British codes) offer recommendations for the Information and Communications Technology (ICT) sector as a whole (Enterprise Strategy Group 2004; Forfas 2003).

Professional bodies have also avoided role distinctions. The Irish Computer Society (2006) is promoting the use of the Skills Framework for an Information Age (SFIA Foundation 2006). This framework provides a list of 78 skills and asks practitioners to assess themselves on each one. They can then plan their development by improving existing skills or by gaining new ones. However, what constitutes an ideal skills profile for a particular role is not discussed.

The next section of this chapter presents the artifact-centric skill framework, the culmination of a three-year research project, where a total of 38 software practitioners were interviewed in order to gain insights into the knowledge, skills, and abilities needed to develop software. With an understanding of the framework, the third section attempts to create artifact-centric job descriptions, for example, job advertisements, including that illustrated above. The concluding section will acknowledge that the framework does not provide a boilerplate for job descriptions; instead it offers a technique that can be tailored by individual organizations.

# 2 The Artifact-centric Skill Framework

Downey and Power (2007) describes a research study that investigated the skills required to develop software. The research design is fully described in Downey (2005) and is only briefly summarized here. A pilot study was carried out to validate the interview instrument used. This highlighted the need to reduce the scope of the project to a single industry. Because the interviewees from a telecommunications background had the best defined process, it was decided to concentrate on this domain. Thus, individual members of project teams in four different telecommunications software companies were interviewed and the resulting data were analyzed qualitatively using a grounded theory approach. As a result, it was found that software development roles differ widely between companies (even between projects) and they also overlap significantly with other roles. It was concluded that software development roles cannot be defined in a generally applicable manner.

Further analysis of the data showed that the activities and the artifacts of the software development process were largely the same across each of the companies studied. Because the companies follow variations of the familiar "V" model, it was clear that the study of project phases would simply explore well covered territory. However, changing the focus to the artifacts associated with the development process proved to be much more informative, leading to a conceptual framework where artifacts are central.

Artifacts have been studied in the software literature before. For instance, Cluts (2003) describes artifacts as the means of relating people and activity systems. Artifacts also hold the history of those relationships within them. Morisio et al. (2002) are concerned with the attributes of software artifacts, arguing that these can be measured and these measurements are used to support the decision-making process. A particular type of artifact, called a "boundary object" is the focus for Mambrey and Robinson's (1997) study. Such objects "inhabit several intersecting social worlds *and* satisfy the informational requirements of each"

(p. 119). Most of the artifacts identified in this study are boundary objects, providing interfaces between the development team and other functions within the organization, or between the organization and external entities.

Artifacts are used throughout a development project to embody stakeholder knowledge and contribute to the development process. No one member of the development team is involved in the creation of all the artifacts. Some are produced by other team members; some originate in other functions within the company and more are externally sourced—customer requests, for instance.

The artifacts are situated in what this chapter calls "organizational functions." The four functions identified in the telecommunications domain are as follows:

1. **Management.** This includes project management and senior management. It also covers the finance and legal departments. Essentially, it is where the major decision-making activities take place.
2. **Front-end customer interface.** Here we find the product managers and the sales and marketing personnel. These people interact directly with the customer and with the marketplace.
3. **Back-end customer interface.** This is where the product is installed in the customer site. The installation and the subsequent maintenance of the product are under the control of the customer-support function.
4. **Development.** This area includes all personnel who contribute directly to the creation of the delivered product. That is, programmers, testers, technical writers, and trainers.

It may be surprising that the purchasing function does not feature in this list. Although some of those interviewed as part of the pilot study were involved with third-party suppliers, there was little or no interaction by the participants from the telecommunications domain.

The position of the majority of artifacts on the boundaries between functions reflects that these artifacts provide a communications mechanism between functions, allowing the practitioners to collaborate. Study of the principal artifacts (the requirements document, the feasibility report, the project plan, and the installed product) also shows how some of them contain data that are needed for decisions—such as the go/no-go decision—to be made. If knowledge, skills, and abilities are now considered in terms of artifacts, it is likely that each artifact will require certain communications, collaboration, and decision-support skills. However, before exploring this possibility, the concept of an artifact needs to be examined further.

# 3 Artifact Dynamics

Artifacts represent milestones achieved during the project. However, they need to be created in a particular order. For instance, in the development projects described during the interviews, the feasibility study cannot take place until the requirements are understood and the construction effort cannot proceed without a project plan. Thus, one major artifact depends on its predecessors, suggesting that development proceeds in a linear fashion. However, for each artifact, a cycle of activity needs to take place, requiring practitioners to

1. Evaluate a trigger event. This could involve simply recognizing a trigger, such as a news story that in some way affects the company, or a scheduled review of a planned artifact, such as a design document.
2. Gather information and build up the knowledge necessary to understand what is required of the target artifact. Sufficient information may be available from existing artifacts, but it might be necessary to create intermediate artifacts to elicit feedback.
3. Design the artifact. This requires the creative, high-level skills needed to devise new concepts. Also required here are the decision-making and negotiation skills mainly associated with management but are required when investigating alternative courses of action. For instance, detailed analysis of a particular requirement may show that the initial estimates were too optimistic. In this case, the design part of the cycle will have to conceive a solution to satisfy the requirements as well as calculating revised schedule estimates. The update to the project plan is triggered by a report from the programmer.
4. Produce and disseminate the artifact. The skills needed for this supplement the creative skills and include technical writing, prototyping, coding, testing, proof-reading, presentation, and reporting.

An artifact should not be considered merely in terms of the skills needed to design it, but also in terms of the knowledge and the other artifacts that must be acquired before any sensible synthesis can take place. Having created, or embodied, the artifact, it must be made available to others on the project team and reviewed by them. Therefore, a single artifact draws on research, analysis, design, implementation, and evaluation skills.

In summary, the artifact-centric skill framework consists of two relationships: how artifacts are located in the organizational context and how knowledge, skills, and abilities are related to phases of the artifacts' lifecycles.

## 3.1 Creating Artifact-Centric Job Descriptions

Because artifacts are central to the project-based work of software development, identification of an organization's artifacts and the specific people who work on them will help to describe individual tasks. In essence, specialized technical knowledge and skills are needed to create artifacts, but communications, collaboration, and decision-making skills are needed to gather information to base the artifacts on and to disseminate them to other team members. Particular technical skills can be identified for each artifact and the person's responsibilities in relation to that artifact—creation, contribution, review, or use—will determine the 'soft', or transferable, skills (communication, collaboration and decision-support) required.

The artifact-centric skill framework gives the creators of job descriptions an awareness of:

- The entire software development lifecycle. Being aware of all the artifacts in the process encourages recruiters to define the scope of the role in a broader manner than if they concentrate on the job title alone.
- The multi-disciplinary nature of the development process. Because so many of the artifacts require contributions from other team members, the need for teamwork and communications skills is brought to the fore. It also identifies the organizational functions the role interacts with, highlighting the need for a wider perspective than a mere technical one.

This can be seen by applying the artifact-centric skill framework to a set of real advertisements, taken from recruitment websites. The systems architect position, advertised in the introduction, does not mention any artifacts explicitly. It simply talks about "solutions," which could be translated into "installed products," The skills mentioned in the advertisement are quite vague—"problem solving skills," "interpersonal skills," "native level fluency in English," and "strong software development experience."

To create a more detailed advertisement, knowledge of the systems architect role gleaned in Downey (2006) is used to identify the artifacts and the phases of the artifact lifecycle the architect is involved with. Table 1 lists the artifacts a systems architect in the telecommunications sector may be expected to work with. Initially, the architect will be asked to generate detailed, measurable, and testable engineering requirements from marketing requirements generated by the product managers. Thus, the marketing requirements document acts as a trigger for the architect's subsequent work.

Marketing requirements are often quite vague and need clarification. To obtain this, the systems architect may ask to meet the customer directly. Clarification is possible in a question or answer session, but more effective results can be obtained by creating simple prototypes or by carrying out scenario modeling—working through use cases, for instance. While the goal of this exercise is a technical one— the creation of the engineering requirements artifact—the architect must demonstrate interpersonal and team working skills. However, the people the architect has to interact with for this exercise are not fellow developers, but sales and marketing personnel as well as customers.

Another artifact the architects get involved with is the feasibility report. Essentially, their responsibility is to assess technical feasibility. If architects are satisfied that a solution to the requirements is possible, they must contribute time and headcount estimates to the finance and project management people, in order to arrive at the development cost estimate. Thus, architects need to have some appreciation of business realities and understand the way development is financed. Again, the architect is called on to display good interpersonal and team working skills, but this team has different perspectives from the market-driven team of the requirements phase.

**Table 1.** Artifact lifecycle phases involving a Systems Architect

| Artifact | Trigger | Analysis | Design | Creation |
|---|---|---|---|---|
| Marketing Requirements | × | | | |
| Prototypes | | × | × | × |
| Scenario Modeling | | × | × | × |
| Engineering Requirements | | × | × | × |
| Functional Specification | | × | × | × |
| Time and Headcount Estimates | | × | × | × |
| Development Cost | × | × | | |
| Feasibility Report | × | × | | |
| Design Documents | × | × | | |
| Unit Tested Code | × | × | | |
| Bug Reports | × | × | | |
| Feature Requests | × | × | × | × |
| Project Post Mortem | | × | | |

Typically, the systems architect provides technical leadership during what McConnell (1993) terms the construction part of the project (design, code, and test)—although some of the interviewees do implement part of their products themselves. Their contributions would be seen in document and code reviews as well as in advice given during the analysis work of the construction artifacts.

Finally, the architect may offer consultancy to the customers in order to tailor the product to meet their needs better. This back-end interaction with the customer may suggest ideas for new features, which the architects will feed back to their marketing people.

This profile of the systems architect shows how the role is significantly more demanding than the line "strong software development experience" suggests. Knowing the artifacts and the other people who contribute to their lifecycles, a clearer job description is possible, as shown:

*Job Description*

- *The architect will work with the sales and product management functions to agree customer requirements and to assess the feasibility of any proposed solution from a technical perspective.*
- *As part of the requirements definition process, the architect will be expected to produce realistic prototypes and scenario models of proposed solutions.*
- *The main contributions to feasibility will be realistic time and headcount estimates and the identification of possible risks associated with proposed solutions.*
- *The architect is responsible for creating engineering requirements documents, functional specifications, and high-level design/architectural documents.*
- *The architect also takes part in the coding, testing, and installation of the product in an advisory/technical lead role.*

*Skills Required*

- *As part of the requirements definition role, the architect will be called upon to deal directly with our international customers. This will require significant listening and comprehension skills, as well as the ability to present prototypes and use-case scenarios in an engaging manner.*
- *The architect works with a team of developers to produce Internet-based software products. However, the architect will also become part of ad-hoc, self-managing teams, created to identify particular requirements and to assess project feasibility.*
- *The company uses object-oriented design, requiring that the architect has competence in these techniques.*
- *The architect must be proficient in the C# and Visual Basic programming languages and familiar with .net, windows forms, and web based development. Knowledge of the XML protocol is also needed.*
- *As this is a start up company, requirements will be quite fluid until the exact market niche is located. Thus the architect must be able to cope with ambiguity and be prepared to re-plan and re-evaluate designs at short notice.*
- *The architect is expected to take a lead role in development, requiring excellent communication and team leading skills.*

This description draws on both our overall knowledge of the architect's role and details from the advertisement.

## 3.2 Project Manager

The most significant feature of the following project manager advertisement is the total absence of a job description. Indeed, it is difficult to know what skills—technical or managerial—are required.

*"Requirements*

- *Degree in Electronic Engineering, Computer Science, or Mathematics with a first class or second class honours grade 1 qualification.*
- *5 years software design experience with some team lead experience.*
- *Ability to work with a team of specialists and provide leadership, motivation, and coherence.*
- *A track record of participation in the commercialisation of complex system products.*
- *Experience of software quality systems and software project planning.*
- *Familiarity with GUI development and networking.*
- *Familiarity with Linux would be an advantage."*

Because there is so little detail, the artifact-centric job description is based entirely on the interviews with project managers. As before, the first steps to take are the identification of the artifacts and the phases of their lifecycles the project manager is typically involved with.

In an ideal world, the project manager would come on board after the requirements have been clarified and a detailed feasibility study has been carried out. Unfortunately, it is often the case that the project manager is tasked with a very vague assignment—implement the latest version of a particular communications protocol,

**Table 2.** Artifact lifecycle phases involving a Project Manager

| Artifact | Trigger | Analysis | Design | Creation |
|---|---|---|---|---|
| Marketing Requirements | × | | | |
| Engineering Requirements | × | | | |
| Functional Specification | × | | | |
| Time and Headcount Estimates | × | × | × | × |
| Development Cost | × | × | × | × |
| Feasibility Report | × | | | |
| Project Plan | | × | × | × |
| Independent Test Plans | × | | | |
| Documentation Plan | × | | | |
| Installation Plan | × | | | |
| Test Report | × | | | |
| Installation Report | × | | | |
| Progress Reports | × | × | × | × |
| Design Documents | × | | | |
| Unit Tested Code | × | | | |
| Bug Tracking Database | × | | | |
| Project Post Mortem | | × | × | × |

for instance. While the specification provided by the standards body should contain all the necessary details, these requirements must be translated into software functionality—i.e. a functional specification needs to be written. Similarly, the need to support emerging standards is vital to business in the telecommunications market. In other words, a feasibility report is unlikely to have been written. This implies that the project manager has to generate time and headcount estimates from scratch.

Thus, Table 2 shows the project manager generating time, headcount, and cost estimates as well as making use of them. Whether or not a project manager has to drive the requirements gathering and feasibility work, the main artifact all project managers are concerned with is their project plan. This will contain a work breakdown structure and an ever-evolving schedule. It should contain detailed risk analysis and it will be informed by other contributors, such as technical writers (documentation plan), testers (independent test plan), and customer support personnel (installation plan).

Progress will be tracked using reports from individual developers, as well as final test reports and the installation report. In turn, the project manager must report on overall progress to senior management. Once the project is complete, the project manager needs to summarize the experience by producing a project postmortem. Some companies hold such reviews at several stages in the project.

The following is a job description reflecting these issues:

*Job Description*

- *The project manager's primary responsibility is the creation and maintenance of the project plan artefact.*
- *This artefact draws on the product roadmap, the combined engineering requirements document, the preliminary functional specification and the time and headcount estimates produced during the various feasibility studies. The project manager is expected to critically evaluate all of these artefacts.*
- *The project manager must ensure that an adequate set of testable and measurable requirements are in place and that an agreed set of software solutions have been investigated. If not, the project manager must work closely with senior designers to ensure that the work breakdown structure for the project can be developed.*
- *Parts of the final product will be supplied by third-party vendors. The project manager contributes to the creation of contracts with these suppliers and also provides clear requirements and tracks their progress as closely as that of the in-house team.*
- *The project manager provides both written and verbal reports to senior management throughout the project.*
- *At the completion of each project, a post-mortem document is written by the project manager in order to improve the development process.*

*Skills Required*

- *Project management skills. Team leading, coordination, negotiation, prioritisation, planning, risk management, estimation, budgeting and the ability to cope with ambiguity.*
- *Strong technical, market and product knowledge is needed along with an awareness of commercial and political issues.*
- *Evaluation and analysis skills. The project manager has to base the project plan on earlier artefacts and must be able to critically assess both technical and commercial documents.*
- *Both written and verbal communication skills are tested in this role. The project manager must create a cogent project plan and be able to defend the decisions contained within it; must also ensure that work assignments are clearly understood as well as ensuring that all stakeholders are updated on progress.*

## *3.3 Programmer (Software Developer)*

*"Requirements*

*Experience with Software Engineering*
*3–4 Years **Java Lifecycle Development** experience*
*Experience with OOA **Design Patterns**, **UML***
*Experience with related Technologies such as **XML***
*Database experience including **Sybase***
*Knowledge/Experience of **Telecoms, 2G, 3G**, ATM/IP*
*Configuration and Build Management processes (Clearcase/ANT etc)*
*Experience with development on Unix and Windows platforms"*

While this advertisement clearly expresses the technologies the company is involved with, the job seeker has no idea which of these technologies are used as tools and which will be developed by the company. The job seeker also has no clear idea of what the job entails. In the study of the telecommunications software domain, it was found that the programmer's role is the most pervasive, particularly in the case of senior people. This role can require a great deal of customer interaction, both at the front-end and back-end.

**Table 3.** Artifact lifecycle phases involving a Programmer

| Artifact | Trigger | Analysis | Design | Creation |
|---|---|---|---|---|
| Prototypes | | × | × | × |
| Scenario Modeling | | × | × | × |
| Engineering Requirements | | × | × | |
| Functional Specification | | × | × | |
| Time and Headcount Estimates | | × | | |
| Design Documents | × | × | × | × |
| Unit Tested Code | × | × | × | × |
| Progress Reports | | × | × | × |
| Bug Reports | × | | | |
| Updated Code | | × | × | × |
| Feature Requests | × | × | × | × |
| Installed Product | | × | | |
| Project Post Mortem | | × | | |

Programmers may feature all through the software development lifecycle (see Table 3). They may assist the systems architect in defining testable and measurable engineering requirements, perhaps by creating prototype systems. They may also help in the production of the functional specification by evaluating parts of proposed solutions. In this effort, the programmer may be in direct contact with the customer and will have to appreciate the business concerns of sales and marketing people, including the product manager.

Once the project has been approved, the programmer is assigned particular features to implement and will carry out design, code, and test activities. The artifacts created in these phases are reviewed by the systems architect and peer programmers. In turn, the programmer is expected to review other construction artifacts.

Once the product has been tested by the programming team, it is handed over to the independent team and the programmers stand by to address bug reports. Usually, some of the programmers move onto other projects at this point and the remaining ones have to field problems associated with other people's code. This situation becomes more demanding when the product is installed at a customer site. Now, one or two programmers may be asked to accompany the installation team and deal with any software problems that may arise. Several of the interviewees cited these visits as cathartic learning experiences. Thus, the programmer can be involved in all aspects of the development cycle and all the organizational functions.

A realistic job description is:

*Job Description*

- *Programmers review the engineering requirements document and contribute to the functional specification by experimenting with alternative potential solutions.*
- *Programmers contribute time and headcount estimates to the project plan for their portions of the development effort.*
- *The programmer will produce a detailed design document using object oriented design techniques, including UML and design patterns.*
- *Once the design has been reviewed, the programmer will produce a unit-tested suite of Java code. A professional development environment is provided including version control (ClearCase/Ant) and automated builds.*
- *The programmer will provide information to the technical writing group as a basis for their documentation.*
- *The programmer will assist the independent test and the customer support teams in diagnosing problems and providing updated code to address any bug reports.*

*Skills Required*

- *A programmer needs to have reasonable product and domain knowledge (telecommunications—2G, 3G and ATM/IP) in order to contribute usefully to the requirements review.*
- *Detailed technical knowledge is also needed to evaluate alternate solutions and to design, code and test software.*
- *A programmer must be capable of estimating how long any assigned task is likely to take.*
- *Strong object-oriented design skills are essential in this role.*
- *Coding is carried out in Java under both the UNIX and Windows operating systems. Familiarity with XML is also useful.*
- *A programmer needs to have a good knowledge of the theory of testing in order to produce comprehensive unit tests.*
- *Strong writing skills are required to produce clear design documents. Also, contributions to the end-user documentation need to make sense to the documentation people who have less technical understanding.*
- *Given the amount of interaction with other roles—project managers, architects, testers and customer support personnel—good communication and teamwork skills are essential.*

# 4 Conclusion

This chapter shows how the artifact-centric skill framework can offer practical assistance to organizations by facilitating better job descriptions in their recruitment advertisements. This is achieved by specifying the people they want to hire in terms of the artifacts they will be expected to contribute to. Because the artifact-centric skill framework also highlights the fact that many of the artifacts are boundary objects, the multi-disciplinary nature of the work is brought to the fore. For potential candidates, the nature of the work they are invited to apply for is much clearer. According to Fernandez-Araoz (1999), "competencies are useless unless they are described in behavioral terms" (p. 117). This view endorses the artifact-centric approach, in that the job descriptions are based on how employees behave in relation to the artifacts and their co-workers.

As can be seen from the sample advertisements, some companies have a very poor understanding of what sort of knowledge, skills and abilities they need for their organizations. Considering the importance of hiring good staff (DeMarco and Lister 1999; Shapero 1985), an effective means of describing the role required is essential. Although it has been shown in the literature (Belbin 2000; Shaw 2000), that generic roles are not possible to define, each organization should be able to identify what roles mean in their own context.

The artifact-centric skill framework provides such a means. An organization needs to identify the key artifacts in its development process and locate them in terms of the company's organizational functions. It then needs to define its current staff in terms of their contributions to each artifact. This exercise should identify gaps in the team profile or areas where emphasis is weak. By understanding what the roles and responsibilities are, employers are in a position to define clearly what sort of additional skills they are looking for. Indeed, these gaps may be filled by expanding the scope of existing roles—providing career progression opportunities for people in these roles.

It should be noted that the examples given in this chapter have not been validated by human resource professionals. Indeed, this application of the artifact-centric skill framework would make an ideal subject for an action-research project, where a company's process would be described in terms of artifacts and each team member's role defined in relation to those artifacts. It is hoped that such an exercise would reveal gaps in the necessary skill sets and provide a basis for either training or recruitment.

# References

Belbin, R. M. (2000). *Beyond the Team*. Oxford, Elsevier Butterworth-Heinemann.

Casteleyn, M. (1996). *Job Descriptions for the Information Profession*. London, Aslib, The Association for Information Management.

Cluts, M. M. (2003). The Evolution of Artifacts in Cooperative Work: Constructing Meaning Through Activity. ACM SIGGROUP 2003, *Florida, USA*, ACM Press 144–152.

DeMarco, T. and T. Lister (1999). *Peopleware: Productive Projects and Teams*, Dorset House.

Downey, J. (2005). A Framework to Elicit the Skills Needed for Software Development. 2005 ACM SIGMIS CPR Conference, *Atlanta, Georgia*, ACM Press 14–16 April, 2005 122–127.

Downey, J. (2006). Systems Architect and Systems Analyst: Are These Comparable Roles? 2006 ACM SIGMIS CPR Conference, *Claremont, California*, ACM Press 13–15 April, 2006 213–220.

Downey, J. and N. Power (2007). An Artifact-centric Framework for Software Development Skills. ACM SIGMIS CPR, *St. Louis, Missouri*, ACM Press 19–20 April, 2007 186–195.

Enterprise Strategy Group (2004). Ahead of the Curve: Ireland's Place in the Global Economy. Dublin, Forfas.

Fernandez-Araoz, C. (1999). "Hiring without Firing." *Harvard Business Review* 77(4): 109–120.

Ford, G. and N. E. Gibbs (1996). A Mature Profession of Software Engineering, Carnegie Mellon University: 1–94.

Forfas (2003). Responding to Ireland's Skills Needs, The Fourth Report of the Expert Group on Future Skills Needs. Dublin, Forfas: 24–33, 86–94.

Hackman, J. R. and G. R. Oldham (1980). *Work Redesign*. Reading Massachusetts, Adison-Wesley.

Irish Computer Society (2006). Irish Computer Society Website. 28 June 2006: http://www.ics.ie

Litecky, C. R., K. P. Arnett and B. Prabhakar (2004). "The Paradox of Soft Skills versus Technical Skills in IS Hiring." *Journal of Computer Information Systems* 45(1): 69–76.

Mambrey, P. and M. Robinson (1997). Understanding the Role of Documents in a Hierarchical Flow of Work. ACM SIGGROUP 1997, *Phoenix, Arizona*, ACM Press 119–127.

McConnell, S. (1993). *Code Complete*. Redmond, Washington, Microsoft Press.

Morisio, M., I. Stamelos and A. Tsoukias (2002). A New Method to Evaluate Software Artifacts Against Predefined Profiles. ACM SIGSSEKE, *Ischia, Italy*, ACM Press 811–818.

Office for National Statistics (2000). *Standard Occupational Classification—Volume 2*. London, The Publishing House.

SFIA Foundation (2006). Skills Framework for an Information Age. 28 June 2006: http://www.sfia.org.uk

Shapero, A. (1985). *Managing Professional People: Understanding Creative Performance*. New York, The Free Press.

Shaw, M. (2000). Software Engineering Education: A Roadmap. 22nd International Conference on Software Engineering, *Limerick, Ireland*, ACM Press 373–380.

# A Method for Rapid Creation of a Virtual Software Development Team

Damjan Vavpotič, Štefan Furlan and Marko Bajec

Faculty of Computing and Information Science, University of Ljubljana, Slovenia
{damjan.vavpotic, stefan.furlan, marko.bajec}@fri.uni-lj.si

**Abstract** Companies dealing with software development are often facing problems related to cadre as a consequence of rapid technology changes and varying project requirements. Frequently, when a new project is commenced additional workforce is required, but after the project is finished these additional employees are not needed anymore. Possible solution for the problem is formation of a virtual development team. Use of virtual development teams in the field of software development is a well established practice. However, such teams are usually assembled for longer periods and their members are relatively permanent. The goal of our research is to create methodological approach that would enable a software development company to rapidly start an ad hoc virtual team when needed. Members of such team would be only temporary and their tasks relatively simple and independent. In our opinion, such approach could offer interesting advantages to certain types of software development companies. This chapter presents the backbone of the approach and its basic properties.

## 1 Introduction and Background

Nowadays, companies dealing with software development are often facing problems related to cadre as a consequence of rapid technology changes and varying project requirements (Turner et al. 2002). Knowledge of the companies' software engineers is quickly becoming outdated and it is virtually impossible for a single developer to master all the latest technologies and approaches in his field of expertise. Consequently, older technologies often remain in use. Yet another difficulty is that cadre requirements of software development companies change from project to project. Frequently, when a new project is commenced additional workforce is required, but after the project is finished these additional employees are not needed anymore.

The usual solution would be to (temporary) employ more people and to additionally educate some of the existing employees. However, it is often difficult to find enough people locally that have suitable knowledge and expertise and therefore additional training of new employees is also required. If these additional employees are not needed after the project is finished, educating them only for the needs of a project is a costly solution.

An alternative solution might be to form a virtual team. The main advantage of such solution is that team members can be selected form a large pool of people having appropriate skills and knowledge (Furst et al. 2004). Nevertheless, different problems have been reported that arise in such teams (Johnson et al. 2001) and many projects relying on a virtual team failed (Furst et al. 2004). The most exposed problems in virtual teams were related to communication (Gould 1999) and different human factors (Townsend and DeMarie 1998). Researchers suggest that people working in virtual teams need special social and communication abilities and should be trained to work in such teams (Gibson and Cohen 2003).

The goal of our research is to create methodological approach that would enable a software development company to rapidly start an ad hoc virtual team when required. A company should be able to use such virtual team to implement a whole system or only parts of a system. As most of the problems in virtual teams arise due to communication and human factors, an important aim of the research is to lessen their influence.

This chapter is organised as follows: after an introduction and providing sufficient background information (Sect. 1), the method for rapid creation of a virtual software development team (RCVT) is presented (Sect. 2). Each component of the RCVT is discussed in a separate subsection. Next, the approach to test the RCVT is presented (Sect. 3) which is followed by a conclusion (Sect. 4).

## 2 The Method (RCVT)

A backbone of the RCVT comprises of core system architecture, project management, core development process, and human resource management. The purpose of the backbone that is managed centrally is to enable synchronization of virtual team members and to assure suitability and quality of the whole system. Figure 1 depicts the model of RCVT. In the following subsections each component of RCVT is explained.

### 2.1 The Core System Architecture

The main purpose of the core system architecture is to facilitate construction of a system from relatively small and independent parts. The backbone of the architecture is a system framework that connects these parts into a functioning system. Small size and independence of system parts is vital for creation of simple and independent tasks that can be assigned to almost any single member of a virtual team, taking into account mostly his technical knowledge. Therefore, we are focusing on using the system architectures that allow one to break the system on smaller and more manageable parts that are also loosely coupled. One such architectural approach, that we tend to use is SOA (Erl 2005).

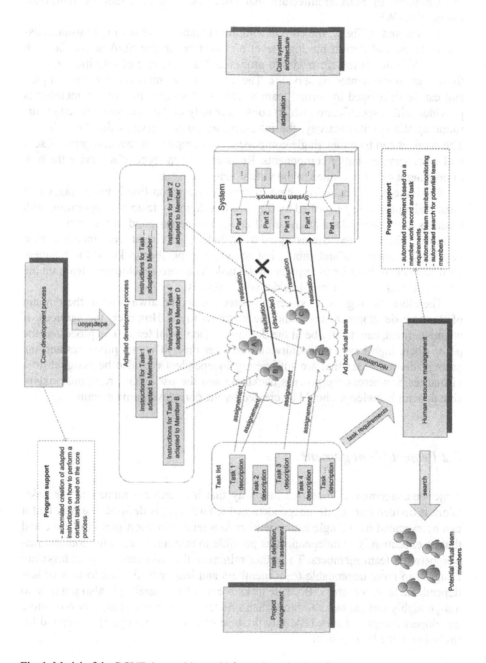

**Fig. 1.** Model of the RCVT that enables rapid formation of a virtual team.

In the SOA realm, the information system is broken down into smaller and independent parts, called services. These services are then used in business processes, providing the business logic in a standardized and reusable manner. One of the variations of SOA architecture that could be used is Windows Workflow Foundation (WF).

As depicted in Fig. 2, the core development team works with the business users to define and design the high level architecture. In the SOA sense the high level architecture is transformed into processes that comprise of activities, and activities are implemented as services. The services are small and loosely coupled and can be developed by virtual team members. A single virtual team member is provided with a specification which consists mainly of the domain knowledge surrounding the specific activity, the interface, and other services that he will use. The services can be either single components or components that comprise of several other services and/or components. Regardless of the type of a service the task of creating it can be assigned to the virtual team member.

The issue here is actually where to draw a distinction line between tasks that must undoubtedly be performed by the core development team in cooperation with business users and tasks that are small enough to be assigned to the virtual team members. The tasks that are assigned to an individual virtual team member must be highly independent and should not require the member to know the business domain in detail in order to implement the task. The core development team on the other side must know the problem domain in details.

Therefore, the high level system architecture should always be in the domain of the core development team and the business users. However, the services, if wisely defined, can mostly be in the domain of the virtual team. The process is the point where high level architecture and services meet. The sub processes and the parts of the processes that are sufficiently independent can also be assigned to a virtual team, whereas the process backbone and the parts that presuppose extensive domain knowledge should be created by the core development team.

## 2.2 Project Management

Project management is modified in a way that it minimizes human factor risks. Work is divided into small independent tasks. Each task is defined in a way that it can be executed by a single team member in a relatively short period of time and that its execution is as independent as possible to minimize needs for communication between team members. To further minimize the risks more critical tasks are assigned to more dependable team members and less critical tasks to new or less dependable team members. Because tasks are relatively small it is also possible to assign highly critical tasks to more than one team member and after two or more developers completed such task only the best solution (system part) is selected for inclusion in the final system.

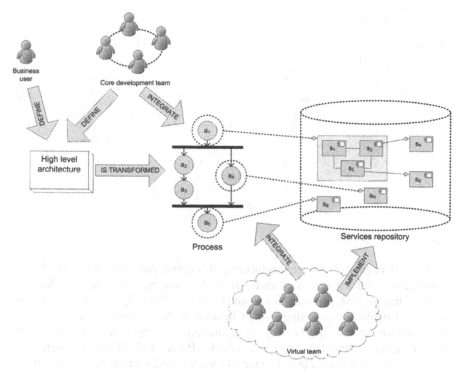

**Fig. 2.** Use of SOA to support core system architecture in the RCVT.

This kind of management style has many similarities to the so-called management by objectives (MBO) which is believed to be suitable for virtual teams (Hertel et al. 2005) and where the role of a project manager is not the same as in traditional settings. One such similarity is goal setting. In our case a task definition is described by an interface (goal) rather than description of how the task must be achieved. The second is feedback, which must be frequent, concrete, and timely, which in our case is achieved via small and very manageable tasks that can be done by one person.

## 2.3 The Core Development Process

The core development process gives detailed instructions on how to perform different types of tasks. To lessen communication problems each team member is given only the instructions that are necessary to perform the type of the task he was assigned. Since not all team members are equally experienced and skilled and their knowledge might vary a lot, the instructions need to be adapted to each particular member. In the RCVT, we suggest that this is done by following the principles of situational method engineering.

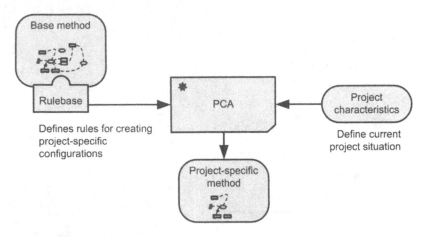

**Fig. 3.** Model of the PCA.

Method engineering is an engineering discipline that deals with the design, construction, and adaptation of methods, techniques, and tools for the development of information systems (Brinkkemper et al. 1996). Specifically popular is situational method engineering, which focuses on how project-specific methods can be created on the fly, either by an adaptation of a single method or by assembling together fragments of various methods (Bajec et al. 2007; Harmsen et al. 1994; Henderson-Sellers 2003; Kumar and Welke 1992). In the literature, various approaches to situational method engineering can be found (for a review see Ralyte et al. 2003). They differ in several aspects, but most notably in the point of departure (a single method or multiple methods), the granularity of method fragments used to create situational methods, and the ability to execute (for the details refer to Bajec et al. 2007). For the needs of the RCVT we adopted the Process Configuration Approach (PCA), which uses a single method as the point of departure, works on a low layer of granularity (thus providing the highest possible flexibility) and provides sufficient details to execute in real practice.

The idea that lies behind the PCA is relatively simple and can be explained as follows (see Fig. 3): for each individual project a specific process configuration (project-specific method) is created. This is done by selecting components from a method that has been specifically designed for the organization and thus reflects its actual performance on the projects (base method). The configuration is done by processing the rules that tell in what circumstances for project situations it is compulsory, advisable, or discouraged to use a particular component. The rules are part of the base method and are defined together with other base method elements.

The most important part of the PCA is a base method which documents how the organization is performing its projects. In an ordinary performance of the PCA for the needs of a particular organization the base method is created by observing how the organization is currently performing its projects and by making necessary improvements so that the created method is technically and socially sound (Vavpotič et al. 2004). This means that by using the PCA we can assure all the fragments (e.g. diagramming techniques, activities, tools, etc.) of the formalized method are technically suitable for the type of projects the organization is typically performing and adopted by its development team.

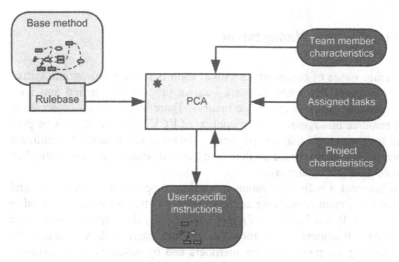

**Fig. 4.** Adoption of the PCA for RCVT purposes.

We believe that the PCA can also be very useful for the needs of the RCVT, as the creation of instructions in the RCVT and the creation of project-specific methods in the PCA shares the same objectives: the created method/instructions must be aligned with the requirements of the project and with the characteristics of the development team (see Fig. 4). The latter is of course much more complicated to achieve in the RCVT, as the development team is created on-the-fly and includes members from inside and outside of the organization. This poses several requirements on the PCA adaptation for the needs of the RCVT. Firstly, the approach must support the creation of instructions on different layers of granularity. For example, for those members who are more experienced and already known to the organization, the instructions might be less detailed while for newcomers and less experienced developers, detailed guidelines are more appropriate. Furthermore, the rules component that is used in the PCA to auto-configure base methods for the needs of a particular project situation becomes more complex in the RCVT, as we cannot focus on the characteristics of the development team as a whole but we have to take into account each particular team member and his/her characteristics. Finally, in the RCVT we are not interested in the complete method that is required for the project performance but only on the parts that are relevant for the performance of the tasks assigned to a particular member.

The use of the PCA in real practice turns out to be quite complicated, predominantly due to the effort that is required for the establishment of a well-defined base method. In addition, there are typically a large number of rules (a hundred ore more) that we have to deal with in the method configuration which makes manual performance of the configuration virtually impossible. For this purpose the PCA comes with a toolset that supports all the necessary activities reducing the burden of method engineers and project managers (for details see Bajec et al. 2007). We believe that not only many adjustments are required for the tool-set to make it useful but also for the need of the RCVT.

## 2.4 Human Resource Management

One of the main issues of composing a virtual team is finding appropriate virtual team members, especially when they are—as we propose—identified and inte-grated into the virtual team in an ad-hoc manner. Therefore, the main objective of the human resource management in the context of RCVT is to create a large pool of potential team members that can perform different kinds of tasks. Recruitment of team members is mainly based on their work record, knowledge, and skills they have in the context of a certain task.

We propose that a software system is used to support this activity. Several ideas on how to go upon composing and managing a virtual team can be found in Norman et al. (2004) and Suter (1999). We are currently developing a web-based application that will automate this process as much as possible. It will be used by companies looking for potential team members and by potential team members who wish to be included in such a team. The application will allow companies to define projects and search for potential team members whose knowledge, skills, and experience match those needed for the project. The potential team members will have to input the information about their past experiences, knowledge, and skills.

The main issue of this application is the authenticity of the information that the potential team members provide. For instance, the data about work experience and knowledge can easily be fabricated to get employed. To solve this problem we will base the application on social networks (Adamic and Adar 2005). Social net-works allow members to link to each other where links usually represent real-life acquaintanceship. Well-known examples of such networks are Facebook (2007), LinkedIn (2007), and MySpace (2007) that focus on students, professionals, and general public, respectively.

In our system, the link between two members will identify either a real-life ac-quaintanceship or cooperation on past project(s). The links will, therefore, enable a company to confirm potential team member's identity and authenticity of the data via mutual acquaintances. With this mechanism it will be able to encapsulate a sound system of trust and therefore minimize the risk of recruiting an unsuitable virtual team member based on the false data.

## 3 Verification and Validation of the RCVT

The RCVT will be tested to verify and validate its usefulness in practice and to gain experience that will serve as the basis for its improvements. Tests will be per-formed in three stages.

In the first stage, preliminary testing will be performed. Its purpose will be to gain additional experience with the RCVT. Based on the experience we will fine-tune the RCVT and try to minimize its deficiencies. Although we expect that during preliminary testing many of the deficiencies will be identified, these tests will not explain how the RCVT actually performs in practice.

Therefore, in the second stage, we plan to perform tests in the university environment. We intend to create an experimental virtual team comprising of university students. To minimize the problems that would arise in a virtual team due to lack of development skills of its members, only senior students who already have knowledge and practical experience in software development will be allowed to participate in the experiment. Although these students will be skilled in development, they will not have any particular knowledge of a chosen business domain. This way we will try to reproduce the conditions of a real environment. The experience that we will gain during pilot testing will be used to further improve the RCVT.

In the third stage, we plan to test the RCVT in a real life environment in cooperation with software development companies. Web system will be created to enable acquisition of team members and coordination of the development team over the Internet. In the beginning, the RCVT will be used to develop less crucial and less complex parts of real projects so that a company will be able to gain confidence and experience with RCVT. Gradually more complex project parts will be introduced.

## 4 Conclusion

So far, we have delineated the backbone for the RCVT and identified its basic properties. In our opinion, the RCVT could offer interesting advantages to certain types of software development companies as it would enable them to quickly assemble a virtual team when additional workforce is needed. It would also minimize the needs for special communication and social abilities of virtual team members, as each member would be given precise instructions on how to perform his tasks and each task would be as independent as possible. However, we are aware that there are many difficulties that will have to be resolved. Currently, the initial tests of the RCVT are in progress. We expect that most difficulties will be identified during these tests and that their results will enable us to understand the advantages and disadvantages of the RCVT more clearly.

## References

Adamic, L. and Adar, E. (2005) How to Search a Social Network. *Social Networks,* 27, 187–203.
Bajec, M., Vavpotic, D., and Krisper, M. (2007) Practice-driven approach for creating project-specific software development methods. *Information and Software Technology,* 49, 345–365.

Brinkkemper, S., Lyytinen, K., and Welke, R. J. (Eds.) (1996) *Method Engineering—Principles of Method Construction and Tool Support,* Atlanta, USA, Chapman & Hall.

Erl, T. (2005) *Service-Oriented Architecture: Concepts, Technology, and Design,* Upper Saddle River, NJ; London, Prentice Hall Professional Technical Reference.

Facebook (2007) [online] [Accessed 2007/4/13]. Available from World Wide Web <http://www.facebook.com>.

Furst, S. A., Reeves, M., Rosen, B., and Blackburn, R. S. (2004) Managing the lifecycle of virtual teams. *Academy of Management Executive,* 18, 6–20.

Gibson, C. B. and Cohen, S. G. (Eds.) (2003) *Virtual Teams That Work: Creating Conditions for Virtual Team Effectiveness,* San Francisco, Jossey-Bass, A Wiley Imprint.

Gould, D. (1999) Virtual Organization, Leading Virtual Teams, http://www.seanet.com/~daveg/Virtual%20Organizing.pdf.

Harmsen, F., Brinkkemper, S., and Oei, H. (1994) Situational Method Engineering for information system project approaches. *IFIP WG8.1 Working Conference on Methods and Associated Tools for the Information Systems Life Cycle.* Amsterdam, Elsevier Science.

Henderson-Sellers, B. (2003) Method engineering for OO systems development. *Communications of the ACM,* 46, 73–78.

Hertel, G., Geister, S., and Konradt, U. (2005) Managing Virtual Teams: A Review of Current Empirical Research. *Human Resource Management Review,* 15, 69–95.

Johnson, P., Heimann, V., and O'Neill, K. (2001) The "wonderland" of virtual teams. *Journal of Workplace Learning,* 13, 24–30.

Kumar, K. and Welke, R. J. (1992) Methodology Engineering: A Proposal for Situation-Specific Methodology Construction. In Cotterman, W. W. and Senn, J. A. (Eds.) *Challenges and Strategies for Research in Systems Development.* New York, Wiley.

LinkedIn (2007) [online] [Accessed 2007/4/13]. Available from World Wide Web <http://www.linkedin.com>.

MySpace (2007) [online] [Accessed 2007/4/13]. Available from World Wide Web <http://www.myspace.com>.

Norman, T. J., Preece, A., Chalmers, S., Jennings, N. R., Luck, M., Dang, V. D., Nguyen, T. D., Deora, V., Shao, J. H., Gray, W. A., and Fiddian, N. J. (2004) Agent-based formation of virtual organisations. *Knowledge-Based Systems,* 17, 103–111.

Ralyte, J., Deneckere, R., and Rolland, C. (2003) Towards a Generic Model for Situational Method Engineering. *15th International Conference on Advanced Information Systems Engineering.*

Suter, B. (1999) The VEGA* Cooperation Platform: Providing Real Support for Virtual Enterprises. In Sieber, P. and Griese, J. (Eds.) *International VoNet—Workshop.* Zurich, Simowa Verlag Bern.

Townsend, A. and DeMarie, S. (1998) Virtual teams: technology and the workplace of the future. *Academy of Management Executive,* 12, 17–29.

Turner, M., Smith, A., and Smith, H. (2002) IT outsourcing: The challenge of changing technology in IT outsourcing agreements. *Computer Law & Security Report,* 18, 181–186.

Vavpotič, D., Bajec, M., and Krisper, M. (2004) Measuring and improving software development methodology value by considering technical and social suitability of its constituent elements. In Vasilecas, O. and Zupančič, J. (Eds.) *13th International Conference on IS Development.* Vilnius, Lithuania, Vilnius: Technika.

# Girls and IT: New Times, New Challenges

Sandra Downes

School of IT, Murdoch University, Perth, Western Australia, s.downes@murdoch.edu.au

**Abstract** With computers and the Internet bringing changes to every aspect of our lives, it is time to re-examine gender issues in Information Technology (IT). Five focus groups involving female and male high school students, male and female high school teachers and female parents were organised during a 4-week period. Each group was asked questions about children's attitudes to IT and the experiences that affect these attitudes, particularly within the context of the school. The data were analysed to find common themes, which are reported in this paper. The common themes identified were (a) lack of computers is no longer an issue; (b) IT is no longer seen as a male-dominated domain; (c) old attitudes still exist, but things are changing; (d) the school, and particularly teachers, can influence students' attitudes to IT and (e) parents have considerable influence on students' positive and negative attitudes to IT. The paper concludes that attitudes to IT amongst males and females are changing and that schools and parents have an opportunity to reverse the trend of females away from IT.

## 1 Introduction

The dearth and ever decreasing number of females from careers in Information Technology (IT) is well known and well documented (Charles and Bradley 2005; Galpin 2002). Given the pervasiveness of IT today, it is essential that more females are encouraged to take up IT and to stay within the discipline (Sanders 2005; Goasduff and Swedemyr 2006). A female perspective on the use of technology (Sanders 2005) as well as more females to address the growing shortage of IT people (Gaudin 2000) is needed. Philip Argy, President of the Australian Computer Society, recently reported as follows:

The reality for the ICT sector is that we need the skills and capabilities that women naturally have as strengths, such as their ability to multi-task, understand complex business problems and work collaboratively to identify solutions that drive change and improve people's lives. If there were as many women as men in ICT, there'd be no shortage. (Argy 2007)

The literature has described many reasons why females have not accepted IT as a possible career option. These include the following:

C. Barry et al. (eds.), *Information Systems Development: Challenges in Practice, Theory, and Education, Vol.1*, doi: 10.1007/978-0-387-68772-8_36,
© Springer Science+Business Media, LLC 2009

- Lack of access to computers (Sanders 1985; Gunn 2003; Linn 2005). For example, Gunn found that females entering university were less likely to own a computer and had less ready access to computers (Gunn 2003). Linn (2005) reported the importance of access to computers at home where a student can get as much access in a week-end as they can in a whole year at school. Clarke (1992) details many research projects in which boys were more likely than girls to participate in computer-related activities and concludes that this leads to girls being less likely to gain further experience with computers and hence be involved in Computer Science.
- Association of IT with males (Seymour and Hewitt 1997; Gurer and Camp 2002) and mathematics (Gressard and Loyd 1987; Munger and Loyd 1989). For example, Clarke (1990) found that gender differences in computer ownership, experience with computers and perceptions of achievement with computers all worked in favour of men.
- Stereotypical attitudes to IT (Arenz and Lee 1990; American Association of University Women Educational Foundation 1998). For example, a 2005 report by the National Center for Women and IT found that high school females associate computer scientists with geeks, isolated cubicles and looking at a screen all day writing code (Dean 2007).
- Social expectations (Collis 1985; Fetler 1985; Turkle 1988), for example those of teachers and parents. Clarke (1992) reported that studies interviewing teachers reported no gender differences in the classroom, whereas studies observing classrooms or interviewing students reported considerable gender differences in the classroom. Kekelis et al. (2005) conducted a study of high school students using interviews and focus groups in 2000–2003. They found that parents were less likely to encourage their female children to consider information communication technology (ICT) than their male children. Shashaani (1994) found that parents encouraged their sons into ICT, but discouraged their daughters.

In Australia most homes have access to a computer and the Internet, with the Australian Bureau of Statistics (ABS) reporting in 2006 that 70% of households had access to a computer, and 60% of households had access to the Internet, and the greatest percentage of households with computers being those with children younger than 15 years (ABS 2006). Therefore the current generation of students, the so-called Millennials (Oblinger and Oblinger 2005), have grown up with computers and in some cases the Internet: technology is a part of their every day life. There is a growing amount of research that indicates that this generation is quite different in many diverse ways (Oblinger and Oblinger 2005; Jonas-Dwyer and Pospisil 2004; Barnes et al. 2007). For example, millennial students are keen to learn new things, but they learn in ways different from those of students from previous generations (Barnes et al. 2007); also, their values are different from those of the previous generations (Jonas-Dwyer and Pospisil 2004).

This research aimed to explore whether the new millennium generation, the increase in computer availability and the changes in the use of computers have led to a change in attitudes to IT. Further, this research intended to examine any changes in the attitudes of females to IT and the possibility that this could be reflected in more females in IT in the future.

## 2 Methodology

A qualitative approach was chosen to gain a rich variety of data about students' attitudes to IT. The aim was to gain data that were not dependent on previous findings. Focus groups are a method that can be used to gain a wide variety of attitudes and opinions from different groups of people (Krueger 1994; Morgan 1998). The richness of the data from focus groups is superior to that gained from surveys, but takes lesser time to conduct than in-depth interviews (Hurworth 1996). This was considered an advantage given the limited access to the participants, especially the high school students.

A large parent-controlled high school was chosen because of the my association with the school and also because the school had students from a wide variety of backgrounds, including metropolitan and country, as well as students from different ethnic backgrounds and socioeconomic groups. With focus groups there is no requirement to use a "statistically random" sample, but a wide selection of participants is more likely to give more variety of attitudes and hence richer data (Hurworth 1996). Student participants were chosen by the Head of IT in the school as a representative group of students. Teachers were invited to attend the focus group by e-mail, and interested teachers participated.

Five focus groups were conducted during a 4 week period. For each of the focus groups all the participants were of the same gender, that is, all male or all female. This arrangement was deliberately chosen to minimise any reluctance to comment by either gender. In two groups the participants were high school students; in two groups the participants were teachers of high school students and in the final group the participants were female parents of high school students. The students and teachers were from the same large parent-controlled school. The parent group consisted of six female parents who all had children who attended the same parent-controlled school, but none were parents of the students in the focus groups. On two occasions, I attempted to arrange a focus group of male parents, but on each occasion only one parent attended. Each focus group of teachers consisted of six participants and included teachers of IT and also teachers of a variety of other subjects. The male high school student group consisted of ten 14–15-year-old boys, all of whom were currently taking at least one IT subject. The female high school student group consisted of nine 16–17-year-old students who were all taking at least one IT subject.

Each group was asked the same basic questions. Slight modifications were made to the questions depending on the participants. For example, the students were asked to what extent they felt the media influenced their attitude to IT, but the parents were asked to what extent they felt that the media influenced their children's attitude to IT.

Each group was offered refreshments before the focus group began. A small room was used and the entire focus group session was recorded. A (human) recorder also made notes for each of the focus groups and these were used to clarify any points not clear from the tape. Each of the tapes from the sessions was transcribed, the names were removed and then the data were placed in a large table.

The data were examined to identify common themes. For one focus group, an independent researcher, who had been present as an observer at the focus group, also identified the themes for that focus group. The two sets of themes were compared and found to be basically equivalent. The themes were codified and then each of the transcripts was examined to find occurrences of these themes. This process is variously named thematic analysis (Zhang 2006), grounded theory analysis (Glaser 1992; Glaser and Strauss 1967) or framework analysis (Lacey and Luff 2001). The aim was to find the themes that emerged from the data. This paper focuses on themes that contradicted some of the previously held suppositions about gender issues in IT. These themes are discussed here.

# 3 Findings

## 3.1 Access to Computers

Access to computers is no longer an issue for females. In this school there are plenty of computers and so there was no issue with female students not being able to get access to a computer. This is contrary to research conducted in previous years (Gunn 2003; Sanders and McGinnis 1988). The students, teachers and parents all reported that at the school there were always ample computer resources for students to use. For example one female student reported as follows:

> "... but at S (the high school) there are so many resources that there is not a problem with computers."

Previous research has reported that boys tend to "hog" the computer, but this was not the case in this school. In fact, one boy reported that girls hog the computers more than boys do because they wanted to talk online.

> "No way! Girls hog computers more than boys to talk online".

Further, in most cases, access to a computer at home was not an issue. Only one student and one parent reported that they did not have at least one computer per person at home. This prevalence of computers at home is confirmed by the ABS (2006) report that 70% of Australian households have access to a computer and 60% have access to the Internet.

Table 1 is reproduced from data in the ABS report and shows that there is no difference between male and female use of computers and the Internet.

**Table 1.** Australian Bureau of Statistics household use of IT (2005–2006), by gender

|  | Male | Female |
|---|---|---|
| Use of Internet (No. 15 years or over) '000 | 7,889 | 8,119 |
| Use of Internet at home (No. 15 years or over) '000 | 4,591 | 4,465 |
| Use of computers (No. 5–14 years) '000 | 1,367 | 1,298 |
| Use of computers at home (No. 15 years or over) '000 | 1,113 | 1,078 |

This is in contrast to a study of females and technology in Australian high schools in 2001, which reported that females used computers less at home (Carey and Baker 2001). In their study this translated into less prior knowledge at school. However, in the current study all groups reported that girls were as knowledgeable as boys in IT. As one female teacher explained:

> "I've noticed a bit of a change, where traditionally or in the past I would have said that IT was a more boy-focused subject, but I have noticed that there is a lot of girls with a particular strength in this subject as well and so it is petering out and becoming more even. That's what I have noticed."

Similarly, another female teacher reported as follows:

> "I think that people tend to assume that boys are better at IT, however I think this assumption is quickly changing."

## 3.2 The Male Domination of IT

Prior research has theorised about the male domination of IT, with some even speculating that technology could be masculine (Hodgkinson 1999). One vociferous male student even exclaimed:

> "I don't want to be sexist, but, man designed computers and man should use it."

The same student later admitted that many of the girls in his class were much more capable with computers than he was! This attitude was not widespread amongst the male students and many of them acknowledged that females were commonly using computers in the school and taking IT as an elective subject. In general, this research found that IT is no longer seen as a male-dominated discipline.

Many of the participants of the focus groups talked about the fact that in the early years of computers they were used for mathematics and hence became associated with males. They then explained that this was no longer the case. This point was especially emphasised by the female students, but also confirmed by both groups of teachers. For example, one female teacher explained:

> *"It has gone from being a mathematical centre, and I don't know if this is the way we are socially trained or just the way we are biologically, but boys are taught that they are better at maths.... and when the computer was sold in that era as a maths tool almost, and you had to learn this equation and this strange mathematical language to be able to continue to use it... whereas I think nowadays the computer is... especially with programs like DreamWeaver, you know like WYSIWYG, so actually it is a far more aesthetically pleasing tool, and you can do something in colour and you can put lovely pictures into it.... you can design stuff... you know girls always like to decorate their book covers in Primary school, and they like to do flash web sites.*

For the focus group participants, the perception of computers as male only is no longer true. Computers are no longer seen as associated with Mathematics, but rather they are seen as communication devices; this is self-evident in that ICT is now used instead of IT. Female students see technology and computers as communication devices, and each of the focus groups mentioned that girls use computers for communication. The merging of technologies, so that a mobile phone can perform many of the functions of a computer, has led to females seeing IT as their domain. The female parents expressed exasperation with their female children who seemed obsessed with using computers for this purpose.

Interestingly, the female students expressed concern that they were using computers for communication with other family members who were in the same house, in a room nearby.

> *"And so, like, family life there is none. Everyone is in their rooms on their computers using MSN. Like, I'm in my room and my sister is in the room next to me on MSN and we are talking to each other"*

Although the female students enjoyed using MSN, they realised that this was inhibiting social interactions within the family and they were concerned about this. The male students made only passing mention about the communication possibilities of IT.

Additionally, all the focus groups except the male students explained that females used the computer as a tool for design and hence a way to be creative. For example, one male teacher reported:

> *"The girls seem to prefer to make use of the IT, in the upper school, certainly... as opposed to the boys... because they can be a bit more creative when they do presentations, as opposed to something that is just a written or a typed up assignment. Because you have the visual aspects in there they can have all the other things in... whereas boys will just try to be clever. You know, and show how well they can manipulate the IT. But certainly the girls have said that, although it takes them longer to do it, they prefer it that way."*

The female students expressed a fascination for MySpace because it allowed them to be creative:

> "I spend lots of time on MySpace. 'Cos you can make differ-
> ent backgrounds and stuff, and you decorate lots of stuff."

The female students also boasted as much as the male students of their ability to use the computer to design various things, for example, Web pages, etc. Because the computer was being used for design and to be creative, they did not have a problem with the technology.

Finally, all the female focus groups mentioned that computers are no longer those large, clunky, grey machines. Being able to buy computers in different colours, even pink, and to "accessorise" your computers was seen by all the female groups as really important. Fun mice and "funky" accessories for your computer are the norm, and females are embracing these features and hence claiming IT as their own. For example, one female teacher remarked:

> "... even the look of a computer in general, you know, you can
> buy iMacs and things like that, you can choose the colours, and
> your mouse can be a colour and there is.... and I like to colour co-
> ordinate things at home and so I like to think what colour will my
> PC be? and what am I going to do? and what colour will my laptop
> be?"

## 3.3 Stereotypical Attitudes to IT

This research found that the old stereotypical attitudes are still there, but that the new generation sees things differently. At some time during each of the focus groups the prevalence of stereotypes in IT, particularly those of the nerd or geek, was discussed. For example, one parent commented:

> "Well, there is a stigma attached to computers... my daughter
> thinks computer people are nerdy people. And doesn't want any-
> thing to do with that.."

Each of the groups recognised that these stereotypes were still widespread but each group also expressed the belief that things were changing. This same parent (whose husband works in IT) also remarked:

> "The mould is breaking...Because if you see the people who
> my husband works with... most definitely.. young, handsome,
> yuppy."

Several groups also argued that being a nerd does not have the same negative connotations that it had previously and that being a successful nerd was an advantage. The situation is summed up by one of the female teachers when referring to the term geek:

> *"Yeah, but geek does not still have the same negative connotations. Computer nerds and computer geeks will call themselves computer nerds and computer geeks."*

The male students were keen to declare that they were all very capable with computers, but that none of them were nerds or geeks:

> *"I might just say, the media doesn't distinguish between computer usage, high usage, and complete nerdism. Because I'll get on the computer and I'll get distracted and I'll be on there for 3 to 4 hours. Like you watch shows like the Simpsons and they'll depict people like that as complete and utter nerds, but I'm not like that, I actually enjoy a game out there doing things."*

The female students were well aware of the stereotypical attitudes, but did not think that they applied to them. They appeared to see through the spurious stereotypical facade constructed by the popular media. As one female student explained:

> *"There's two sides to IT, like, there's the real side and then there's the stereotypical 'I love my computer; I sit at my desk all day.'"*

This change in attitude could bode well for the future of females in IT.

## 3.4 The Influence of the School and Teachers on Students' Attitude to IT

This research found that the school, and in particular the teacher, can have an important influence on students' attitude to IT. All focus groups confirmed that the gender of the IT teacher is not important; rather the students were more interested in what the teacher was like. Both focus groups of students (male and female) stated that the main reason they enjoyed IT was because of the teacher – in this case a male. They also liked the fact that the teacher gave them lots of choice in the work they had to complete. As one female student commented:

> *"I really like his way, that's why I like his class. He just gives us the work and he just sets it there and gives us like that outline and he trusts us to do it at our own pace."*

Similar comments were made by the male students and the parents. For example one male student recounted:

> *"Also, teachers that let you know the things in IT that really help you… then that gives you a real boost because you know you can do something that other people can't do, and you can do it well … and that really helps… 'cos with the things you know you can really go places."*

The IT teacher also encouraged them to use IT in other areas, for example, in other subjects. One female student explained:

> *"I actually got offered a job to design a company's web page. At first my Mum had spoken to me about it; it was through someone at her work. And I felt like I couldn't do it. And I told Mr L and he sat down and explained everything to me from 'woe to go'. And I showed the lady a few of my web pages that I have done before and she is willing to pay me to design the whole web site for her business. And I just know that from that other doors are going to open up.*

The one problem that all the focus groups spoke about was the issue of keeping the curriculum up to date, with IT changing so quickly. They all recognised that if the material covered in class was knowledge and skills that the students already possessed, then this was a problem as the students would soon become bored. Similarly, if the teacher did not have the knowledge and skills required to teach IT, the students soon realised this and became quite dismissive of them, as one male teacher pointed out:

> *"Because there are some teachers who know for a fact that the kids know more than them... and so in some places that can actually be.... you know, the kids take advantage of it."*

This problem has been reported by other researchers (Cohen 2002) and will continue to be a problem because the pace of change in technology is not going to change.

## 3.5 Parents' Influence on Students' Attitude to IT

This research found that parents have an important influence on students' attitudes to IT. The focus group participants reported two kinds of influence by parents: one positive and one negative. Predominantly positive influences on students were expressed by all focus groups when the parents were computer literate. However, even non-computer-literate parents could have a positive influence when they were prepared to work with their children, as explained by one female parent:

*"Because I'm not very good at computers that doesn't mean that I'm not interested, I just don't have the knowledge thing. I find that I get quite excited when J (her son) has an assignment and we manage to find the information... and I think 'wow, J, look at this'... and we scroll down and we read stuff and he gets excited because I am excited about it... I'm learning something new and he's learning something new and so the kids feed off you.... they can think... Oh, Mum thinks this is really good you know... and so it is really important to show that you are interested... and also that you are excited.... because you are learning something; 'cos kids aren't the only ones who are learning something."*

Negative influences were related by the focus group participants when parents did not have a lot of knowledge about computers. After seeing media reports about the negatives of computer, and especially Internet use, parents were protective of their children, in particular their use of the Internet. This protectiveness of parents was also described by the students and the teachers. For example, one female parent who worked in IT reported:

> *"The media reports on the negatives... the dangers that young kids are involved in chat lines and chat rooms and whatever. But that doesn't affect the kids' attitude to it. It's just the parents. Like J (her daughter), I'm always on her, like, when she's on the chat line. Telling her about the latest news report, they've said this, this and this. She just says 'Oh yeah, that doesn't apply to me. You know. I'm not that stupid'".*

The female parents seemed to be more protective of their female children; for example, one parent said that there were games that she would let her son play, that she would not let her daughter play, despite there being only 1 year difference in age. Similarly, another parent allowed her two sons to have a computer each and access to the Internet, but her 15-year-old daughter was allowed to have a computer, but no Internet connection; when she wanted to access the Internet, she had to do it from the parent's computer so that they could monitor her.

# 4 Conclusions

This research found that for the focus group participants access to computers at school and home is no longer a problem when considering gender issues in IT. Additionally, females' increasing perception of IT as a communication device and a design tool has led to them seeing IT as neutral and not necessarily male-dominated. These factors, combined with the accessibility of aesthetically pleasing computers and accessories, mean that females are using computers at least as much as males do and see themselves as equally competent in IT.

This research also examined the influence of the school, teachers and parents on students' attitudes to IT. It concluded that for the focus group participants the personality of the teacher (of IT) was more important than the gender of the teacher. Also important was that the knowledge and skills of the teacher were sufficient to teach the students and that the curriculum was up to date. Finally, all students enjoyed IT when there was flexibility and choice in the tasks to be completed. To conclude, this research described possible positive and negative influences of parents.

This research is constrained by the decision to use focus groups to gather the data and thematic analysis to analyse the data. The findings of this group cannot be used to generalise about the general population. Generalisability is not the goal of focus groups or the analysis method used. However, the data collected can be used as a basis for future research in this area.

There is a need for further research in this area. I have conducted several focus groups in other schools, and anecdotal evidence from these indicate that the findings reported here are evident at other schools. However, I intend to organise more focus groups in different schools to confirm these findings. A further study involving classroom observations is planned, as well as in-depth interviews with the IT teachers. There is evidence that girls as young as primary school age make decisions not to study IT (WEEA Equity Resource Center 2000), and so focus group studies with primary school students, teachers and parents would also be of interest. I intend to conduct focus groups at several primary schools to obtain data from different age group students. These studies will facilitate validation of the findings reported here.

# References

ABS (2006) Household Use of Information Technology. ABS, Canberra.

American Association of University Women Educational Foundation (1998) Gender Gaps: Where Schools still Fail our Children. Washington.

Arenz, B. W. and Lee, M. J. (1990) Gender Differences in the Attitude, Interest and Participation of Secondary Students in Computer Use. American Educational Research Association, Boston.

Argy, P. (April/May 2007) Demand for ICT Professional Skills Reaches All-Time High. Information Age. 2–3. http://www.infoage.idg.com.au/index.php/id;925882996;fp;4;fpid; 1804200527. Accessed 17 April 2007.

Barnes, K., Maratro, R. C. and Ferris, S. P. (2007) Teaching and Learning with the Net Generation. Innovate. 4, 2.

Carey, P. and Baker, S. (2001) Girls and Technology in the Secondary School. Catholic Education Office of Western Australia, Western Australia.

Charles, M. and Bradley, K. (2005) A Matter of Degrees: Female Underrepresentation in Computer Science Programs Cross Nationally. In: J. M. Cohoon and W. C. Aspray (Eds.), *Women and Information Technology: Research on the Reasons for Underrepresentation.* The MIT Press, Cambridge MA, pp. 183–204.

Clarke, V. A. (1990) Sex Differences in Computer Participation: Concerns, Extent, Reasons and Strategies. Australian Journal of Education. 34, 52–66.

Clarke, V. A. (1992) Strategies for Involving Girls in Computer Science. In: C. D. Martin and E. Murchie-Beyma (Eds.), *In Search of Gender Free Paradigms in Computer Science Education.* International Society for Technology in Education, Oregon, pp. 71–86.

Cohen, E. B. (2002) *Challenges of Information Technology Education in the 21st Century.* Idea Group.

Collis, B. (1985) Psychosocial Implications of Sex Differences in Attitudes Towards Computers: Results of a Survey. International Journal of Women's Studies. 8(3), 207–213.

Dean, C. (2007) Computer Science Takes Steps to Bring Women to the Fold. New York Times, April 17, 2007.

Fetler, M. (1985) Sex Differences on the California Statewide Assessment of Computer Literacy. Sex Roles: A Journal of Research. 13(3), 181–191.

Galpin, V. (2002) Women in Computing Around the World. SIGCSE Bulletin. 34(2), 94–100.

Gaudin, S. (2000) Women, Minorities Could Fill More High-Tech Jobs. Network World. 17(29), 6–16.

Glaser, B. G. (1992) *Basics of Grounded Theory Analysis.* Sociology Press, California.

Glaser, B. G. and Strauss, A. L. (1967) *The Discovery of Grounded Theory: Strategies for Qualitative Research.* Aldine, New York.

Goasduff, L. and Swedemyr, C. (2006) Gartner Advises IT Leaders to Recognise Complementary Gender Strengths. Press Release, France, Cannes, November 6, 2006. http://www.gartner.com/it/page.jsp?id=498223

Gressard, C. P. and Loyd, B. H. (1987) An Investigation of the Effects of Math Anxiety and Sex on Computer Attitude. School Science and Mathematics. 87(2), 125–135.

Gunn, C. (2003) Dominant or Different? Gender Issues in Computer Supported Learning. Journal of Asynchronous Learning Networks. 7(1), 14–30.

Gurer, D. and Camp, T. (2002) An ACM-W Literature Review on Women in Computing. ACM SIGCSE Bulletin. 34(2), 121–127.

Hodgkinson, L. (1999) Is Technology Masculine? Theorising the Absence of Women. Technology and Society, 1999. International Symposium on Women and Technology: Historical, Societal, and Professional Perspectives. pp. 121–126.

Hurworth, R. (1996) Qualitative Methodology: Common Questions about Running Focus Groups during Evaluations. Evaluation News and Comment. 5(1), 48, 49, 52.

Jonas-Dwyer, D. and Pospisil, R. (2004) The Millennial Effect: Implications for Academic Development. HERDSA Conference, Sarawak, Malaysia.

Kekelis, L. S., Ancheta, R. W. and Heber, E. (2005) Hurdles in the Pipeline: Girls and Technology Careers. Frontiers: A Journal of Women Studies. 26, 1.

Krueger, R. A. (1994) *Focus Groups: A Practical Guide for Applied Research.* Sage, Thousand Oaks, CA.

Lacey, A. and Luff, D. (2001) Trent Focus for Research and Development in Primary Health care: An Introduction to Qualitative Analysis. Trent Focus.

Linn, M. C. (2005) Technology and Gender Equity: What Works? In: N. F. Russo et al. (Eds.), *Women in Science and Technology.* American Psychological Association, New York.

Morgan, D. L. (1998) *The Focus Group Guidebook.* Sage, Thousand Oaks, CA.

Munger, G. F. and Loyd, B. H. (1989) Gender and Attitudes Toward Computers and Calculators: Their Relationship to Math Performance. Journal of Educational Computing Research. 5(2), 167–177.

Oblinger, D. G. and Oblinger, J. L. (2005) *Educating the Net Generation.* Educause, Colorado, Boulder.

Sanders, J. (2005) Gender and Technology: A Research Review. Center for Gender Equity. Seattle.

Sanders, J. S. (1985) Making the Computer Neuter. The Computing Teacher. 12(7), 23–27.

Sanders, J. and McGinnis, M. (1988) Computer Equity for Girls. In: A. O. B. Carelli (Ed.), *Sex Equity in Education: Readings and Strategies.* Charles C Thomas Pub Ltd, Springfield, pp. 157–172.

Seymour, E. and Hewitt, N. M. (1997) Issues of Gender. In: *Talking about Leaving: Why Undergraduates Leave the Sciences.* Westview, Boulder, pp. 231–318.

Shashaani, L. (1994) Socioeconomic Status, Parents' Sex-Role Stereotypes, and the Gender Gap in Computing. Journal of Research on Computing in Education. 26(4), 433–451.

Turkle, S. (1988) Computational Reticence: Why Women Fear the Intimate Machine. In: C. Kramarae (Ed.), *Technology and Women's Voices.* Routledge & Kegan Paul, New York.

WEEA Equity Resource Center (2000) Facts on Women's and Girl's Educational Equity. WEEA Equity Resource Center, Newton, MA.

Zhang, Y. (2006) Content Analysis (Qualitative, Thematic). http://www.ils.unc.edu/~yanz/Content%20analysis.pdf. Accessed 11 April 2007

# A Theoretical Investigation of the Synergy Between Enterprise E-Learning and Knowledge Management

Brenda Mallinson and Lindsay Vos

Department of Information Systems, Rhodes University, Grahamstown, South Africa,
B.Mallinson@ru.ac.za, voslin@gmail.com

**Abstract** Organizations wishing to achieve and sustain competitive advantage need to improve the knowledge and skills of their workforce. E-learning and knowledge management are distinct disciplines that both aim to serve this purpose. The primary focus of this paper is to investigate the fields of e-learning and knowledge management within an organizational context, in order to determine whether the two disciplines can leverage off one another for the purpose of improved learning in organizations. The manner in which organizations currently implement learning is addressed. Both fields are investigated in terms of their characteristics, benefits, environment, and implementation issues. A number of similarities are found to exist, and it is concluded that the two fields can leverage off one another in order to improve organizational learning. Current models of enterprise learning are explored, and inform the creation of a proposed framework to guide organizations wishing to improve learning, by synergizing aspects from the disciplines of e-learning and knowledge management.

## 1 Introduction

A knowledge-hungry generation has emerged with a need for fast access to knowledge and learning resources. Traditional classroom learning can be assisted by e-learning (EL), which makes use of information and communication technology applications to train employees, in order for them to become more productive and knowledgeable workers. Wild et al. (2002) define EL as the creation and distribution of knowledge through the online communication and delivery of information, education, and training.

Knowledge management (KM) aims to leverage the intellectual capital of an organization by collecting, organizing, and sharing the information and experiences within an organization in order to facilitate the creation of additional organizational value (Sveiby 2000). There is an increasing interest in bridging the current gap between enterprise EL and KM (Asgarkhani 2004). Both EL and KM are emerging disciplines, operating in environments that appear to be of a similar nature, and evidence of a common ground between the two fields exists, with a likelihood of the two areas leveraging off one another. This paper aims to shed light on these disciplines and their possible synergy, in order to improve learning in organizations. Current models of enterprise learning are explored, and pertinent elements are drawn from each of these models to create the proposed framework.

## 2 Current Learning Practices in Organizations

A learning organization strives to improve the knowledge and skills of its work-force. An organization's competitive edge is heavily dependent upon the knowledge and skills of its professional staff, and to address this, some form of learning strategy needs to be in place within the organization (Finn 2002). Piskurich and Sanders (1998) identified organizational learning methods as instructional (for example, case studies and demonstrations), presentational (for example, audio and video), and distributional (for example, DVD and the WWW).

Örtenblad (2004) advocates the integration of his four aspects of the learning organization: organizational learning, learning at work, positive learning climate, and learning structure. Organizational learning comprises an awareness of a variety of learning levels, and the organizational storing and use of knowledge. Learning in organizations needs to be supported by learning structures, and the organizational culture needs to be geared towards such practices. The members of the organization should be continuous learners in order to be able to manage customer's changing needs, wants, and demands (Örtenblad 2004). A learning structure should be flexible and organic as opposed to bureaucratic, seeking to replace rigid with adaptable approaches to working-as-learning. A decentralized structure places importance on the organization's members making their own decisions, and fosters team work where members are encouraged to learn each other's roles and multitask. In addition, an organization's customers are a key source of functional knowledge, enabling the organization to benchmark its working practices against competitors and industry leaders (Örtenblad 2004).

Thorne (2003) describes the emergence of a blended learning (BL) approach that interleaves online learning with more traditional classroom methods. She maintains that while classroom training will not completely disappear, EL will have a significant effect on training. BL has proven to be more effective than any single delivery method (Finn 2002). In a study of more than 950 organizations, Van Buuren (2001) identified trends in organizational learning methods, including those of organizations delivering less and less of their training in the classroom, with a corresponding increase in technology-delivered training or EL. This approach uses the strengths and supporting competencies of traditional classroom training, presentations, stand-alone interactive online training, and asynchronous and synchronous Web-based training (Reay 2002), to provide a tailored solution to fit both the learner's need and style (Thorne 2003). A blend of instructor-facilitated, synchronous and asynchronous, self-directed, self-paced approaches can be used to meet learner needs (Reay 2002; Thorne 2003; Rosenberg 2006);

**Table 1.** Elements of successful e-learning (EL) and knowledge management (KM)

| EL – Characteristics – KM | |
|---|---|
| • Networked infrastructure and communities; delivered via a computer using standard Internet technologies and focused on the broadest view of learning (Rosenberg 2001; Hansen 2001)<br>• Builds new knowledge and skills linked to individual learning goals or improved organizational performance (Clark and Mayer 2003)<br>• Incorporation of a variety of digital media, interaction, competition, and skill-building challenges; course objectives and relevance should be specific and known (Hansen 2001) | • Create value from intangible assets; manage the environment, not the knowledge (Sveiby 2000)<br>• Strategy-driven; aim to achieve organizational goals; motivate and facilitate the workforce (Henczel 2004; Tiwana 2000; Uit Beijerse 1999)<br>• Systematic processes to identify, create, capture, share, and leverage knowledge (Henczel 2004) |
| **EL – Benefits – KM** | |
| • Cost savings/avoidance; reduced time out of workplace (Asgarkhani 2004; Hall 2002)<br>• Increased accessibility, flexibility, productivity, and efficiency; shorter development cycles to contend with the rapid pace of business change (Hall 2002; Wild et al. 2002)<br>• Customized and consistent content; timely and dependable information; enhanced business responsiveness; universality; scalability (Rosenberg 2001)<br>• Increase in benefits, value, usage, and attitude of stakeholders (Harris 2004)<br>• On-demand availability; self-pacing; interactivity; timely material updates; certification and completion proof; expert knowledge captured (Asgarkhani 2004) | • Enables dealing with complexities accompanying the emergence of the knowledge-based economy: improved efficiency, market position, and relevant competencies; enhance continuity and profitability; enable more efficient and effective learning; enable better decision-making; improved communication and synergy; improved worker retention; focus on core business and critical knowledge (Uit Beijerse 1999) |
| **EL – Environments – KM** | |
| • High performance networks; technical skills; change management; marketing (Harris 2002)<br>• Web-based environments should be interactive; learner controlled; device- and time-independent; globally accessible; and address a variety of learning styles (Khan 1997)<br>• Organizational vision and strategy; sponsorship and active executive support and enterprise awareness of value and role; governance board; change management to develop a learning culture; adequate funding; distinguish between career development and skills development, and view EL as an ongoing program; integration into core business processes measured against business objectives; exploit emerging technology early and aggressively (Harris 2004) | • A holistic environment encompassing processes of knowledge identification/discovery, knowledge creation/acquisition, knowledge capture/retrieval and knowledge sharing/transfer/flow; espousing a sharing culture, value based, people focused, motivated, committed, proactive, resources supported, and technology enabled (Henczel 2004)<br>• Creation of organizational knowledge via interaction between tacit and explicit knowledge i.e. knowledge conversion (Nonaka and Teece 2001) |
| **EL – Implementation Issues – KM** | |
| • Strategic foundation comprising new approaches to learning; learning architectures; learning culture; management, ownership, and change management; sound business case; infrastructure, Internet access, materials portal; interoperability; focus on delivering instruction/information and enabling collaboration (Rosenberg 2001, 2006)<br>• Clear, purposeful, compelling vision of learning, knowledge and performance; stakeholder communication; develop strategy; select content (Engelbrecht 2003; Hall 2002)<br>• Guiding principles of appropriateness and readiness, interaction and evaluation criteria (Blass and Davis 2003; Hall 2002) | • Creating awareness, performing benchmarking, developing a knowledge taxonomy, a KM strategy, and identifying target areas; selection of KM technologies and tools, infrastructure; communities of practice (Liebowitz and Megbolugbe 2003)<br>• Identify the knowledge users, authors, and analysts; encourage a sharing culture; create and manage data, information and knowledge; appropriate technical infrastructure (Stacey 2000) |

BL should be relevant and demand a holistic strategy leveraging the best characteristics of all learning interventions (Reay 2002).

## 3 Investigating E-Learning and Knowledge Management

Learners want and need knowledge, and EL is an efficient and potentially fruitful means to this end (Wild et al. 2002). Professional training organizations have acknowledged the strategic importance of using online technology-based learning (Asgarkhani 2004). Rosenberg (2006) redefines EL as "the use of Internet technologies to create and deliver a rich learning environment that includes a broad array of instruction and information resources and solutions, the goal of which is to enhance individual and organizational performance". KM is ultimately about "delivering the right knowledge to the right people at the right time" (Rossett and Sheldon 2002). Table 1 summarizes the characteristics, benefits, environments, and implementation issues associated with EL and KM.

## 4 Areas of Synergy Between E-Learning and KM

Enterprise EL and KM are both relatively new *emerging disciplines*, still thought to be very much in their infancy (Hansen 2001) and accompanied by continuing discussion over how best to use the power of each discipline. As they become better understood, the apparent similarities will perhaps show how the two fields can leverage off one another. This may be seen as a natural step towards better organizational results, and learning management and KM should be combined into one integrated program, process, philosophy, and approach, resulting in a more powerful intellectual capital management (Brandon-Hall 2001). Wild et al. (2002) liken *organizational readiness* in EL to determining organizational needs and the knowledge gap in KM.

KM and enterprise EL both aim to achieve strategic organizational goals, and strive to enhance human knowledge and its use within organizations (Brandon-Hall 2001). Organizations with successful EL adoptions reported training as being integral to overall strategy (Hall 2002). The primary objectives of KM are to identify and leverage the collective knowledge in an organization to achieve the overriding goal of helping organizations compete and survive (Choo 1996 in Wild et al. 2002).

A strategic foundation is necessary for both EL and KM when solutions are planned and developed. Asgarkhani (2004) states that both KM and EL solutions should take a holistic approach, and address fundamental issues from a strategic point of view. Knowledge is considered to be the most strategically important resource and learning is the most strategically important capability for business organizations. Both disciplines need to secure top management support, align their goals with business strategies, define an information vision and architecture, and develop strategic, tactical, and operational plans for the implementation of an information vision and architecture for EL and KM solutions (Asgarkhani 2004).

Both EL and KM provide knowledge in different ways to the employee. KM identifies and leverages the collective knowledge in an organization for timely access. The premise of EL is that it provides knowledge to the learner, anywhere, anytime, through online courses (Rosenberg 2001). Professionals in both fields seek ways to categorize and store knowledge, using database architecture as a foundation (Brandon-Hall 2001). The primary goal of both EL and KM is to share information (Clark and Mayer 2003). The trend of a blended means of distributing knowledge is expanded by Rosenberg (2006) to include both formal and informal settings that support KM, Performance Support, and Mentoring.

The challenges of implementing EL mirror those of conducting KM. Both initiatives require appropriate technological infrastructures to be developed, and organizational behavior and culture need to be shifted to accommodate and encourage EL and KM within the organization. Building senior management support for the change in culture becomes increasingly important. An enterprise-wide knowledge strategy needs to be designed and communicated throughout the organization and economic investments are required for both initiatives (Wild et al. 2002). Ardichvili et al. (2006) found a lower than expected importance of several cultural values in sharing knowledge patterns in an online environment. Nevertheless, they recommend that cognizance should be taken of organizational and national values and cultural preferences when engaging in sharing knowledge.

The benefits of EL complement and strengthen KM activities (Wild et al. 2002). EL assists KM as it incorporates education and technology to capture, disseminate, and share knowledge. Learning content management systems (LCMS) aid the fusion of EL with KM. The alignment of EL with KM is both obvious and beneficial, and it is a trend that will lead to a "powerful fusion of processes, material, systems and strategies bringing together all the know-how, skills and information an organization needs in order to flourish" (Reay 2002). Rossett et al. (2002) suggest that training professionals should claim more of a leadership role in managing the wealth of intellectual resources in the organization.

Rosenberg (2001) reveals that the "implications of KM on e-learning are huge." By providing access to information that contains the collective wisdom of the company, the organization is providing the workforce with an additional valuable tool; organizational needs can be met via instruction or information as appropriate. As EL grows in diversity, it will generate and disseminate information and directly support performance in the workplace via business processes (Rosenberg 2001). San Diego State University (1999) reports that KM assists EL initiatives as it makes it easier for trainers to situate learning and growth on the job, and deliver content as it is needed.   Just-in-time training is possible through just-in-time KM. KM can also identify the most current and viable content for the EL initiative. KM promotes continuous access to information, learning, and professional growth for employees who want to develop their skills horizontally within a profession.

The identified areas of synergy between enterprise EL and KM include their roots in strategy and their desired explicit link to business strategy, targeting organizational goals such as increased performance and long-term competitive advantage. Both disciplines share the common goal of knowledge sharing and making it available to the right people anywhere, anytime. Surrounding implementation issues are similar as both involve technological, cultural, economic, and strategic initiatives. EL helps capture, disseminate, and share knowledge throughout the organization and aids KM by fusing all the collective skills and information of the organization. KM complements EL by making well-structured information and content available as it is needed and providing access to the collective wisdom of the organization. Both fields complement each other, and the areas of synergy show the possibility of merging the two fields into a single discipline for organizational learning.

## 5 Current Models

Four models were explored and are briefly described: the Framework for Enterprise Learning (Finn 2002), the Framework for EL as a Tool for KM (Wild et al. 2002), Guidelines for using KM Perspectives during Training in Organizations (Rossett et al. 2002), and Rosenberg's (2006) Learning and Performance Architecture.

Finn (2002) proposes a framework for enterprise learning and explains the components that inform a learning strategy. An organization seeking to adopt this framework for enterprise learning needs to build an architecture that supports every aspect of learning and is mapped to critical business processes. Learning must be embedded in the culture of the organization and the company must redefine learning as a continuous activity and as a process, not a single event. An enterprise learning system is composed of multiple tasks that work together to meet the organizational learning goals: enterprise learning and program planning; content creation and management; knowledge delivery and assessment; program and learner management.

Wild et al. (2002) provide a framework for the EL process that is tied to the processes in the knowledge value chain. The model states that EL creates a growing repository of knowledge that will continuously deliver to employees just what they need, when they need it. EL permits the participant to acquire knowledge, pass it on, apply it to organizational problems/opportunities, and store that knowledge for future use. This is familiar to KM; both fields are about generating, storing, distributing, and applying knowledge. This framework addresses important planning and implementation considerations that will help to ensure the success of the organization's EL initiatives. The KM chain comprises the following steps: Determine Strategic Knowledge Management Needs; Determine the Knowledge Gap; Close the Knowledge Gap; Disseminate and Apply Knowledge Acquired.

Organizational readiness in the Wild et al. (2002) EL value chain is directly tied to the first two processes in the KM value chain; i.e., it requires the determination of strategic knowledge requirements and an assessment of the current organizational knowledge gap. The last two processes in the knowledge value chain are aligned with the last three phases of the EL value chain. The design of knowledge content and presentation, and the subsequent EL implementation are intended to close the knowledge gap and disseminate the knowledge required to promote organizational survival and competitive position. The EL value chain comprises the following: assess and prepare organizational readiness, design appropriate content, design appropriate presentation, and implement e-learning.

Rossett et al. (2002) move towards a definition of training that includes KM perspectives, services, and products. Training professionals must claim a leadership role in managing the extant wealth of organizational intellectual resources. Guidelines for adopting a KM perspective include the following: create a rich environment, bust the boundaries of the classroom, establish broader access to information, nurture relationships, establish alliances, attend to social and tacit aspects, contribute to a sharing and positive culture, attend to individuals not yet ready to be self-reliant.

Rosenberg (2006) describes his Learning and Performance Architecture as necessary for the "smart enterprise." This architecture encompasses all of the desirable components to implement true BL/training in the workplace. His inner KM area comprises linked *Information Repositories, Communities and Networks,* and *Experts and Expertise.* Each of these three components also links to the exterior EL elements of *Online Training* and *Performance Support.* The view is holistic as all of these components operate within the context of *Workplace Learning and Training* in both *Formal* and *Informal Workplace Settings.*

## 5.1 Critical Analysis of Current Frameworks and Guidelines

Finn (2002) provides a sound framework for enterprise learning and identifies critical elements that come together to form an enterprise learning strategy. The four building blocks described for enterprise learning are simple and intuitive, and cover the fundamental aspects of planning, creating, delivering, and managing learning programs. However, the framework focuses primarily on EL initiatives and ignores traditional learning methods, which are also important aspects for consideration. The concept of BL, which could strengthen the model, is absent.

Finn (2002) clearly states that organizations seeking to adopt a framework for enterprise learning must build an architecture that supports every aspect of learning and take a strategic view. Although she emphasizes the incorporation of the learning strategy into the business infrastructure, it is not reflected in the model. Even though Wild et al. (2002) explain that the strategic knowledge requirements need to be identified during the first phase of their EL value chain, this model does not define EL and KM as elements tied to the organizational strategy. Rossett et al. (2002) make no mention of a strategic aspect in their model.

Wild et al. (2002) take a logical step linking the KM value chain with the phases of the EL planning process. The model, similar to Finn's (2002), covers some important planning aspects of organizational readiness, as well as designing content, presentation, and implementation issues for EL initiatives. Wild et al. (2002) include the concept of bended learning in their model, which is a crucial aspect to consider when designing the presentation style for learning in the organization.

Both Finn (2002) and Wild et al. (2002) include the discussion of content in their models. Rossett et al. (2002) fail to mention content in their model. However, the model does take the angle of using KM perspectives during training. Rosenberg (2006) incorporates content in his information repository.

Rossett et al. (2002) have identified promising opportunities for training professionals when implementing learning in the organization using a KM perspective. This approach is similar to the framework of Wild et al. (2002), and although these guidelines are adequate and possible, they focus mainly on the softer issues surrounding training and tend to ignore the physical, technological, and infrastructural aspects of implementing EL. Both the Wild et al. (2002) and Finn (2002) models focus on the components that create a learning strategy. However, the softer issues mentioned in the Rossett et al. (2002) model are of critical importance, and all three models mention how the creation of a sharing culture is necessary when implementing EL and KM initiatives. Rosett et al. (2002) also emphasize that learning should include both traditional classroom instruction as well as technology-based training. The Rossett et al. (2002) guidelines could be more comprehensively summarized and most of the guidelines could be grouped into one or two "soft" issues.

Rosenberg's (2006) Learning and Performance Architecture expands the view of BL where the course is no longer the exclusive container for the solution. He acknowledges the value of both formal and informal, traditional and online training, performance support and mentoring, and the availability of both instructional and informational resources. The inclusion of the informal workplace learning in his architecture encourages a move from exclusive push learning to incorporate pull learning. Users can therefore exercise more control over their learning and information gathering, and a more flexible learning culture is developed. It is debatable that the KM area should be totally subsumed within the EL environment.

Each model looks at a distinct, valuable aspect of this research area. Finn's (2002) framework highlighted the importance of enterprise learning and program planning, content creation and management, knowledge delivery and assessment, and program and learner management. These crucial building blocks provide a foundation for building successful and strong enterprise learning frameworks on the basis of business goals and organizational strategies. Wild et al. (2002) showed that EL is an effective tool for KM and addressed important planning and implementation considerations that will help ensure the success of the organization's EL initiatives. By tying the implementation considerations of EL to the processes in the knowledge value chain, the framework successfully illustrated how EL can be used as an important tool in KM. Finally, Rossett et al. (2002) comprehensively identified how KM can be used by training professionals to manage intellectual capital in the organization, and the opportunities available to trainers using a KM perspective. Rosenberg's (2006) Learning and Performance Architecture provides a comprehensive structure to implement KM and EL within the "Smart Enterprise". Although each model has a unique focus, collectively they all contribute to the greater area of study, which is how EL and KM complement and overlap each other.

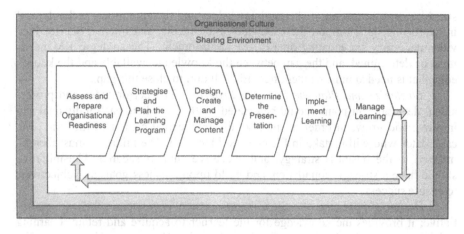

**Fig. 1.** A framework for implementing enterprise learning

# 6 Proposed Framework for Enterprise Learning

The proposed framework (Fig. 1) aims to provide a guideline for organizations wishing to develop the knowledge and skills of their workforce by improving learning in the organization. Although the framework is unique, the steps in the process are based primarily on a combination of Finn (2002) and Wild et al. (2002) models, and include softer aspects from the guidelines set out by Rossett et al. (2002). Additional aspects (Table 1) are drawn from the fields of KM and EL to improve existing organizational learning, or to help organizations create learning. The particular issues that have been adapted include the importance of aligning learning with strategic foundations, the concept of BL, and the softer implementation issues such as organizational culture and a positive, sharing environment.

The framework suggests a number of steps to create organizational learning, contextualized within the organization's environment and culture. A brief description of each step of the framework is provided and so is a discussion on the "sharing environment" and "culture", which are not considered steps, but rather other organizational factors to consider. The model has a directional arrow returning to the first step, which shows that learning in an enterprise is continuous. The completion of one program should offer opportunities for ongoing professional development.

## 6.1 Framework Stages and Environment

*1. Assess and Prepare Organizational Readiness:* Prior to implementing organizational learning initiatives, a readiness assessment must be conducted. The employees should accept the notion of sharing knowledge, and the appropriate technological infrastructure must support the bandwidth, multimedia, and Internet Service Provider necessary for creating an EL/KM environment. The strategic KM needs must be determined, and the gap between the knowledge available and the knowledge that is needed must be identified. EL will aim to close this gap.

*2. Strategize and Plan the Learning Program:* The performance and professional development plans should be created, outlining where each individual can improve and grow, in order to improve the intellectual capital of the firm. The candidates who will partake in EL must be identified. The initiative must then be mapped to the business strategy, and executive support secured. The initiative should have a strategic foundation, and build upon business goals and objectives, to ensure success.

*3. Design, Create, and Manage Content:* Content is crucial for the learning initiative; it provides the knowledge for the learner to acquire and retain. Learning objects must be identified for reuse through various learning environments. The content design should be guided by the strategic knowledge requirements. Although the nature of content will vary, EL should aim to communicate the tacit knowledge of all the employees. Explicit knowledge or training is also communicated so that workers can improve work performance and assist in improving products and services. Content designers should aim to use a variety of innovative, dynamic, and informational materials to ensure that learning objectives are met and knowledge retention is high. Subject matter experts should have the knowledge, appropriate skills, and experience to develop content for any delivery method. A learning content management system provides a technical solution to storing and organizing content in an easily searchable central repository. Content should also adhere to packaging standards; this ensures that the content is useful within a variety of delivery methods, and ensures interoperability.

*4. Determine the Presentation:* Combining the characteristics of classroom learning with online learning creates a rich and varied presentation environment that should satisfy the needs of the learners. Learning management systems, electronic performance support systems, Web portals, and catalogues are some effective ways to provide access to learning materials. Instructors should ensure that their knowledge and expertise are available to the learners; and synchronous and asynchronous forms of delivery also must be considered at this stage. This step should be heavily dependent on a sound learning architecture such as that described by Rosenberg (2006).

*5. Implement Learning/Knowledge Program:* This involves implementing a properly planned, provisioned, and maintained network, setting up the appropriate content application and software tools, and creating a learning map that will help to direct the EL process and assess its success. A pilot group can be used when implementing a new learning plan and these results are often useful in improving the program, prior to enterprise-wide implementation.

*6. Manage Learning/Knowledge Program:* Both the learners and the program need to be managed after the implementation. Results of the new learning style must be analyzed to determine whether it has achieved the desired goals set out in the strategy. When managing learning, the person or team in charge of organizational learning must return to the beginning of the process, and reconsider each step in the process to ensure that organizational learning is continuous.

7. *Sharing Environment and Organizational Culture:* A learning culture must be in place within the organization, where learning is encouraged and facilitated. The organization must also ensure that the employees view knowledge as something that must be shared, not hoarded. They should strive to achieve a rich environment where the social aspects (such as collaboration and cooperation) are taken into consideration along with the content. If organizations do not encourage sharing, the knowledge base will suffer, no matter the investment in technology. Organizations should view knowledge as an asset, and develop organizational norms and values that support the creation and sharing of knowledge.

## 7 Conclusions

To create and sustain competitive advantage, organizations need to develop the knowledge and skills of their workforce. This theoretical investigation shows how enterprise EL and KM can leverage off one another, and be combined into a single program, to aid organizational learning.

The proposed framework can be used by organizations wishing to improve learning, so that organizations will have a stronger knowledge base, retain intellectual capital and employees who are better equipped to deal with organizational problems or opportunities. This should result in organizations having improved products and services, and ultimately competitive advantage, which is what both EL and KM aim to achieve. The framework draws on aspects from the fields of KM and EL to create a unique framework that comprises six fundamental steps: Assess and prepare organizational readiness; strategize and plan the learning environment; design, create, and manage content; determine the presentation; implement learning; and manage learning. Learning in an organization is a continuous process that is illustrated by the iterative nature of the framework. Organizational culture and a sharing environment are deemed crucial for the success of any organizational learning strategy. The framework for enterprise learning harvests the principal issues from the fields of EL and KM. This framework can be used as a set of guidelines to help the organization create or improve its learning and knowledge.

## References

Ardichvili, A., Maurer, M., Li, W., Wentling, T. and Stuedemann, R. (2006) Cultural Influences on Knowledge Sharing through Online Communities of Practice. *Journal of Knowledge Management*, 10(1), 94–107.
Asgarkhani, M. (2004) The Need for a Strategic Foundation for Digital Learning and Knowledge Management Solutions. *Electronic Journal of E-Learning*, 2(1), 31–42.
Blass, E. and Davis, A. (2003) Building on Solid Foundations: Establishing Criteria for E-Learning Developments. *Journal of Further and Higher Education*, 27(3), 227–245.

Brandon-Hall (2001) Learning Management and Knowledge Management. http://www.brandonhall.com/public/whitepapers/lmkm/whitepaper_lmkm260101.pdf

Clark, R.C. and Mayer, R.E. (2003) *E-Learning and the Science of Instruction*. San Francisco: Pfeiffer

Engelbrecht, E. (2003) A Look at E-Learning Models: Investigating Their Values for Developing an E-Learning Strategy. *Progressio*, 25(2), 38–47.

Finn, A. (2002) Building a Framework for Enterprise Learning. *Centra Learning Officer*. http://www.centra.com/docs/card.asp?mproject=web

Hall, B. (2002) Six Steps to Developing a Successful E-Learning Initiative: Excerpts from the E-learning Guidebook. In: Rossett, A. (Ed.), *The ASTD E-Learning Handbook*. Madison: McGraw-Hill.

Hansen, L. (2001) E-Learning – Separating the Myths from Reality. *Knowledge Management Review*, 4(3), 34–37.

Harris, K. (2002) E-Learning: Value, Benefits and Investment. Gartner. DF-18-3842.

Harris, K. (2004) Use a Maturity Model to Make the Most of E-Learning. Gartner. DF-22-3036.

Henczel, S. (2004) Supporting the KM Environment: The Roles, Responsibilities, and Rights of Information Professionals. *Information Outlook*, 8(1), 13–18.

Khan, B.H. (1997) *Web-Based Instruction*. New Jersey: Educational Technology Publications.

Liebowitz, J. and Megbolugbe, I. (2003) A Set of Frameworks to Aid the Project Manager in Conceptualizing and Implementing Knowledge Management Initiatives. *International Journal of Project Management*, 21(3), 189–198.

Nonaka, I. and Teece, D.J. (2001) *Managing Industrial Knowledge*. London: Sage.

Örtenblad, A. (2004) The Learning Organization: Towards an Integrated Model. *The Learning Organization*, 11(2), 129–144.

Piskurich, G. and Sanders, E.S. (1998) *ASTD Models for Learning Technologies: Roles, Competencies and Outputs*. Alexandria, Virginia: ASTD.

Reay, J. (2001) Blended Learning: Fusion for the Future. *Knowledge Management Review*, 4(3), 1–6.

Rosenberg, M.J. (2001) *E-Learning: Strategies for Building Knowledge in the Digital Age*. Madison: McGraw-Hill.

Rosenberg, M.J. (2006) *Beyond E-Learning: Approaches and Technologies to Enhance Organizational Knowledge, Learning and Performance*. New York: Wiley.

Rossett, A. and Sheldon, K. (2002) How Can We Use Knowledge Management? In: Rossett, A. (Ed.), *The ASTD E-Learning Handbook. Best practices, strategies and case studies for an emerging field*. Madison: McGraw-Hill.

San Diego State University. (1999) Knowledge Management and Training. http://defcon.sdsu.edu/1/objects/km/home/index.htm

Stacey, P. (2000) E-Learning. http://www.bctechnology.com/statics/pstacey-oct2700.html

Sveiby, K.E. (2000) Knowledge Management: Viking Way. http://www.sveiby.com/library.html

Thorne, K. (2003) *Blended Learning*. London: Kogan Page.

Tiwana, A. (2000) *The Knowledge Management Toolkit*. New Jersey: Prentice-Hall.

Uit Beijerse, R.P. (1999) Questions in Knowledge Management: Defining and Conceptualizing a Phenomenon. *Journal of Knowledge Management*, 3(2), 94–110.

Van Buuren, M. (2001) *State of the Industry: 2001 Report*. Alexandria, Virginia: ASTD.

Wild, R.H., Griggs, K.A. and Downing, T. (2002) A Framework for E-learning as a Tool for Knowledge Management. *Industrial Management and Data Systems*, 102(7), 371–380.

# KNOC: A Knowledge-Oriented Cooperative Software Development Process

Claudine Toffolon[1] and Salem Dakhli[2]

[1] LIL Laboratory, Littoral University, Calais, France, Claudine.Toffolon@dauphine.fr

[2] CERIA Laboratory, Paris-Dauphine University, Paris, France, Salem.Dakhli@dauphine.fr

**Abstract** Software systems have become one of the most valuable assets of modern organizations, where they play a critical role in supporting operational and decision processes. Nevertheless, despite the large part of organizations' resources invested in information technology, development of software systems faces many problems recognized by the term *software crisis*. To reduce the economic and social impacts of this crisis, one widely acknowledged approach has been to improve software processes and software development methods supporting them. However, as stressed by many authors, such solutions of the software crisis are partial and incomplete and present many weaknesses related to their technical orientation. In this paper, we present a knowledge-oriented and cooperative software development framework process in order to improve the existing solutions of the software crisis. This framework considers software systems as an accumulation of knowledge. It proposes a cooperative guidance to gather the knowledge necessary for designing to software products that is distributed among various stakeholders.

## 1 Introduction

With the ever-increasing penetration of information technology into the daily functioning of society, software systems have become one of the most valuable assets of modern organizations, where they play a critical role in supporting operational and decision processes. Indeed, modern organizations need software systems that provide them with instruments to leverage core business competencies, accelerate innovation and time to market, improve cycle times and decision-making, strengthen organizational commitment, and build sustainable competitive advantage. Moreover, software artifacts appear in almost every aspect of life, from the desktop, to the car, to the living room. Some of these artifacts are used in mission-critical and real-time situations where human lives are at stake. However, despite the large part of organizations' resources invested in information technology,

C. Barry et al. (eds.), *Information Systems Development: Challenges in Practice, Theory, and Education, Vol.1*, doi: 10.1007/978-0-387-68772-8_38,
© Springer Science+Business Media, LLC 2009

development of software systems faces many problems recognized by the term *software crisis* (Gibbs 1994; Neumann 1995; Pressman 2004). In particular, the "productivity paradox" (Solow 1987; Dedrick et al. 2003), which states that the links between information technology and white-collar workers' productivity have historically been weak, is partly related to the software crisis. To reduce the economic and social impacts of the software crisis, one widely acknowledged approach has been to improve software processes and software development methods supporting them. Nevertheless, as stressed by many authors, such solutions of the software crisis are partial and incomplete and present many weaknesses related to their technical orientation. In particular, well-established processes and methods neglect many important aspects of software, notably economic, organizational, and human aspects (Abdel-Hamid and Madnick 1991; Boehm 1988; Toffolon 1996; Fitzgerald 1996, 1998). To improve the quality of software products, many academics have noticed the multidimensional nature of IS and the multiplicity of the organizational actors involved in their development, maintenance, and use (Kling 1996; Lyytinen 1987; Toffolon 1999; Toffolon and Dakhli 2002). According to these authors, situated software development processes and methods taking into account all the aspects of software are required to build effective software systems that meet modern organizations' needs. We think that to effectively support operational and decision-making processes within modern organizations, software systems must integrate the knowledge distributed among the various stakeholders concerned with these systems. In this paper, we present a knowledge-oriented and cooperative software development process framework, called KNOC, in order to improve the existing solutions of the software crisis. This framework considers software systems as an accumulation of knowledge. It proposes a cooperative guidance to gather the knowledge necessary to software products design and distributed among various stakeholders. The rest of this paper is organized as follows. Section 2 describes the relationship between software and knowledge and explains why a knowledge-oriented and cooperative software development framework process may provide a significant contribution to software engineering. In Sect. 3, we present synthetically the theoretical foundations of our framework. Section 4 is dedicated to the detailed presentation of the proposed framework. In Sect. 5, we conclude our paper by listing future research directions.

## 2 Software and Knowledge

Software is a set of items or objects that form a configuration that includes programs, data, and documentation. Software products may be developed for a particular customer or may be developed for a general market. They may be generic or customized. Generic software is developed to be sold to a range of different customers while customized software is developed for a single customer according to his specifications. Software plays a dual role in modern organizations and daily life. On the one hand, software is a product that delivers computing potential and produces, manages, acquires, modifies, displays, or transmits information. On the other, software is a vehicle for delivering a product. It supports or directly provides systems functionality, controls other programs (e.g., an operating system), manages communications (e.g., networking software), or helps build other software (e.g., software tools, COTS). Among the various applications of software, the most important are system software, application software, engineering and scientific software, artificial intelligence software, embedded software, and product-line software.

The term *knowledge* is often used to refer to three different meanings: explicit knowledge, "know how," and "know about". Explicit knowledge refers to a body of knowledge that has been articulated and captured in the form of books, papers, formulas, procedure manuals, computer code, etc. "Know about" corresponds to a state of knowing, by which we also mean to be acquainted or familiar with, to be aware of, to recognize or apprehend facts, methods, principles, techniques, etc. "Know how" refers to an understanding or a grasp of facts, methods, principles, and techniques sufficient to apply them in the course of making things happen. "Know about" and "know how" are generally designated by the expression "tacit knowledge." Davenport and Prusak (1998) draw distinctions among data, information, and knowledge. Data and information correspond to a body of knowledge that exists apart from people and therefore fit within explicit knowledge. These authors define working knowledge as "a fluid mix of framed experience, values, contextual information, and expert insight that provides a framework for evaluating and incorporating new experiences and information. It originates and is applied in the minds of knowers. In organizations, it often becomes embedded not only in documents or repositories but also in organizational routines, processes, practices, and norms." The relationship between software and knowledge may be analyzed from two perspectives related either to the nature of software or to the organizational domains supported by software.

## 2.1 The Nature of Software

As demonstrated by many authors, software is situated (Lycett et al. 2003; Highsmith 2002; Cockburn 2002). The situated software concept means that the software development process must be tailored to meet each project's contextual needs. Besides, software development and use depend on organizational priorities and constraints, resources, and external environment. Consequently, understanding the nature of software requires modeling organization. Hence, prior to analysis of the nature of software, we present a model of organization. According to Leavitt's model modified by Stohr and Konsynski (1996), an organization is composed of five interconnected elements (structure, tasks, people, production technology, information technology) which interact with environment. This model provides us with a static view of organizations. To take into account the behavioral aspects of the organization's components, Toffolon (1996) improves this model by using the economic agency theory (Alchian and Demsetz 1972) and the transaction costs theory (Coase 1937; Williamson 1981) to describe the information flows sent and received by the organizational entities. There are three categories of organizational entities (actors, resources, tasks) which exchange three types of information and physical flows related to decisions, contracts, and products. The organization's actors are people involved in operational or decision-making processes. They are either producer or consumer of goods and services within the organization. Actors use resources to carry out the organization's business processes composed of tasks. Resources are either technology or organizational structure (rules, protocols, etc). We use this model of organization to point out that the relationship between software and knowledge may be analyzed at three levels: static, dynamic, and organizational. The static level refers to artifacts exchanged by organizational actors while carrying out the organization's operational and decision-making processes. Such artifacts include software that pervades nowadays an increasing number of products and services used or issued from operational processes. Baetjer (1998) makes use of the theory of capital as developed in the Austrian economic theory to point out that software products embody knowledge in the same way as all capital goods embody knowledge. As such, software grows by the continual upgrading of the capabilities it embodies. Therefore, software systems are accumulation of knowledge. Armour (2000) argues that software development process is a communication medium that must translate tacit, evolutionary, and often undefined knowledge embodied in informational digital goods. In addition to basic grammar, syntax, and rules, the translation involves also contextual and subjective semantic issues of meaning (Eischen 2002). Lycett et al. (2003) conclude that software development is a knowledge-acquiring as well as a product-producing activity, and its structure must address a communication medium's demands. The dynamic and organizational levels stress that before being embodied in software artifacts, knowledge is specialized, disparate, and distributed among existing artifacts and stakeholders (organizational level) who gather it, combine it, and transform it through a social learning software development process (dynamic level) that delivers new software artifacts.

## 2.2 The Organizational Domains Supported by Software

Modern organizations' operational and decision-making processes take place in knowledge-intensive domains characterized by multiple and heterogeneous information sources. Organizational actors involved in these processes rely on external information resources to augment their mental abilities to comprehend and solve complex problems. However, they often encounter many difficulties accessing the information they need when they need it. Besides, the amount of information available to these actors makes it difficult to find relevant information needed. By another way, the amount of knowledge required to do work in knowledge-intensive domains is vast and constantly changing. Another important characteristic of the knowledge-intensive domains is related to problem-solving activities. Such activities need contextual information which cannot be predicted a priori, but instead is determined by the demands of the particular problem-solving situation. Information sources are therefore necessary for learning while working, but the essential challenge is to find information when it is needed to solve a problem. Finally, for many knowledge-intensive domains, the temporal dimension, materialized by severe time constraints, plays a critical role while carrying out operational and decision-making processes which require that needed information be found very quickly. This class of domains includes telephone-based consulting (e.g., hot-line services, call centers) in which organizational actors interact with customers over the telephone and must locate and use information within the context of real-time conversation with these customers.

The previous analysis points out three main facets of software. On the one hand, a software system is an accumulation of knowledge related to the operational and decision-making processes it supports. In particular, the ten dimensions of software identified by Toffolon (1999) reflect the multidimensional nature of knowledge embodied by software systems. Moreover, the value added by software artifacts to organizations results from the knowledge they embody. On the other hand, knowledge to be integrated in software systems is either articulated or tacit, constantly changing, and distributed among organizational entities composed of stakeholders, resources, and tasks. By another way, to build software systems that effectively support organizations' operational and decision-making processes, software development processes must be able to gather vast amounts of knowledge dispersed among organizational entities. Finally, since stakeholders do not have a clear idea of what software system they need, software development may be considered as an ill-defined problem. Therefore, the software development process is iterative and consists in defining simultaneously the scope of computerization (the problem) and the computer solution. Consequently, software engineering relies on social, cooperative, and knowledge-oriented situated processes.

# 3 Theoretical Foundations

To take into account the social, situated, and multidimensional nature of software engineering, the framework proposed in this paper rests on the software dimensions theory (Toffolon 1999) and the software global model (Toffolon and Dakhli 2002). To take into account the cooperative, knowledge-oriented nature of software engineering, our framework draws on the distributed constructionism theory (Resnik 1996).

## 3.1 The Software Dimensions Theory

Toffolon (1999) identified ten major aspects of software or dimensions. These dimensions have been determined on the basis of a deep analysis of the effects of the software crisis and organizations' structure (Leavitt 1963). Those ten dimensions concern altogether the software process and the artifacts produced by this process. The process's dimensions (cost, delay, technical, communication, and organizational dimensions) and the product's dimensions (functional, human, economic, organizational, and temporal dimensions) demonstrate that a same software may reflect many different realities which depend on the organizational, social, and economic contexts of its use and exploitation. So, any solution should be global and take into account these dimensions. In particular, characteristics and constraints corresponding to the "human" and "organizational" dimensions must be emphasized by any global solution of the software crisis. We notice that most of the time, software development methodologies in use concentrate on technical aspects and ignore these dimensions.

## 3.2 The Software Global Model

Toffolon and Dakhli (2002) notice that software development methodologies in use make a confusion between four businesses: the stakeholder/customer's business, the end user's business, the developer's business, and the architect's business. Elimination of this confusion leads to identification of four different spaces representing respectively these four businesses:

1. The problem space where are defined the customers and users problems and their organizational solutions. This space represents the stakeholder/customer's business.
2. The solution or architectural space where are defined the computer solutions of the customer/user's problems. This space represents the architect's business.
3. The construction space where these solutions are implemented. This space represents the developer's business.
4. The operation space where are evaluated the software's usability from the user's perspective as well as its contribution to the organization's competitiveness. This space represents the end user's business.

Besides, each actor may have two categories of roles: producer (agent) or consumer (principal) of software artifacts. A role played by a project's actor in one of the four spaces is either principal or secondary. In each space, it is possible that a project has many actors assuming secondary roles, but there can be only one project actor involved in a principal role; moreover, an actor can play a secondary role in many spaces, but a principal role in only one (every actor plays the principal role in some space). For example, in the problem space, the customer plays the principal role while the user and the architect play secondary roles.

The transition between the four spaces is based on the iterative software development meta-lifecycle, designated by the acronym PACO (problem-architecture-construction-operation): the definition of a computer solution of an organizational problem permits the transition from the problem space to the solution space. The implementation of this solution expresses the transition from the solution space to the construction space. The installation of the software artifacts built in the construction space results in the transition from this space to the operation space. The description of problems and needs generated by the use of the software installed permits the transition from the operation space to the problem space. The software global model refers to the software dimensions theory proposed by Toffolon (1999) and points out that project space is associated with a subset of the ten software dimensions.

## 3.3 The Distributed Constructionist Theory

The constructionist theory is based on two hypotheses. First, it asserts that individuals build knowledge from their experiences in the world. In that way, this theory refers to constructivism. The second hypothesis stresses that the effectiveness of the knowledge construction process depends on the creation of personally meaningful products. Resnik (1996) defines distributed constructionism as an extension of the constructionist theory which focuses on situations in which many individuals contribute to knowledge construction activities. He refers to the distributed cognition theory (Salomon 1994), which states that cognition and intelligence result from interactions of a person with the surrounding environment, including artifacts, other persons, organizational context, etc. Since knowledge may be considered as the raw material of software design teams (Walz et al. 1998), the distributed contructionism theory seems to be appropriate to model the social knowledge-oriented facet of software engineering.

## 4 The KNOC Framework

In this section, we analyze the KNOC framework from three perspectives: static, dynamic, and organizational. The static perspective is related to the inputs and outputs of the software engineering process. Inputs are composed of working structure (project spaces) and resources (existing artifacts, tools, etc.) while outputs consist of software artifacts issued from the software engineering process activities. The dynamic perspective describes the software engineering process as a nexus of cooperative, knowledge-building, and iterative activities. The organizational perspective is concerned with organizational actors involved in software engineering and describes their roles and behavior.

## 4.1 The Organizational Perspective

According to the software global model (Toffolon and Dakhli 2002), software engineering may be modeled as a nexus of principal/agent contracts linking organizational actors who belong to four categories: customer, end user, architect, and developer. Agency contracts determine the behavior of the organizational actors they link. These contracts are either vertical or horizontal. Vertical agency contracts link organizational actors who belong to the same category and thus they are realized within one project space. Horizontal agency contracts link organizational actors who belong to different project spaces. Such contracts are materialized by an exchange of software artifacts between two organizational actors who play the principal role in two different project spaces. Since an organizational actor can play a secondary role in many project spaces, but a principal role in only one project space, vertical and horizontal agency contracts are dependent of each other. Consequently, to be successful, the software engineering process has to be managed at two levels: vertical and horizontal. The former expresses the efficiency and the latter the effectiveness of the software engineering process. Therefore, the success degree of the software engineering process can be described by two coordinates $(n, m)$ which measure the software engineering process efficiency and effectiveness.

## 4.2 The Static Perspective

As stressed in a previous section, software systems needed to support decision-making and operational processes of modern organizations are accumulation of knowledge. Such a knowledge, either tacit or articulated, is distributed among stakeholders, existing software artifacts, and other external and internal sources. Inputs of the software engineering process are based on tacit and articulated knowledge extracted from these three sources. Outputs issued from this process are materialized by a sequence of specifications $S_n$ which accumulate knowledge resulting from processing and combining inputs knowledge. The transformation of specifications $S_n$ results in specifications $S_{n+1}$ which are more formal and more complete than specifications $S_n$. As a result, software engineering may be viewed as a nexus of activities which establish specifications and transform them into a final software system by building a sequence of more and more formal versions of the stakeholders requirements and needs. The final software system delivered to users is the most formal version of specifications. The failure in gathering inputs knowledge and the losses or misinterpretations of knowledge while transforming specifications $S_n$ into specifications $S_{n+1}$ are among the main causes of deviations and inconsistencies inherent in software engineering (Cugola et al. 1996). Besides, as specifications play a critical role in building software systems, establishing and mastering them are the core activities of the software development process. There are four types of specifications – $S_0$, $S_1$, $S_2$, and $S_3$ – which include the minimum amount of knowledge necessary to be integrated in the final software system. Specifications $S_0$ describe the stakeholders' requirements, needs, and problems using natural language. They are established in the operation space by the end user. Specifications $S_0$ are a horizontal agency contract between the end user (the principal) and the customer (the agent). Specifications $S_1$ describe systems requirements and consist in a more formal version specifications $S_0$ with adjunction of information related to the required behavior of the future software (performance, availability, etc.). Specifications $S_1$ correspond to the software problem. They are established in the problem space by the customer and constitute a horizontal agency contract between the customer (the principal) and the architect (the agent) who uses them to establish specifications $S_2$. These specifications describe the computer solution, i.e., the architecture of the future software system. They are carried out within the solution space and constitute an agency contract between the architect (the principal) and the developer (the agent). Specifications $S_2$ may be decomposed into two parts: $S_{21}$ and $S_{22}$. The former describes the global architecture of the final software system in terms of components and connectors. The latter provides the detailed architecture of each component and connector in terms of algorithms, interfaces, data flows, etc. In this case, specifications $S_{21}$ may be viewed as a vertical contract between two software architects while specifications $S_{22}$ are a horizontal contract between the architect and the developer. Finally, specifications $S_3$ are an agency horizontal contract between the developer and the end user. They consist of the final software system built by the developer in the construction space according to specifications $S_2$ and delivered to the end user.

## 4.3 The Dynamic Perspective

The goal of the dynamic perspective of the KNOC framework is to gather, combine, and transform knowledge into a software system through a sequence of specifications with an increasing degree of formalism. Therefore, the core activities of the software development process are dedicated to cooperative and iterative knowledge engineering. The cooperative nature of the knowledge engineering process is due to two types of asymmetries. On the one hand, the dispersion of knowledge across stakeholders and existing software artifacts creates an asymmetry of know-how, i.e., tacit and articulated knowledge owned by human actors. For example, there is a know-how asymmetry between organizational actors belonging respectively to the problem side (end user, customer) and the solution side (architect, developer). The customer and the end user are domain experts who understand the practice and know implicitly what the system is supposed to do. They do not know the technological possibilities for supporting their work. The architect and the developer know how the technology can do it but they ignore whether the technology they create will be appropriate for the support of operational and decision-making processes. On the other hand, the second type of asymmetry, called understanding asymmetry, results from the differences between stakeholders' understanding of knowledge accumulated in existing software artifacts, and between their perspectives of what the future software system should be. The major challenge of the development process knowledge-oriented activities consists in building a shared vision of the future software system included in the four specifications types. This challenge is difficult because of the know-how and understanding asymmetries. That is the reason why the development process knowledge-oriented activities must be cooperative; i.e., stakeholders work together to reduce asymmetries and build a common view of the required future software system. Such a view is based on knowledge embedded in existing software artifacts or owned partially by stakeholders combined and transformed through the knowledge engineering process. Effective cooperation of stakeholders results in software prototypes which either permit uncertainty reduction or are pieces of the final software system. In the first case, informative prototypes are built to extract knowledge embedded in existing artifacts or owned by stakeholders and to illustrate a common understanding of requirements and needs. In the second case, final versions of software modules, called operational prototypes, define and implement the stakeholders' common view of what the final software system should be. Operational prototypes are parts of the software system version delivered to end users. Informative prototypes reduce uncertainty inherent in requirements and generated by know-how and understanding asymmetries. They may be considered as communication tools related to the software problem. Operational prototypes are communication tools related to the software solution. The volatility and the fuzzy nature of requirements and needs, and the knowledge asymmetries are the main causes of the iterative nature of the knowledge engineering process, i.e., the software process knowledge-oriented activities. During each iteration, informative prototypes are built, discussed, and assessed by stakeholders working together prior to developing a version of the final software system composed of operational prototypes. Therefore, each version of the final software system, issued from an iteration of the software development process, reflects the state of the vision of the software problem and solution shared by stakeholders. Besides, an evolution of a software system may be viewed as an evolution of the stakeholders' shared understanding of the problem and the solution.

During an iteration of the software development process, the key knowledge engineering activities are as follows:

- Discovery of knowledge embodied in existing software artifacts and other internal and external sources, or owned by stakeholders
- Shared understanding of existing knowledge
- Construction of a common vision of the computer solution
- Assessment of this solution

The knowledge engineering process takes place cooperatively in the four project spaces according to the following four-stage lifecycle called DUCA (Discover–Understand–Construct–Assess). The Discover stage consists in gathering knowledge owned by stakeholders or embodied in existing artifacts. Such knowledge is used during the Understand stage to build a shared understanding of the problem using articulated knowledge and informative prototypes. During the Construct stage, the stakeholders work together by combining and transforming their knowledge in order to define a shared vision of what the future system should be. During this stage, the stakeholders generally build a sequence of informative prototypes in order to elicit and conciliate their points of view. Such a common vision is embodied in a set of operational prototypes which make up a version of the required software system to be used and evaluated by users during the Assess stage. Figure 1 illustrates the DUCA lifecycle.

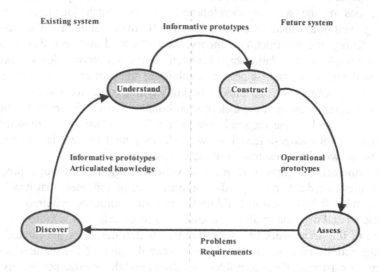

**Fig. 1.** The DUCA lifecycle.

The DUCA lifecycle is compliant with the PACO meta-lifecycle as these two lifecycles play complementary roles. As noticed previously, the PACO meta-lifecycle provides an iterative framework to manage the transition between the four project spaces and the relationships between stakeholders. The DUCA lifecycle describes the key knowledge-oriented activities carried out by stakeholders within each project space in order to build specifications. The progress of the PACO meta-lifecycle depends on the effectiveness of the DUCA lifecycle.

## 5 Conclusion and Future Research Directions

In this paper, we have presented a theoretical software development process framework that considers software systems as an accumulation of knowledge. It proposes a cooperative guidance to gather the knowledge necessary to software products design and distributed among various stakeholders. According to this framework, building software systems that effectively support organizations' operational and decision-making processes is necessarily cooperative and knowledge-oriented. Besides, it postulates that knowledge engineering activities are based on an iterative lifecycle called DUCA composed of four stages: (1) discover existing knowledge, (2) build a shared understanding of existing knowledge, (3) construct a shared vision of the future software system and embody it in the software system, and (4) assess the software system.

This paper makes contributions at two levels: First of all, it provides theoretical foundations of the software development process. Such foundations rely on existing well-established theories belonging to many domains. The economic agency theory, the constructionist theory, the software dimensions theory, and the Baetjer's work on the relationships between capital and knowledge are examples of such theories. Second, it permits explaining the software crisis in terms of stakeholders' know-how and understanding asymmetries. So, a software system may be rejected because of the lack of stakeholders' shared visions of the problem to be solved and of the required computer solution. That is the reason why a cooperative, knowledge-oriented software development process is appropriate to improve the well-known solutions of the software crisis.

Nevertheless, our framework must be validated against real world projects or case studies in order to convince the community of practitioners that it will be effective and will help them in building the software solutions required to support operational and decision-making processes. To reach this goal, a more operational version of this framework has to be defined, which describes the mutual understanding activity and the construction of a shared vision of the required software system. In particular, the stakeholders' conflicts and the approaches to solve them must be described.

# References

Abdel-Hamid, T. and Madnick, S.E. (1991) Software Project Dynamics: An Integrated Approach. Prentice-Hall, Englewood Cliffs, NY.

Alchian, A.A. and Demsetz, H. (1972) Production, Information Costs and Economic Organization. *American Economic Review*, Vol. 62, No. 5, pp. 777–795.

Armour, P.G. (2000) The Case for a New Business Model. *Communications of the ACM*, Vol. 43, No. 8, pp. 19–22.

Baetjer, H., Jr. (1998) Software as Capital: An Economic Perspective. The Institute of Electrical and Electronics Engineers, Piscataway, NJ, 194 pp.

Boehm, B.W. (1988) A Spiral Model of Software Development and Enhancement. *IEEE Computer*, Vol. 21, No. 5, pp. 61–72.

Coase, R. (1937) The Nature Of The Firm. *Economica*, Vol. 4, pp. 386–405.

Cockburn, A. (2002) Agile Software Development: Software Through People. Addison-Wesley, Reading, MA.

Cugola, G., Di Nitto, E., Fuggetta, A., Ghezzi, C. (1996) A Framework for Formalizing Inconsistencies and Deviations in Human-Centered Systems. *ACM Transactions on Software Engineering and Methodology*, Vol. 5, No. 3, pp. 191–230.

Davenport, T. and Prusak, L. (1998) Working Knowledge. Harvard Business School Press, Boston.

Dedrick, J.V., Gurbaxani, V., Kraemer, K.L. (2003) IT and Economic Performance: A Critical Review of the Empirical Evidence. *ACM Computing Surveys*, Vol. 35, No. 1, pp. 1–28.

Eischen, K. (2002) Software Development: An Outsider's View. *IEEE Computer*, Vol. 35, No. 5, pp. 36–44.

Fitzgerald, B. (1996) Formalized Systems Development Methodologies: A Critical Perspectives. *Information System Journal*, Vol. 6, No. 1, pp. 3–23.

Fitzgerald, B. (1998) An Empirically-Grounded Framework for the IS Development Process. *Information and Management*, Vol. 34, pp. 317–328.

Gibbs, W. (1994) Software's Chronic Crisis. *Scientific American*, pp. 72–81.

Highsmith, J. (2002) Agile Software Development Ecosystems. Addison-Wesley.

Kling, R. (1996) Computerization and Controversy: Value Conflicts and Social Choices, 2nd edition. Academic, San Diego.

Leavitt, H.J. (Ed.) (1963) The Social Science of Organizations: Four Perspectives. Prentice-Hall, Englewood Cliffs, NJ.

Lycett, M., Macredie, R.D., Chaitali, P., Paul, R.J. (2003) Migrating Agile Methods to Standardized Development Practice. *Computer*, Vol. 36, No. 6, pp. 79–85.

Lyytinen, K. (1987) Different Perspectives on Information Systems: Problems and Solutions. *ACM Computing Surveys*, Vol. 19, No. 1, pp. 5–46.

Neumann, P.G. (1995) Computer Related Risks. ACM Press, New York.

Pressman, R.S. (2004) Software Engineering: A Practitioner's Approach, 6th edition. McGraw-Hill Series in Computer Science.

Resnik, M. (1996) Distributed Constructionism. In Proceedings of the 1996 International Conference on Learning Sciences, Evanston, Illinois, pp. 280–284.

Salomon, G. (Ed.) (1994) Distributed Cognition. Cambridge University Press, Cambridge, UK.

Solow, R. (12 July 1987) We'd Better Watch Out [Book Review]. *The New York Times*, p. 36.

Stohr, E.A. and Konsynski, B.R. (1992) Information Systems and Decision Processes. IEEE Computer Society Press.

Toffolon, C. (1996) L'Incidence du Prototypage dans une Démarche d'Informatisation. Thèse de doctorat, Université de Paris-IX Dauphine, Paris.

Toffolon, C. (1999) The Software Dimensions Theory. In Enterprise Information Systems, Filipe, J. (Ed.). Kluwer, Dordrecht. Selected papers book.

Toffolon, C. and Dakhli, S. (2002) The Software Engineering Global Model. In Proceedings of the COMPSAC'2002 Conference, Oxford, UK, 26–28 August.

Walz, D.B., Elam, J.J., Curtis, B. (1998) Inside A Software Design Team: Knowledge Acquisition, Sharing, and Integration. *Communications of the ACM*, Vol. 36, No. 10, pp. 63–77.

Williamson, O.E. (1981) The Modern Corporation: Origins, Evolution, Attributes. *Journal of Economic Literature*, Vol. 19, No. 12, pp. 1537–1568.

# Resolving Emergent Issues in Complex Projects: A Knowledge Management Approach

**Jill Owen[1] and Henry Linger[2]**

[1]School of Business, Australian Defence Force Academy, University of New South Wales, Sydney, Australia, j.owen@adfa.edu.au

[2]Faculty of Information Technology, Monash University, Australia
Henry.Linger@infotech.monash.edu.au

**Abstract** Complex projects are characterised by structural complexity, ambiguity about the goals of the project and uncertainty about the means to achieve those goals. This is compounded when the project is conducted in an unstructured or volatile context and aims to deliver innovation for the client. In this paper we argue that in this context project management should be seen as a knowledge-based practice and that knowledge management principles need to be explicitly integrated into project management practices. We introduce a theoretical framework that incorporates knowledge management techniques to manage emergent issues, to escalate these issues and to resolve them as well as accommodates learning and the evolution and adaptation of project management practices. The framework is illustrated through two studies that show the impact of knowledge processes on projects.

## 1 Introduction

For organizations to remain competitive, build market share or develop a new capability, they need to innovate (Drucker 2006). Such innovations are complex and inevitably involve uncertainty and ambiguity. Innovation usually has an element of technical uncertainty, may require experimentation, may change in scope (Deakins and Dillon 2005), or is crucially dependent on technological development (Turner and Keegan 2004). Implementation of innovation often requires an iterative or experimental approach (Eisenhardt and Tabrizi 1995) and usually involves rapid change in the organization. Innovation is usually implemented via projects (Cleland and Ireland 2007) and requires a variety of knowledge areas from different sources and backgrounds (Project Management Institute [PMI] 2004).

Projects that implement innovation tend to have unclear objectives, uncertainty in how these objectives will be met (Williams 2002), and usually have a number of stakeholders with differing agendas and understanding of the scope of the project and how it should be delivered (Alderman et al. 1995). This is compounded when the project is conducted in an unstructured context where the future is uncertain

C. Barry et al. (eds.), *Information Systems Development: Challenges in Practice, Theory, and Education, Vol.1*, doi: 10.1007/978-0-387-68772-8_39,
© Springer Science+Business Media, LLC 2009

(Prahalad and Hamel 1990). The combined effect of these situations can influence the complex, uncertain and ambiguous nature of projects. Complex projects are therefore characterized by structural complexity (the size of the project and the interdependence of the elements) and ambiguity about its goals and uncertainty about the means to achieve those goals.

Although uncertainty and ambiguity exist to some extent in all projects, the defining character of complex projects is that when these issues emerge during the project life span, they cannot be resolved within the confines of the project. The issues need to be escalated to a forum that has the expertise and experience to resolve the issues. This acknowledges and recognizes the importance of knowledge in resolving ambiguity and uncertainty. Yet the role of knowledge in a project environment is an area that has been paid little attention in the research agenda for project management (Love et al. 2005). Consequently, there is a lack of theories, models and/or frameworks that explicitly incorporate knowledge processes into project management practice. Such theoretically grounded models are necessary to provide an adequate understanding of the complexity of projects (Winter et al. 2006) as well as guidance for project management practice.

In this paper we explore the role that knowledge management can play in managing complex projects and emergent issues. We introduce a theoretical framework that shows how these emergent issues are escalated and resolved. The framework is derived from the task-based knowledge management approach (Burstein and Linger 2003) and is based on the viable systems model (Beer 1995). The framework incorporates knowledge management techniques to manage emergent issues, to escalate these issues and to resolve them (Owen 2006; Owen and Linger 2006) and accommodates learning and the evolution and adaptation of practice. The framework is illustrated through two case studies that show the impact of knowledge processes on projects.

## 2 Complex Projects

Businesses are improving their capability by using projects to implement their strategy and change (Cleland and Ireland 2007), and consequently structure their organization around projects rather than along functional lines (Ibbs et al. 2004). An important feature of the business environment today is complexity (Frame 2002), which creates an atmosphere of uncertainty and risk. Contributing to this complex environment are political pressures and stakeholders with differing agendas (Jaafari 2004). Complexity in projects is due to three elements: contextual complexity (the environment and stakeholders), structural complexity (number of project elements and their interdependencies) and functional uncertainty (in terms of methods, goals, technology and practice) (Williams 2002). Thus complex projects consist of many interrelated parts in terms of differentiation and interdependency (Baccarini 1996) and the need to deal with risks and uncertainty in all facets of managing the project (Frame 2002). Consequently, such projects need to adapt and evolve dynamically throughout the project life span (Jaafari 2004).

All projects are complex to some degree because of the interdependence of issues that characterize them, the dynamic nature of their environment as well as the conduct of the project. Uncertainty can be understood as the difference between what is known in a project and what is required to complete the project. Ambiguity arises when differing and conflicting interpretations of a situation lead to a lack of shared understanding about a given situation between project stakeholders (Thiry 2002; March 1999) and the realisation that this understanding will change over time as additional knowledge about that situation becomes available (March 1999; Robertson and Swan 2003). The nature of projects means that these factors, uncertainty and ambiguity, emerge throughout the life span of a project (Thiry 2002; Atkinson et al. 2006).

Traditionally, existing project tools and techniques, such as project management processes, planning, budgeting and risk management techniques, can be used to reduce or manage uncertainty. Uncertainty is addressed in the planning stage of a project where a shared understanding of the project between all stakeholders is established. This involves defining the scope of a project, allocation of appropriate resources in terms of personnel, skills and expertise, and the development of risk mitigation strategies to anticipate uncertainty through quantifiable control processes. Conflicting understanding of a current situation gives rise to ambiguity. But resolving ambiguity is problematic as it requires sense-making processes, acknowledgement of existing and changing power structures and negotiation rather than relying on a rational decision-making process (March 1999).

In complex projects, emergent issues cannot be resolved within the confines of the project through existing project management tools and techniques. In these situations existing approaches are applied and the issues are apparently resolved as with other projects. What is not acknowledged is the work done at the periphery of the project in order to reach a shared understanding and make judgements that enable the project to adapt and practices to evolve. These "invisible" and undocumented activities have now given rise to programme and portfolio management as meta-level venues for processes to resolve emergent issues (Thiry 2002; APA 2006) outside the confines of the project.

Emergent issues that are escalated beyond the confine of the project are resolved through knowledge processes that draw on a broader knowledge base, a "meta-level" understanding of the issues (Beer 1995) and draw on explicit experiential learning. Resolving these emergent issues requires innovation and flexibility (March 1999) and even experimentation since these issues cannot be resolved using existing methodologies or standard processes. Knowledge management techniques become key elements of managing complex projects throughout the project life span (Atkinson et al. 2006; Owen 2006; Owen and Linger 2006; Thiry 2002).

## 3 Project Management as Knowledge-Based Practice

We argue that project management is a knowledge-based practice and a profession based on that practice. The difficulty with this assertion is that all work requires knowledge to some extent (Beyerlein et al. 1995) and all work is social (Schmidt and Bannon 1992) and cooperative in some respect (Ngwenyama and Lyytinen 1997). Our approach is to view project management as a profession from the perspective of knowledge work (KW).

Although the concept of KW is discussed in literature across a range of disciplines (organizational theory, management, information systems, knowledge management), it is still used widely as a slogan about work. In this paper we use Iivari and Linger's (1999) characterization of KW as work that is based on a body of knowledge (BoK), involves working with representation of the object of work rather than the objects themselves, requiring a deep understanding of those objects and assumes knowledge is an element of the output of that work. The BoK is knowledge about relevant phenomena that is the subject of KW and comprises relevant facts, rules, techniques, case histories (cases), stories, theories, hypotheses, philosophies, metaphors, etc. Significantly the BoK is not constraint to codified knowledge, does not need to be scientifically valid and may include experiential knowledge (Iivari and Linger 1999). Moreover, the BoK relates to both the objects of work and the work processes. This characterization of KW focuses on BoK and its relationship to the objects of work, rather than knowledge. This orientation ensures that it is work practice, rather than abstract concepts, that is central to understanding KW.

This characterization of KW overlaps with working definitions of professions, particularly the more traditional ones such as medicine. A very loose definition of a profession is an occupational group that applies somewhat abstract knowledge to particular cases (Abbott 1988; Macdonald 1995) and has autonomy to control the "substance" (the objects of work) and "technique" (work processes) of their own work (Freidson 1988) as well as the BoK. In this sense the profession is the authority that determines what is or is not valid knowledge. Importantly, this characterisation views the occupation in terms of KW and illuminates something essential of their work. It also allows occupational groups such as managers, systems developers and project managers to be viewed as a profession even though their professional status may be doubtful on different grounds (Iivari and Linger 1997).

Project management conforms to this loose definition of a profession. It has a defined BoK (PMI 2004; APA 2006) and authority over its BoK. The BoK is to some extent abstract and experientially based and is applied (by definition) to particular cases. Project management also has the mostly external and institutional trapping necessary to be identified as a profession. It has established the necessary apparatus of professional bodies (national and international) to allow them to control entry into the profession through certification. Certification provides evidence of mastery of the BoK. These bodies also engage with universities to ensure their BoK can be taught at a tertiary level to distinguish the profession from a body of skills acquired only through experience and apprenticeship. This latter aspect is significant in that it assumes that the BoK has theoretical grounding that can inform academic research as well as professional practice.

This perspective allows project management to be conceptualised in the domain of KW. Project managers undertake their activities by applying authorised tools and techniques that are consistent with the BoK, while the documentation of the project is a representation of the object of work; the project itself. The project is an instantiation, a particular case, that often requires the application of the manager's experiential knowledge to deal with the complexity, uncertainty and ambiguity inherent in the project. Project performance provides the managers with an opportunity to learn and enhance their knowledge and potentially share this new knowledge in the social context of their relationship with their peers (Fincham 2006; Blackler 1995).

# 4 Integrating KM Practices into Project Management

In complex projects, the ability of the manager to address emergent issues is challenged. The recourse is to escalate the issues so that they are able to be considered at a more abstract, theoretical or meta level. This escalation removes the issues from the imperatives of the project, allowing them to be re-conceptualised, reflected on and understood through a process of collective sense-making in the context of peer review. This allows participants to provide different interpretations based on their individual expertise and experience and opportunities to share knowledge, build on existing knowledge and potentially construct new knowledge (Linger and Ivari 1999; Hardwig 1991). Usually, this escalation is to a formal or informal structure within the project organization that allows a broader collective knowledge and experience to be brought to bear on the issues. Importantly, this structure must have the necessary authority to resolve the issue. This escalation is consistent with the reflective nature of KW and contributes to continuous learning and improvement (Schön 1988; Burstein and Linger 2003) in the project environment.

Emergent issues in complex projects are initially addressed by staff who bring to bear their experience, knowledge and skills as well as their collective understanding of the current situation. However, the complexity, uncertainty and ambiguity of the situation often mean that the tools, techniques and knowledge available to the project team are insufficient to resolve the issue to get the project back on track. Alternatively, project staff do not have the authority to resolve the issue as it might require fundamental changes in the scope and/or objectives of the project or resources available to the project.

Within the project, staff rely on their intimate understanding of their BoK in order to apply this knowledge to the issues. The BoK applies to the project, work processes and the management of those processes. The management of the project is mediated by the methodology adopted for this project that defines activities and work processes. To resolve issues internally, the issue is escalated to the project team who can draw on the specialised knowledge of the subject of the project and/or methodological aspects, while professional knowledge applies to the broader issues of managing the project. However, these are not independent areas but are highly interdependent, and project staff often have roles in all three areas simultaneously.

Knowledge management principles are key to the resolution of emergent issues (Thiry 2002; Atkinson et al. 2006). Whatever the nature of the emergent issues, staff are involved in learning, sense-making and exploiting organizational memory as well as their own experiential knowledge. These knowledge processes allow staff to exercise professional judgement and take action to bring the project back on track. These decisions usually relate to the three constraint of projects: costs, time and resources. Such activity is typical for project management. However, reflection on these decisions and action can also result in revision of project methodology for such projects to improve future practice. Typically such reflection is part of project closing. From a knowledge management perspective, these decisions, actions and their justification need to be documented contribute to the construction of the organizational memory, and subsequently to support learning, knowledge construction and improvement in practice through knowledge reuse (Burstein and Linger 2003).

Yet not all issues can be resolved in this way and those that cannot need to be the subject of another forum. Moreover the resolution of issues internally within the project can in itself raise other issues that need to be escalated for resolution at a meta-level. When intervention is required, an escalation process presents the issues to another forum where a broader collective knowledge and experience can be brought to bear on the issue as well as the necessary authority to resolve the issue. Programme management (PMI 2004) is typically such a forum. This level of project organization is either formally constituted or can exist as an informal and/or ad hoc structure to support project management. It provides a different, usually more business-oriented, perspective of the circumstances of the project and the situation that gave rise to the issues that emerged in the performance of the project. As such, participants in the programme can make sense of the issues and resolve them from the perspective of this meta-level understanding. However, this resolution needs to be expressed in terms that are consistent with the parameters of the project and the management of the project.

The process of resolution in this forum is, in an abstract sense, identical to the project level resolution process. What distinguishes this forum is the object of work, the BoK that underpins that work, the methods used to perform that work and the specialist and professional knowledge needed to make sense the subject of that work.

In Fig. 1 we introduce a framework that extends project management to incorporate knowledge management principles in order to deal with emerging issues. The framework is a theoretical construct derived from the task-based knowledge management approach (Burstein and Linger 2003). The inner loop of the framework work incorporates the operational aspects of project management that deal with emergent issues within the confines of the project and the methodology applied to that project. The outer loop applies to emergent issues that cannot be resolved operationally and escalates them to a level where broader knowledge, experience and authority can be brought to bear to resolve the issues. Reflective practice, learning and collaboration are integral to the framework and are the core processes by which knowledge management supports project management. These aspects are encapsulated in the framework as the KW element of the management box. The significance of the framework lies in its focus on knowledge transfer and reuse in the task of managing projects and the formal acknowledgement of organizational KW to support that task.

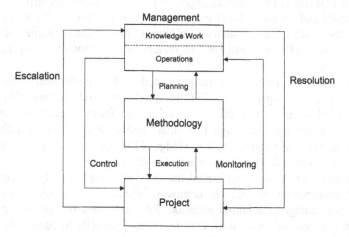

**Fig. 1.** A framework for resolving emergent issues.

# 5 Illustrative Case Studies

The two studies discussed here illustrate the impact of knowledge management practices and their absence. The bridge study uses secondary sources in the form of a Royal Commission report. This is a rare opportunity to study project failure as the report provides voluminous data on all factors contributing to the failure, collected under oath and subject to judicial review. The Engineering study on the other hand was an empirical study of the company. We were provided with unlimited access and were able to triangulate our finding through observations, interviews and access to documentation.

## 5.1 The West Gate Bridge

The West Gate Bridge, an innovative engineering construction project, was designed to provide a road link between eastern and western regions of metropolitan Melbourne in Australia. Two years into the construction of the bridge, on 15 October 1970, a 112-m box girder span between two piers collapsed and fell 50 m to the ground, killing 19 workers. This disaster was investigated by a Royal Commission, an ad hoc judicial body established by the State government with defined terms of reference and coercive powers beyond the usual judicial system. This case study uses the Report of the Royal Commission into the Failure of West Gate Bridge (1971) to explore how emergent issues were addressed.

There was a coterie of actors involved the West Gate Bridge. The Lower Yarra Crossing Authority was established by an act of parliament with the responsibility of overseeing the design and construction of the bridge. Maunsell and Partners were the initial design consultants while the UK engineering designers Freeman,

Fox and Partners (FFP) were engaged to provide specific expertise unavailable to Maunsell and Partners. Steel construction was carried out by World Services Construction (WSC), a subsidiary of a Norwegian company, while John Holland Constructions (JHC) was engaged to undertake the concrete component of the construction.

Maunsell and Partners were inexperienced in the type of steel construction required and lacked expertise; so, FFP accepted increased responsibility. The Authority failed to define respective areas of responsibility between the two organizations. In designing the bridge FFP made certain assumptions which extended beyond the range of engineering knowledge. FFP failed to give proper and careful consideration to the design and process of its construction.

The schedule of work performed by WSC was significantly impacted by industrial problems on the site. The company failed to place anyone in control who could have managed the labour situation. Site staff were inexperienced, and with frequent absences of senior staff, they lacked the capacity to control the situation. As such the contract was renegotiated allowing WSC to continue with the fabrication of the box girders but broadening JHC's scope to erect the boxes and construct the steel portion of the bridge. JHC did not have any experience with steel construction and were not conversant with the design or erection calculations. They took the view that they would do what FFP and WSC told them and would not take any responsibility unless there was gross negligence on their part. At that stage, WSC had not worked out how to erect and construct the bridge. Nevertheless, a procedure manual for construction was drawn up documenting an unusual method of construction. Although JHC was involved in producing the manual, it did not always follow the specified procedures.

With three parties being involved in the design and construction, there was a failure to insist on joint reports from the parties, nor proper detailed periodical reports from the joint consultants. Significant matters were missing from the reports.

The reasons for the collapse of the West Gate Bridge are to be found in the acts and omissions of those entrusted with building a bridge using new, untested and sophisticated structures. In the design and construction of steel spans there were mistakes, miscalculations, errors of judgment, failure of communication and sheer inefficiency (Barber et al. 1971). The Royal Commission attributed the failure of the bridge to two causes: the structural design by designers FFP and an unusual method of erection by WSC, the original contractors of the project (Barber et al. 1971). There were two earlier failures of similarly constructed bridges before the West Gate disaster. However, the knowledge from these earlier disasters was not used to mitigate risks.

The evidence revealed by the Royal Commission shows a breakdown in process and communication, compounded by personality clashes and industrial and professional conflicts. What is apparent from the findings is that there was no mechanism to identify emergent issues, nor procedures to escalate these issues. The deliberate acts to suppress issues as they emerged extended to the absence of a forum and processes to formally deal with the issues. Each party retreated to their contractual obligations, as they interpreted them, and created knowledge silos where nothing was shared between the consultants. What is even more revealing is the inability of all the consultants to recognise the limits of their knowledge, expertise and capabilities and to take actions to meet those gaps. The Commission report clearly shows the inextricable spiral that entrenched the destructive behaviours of the consultants.

## 5.2 Engineering Consulting Company

The engineering project management firm consults globally on projects to international organizations. The culture of the company is open and encourages everyone to achieve their full potential. The culture was developed by the founders of the company and evolved with extensive staff consultation. Staff are encouraged to network and share information within this culture. They work with the client to understand the business and then utilize the best people for the job in terms of skills and knowledge (both technical and local).

An exploratory case study methodology was used to provide an insight into the ability of the firm to resolve emergent issues (Marshall and Rossman 1995). The study used various analytical techniques such as document analysis, analysis of internal and external business processes and in-depth interviews. These techniques provided different perspectives and enabled cross-checking (Sabherwal et al. 1998). Two linked projects were analysed.

The company follows a project management methodology. Each project has a Project Director who provides a mentoring role and is responsible for stakeholder management, project control, performance and risk management. Reviews occur throughout the project to assist in managing the project risks. The Project Director mentors the Project Manager by meeting with the Project Manager to discuss the project. Roadblocks, issues, potential risks and risk mitigation strategies are discussed in these meetings. Project team members, especially those who have worked with the organization for a number of years, have created strong informal networks within the organization and so they have access to other projects within the company.

Knowledge is reused between projects as both the company culture and its systems and methods encourage this type of behaviour. At the planning stage of a project the company uses explicit knowledge in the form of tenders, proposals, project plans, and technical documentation from earlier projects. It also relies on the team members' knowledge and understanding that they have gained form their previous project engagements or their networks. The company provides such forums throughout the project in order to tap into the personal knowledge and networks (both formal and informal) so as to resolve emergent issues. Even though the company does not have a formal programme management, these forums effectively serve this purpose. Moreover, the culture of the company ensures that staff are empowered as they are all encouraged to participate in the processes to resolve emergent issues and their contributions are valued.

## 6 Discussion

Contrasting these two cases provides an excellent opportunity to examine how and when knowledge is used to overcome emergent issues leading to successful outcomes and project success as shown in Table 1.

**Table 1.** Handling of emergent issues

| Type of issue | Project failure – West Gate Bridge | Project success – Engineering Consulting Company |
|---|---|---|
| Resolution of ambiguity | • Technical solution was untested<br>• No identification or buy in of stakeholders<br>• No resolution of ambiguous situation via group collaboration | • Resolution via group collaboration – informal and formal |
| Resolution of uncertainty | • Regular and frequent inspections did not occur<br>• No knowledge reuse<br>• No formal signoff of project deliverables<br>• Risks were not documented and managed as they arose | • Reviews at key points in the project<br>• Use of embedded knowledge – knowledge from earlier projects reused<br>• Existing tools and techniques used |

The main cause for the West Gate Bridge disaster was a lack of communication and collaboration and a collective inability to construct a shared understanding of the issues. In their design, FFP did not consult or collaborate to resolve the issues in their design that emerged during construction. Even though there was a procedure manual, JHC chose to use their concrete experience rather than drawing on the BoK and experience of FFP and WSC to understand and resolve issues, especially those relating to the misalignment and gaps between girders. In both cases the actions taken were in the absence of a collective understanding of the issues and reference to, or cooperation of, other stakeholders. Yet the resolution of emergent issues in complex projects relies on a shared understanding of those issues, both within the project and the broader, meta-level forum. In the case of the West Gate Bridge, the complexity of the project, coupled with the uncertainty and ambiguity arising from the innovative design, was compounded by the lack of collaboration between stakeholders, inability to work towards a shared understanding of the situation and the absence of reflective practice. This case highlights the deadly consequences if projects do not have the ability to adequately resolve all emergent issues. In particular, this case focuses on the need to implement knowledge management practices to resolve a clear gap in knowledge required by the project.

By contrast, in the engineering company collective sense-making is built into their project management processes. Project organization allowed collaboration between staff across projects in order to gain a broad but shared understanding based on their experiential knowledge. The company enabled staff to form networks (either formal or informal) each time an issue emerged that could not be resolved internally by the project. These networks were dynamic and were disbanded when the issue was resolved. Such focused networks provided the basis for longer term personal networks and more generally allowed staff to broaden their personal understanding of industry and application knowledge as well as a much clearer understanding of the organization's work programme and internal expertise.

# 7 Concluding Remarks

The insights of the illustrative case studies, both positive and negative, are typical for the escalation and resolution of issues through collaboration using sense-making and experiential knowledge. Our framework formalizes the processes to resolve issues that emerge as a consequence of complexity, ambiguity and uncertainty. The basis for the framework lies in conceptualizing project management as knowledge-based practice and explicitly incorporating knowledge management principles into that practice. The contribution of the research is to make knowledge management processes and structures an explicit part of the overall BoK of project management.

Our current research involves an action research project to apply the framework to a project management company. The objectives of this study are to change the organizational structure and processes of the company to enable the company to be more effective in the marketplace. Moreover, the company intends to reflect on and learn from their experiences in order to develop new services and products.

# References

Abbott, A. (1988) *The System of Professions: An Essay on the Division of Expert Labor*. The University of Chicago Press, Chicago.

Alderman, N., Ivory, C., McLoughlin, I. and Vaughan, R. (1995) Sense-making as a process within complex service-led projects. *International Journal of Project Management* 23(5), 380–385.

Association for Project Management. (2006) APM Body of Knowledge, High Wycombe, UK.

Atkinson, R., Crawford, L. and Ward, S. (2006) Fundamental uncertainties in projects and the scope of project management. *International Journal of Project Management* 24(8), 687–698.

Baccarini, D. (1996) The concept of project complexity – a review. *International Journal of Project Management* 14.

Barber, E. H. E., Bull, F. B. and Shirley-Smith, H. (1971) *Report of Royal Commission into the Failure of West Gate Bridge*. C. H. Rixon, State of Victoria Government Printer, Melbourne, Australia.

Beer, S. (1995) *Brain of the Firm*. Wiley, Chichester.

Beyerlein, M. M., Johnson, D. A. and Beyerlein, S. T. (Eds.) (1995) *Knowledge Work in Teams*. JAI Press, Greenwich, CT.

Blackler, F. (1995) Knowledge, knowledge work and organizations: an overview and interpretation. *Organizations Studies* 16(6), 1021–1046.

Burstein, F. and Linger, H. (2003) Supporting post-Fordist work practices: knowledge management framework for supporting knowledge work. *Information Technology and People* 16(3), 289–305.

Cleland, D. and Ireland, L. (2007) *Project Management Strategic Design and Implementation*. McGraw-Hill, USA.

Deakins, E. and Dillon, S. (2005) A helical model for managing innovative product and service initiatives in volatile commercial environments. *International Journal of Project Management* 23(1), 65–74.

Drucker, P. (2006) *Classic Drucker: Wisdom from Peter Drucker from the Pages of Harvard Business Review*. Harvard Business School Press.

Eisenhardt, K. and Tabrizi, B. (1995) Accelerating adaptive processes: product innovation in the global computer industry. *Administrative Science Quarterly* 40(1), 84–110.

Fincham, R. (2006) Knowledge work as occupational strategy: comparing IT and management consulting. *New Technology, Work and Employment* (21).

Frame, J. (2002) *The New Project Management: Tools for an Age of Rapid Change, Complexity and Other Business Realities*. Jossey-Bass, San Francisco, CA.

Freidson, E. (1988) *Professions of Medicine: A Study of the Sociology of Applied Knowledge*. The University of Chicago Press (First published 1970).

Hardwig, J. (1991) The role of trust in knowledge. *The Journal of Philosophy* 88(12), 693–708.

Ibbs, C. W., Reginato, J. M. and Kwak, Y. H. (2004) Developing project management capability: benchmarking, maturity, modelling, gap analysis and ROI studies. In: Morris, P. W. G. and Pinto, J. K. (Eds.) *The Wiley Guide to Managing Projects*. Wiley, Hoboken, NJ.

Iivari, J. and Linger, H. (1997) What is Knowledge Work: Initial Thoughts. *Proceedings of the Australian Workshop on Intelligent Decision Support, IDS'97*, Monash University.

Iivari, J. and Linger, H. (1999) Knowledge Work as Collaborative Work: A Situated Activity Theory View. *Proceedings of the 32nd Hawaii International Conference on System Sciences*.

Jaafari, A. (2004) Modeling of Large Projects. In: Morris, P. W. G. and Pinto, J. K. (Eds.) *The Wiley Guide to Managing Projects*. Wiley, Hoboken, NJ.

Love, P. E. D., Fong, P. S. W. and Irani, Z. (2005) *Introduction in Management of Knowledge in Project Environments*. Elsevier.

Macdonald, K. M. (1995) *The Sociology of Professions*. Sage, London.

March, J. G. (1999) *The Pursuit of Organizational Intelligence*. Blackwell Business.

Marshall, C. and Rossman, G. B. (1995) *Designing Qualitative Research*, 2nd Edition. Sage, London.

Ngwenyama, O. K. and Lyytinen, K. J. (1997) Groupware environments as action constitutive resources: a social action framework for analyzing groupware technologies. *Computer Supported Cooperative Work* 6, 71–93.

Owen, J. (2006) Integrating knowledge management with program management. *The International Journal of Knowledge Management* 2(1).

Owen, J. and Linger, H. (2006) The Nature of a Program Through a Knowledge Management Lens. *IRNOP Project Research Conference*, Xi'an, China, Oct. 2006.

Prahalad, C. K. and Hamel, G. (May–June 1990) The core competence of the corporation. *Harvard Business Review*, 68(3), 79–91.

Project Management Institute. (2004) *A Guide to the Project Management Body of Knowledge*. Project Management Institute, USA.

Robertson, M. and Swan, J. (2003) Control – what control? Culture and ambiguity within a knowledge intensive firm. *Journal of Management Studies* 40(4).

Sabherwal, R., Hirschheim, R. and Goles, T. (1998) The dynamics of alignment: a punctuated equilibrium model. *Organization Science* 12(2), 17.

Schmidt, K. and Bannon, L. (1992) Taking CSCW seriously: Supporting articulation work. *Computer Supported Cooperative Work* 1, 7–40.

Schön, D. A. (1988) *Educating the Reflective Practitioner*. Jossey-Bass, San Francisco, CA.

Thiry, M. (2002) Combining value and project management into an effective programme management model. *International Journal of Project Management* 20(3).

Turner, R. J. and Keegan, A. E. (2004) Managing Technology: Innovation, Learning, and Maturity. In: Morris, P. W. G. and Pinto, J. K. (Eds.) *The Wiley Guide to Managing Projects*. Wiley, Hoboken, NJ, pp. 567–590.

Williams, T. (2002) *Modelling Complex Projects*. Wiley, UK.

Winter, M., Smith, C., Morris, P. and Cicmil, S. (2006) Directions for future research in project management: the main findings of a UK government-funded research network *International Journal of Project Management* 2, 385–430.

# Leadership Issues in ERP Implementation: Insights from Field Study

Piotr Soja

Department of Computer Science, Cracow University of Economics, Cracow, Poland,
eisoja@cyf-kr.edu.pl

**Abstract** This study examines leadership issues in the context of ERP implementation projects. It discusses how leadership issues are present in success factor models, and, considering the factors describing leadership from a selected model, investigates how ERP leadership occurred in business practice. On the basis of research conducted among enterprises introducing ERP into their organisations and experts dealing with ERP projects from the system supplier perspective, this paper studies the practitioners' opinions about the importance of "leadership" factors and examines the influence of these factors on implementation success. The analysis considers three different perspectives: enterprise size, implementation scope and implementation duration. The results demonstrate the greater role of leadership for projects conducted in large enterprises, for partial-scope implementations, and, to a certain extent, for long-lasting projects. The research outcome also reveals some differences in comprehension of leadership between experts representing the system supplier and employees of the company implementing ERP system.

## 1 Introduction

Among the many conditions and dimensions of an ERP implementation project, the issues connected with project leadership draw the attention of numerous researchers. The authors present the issue of project leadership by describing various aspects such as those connected with the rules of effective leadership, the skills of a leader or the duties that are expected to be fulfilled by a leader. The researchers are talking about "visionary leaders", "transformational leadership" and "active leadership", stressing the dominant role of leadership for the project outcome (e.g., McLean and Smits 2003; Stewart et al. 2000).

Leadership can be defined as the use of non-coercive influence to direct and coordinate the activities of group members toward goal attainment (McLean and Smits 2003). Leadership is about coping with change through setting a direction and aligning people to a vision of an alternative future. It is connected with empowering and motivating people to meet the challenges created by the vision (Kotter 1990).

C. Barry et al. (eds.), *Information Systems Development: Challenges in Practice, Theory, and Education, Vol.1*, doi: 10.1007/978-0-387-68772-8_40,
© Springer Science+Business Media, LLC 2009

The researchers emphasise the need for sustained leadership in an ERP project. Mandal and Gunasekaran (2003) list strong leadership as one of the basic requirements that should be met for successful ERP implementation. Al-Mashari and Zairi (2000) state that an organisation needs a strong project management infrastructure which should ensure a disciplined and structured project leadership. Fitz-Gerald and Carroll (2003) emphasise the role of governance in ERP implementation defined as providing strategic direction, planning and controlling projects and people.

Leadership is also perceived as a key human/organisational issue in an ERP implementation project. Sarker and Lee (2000) illustrate that strong and committed leadership at the top management level, at the project management level, and of the IS function must be given significant priority throughout the life of an ERP implementation project. Sumner (1999) points out that in order to decrease the risk of project failure, an organisation should obtain top management support for the project and a commitment to establishing and supporting project leadership.

Empirical research demonstrates the serious negative consequences resulting from the problems connected with IT project leadership. Davis and Wilder (1998), discussing the results of a survey conducted among IT managers, state that inadequate project management and leadership was one of the most important causes of the failure of IT-related projects. Gould (2004) reveals that the most common reason why ERP projects fail to achieve their business goals is inadequate executive leadership (26%), followed by vendor over-promising (21%), runaway professional service costs (20%) and buggy vendor code (19%).

The main goal of this paper is to examine the issues connected with leadership in the context of ERP implementation projects. Considering the factors describing leadership from a selected success factors model, this study tries to investigate the influence of leadership on the project success. Moreover, the analysis takes into account different project types and stakeholder perspectives, examining the opinions of people from organisations introducing an ERP package and the views of the experts representing system suppliers.

## 2 ERP Leadership Among Success Factors

### 2.1 Literature Review

There are several models of critical success factors (CSF) for ERP implementation that attempt to reflect various conditions influencing the outcome of an ERP project. The majority of those models emphasise the idea of ERP leadership and propose various factors describing different facets of this concept. The results of some major research on ERP implementation success factors have been described below, concentrating on leadership factors and their importance for project success.

The discussed studies on CSFs are summarised in Table 1, which provides details about sampling method, sample size, respondents, and number of CSFs in the model. Leadership factors are listed together with achieved ranks on the basis of appropriate studies, where it was applicable.

**Table 1.** Leadership factors among selected critical success factors (CSF) models

| Study | Sampling method/sample size | Respondents | No. of CSFs | Leadership factors | Rank |
|---|---|---|---|---|---|
| Somers and Nelson 2001 | Questionnaire 86 | IS executives | 22 | • Top management support<br>• Project champion presence<br>• Use of steering committee | 1<br>8<br>13 |
| Nah et al. 2003 | Questionnaire 54 | CIOs | 11 | • Top management support<br>• Project champion | 1<br>2 |
| Holland and Light 1999 | Case study 8 | Key (business and IT) company personnel | 12 | • Top management support | |
| Brown and Vessey 2003 | Case study 3 | IS leaders, business managers, business users | 5 | • Top management is engaged in the project, not just involved<br>• Project leaders are veterans, and team members are decision-makers | |
| Parr et al. 1999 | Interview 10 | Implementation project managers (employees and external experts) | 10 | • Management support<br>• Empowered decision-makers<br>• Presence of a champion | |
| Esteves and Pastor 2000 | | | 20 | • Sustained management support<br>• Adequate project champion role<br>• Empower decision-makers | |
| Al-Mashari et al. 2003 | | | 12 | • Management and leadership | |

There are two studies based on surveys conducted among a few dozen IS executives involved in ERP projects. The first study, performed by Somers and Nelson (2001), provides 3 factors linked to ERP leadership among their broad list of 22 CSFs. The second research, conducted by Nah et al. (2003), uses a model of 11 CSFs with 2 factors related to leadership. Both studies present factors' rankings and unanimously reveal the topmost significance of top management support. A factor connected with project champion presence is ranked very high or high by both studies, while use of a steering committee is perceived as moderately significant by the first study.

Two studies are based on case studies among companies introducing ERP into their organisations. Holland and Light (1999) use a CSF model with 12 factors, which include one leadership factor (top management support). Brown and Vessey (2003) have studied a dozen ERP implementations in depth and concluded that there are five success factors for ERP projects. Among those five factors, as many as two are related to project leadership, which suggests the special attention paid to the idea of ERP leadership. The authors of both studies illustrated the factors' significance with the use of several ERP implementations case studies; however, they did not formulate conclusions regarding factors' ranking.

A study by Parr et al. (1999) is based on a series of interviews conducted among project managers who participated in ERP projects as a company's employees or external experts. The authors elicit 3 CSFs related to project leadership among the total of 10 factors and report that most interviewees acknowledged the crucial role of these leadership factors.

Finally, two papers are based on literature review. The first, by Esteves and Pastor (2000), suggests the list of 20 CSFs which contains 3 factors related to leadership. The second, by Al-Mashari et al. (2003), presents a taxonomy of 12 CSFs divided into 3 dimensions related to the stages of an ERP project (setting-up, deployment and evaluation). The CSF model includes one leadership factor placed in the setting-up phase of the project.

The major weakness of previous ERP studies is that they usually cover only one of two sides involved in implementation projects – either people from within the company introducing ERP into its premises (adopters), or external consultants providing implementation services from the system supplier side (experts). In particular, the majority of the above-mentioned studies take into account the organisation's perspective. Meanwhile, it is valuable to understand and compare the opinions of both groups.

Moreover, ERP implementation projects form a very diverse population, and in order to compare particular implementations, one has to keep this diversity in mind so that such a comparison is reasonable (e.g., Stensrud and Myrtveit 2003). Thus, it seems appropriate to purposefully group implementation projects into homogenous collections, where the comparison of projects is feasible and sensible (Soja and Put 2007). In particular, the ERP implementation projects differ in enterprise size, implementation scope and project duration. Hence, it is interesting to examine how ERP project leadership depends on the implementation type.

## 2.2 Success Factors Model Adopted

The results of research dealing with ERP implementation success factors show that there is a variety of models employing various levels of factors' generalisation, using different categorisations, and there does not appear to be any single generally accepted success factors model. Therefore, this study uses a general model of potential success factors defined in Soja (2004, 2006), where 26 factors are divided into groups related to implementation participants, top management involvement, project definition and organisation, project status and information systems.

The factors describing ERP leadership contain a total of 3 factors related to top management involvement and 2 factors placed in other groups – project manager presence and project team empowerment. Among the factors describing top management involvement, apart from the widely cited top management support, the factor illustrating top management awareness about the project's importance and complexity was separated. Furthermore, given the uttermost importance of the project's goals and schedule for further implementation works run, the factor connected with top management's participation in the project schedule and goals definition was formulated. The description of the factors is presented in Table 2.

**Table 2.** Success factors connected with ERP leadership (adapted from Soja 2004, 2006)

| Factor | Factor description |
|---|---|
| *Related to the implementation participants* | |
| Project manager | The project manager is the person from the enterprise who sacrifices most of his working time to implementation duties |
| *Related to the top management involvement* | |
| Top management support | The top management support for the project and the management members involvement in implementation duties |
| Top management awareness | Top management awareness regarding the project goals and complexity, demanded labour, existing limitations, required capital investment and project inevitability |
| Top management participation | Top management participation in the project schedule and goals definition |
| *Related to the project status* | |
| Project team empowerment | The project team members empowerment to decision-making and their high position in the enterprise hierarchy |

# 3 ERP Leadership in Practice

## 3.1 Research Data

The research of ERP system implementation projects was twofold: first from the viewpoint of enterprises that had decided on an ERP system implementation (adopters), and second from the perspective of ERP systems and services suppliers. In the first case, the research sample consisted of Polish enterprises implementing an ERP system in their organisations. In the second case, the research sample comprised the consultants and experts representing various suppliers of ERP systems in Poland.

The research done on adopters was conducted with the use of a questionnaire directed toward the people playing leading roles in the implementation. During the research, 223 enterprises were contacted and 68 (30%) answers were obtained from enterprises representing the whole country and various industries. Practically all researched companies completed the actual implementation phase and were at the stage of ERP deployment or evaluation. The companies represent mainly manufacturing enterprises (75%). The researched firms implemented various ERP packages, and the most popular solution was SAP (25%) and IFS Applications (10%).

To examine the experts' opinions, the research questionnaire was directed to specialists with experience in implementing various ERP systems in many companies from the supplier perspective. Therefore, they provide a broader view of the projects' conditions and their opinions, representing another party of project participants, and their opinions can be compared with the adopters' viewpoint. During the research, 45 people were questioned, and in the end, opinions of 31 (69%) experts were gathered. The experts represented 22 firms supplying ERP systems and implementation services.

The analysis of data from the respondents from enterprises was done from three perspectives, using the following criteria: enterprise size, implementation scope and implementation duration. For the analysis, enterprises were divided into small and large companies. The small firms comprised enterprises employing less than 300 people (29 companies); the remaining companies formed the group of large enterprises (39). The division regarding implementation scope took into consideration the modules implemented of the ERP system, and yielded a group of full-scope implementations (31 projects) and a group of partial implementations (37). In the division taking into account project duration, short implementations were defined as projects lasting up to 1 year (33 projects), and those lasting more than 1 year were marked as long implementations (33).

## 3.2 The Importance of ERP Leadership in Practice

The importance of ERP leadership is researched by gathering the respondents' opinions about the importance of the factors related to leadership in the implementation process. In their judgement of factors' importance, the respondents from enterprises used a scale from 0 (*no importance at all*) to 5 (*the highest importance*). In the next step, they estimated the level of occurrence of each factor (on a scale from 0 to 5) in their ERP projects. Similar to the adopters, the experts expressed their opinions regarding the importance of the factors suggested in the implementation process. Additionally, they were asked to mark the factors whose occurrences are necessary for a successful implementation.

To illustrate the respondents' opinions regarding the importance of the proposed factors, an average was calculated for each factor. These calculations have been made for all researched enterprises as well as for defined groups using the adopted criteria (i.e., size, scope and time). The calculation effect limited to the factors related to ERP leadership is shown in Table 3. The average importance is presented in column *Avg* and column *Rank* contains the rank obtained by the factor within a specific group on the basis of decreasing average importance calculated within a given group.

Considering the responses from all queried enterprises, project manager presence is perceived as a factor of moderate importance, which is considerably higher in the case of small companies. Top management support has an average importance among all queried companies, but is important for projects in large companies and with long duration, as well as for those of partial scope being implemented. Top management awareness about the project is perceived as a very important factor in overall ranking and among small companies and full-scope projects, while for other types of projects this factor is quite important. On the other hand, top management's participation in the project schedule and goals definition is perceived as completely unimportant in overall ranking and regardless of the division into groups. Finally, project team empowerment is regarded as moderately important regardless of division into groups, except for large enterprises, where it appears to be more important, compared with small companies.

The experts, on average, considered project manager presence as the most necessary and second most important factor for implementation success. As the most important factor, they considered top management support, which was also perceived as quite necessary for project success. They regarded top management awareness as a factor of moderate importance and necessity and perceived top management's participation in the project definition as unimportant and unnecessary. Finally, the experts perceived project team empowerment as quite important.

**Table 3.** Factors' importance in the opinions of respondents (adapted from Soja 2004, 2006)

| Factor | Respondents from enterprises | | | | | | | Experts | |
|---|---|---|---|---|---|---|---|---|---|
| | All | Enterprise size | | Implementation scope | | Project duration | | Importance | Necessity |
| | | Small | Large | Full | Partial | Short | Long | | |
| | Rank | Rank | Rank | Rank | Rank | Rank | Rank | Rank | Rank Number |
| | Avg | Avg | Avg | Avg | Avg | Avg | Avg | Avg | |
| Project manager | 12 | 13 | 13 | 10 | 13 | 9 | 15 | 2 | 1   23 |
| | 4.23 | 4.07 | 4.34 | 4.37 | 4.11 | 4.33 | 4.06 | 4.61 | |
| Top management support | 8 | 10 | 5 | 11 | 6 | 12 | 5 | 1 | 5   18 |
| | 4.40 | 4.21 | 4.54 | 4.35 | 4.43 | 4.21 | 4.55 | 4.65 | |
| Top management awareness | 3 | 2 | 4 | 3 | 5 | 6 | 4 | 10 | 10   14 |
| | 4.51 | 4.45 | 4.56 | 4.58 | 4.46 | 4.42 | 4.61 | 4.26 | |
| Top management participation | 22 | 22 | 22 | 24 | 22 | 23 | 20 | 22 | 17   6 |
| | 3.66 | 3.45 | 3.82 | 3.68 | 3.65 | 3.45 | 3.85 | 3.26 | |
| Project team empowerment | 10 | 11 | 7 | 8 | 7 | 8 | 9 | 6 | 6   18 |
| | 4.40 | 4.21 | 4.54 | 4.42 | 4.38 | 4.39 | 4.36 | 4.42 | |

Although, in general, the respondents from enterprises quite agree with the experts as regards factor importance, there are some differences of opinions regarding leadership factors. The respondents from enterprises tend to underrate the importance of project manager presence and top management support, which, in turn, are recognised as most important and necessary by the experts. The latter, on the other hand, underestimate top management awareness about the project.

The examination of chosen success factors occurrence in researched projects gives us insight into how the aspects of leadership captured by the factors were present in the projects. Table 4 contains the calculation effect as regards factors' occurrence arranged in a similar style as Table 3 does in the case of factors' importance.

The factor project manager achieved a very high level of occurrence in the overall calculation and regardless of the division into groups. It is worth noting that in the case of full-scope implementations this factor reached the highest level of occurrence among all factors. Top management, on average, moderately supported researched projects, in overall view as well as in all divisions into groups. Top management awareness about the project was slightly weaker than their support for the project, with the exception of full-scope implementations. Judging by the low level of occurrence of factor top management participation (ranks from 19 to 23), one could say that top management practically did not participate in the definition of schedule and goals for researched projects. Finally, the project team was moderately empowered to make decisions for all types of projects with the exception of projects in large enterprises to some extent, where project team empowerment was slightly stronger.

**Table 4.** Factors' occurrence in researched ERP projects

| Factor | All | | Enterprise size | | | | Implementation scope | | | | Project duration | | | |
|---|---|---|---|---|---|---|---|---|---|---|---|---|---|---|
| | | | Small | | Large | | Full | | Partial | | Short | | Long | |
| | Rank | Avg | Rank | Avg | Rank | Avg | Rank | Avg | Rank | Avg | Rank | Avg | Rank | Avg |
| Project manager | 3 | 3.92 | 5 | 3.75 | 3 | 4.05 | 1 | 4.37 | 6 | 3.56 | 3 | 3.94 | 6 | 3.84 |
| Top management support | 9 | 3.51 | 8 | 3.59 | 10 | 3.46 | 12 | 3.48 | 8 | 3.54 | 9 | 3.36 | 9 | 3.64 |
| Top management awareness | 13 | 3.35 | 13 | 3.31 | 13 | 3.38 | 8 | 3.61 | 13 | 3.14 | 14 | 3.21 | 12 | 3.52 |
| Top management participation | 23 | 2.76 | 19 | 2.97 | 23 | 2.62 | 21 | 3.00 | 23 | 2.57 | 23 | 2.76 | 21 | 2.82 |
| Project team empowerment | 12 | 3.44 | 14 | 3.31 | 9 | 3.54 | 10 | 3.55 | 12 | 3.35 | 12 | 3.33 | 11 | 3.55 |

## 3.3 The Influence of Leadership on ERP Project Success

In the proposed model, implementation success is perceived as the completion of assumed goals and implementation scope within a planned time and budget, while achieving user satisfaction. To prove the influence of the factors identified on implementation outcome, a synthetic measure of implementation success was worked out based on five partial measures: (1) the actual scope of an implementation with respect to the planned implementation, (2) the actual duration with respect to the assumed duration, (3) financial budget with regard to the planned budget, (4) users' level of satisfaction from the system introduced and (5) the existence and achievement of project goals (Soja 2006).

After the calculation of implementation success measure, for each success factor, the correlation coefficients between the level of factor occurrence and the success measure were calculated for researched projects. This computation was done in order to determine the impact of a factor's occurrence on the successfulness of an implementation project. Thus, taking into consideration the factors related to ERP leadership, we are able to assess in what way the project guidance affected an implementation success. The calculation results are presented in Table 5 including factors' correlation coefficients and ranks.

Taking into account all researched enterprises (column *All*), the influence of factors' occurrence on project success is not great, because the highest correlation value among leadership factors is equal to 0.38. However, when we take into account the projects' division into groups, the correlation values are considerably greater.

**Table 5.** Correlation between success and factors' occurrence (adapted from Soja 2006)

| Factor | All | | Enterprise size | | | | Impl. scope | | | | Project duration | | | |
|---|---|---|---|---|---|---|---|---|---|---|---|---|---|---|
| | | | Small | | Large | | Full | | Partial | | Short | | Long | |
| | Rank | Correlation | Rank | Correlation | Rank | Correlation | Rank | Correlation | Rank | Correlation | Rank | Correlation | Rank | Correlation |
| Project manager | 23 | .17 | 11 | .20 | 23 | .14 | 14 | .28 | 23 | .15 | 22 | .20 | 22 | .19 |
| Top management support | 6 | .38* | 17 | .13 | 3 | .57* | 21 | .16 | 2 | .54* | 13 | .34 | 7 | .40^ |
| Top management awareness | 8 | .36* | 22 | .00 | 2 | .62* | 8 | .35 | 8 | .39^ | 17 | .33 | 8 | .39^ |
| Top management participation | 17 | .24^ | 26 | -.16 | 7 | .55* | 20 | .20 | 14 | .29 | 21 | .26 | 12 | .32 |
| Project team empowerment | 12 | .34* | 7 | .23 | 13 | .43 | 2 | .50* | 19 | .22 | 9 | .36 | 20 | .25 |

$*p < 0.01$, $^p < 0.05$

Project manager presence, having no influence in overall ranking, has some impact on project success, compared to other factors, only in the case of small enterprises (rank 11) and for full-scope implementations (rank 14). However, the influence in both cases is very weak since correlation coefficients reached barely 0.20 and 0.28 respectively.

Top management support is the most influential among leadership factors in overall ranking. It has strong influence in the case of large companies, while it practically does not affect project outcome in small enterprises. Similarly, top management support has a strong effect on partial-scope implementations, having no impact on full-scope projects. Taking into consideration the duration of a project, top management support reveals slightly stronger influence on long projects.

Top management awareness about the project, having a moderate influence in overall ranking, strongly influences projects in large companies and has no impact at all on projects in small companies. The influence of this factor does not depend on implementation scope. On the other hand, in the case of long projects, it has a slightly stronger influence than for short projects.

Top management's participation in the project schedule and goals definition has a weak influence in overall ranking. However, it quite strongly affects projects in large enterprises, having no influence whatsoever in small companies. It has some influence on partial implementations and long projects, but this influence is not strong.

Project team empowerment, in overall ranking, moderately influences the project outcome. In the case of small enterprises, its influence is very weak (correlation, 0.23); however, this influence is moderate when compared to other factors (rank 7). On the other hand, in the case of large companies, this factor plays an average role among other factors (rank 13) but its influence on project success is almost two times stronger that its impact on projects in small companies. Taking into account implementation scope, project team empowerment has a strong influence on full-scope projects and does not affect partial-scope implementations. Its role depends on project duration and is more significant in the case of short implementations.

## 4 Discussion of Findings

The research described portrays the paramount role of leadership during ERP implementation project run. We can learn from practice by examining how various aspects of leadership, described by selected success factors, influenced the ERP projects outcome. On the basis of this experience, we can draw conclusions and formulate recommendations toward the improvement of ERP projects leadership.

The practitioners tend to overestimate project manager presence, which is exceptionally evident in the case of experts representing the supplier perspective. In fact, although project manager presence occurred in all researched projects, it did not have any influence on the implementation success. Therefore, although the presence of a project manager is a necessary element for an ERP project, it is not a sufficient condition for the project success. Hence, an organisation should not expect that by appointing a project manager it will assure the ultimate success. The results suggest that the project managers were not used effectively in the researched ERP implementations and illustrate the need for improvement.

The respondents accurately perceive the higher importance of top management support in the case of larger companies and also among partial implementations. In those cases, this factor had the leading influence on project success. Moreover, similar rule applies to longer projects, where top management support had a slightly larger influence on project outcome and a slightly higher importance assessed by the respondents from enterprises.

The experts have a tendency to underestimate the role of top management awareness about the project, while the respondents from enterprises tend to overestimate its importance in the case of small companies and, to some extent, short implementations. Meanwhile, it turned out that this factor has a paramount influence only in the case of large companies.

Top management's participation in the project schedule and goals definition is unanimously perceived as completely unimportant regardless of project type by both experts and respondents from enterprises. However, the role of this factor should not be disregarded, especially in the case of projects in large companies, where it revealed to have quite a strong effect on project success.

The respondents recognise the average importance of project team empowerment; however, they should be very cautious in the case of full-scope projects, where the paramount influence of this factor on project success was observed.

Taking into account the results of previous research, we can state that they are partially supported by this study's findings. In particular, this study confirms the vital significance of top management involvement during the project – the factor present in practically all CSF models and regarded as topmost by two discussed studies. While emphasising the importance of top management involvement in projects conducted in large companies, this study's findings also illustrate how its significance varies depending on project and company type. As regards other leadership factors discussed by this study, it is difficult to compare this study's outcome with those of other research works because of the different scope and meaning of factors employed or the lack of factors' ranking.

The main limitation of this study is connected with the fact that the research has been conducted in Poland, an example of an emerging economy. Implementation projects in such countries can be characterised by restricted resources, often weak computer infrastructure and workers' inappropriate preparation for work in a complicated integrated system environment (e.g., Huang and Palvia 2001). Therefore, the scope of this study's findings seems to cover first and foremost countries from Central and Eastern Europe, which are now experiencing economic transition, especially those that joined the European Union in 2004.

# 5 Conclusion

This study discusses the practitioners' opinions about leadership issues in ERP projects and examines their influence on implementation success. The unique contribution of this research is that it demonstrates that the influence of ERP leadership varies with implementation project type. Additionally, the results shed light on the understanding of leadership in ERP implementation by illustrating the viewpoints of the two main parties involved in a project – stakeholders from companies introducing an ERP package and experts representing the system supplier.

Taking into consideration the results of the research, we can state that effective ERP leadership is far more important for large companies, in comparison with small firms. In the first case, all factors describing ERP leadership, except for project manager presence, had significantly stronger influence on project success than they did in the case of small companies. On the other hand, top management involvement captured by three discussed factors is more significant for partial-scope projects than for full-scope implementations, while, in the latter case, project team empowerment is of much greater significance. Similar rule applies to the division on the basis of project duration: top management involvement is more important for long projects, while project team empowerment is more significant for short implementation.

The results of the research can be a suggestion for practitioners dealing with ERP implementation projects. They should pay special attention to various aspects of leadership depending on project type and conditions. However, it has to be stressed that none of the described leadership facets should be disregarded, even those considered as completely unimportant or without any influence in particular situations. The conclusions drawn should be treated as hints in working out particular ERP strategies, establishing the whole project infrastructure and managing day-to-day implementation tasks.

# References

Al-Mashari, M. and Zairi, M. (2000) The effective application of SAP R3: A proposed model of best practice. *Logistics Information Management*, 13(3), 156–166.

Al-Mashari, M., Al-Mudimigh, A. and Zairi, M. (2003) Enterprise resource planning: A taxonomy of critical factors. *European Journal of Operational Research*, 146, 352–364.

Brown, C.V. and Vessey, I. (March 2003) Managing the next wave of enterprise systems – Leveraging lessons from ERP. *MIS Quarterly Executive*, 2(1), 65–77.

Davis, B. and Wilder, C. (1998) False starts, strong finishes – Companies are saving troubled IT projects by admitting their mistakes, stepping back, scaling back, and moving on. *Information Week*, 30 November, 41–43.

Esteves, J. and Pastor, J. (2000) Towards the Unification of Critical Success Factors for ERP Implementations. In *Proceedings of 10th Annual BIT Conference*, Manchester, UK.

Fitz-Gerald, L. and Carroll, J. (2003) The Role of Governance in ERP System Implementation. In *Proceedings of the Australasian Conference on Information Systems*.

Gould, J. (2004) ERP ROI: Myth and reality. A Peerstone research report, http://www.peerstone.com.

Holland, C. and Light, B. (May/June 1999) A critical success factors model for ERP implementation. *IEEE Software*, 30–36.

Huang, Z. and Palvia, P. (2001) ERP implementation issues in advanced and developing countries. *Business Process Management Journal*, 7(3), 276–284.

Kotter, J.P. (1990) What leaders really do. *Harvard Business Review*, 68(3), 103–111.

Mandal, P. and Gunasekaran, A. (2003) Issues in implementing ERP: A case study. *European Journal of Operational Research*, 146, 274–283.

McLean, E.R. and Smits, S.J. (2003) A role model of IS leadership. In *Proceedings of 9th Americas Conference on Information Systems*, Tampa, FL, pp. 1273–1282.

Nah, F., Zuckweiler, K.M. and Lu, J. (2003) ERP implementation: Chief Information Officers' perception of critical success factors. *International Journal of Human–Computer Interaction*, 16(1), 5–22.

Parr, A., Shanks, G. and Darke, P. (1999) Identification of necessary factors for successful implementation of ERP systems. In O. Ngwenyama, L.D. Introna, M.D. Myers and J.I. DeGross (Eds.), *New Information Technologies in Organizational Processes – Field Studies and Theoretical Reflections on the Future of Work*. Kluwer, Boston, 99–119.

Sarker, S. and Lee, A.S. (2000) Using a case study to test the role of three key social enablers in ERP implementation. In *Proceedings of the International Conference on Information Systems*, Brisbane, 414–425.

Soja, P. (2004) Important factors in ERP systems implementations: Result of the research in Polish enterprises. In *Proceedings of the 6th ICEIS*, Porto, Portugal, 84–90.

Soja, P. (2006) Success factors in ERP systems implementations: Lessons from practice. *Journal of Enterprise Information Management*, 19(4), 418–433.

Soja, P. and Put, D. (2007) Learning from model ERP projects. *International Journal of Enterprise Information Systems*, 3(2), 50–67.

Somers, T. and Nelson, K. (2001) The impact of critical success factors across the stages of enterprise resource planning implementations. In *Proceedings of HICSS*.

Stensrud, E. and Myrtveit, I. (2003) Identifying high performance ERP projects. *IEEE Transactions on Software Engineering*, 29(5), 398–416.

Stewart, G., Milford, M., Jewels, T., Hunter, T. and Hunter, B. (2000) Organisational readiness for ERP implementation. In *Proceedings of Americas Conference on Information Systems*.

Sumner, M. (1999) Critical success factors in enterprise wide information management systems projects. In *Proceedings of 5th Americas Conference on Information Systems*, 232–234.

# A Decision Support System for Enterprise Engineering

O. Noran

School of ICT, Griffith University, Australia, O.Noran@griffith.edu.au

**Abstract** This paper describes the design principles of a system aimed to support decision-making in Enterprise Engineering projects. The system proposes a novel approach based on the analysis of the interactions between project participants in the context of their life cycles. An outline of the theoretical foundation is followed by the requirements, architectural and detailed design descriptions of the proposed support system.

## 1 Introduction

The business environment is undergoing a fundamental change. Underpinned by the fast-evolving capabilities of the communications infrastructure, business opportunities are becoming accessible to worldwide tenders. Cooperation and competition have gathered a global dimension; more than ever before, businesses must become agile and ready to cooperate irrespective of location (such as by forming virtual organizations) and in a timely manner, in order to meet project bidding scope and deadlines. Typically however, the tasks involved in creating or evolving organizations (an endeavour often called Enterprise Engineering (EE)) are complex, potentially lengthy and often ill-defined. Therefore, EE project managers must promptly understand the current situation, clarify and choose the future alternative, grasp the scope and content of the change process required, gather knowledge of useful artefacts, and importantly, adequately communicate and justify their way forward to the organization(s) involved. Current systems such as Executive Dashboards, based on the Executive Information Systems principles as described by Volonino and Watson (1990), focus more on presenting existing data rather than on actively assisting the decisional effort.

This paper describes the principles of a system aimed to support decision-making in EE projects by using the analysis of the interactions between EE project participants in the context of their lifecycles. The system elicits and transforms the tacit domain know-how of the project stakeholders into new knowledge. Mainstream Architecture Framework (AF) elements and supporting tools are then used by the system to model this knowledge and help the participant organization(s) understand and internalize it.

C. Barry et al. (eds.), *Information Systems Development: Challenges in Practice, Theory, and Education, Vol.1*, doi: 10.1007/978-0-387-68772-8_41,

## 2 The Theoretical Base of the Support System

The foundation of the proposed support system originates in research attempting to assess the feasibility and define the principles of a method to create methods (meta-methodology) guiding specific projects in the collaborative network and virtual organization areas (Noran 2004a, b, 2005b, 2006a). The main result of the meta-methodology application to a specific project is a method expressed in an activity model depicting tasks necessary to accomplish that project.

Importantly, the research has found that in order to be able to describe the necessary tasks, the project stakeholders must first understand the problems of the current state, reason about possible ways to solve them and select the optimal solutions. This requires modelling of additional aspects using appropriate views, formalisms, reference models and modelling frameworks (MFs). Thus, in fact the meta-methodology assists stakeholders in using their (often tacit) domain knowledge (Fig. 1, left) to infer new facts, within a guided process of business modelling (Kalpic and Bernus 2006). This new knowledge is explicit (expressed in the models created) and used primarily to accomplish the project. In addition, it is internalized by other stakeholders and reflected in future decision-making, thus completing the knowledge lifecycle within the participant organization(s).

### 2.1 Stages and Sub-steps

As can be seen from Fig. 1, currently the meta-methodology comprises three major stages and a set of sub-steps. In the first stage, the user is prompted to create a list containing entities of interest to the project in question, making sure to include project participants, target entities (organizations, other projects) and importantly, the EE project itself. The second stage comprises the creation of business models showing the relations between the previously listed entities in the context of their lifecycles, i.e., illustrating how entities influence each other within each life cycle phase. The third stage assists the user in inferring the set of project activities by reading and interpreting the previously represented relations for each life cycle phase of the target entities. The activities must be detailed to a level deemed as comprehensible (and thus usable) by the intended audience. This task is assisted by other models and artefacts built and adopted during the second stage (as further exemplified).

The first meta-methodology sub-step calls for the selection of suitable aspects (or views) to be modelled in each stage; the life cycle aspect must be present since it is essential to the meta-methodology. The selection of a MF is also recommended, as MFs typically feature structured collections of views that can be used as checklists of candidate aspects and their intended coverage. This sub-step also calls for the identification and resolution of any aspect dependencies.

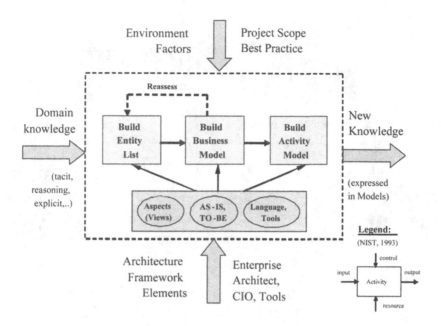

**Fig. 1.** Simplified meta-methodology concept

The second sub-step asks the user to determine whether the present (AS-IS) state of the views adopted previously needs to be shown and whether the AS-IS and TO-BE (future) states should be represented in separate or combined models. The third sub-step requires the selection of suitable modelling formalisms and modelling tools for the chosen aspects.

Note that all the above-described stages and sub-steps have underlying logic guiding the user in the decision-making process. A sample subset of this logic (refined and implemented as rules and facts in the system detailed design) is presented in Sect. 3 in a simplified format.

## 2.2 A Structured Repository of AF Elements

The meta-methodology concept relies on creating and interpreting models depicting various aspects of the EE project participants. This modelling effort requires the selection of methods, languages, tools, MFs and reference models according to specific project requirements and best practice. As such artefacts are typically structured in AFs, the question is in fact how to find suitable sets of AF components for given projects. A possible answer is to construct ranked lists of suitable AF elements and assist the stakeholders in selecting the most appropriate ones for the EE task at hand, based on their domain knowledge.

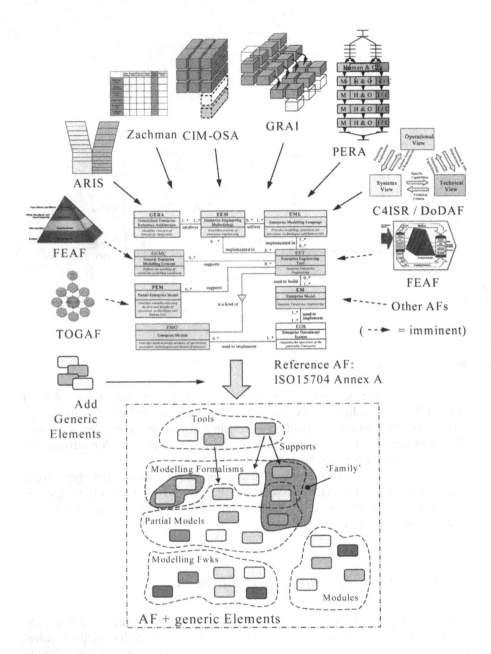

**Fig. 2.** Building the Structured Repository of Architecture Framework elements

For this to be possible, AFs must first be decomposed in elements assessed on their scope, integration, dependencies, etc., and organized in a coherent collection using a set of consistent criteria.

In this case, the organized pool of AF elements (hereafter called a structured repository, or SR) has been obtained by assessing and decomposing mainstream AFs with respect to ISO15704 Annex A – the Generalized Enterprise Reference Architecture and Methodology (GERAM) (ISO/TC184 2000), which is neutral with respect to all assessed AFs and contains most criteria necessary for AF element classification.

PERA[1], GRAI-GIM[2], CIMOSA[3], ARIS[4], Zachman[5] and DoDAF[6] have thus been decomposed using GERAM's elements (Noran 2003, 2005a) (see Fig. 2). Other AFs, such as TEAF[7], FEAF[8] and TOGAF[9] are also being analysed and mapped onto GERAM with the resulting components being added to the repository.

Previous research and testing has determined that, although originating in the collaborative network/virtual organization area, the meta-methodology is in fact applicable to *any* EE project type, due to its open character and neutral approach towards all major AFs (Noran 2007).

# 3 Design of the Decision Support Framework

## 3.1 Identifying the Need for Support: Knowledge and Decision-Making

Knowledge is present in all organizations in various forms (explicit, tacit, descriptive, procedural, reasoning), but is also continuously produced (or converted (Nonaka and Takeuchi 1995)) as a consequence of knowledge-intensive decision-making processes (Holsapple and Whinston 1996). Knowledge is an enabler of organizational agility, ensuring survival and competitiveness; thus, its capturing, representation, processing and the selection of supporting technology and infrastructure (Davenport and Prusak 1998) are major concerns of management. The use of enterprise-wide management and executive information systems, expert systems, decision support systems (DSS) and their business performance-related derivatives (e.g., balanced scorecards and executive dashboards) promotes organi-

---

[1] The Purdue Enterprise Architecture Framework (Williams 1994)

[2] Graphs with Results and Activities Interrelated (Doumeingts 1998)

[3] Open System Architecture for Comp. Integrated Manufacturing (CIMOSA Association 1996)

[4] ARchitecture for Information Systems (Scheer 1992, 1999)

[5] The Zachman Architecture Framework (Zachman 1987)

[6] Department of Defence Architecture Framework (DoDAF Working Group 2004)

[7] Treasury Enterprise Architecture Framework (Treasury CIO Council 2000)

[8] Federal Enterprise Architecture Framework (The CIO Council 1999)

[9] The Open Group Enterprise Architecture Framework (The Open Group 2006)

zational learning; this results in improved decision-making, which will enrich and refine the existing body of knowledge (Klein and Methlie 1995; Power and Karpathi 1998).

EE tasks (activities) often present a semi-structured character due to insufficient information and the inherent complexity of organizational change processes. This requires EE project managers to make "semi-programmed" decisions (Simon 1977) that are difficult to encode in a program that can be facilitated by a DSS (Keen and Scott-Morton 1978). This obvious need for decision-making guidance and support in EE has led to the idea of materializing the knowledge acquisition, structuring and transformation capabilities of the meta-methodology in the form of a DSS for EE that would help stakeholders such as enterprise architects, project managers and chief information officers identify problems, find suitable solutions and define change processes to implement them.

## 3.2 Defining System and User Requirements

Successful support systems initially aimed at the executive level are likely to gain increasing acceptance and gradually expand into an enterprise-wide system embraced at several organizational levels (Wheeler et al. 1993). This scenario suggested designing scalability into the proposed system (Power 2002) and considering the possibility of future (semi-)automated learning to alleviate the anticipated knowledge acquisition bottleneck (Fogel et al. 1993).

EE decision-making involves problem-solving in addition to using well-defined procedures. This mandates a cooperative and interactive support system, allowing the users to address the part of the problem that cannot be structured and to use their own insights to modify and/or refine the solutions proposed by the system (Turban 1995). In this specific case, the users must be able to review and accept or override the ordering in the ranked lists of modelling elements suitable for the EE problem at hand. Interactivity and cooperation promote acceptance of the system; equally important, they put to use natural knowledge management skills and talents that cannot be programmed into a machine (Holsapple and Whinston 1996).

Finlay (1994) has defined some basic requirements for DSS-es, which are reflected in the proposed system's functionality: help detect existing problems, model a problem situation to clarify it, provide the means to consider various options (e.g., via simulation) and help with implementation of change (by assisting in the modelling of the TO-BE states). The system must also allow the user to bookmark important decision points so as to be able to backtrack if the decisions made have led to unsatisfactory outcomes. This would allow the analysis of various scenarios and cycling until an acceptable solution is obtained (Hättenschwiler 1999).

Other typical DSS requirements such as robustness and ease of use and control (Little 1970) can be satisfied here by using tested off-the-shelf (but highly configurable) components providing most necessary services, such as Web-based shells. This allows focusing the effort towards the knowledge repository development and user interface improvement, rather than on the intricacies of implementation.

The knowledge captured by the system should be easily accessible for debugging and upgrading – thus preferably stored in plain text format.

## 3.3 The Concept and Architectural Design of the Proposed System

The close connection between EE decision-making and knowledge management has suggested a rule-oriented knowledge-based paradigm (Holsapple and Whinston 1996) for the proposed support system. The adopted structure builds on previous mainstream research in this area. Thus, essential elements of knowledge-based DSS frameworks described by Sprague (1980), Sprague and Carlson (1982) and Marakas (1999) are present in the design of this system – such as a database (a rule-based knowledge base (KB), if database elements are represented as facts and rules), a model base (reference models of the AFs or abstracted from previous projects) and a dialog generation mechanism (possibly provided by the inference engine).

Figure 3 presents the KB approach adopted for the SR described in Sect. 2.2, containing rules for element selection (e.g., via pattern matching) and ordering (for ranked lists), fixed facts (e.g., AF element representations) and other rules

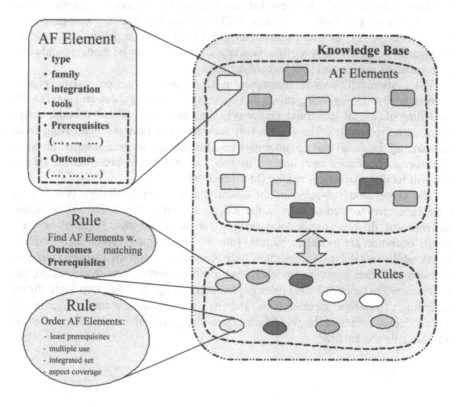

**Fig. 3.** Structured repository in knowledge base format

containing the logic necessary for system operation. Typically, rules take a form similar to IF/THEN statements (implemented depending on the specific inference engine used).

For example, the rule to decide whether to model the present state (AS-IS) in an EE project could take the following form:

$$\text{IF ((TO-BE\_obtained\_from\_AS-IS) OR (AS-IS\_not\_understood))}$$
$$\text{THEN (model\_AS-IS)} \tag{1}$$

Thus, the "model the present state" rule will fire if the user asserts the fact that the AS-IS is not understood or the fact that the TO-BE will be obtained from the AS-IS. Another example:

$$\text{IF (undecided\_TO-BE)  THEN (several\_TO-BE)} \tag{2}$$

and as a likely consequence:

$$\text{IF (several\_TO-BE)  THEN (separate\_AS-IS\_TO-BE)} \tag{3}$$

Thus, if the TO-BE will be derived from the AS-IS (e.g., no radical changes are to be made) or if stakeholders do not have a clear and common view of the future state of the enterprise and assert this at run-time (1), then several TO-BE states will be required (2) and it is likely that they will need to be shown separately from the AS-IS state (3). Note that although (3) is a recommended ("best-practice") consequence of (2), the user can override (3) if there is a compelling reason to do so. Generally, various levels of interactivity and control can be made available so as to match the needs and skill level of the user.

The system will provide assistance in all essential decision-making phases (Simon 1977): intelligence gathering (via AS-IS modelling), design (via TO-BE modelling of several scenarios), choice (via simulation) and review (via the analysis of scenario results). The system will seek to apply best practice (using rules and ranking the facts) and consider user insights (using run-time asserted facts) to construct a set of solutions, ordered by their suitability and presented in a form that will facilitate decision-making (Mallach 1994).

The stages and sub-steps of the underlying meta-methodology (see Fig. 1) have been incorporated as rules in the KB, as shown in Fig. 4, left. Thus, in the current form, the meta-methodology stages, sub-steps and logic required for their proper operation are modelled by rules (the AF elements are represented by fixed facts), while user decisions (accept or override system recommendations) and motivations and other input are modelled via run-time asserted facts. As expected, the solutions are to be built by (a) rules implementing stage and sub-step logic, firing according to run-time asserted facts, and (b) pattern-matching routines, ensuring that all dependencies of the fixed facts representing recommended and/or selected AF elements are satisfied.

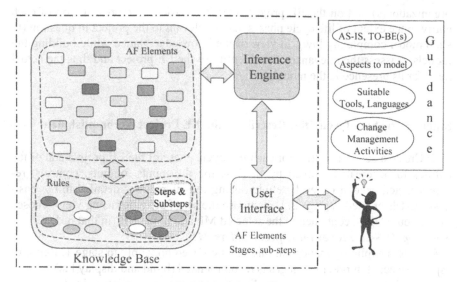

Decision Support System

**Fig. 4.** Decision support system architecture and possible outcomes of a consultation

## 3.4 Detailed Design: Main Steps of the Proposed Support System

Owing to space constraints, detailed design descriptions have been limited to the components reflecting the original meta-methodology stages and sub-steps described in Sect. 2.1. To facilitate the understanding of the system operation, the level of detail has been kept low and plain text has been used to describe rule components.

### Stage 1: Create a List of Entities Relevant to the EE Project

*System Explanation/Recommendation (E/R):* At this early stage, type and granularity consistency of the entities relevant to the project is not important. Thus, the set may contain documents, entire organizations, individuals, policies, etc. The target organization(s) (i.e., that are being created or evolved) and the EE project itself must be included in the list.

### Stage 2: Business Models of Entity Relations in a Life Cycle Context

*E/R:* Represent the interactions between the entities listed, in the context of their life cycles (i.e., for each life cycle phase of the target entities). Focus on the target organization(s) and on the EE project. Ideally, restrict the representation of each entity to the extent of life cycle phases that is relevant to the project in question (to keep model complexity low). In view of the knowledge gained while building the models, reassess the relevance of each entity to the EE project and thus the actual need for its presence in the models.

## Stage 3: The Set of Activities Describing the EE Project Accomplishment

*E/R:* Create a set of activities for each life cycle phase of the EE project and of the entities to be created/evolved by it. Describe the inputs, outputs, controls, resources, etc., needed for each activity, using the interactions detailed in the business models created in stage 2. Decompose the set of activities using views chosen in previous stages, contained in the selected MF and in the KB (in that order).

*Sub-Step A: Select Relevant Aspects and an MF*
*E/R:* Unless explicitly mandated, this sub-step need not apply to stage 1. Reuse of aspects selected in previous stages is recommended (build and display list).
*Rules:* Life cycle aspect mandatory. Functional aspect is mandatory in stage 3. Select an MF (a) as mandated, (b) according to existing skills or (c) containing most of the aspects required by the project scope. Some typical aspects are as follows: management (or control)/service (or production, depending on enterprise profile), human extent, decisional, organizational, functional, resources, informational, stakeholder, concern, hardware/software. Attempt to recommend MF according to project scope; default on the MF used to organize the original SR (the MF of GERA – Generalized Enterprise Reference Architecture (ISO/TC184 2000), a component of GERAM) as most comprehensive; recommend complementary views if selected MF lacks them.
<Stakeholder input: accept/override recommendations>
*Rules:* Dependency/overlap check of selected aspects; warn and ask user if overlaps detected or additional aspects required. Record decision, bookmark decision points.

*Sub-Step B: AS-IS Required? Type of AS-IS and TO-BE Representation?*
*E/R:* Unified representation is recommended in stage 1. In stage 3, use the same representation type as in stage 2 unless otherwise mandated.
*Rules:* Apply this sub-step for all aspects selected in sub-step A. TO-BE representation is *mandatory*. AS-IS must be represented if there is no clear common understanding of the present state by stakeholders, or if the TO-BE state must be evolved from the AS-IS. Represent AS-IS and TO-BE separately if there are obvious benefits (allow discerning between various scenarios, clarity, etc.).
<Stakeholder input: accept/override recommendations, make decision>
*Rules:* Record decision, set bookmarks.

*Sub-Step C: Modeling Formalisms, Tools*
*E/R:* Choose formalisms (modelling languages) that best support the aspects selected in sub-step A and choose tools supporting these formalisms (ranked lists are provided). Within stage 1, keep things as simple as possible (e.g. text editor).

*Rules:* Create ranked lists of suitable formalisms and tools for aspects selected in sub-step A, using best practice criteria – e.g., used in previous stages (priority criterion), potential multiple use, aspect coverage (or fit) factor, part of an *integrated* set (e.g., via underlying metamodels), etc.
<Stakeholder input: accept/override recommendations>
*Rules:* Perform dependency check for chosen elements, record decision; bookmark.

## 3.5 Implementation

The main research is directed towards extending the SR and developing and testing the support system rules in real case studies until reaching a maturity level suitable for full-scale implementation. Nevertheless, prototype implementations of the system have been attempted using the expert system shells, e.g. JESS (Friedman-Hill 2007).

## 3.6 Testing of the Proposed Support System

The behaviour of the proposed system can be tested before reaching the full implementation phase since most of the essential rules and facts are known at this stage. Thus, a facilitator familiar with the rules and facts present in the KB can perform the functions of the user interface and the inference engine, applying rules, asserting facts to reflect stakeholders input, building ranked lists and assisting in the creation, presentation and interpretation of the results.

A test of the rules composing the proposed support system has been accomplished within a case study that has also validated the theoretical framework (Noran 2006b, 2007). Space limitations do not allow presenting the practical rule application results; they will be published elsewhere.

## 4 Conclusions and Further Work

In setting up and managing EE projects, stakeholders are sometimes confronted with a complex present, an incomplete picture of the future and with quandaries of "what needs to be done next", what artefacts to use, and how to clearly communicate their vision to the organisation(s) involved. This paper describes the design principles of a system aiming to guide and assist the stakeholders in using their domain knowledge to address these essential issues.

The proposed system has several distinct features with respect to other approaches. Thus, the system is underpinned by a sound and original theoretical basis, tested in several case studies. Second, the paradigm used by the system is based on a *life cycle*, rather than "snapshot" approach, covering all relevant life cycle phases of the analysed entities rather than just a particular one. This approach is suitable for the dynamic nature of organisations. Finally, the system uses a collection of elements belonging to well-known AFs and tools, structured using a *neutral* framework. Thus, the system can be extended with elements of other AFs in order to maintain its relevance in the future.

Substantial work lays ahead for the proposed system. The system may be implemented in a myriad of ways, e.g., local or Web-based, stand-alone or as a decision support add-on to existing project management systems. Irrespective of this however, the repository and associated knowledge base need to be enriched with elements of other major AFs as previously described. In addition, more case studies are necessary in order to test and refine the rules – before and after full implementation. In fact, the knowledge acquisition, rule base update and testing processes must be *on-going* for the system to reflect the state of the art in EE and thus to remain an effective management tool.

# References

CIMOSA Association. CIMOSA – Open System Architecture for CIM. Technical Baseline, v. 3.2. Private publication, 1996

Davenport, T., Prusak, L. Working Knowledge. Boston: Harvard Business School Press, 1998

DoD Architecture Framework Working Group. DoD Architecture Framework, v. 1.0. Available at http://www.dod.mil/cio-nii/docs/DoDAF_v1_Volume_II.pdf, 2004

Doumeingts, G. GIM, Grai Integrated Methodology. In A. Molina, et al. (Eds.), Handbook of Life Cycle Engineering – Concepts, Models and Methodologies (pp. 227–288). Dordrecht: Kluwer, 1998

Finlay, P. N. Introducing Decision Support Systems. Manchester: Blackwell, 1994

Fogel, D., et al. The Impact of Machine Learning on Expert Systems. Proceedings of the 1993 Conference of the ACM on Computer Science (pp. 522–527). Indianapolis, Indiana, US: ACM, 1993

Friedman-Hill, E. JESS – The Rule Engine for the Java Platform. Distributed Computing Systems. Available at http://herzberg.ca.sandia.gov/jess/, 2007

Hättenschwiler, P. Neues anwenderfreundliches Konzept der Entscheidungsunterstützung. Gutes Entscheiden in Wirtschaft, Politik und Gesellschaft. Zurich: vdf Hochschulverlag AG, 1999

Holsapple, C. W., Whinston, A. B. Decision Support Systems: A Knowledge-Based Approach. Minneapolis/St. Paul: West, 1996

ISO/TC184. Annex A: GERAM, ISO/IS 15704: Industrial automation systems – Requirements for enterprise-reference architectures and methodologies, 2000

Kalpic, B., Bernus, P. Business process modeling through the knowledge management perspective. Journal of Knowledge Management, 10(3), 40–56, 2006

Keen, P. G. W., Scott-Morton, M. S. Decision Support Systems: An Organizational Perspective. Reading, MA: Addison-Wesley, 1978

Klein, M., Methlie, L. B. Knowledge-Based Decision Support Systems with Applications in Business. Chichester, UK: Wiley, 1995

Little, J. D. C. Models and managers: The concept of a decision calculus. Management Science, 16(8), B466–B485, 1970

Mallach, E. G. Understanding Decision Support and Expert Systems. Illinois: Richard D. Irwin, 1994

Marakas, G. M. Decision Support Systems in the Twenty-First Century. Upper Saddle River, NJ: Prentice Hall, 1999

Nonaka, I., Takeuchi, H. The Knowledge-Creating Company. How Japanese Companies Create the Dynamics of Innovation. Oxford: Oxford University Press, 1995

Noran, O. A Mapping of Individual Architecture Frameworks (GRAI, PERA, C4ISR, CIMOSA, Zachman, ARIS) onto GERAM. In P. Bernus, et al. (Eds.), Handbook of Enterprise Architecture (pp. 65–210). Heidelberg: Springer-Verlag, 2003

Noran, O. A Meta-Methodology for Collaborative Networked Organizations. Doctoral thesis, School of CIT, Griffith University, 2004a

Noran, O. A Meta-Methodology for Collaborative Networked Organizations: A Case Study and Reflections. In P. Bernus, et al. (Eds.), Knowledge Sharing in the Integrated Enterprise: Interoperability Strategies for the Enterprise Architect. Toronto, Canada: Kluwer, 2004b

Noran, O. An analytical mapping of the C4ISR architecture framework onto ISO15704 Annex A (GERAM). Computers in Industry, 56(5), 407–427, 2005a

Noran, O. Managing the Collaborative Networks Lifecycle: A Meta-Methodology. In A. G. Nilsson, et al. (Eds.), Advances in Information Systems Development – Bridging the Gap Between Academia and Industry. Proceedings of the 14th International Conference on Information Systems Development (ISD 2005) (Vol. 1, pp. 289–300). Karlstad, Sweden: Kluwer, 2005b

Noran, O. Refining a meta-methodology for collaborative networked organizations: A case study. International Journal of Networking and Virtual Organizations, 3(4), 359–377, 2006a

Noran, O. Using Reference Models in Enterprise Architecture: An Example. In P. Fettke, P. Loos (Eds.), Reference Modeling for Business Systems Analysis. Hershey, USA: Idea Group, 2006b

Noran, O. Discovering and Modelling Enterprise Engineering Project Processes. In P. Saha (Ed.), Enterprise Systems Architecture in Practice. Hershey, USA: Idea Group, 2007

Power, D. Decision Support Systems: Concepts and Resources for Managers. Westport, CT: Quorum, 2002

Power, D. J., Karpathi, S. The Changing Technological Context of Decision Support Systems. In D. Berkeley, et al. (Eds.), Context-Sensitive Decision Support Systems. London: Chapman & Hall, 1998

Scheer, A.-W. Architecture for Integrated Information Systems. Berlin: Springer-Verlag, 1992

Scheer, A.-W. ARIS-Business Process Frameworks (3rd ed.). Berlin: Springer-Verlag, 1999

Simon, H. The New Science of Management Decision (3rd ed.). Englewood Cliffs, NJ: Prentice-Hall, 1977

Sprague, R. H. A Framework for the development of decision support systems. Management Information Systems Quarterly, 4(4), 1–26, 1980

Sprague, R. H., Carlson, E. D. Building Effective Decision Support Systems. Englewood Cliffs, NJ: Prentice-Hall, 1982

The CIO Council. Federal Enterprise Architecture Framework, v 1.1. Available at https://secure.cio.noaa.gov/hpcc/docita/files/federal_enterprise_arch_framework.pdf, 1999

The Open Group. The Open Group Architecture Framework, TOGAF, v 8.1.1, 2006

Treasury CIO Council. Treasury Enterprise Architecture Framework, v. 1. Department of the Treasury Chief Information Officer Council. Available at www.eaframeworks.com/TEAF/teaf.doc, 2000

Turban, E. Decision Support and Expert Systems: management Support Systems. Englewood Cliffs, NJ: Prentice Hall, 1995

Volonino, L., Watson, H. J. The strategic business objectives method for guiding executive information systems development. Journal of Management Information Systems, 7(3), 27–39, 1990

Wheeler, F. P., et al. Moving from an executive information system to everyone's information system: Lessons from a case study. Journal of Information Technology, 8(3), 177–183, 1993

Williams, T. J. The Purdue Enterprise Reference Architecture. Computers in Industry, 24(2/3), 141–158, 1994

Zachman, J. A. A Framework for information systems architecture. IBM Systems Journal, 26(3), 276–292, 1987

# Why Focus on Roles when Developing Future ERP Systems?

**B. Johansson**

Center for Applied ICT, Copenhagen Business School, Frederiksberg, Denmark,
bj.caict@cbs .dk

**Abstract** In this paper the question "Why software vendors focus on roles when they aim at developing the future enterprise resource planning (ERP) systems?" is discussed. At the moment there is increasing interest in developing ERP systems that support a person's different working roles in the organisation, which could be described as role-based ERPs. It could be asked whether this is a reaction to the well-known problem of misalignment between users' requirements for ERP systems and what functionality ERP systems de facto support the organisation with. The question also relates to a discussion about the impact ERP systems have on users and how they are affected by the implementation, as well as the resistance to change that is often seen in an ERP implementation. One conclusion is that ERPs can have different influencing roles in an organisation, which range between increased control and increased agility. This can definitely be seen as an influencing factor for why role-based ERPs are in focus. The main conclusion delivered is that development of future ERPs could benefit from having a role-based perspective, but it is necessary to combine this with a business process perspective; if not, the gap between delivered functionality and needed functionality will still exist.

## 1 Introduction

Enterprise resource planning (ERP) systems had their introduction in the 1950s and 1960s when computers were introduced in organisations (Møller 2005). ERPs are often defined as standardized packaged software designed with the aim of integrating the entire value chain in an organisation (Lengnick-Hall et al. 2004; Rolland and Prakash 2000). ERP has its origin in the manufacturing industry where the first generation of ERP systems were introduced (Kumar and Van Hillegersberg 2000). According to Kumar and Van Hillegersberg, development of the first-generation ERP systems was an inside-out process going from standard inventory control packages, to material requirements planning, material resources planning (MRP II), and then further on expanding to a software package that aims at supporting the entire organisation (second-generation ERPs). This evolved software package is then described as the next-generation ERP labelled as ERP II, which according to Møller, is the next-generation enterprise systems. By stating that it is an enterprise system and not an ERP, the focus on the entire organisation and all its business processes is clearer.

ERP as a concept probably had its invention in the 1990s, with the introduction of, for instance, SAP R/3. SAP R/3 followed SAP R/1 and SAP R/2. SAP R/1 was a financial accounting system in which the R stands for real-time processing. R/1 was replaced by R/2 at the end of 1970s. The R/2 introduced the mainframe as a delivery form for the software, and had a focus on large multinational European organisations. This software aimed at supporting users with real-time business applications in which multilanguage and multicurrency capabilities were built in. The difference between R/2 and R/3 is then that R/3 uses the distributed client/server architecture and this change resulted in that R/3 can be managed on multiples platforms and operating systems. R/3 consists of distinct functional modules, which have a focus on best practices and therefore it more or less forces the adopting organisation to change its business processes (Koch 2001). The evolution of SAP to a great extent also describes the evolution of other ERPs, both when it comes to focus on best practices as well as the structure of functional modules. It also relates to the definitions of ERPs and the ways ERPs are described.

A major problem with existing ERPs is the "misfit" between delivered functionality and needed functionality, described as a gap between the processes the ERP supports and the processes the organisations work by. This misfit has many causes, for example, increased costs of customizing and upgrading ERP systems, leading to unwillingness to adapt the system to the organisation. In part, the misfit is also due to a poor process of defining exact requirements for the system. This has created an interest among ERP vendors to improve future ERP systems so that the architecture better supports coordination between users' perceptions of the system and their work tasks and thereby minimizes the misfit between the system and the organisation.

Microsoft (Microsoft Dynamics 2006) and SAP (SAP 2007) have recently focused on "role-based ERPs". When SAP describes mySAP and SAP NetWeaver, they focus a lot on describing roles and how their ERP aims at being a role-based one. The same can be said about Microsoft Dynamics (2007), which describes it as "Role Tailored Business Productivity", gained by software designed for your people.

The question then is, why do software vendors focus on roles when developing the future ERP systems? This is the question discussed and the aim is to describe and suggest some future research area related to this question.

The rest of the paper is organised as follows: first, ERPs and the misfit problem are discussed, followed by a discussion on how to solve the misfit problem; three different directions for doing this are discussed. The paper then ends with a concluding discussion that suggests some questions for future research related to development of role-based ERPs and how to close the functionality gap, which in the paper is described as the misfit problem.

## 2 Existing ERPs and the Misfit Problem

There is a great extent of ERP research such as Shehab et al. (2004), Esteves and Pastor (2001), and Botta-Genoulaz et al. (2005). Reviewing these reports gives the impression that a major part of the research is on implementation of ERP systems. It also shows that the main problem presented is the misfit between ERP functionality and business requirements. Soh et al. (2000) describe this as a common problem when adopting software packages. The problem of misfit means that there is a gap between functionality offered by the package and functionality required from the adopting organisation. Askenäs and Westelius (2000 p 433) describe this in the following way: "Many people feel that the current ERP system has taken (or been given) a role that hinders or does not support the business processes to the extent desire". Another way of describing this is as said by Bill Swanton, vice president at AMR research, saying that only 35% of the organisations are satisfied with the ERP they use at the moment, and he says the reason for the dissatisfaction is that the software does not map well with the business goals (Sleeper 2004).

The question is then whether it is possible to describe more clearly what this misfit is about. One way could be to use the categories of misfits between ERP functionality and business requirements that are described by Soh et al. (2000), and relate the categories of misfit to architecture of the specific software, IT architecture and business architecture. Soh et al. group the observed misfits into three broad categories: data, process, and output.

Misfits in *data* arise from incompatibilities between business requirements and the ERP package regarding the data format as well as the relationships among entities in the underlying data model, which probably could be compared to the data model that is the base for the specific software architecture.

*Process* misfits are described as functional misfits involving three different dimensions. (1) Access misfits, which mean the users do not have access to the functionality they need or that the organisation lacks enough licenses for the used software. If it is a lack of licenses the customer organisation can relatively easily negotiate with the vendor for additional licenses. If it is lack of access to a specific function the customer organisation also needs to negotiate with the vendor for maybe buying this functionality or alternatively developing this functionality by themselves or with the help of a solution provider. (2) Control misfits, which mean that the ERPs' source code does not allow the introduction of validation routines without changing the source code. (3) Third, operational misfits, which are present when the ERP does not support normal operational steps or the support is inappropriate.

*Output* misfits are described by Soh et al. as the most prevalent form of misfit. This misfit is strictly about the users not getting the information they want to have regarding both the presentation as such or the content of the information. It is stated that this to a great extent can be managed by the ERP system's report writer. However, the report writer is often hard to handle and it quite often needs to have an external solution partner to help the customers create the report they need. Output misfits could be compared to the business architecture, and the reason this misfit occurs is because the ERP does not support the business model and/or the business processes in the organisation to the degree that expected.

The misfits can be related to the fact that when an organisation implements an ERP it has to either change its business processes or customize the software. In most cases what happens is that organisations do a little bit of both, which means that they customize the software to some extent and they change the business processes to some extent. There are disagreements as to whether this is good or bad, but what can be stated is that it costs a lot of money for the adopting organisation both during the implementation and during upgrades of new versions of the software in the future (Koch 2005). The duality in changes relates to the main misfit problem described by Soh et al. (2000) as the misfit between ERP functionality and business requirements; they also state that this is a common problem when adopting software packages.

One reason why this problematic situation shows up is that there exist different views of what actually is required. Alvarez (2002) describes this as a conflict from a "communication problem" between business analyst and customer. According to Daneva and Wieringa (2006), most vendors have their "standard" process for requirements engineering that they use in establishing new ERP projects. Luo and Strong (2004) state that a key issue in ERP implementation is how to find a match between ERP functionality and the organisations' business processes. The question is then how to find the requirements as well as how to find the functionality that the ERP delivers. A crucial question that Schindler (2007) raises is that right people should define the requirements. What Schindler claims is that it is often the wrong people who identify the requirements and then "throw it over the wall". This metaphor emphasizes the fact that it is often business analysts who identify the requirements and these requirements are then very weakly presented to the development staff in an ambiguous way. The development staff then work from the requirements without questioning these, nor do they try to influence requirements that they think are wrong.

Rolland and Prakash (2000) identify four views of ERP functionality: content view, form view, purpose view, and the customizing process view. The framework they suggest from these different views can probably be used to evaluate ERPs from a functionality perspective, but it could also be used as a way of identifying business requirements on ERPs. The different views are described in the following way by Rolland and Prakash (2000): "Content refers to the knowledge that is included in the representation system, form refers to the structure and notation used, purpose refers to the objective fulfilled by the representation system and the kind of use which it facilitates, customization process refers to the process by which the ERP functionality is customized to meet specific organisational needs" (p 188). Both Rolland and Prakash's as well as Luo and Strong's call for the importance of matching the organisation's need with the ERP-system functionality makes it mandatory to further look into how to identify and present business requirements for *the* future ERP.

# 3 How to Solve the Misfit Problem

The question then is how to solve the misfit problem, and it can be asked whether any of the three different ways (1) better integration between ERPs and the enterprise architecture (EA), (2) development of role-based ERPs, and (3) change users' perception of ERPs, which are presented below, could solve the misfit problem.

## 3.1 Better Integration Between ERP and EA

One way to discuss this is to look into the concepts enterprise architecture and enterprise architecture integration (EAI) and discuss whether EAI and better integration can close the functionality gap. Bucher et al. (2006) describe enterprise architecture as consisting of five different layers: business architecture, process architecture, integration architecture, software architecture, and technology or infrastructure architecture. Bucher et al. describe software architecture as the fundamental organisation of software artefacts. However, since ERPs are much more than software artefacts it can be argued that they also influence the integration architecture as well as the rest of the different architectures. According to Bucher et al. (2006), ERP represents the integration architecture, the integration of information systems components in the relevant enterprise context. This means that ERPs consist of both the software as well as the integration architecture since ERPs are systems that aim at integrating the entire organisation's business processes. This also means that there seems to be a close relationship between ERP systems' basic architecture, business processes, and the business architecture. The interesting issue is then to consider how ERPs impact and influence the totality of the architecture. Bucher et al. state, by referring to the hierarchical, multi-level systems theory approach, that each layer of architecture influences each other. The basic thinking they suggest is that each layer reduces the freedom of action of the subsequent layer. This means that ERPs to a great extent integrate the different layers of architecture in an organisation. Melin (2003) states that implementation of ERPs is dependent on the architecture of the ERP. He argues that since ERPs more or less build on the assumption that all data are stored in one "bucket", it suggests a high level of centralisation and standardisation. This means that an organisation when implementing an ERP solution most likely goes for an increase of centralisation and standardisation.

This indicates that ERP is one way to integrate different layers in enterprise architecture. Another possibility to integrate the different layers is, according to Lee et al. (2003), EAI, and they claim that EAI automates the integration process with less effort than required with ERP. Lee et al. describe ERP as an approach that addresses operational integration aiming at supporting daily operations in organisations. Data warehousing is also described as an approach aiming at integration, but it focuses on informational integration supporting decision-making (Lee et al. 2003). They describe EAI as an approach of integrating existing applications with some kind of middleware, and they label it an externalization approach. The opposite, according to Lee at al., is the internalization approach, which is made when an organisation implements an ERP solution. They also state that the biggest challenge in integration is not the technical integration; instead, it is the behavioural integration. It can be argued that by developing an ERP towards being role-based, the behavioural integration would probably be better, and in that way a role-based ERP could also be seen as an externalization approach for integration.

According to Carlsson and Hedman (2004), the development of ERPs has made organisations truly integrate different sources of data, and the ERP vendors have recognized that the client/server architecture did solve the problem with inflexibility that the mainframe architecture had. But, when solving this inflexibility problem another problem with non-integrated client/server solutions surfaced. Carlsson and Hedman state that client/server solutions have resulted in many organisations developing into an incoherent collection of disparate subsystems. The incoherent collection of disparate subsystems can be seen as one reason for the development of enterprise portals and maybe it is a reason for developing role-based ERPs.

## 3.2 Development of Role-Based ERPs

The aim of developing a role-based ERP is, according to Sleeper (2004), that the software vendor tries to think in terms of functions and transactions for the overall structure, but through the eyes of a particular person who has a particular responsibility. Sleeper suggests the need for less training as the main benefit with a role-based ERP. He states that one of the major drawbacks of existing ERPs is that they demand a huge amount of training if they should be as useful as they could be. He also states that the role-based ERP could be compared to self-services applications which demand zero training, and claims that if ERPs can be completely intuitive, the organisation will be better off (Sleeper 2004).

One way to solve the misfit problem could be to use *roles* as the base for finding the requirements, by identifying different roles' work task and how they execute the tasks, but that probably depends on how role's are defined. Microsoft Dynamics (2006) defines roles in the following way: "A role is a specific grouping of tasks that a persona is responsible for or participates in" (p 8). Personas in this context should then be understood as a representation of a typical view of the people that can occur within an organisation defined by the collection of roles they have. This indicates that a persona can have or has different roles. Looking at business requirements from a role-based perspective means that the ERP should have the technical solution to fulfil new business requirements that organisations have with the feature of having one-point access for different work roles in an organisation.

An extension of the role analysis is to look into the roles/composite roles that exist in different organisations as well as the kinds of combinations of roles that exist. The roles could be categorized into task-oriented roles or managerial roles, and do a reverse engineering approach of what different access rights there are. Finally, another direction of looking into roles and how these roles influence business requirements could be to categorize what decisions and what kinds of decisions are made in different organisations.

Role-based ERPs can be compared to enterprise portals (EPs), since EPs focus on designing a specific user interface for a specific role. EPs are defined by Carlsson and Hedman (2004) in the following way: An EP is designed as a single access point to an organisation's external and internal information and communication technologies (ICTs). They describe EP as a technical solution to fulfil new business requirements that organisations have on ICT with the feature of having one-point access for different work roles in an organisation. According to Carlsson and Hedman, an EP differs from other corporate information systems in three ways. First, EP provides the user with a single access point to all computer-based data and information the user needs to fulfil the work tasks. Second, EP provides the user with services, which do not necessarily have to be strictly connected to the users' work tasks. Carlsson and Hedman describe this as self-employee services and give the example of employees paying their own bills from the portal they use at their working place. Third, EP gives the possibility to personalization. The last mentioned difference is the one that can be said to give the basic thinking of role-based ERPs. Carlsson and Hedman state that SAP introduced the concept of roles to support the implementation of portals. They describe roles as something that determines what information, application, and service a user can access or need to have access to when carrying out the tasks and activities. According to Carlsson and Hedman (2004), SAP defines roles as follows: "a collection of activities that an employee carries out in one or more business scenarios of an organisation. Users access the transactions, reports and web-based applications in a role via a series of menus. Roles are specific to individual employees and match their specific tasks and service/information needs" (p 268).

It could be said that ERPs are process-based or at least have the capacity to be process-based. According to Koch (2001), the basic architecture building on a department/stab model as for instance SAP R/3 makes ERPs not supporting the idea of business processes and thereby not the integration between different departments in an organisation. Koch states that it does not help that the software vendor attached some words about business processes and so on to their ERP products, since the basic architecture does not support business processes.

It can also be said that by focussing on being process-based the characteristics of human agents are missing. The reasons why an organisation wants to have alignment of its business processes, its enterprise systems architecture, and its ERP system are several. One reason could definitively be that the organisation wants to have a competitive advantage over its competitor.

According to Worley et al. (2005), the concept of role is particularly valuable when describing the interaction between information systems and its users. It is of special interest in ERPs since they are information systems supposed to support all concerned functions of an organisation. That it is highly intertwined means that ERPs have to support a lot of different roles in an organisation and the work tasks these roles have. Worley et al. describe roles as a group of functions aiming at achieving a specific purpose, and according to them there are four generic classes of roles found in all organisations: interpersonal, informational, decisional, and operational roles. These roles have specific needs to the software that is supposed to support them. Worley et al. conclude that this means that optimization of ERPs therefore is hard to make since it demands both a change in the system as well as a change in the role. The change in role is to change the way people work and change the process that they conduct.

## 3.3 Change Users' Perception of ERPs

The third way of solving the misfit problem can be compared to the discussion about the relation between information technology (IT) and organisational change suggested by Markus and Robey (1988). Melin (2003) has this as a starting perspective, when he describes the relationship between technology and human agents, and by referring to Orlikowski (1992) he states that there exist two different modes, the design mode and the use mode, for the interaction. The design mode means that the user of the technology builds certain interpretive schemes when using the technology. The use mode means that the user assigns intersubjective meaning from the usage of the technology. The technology then mediates user activities at the same time as it constrains performance by facilitating the usage in a particular manner. But, as described by Markus and Robey (1988), technology does not determine social practices; it only conditions social practices according to Melin (2003). Markus and Robey (1988) describe three different directions of what they call causal agency between IT and organisational change: the technical imperative, the organisational imperative, and the emergent perspective. These differ according to the role of IT as a driving force or as a causal agent for the change. The technical imperative views technology as the driving force, the organisational imperative views human agents as the driving force, and the emergent perspective views the change as a reaction to the interaction between technology and human agents.

Askenäs and Westelius describe five different roles an ERP could have. The description builds on the fact that they see ERPs as having an "actor" role in organisations. The roles are labelled as bureaucrat, manipulator, consultant, administrator, and dismissed. The last role is actually not a role and it is described by Askenäs and Westelius as the status when the ERP is not used or is used only partially by some users. This means that the impact of an ERP that has the role "dismissed" is close to zero. However, the other roles influence and impact the organisation and its employees in different ways. Figure 1 describes the direction of impact different roles have according to Askenäs and Westelius. The figure shows the role an ERP can have from two different directions – first, direction of control, and second, the fit the ERP has with the existing structure of the organisation.

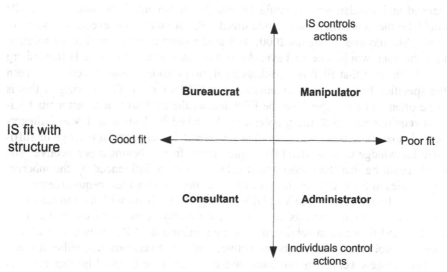

**Fig. 1.** Four roles ERP can have (Askenäs and Westelius 2000, p 427)

Staff (2006) describes mySAP as the next generation of ERPs, and says that this software is fast, flexible, and an efficient foundation offering organisations new functions, greater productivity, and integrated analytical insights into business processes which increase the flexibility to design the software so that it meets customer requirements. This is described as role-specific development aiming at increasing employee productivity by supporting them with a tool tailored to their specific work tasks. This contradicts the statement by Melin (2003), who states that implementation of an ERP is a strategy aimed at implementing a highly standardized information system. The statement from Melin is supported by Millman (2004), who states that one of the biggest mistakes an organisation can make is to customize the ERP so that it fits their processes instead of changing their processes to fit the software. However, it could be asked how and whether development of role-based ERPs could support increased flexibility at the same time as it suggests standardisation. Millman states that organisations often want to have a customisation of a "bad" process, and since the consultant earns money on customisation it happens that the ERP is adjusted to the bad process. Experience shows that it is not the customised ERP that makes organisations increase their profit; instead it is the reengineering of existing business processes that make it happen (Millman 2004).

# 4 Concluding Discussion

Melin (2003) states that the opinions from executives are that ERPs should be centralised and standardised. It could be asked whether and how role-based ERPs could be the centralised and standardized ERP solution that executives want to have (Askenäs and Westelius 2000), and at the same time be the flexible solution that the user would like to have. According to Kumar and Van Hillegersberg (2000), the fact that ERP is a packaged solution creates a disconnection between the specified business requirements and the ERP solution. The solving of this is quite often that an "expert" on the ERP adjusts the ERP so that it better fits business requirements. But, the problem, as described by Kumar and Van Hillegerberg, is that there is no guarantee that the expert has enough knowledge or sufficient knowledge to understand the requirements from a business perspective. The result could be that the implemented solution is more influenced by the inherent capabilities in the ERP than from the actual underlying business requirements.

According to Kumar and Van Hillegerberg, the problem with the mismatch between business requirements and ERP functionality is focussed on by the ERP vendors and they aim at solving this by customizing the ERP. However, this creates new problems in the migration between different versions, and either it could be that the new version is not backward compatible or it could be that the customer organisation has made modifications of the ERP, and these modifications do not automatically adjust to the new version of the ERP.

Askenäs and Westelius (2000) state that it is not possible to adjust or configure an ERP so that it fits all users' needs. There are at least two different reasons why this is the case. The first is that users to a high extent are different and even if they perform the same work tasks they do it differently from each other. The other reason is that an ERP builds on an architecture that make it hard to do the necessary changes in the configuration. It is not possible to do much about the first reason – it is hard to change people's behaviour, but the second reason could be taken care of. It may be argued that ERPs have the intention of changing working behaviour which can be compared with Markus and Robey's (1988) description of change through technical imperative. This attempt to change can probably be seen as one reason for ERPs implementation problems. The difficult question is to find out how the architecture should be constructed or changed to make it possible to have that high flexible solution that a totally role-based ERP demands.

Gammelgård et al. (2006) describe the following quality attributes of IT systems: availability, reliability, data quality, functional fit, information security, interoperability, modifiability, performance, safety, usability, and user productivity. All these could be described as capabilities received from IT systems or specifications of demands on IT systems. The question would then be how an ERP system and specifically a role-based ERP relate to these attributes. It can be stated that an ERP aims at fulfilling all these; however, the role-based ERP can be said to aim at making a difference in availability, reliability, functional fit, modifiability, usability, and user productivity. But, to do so, it probably has to change its basic architecture and maybe aim at what Kumar and Van Hillegerberg describe as component-based

ERP architecture. It can be argued that role-based ERPs aim at increasing the level of adoption among users in organisations and that the result of having the role that Askenäs and Westelius describe as dismissed ERP should be avoided. The focus on role-based ERP and the aims at being customized are interesting to further follow, and it could be asked whether role-based ERPs are the solution to the negative reaction that users often have when ERP is introduced and it can be asked whether and how role-based ERP changes the adoption rate of ERPs. It could also be asked whether the attempt of developing role-based ERPs is a solution to the problems that exist between ERPs and the organisations' desire for customization of ERPs.

# 5 Conclusions and Future Studies

The question asked in this paper was, why do software vendors focus on roles when developing the future enterprise resource planning (ERP) systems? The answer to that question can be described as follows: software vendors focus on roles since they see this as a way for closing the functionality gap existing within ERPs. But, it can be concluded that the main problem with doing this is to identify and describe relevant roles and the work tasks in which these roles need and use an ERP to fulfil the task. This indicates that further research is needed when it comes to how to find the roles as well as how to make sure that the roles are reflected in the ERP in the correct way. This emphasises on the specific problem that exists when developing a role-based ERP that suites small- and medium-sized enterprises since there are fewer people. But that kind of organisations probably more or less have the same amount of roles as in bigger organisations, which means that one person has several roles or do the work tasks that belong to several roles. This means that the ERP needs to support different roles in the same user interface or have the possibility to be very easy to shift between different user interfaces developed for different roles.

Although software vendors of ERPs started to talk about role-based ERPs in the late 1990s, they have not really taken off. A question to ask is then why? It could be that it is not the way to go for the development. However, the indication from the discussion in this paper does definitely support role-based ERPs as the way to go. Another reason could be that the software vendors have not really solved the technical side of role-based ERPs or that they have not really found the business requirements needed to be able to develop a role-based ERP. It can also be concluded that, as described in Fig. 2, several factors, architecture, new business requirements, and users perception of ERPs influence the development at the same time as these factors influence each other, and this definitely complicates the development of a role-based ERP.

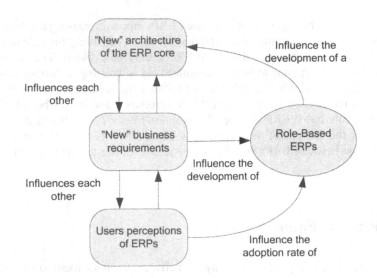

**Fig. 2.** Influencing factors on development of role-based ERPs

Another direction of future research on role-based ERPs could be to analyse whether and how role-based ERPs aim at being more of a "consultant" from the user perspective while at the same time keeping a high level of control from the entire organisation perspective. This change of ERPs definitely impacts the entire enterprise architecture and it could be asked how the future architecture of ERPs should be constructed so that it supports this change.

The interesting issue that deserves further research is in what direction this role-based ERP aims. Are ERPs heading for having a clearer role as a bureaucrat, manipulator, administrator, and/or consultant? In other words, do future ERPs aim at increasing control or increasing agility or increasing control and agility at the same time? Role-based ERP seems to go in the direction of being more of a consultant. Simultaneously, the development of role-based ERPs impacts the future enterprise architecture of organisations. But, the question remains whether this is the way to go for ERP development if future ERP investments should decrease the gap between desired requirements and delivered functionality and thereby become a more successful investment for organisations.

One reason why role-based ERPs have not yet seen the light could be said is dependent on difficulties with eliciting business requirements for a role-based ERP. However, the most apparent reason is probably a combination of technical problems and lack of understanding about business requirements. The role-based ERP probably needs a totally new architecture, which is probably to a high extent dependent on what the business requirements are. This combination of problems is difficult to solve and emphasises that further research on both ERP architecture as well as ERP business requirements is needed before alignment between requirements and functionality becomes a reality.

# References

Alvarez, R. (2002) Confessions of an information worker: A critical analysis of information requirements discourse. Information and Organization 12 (2), 85–107.

Askenäs, L. and Westelius, A. (2000) Five roles of an Information System: A social constructionist approach to analyzing the use of ERP systems. In 21st International conference on information systems, pp. 426–434. Association for Information Systems, Brisbane, Queensland, Australia.

Botta-Genoulaz, V., Millet, P. A. and Grabot, B. (2005) A survey on the recent research literature on ERP systems. Computers in Industry 56 (6), 510–522.

Bucher, T., Fischer, R., Kurpjuweit, S. and Winter, R. (2006) Enterprise architecture analysis and application – An exploratory study. In TEAR 2006 workshop.

Carlsson, S. A. and Hedman, J. (2004) From enterprise resource planning systems to enterprise portals. In The enterprise resource planning decade: Lessons learned and issues for the future (Adam, F. and Sammon, D., Eds), pp. 263–287. Idea Group, Hershey, PA.

Daneva, M. and Wieringa, R. J. (2006) A requirements engineering framework for cross-organizational ERP systems. Requirements Engineering 11 (3), 194–204.

Esteves, J. and Pastor, J. (2001) Enterprise resource planning systems research: An annotated bibliography. Communications of AIS 7 (8), 1–51.

Gammelgård, M., Lindström, Å. and Simonsson, M. (2006) A reference model for IT management responsibilities. In TEAR 2006 workshop.

Koch, C. (2001) ERP-systemer: Erfaringer, ressourcer, forandringer. Ingeniøren-bøger, København.

Koch, C. (2005) The ABCs of ERP. CIO. http://www.cio.com/article/14605/The_ABCs_of_ERP.

Kumar, K. and Van Hillegersberg, J. (2000) ERP experiences and evolution. Communications of the ACM 43 (4), 22–26.

Lee, J., Siau, K. and Hong, S. (2003) Enterprise integration with ERP and EAI. Communications of the ACM 46 (2), 54–60.

Lengnick-Hall, C. A., Lengnick-Hall, M. L. and Abdinnour-Helm, S. (2004) The role of social and intellectual capital in achieving competitive advantage through enterprise resource planning (ERP) systems. Journal of Engineering and Technology Management 21 (4), 307–330.

Luo, W. and Strong, D. M. (2004) A framework for evaluating ERP implementation choices. IEEE Transactions on Engineering Management 51 (3), 322–333.

Markus, M. L. and Robey, D. (1988) Information technology and organizational change: Causal structure in theory and research. Management Science 34 (5), 583–598.

Melin, U. (2003) The ERP system as a part of an organization's administrative paradox. In 11th European conference on information systems, Naples, Italy.

Microsoft Dynamics. (2006) Roles-based business productivity – Software designed for your people. http://www.microsoft.com/dynamics, pp. 1–57.

Microsoft Dynamics. (2007) Microsoft dynamics role tailored business productivity – Software designed for your people. http://download.microsoft.com/download/9/3/3/933042ed-61f4-4c24-8f22-cb6deaab9404/Microsoft_Dynamics_RoleTailored_Business_Productivity_whitepaper.doc.

Millman, G. J. (May 2004) What did you get from ERP, and what can you get? Financial Executives International 5, 15–24.

Møller, C. (2005) ERP II: A conceptual framework for next-generation enterprise systems? Journal of Enterprise Information Management 18 (4), 483–497.

Orlikowski, W. J. (1992) The duality of technology: Rethinking the concept of technology in organizations. Organization Science 3 (3), 398–427.

Rolland, C. and Prakash, N. (2000) Bridging the gap between organisational needs and ERP functionality. Requirements Engineering 5 (3), 180–193.

SAP (2007) User productivity enablement with SAP netweaver. http://www.sap.com/belux/platform/netweaver/pdf/BWP_SB_User_Productivity_Enablement.pdf.

Schindler, E. (2007) Getting clueful: Five things CIOs should know about software requirements. CIO.com.

Shehab, E. M., Sharp, M. W., Supramaniam, L. and Spedding, T. A. (2004) Enterprise resource planning: An integrative review. Business Process Management Journal 10 (4), 359–386.

Sleeper, S. Z. (2004) AMR analysts discuss role-based ERP interfaces – The user-friendly enterprise. SAP Design Guild.

Soh, C., Kien, S. S. and Tay-Yap, J. (2000) Cultural fits and misfits: Is ERP a universal solution? Communications of the ACM 43 (4), 47–51.

Staff, C. (2006) SAP's next generation ERP software enhances and improves business processes. Caribbean Business.

Worley, J. H., Chatha, K. A., Weston, R. H., Aguirre, O. and Grabot, B. (2005) Implementation and optimisation of ERP systems: A better integration of processes, roles, knowledge and user competencies. Computers in Industry 56 (6), 620–638.

# Index